Man in the Spangled Pants

**Jack Ragotzy
and the First Fifty Years of the Barn Theatre**

Betty and Jack Ragotzy, circa 1965

Man in the Spangled Pants

Jack Ragotzy and the First Fifty Years of the Barn Theatre

by
Joe Stockdale

Edited by Ruth Heinig

The Priscilla Press
Allegan Forest, Michigan
2002

© Joe Stockdale 1997, 2002

No part of this manuscript may be reproduced or transmitted in any form by any means electronic or mechanical, including photocopy, recording or any other information storage or retrieval system now know or to be invented, without permission in writing from the author (or his designee), except by a reviewer who wishes to quote brief passages in connection with a review written for inclusion in a magazine, newspaper, or broadcast.

ISBN 1-886167-17-6

For
Jack and Betty,
audiences, critics and theatre workers who have made
The Barn Theatre, Augusta, Michigan
the quintessential summer stock theatre in America.

Table of Contents

Acknowledgements . . . . *x*
Foreword . . . . *xi*
Part I 13
Part II 121
Part III 202
Appendix: Barn Theatre Productions 1946-1995 223
Index 280
About the Author 287

Acknowledgments

First and foremost to Robin Stockdale, a tough broad, who, during the year and a half it took to research, write and re-write this book, must have gone over the manuscript a hundred times, editing and proofing and giving me maddeningly ill-considered advice (most of which was eventually incorporated into this final draft), instead of the unconditional praise I so desperately wanted, and who patiently bore the consequences of her beliefs — through my snits, pouts, sulks and piques. Without her help this book would not have come into being.

Thanks also to Jack (who gave hours of time for the necessary taped interviews); to Brendan Ragotzy for giving me full access to the Barn's files, programs and scrapbooks; and to Howard McBride for facilitating this permission which allowed me the freedom to write this book "on spec" and to hold the copyright so that its viewpoint could remain wholly my own without undo influence. Special acknowledgment to Betty Ebert Ragotzy for respecting history and making the effort to save it in scrapbooks filled with photos she took as well as photos taken by official Barn photographers: Lance Ferraro of Kalamazoo and from Battle Creek – Corwin "Corky" Wherrett and John Charles of LA Images.

Part III of this book cannibalizes some of my article "Straight from the Heartland: Michigan's Barn Theatre," published in *TheaterWeek*, August 7, 1995. In addition, I have used quotations from the theatre critics' reviews along with news items by reporters from: the *Kalamazoo Gazette*, *The Battle Creek Enquirer News*, *The Grand Rapids Press*, *The Jackson Citizen-Patriot*, *The Homer Index*, *The South Bend Tribune*, *The Detroit News*, *The Lansing State Journal*, *The Detroit Free Press*, *The* (Glenn Shores) *Commercial Record*, *Encore*, *The New York Post*, *New York Times*, *The Daily News*, *The New Haven Register*, *The Morning Telegraph*, *The New York Post*, the *village Voice*, *Variety*, *The Newark Evening News*, *The Boston Record American*, *The Saturday Review*, *The New Yorker*, *Newsweek*, *Newsday*, *New York* magazine, *The New York World-Telegram and Sun*, *The New York Mirror*, *Women's Wear Daily*, *The New York Journal American*, and the (New York) *Herald Tribune* for which credit is given in the text.

In addition, I am indebted to the many Barnies who read the manuscript and made suggestions and corrections: Joe Aiello, Penelope Alex, Becky Ann Baker, Scott Burkell, Dick Fuchs, Robin Haynes, Dale Helward, Wayne Lamb, Merle Louise, Angelo Mango, Barbara Marineau, Marin Mazzie, Robert Newman, George McDaniel, Shay Moore, John Newton, James Pritchett, Brendan Ragotzy, Jack Ragotzy, Dusty Reeds, Peter Simon and Tom Wopat, along with non-Barnie Page Karling

Finally, I wish to acknowledge the staff at The Billy Rose Collection at Lincoln Center in NY, The NY Public Library at 42nd Street and Fifth Avenue, Galen Rike, David Isaacson, and Aedin Clements of Waldo Library, Central Reference at Western Michigan University. Thanks also to Lyda Stillwell, Professor Emerita of Theatre at WMU for her encouragement, and of course, special thanks to my editor, Ruth Heinig, Professor Emerita of Communication at WMU for her knowledge, work, support and constant encouragement and getting my manuscript to the publishers, Larry and Priscilla Massie. If it had not been for Ruth Heinig, the manuscript would not have been published.

Joe Stockdale

Foreword

About the time the Barn Theatre was readying itself for its 50th anniversary, I was living in NYC and one afternoon decided to see Woody Allen's *Bullets Over Broadway*. In the men's room after the show, a New Yorker cozied up to the next urinal and nasally twanged, "Great show, ain't it? But it'll never play Kalamazoo!" meaning, one supposed, that *Bullets* was too sophisticated for that Michigan city.

Augusta, the home of the Barn Theatre, is only a dozen miles from Kalamazoo, and its existence is at least one good reason why Mr. Know-It-All New Yorker should rid himself of the notion that every place west of the Hudson is some kind of cultural backwater interested only in the Chautauqua circuit and dumb and dumber Toby Shows.

Man in the Spangled Pants is the story of this theatre, from its inception in '46 through a celebration of its first 50 years in '95. It's also the story of Jack P. Ragotzy, who had both an off-B'way and B'way career in addition to being producer and director of the Barn.

In writing Jack's and the Barn's story, neither space nor reader's time permitted even a cursory discussion of every production of the fifty seasons. A decision was made at the outset to limit discussions to one or two productions a season, and the choice would be Ragotzy's. These choices are starred with an asterisk in the text box appearing in the left margin at the beginning of each season.

In '46 there was one critic covering the Barn beat, and in '95 there were ten. We limited our choice to two, or at most three, reviews that represented the majority opinion but adding, of course, minority viewpoints so the reader would have an overview of the production's reception. The exception to this procedure are the detailed, critical analyses of new plays premiering at the Barn and of Ragotzy's NY productions.

We have put all shows directed and/or produced by Ragotzy and all shows produced at the Barn in boldface type so that readers can quickly thumb through the book to find specific titles. Italics are used for all other titles, including plays, films, novels, and TV series. For individual titles within a TV series, we have used quotation marks.

We avoided duplication of plot synopses in quoting critics. For titles such as **You Know I Can't Hear You When the Water's Running**, we substituted "**Water**," "the show," or "it." We have avoided the use of [sic] to indicate typos, misspellings, or the occasional use of incorrect words by newspaper critics writing against a deadline. Instead, we corrected the errors and changed the words to what we believe the critic intended them to be.

In quoting critics, there were the following possibilities: a) quote in full, b) use an ellipsis(. . .) when cutting from the quotation, c) or quote and cut (without the ellipsis) but not out of context. Choice a) would have made the book far too long and repetitious b) would have impeded the flow and readability and c) might have created distortion. Regardless of the danger of distortion, we chose method c. This is exemplified by the following quote, in which we have italicized and bracketed those words cut:

The first paragraph of a review of **West Side Story** reads: "Members of the [*Augusta Barn Theatre*] company, taking on what probably is the toughest assignment of their 16 years [*of entertainment in these parts,*] came up [*Tuesday night*] with a pleasing, if slightly rough, premiere of [*the B'way and London smash musical hit,*] **West Side Story**."

For ease in reading we have shortened titles of all Michigan newspapers whose reviews are most often quoted. The *Kalamazoo Gazette* is called *Gazette*; *The Battle Creek Enquirer and News*, which was later changed to *The Battle Creek Enquirer*, is called *The Enquirer*; *The Grand Rapids Press* is called *The Press*; *The Jackson Citizen Patriot* is called *The Citizen Patriot*. Big city papers in both NY and LA are identified by either LA or NY prior to a shortened version of the newspaper's name. For example, *The New York Times* becomes *NYTimes*. Publications with brief titles remain the same, as do newspapers and magazines which are quoted only a few times. The first time a critic's name is mentioned, we use full name; thereafter, last name only. In addition, we use "NY" for New York, "'96" for 1996 etc., and "B'way" for Broadway.

Our hope has been to avoid a ponderous scholarly style and to make *Man* an enjoyable and easy read.

JS and RH

Part I

Angela, with Geraldine Page, directed by Jack Ragotzy, opened on Broadway in 1969.

"Before **Angela** closed on Saturday and Sumner [Arthur Long], his wife, Beulah, Betty and I caught the red-eye back to California, I went backstage to Geraldine's dressing room," Ragotzy said.

"The show had opened on Thursday and this was the fourth and final performance. The reviews were there on her dressing room table and Geraldine said, 'Isn't it a shame that we worked so hard and this is the result?' I wanted to kick her in the teeth, but tears were in her eyes. She seemed to really mean what she said, so I almost forgave her all the problems.

"We had originally wanted Maureen O'Sullivan. And she wanted to do it in March of the previous year. But there was a theatre jam on at that point and the producers, Elliott Martin and Mike Ellis, were afraid they couldn't get a theatre because O'Sullivan wasn't a big enough star. I thought why? Damn it! She's already been a hit in *Never Too Late*.

"And the irony is, *I* was the one who finally got Geraldine Page. I went to Hollywood to talk to her. She was living in Redwood with her kids. I waited while she got ready to go to the studio and the chauffeur sat outside in one of those long limos. She was deciding whether or not she was going to do **Angela**. At that time she was getting fat and I thought, 'Goddamn! Why am I asking her to play this role?'

"I called her husband, Rip Torn, who was in Sonora, Mexico — they were having marital problems — and Rip said he didn't want her to do it. He said it was a lousy part for her. Her role was not the lead. The lead was the boy.

"Gerry was about my age, and I liked her personally. I just thought she wasn't right for the show, and I was stupid for letting myself be pressured into casting her. At first I rationalized and thought she'd lose weight and eventually be wonderful, but it didn't happen. Maureen O'Sullivan would have been so darling. I got Gerry and the irony is that none of them — writer or producers — could get her. *I* got her! I was being the big hero, you know, getting her so they could get a theatre.

"Then I found out. She couldn't play comedy!"

*****

August '69, during the end of a very successful summer stock season at the Barn Theatre, director Jack Ragotzy's mind was on his forthcoming B'way production of **Angela**. After all the years of struggle — the world premieres, the near misses — he felt maybe this time a show that had been enormously successful at the Barn would make it on B'way.

The production would start rehearsals in NY on September 15, go to New Haven for the out-of-town tryout, follow with another preview at Boston's Wilbur Theatre, and then open on October 30 at the Music Box, one of B'way's finest theatres.

"Dale Helward, who played the leading male role at the Barn where the show had its world premiere during the summer of '68, was our choice for the boy," Ragotzy explained. "He had been flown to California to be interviewed by Page when she was making the film, *Whatever Happened to Aunt Alice?* In her dressing room she didn't give Helward much more than five minutes before dismissing him. Since Dale had made the long trip from NY, I insisted that she give him a bit more time. Even when she did, Helward was certain she didn't want him."

So the actor cast as the TV repairman — Miss Page's onstage lover — was Rob Anthony.

"Rob was a stage manager who really couldn't act," Ragotzy continued, "but Gerry wanted him. He gave a damn good first reading, but he never got any better. I worked my ass off with him, but as we neared the end of the rehearsal time before going out of town, Sumner had convinced the producers to replace him. Sumner wanted Dale Helward. So Rob was let go and I put Dale in the show on a Sunday rehearsal. He opened in New Haven on Tuesday and for a while there things looked good."

How did critics react? "The author has the ability to create comedy we can all identify with and to build a solid play along classic lines," wrote Marshall Hahn of *The New Haven Register*. "Geraldine Page plays with a cuteness, a coyness, a sexy, sultry maturity that could have been sleazy with a lesser actress. Her 24-year-old lover [is] played with great comic effect by Dale Helward. Though the third act faltered somewhat, much can be said for the steady directorial hand of Jack Ragotzy."

Florence Johnson of the *New Haven Journal-Courier* wrote, "That beguiling lady of the theatre, Geraldine Page, came to the Shubert in **Angela**. A generous-minded audience applauded her efforts, but the play is, at this point, something less than a success. Miss Page and Dale Helward wade through a cumbersome script as best they can. There are some rare moments of light comedy, but sharp sophisticated wit is sadly lacking."

Variety called **Angela**, "a potentially sparkling comedy," and predicted that it "should not be too difficult to polish for big time exhibition." Of the acting and directing the critic observed, "Geraldine Page is the personification of graciousness and the role seems a natural for her. Dale Helward gives a straightforward interpretation of the young repairman. Jack Ragotzy's staging involves comparatively few lulls and capitalizes well on the overall comedy content of the script. **Angela** could make an entertaining film."

"After those reviews, we thought maybe Geraldine would accept Dale," Ragotzy went on. "We thought she would agree to having him play the part because he was obviously doing a hell of a good job."

But Page insisted that another actor be cast in the role. In fact, Helward heard his lines being read from the stage right after his opening night performance in New Haven.

One of the actors called to New Haven was David Carradine. He was asked to take over the role, but after seeing Helward's performance, he objected, saying, "I can't do it better than he can. You've got an awfully good young man there. Why do you want to replace him?"

But Page insisted that the role be recast, so Tom Ligon, a young Yale Drama School graduate, was hired. Ligon watched every performance in New Haven plus the first week in Boston and then remarked to Helward, "I don't know why they want to replace you."

Ragotzy went on with his story. "The new kid who took over as the male lead turned out to be not nearly as good as Helward. And Geraldine didn't like *him* after a while. Actually at that time, Gerry — God bless her — wanted someone to sleep with. I think at first she thought she had somebody until she realized he had a close friend."

When Ligon took over the role, Helward continued to understudy but was not even allowed to play the small role of the *second* TV repairman. Instead, Angelo Mango, who had played it at the

Barn, was brought in and approved by Page.

Ragotzy analyzed her lack of comedic ability this way: "Geraldine didn't know she had to wait for laughs. She literally didn't know when the laugh peaked and then started to die down. I'd say, 'As soon as they start to laugh, count to ten before you say your next line.' But she just didn't understand.

"She worked hard at it, but she didn't grasp the fact that the audience was a part of the communication triangle. I tried to explain it to her this way, 'You've got to wait for that third person to play his part in the scene. You must listen to that person because he is telling you he is on your side, and you must enjoy the fact.' But she just didn't get it! So she'd stand there doing things with the phone cord. I wanted to pull a Kazan, or Clurman or whoever and yell, 'Don't just *do* something, *stand* there!'"

In addition to cast replacements in New Haven, the producers called in James Hammerstein, "ostensibly to help with rewrites," Ragotzy said years later. However, two cast members reported that Jack had actually been replaced as director, even though the show came in under his name.

"I had no idea who Jim Hammerstein was," Jack said. "All I knew was that they said they needed someone to come in because Sumner wouldn't write anymore. Jim would want to rewrite and Sumner would just go sit. So the producers worked it out.

"I would sit up all night with Sumner, who drank constantly — and who could blame him? — and we would make up new lines. I would write them out in longhand and then he would type them, which he could do drunk or sober. Then in the morning I'd go to breakfast with Hammerstein, discuss the rewrites, and he would put in the new material. I'd sleep during the day and go watch the show at night, give notes, and then we'd go back to rewriting with Sumner. This happened for about a week, but the show got nothing but worse.

"Writing stuff to give Page more laughs was a lost cause. Not only couldn't she play a laugh line, she didn't understand that her laughs were in reaction to the boy's. The producers and Jim Hammerstein couldn't understand it either."

When the show got to Boston, it was reviewed by the "Dean of American Drama Critics," Elliot Norton, who called **Angela** "empty and silly" and concluded that the play sounded "very much like one of those summer theatre tryouts which amuse friendly audiences in the haybarns in July and which are then repaired and revised and patched in the hope they will be strong enough for B'way in the winter." Of Page he remarked, "She manages to give a glow of life and a hint of humor to scenes that are dubious and dull."

Jack remembers it this way: "When we opened in New Haven, I was sure we were a hit. It went great and it was a funny show. But out of lots of major guffaws opening night, there were only seven big laughs left when we finally got to B'way! We had a rehearsal on Tuesday and a preview on Wednesday. After the preview, Jim Hammerstein came up to me and said, 'It's too bad, but you were right. It's the boy's show. We should never have made the changes.'"

'*Too bad*,' Jimmy?" Ragotzy snorts. "Too bloody late!

"For crissakes! I never questioned from the beginning that it was the boy's show. The woman is there, but *it's the boy's show*! When she gets laughs, hers are *reaction laughs* to what he has done or said. It's all reflective. She can steal laughs like crazy, but she must let both the boy and the husband — played by that wonderful actor, Simon Oakland, who also got very frustrated with Gerry — play their parts."

*****

The reviews, which lay on Geraldine Page's dressing room table when Jack went back to see her after the final performance, were devastating.

Leo Mishkin of *The (NY) Morning Telegraph* compared the situation in **Angela** to *Forty Carats*, running just a few doors down the block. "The only trouble with **Angela**," Mishkin concluded, "is that it doesn't do anything better than *Forty Carats*. In fact it does everything much worse. If *Forty Carats* is to be held as a measuring standard for gold, **Angela** is pure dross."

Daily News critic John Chapman concurred: "**Angela** is a slender, one-joke situation stretched into six scenes and two short acts, and not all the artful mannerisms and vocal tricks of the star, Geraldine Page, can save it from almost literally boring itself to death."

Clive Barnes of the *NYTimes* observed, "The staging by Jack Ragotzy proved moderately unimportant. It didn't save the show, but even the United States Cavalry couldn't have done that. Miss Page acted with an understandably abstracted charm. Tom Ligon does his best as the repairman but the play didn't need a repairman: it needed a miracle."

Writing for the *NY Post* Richard Watts, Jr. felt the play "proved to be totally without humor, charm or anything in the way of dramatic interest." Page, he said, "is bogged down in an unrewarding role despite her charm and artfulness."

Variety noted, "It was probably inevitable after the popular reception of *Forty Carats* that someone would try to cash in again on the ladies' matinee come-on of a comedy about an older woman with a young lover. It may have seemed an inspiration in prospect, but it's yawn time in a B'way theatre."

Newsday critic George Oppenheimer wrote, "Once again Miss Page is playing comedy and, although she has improved considerably, I still feel that this is not yet her forte. In justice, I doubt if any comedienne could do much for Mr. Long's far-fetched effort, but Miss Page seems not to have the skill that can turn a sow's ear into at least an imitation silk purse. The direction by Jack Ragotzy seems at best ragged, and only an attractive boudoir setting by Robert Randolph impressed me."

Leonard Harris of WCBS TV 2 labeled the production a "disaster." Edwin Newman of NBC4 TV called it an "intolerably bad play," and John Bartholomew Tucker of WABC-TV 7 joked: "If you have only two hours to live, spend the time watching **Angela**. It'll seem like two years."

John Simon of *New York* magazine, cutting right to the chase, opined, "What was truly painful here was Miss Page's performance. The actress is an expert of the whine-and-flutter school of acting, which is the distaff side of the scratch-and-grunt school, both, of course, the bequest of the Actors Studio. It is distressing that Miss Page should have become accepted as one of our two or three leading actresses — almost as if the triangle were to become the main instrument in the symphonic orchestra."

Angela's closing was the defining moment in Jack Ragotzy's theatre career. It was his last hurrah. At the age of 48 he had spent 17 years devoting every effort to making it in the big time world of NY show biz and, as he said 28 years later, "Jim Hammerstein's words after that Wednesday preview made me realize that directing for B'way wasn't all that important. I'm not saying **Angela** is a great play, but I *am* saying that if B'way was not so riddled with show-biz ideas — especially the one mandating the necessity of a 'star' — and if Maureen O'Sullivan and Dale Helward had played the show, I doubt that **Angela** would have been the disaster it was. It probably would not have been a hit because of the *Forty Carats* comparison, but it would not have closed after only four performances. If it had *had* even a *moderate* run like John Patrick's *The Curious Savage*, which also got bad reviews, it would have gone on to play summer stock and community theatres and garnered substantial royalties in which everyone would have shared."

As he flew back to LA on the red-eye, Jack thought back over his life. There was a vivid memory of the circus when he was a kid in Kalamazoo.

The tall figure pranced down the street ahead of the band — ahead of the people, the elephants, camels, and a tiger in a cage — followed by the baggy pants clowns. The tall man moved with a kind of ease and assurance that told of total command of those who followed.

He was dressed in a stovepipe hat with a band of stars and wore a blue swallow-tailed coat. Attached to his pants were circular pieces of red and silver metal that formed vertical stripes. Their movement caught the sun and reflected stars into the eyes of the boy who stood on the sidewalk. That man's life must surely be better than what the kid saw all around him.

*****

Jack P. Ragotzy, the son of Mary Louise Gordon and Floyd Charles Ragotzy, was born at home in Kalamazoo on December 16, '21 — and *not* with a silver spoon in his mouth. He grew up in a not-so-good neighborhood — the washed-out center of downtown Kalamazoo with its roadways, electrical wires, and not-too-distant paper mills — on Sheldon Street, a couple of blocks and two railroad tracks east of Portage.

His 16-year-old mother had run away to

Ohio to be married because that state had no age limit. His father, Floyd Ragotzy, only 18, was soon to be the youngest man ever to get a divorce in Kalamazoo County. Mary Louise insisted Jack keep his father's name in the hope of collecting alimony. Raised mostly by his maternal grandparents, Jack, at age ten, was given a stepfather when his mother married M.W. Fisher.

According to Jack, his paternal grandfather was Charles Rakoczy, from Alsace-Lorraine in northeast France, whose name got changed to Ragotzy, standard procedure at the time as part of the "greenhorn's" assimilation into the melting pot. Charlie, a carnival worker and chronic alcoholic, was eventually committed to the state mental hospital in Kalamazoo. Jack remembers visiting him in the "snake pit up there on the hill where he died of unnatural causes."

His maternal grandfather, Peyton Gordon (from whom he inherited the initial "P" in his name), was mistaken for a man who had taken money from a racetrack and was shot in a barroom brawl in Owensboro, Kentucky, years before Jack was born. "My grandmother, the matriarch of the family, then married — if you can believe the name — Nick Faust. He was a bit of a drinker, but this was my 'grandfather.'" Jack said, "He taught me baseball. He was the grandfather I lived with and remember. I called him 'Potty.'"

Asked if he had any contact with his father when he was growing up, Ragotzy paused and, in a deep but controlled voice, said, "Apparently I saw him when I was three years old and went fishing with him or something. I have a picture someplace with him in a boat. It's the only picture of him I have."

Does he know what happened to his father?

"One night a few years ago, after a show, a man came up to me and said he'd worked with my dad as a pressman on the *Gazette* in the early 20's and that he was something of a — he used the word 'genius' — at mechanics. Apparently he invented something they still used in the pressroom. He never got anything for it. The man characterized him as 'likeable' and said he was surprised when he left town. Dad probably left town to avoid my mother. If he had ever reappeared on the scene, she was determined to get her back alimony. It was her cry through life, 'my back alimony.' My dad didn't want a family. He just couldn't face the fact that he was a father."

Again Ragotzy pauses, ridding himself of feelings from almost seventy years earlier. When he speaks, his voice is without emotion. "I didn't think to get the guy's name so I could sit down and ask what he knew about my dad. I'm sure that somewhere in their records the *Gazette* has something. But I never tracked it down."

When asked about growing up during the Depression, Jack replied, "They were hard times, but I have a distinct and fond memory of when the Barnum and Bailey circus came to town and had a parade up Burdick Street. For fun, there was baseball during the summer at Edison Elementary School and at Washington Junior High. We didn't go on welfare because everyone in my family worked, including my grandmother and mother, who were seamstresses for the Kalamazoo Pants factory. Money wasn't plentiful." He paused to control his emotions and then said, "There *were* bad times — especially the day the family ate my pet rabbit."

Entering Kalamazoo Central High School, which housed grades ten through 12, in September '36, wrong-side-of-the-tracks-Jack found that acceptance in the theatre depended on talent rather than social or economic origin. Central was similar to most high schools at that time with heavy emphasis on sports: football, basketball, baseball, track, wrestling, swimming, tennis and golf — these activities taking most of the space in the school's yearbook, the *Delphian.*

But there was also something unique about Central.

According to the *Gazette,* the school's auditorium was "considered for many years the best-equipped high school theatre in the nation," which may have had something to do with the fact that Superintendent of Schools Loy Norrix was a theatre buff. And the head of the drama department, "the only such full-time department in secondary education in the U.S.," was a man named Howard Chenery.

Chenery had been a professional actor and a playwright, writing *The Ferguson Family*, which played for a substantial six-month run on B'way during the '28-'29 season. Later he wrote *The Courageous Mrs. Hardy*, which closed in Boston, never making it to NY. But his *The Dev-*

il of Pei-Ling opened in February '36 on B'way and ran for 11 performances. In addition, he wrote several plays geared for high school production, showcasing them at Central and giving his students the opportunity of working on a world premiere.

Chenery was also a founding member of a theatre that performed at Kalamazoo's Lincoln Auditorium, producing nine shows on a one-a-week schedule in the late summer of '29. This summer stock effort was soon institutionalized into a permanent organization known as the Kalamazoo Civic Players, supported and nurtured financially by Dr. W. E. Upjohn of the drug company (now Pharmacia), who had been sensitized to theatre's importance by his daughter, Dorothy.

Dr. Upjohn's gift of $300,000 financed the building of the Civic Auditorium, it was rumored, to bring his daughter back home from the wilds of the NY Theatre to the more civilized clime of Kalamazoo. The building was opened on October 12, '31, and when NY's Theatre Guild presented their production of George Bernard Shaw's *The Apple Cart* at the Civic on March 5, '32, Bram Nossen, writing for the *NYTimes,* described it as "probably the loveliest and best equipped theatre in America."

One has only to read Sinclair Lewis' *Main Street* to understand the small mindedness and bigotry that existed in provincial America at the time. Despite the United States being a fiercely democratic nation, there existed a class system as rigid as that of England's. The side of town you were born on counted, and who your parents and grandparents were counted. And regardless of how strange it may sound today, when almost half the births are from single mothers, coming from a divorced family counted.

Jack was eight years old when Wall Street — as *Variety*'s famous headline informed the world — "laid an egg." Two years before, Al Jolson made *The Jazz Singer*, a partly-talking motion picture. Ticket prices for kids under 12 at the Kalamazoo movie houses — The New and The Orpheum — cost a dime; prices at the State, Michigan, Fuller, Uptown, Capital and Regent (which still played "legit") cost more. Occasionally, even poor kids could afford 25 cents if what was playing was something special. What was special to the impressionable young Ragotzy during the 30's was the actor, John Garfield. He liked any movie that John Garfield, the tough but sensitive NY street kid, acted in.

So even before entering Central High School and meeting Howard Chenery, Jack's interest in show business had been whetted. He was developing an imagination, a beginning theatrical know-how, and an understanding of the joy in make-believe. He saw the theatre as a means to recognition and a way of escaping his past and present.

Drama "coach" Howard Chenery was childless and took an interest in young Ragotzy, perceiving a budding theatrical talent. Jack credits Chenery with giving him his theatrical foundation. "He let me work on almost every show while I was in high school. All of these productions were done on the big auditorium stage with full-scale sets, lights, costumes — the whole beautiful ball of theatrical wax."

True, he wasn't the first to be asked out after rehearsals and performances because he "didn't have the money to go to the places the rich kids went to." But he *was* asked because of his contribution to the shows.

During Jack's three years at Central, Chenery produced 12 shows, including such B'way hits as *The Night of January 16th*, *The Torch-Bearers*, *Big-Hearted Herbert*, *A Murder Has Been Arranged* and *Seven Keys to Baldpate*. In addition to performing in most of the plays, Jack also saw and admired the Kalamazoo Civic Players' productions. The Civic's stable of actors was comprised of Virginia and Helen Burdick, Louise Carver, Howard Chenery, Pauline DeCrocker, Dorothy Upjohn DeLano, Paul and Dorothy Fuller, Sylva Gilmore, Jean Henderson, Ruth Hartman, Tom Jones, Larkin and Ruth Noble, Howard Snow, Abbie Smith and Ethel West, to name only a few. And Jack saw and admired them all.

Allan B. Hobsen, first president of the Players, wrote at the time, "In the spirit of the amateur, *and without regard for class or status*, literally scores of players unite [at the Civic]." The first three directors — Paul Stevenson, Sidney Spayde and Gerhardt Lindemulder — were first-rate and naturally wanted to produce the best possible production. But since there was such a large number of fine actors of professional quality in the casting pool, it was difficult for the outsider to break in.

In March of '38, after trying out for the lead in the high school's production of *Big-Hearted Herbert* and not being cast, Jack auditioned for the Civic's 100th production, Robert E. Sherwood's *The Road to Rome*, and was rewarded for his *chutzpa* by being cast as one of the guardsmen. Whether Chenery was covetous of his own stable of talent or whether he felt a proprietary interest in his charge and believed the Civic crowd was too sophisticated, "he kicked my butt," Jack said. "But it didn't keep me away from the Civic because in my senior year I read for, but was not cast as, Richard in *Ah, Wilderness!* Later I did get the role of an office boy in *Counselor at Law*."

Did Jack have any other interests in high school besides the theatre?

"I started out playing baseball in grade school, continued it in junior high, and while in high school played Legion Junior baseball on a team which went to the state finals. Even after high school, I played city league baseball. I was a damned good catcher."

Any other interests?

"Girls!"

Jack's senior picture is in the *Delphian*, the class yearbook, along with the obligatory write-ups on all 491 graduates. Jack's mention — "Mary Rosso was seen in *Seven Keys to Baldpate*. Jack Ragotzy was in that play too, and in practically all the plays" — is only slightly backhanded.

Graduating in June of '39 in the largest class Central High had yet produced, Ragotzy was *not* listed as one of the five "outstanding" males, most of whom were letter winners in football and basketball. In a random sampling by a reporter from the *Gazette* of some 65 members of the class, Jack, along with 32 others, said he would be attending Western State Teachers College (Kalamazoo) in the fall.

Instead, he went to work.

His first job was for "Two Legs, Inc.," a company within the Kalamazoo Pant Company family with a chain of 21 stores throughout the Midwest. Jack was trained at the Kalamazoo store and then sent to Louisville, Kentucky, for instruction in store management. He was then given an assistant manager's job in Evansville, Indiana, which he said "was great because it was my family's home town and it had a much talked-about red-light district."

The company soon sent him to Chicago where he met Virginia Nemer. "She worked the notions counter in a Woolworth store next to Two Legs. 'A gal from the five and ten cent store,'" he sings in his George Burns' rasp. "We eventually married."

Not long after the marriage, the manager of Windy City's Two Legs accused Jack of stealing $8.98. "He was short that amount and he tried to get me to make it up," Jack said. "I came back to the home office in Kalamazoo to complain, but the owner's son said the manager would not have accused me unless he believed it was true. So he fired me. I didn't want to work for the bastard anyway. I knew this wasn't what I wanted to do with my life, so I got a job with Montgomery Ward. Virginia and I moved to Kalamazoo, and I headed straight for the Civic Theatre."

"'Ginny' was a good seamstress and could have helped out there, but she refused. And, although she was sociable, my mother and stepfather didn't much care for her. She was Catholic and I had joined the church when we married, but I didn't attend. And since my life was at the Civic and Virginia hated the theatre, we separated. She went home to Chicago and we later got a divorce."

In November '40, Ragotzy got his big chance at the Civic playing "Siggie" in Clifford Odets' *Golden Boy*, the same role played by John Garfield for The Group Theatre on B'way. In January, he was in *I Killed the Count*, a show he also stage-managed and helped direct when director Sidney Spayde was out of town for two weeks. In February he played the role of Bill Clary in E.P. Conkle's *Prologue to Glory*.

Then he didn't appear in another Civic show until May '42, when he played David Lloyd George in Howard Koch's *In Time to Come*. One reason for this hiatus was that, during the production of *Prologue to Glory*, he had a falling out with the Civic's mainstay, described as "a conservative New England Yankee," who had been the business manager since the theatre opened.

Jack tells the story as follows: "There was a girl I knew who had a crush on one of the actors. She had come down to the theatre one night to help me out while I was making coonskin caps for *Prologue to Glory*. She later bought the actor a

$12.50 cigarette lighter. One of the actresses had been working earlier and, unbeknownst to me, left her purse. The next day I was accused of stealing $10 from it."

Spayde, a brilliant director, considered Jack a kind of protégé and managed to smooth the troubled waters. As a result, not only did Jack do the Koch play, but he was back for *Ladies of the Jury* in February '43. Then in April, the program for *The Man Who Came to Dinner*, in a new column called "Honor Roll," listed "Air Cadet Jack Ragotzy's" address as "Squadron 107, Barracks 1699, AAF, Classification Center, San Antonio, Texas, Aviation Cadet Center."

Seven months after the bombing of Pearl Harbor, Jack had enlisted in the Army Air Force but wasn't called to cadet training school until February '43 — just after the final performance of *Ladies of the Jury*.

Graduating with lieutenant's bars, he spent the next 15 months in Texas, another three months at Ellington Field and Laredo, and over a year at Midland Air Force Base. At Midland he met Sergeant Art Cole, who, on off hours, worked with the Midland Community Theatre. The two men became friends, and Cole cast Jack in Maxwell Anderson's *The Eve of St. Mark*. Later, Jack was asked to direct **You Can't Take It With You** for the group. Jack also worked on "soldier shows" — musical revues — for which he helped write the skits. After leaving Midland, he met Art once again, briefly on Guam, and the two swore they would see one another again, but never did.

All of this theatre activity at Midland intensified Ragotzy's desire to go into the theatre in one capacity or another. His real job, however, was as a bombardier instructor. He had earned that position by graduating as one of the top three in his class. "The Major recommended me as a teacher in ground school. It was this experience that gave me the idea that after the war I might like to teach. Also, teaching kept me from having to fly student bombing missions with those crazy pilots."

But safe harbor at Midland was not to be, and in the fall of '44 Jack was transferred to Langley Field, Virginia, for instruction as a radar bombardier. Four months later, in February '45, he was sent overseas to Hawaii, Guam and finally Tinian, one of the islands in the Northern Marianas where the war in the Pacific was gearing up for a decisive climax. Tinian was, in fact, the very island from which the atom bombs were carried to Japan.

Years later, Ragotzy described those last months of the war: "As we took off from Tinian, I'd look back and hope to hell to see land again. Then I'd settle in for the long flight over the Pacific toward our target." He remembers flying over Yokohama when the B-29 on which he was bombardier "led the entire wing. And when the flack from the Japanese antiaircraft started up, it reminded me of riding over an old-fashioned corduroy road back in Michigan."

On another flight, this one over Tokyo, antiaircraft fire hit the No. 3 engine of the B-29, stripping the gears which operated the propeller. "The propeller, running idle, continued picking up speed until it was running two or three times faster than normal and creating so much heat that it intermittently set the motor on fire. This continued for two and a half hours until we made it back to Tinian."

Having completed 20 missions, Ragotzy got leave to visit Kalamazoo. Returning to his base at Tinian, he flew three more missions, the last one on the morning of August 14, '45. "We were told when we took off that we might be ordered back," he recalled, "because the United States had already dropped the atomic bomb on Hiroshima on August 6 and another on Nagasaki on August 9. The war was winding down real fast." It was not until he was back at Tinian that he knew the war had ended hours before. "Since our plane was last in the flight pattern, I guess we were the last combat plane against the enemy."

The next time he flew over Japan was in a show of support and strength on the day the peace treaty was signed aboard the *USS Missouri*. Because U.S. fire bombings were done mostly at night, it was the first time he had seen the enormous damage done to Tokyo. He was appalled.

In November '45, Jack took part in a mass flight of B-29s back to the United States, and in late December he was home on terminal leave. The first thing he did was go to the Civic. "It was a snowy December evening," he recalled. "I had on my uniform — the only suit I had. Walking in the back door of the theatre was my homecoming. Someone asked, 'Are you back for good?' And I

At Turnabout Theatre, Betty Ebert acted and also worked the light board. (Photo for *Collier's* by Curt Gunther)

said 'Yes.'

"It just so happened that a character man had dropped out of Oliver Goldsmith's *She Stoops to Conquer*, which was being rehearsed for an early January opening, and after a quick audition for director Gerhardt Lindemulder, I was cast." Ragotzy played two roles: "Muggins," the "fourth shabby fellow" in the alehouse with one line, and "Sir Charles Marlow," who appeared in the fifth and final act with 20 lines. Although not an auspicious reentry into the theatre world, it was compensated for by the fact that in the cast, playing the second ingenue, was an attractive young woman named Betty Ebert.

*****

During the summer of '45, the director and board members of the Civic decided to instigate a program they had long been planning—to bring a college graduate to Kalamazoo to apprentice with the Players. To facilitate this program, which was supported by Dorothy Upjohn Dalton, they sent out applications to the heads of various drama departments.

The apprentice would work nine months, "taking successive assignments in all departments, assisting with direction, stage management, set construction and painting, lighting and sound, play selection, children's theatre, and all other phases of community theatre work including business management." Several candidates were proposed, and a committee of Players selected Betty Jane Ebert.

Born in Hitchcock, OK, on April 5, '23, Ebert had moved with her family to San Bernardino, CA, two months later in a Model T Ford along a dirt road known as Route 66, emigrating to the "Golden State" a decade ahead of the dust storms that would drive so many "Okies" there. Betty loved the theatre and participated in high school productions at every opportunity, winning an outstanding actress award in her senior year. She was also an associate editor of San Bernardino High School's weekly newspaper and graduated in '40.

After receiving her associate's degree from San Fernando Valley Community College, she entered the University of California at Los Angeles as an English literature major, graduating in June of '44. While there, she participated in the theatre department's productions, and for her senior project directed playwright Susan Glaspell's '30-'31 Pulitzer Prize drama, *Alison's House*.

Betty then went to work at Hollywood's unique 160-seat Turnabout Theatre, owned and operated by the Yale Puppeteers. Shows were staged at both ends of its auditorium: first a puppet show, and after the trolley seats were reversed, a musical revue. Audience members consisted of such luminaries as Albert Einstein, Greer Garson, Rudy Vallee, Shirley Temple, Ingrid Bergman, Marlene Dietrich and Frank Sinatra.

In February '46, Turnabout received national publicity in *Collier's* magazine, which featured a picture of Ebert running the light board. She also functioned as a performer in revues that starred Elsa Lanchester (Mrs. Charles Laughton, remembered for the title role in *The Bride of Frankenstein*.)

Ralph Freud, who headed UCLA's theatre department, passed along the information about the Kalamazoo Civic's apprenticeship, which paid $900 for nine months. Betty applied. Since the position was clearly advertised as providing opportunity in *community theatre,* "as distinguished from commercial, educational, art, little theatre and other types of stage enterprise," it perfectly matched Betty's objective of learning about the operation of such a theatre, rather than being merely a stopgap job on the way to B'way.

Interviewed by a *Gazette* reporter, she declared she found Kalamazoo's "interest in theatre refreshing and very genuine compared to some of the Hollywood fringe activities." She went on to say, "Community theatre is one of the theatre's most progressive branches and performs a real service. Theatre is for everyone. But everyone can't go to NY to see a show. And theatre is something for everyone to be in — not just to see."

*****

It was during that snowy December night when Lt. Jack Ragotzy returned to the Civic that the future director/producer and Betty Ebert met. She was very pretty, and dating at the time, but then the man took a job at Charleston's Dock Street Theatre. "And the moment he was out of town, I asked for a date," Jack chuckled.

Everyone at the theatre was aware of the budding romance. Although Jack did not know it at the time — "Betty would not have told me" — she received an anonymous letter warning her "not to get involved with Ragotzy, who is just a clerk at Montgomery Ward."

First meeting of Village Players at the Ragotzys' tiny apartment, May, 1946. (L to R) Joe Stockdale, Jack Ragotzy (in back), Margaret Ann Curran and Betty Ebert

Since Betty's mother worked for Montgomery Ward in San Bernardino as head of the catalogue order department, this was an unfortunate choice of deterrent. Jack said they found out later that Ruth Chenery, his high school mentor's wife, wrote the letter. "And she was probably more right than wrong in her assessment," Jack admitted. "I was no angel."

But more damaging words of his "bad character" came from a staff member at the Civic, who called Betty into his office "and advised her not to get involved with me, since I was hardly from the right side of the tracks and had stolen money at the theatre."

Jack, who had been cast in the leading male role in *Kind Lady*, was at the theatre daily and could not help but feel the hostility. But at age 24, with his background in survival, such resistance only spurred him on. It was not long before he proposed.

Jack Peyton Ragotzy and Betty Jane Ebert were married in a civil ceremony on February 5, '46, by a justice of the peace, less than a month after they met.

*****

Betty Ebert — 1946

During her apprenticeship at the Civic, Betty was given program credit for sound, lights, construction, painting, properties, stage managing and acting. She also produced and directed her own version of *The Ghost of Benjamin Sweet*. But since Betty had acted in only one production, that spring she began talking about going East to summer stock to gain some acting experience. Jack, who had started his degree at Kalamazoo College, was still thinking of combining theatre with the more secure profession of teaching. "K" did not offer summer courses, so Jack decided to go to summer school at Western Michigan College of Education (now Western Michigan University) because the transferred credits would shorten the time it would take to get his degree. Funds were low. Having spent $600 of their $900 bank account on a car, he needed the monthly income provided to veterans going to school on the GI Bill. "It was then that I dreamed up the idea of forming a summer stock company to keep Betty in town and me in college." It was a pretty gutsy plan for a couple of kids in their early 20s.

Deciding who might be a part of the company was not difficult. Betty knew some excellent technicians who were not on the Civic staff and who wanted to be more actively involved in theatre. Since Jack had worked two shows that winter, both were aware of young would-be actors who were generally cast only in small roles because the Civic's backlog of experienced players of all ages, not unexpectedly, got the best roles.

Jack and Betty called a meeting of talented young hopefuls, including myself and my future wife, Robin Fastenrath, along with ten others — Robert Baker, Grant Baxter, Frank Bradley, Jr., Evelyn Buerger, Art Crain, Margaret Ann Curran, Lance Ferraro, Robert Finley, Marjorie Taintor and Freda B. Winters. We incorporated into a partnership known as The Village Players.

1946 – 1955

Jack discovered a former Methodist church that had been turned into a community hall in the village of Richland, about ten miles northeast of Kalamazoo. The building, with its high ceilings, nave and lobby, was perfect for conversion into a theatre. The village was willing to rent

Jack P. Ragotzy — 1946

it for $30 a week. It had bathrooms, which were kept clean and furnished with paper towels, and there was even a complete kitchen. In short, it was a functioning building, but not yet a theatre. Much remained to be done.

In those days, highly motivated veterans going to school on the GI Bill were often given permission to exceed the normal 15 credit-hour semester. Even though Ragotzy was finishing a grueling 20 credit-hour first semester at Kalamazoo College and Betty was completing her apprenticeship at the Civic, they succeeded in selecting a season of five plays. Under the leadership of Ragotzy and technical director Art Crain, the Players began to gather lumber needed to build the stage.

Obviously, buying lumber was not an option. But street-savvy Jack found a supply from an old warehouse that was being torn down, and the Players, armed with hammers and crowbars, went to work ripping the planks from the building's floor. Some straightened nails for re-use and did other odd jobs under Betty's watchful eyes. Known for her frugality and insistence that every-

one be kept busy, Betty did not believe in either waste or idle hands.

They hauled the lumber to Richland and constructed the stage of 3-foot high, 4 by 4-foot parallels, covered with 3/4 inch plywood lids. These platforms were fastened together to form a stage 20-feet wide and 16-feet deep.

If young people were making a theatre today, they would probably choose the easier configurations of 3/4 round, thrust, or in-the-round. But 50 years ago, theatre, with all that word implied, was dependent on a proscenium arch, in front of which was the audience and behind which were hidden all the mechanisms necessary for the creation of magic. *Magic was created when the man in the spangled pants danced his way down Burdick Street in front of the band. Magic was when the house lights dimmed and the curtain opened.*

Art Crain, a first-rate scene painter, created the proscenium arch. Suspended from free-standing 12-foot high, right and left proscenium "walls," he built a beautiful contoured arch over the stage. Looking like solid wood, in reality it was built from two pieces of cardboard fastened in the middle. It was designed to hide the backstage fly space in order that painted drops — which had to be "tripped," that is, folded rather than hung flat — could be flown out of sight of the audience. This method of changing scenery would quickly prove invaluable in the production of shows with more than one set.

A main curtain was needed, but the Players could not afford to buy material. Betty re-

Indispensable technicians: Paxton Stratton, Art Crain and Grant Baxter — 1946

(L to R) Peggy Stroud, Lloyd Kaechele, Robert Cass (on ladder), Jack Ragotzy, Lance Ferraro, Loy Norrix and Robin Fastenrath get the community hall ready.

membered that the small stage upstairs at the Civic had two curtains, one black, one gold, and she managed to persuade the Civic's powers-that-be to loan them to the fledgling theatre group. In Richland, unbeknownst to the Civic's management, the curtains were taken apart and put back together as alternate gold and black panels to form the main curtain.

The lighting system was designed by Grant Baxter and Paxton Stratton, who made strip, foot and border lights ingeniously from various-sized tin cans. Spot lights, lekos, and fresnels (theatrical lighting instruments) were "borrowed" from the "K" College Theatre and used for area lighting. Sixteen such instruments — either hung from an iron pipe suspended from the auditorium's ceiling or attached to freestanding iron pipes (light trees) — were used to cover four downstage and four upstage areas of the stage. The lighting control board was jerryrigged. That God was on the side of The Village Players is attested to by the fact that the old church did not burn to the ground that first summer.

Once the stage, proscenium arch, front curtain, tormentors, teasers (curtains used to mask backstage areas) and lights were in place, it was only a matter of setting up folding chairs in the auditorium and putting up the sign on the marquee and The Village Players were ready for business.

Program credit for directing the first show, Brandon Thomas' 1890s farce, **Charley's Aunt**, was given to Betty. Forty-eight years later she recalled: "I'll never forget it. I didn't know how to write down blocking and business in the script. I was an English literature major! Besides, I don't have a visual memory. I simply didn't know what

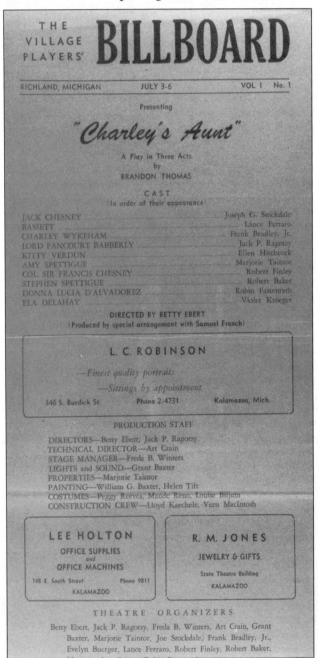

Joe Stockdale — 1946

I'd told the actors to do the day before. To this day I can feel the panic. But somehow we managed to get through."

> **1946 The Village Players, Richland**
> Charley's Aunt
> The Bishop Misbehaves
> Pure as the Driven Snow
> *Morning's at Seven
> Goodbye Again

The reason that Jack, who did have directing experience, did not take over was that he was playing the leading role. So "getting through" involved calling in Howard Chenery, whose directing style included acting out the roles himself for the actors to imitate. I was playing the role of Chesney, and after repeating a particular scene several times, I exploded. "I can't imitate you. I have a different body and voice — a different mind." Chenery quickly backed off. Regardless of the difficulties involved, including several of the actors taking college classes at 7:40 a.m., the curtain opened on July 3, '46.

Jack played the lead, Lord Fancourt Babberly, who gets most of the laughs. The one who gives the exposition — the "feeder" for the laughs, the straight man and engine for the production's pacing, with almost 400 lines — is Jack Chesney. "Luckily," Ragotzy remarked later, "Joe Stockdale and I knew what to do and the show played well."

Charley's Aunt, a remarkably apt choice for the opener, tells the story of two Oxford undergraduates who invite their sweethearts to their rooms in order to propose marriage. Their plan is thwarted when news comes that Charley's aunt, Donna Lucia D' Alvadorez from Brazil, "where the nuts come from," who was to chaperon the couples (remember, the show is set in Victorian England) is detained. The girls arrive, but leave when they discover the aunt is not yet present. Fancourt, who happens to be playing the female role in a production at the Oxford Dramatic Society, drops in on the boys to ask advice about his costume. The girls return, and the boys force Fan-

Jack P. Ragotzy as Lord Fancourt Babberly, dressed in Queen Victoria lookalike basic black. **Charley's Aunt** — 1946 (Photo by Lance Farraro)

court into taking the real aunt's place. The resulting antics, which include two proposals of marriage to the surrogate aunt, prior to the real one showing up, proves to be one of the most popular farces ever written. Unfortunately, it is rarely produced today because so few know how to read and *visualize* farce, let alone act it.

Because of the limited space backstage, the set had to be butted up against the back wall, leaving no room for crossover behind it. In the scene where Lord Fancourt, dressed in Queen Victoria lookalike basic black, is being pursued by the girl's ward, Mr. Spettigue, the action requires several fast exits and entrances. To facilitate these, Ragotzy had to exit stage left, run around the building, climb up a step ladder and go through a window prior to making his breathless re-entrance, stage right. Fortunately, he never met the Richland constable while executing this maneuver in full Victorian drag.

*****

Paul Osborn, author of **Morning's at Seven**, was from Kalamazoo and his play contained real-life family prototypes. Rights to produce it were accordingly restricted for a radius of 75 miles. But it was a play Ragotzy loved, and he managed to persuade the leasing agency to let The Village Players do it by being vaguely inaccurate about the village of Richland's proximity to Kalamazoo.

Morning's — a character-driven play that concerns the lives of four sisters in a small town — has several Chekhovian (it might have been called *Four Sisters*) subplots and all the theatrical

(L to R) Don Griffith as the hero tied to RR tracks, Margaret Ann Curran as villainess and Joe Stockdale as the villain in **Dirty Work at the Crossroads** — 1947.

elements that appealed to Ragotzy. First and foremost, as the highly successful '80 all-star B'way revival revealed, it has humor in abundance. But in addition, the characters are deeply etched, and the story of their relationship and misunderstandings is poignant. As the *Gazette* write-up correctly pointed out, "As directed by Ragotzy, the production sustains a restrained mood, but one in which underlying pathos is never allowed to mar the prevailing comic vein."

The setting, designed by Ragotzy and Art Crain and lit by Paxton Stratton and Grant Baxter, included the back porches and yards of two of the sisters' homes. In such limited space, it proved to be a major accomplishment.

Betty is credited with directing the third production, **Pure as the Driven Snow or A Working Girl's Secret**, a "mellerdrama" that satirizes the melodramatic style of production. She had a good grasp of this style, which she had demonstrated in acting a minor role in the Civic's production of *She Stoops to Conquer* and from her revue experience with Elsa Lanchester at Turnabout.

Goodbye Again was Betty's last attempt at directing. Since Jack again had a rather large role in the production and was unable to take over the directing, the program rightly gives the following credit: "Directed by Betty Ebert and Jack P. Ragotzy, who give a very special note of thanks to Howard Chenery."

The Village Players started with $350 supplied by the 14 partners who kicked in $25 apiece. Ticket prices were 75 cents for Wednesday and Thursdays and 90 cents Fridays and Saturdays, and there was a 20 percent federal entertainment tax. The season ended with a total attendance of 2,359, the lowest night being 56 and the highest 222. All bills were paid, and at the end of the season each partner not only received back his $25 investment, but made $8.40 profit.

*****

Don Griffith as Curley, Betty Ebert as Laurey and Delphine Stratton as Aunt Eller in **Green Grow the Lilacs** — 1947

With the summer season over, Betty got a job as secretary in the public schools and Jack was again a student at "K." They moved to veterans' housing on campus, and in spite of taking an overload of credit hours, Jack directed **Morning's at Seven** at Dowagiac, worked as a paper tester at one of the paper mills and as an anouncer at radio station WGFG.

1947
Kiss and Tell
Dirty Work at the Crossroads
Laburnum Grove
*Green Grow the Lilacs
Boy Meets Girl

For their second season, seven of the original members (Baxter, Curran, Crain, Ebert, Fastenrath, Ragotzy and Stockdale) returned. In addition, eight new partners—Robert Bonfoey, Donald Clark, Sue DeLano, Richard Gregg, Donald Griffith, Donald Keil, Delphine Stratton and Richard Snyder—each chipped in $25 to start the season. The ex-GIs again went to both six-week summer school sessions and 7:40 a.m. classes.

The best of the '47 season was Lynn Riggs' folk play, **Green Grow the Lilacs,** which Jack advertised as "the play on which the musical *Oklahoma!* is based." The cast of 20 and the scenic requirements — a combination interior-exterior set for the home as well as insets for the smoke house and Old Man Peck's place — strained the Players' meager resources; but critic George Dolliver of *The Enquirer* called the set "a work of art." He went on to proclaim that the Players "reached new heights." Of the play he commented, "The old Indian Territory folk-songs, with their combined simplicity, robustness and at times droll sadness, are introduced freely and appealingly." He concluded by saying, "There is more substance to **Green Grow the Lilacs** than there is to the musical version."

Under Ragotzy's direction, Betty Ebert in the role of Laurey gave her best performance to date. Dolliver asserted, "She does a beautiful job. She has the attractiveness, the sweetness, and naivety and the all-round histrionic capabilities that the role calls for, and her performance is a delight."

The critic for the *Gazette* was equally laudatory, saying that the production was "completely enjoyable" and that Betty Ebert showed "a professional ability in the handling of a challenging and complicated role."

Robin (Fastenrath) Stockdale — 1948

The second season ended with a total attendance of 4,035 — nearly doubling that of the first year. The lowest night's attendance was 99 and the highest 307, which filled the theatre's auditorium to the breaking point. Ticket prices were upped to 90 cents for Wednesdays and Thursdays and $1 for Fridays and Saturdays. Total seasonal income, including advertising, was $4,497.60. Cost of the five shows was $2,370.23. After paying back the partners their $25, the net profit was $1,752.37 — less salaries of $450 to Ragotzy, $300 to Betty Ebert, $300 to technical director Art Crain and $150 to me as secretary/assistant. The total profit of $552.37, minus $1.87 to cover writing the final checks split among 15 partners, was $36.70, or $3.05 a week.

Putting a positive spin on it, the investors made almost five times as much as those of the first season.

*****

Jack graduated from prestigious Kalamazoo College in the spring of '48 after only two and a half years. Early graduation was possible because, in addition to having been granted ten credits in science for his radar work in the Air Force, he went to summer school at Western and took overloads at "K." And not to take away from his intelligence but to acknowledge a debt, he was helped by Betty — just as so many veterans, me included, were helped by their wives. Betty not only helped support Jack financially, but having received her degree in English literature, helped him with his.

Jack's senior photograph in *The Boiling Pot*, "K" College's yearbook, reveals a handsome young man with a confident and determined look. The accompanying credits list him as a member of the College Players, the French Club and a participant in the Michigan State Interpretive Contest. He is pictured with *Le Cercle Francais*, in two pictures from the commencement play (Maxwell Anderson's *The Star Wagon*) in which he played the lead, and is pictured as one of ten students elected by the faculty to represent "K" in *Who's Who Among Students in American Universities and Colleges* — "students chosen for their leadership, character, scholarship and potential value without doubt, the highest of all Honor's Day tributes."

In their third season at Richland, Jack decided there would be only eight partners: Baxter, Curran, Crain, Ebert, Handley, Ragotzy and Paxton Stratton along with new partner, Loy Norrix. Each put up $50. Robin and I were not partners that year because we were asked to open the newly organized Saugatuck Summer Theatre (later called The Red Barn — still in existence), playing the leads in *Angel Street*. We then played two shows for Ragotzy, **Love Rides the Rails** and **Petticoat Fever**, before taking a belated honeymoon to the West Coast.

The show of the season was **Ah, Wilder-

(L to R) Robin (Fastenrath) Stockdale, Walter Wagner, Jack Ragotzy, Harry Travis and Joe Stockdale in **Boy Meets Girl** — 1948

In 1951, Jack started the practice of giving a pre-show curtain speech to praise the current production and generate excitement for the next. He still does it.

ness!**, Eugene O'Neill's only comedy. Taking place in New London, Connecticut, in '06, it required period costumes, one exterior and two interior sets, and a cast of 15. The story concerns budding anarchist Richard, an O'Neill prototype, played by Ragotzy. Critic Jack Bell of the *Gazette* wrote of Howard Chenery, who played Nat, "He literally 'wraps it up' in a performance that is a distinct pleasure to behold." He went on to say, "Delphine Stratton keeps close pace as the mother. In the play's nominal lead, Jack P. Ragotzy gives a nicely restrained portrayal as the son." Dolliver of *The Enquirer* added: "The star performance is given by Howard Chenery. His delineation of Nat Miller is worth going miles to see. Delphine Stratton does an excellent job. Jack Ragotzy is well cast as the moody young Richard." In addition to acting that season, Ragotzy directed all five shows with a big assist on **Ah, Wilderness!** from Howard Chenery.

1948
See My Lawyer
Love Rides the Rails
Petticoat Fever
*Ah, Wilderness!
The Male Animal

By now Jack began to realize that if he combined his passion for theatre with teaching at a university, he would need an advanced degree. So as soon as the season was over, he and Betty moved to Los Angeles, where he had been admitted to UCLA as the first master's degree candidate in the Theatre Department headed by Kenneth Macgowan. Once ensconced, Jack pursued his degree with the same kind of fervor he had pursued his studies at "K." What drove him was the anticipation that he would be returning to Richland for the summer. As spring rolled around, he and Betty began planning the season's schedule.

In answer to their renewing-the-lease letter came a reply saying that the old church turned community hall in Richland would probably not be for rent that summer. Jack was stunned. Since he was on spring break, he took off across country. "I never drove so fast so far," he said. "And the roads were not all that good — not four lanes like today. When I arrived, I went out to the farm of the village official in charge of renting. He was plowing for spring planting, and I followed his furrows most of the afternoon explaining how much we needed the hall. This guy was about as talkative as Percy Kilbride's 'Pa Kettle,' but by the end of the day, I felt he was on our side.

"I got back to California, and two weeks later got a postcard. I still have it. It's framed and hangs in my office. It reads: 'Dear Mr. Ragotzy' and in the center of the card was printed, 'No.'

"There wasn't a hell of a lot to do about it. I finished the second semester with 30 credits, including six for my written thesis, which was an original play, and passed my written and oral exams. The only thing I hadn't done was pass my French exam.

"Betty and I thought a lot about what we were going to do and finally decided to come back to Kalamazoo and look for another building. We had too much of a good thing going after three summers of hard work, and so we drove back and went on a shopping tour to find a barn. It was about the time that barn theatres were springing up all over the country, giving rise to what was dubbed 'the straw hat circuit.'

"We searched and searched, but most of the ones that were vacant were falling down, full of hay or reeked of cow manure. We'd about decided to give up but made one last trip to the Upjohn Farm. When the guy said he didn't have anything, we figured our dream of having a theatre was over. We walked away, got in the car, started down the driveway, and then heard the guy calling. He ran up to us and said he just remembered there was a barn near Augusta that had been built by a guy named Cook.

"We went immediately to Augusta.

"The barn had been built for dairy cattle but had never been used for that purpose. A few horses had been stabled in it and there was about a foot of hay on the floor. The doors were hanging off their tracks. But it was just five years old and had been left unfinished and unpainted. The water supply was from a single faucet. There was no indoor plumbing, but it was 40-feet wide and 90-feet long, with concrete walls. It was beautifully constructed with curved, laminated timbers and a hayloft designed to hold 90 tons! We knew it was perfect!"

At a cost of $300, Jack and Betty incorporated, thus assuming sole financial responsibility. Jack explained later: "We tried to get everyone who was a partner the year before to incorporate with us, but no one wanted to. They all continued to work at the theatre, and Art, Grant, and Paxton continued to share as partners. But everyone seemed afraid of incorporation. Our lawyer insisted that someone assume legal responsibility since we had a barn in the middle of nowhere with limited fire department protection. We took the full responsibility by default. And that's the way it has remained."

The barn was discovered on July 5, about the time the season usually opened, but it bore no resemblance to a functioning theatre. Jack and Betty immediately SOSed various UCLA actors and technicians, telling them the theatre was going to open and to come as soon as possible.

The stage manager came up from her home in Indiana; an actor hitchhiked and hoboed his way from Oregon, where he was with the Ashland Shakespeare Festival. Three others from LA piled into an old Buick that blew its engine somewhere in Arizona. These five, along with Drew Handley, who was in his second year as technical director, two actors from the previous season and Jack himself, made a total of nine from UCLA's theatre department — along with one alumna, Betty.

Jack immediately announced a six-show, one-a-week, summer season — a big change from the four performances of five shows presented every other week, which had been their schedule for the three previous years. He also upped the number of performances by one, which meant the Players would open on Tuesdays, strike the set on Saturdays after their final performance and spend Saturday night and Sunday morning setting up the next show. Sunday evening they would do a technical run-through, while also setting lights and sound. Mondays would be devoted to finishing the set(s). In the evening there would be a dress rehearsal, which usually lasted until well after midnight. After a few hours' sleep, they would complete the set, costumes, lights and sound on Tuesday morning, have the final dress rehearsal that afternoon, and open that evening — barely minutes before the patrons started arriving. The next day, they would block the first act of the following week's show and play an evening performance of the current offering. This was the old-time, summer stock schedule, in which only the fittest survived.

Getting the shows ready was difficult enough, but there was also the awesome job of turning the barn into a theatre. Fortunately, Jack and Betty, as well as Art Crain, Paxton Stratton and Grant Baxter, had been through it before at Richland. Moreover, Drew Handley, the company's leading man, was also a first-rate technical director. Work started. The floor at one end of the barn was ripped up and a stage erected; proscenium walls and an arch built; drapes hung to mask the backstage; a fly loft with a pulley system built to fly scenery; and a main curtain strung.

Jack remembered some old plate dimmers he had seen when he was directing at Dowagiac. "The dimmers and control panel were in the back of a restaurant, and the manager said we could have them if we could get the damn things out. From this basic equipment, Art built the light board and Grant wired it."

Steps up the hill to the theatre's entrance were dug, posters printed, ads placed in the various newspapers announcing the season, parking lot lights installed, the surrounding acres mowed and the hay hauled away. A road sign was built and "The Village Players" painted on the steeply-

Pax Stratton and Grant Baxter checking the dimmers and control panel on the light board donated by a restaurant manager in Dowagiac (Photo by Lance Farraro)

Putting up the Village Players' marquee at Barn's entrance — 1949 (Photo by Lance Farraro)

Present-day apprentices who gripe about lawn detail should know that back in '49, actors weren't riding a gas-propelled mower!

raked roof of the barn. Folding chairs were obtained. And while all these things were happening, rehearsals progressed under Ragotzy's direction amid the sound of construction at the other end of the barn.

Theatre buffs and stalwarts from Kalamazoo, Battle Creek and Augusta, sensing high-level energy in the vicinity, pitched in and helped. The Loy Norrix family brought food — huge pots of chili to feed the hungry workers.

Just five days before the opening, a rehearsal break was called so that all hands could help move the new light board. During the process, Jack slipped and fell. As soon as it happened, he knew he had injured himself badly, but he said nothing and resumed rehearsals in the heat of the day. It was not until the next morning, when he arrived with his arm in a plaster cast, that the company knew he had broken the bones in his hand. But nothing was going to keep his theatre from opening. On July 19, a large crowd assembled for the 8:30 curtain of **Room Service** and the Barn Theatre officially opened.

As if opening a new theatre were not enough, Jack scheduled two world premieres. The first, **Verily I Do** by Gladys Charles and George Savage (a UCLA professor), was reportedly being considered for B'way by actor/producer Eddie Dowling. It was a comedy of the hill country with music. Jack, remembering the success of **Green Grow the Lilacs** and the recent B'way

1949
AUGUSTA
Barn Theatre, Inc.
Room Service
Night Must Fall
Pure as the Driven Snow
The Milky Way
*Verily I Do
*Country Mile

Drew Handley and Betty Ebert in **Pure as the Driven Snow** — 1949

production of *Dark of the Moon,* obtained a special pre-B'way release. If the show were to hit the "Main Stem," he knew his Barn Theatre would receive considerable recognition.

The *Gazette* noted that more than 200 — the largest opening-night audience of the season — viewed the first performance. The critics lauded the Players' "keen sense of fitness" for not making a burlesque of mountaineer characters and said that Betty Ebert, who was "literally shoved" into a character role at the last moment, "submerged her beauty in gray make-up" and spoke her lines "clearly and convincingly."

Now, if **Verily** could be optioned for B'way, Jack thought, why not a play by Ragotzy? After all, his master's thesis had received a lab production at UCLA as part of the requirements for his degree. Theatre Chair Kenneth Macgowan was a man who had long encouraged the creative thesis (including the writing of plays), as opposed to traditional scholarly research. "I was his favorite child," Jack explained, "because even though I didn't take his playwriting class, I was the only one to write a play."

Actually, the writing of the play came about by accident.

Jack's first choice for a creative thesis was to direct *Balloon* by Irish playwright-poet, Padraic Colum, in the large theatre on UCLA's campus. *Balloon* had a cast of 47, seven settings, and its original production at Ogunquit, Maine, included mobiles by American sculptor Alexander Calder. However, this derring-do project never got off the ground. "I had converted a World War II barracks on campus into a 75-seat theatre, and it became so popular the faculty decided that's where all the thesis productions would be done," Jack continued. "But the height of the proscenium was only

Dressing rooms were primitive in '49. Actors usually made up backstage near the light board.
(Drew Handley standing and Ollie S. McQueen seated) (Photo by Lance Farraro)

eight feet. Obviously I couldn't do *Balloon,* so I spent six days during the Christmas holidays writing **Country Mile.** I'd heard that William Saroyan wrote *The Time of Your Life* in seven, and I wanted to beat his record!"

Eight months later, the play was to get a full production with Ragotzy directing, playing a role, and taking his French exam (*in absentia*) in order to receive his master of arts degree. He began to wonder if his ticket to B'way would be as a writer.

Country Mile opened on August 23 as the last production of the Barn's first season. Its setting is a drab tourist cabin near Scottsbluff, Nebraska. Six hard-working magazine salesmen and their slave-driving boss are the play's key figures.

Dolliver of *The Enquirer*, noting that premieres were rare in the Kalamazoo/Battle Creek area, proclaimed that **Country Mile** "was as sordid as *A Streetcar Named Desire*, but is an intriguing drama dealing with a segment of American life — door-to-door magazine salesmen — that has seldom, if ever, been portrayed on the stage. It is a coarse story, with dialogue that reeks with profanity and suggestive words. But Ragotzy has concocted a strong document. Whether it will ever reach B'way is problematical. Before it does, it will have to undergo cutting, polishing and some reinforcing."

The opening, he continued, "was charac-

Betty in the field studying her lines for the next show.

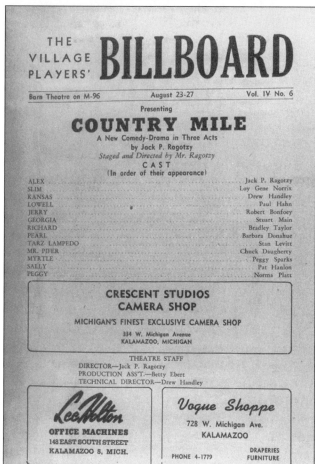

(L to R) Jack, Stuart Main, Loy Norrix and Drew Handley in **Country Mile** — 1949

terized by unusual first night attendance and the crowd seemed to like the show immensely, guffawing at the torrid language and finding the beer-drinking scenes funnier than they seemed to this writer.

"Despite its sordidness," he concluded, "**Country Mile** is well written and in no way smacks of amateurism, in authorship or interpretation. Why a modern world takes to this type of drama is a mystery, but Mr. Ragotzy seems to have sensed that it does. People who are not too greatly upset by foul language and coarse behavior on the stage will find **Country Mile** interesting dramatic fodder."

It is worth noting that the Barn's first season in Augusta ended with a total attendance of 7,444 and **Country Mile** played to 1,700 — the largest attendance of the season.

Willy Sutton claimed he robbed banks because that's where the money was. Similarly, after the season, Jack and Betty headed for NYC because that was where the theatre was. At the same time he would attend NY University on the GI Bill of Rights and work on a doctorate. Why not? He was on an educational roll. They got an apartment on West 74th Street, and it was from there that Betty wrote me in the early winter of '49: "Jack is now almost a semester gone on his Ph.D. and has passed his preliminary examinations. I'm working for a man and wife in their joint office near the Museum of Modern Art. He's in the fashion promotion business and she's a producer. We have an apartment — two rooms with 'shared' bath — and our black Cocker Spaniel, Little Jo, is the only one who really seems to like 'living' in NY. But it's wonderful to see all the shows. By the way, yesterday we turned down a chance to buy the set for *The Father* (designed by Donald Oenslager) for $100. Transportation would be just too costly. Whoops — the boss just came in!"

In the spring of '50, when I was teaching my first semester at Purdue University, Jack wrote: "We've decided to become a professional stock company and the letters have been pouring in. I've spent all of yesterday and today writing answers most of which were 'no.'" He went on to say that he would "hire twelve people, each of whom will receive salaries ranging from $10 to $25 a week, the latter going to those persons whose skill and faith to the organization have been proven. Naturally you fall into that category. Drew Handley, Betty and I, form the governing nucleus. Drew in the technical and production end, and you know what Betty and I do — almost anything and everything. Ours has become more than a seasonal job — one that, like a ghost, haunts us twenty-four hours a day all year long." His letter ends: "If your answer is in the affirmative, I shall forward a contract — nothing formal, but something which, when operating in our present incorporated state, we must observe."

For the season of '50, ten shows were scheduled, the first opening June 26 and the last closing on September 2. Instead of playing five nights a week, Jack decided to open on Monday evenings, giving each show a six-performance

The Barn — circa early '50s

The Barn's interior — circa early '50s — where the sound of construction could be heard during rehearsals
(Photo by Lance Farraro)

run. He directed all ten shows.

The opening production was Robert McEnroe's **The Silver Whistle,** for which Jack obtained the first stock rights. Most of the characters are elderly and confined in a home for the aged. For a producer to choose this play for a company of young actors would seem foolhardy today. But '50 was still a time of Stein's stick greasepaint, when young actors were trained in stage makeup. Jack himself was taught the art of makeup by director Sidney Spayde of the Civic and spent an hour and a half before every performance of *In Time to Come,* turning himself into elder statesman David Lloyd George. Playing what you were *not* was considered an actor's job in those days.

Jack makes up for a bald role.

1950
*The Silver Whistle
Three's a Family
Apple of His Eye
See How They Run
The Curse of an Aching Heart
But Not Goodbye
Of Mice and Men
Hooray for the Madam
Harvey

So it is no wonder that the *Gazette* review was headlined: "'**Silver Whistle**' Marked by Some Superb Acting." The critic went on to say that, although the play "may have been short of outstanding, the work turned in by Director Ragotzy's cast made the text secondary."

For the second season at Augusta, Jack decided he had to make some structural changes in the Barn to aid sight lines. During the opening season, folding chairs had been placed on the flat floor. Prior to opening the second season, Rows A through J were raised 16 inches, and from row J, the floor was raked so that the back row of the

Young actors made up as oldsters in **The Silver Whistle** — 1950

41

Carol Ann Stover and Howard Chenery (both seated) with Richard Thrall and Ann Butterfield (both standing) in **Apple of His Eye** — 1950

William Miles and Drew Handley in **Of Mice and Men** — 1950

house was three feet higher than the floor at the front of the auditorium. Attendance for the ten productions in ten weeks reached 12,406.

In the spring of '51, Jack had completed all course work, language exams, and now needed only to write the dissertation for his doctorate. His resident company would be comprised of local actors, plus those selected from more than three hundred applicants. Among them was Milt Hamerman, who would much later become a vice president and casting director for Universal Pictures. Jack also hired Earl Clason of Kalamazoo as advertising representative for the theatre.

The most anticipated production of the season was Tennessee Williams' **A Streetcar Named Desire**, in which Betty played Blanche Dubois. Jack had fought hard for the release. It would be the first Michigan production of Williams' hit B'way play. In anticipation of large crowds, he scheduled a two-week run. Then he changed his mind and rescheduled the play for "one week only," knowing full well the advantages of getting the crowd in early, then holding the show over a second week and advertising it "by popular demand."

Bell of the *Gazette* exclaimed, "The Players have never known an opening night like it, nor is it likely that Barn Theatre patrons have viewed a more ambitiously-staged presentation by the group. Every one of the theatre's 440 seats was occupied, and 20 patrons viewed the proceedings from benches and chairs hastily moved into the auditorium, while 200 customers were turned away."

Anyone recognizable to readers in this audience? — circa early '50s

1951
Mr. Barry's Etchings
Papa Is All
Dirty Work at the Crossroads
The Voice of the Turtle
*A Streetcar Named Desire
The Curious Savage
The Show-Off
*Tobacco Road
Come Back Little Sheba
Springtime for Henry

He went on to report that the play "did not meet with unanimous favor." Calling it "earthy and profane," he claimed the production was "frequently overacted." But he noted that "hardly anyone left before the final curtain — and this despite a three hour and ten minute running time in heat so stifling the Barn could very well have been situated in the sticky-hot, New Orleans locale of the play.

"Just as the NY production was a personal triumph for Marlon Brando, so The Players' version is a walkaway for Jerome Gardino, who manages to dominate the proceedings even when he is in the background. Gardino's expertness in the role virtually makes it his play."

Of Betty's performance Bell commented,

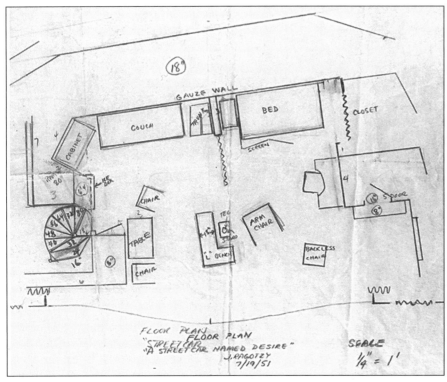

Once a show's floor plan is conceived, all blocking related to furniture, entrances/exits and offstage spaces is predetermined. Jack drew floor plans (like this one for **Streetcar**) for all his productions.

"She gives a sensitive but heavily-animated reading. All in all she does a convincing, sympathetic piece of work, although there is a need here for more vocal volume."

Dolliver of *The Enquirer* warned his readers that the Williams' play "is strong diet for summer theatre customers, but nobody can say he does not attract them." He also commented on Ebert's difficulty with vocal projection. "Her voice did not carry to the 'outskirts' of the theatre, except at rare intervals, and many of her lines were lost. Before the play ended she found the vocal focus and retained it most of the time. The best work is done by Jerome Gardino. He looks the part, acts it vehemently, and never creates an impression of over-acting."

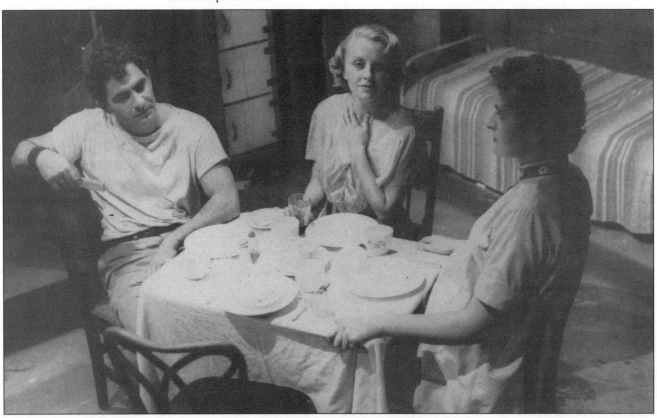

Birthday party scene in **A Streetcar Named Desire** with Jerome Gardino as Stanley, Betty Ebert as Blanche and Charlotte Shoaff as Stella — 1951

Blanche drinks to escape the sense of disaster that is closing in on her. (Photo by Lance Ferraro)

The big event of the '51 season, however, did not take place on stage. On August 16, Jack, along with eight company members, lined up at Kalamazoo's First National Bank and Trust Company to obtain certified checks covering their $100 initiation fee and biannual dues in Actors' Equity Association.

Becoming union members was a big step for each actor and a huge step for Jack and Betty as producers. Negotiations with Equity had begun in the spring a year after Jack wrote a letter to me saying they were going professional.

Up to this time, Ragotzy was the only non-Equity member of the Stock Managers Association, an organization of dramatic stock officials operating out of NY. Joining Equity would give him more clout in the Association, and the Barn would became the only Class A Equity summer stock theatre located in Michigan — the other being imported from NY for the annual Ann Arbor Drama Festival.

"Going Equity," Jack explained, "was the only way to get solid, first-rate professional performers. When we joined, the minimum weekly salary was $55 and there were no fringe benefits. The big expense was putting up 'bond' — two weeks' salary for every union member employed

Helen Burdick in **The Curious Savage** — 1951

Joining Actors' Equity are Jack (in front of Milt Hamerman), Joan Creears, Jerome Gardino, Loy Gene Norrix (behind Gardino), Charlotte Shoaff, Leon B. Stevens, Betty Ebert and Arvid Nelson — 1951

— a lot of money for us back then. But Betty and I wanted to be Equity members so we could audition in NY during our off-season. In those days, as opposed to now when there are mandatory 'open calls' for non-union actors, you couldn't get to read for a producer unless you were in the union.

"Also, by joining Equity, we could get top apprentices. Obtaining Equity membership wasn't easy in those days. The best of the college kids needed to become union to continue their careers, and they could get in by apprenticing. By the third show of their second season or first of their third, they had to be made an Equity member.

"We had some problems over the years with Equity, especially in relationship to the number of non-Equity to Equity members we could use, because they changed the rules after we joined. But those disagreements were resolved amicably. Now, of course, there are added fringe benefits – health and retirement – which really ups the ante. But on the other hand, look at the benefits. I get a pension of $900 a month from Equity. And think of the health insurance benefits received!

"Being an Equity company is also helpful in securing rights to shows because there are amateur rights and professional rights, and the latter get first dibs on new releases. In addition, once we acquired rights to a show, we could stop any other production within a 75-mile radius.

"The union demands certain professional standards, such as: the amount of time and the conditions under which actors rehearse (including rehearsal breaks), floor and bathroom requirements, cleaning of costumes, and the time between shows on matinee days. But most of the rules are sensible, and Equity will waive those that are not applicable to our situation. So all in all, we believe joining Actors' Equity Association was a wise choice." Joining Equity took place on a Friday, and on Monday the Players opened their first professional show, Erskine Caldwell's **Tobacco Road**.

Bell of the *Gazette* remarked, "Judging from a capacity-business opening night, the Players have come up with another assured box office success. Last night's presentation was a complete sell-out, a situation that generally forecasts a series of full houses for the entire run. The play has real impact and under Ragotzy's direction the cast does a generally excellent job."

Dolliver of *The Enquirer* contended that the play was "marvelously well preserved," but called it "sordid, profane and blasphemous." Nevertheless, he noted that for "all its coarseness, it has an appeal" and that, as Jeeter Lester, Milt Hamerman "does his best work of the season." He noted, with some surprise, that the setting "not only reveals the Lesters' dilapidated cabin with its worn porch and unrepaired shutters, but it has real earth — not the red clay imported from Georgia for B'way, but Michigan dirt, right off the Barn premises. The dust that plays quite a part in the play is real." He ended his review wondering, "Whether the customers can all get into the Barn in one week remains to be seen."

They couldn't.

The production became the biggest hit the Players had to date. Ragotzy immediately scheduled it for a second week, which made a 12-week season, the longest and most successful in their six-year history. Nearly 4,500 people saw **Streetcar**, but **Tobacco Road** broke that record.

Back in NY in the fall, Jack continued working on his doctoral dissertation, for which he had a 40-page outline approved by his major professor. "I was tired after the season, and was naturally thinking about plays for the next season — our first full season as a professional company which would involve advertising for apprentices. One evening when I was cussing a lot, I said, 'For two cents I'd quit this whole damn thing.' Betty put two cents on the typing table and that's all I needed. I didn't write the dissertation. I had my doubts about the NYU doctorate in drama anyway. I was tired of the academic approach — a sneer for everything on the professional stage." Now he could focus on what he had always really wanted — to become a director/producer in the NY theatre. And he could use the Barn as a tryout house. Twenty-five years later, the major regional theatres in the United States would do the same.

Louis Cutelli as the leprechaun Og and dancer Alicia Krug as Susan in **Finian's Rainbow** — 1952

1952
Twentieth Century
Rain
Season in the Sun
Burlesque
Clutterbuck
*Finian's Rainbow
The Great Big Doorstep
The Gorilla
The Rose Tattoo
The Orangutang
The Respectful Prostitute

The season of '52 saw the Barn's first musical, **Finian's Rainbow**. Bell of the *Gazette* called it the Players' "most ambitious job to date and a rousing success."

Dolliver of *The Enquirer* found the production "almost flawless" noting, "Curtain call after curtain call attested to the audience's appreciation." He had high praise for William Flatley, who not only played the title role "to perfection," but also directed. He called Alicia Krug's dancing "superb — a highspot" and her acting "ingratiating." He went on to marvel, "In her closing number when her bare heel was penetrated by a tack left on stage, she paused a moment, removed the tack and finished the number. First aid came later."

Of the scenery he commented that, in place of the expensive backdrop of tobacco fields from the B'way production, the Barn's was "impressionistic hills." He added that Mike Schacht, a recent

Michael Capanna, (Margaret) Ann Curran and Teri Robin in **The Rose Tattoo** – 1952

48

German immigrant, handled the Steinway — and indeed it was a Steinway, secured for the occasion — "beautifully. He plays the **Finian's** score so well that one forgets that on B'way there was a whole orchestra." Dolliver closed his review by advising that the production "should not be missed."

Finian's was followed by **The Rose Tattoo**, directed by Ragotzy, which was notable for the fact that young Ann Curran (the name Margaret was dropped when she went Equity) was cast in the leading role of Serafina Della Rose. "J.F.S." (actually, Frances Jane Sims) of *The Enquirer* declared: "A near capacity audience turned out for the first night. There were several curtain calls and thunderous applause for Ann Curran, who carried off the female lead with a precision and finish which would have done credit to an actress older in years (she is 23) and in stage experience. But Miss Curran was not alone on the stage. One should include Michael Capanna as Alvaro Mangiacavallo, the lover, who brings the bloom back to Serafina's cheeks, and to her chest as well. **The Rose Tattoo** will long be regarded as a highlight of the Village Players' history."

The season ended with an unusual double bill of an original one-act curtain raiser, **The Orangutang** by Tom Tiler, a University of Southern California student, followed by Jean Paul Sartre's **The Respectful Prostitute.**

Back in NY after the very successful season and no longer saddled with work on his doctorate, Jack was now free to pursue both acting and directing. On March 20, '53, he opened his first NY production for the Equity Library Theatre. The show, Dorothy and Dubose Heyward's **Mamba's Daughters**, was staged at the DeWitt Clinton Community Center in the Bronx and went on to play two weekends at the Bryant Adult Youth Center in Queens. Since the theatre was so far uptown, critics had to view the production's dress rehearsal in order that their review could appear the day after the opening.

Vernon Rice of the *NYPost* lauded the "enormous potentialities of gifted performer, Fredye Marshall," who played Hagar. He went on to say, "Miss Marshall and the others in the cast have had the good fortune to have Jack P. Ragotzy as their director."

Variety added: "Under Jack P. Ragotzy's sensitive, telling direction, the large cast is accomplished in acting and singing. Ragotzy uses these South Carolina field workers as a chorus to mirror the hopes and fears of the race and as individuals who respond to the plight of the central character, Hagar."

Perhaps one of the best, if not *the* best, critics in the country at the time was Brooks Atkinson of the *NYTimes*. In his review he credited "John [*sic*] P. Ragotzy, director of the production," for finding Fredye Marshall, who gave "a poignant performance of considerable stature."

Jack now had every reason to believe he would soon break into the big time show-biz world of NY. When he returned to Augusta for the

'53 season, the most important production was **Point of No Return** by Paul Osborn (adapted from the novel by John P. Marquand). This production was notable inasmuch as Ragotzy rewrote the B'way version and included new material, not only from the novel but from his own imagination. No doubt he was allowed to do so because he convinced those in charge of leasing the property that the B'way script would not be staged by summer stock and community theatres around the country — a major source of royalties — unless it were rewritten with simplified scenery and staging.

1953
Stalag 17
The Moon is Blue
*Point of No Return
Season in the Sun
Summer and Smoke
I Am a Camera
The Member of the Wedding
The Male Animal
The Shrike
Separate Rooms

The B'way version, which cost $125,000, a considerable amount in the early '50s, called for three interiors, an exterior and an inset. Rather than realistic scenery, Jack decided to use an *Our Town* technique in which a character paints the scenery via narration. To do so, he had to create a narrator.

Dolliver of *The Enquirer* suggested that Barn theatregoers would now realize that Ragotzy could write, as well as direct and act. "Few of those present could differentiate between his lines and those originated by the combination of Marquand and Osborn." He continued his praise by saying, "The Players give an almost perfect performance. John Dutra contributed a convincing portrayal, and Betty Ebert presents a properly repressed picture of Mrs. Gray. With scenery eliminated, the Barn's production seemed to many like a reading of the book — and a very capable reading — by artists who know the values of clear diction and proper shading of words and sentences."

In today's computer- and TV-oriented climate, getting people to read anything is extreme-

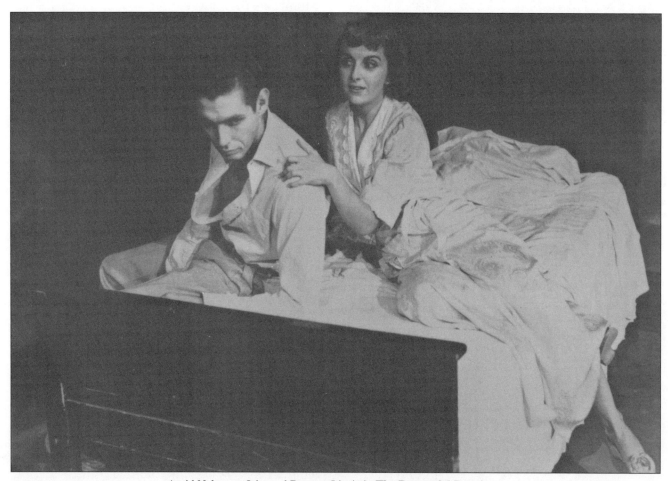

Arvid Nelson as John and Betty as Lizzie in **The Respectful Prostitute**

John Dutra and Betty Ebert in **Point of No Return** — 1953

ly difficult. Dolliver's comment reveals reading habits of an earlier time: "There is something intensely human about the novel that many a person has read two or three times."

Philip Mayer's *Gazette* review was less laudatory. His major objection was that it was impossible to condense the 559-page character study of banker Charles Gray into two and a half hours. He felt that Betty Ebert did "the best work of the evening" and ended by stating, "The Barn is certainly to be congratulated on their courageous and effective use of a 'cinematic' form of production that moved easily from scene to scene."

Jack had used a cyclorama, nine identical chairs and three tables. In NY, Arthur Miller's *The Crucible*, which was not a resounding hit, had abandoned its realistic Salem settings as a cost reduction measure toward the end of its B'way run and substituted a cyclorama. Ragotzy had simply, but cleverly, combined this idea with an *Our Town* narrator and his knowledge of the Elizabethan thrust stage (where "scenery" is created by the imagery within the lines) to move the many scenes in the Marquand work swiftly and seamlessly.

Still another Ragotzy-directed production that had strong appeal in the '53 season was Joseph Kramm's Pulitzer Prize drama, **The Shrike**. It is the story of a man who, out of despair, unsuccessfully attempts suicide and is committed to a city hospital's mental ward. His wife, the Shrike (a predatory bird that impales its victims), bitter because he has been unfaithful, is his only hope of release. But the price he must pay for freedom is to be under her domination for the rest of his life.

It was certainly not the average laugh-a-minute summer stock offering.

In the Equity company for the first time was Louis Girard, who had appeared as the Judge in Ragotzy's production of **Mamba's Daughters** in NY. Girard played the leading role in **The Shrike** "magnificently," according to Bell of the *Gazette*, who also declared that Girard's performance "stamps the actor as one of exceptional talent." Of Betty, who played the title role of the unsympathetic wife, Bell noted that she makes the character "conniving" and "coldly calculating" and, at the same time, "pathetic."

Dolliver of *The Enquirer* asserted that Girard came through with a "perfect performance" and added that the actor "seemed to be living rather than acting." After the company call, Girard "was given a solo recognition that turned into an ovation." The reviewer also noted, "Betty Ebert rises to new heights as the scheming wife."

Dolliver concluded by suggesting, "Mr. Ragotzy did the patrons of the Barn a real favor when he took the risk of presenting Joseph Kramm's drama of life behind the barred windows of a mental hospital. **The Shrike** is not what might be called entertainment, but it is drama with a punch. It sends an audience home thinking."

The '53 season was distinguished by other Ragotzy-chosen shows of real quality: Tennessee Williams' **Summer and Smoke**, John van Druten's **I Am a Camera** and Carson McCullers' **The Member of the Wedding**, none of them the usual one-a-week summer stock fare.

During the winter, Jack acted in a TV soap, *Portia Faces Life*; and although he returned early for the '54 Barn season, he had to go back to NY "to be shot to death at noon, June 11, over CBS TV." Asked to return again the following week so he could be his own corpse, he told the director, "Get an understudy!"

This was a big year for both Jack and the Barn. He had decided to add a new wing — referred to as "the Growth" — an 18- by 30-foot rehearsal space. Up to this time, rehearsals had been held in the auditorium after the folding chairs nearest the stage were removed. The new addition could also be used to provide extra space for scenery and prop storage. The Ragotzys would also acquire new and more comfortable seats from a Saginaw theatre for the down-front customers. "But the Growth and new seats would make the property worth a hell of a lot more," Jack reasoned, "so we decided we'd better buy the Barn before we improved it."

The Barn and a little over six acres of land cost Jack and Betty $16,500, major money in '54. But it was a gamble that paid off, and the mortgage was burned just six years later.

1954
Mister Roberts
*Rhom
My Three Angels
The Fourposter
*Desire Is a Season
For Love or Money
Mrs. McThing
Anna Lucasta
Petticoat Fever
The Little Hut

The '54 season boasted 13 stellar resident Equity members, 11 apprentices, and featured 19-year-old ingenue, April Kent, daughter of actress June Havoc and niece of Gypsy Rose Lee. Kent had already had summer stock experience, had been on the Steve Allen and Virginia Graham TV shows and as a child appeared on B'way in *Mexican Hayride*. In the spring of '54, she completed a stint at NY's Copacabana nightclub. Just before coming to the Barn, she was featured in color on the cover of the *NY Mirror's* Sunday magazine, which devoted an inside page to the story of her life.

James T. Pritchett, who had graduated from law school at the University of North Carolina and would eventually portray Dr. Matt Powers on NBC's *The Doctors* for 20 years — winning TV's coveted Emmy Award as outstanding actor in a daytime dramatic series — had spent the winter in stock in Erie, PA. Leon B. Stevens, William Bramley (who would create the role of Officer Krupke in *West Side Story* on B'way) and Mary Van Fleet were back, along with Dirk Wales, who was technical director/actor and had just completed his degree at UCLA. Norman Kean was an apprentice I recommended from the University of Denver,

James T. Pritchett — 1954

John Newton — 1954

where I was working on my doctorate.

Another newcomer, along with wife Dusty and infant son Robin, was John Newton. John had five seasons of summer stock under his belt, including two summers in Colorado Springs where he operated his own company, and would eventually appear in 12 B'way shows.

Ragotzy's production of **Mister Roberts** was notable, not only because it was a smash hit, but because it introduced and starred Jim Pritchett. The season was further distinguished by two world premieres, both of which B'way-minded Ragotzy had optioned for possible NY production. The first was **Rhom** by Air Force veteran Gordon Russell, who had met his co-author, Navy veteran Larry Ward, at NY's American Theatre Wing. Since both worked on B'way and in TV, it had taken a year to finish the first draft of their play, followed by two years of revisions prior to the Barn's premiere.

Bell of the *Gazette* reported, "Up to a few hours before curtain time the play was still being revised, and the cast did a commendable job with the material at hand. But **Rhom**, while it has some interesting moments, doesn't seem worth the effort." Dolliver of *The Enquirer* agreed, saying, "**Rhom** is a good play, though it is not yet ready for B'way."

The *Variety* review spoke of the full, almost 400-seat house and praised James T. Pritchett in the title role, along with William Bramley and director Ragotzy, but said the play "is a disappointment, over-long, frequently clumsily and obviously motivated." The reviewer concluded, "At this point it appears to be a questionable bet for B'way."

Undaunted, two weeks later Ragotzy produced a second world premiere, a show I had written at age 28 and which was based on my observations while performing in the outdoor drama, *Unto These Hills*, on the Cherokee Indian Reservation in North Carolina. Jack produced the play under the title **Desire Is a Season**.

Mayer of the *Gazette* gave the following

(L to R) James Pritchett, William Bramley (on ground) Betty Ebert, Ginger Russell and Norman Kean in world premiere of **Desire Is a Season** by Joe Stockdale — 1954

account: "Stockdale's frequently moving, tragic story of a Cherokee Indian family in North Carolina is more than a big play. It sprawls, moving in 'giant steps' from skillfully done propaganda about the very real problems of the Indians' racial twilight to the sheer theatrics of an onstage suicide and an over-wrought seduction scene. It's strong stuff ably written but done with more courage than discretion. Characterization is bold and pitilessly detailed. Stockdale knows playwriting and he seems to know his Indians. But I think he knows a good deal less about audiences. His play has a large dose of interesting sociology and too much 'kick 'em in the gut' melodrama. That's a large order to force feed any audience. Eugene O'Neill tried it over and over again — and failed as many times as he succeeded. When the show's at its best it recalls some of Tennessee Williams' tinted realism. But the play ran aground on the shoals of Mickey Spillane, and beached on *Tobacco Road*."

Dolliver of *The Enquirer* observed: "Old-timers who turned the police on *Sappho* because her lover carried her upstairs to her bedroom, or were shocked by *Tobacco Road*, would probably pass out completely upon contact with **Desire Is a Season**. In many years of playgoing, this writer can recall no scene as sexy as the mutual seduction of hero and heroine in Act II and no scene more morbid than the suicide in the same act. It is doubtful that even blasé B'way would accept either for public presentation.

"The Players give excellent portrayals. Betty Ebert is a reasonable facsimile to an educated Indian girl; James T. Pritchett is manly and appealing. But in a way Norman Kean, a less known member of the company, steals the show as the brother who doesn't intend to be downtrodden because of his race. He looks like an Indian, acts like an Indian, and displays a fine conception of the role.

"The main setting, depicting the dump that

Gordon Russell and Ginger Russell in **Desire Is a Season** — 1954

Jack and Betty greet Gov. G. Mennen Williams and family at the Barn for 10th anniversary season.

the Chief calls a 'trading post,' with the rear end of a bus station on one side, is beautifully designed by director Ragotzy. The first night audience was large and seemed to accept sexiness and stark realism as if accustomed to it. Applause was generous and there were several curtain calls."

The *Variety* review suggested: "There is a promise of commercial possibilities in this new play. An unusual theme and background, with which the author is obviously familiar, heighten audience interest, although there is a tightening and sharpening of some of the characterizations to be done. The story involves an educated Indian girl's love for a white man whom she met in NY, and her discouragement at her race's lot in this period between a great past and a progressively dimmer future. She calls it 'the time between the end and the beginning' (the play started under the title of *The Time Between* — the switch being made for box office draw.)

"Most of the Barn's Equity and apprentice company is used," *Variety* continued, "with Betty Ebert doing a stand-out job as the Indian girl who wants to escape her destiny but fears she is trapped. James T. Pritchett is impressive as the white lover. Norman Kean, an apprentice, is outstanding as a rebellious student at the reservation school.

"**Desire Is a Season** warrants more work by the author."

The following season, the Players' tenth, was distinguished by a visit to the Barn by Governor G. Mennen Williams and his family and the fact that Ragotzy had decided to produce another musical.

To direct **Guys and Dolls**, Jack brought in 26-year-old nightclub pianist and entertainer, actor and composer, Rinaldo Capillupo, a Phi Beta Kappa graduate from the University of Denver. Wayne Lamb, a featured dancer from B'way and TV, was hired as choreographer and principal dancer. Lamb would become a major player in the Barn's history.

Adelaide was played by jobber Carol Doughty. A native of Denver, she had been a child entertainer and after graduating from the U. of Denver, appeared with *The Denver Post* Opera Company and worked with the famed Pioneer Players at Central City. Cindy Arnold — later to become Mrs. James T.

Wayne Lamb — 1955

1955
Oh, Men! Oh, Women!
Dial "M" For Murder
*Guys and Dolls
The Caine Mutiny Court-Martial
The Remarkable Mr. Pennypacker
Gigi
Dear Charles
The Fifth Season
The Rainmaker
Tobacco Road
The Tender Trap

Jim Pritchett as Sky Masterson with cast of crap shooters that includes John Newton (on floor L of Pritchett) in **Guys and Dolls** — 1955

Harry Dorman as Dude (standing left), Ruth Clason as Pearl and Jim Pritchett as Lov (both sitting at left), Dusty Reeds as Ada Lester, John Newton as Jeeter Lester and Betty Ebert as Grandma Lester in **Tobacco Road** — 1955

Pritchett — a local performer hired to play Sarah Brown, had appeared previously at the Barn and also played leading roles at the Kalamazoo Civic Theatre.

The role of Nicely-Nicely Johnson would be played by Otto Lohmann of NY. His credits included summer circuit tours, nightclubs, TV shows, and an off-B'way production of *October in the Spring*, a play I had written as my master's thesis and which was produced by The Playmakers at the University of North Carolina, Chapel Hill. The last of the half dozen imports was 6-foot-4-inch Ray Barbata from Brooklyn, who played "Big Jule." Barbata was a pianist as well as an actor and had sung in opera and acted in summer stock.

Mayer of the *Gazette* opened his review by calling **Guys and Dolls** "bright and tuneful," "breakneck paced entertainment," and added, "the finale set off applause that topped anything heard before at the summer playhouse."

He called the performances of Cindy Arnold, John Newton, Jim Pritchett, and Carol Doughty "outstanding," and added that Jack Ragotzy was "especially good" as Benny Southstreet teamed with Otto Lohmann and Boyd Dumrose (who would later become a major NY stage and TV designer) in "Fugue for Tinhorns."

The Enquirer critic, J.F.S., said the show was "magnificent, likely the best thing the Players have done in ten seasons," and had the audience "rolling in the aisles."

Ironically, newspaper layout and headline writers also got in the act. Right below *The Enquirer* review was an article about six local guys who were arrested for shooting craps headlined: "Dice Shooters Get Fines, Jail Terms."

1956 - 1965

1956
Reclining Nude
A Girl Can Tell
Champagne Complex
Annie Get Your Gun
*The Painted Days
The Seven Year Itch
Tea and Sympathy
*Where's Charley?
A Streetcar Named Desire
Bus Stop
Anniversary Waltz

The second decade opened with a bang! **Annie Get Your Gun** was one of two musicals scheduled that season as a follow-up to the success of the two musicals presented during the first decade. When Jack and Betty returned from another winter in NY on May 1, '56, they announced the largest company in the Barn's history. The 25 apprentices were comprised of outstanding theatre students from Butler, Syracuse, UCLA, the Universities of Denver, Illinois, Kansas, Michigan, Texas and NY's American Theatre Wing.

The newspaper hype, however, was on the new Equity ingenue, Jane McArthur, described by one reporter as "a cute little trick" from Virginia. She graduated from California's Stanford, studied at NY's Neighborhood Playhouse, had made her B'way debut in *The Rehearsal,* and was also on the Main Stem in *The Young and the Beautiful.* TV credits included *Phillip Morris Playhouse, Kraft TV Theatre, Armstrong Circle Theatre* and a soap opera, *Three Steps to Heaven*. She would go on to play Emily in the critically acclaimed Circle in the Square production of *Our Town* in NY.

Levi Newton & Son Construction Company, who did much of the building the first 20 years, put up the new box office — circa mid '50s. Jack (in white sweat shirt) always worked right alongside the hired help in such projects.

Given less pre-season hype was the leading man, Jon Cypher, who would soon gain national attention.

This was also the first season for Angelo Mango, who would play Tommy in **Annie Get Your Gun** and eventually play a very important role in the future of the Barn.

Annie Get Your Gun was a big-bang hit that introduced new talent to the Barn and drew a capacity first-night crowd of more than 500. Bell of the *Gazette* called it "three hours of flashy, fine show," "skillfully blended by Rinaldo Capillupo and Wayne Lamb." He noted Dusty Reeds' "colorful costumes," Boyd Dumrose's "simple and effective stage settings," and predicted, "It can hardly miss being one of the Barn's all-time biggest hits; advance sales already indicate a hold-over run. It fully deserves such success."

Jon Cypher — 1956

Carol Doughty and Angelo Mango in
Annie Get Your Gun — 1956

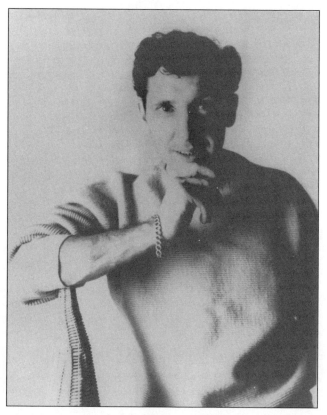

Angelo Mango — 1956

Jon Cypher as Frank Butler and Carol Doughty as Annie in **Annie Get Your Gun** — 1956

In a like manner, Dolliver of *The Enquirer* declared, "**Annie** qualifies as one of the big shows of all time for the Barn. A standing-room only opening night audience treated the entire company to thunderous applause when the final shot had been fired." He added that Carol Doughty "worked magic" in the title role; Jon Cypher was "excellent"; and predicted "a hold-over."

As indeed it was.

A second production that season merits special remembrance — the world premiere of John Byrne's **The Painted Days**. The title refers to the sightless days of a sensitive girl who sees the world and people in her imagination more beautifully than they exist in real life. When an operation restores her sight, she must face the real world.

"Magnificent!" "Splendid!" Bell of the *Gazette* called both the play and the production. "Mr. Byrne emerges as a theatre writer of considerable promise, one able to compose realistically and dramatically and, at the same time, with a delicate poetic grace. Under Ragotzy's probing thoughtful direction, the cast gives exciting, often electrifying, performances. Jane McArthur's portrayal of the central figure retains a firm grip on the onlooker's emotions in her intense, always believable, characterization."

Bell reported that after the opening night, Adna Karns, the NY producer who held a stage option on the play which had already been sold to 20th Century-Fox, indicated renewed interest in a B'way production. There was also a possibility that the author would fly out from Hollywood for one of the closing performances.

J.F.S. of *The Enquirer* called John Byrne "a fine new voice in the theatre" and claimed that he spoke "lyrically with majesty of language" and "the power to make an audience alternately laugh and weep." The audience was "ecstatic," she noted, and the final curtain brought "frenzied applause and a dozen curtain calls." However, "the applause was not for the author only. It was tribute to the players, and to what must rank as Producer-Director Ragotzy's most sensitive directing accomplishment."

She went on to report that playwright Byrne, a former radio-TV and public relations writer, was now with 20th Century-Fox where he adapted *Jane Eyre*, and that **The Painted Days** was being produced in both England and Ireland by the British subsidiary of 20th Century-Fox. She ended her review by calling the production "magnificent" and rating it "among the half-dozen best" the Village Players had done.

The *Variety* review was equally laudatory, reporting that Jane McArthur gave "an intense, touching performance" and John Newton "a solidly convincing portrayal." It ended with a prediction that the play "should stand a good chance for bigger showcasing."

Betty also scored during the season in

(L to R) Al Hinckley, Jon Cypher, Jane McArthur, Dusty Reeds and Harry Dorman in the world premiere of John Byrne's **The Painted Days** — 1956

Robert Anderson's **Tea and Sympathy**, for which Jack had acquired the first Michigan stock rights. Advertising it as "Definitely Not for Children" and capitalizing on J.F.S.'s provocative review in *The Enquirer* that opened with the H word — "the love that dare not speak its name" — the Barn held the play over a second week. In addition to the homosexual theme, the critic pointed out another theme of "guilt by association," the legacy of Senator McCarthy's Communist witch hunt that had decimated the theatrical world.

And if such laudatory reviews were not enough bang for the Barn, there were a couple more during the musical, **Where's Charley?** As J.F.S. of *The Enquirer* wrote: "The Barn Theatre has done it again! Once more it has produced an evening of hilarious, leg-slapping, roll-'em-in-the-aisle entertainment opening last night to a capacity crowd, which, after a two-minute warm-up, stamped feet, guffawed and applauded for two and one-half hours.

"Hardly enough can be said about John Newton, who, as Charley *and* his aunt, laughed, sang, danced, smirked, pranced and galloped his way even deeper into the audience's heart. As regular Barn goers learned long ago, 'Once in love with Newton, always in love with Newton,' and there seems to be no end to his versatility. His charm as he dances and sings is unbeatable."

"The applause lasted for six curtain calls," she reported and then went on to predict, "This will probably be one of the most successful of the Barn productions." She pointed out that **Charley** "is one show to which you may take your family, but beware, all the women from eight to eighty will fall in love with John Newton and want to take Angelo Mango home in their pockets."

The *Gazette* review was more of the same lovefest.

But, as if the production were not a big enough bang in itself, there was another bang during the September 2, Sunday evening performance. Although a few audience members would later claim they heard a shot, not even the following "Dragnet" scenario interrupted their enjoyment of the hilarious onstage high jinks.

*****

It was just another Sunday night at the Barn. Below in the basement, Betty Ebert was in her office doing the usual: typing up news releases while waiting to go on stage. Jack Ragotzy was in an adjoining office counting ticket stubs. Accountant Gayle Hinckley was in the box office counting money. Across the passageway, full-figured, blonde apprentice-actress Gay Kleimenhagen was in her dressing room, readying herself for an entrance. Dusty Reeds was in yet another dressing room down the passageway, the curtains over the door shielding her from direct view of the offstage drama which was about to take place.

It happened in less than five minutes and occurred just after nine o'-

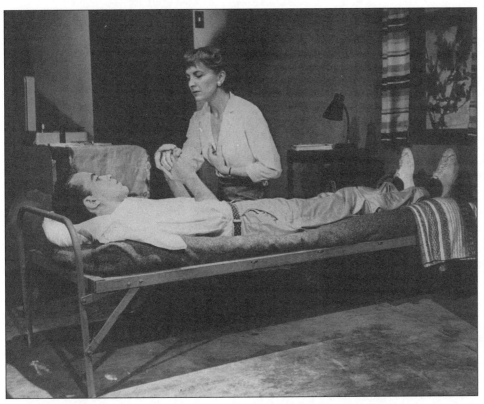
"Years from now. . .when you talk about this. . .and you will. . .be kind. (Gently she brings the boy's hands toward her open blouse, as the lights slowly dim out. . .and. . .the curtain falls.)" Betty Ebert and Harry Dorman in **Tea and Sympathy** — 1956

clock during **Charley's** noisiest number, "The New Ashmolean Marching Society and Student Conservatory Band," featuring the rowdy singing and marching of the Oxford undergraduate characters accompanied by a snare drum. Precisely at the sound that signaled the start of this big production number, two men entered the Barn's basement door facing the parking lot. They were armed — the larger one with what was thought to be a .45-caliber revolver and the smaller one, a snub-nosed pistol, possibly a .38. Both men were grotesquely masked with black silk stockings held in place by visored baseball caps. Ebert and Kleimenhagen were later to describe the shorter one's mask as having eyehole cuts and the larger man's mask as "having runs in the stocking just around the eyes."

Both men wore khaki shirts.

Thus costumed, "and operating with almost theatrical-like finesse," wrote the *Gazette* reporter, the larger of the masked men turned into Ebert's office, while the smaller made his way toward Kleimenhagen's dressing room just as she was about to don her blouse. Ebert later reported to Police Detective Charles Conn: "I heard this man say, 'Come with me and be good or you'll be killed.' Looking up, I saw this fellow standing in the doorway. I couldn't believe what I was seeing. He said it was a holdup.

"'You're kidding,' I said. He appeared to be young and I thought perhaps he was a kid with a toy gun. I grabbed for the gun. He hit me, I screamed, and the gun went off." The "glancing blow to the left side of her head" apparently triggered the gunman's pistol, the bullet whizzing past Betty's head, thudding against the cylinder of the mimeograph machine and ricocheting to the cement wall of the office before it fell to the floor. "I don't think he meant to shoot me," Betty said. "Then I heard Jack's voice and I yelled, 'There's a fool in here with a gun.'" The bandit then pushed Betty down the hallway and into the box office.

In the meantime, the smaller of the bandits had entered Kleimenhagen's dressing room. Seeing him, she yelled. He grabbed for her, ripping her blouse. Upon hearing Kleimenhagen's scream, Ragotzy went to the door of his office, only to be

Angelo Mango, John Newton and Al Hinckley in **Where's Charley?** — 1956

met by the smaller of the bandits who hissed menacingly, "Get back in the room!" Jack immediately called to the box office saying, "Give the man all the money without argument." Hinckley did not reply, for, having heard the gunshot, she was crouched under the ticket counter.

The smaller holdup man then moved into the ticket office. Standing within inches of the crouching Hinckley, he scooped up the night's receipts of $952. "Where's the rest?" he demanded gruffly. Ragotzy responded by handing over his billfold, from which the bandit extracted $30.

While all this was happening, the larger bandit ushered Ebert into the ticket office and was holding her at gunpoint against the wall while she berated him for not working for a living. Ragotzy finally told her to shut up and then politely implored the bandit "not to hurt my wife."

No longer the focus of the smaller bandit's attention, Kleimenhagen "stood unmoving for a moment" and then stole quickly down the passageway and slipped into the boys' dressing room. Seeing no one, she ducked into the girls' and found Dusty Reeds, who had witnessed part of the drama through an unseemly rent in the dressing room's curtain.

In huddled whispers, they decided that Kleimenhagen should run upstairs to the stage and tell someone the awful news. "I had to run the full length of the basement, and as I was making my break, I heard one of the gunmen yell at me. I yelled back, 'I've got to make an entrance,' and ran on." Halfway up the steep stairs, Kleimenhagen met Robert Cadman, actor, assistant technical director and a fellow student at UCLA.

Making his way stealthily toward the box office, Cadman met the two bandits as they were about to leave. The larger of the two pointed his gun at Cadman, motioning for him to enter the room adjoining the box office. After warning the show folks not to move for five minutes, the gunmen fled.

Not heeding their advice, Ragotzy looked out the box office window and saw the two enter a "red and yellow" car and drive away at great speed, but not before he jotted down the automobile's license number. The red and yellow getaway vehicle (actually it was black and yellow, which may say something about Ragotzy's color vision) was later identified as a Cadillac hardtop convertible. It belonged to the President of General Gas & Light Co., George A. Humphrey of Kalamazoo, and had been stolen about an hour and a half before the robbery from the Gull Lake Country Club.

Ragotzy's call to police headquarters was in before the escape car skidded onto the highway. A quick-witted policeman ordered half a dozen roadblocks to be thrown up at intersections leading from the Barn, which resulted in

Betty at her trusty Smith-Corona points to the mimeograph machine that took the bullet for her.

several hundred automobiles being checked by state, county and city officers after the show.

Investigating the crime were two sheriff's deputies, two state police detectives and a master sergeant of the Battle Creek unit of the National Guard. Six suspects, all "out-of-towners," were arrested and jailed because they "could not account for guns found in their cars." In addition, "patrol cars gave chase to at least three suspicious cars which were seen being operated at high speed through the city and on county roads."

Kalamazoo — a "quiet little town" — who sez?

Next day, front-page *Gazette* headlines screamed: "Armed Bandits Rob Barn Theatre," revealing either the editor's assessment of the readers' fondness for the theatre or perhaps merely reflecting the dearth of international or national news.

The loss of 952 smackers — a considerable amount in '56 dollars — was Filene bargain-basement rates for the enormous amount of copy the Barn's publicity department — Betty — generated. Quickly setting up photo-op sessions for the press the following day, she posed, sitting at her typewriter and pointing her right index finger toward the mimeograph machine from which the bullet ricocheted. Gayle Hinckley recreated her crouch under the counter with Delsartian facial expression and gesture. Ragotzy, as a Jack Webb lookalike, pointed toward where the bandit had stood in the box office's doorway, while Kleimenhagen recreated the horror felt as the masked bandit broke into her dressing room.

Indeed, as viewed from a distance of some 40-odd years and the moral low road of a former academician, I might be tempted to think that master showman Ragotzy, using a couple of apprentices, had staged the entire heist. This theory, however, is quickly dispelled when one remembers that if master publicity-hound Ragotzy had planned the incident, he would have staged it at the beginning of the season in order to reap its full effect.

Although Ragotzy theorized the gunmen must have known the physical layout of the Barn's interior and, indeed, the climax of the end of the first act of the show playing onstage, it should be reported that neither of the gunmen was ever apprehended, nor was the money ever retrieved.

Case closed.

Following **Charley** came a revival of **A Streetcar Named Desire.** This time it was Blanche, rather than Stanley, who walked away with the reviews. Again, a capacity audience was there for the opening. J.F.S. of *The Enquirer* said Betty "gave one of her best performances," commenting that the role could be ruined by overacting, but that "Miss Ebert handles it beautifully." She went on to remark that Jon Cypher as Stanley "gives the impression of Marlon Brando imitating Elvis Presley."

It was in the winter of the following year, however, that the leading man of the '56 season made a spectacular entrance into the world of national show biz. Brooklynite Jon Cypher, a graduate of the American Theatre Wing, had credits that ranged from musicals to Shakespeare. Prior to his summer season at the Barn, he had performed on the *Arthur Godfrey Show*, NBC's *Television Opera Theatre,* toured as a soloist with

Gayle Hinckley (crouching) and Ragotzy (as a Jack Webb lookalike) recreating the scene of the crime

Fred Waring's Pennsylvanians and worked in several seasons of stock.

Returning to NY after the season, he found work on TV. In late January, he auditioned for the casting director of "Cinderella," Rodgers and Hammerstein's first TV musical. A few days later, he was called back to sing for R&H. He finished, they said thank you, and he figured that was it. But as he was leaving the theatre, they ran after him and asked him back. During the next two weeks, facing fierce competition from both B'way and Hollywood, he sang five more times and eventually got the part.

Casting a virtual unknown, especially to play opposite Julie Andrews, was unusual; but after it happened, the producers considered the fact an "exploitational element." Cypher was selected, R&H told the media, "because the show calls for singing and acting of a high order and we think Cypher has it." Press agents predicted the role of Prince Charming would make him an overnight star — a lot of pressure to put on a nice guy who lived frugally in a tiny Manhattan apartment, the style of which he called "early Bowery."

Of course, it didn't quite turn out as the pundits predicted, but that's another story.

About the time Cypher was being called "stiff" and "wooden" by TV critics for his "Prince Charming," B'way-bound Ragotzy was having a second show, **Point of No Return**, produced in NY by the Equity Library Theatre both in the Bronx and Queens.

Critic Louis Funke of the *NYTimes* alleged that "under the expert direction of Jack P. Ragotzy," it was one of ELT's "most gratifying productions." He added, "The current production is on a stage that is bare except for a few chairs and tables and a cyclorama for a backdrop. The simplicity of the production is an inspiration. It allows the play full reign and the pace to be brisk."

Ragotzy was, in fact, using the same script and staging, as well as some of the actors, he had used in the summer of '53. It was a "Barn East" production, only NY didn't know it.

Funke had nothing but praise for the actors: "As Charles Gray, John Newton is giving a winning performance, superbly reflecting the earnestness, aspirations and torments of the past. Betty Ebert's portrait of the wife is simple, forthright and altogether in the right key. Louis Girard is brisk and amiable and conveys a pleasant sense of informality. Indeed, in a cast too numerous to mention, there is not a faulty piece of work."

Variety also noted the unique staging and declared, "Because Ragotzy has recruited a good company, and because his staging is consciously precise, **Return** emerges as one of ELT's better '56-'7 evenings."

Staged adulation for macho cop who will, hopefully, solve the crime. (L to R) Bob Cadman, Gayle Hinckley, Officer Charles Conn, Jack and Betty Ragotzy, Gay Kleimenhagen and Dusty Reeds

Louis Girard, Diane Ladd and John Newton (as a lookalike Tom Ewell) in **Will Success Spoil Rock Hunter?** — 1957

1957
Will Success Spoil Rock Hunter?
A Hatful of Rain
Inherit the Wind
The Pajama Game
*States with Pretty Names
*South Pacific
The Desk Set
Twin Beds
Janus

With such NY reviews behind him, Jack planned the '57 season to open earlier than ever before — on June 4. He had acquired an option on a new play titled **States with Pretty Names,** and depending on what happened at its Barn tryout, he was thinking of taking it to B'way. With well-earned confidence, he announced a 14-week season with the largest company — 30 — in the Barn's history, that number increasing with the production of two musicals.

A newcomer that season was Diane Ladd, who was "quite an actress as well as an eyeful," according to a local reporter. Ladd was scheduled to play the leading roles in **Will Success Spoil Rock Hunter?**, to be held over a second week, and **A Hatful of Rain,** in which she had just finished a national tour with Ben Gazarra and Vivian Blaine. She never got to play in the second production.

Barnlore has it that when Jack went backstage between the first and second act of **Rock Hunter** to yell, "What the hell are you doing to my show?" Ladd explained, "Oh, Jack! When I got out on stage, I realized I'd forgotten my cleavage and it just *threw* me!" Obviously she found it, since she later received Academy Award nominations as best supporting actress for *Alice Doesn't Live Here Anymore*, *Wild at Heart* and *Rambling Rose*.

Also new to the company was Stan Watt, a Carnegie Tech grad who had appeared in Jack's NY production of **No Return**, as well as actor/designer Royal Eckert. For the first time, choreographer Wayne Lamb and singer/actor Angelo Mango would sign for the full season. Returning after an absence of several seasons was Louis Girard. Carol Doughty would be singing the leads in both musicals and, for the first time, appearing in straight plays along with other Barn regulars: John Newton, Betty Ebert, Al Hinckley, Dusty Reeds and Boyd Dumrose.

There were 16 apprentices. Many had seen the Barn's ad in the April issue of the prestigious

Angelo Mango, Betty Ebert and Wayne Lamb in the "Steam Heat" number from **The Pajama Game**

national magazine, *Theatre Arts*, and were eager to join the company. Jack had also secured first rights for **Inherit the Wind** while it was still playing on B'way, along with the rights for the musicals **The Pajama Game** and **South Pacific**.

Bell of the *Gazette* hailed the production of **Pajama Game** and added that it was destined to become one of the Barn's top successes, for which he credited director Rinaldo Capillupo and choreographer Wayne Lamb. He also noted that "Miss Ebert, Wayne Lamb and Angelo Mango team up for the feverish 'Steam Heat' dance number and make a pretty good thing of it. A hold-over seems likely."

Following the two-week run of **Pajama Game** was the world premiere of **States with Pretty Names**. When asked what connection the title had with the play, playwright Elliott Baker explained, "It goes back to the old joke about the fellow who said 'paranoia' is the most beautiful of all the states. The 'states' in the play are the different states of the mind."

Ragotzy told the press he thought the play was "the most stimulating new comedy he had read in a long time" and that it had "the best chance of hitting the NY stage. It's lively, tightly-constructed and has something to say worth listening to." Ragotzy and the playwright spent time after each rehearsal, seeking to clarify and tighten the show. There was talk — and Jack hoped it would come true — of a London tryout prior to B'way.

What did the critics think?

Bell of the *Gazette* called it "a smart and sophisticated lightweight melange of sex and psychoanalysis, a witty and good-natured assault on the 'head shrinking' profession. As Ragotzy has directed it, and as some of the Barn's most expert performers play it, the show rolls along merrily and, for the most part, quite logically. Royal Eckert's stage setting is a joy. And the actors! John Newton is sensational."

Dolliver of *The Enquirer* echoed Bell, calling John Newton "superb."

Variety considered the script "a potential bet for B'way," playwright Baker having "laid out a crowd-pleasing, sophisticated narrative which is fairly heavy on sex and which develops some good-natured ribbing of current psychiatry addicts, practitioners and followers alike. With some sharp rewriting, **States** would seem to have a future in the bigger time."

Following this world premiere was another of the Barn's biggies.

"**South Pacific,** one of the truly great musicals of our time gives Jack P. Ragotzy's Barn Theatre what is unquestionably one of the biggest successes in the theatre's 12-year history," Bell of the *Gazette* declared. He went on to praise Rinaldo Capillupo's direction, Wayne Lamb's choreography and Boyd Dumrose's "lush and colorful sets." Of the actors he observed that, although John Newton was untrained as a singer, he did "a pleasing, acceptable and frequently surprising job

Gay Kleimenhagen, Flo Rasbury (Di Re) and Angelo Mango in **South Pacific** — 1957

on the vocal chores. He is completely winning as the French Planter." Bell declared Carol Doughty "a performer of unusual ability," who "captivates" as Ensign Nellie Forbush.

Dolliver of *The Enquirer* reported that **South Pacific** was "splendidly presented by Ragotzy's playhouse. Applause was almost perpetual and there was no doubt that the capacity audience was well pleased. The staging proved remarkably effective."

The year Jack got his first taste of working on the Main Stem, '58, could be called his "year of the cuckoo." After the Philadelphia tryout of B'way-bound **Portofino**, *Variety* concluded the show was "beyond doctoring." Karl Genus, a former Kalamazoo Civic Theatre director, who had at one time been director of the incoming **Portofino** but quit, was called in by producer Richard Ney to help save the show. Genus agreed to take the assignment on the condition that Ragotzy be hired as assistant director to do the rewrites. So sometime in late January, Ragotzy, having rewritten two acts, was rewriting the third for a February 21 opening. Ney discarded all but four lines the day before the opening, but Ragotzy still got his $1,000 and the show limped onto B'way, lasting only three performances.

On March 26, Jack's third NY production opened at the Lenox Hill Playhouse on East 70th Street. Equity Library Theatre's new policy mandated that all its productions be directed by members of their directing pool, of whom Jack was one of seven, and his production of **The Time of the Cuckoo** was the initial entry under the new policy. *Variety* reported that Ragotzy "staged the production with both an eye and ear for atmosphere, with an awareness for the piece's sensitive nostalgia," and added that Jack had "created a hot Italian summer's sleepiness without letting the play's pace slip over into somnolence." Author Arthur Laurents saw the production and announced that Jack "caught the real values of the script," which resulted in show-biz buzz of the play's returning to B'way.

Other "Barnie" (as people who have been part of the Barn's resident company are called) news was that Cindy Arnold and James Pritchett were married that spring and spent their honeymoon at Skidmore College, where Jim was guest artist playing the lackey stud in August Strind-

Jack and Tallulah Bankhead — 1958

berg's *Miss Julie*. Dusty Reeds and John Newton had their second child, John Michael, in NY City and expected to be back at the Barn in the summer.

In late May, local papers carried feature articles on "Co-Star," a new "Record Acting Game" that entrepreneurial Jack had been working on for several months with his NY neighbor. They had convinced Roulette Records of the game's saleability, and the first record was to be marketed nationwide in June.

The idea of Co-Star was to have such well-known actors as June Havoc, Sir Cedric Hardwicke, Vincent Price, Paulette Goddard, Pearl Bailey, Don Ameche, "Slapsie" Maxie Rosenbloom and Tallulah Bankhead (all of whom were involved to some extent), read the star's lines, while Jack or Betty would read the other role without their voices being recorded. This left a space of silence on the disk that could be filled in by the record buyer, thus allowing anyone in America to "act" with a star.

The targeted markets? Parlor game addicts, would-be actors and incurable egomaniacs.

And this was well before Warhol claimed everyone would have 15 minutes of fame. Records were cut, with scenes either being written by Ragotzy or taken from well-known works in the public domain. "I did a rough translation, looked over other translations and lifted a lot, and Tallulah Bankhead read my pastiche of *La dame aux Camelias*," Ragotzy said. "She had played the role in London early in her career, but now she was in her mid-fifties. We were in this big studio and there was this little lady sitting onstage, but when she read, it was like the removal of 40 years. She was wonderful." For the promo both Jack and Betty were pictured with Bankhead and Jack with Ameche.

Was this a cuckoo idea or what?

At the time of this writing, billionaire Bill Gates and on-line Microsoft Network is attempting something of a similar nature to create a new interactive relationship between on-liners and the Web. One gimmick is that four novelists would write the beginning of a story and let Webbers interact with suggestions, making them feel more creative.

Years later, when I asked Ragotzy whatever happened to the venture, he responded, "It never made any money." But, he said, he still has the records in his California home.

Natalie Ross — 1958

1958
Visit to a Small Planet
The Waltz of the Toreadors
Cat on a Hot Tin Roof
Damn Yankees
Gentlemen Prefer Blondes
*The Time of the Cuckoo
Picnic
No Time for Sergeants
The Happiest Millionaire
Fair Game
Nothing But the Truth

In early May, '58, Betty arrived in Augusta and Jack followed a week later to get ready for the opening on June 3. The hype was on a new leading lady, Natalie Ross, a University of Washington grad who won a Fulbright Scholarship to London's Royal Academy of Dramatic Arts, afterwards performing in Europe. When she came back to the United States, she did a variety of show-biz jobs including a nightclub stint with Jimmy "the Schnoz" Durante, weather forecasting, summer stock for Madge Skelly at Manistee, MI, (where James Earl Jones got his start) and acting at Erie (PA) Playhouse, from which so many other Barnies, including Jim Pritchett, came. Natalie would be able to do musicals as well as straight plays, including such whoppers as **Cat on a Hot Tin Roof.**

Gazette critic Louis Bockstanz called Ross' Maggie the Cat "superb." Dolliver of *The Enquirer* thought the production "compared favorably with the B'way version" and also called her "superb," while Craig Huebing was "perfectly cast" as Brick.

Naturally the show was held over, but during the second week, Huebing collapsed after the second act. Jack came before the curtain to ask, "Is there a Doctor in the house?" There was, and after some delay, the show continued. After the performance, Huebing was taken to the hospital, treated for an injured rib and released.

The Thursday before **The Time of the Cuckoo** opened, its author, Arthur Laurents, arrived at the Barn from Denver where he had been spending time with Ethel Merman on the book for a new musical, *Gypsy*, scheduled to go into rehearsal in the fall. Sitting down for a dinner interview with local critic, Jack Bell, Laurents talked of a "cycle" of his plays to be presented off-B'way in the fall, all to be directed by Ragotzy. Included would be **Cuckoo**, **A Clearing in the Woods**, *The Home of the Brave* and *The Bird Cage*, which had petered out on B'way after only twenty-one performances.

This was a dream come true for Ragotzy — big-time acceptance from the playwright whose first book for a musical was *West Side Story*, at that time the longest-running hit on B'way, and which had just been sold to the films for 350,000 big ones.

Dolliver of *The Enquirer* reported that **Cuckoo** was "amazingly good" and that the audience was "the largest the Barn ever had at an opener for a non-musical show." Of NY actress Margaret Draper, jobbed in for the leading role, he observed that she was "an audience favorite," "attractive, with perfect poise, a sense of humor, and genuine acting ability." He added that she had "notable assistance" from John Newton, who was "excellent." Of the other actors, he wrote, "Natalie Ross makes the young wife a delicious bit of instability, and Craig Huebing is convincing as the unfaithful husband." He concluded by saying, "The one setting is well done. It differs entirely from the B'way setting, but in some respects is an improvement."

Bell of the *Gazette* suggested that Augusta was becoming a sort of tryout town for NY. The production, he noted, "won one of those rare ovations usually reserved for a top musical production. Then after acclaiming the work of the actors, the patrons would not vacate the big red showplace on M-96 until the playwright appeared to take a bow."

Among the apprentices that season was a hunky, young actor who took the stage name of James Barrie (in honor of the author of *Peter Pan*?). He did the usual apprentice work and appeared in six shows, his biggest role being that of Joe Hardy in **Damn Yankees**. Much later he changed his name back to the original, Jim Sikking, and was fea-

Margaret Draper, Jack, and Arthur Laurents, author of **The Time of the Cuckoo** — 1958

tured prominently on TV's *Hill Street Blues*, and, at the time of this writing, is on *Brooklyn South*.

After a week's run of **Picnic,** John Newton starred in **No Time for Sergeants**, which was so successful it was extended for a second week. **The Happiest Millionaire** played the following week, marking Newton's 50th role and his 75th week of acting during five seasons, meriting a *Gazette* feature story. "Newton has been the star of the company, so far as the patrons are concerned, virtually from the day he first set foot on the stage at the Barn," the article pronounced. "He is easily the most versatile actor ever seen in the area."

As soon as Jack was back in the City, he was busy readying **Cuckoo** for off-B'way's Sheridan Square Playhouse. It was another "Barn East" production, produced by Paul Michael and Gayle Hinckley, set designed by Boyd Dumrose, lighting designed by Robert Cadman and stage managed by Michael Gleason and assistant, Alfred Hinckley. Also in the cast were Craig Huebing and Louis Girard.

The production received considerable attention. This was a revival of a play that had appeared just six years earlier at B'way's Empire Theatre, directed by Harold Clurman, designed by Ben Edwards and acted by mega-star, 45-year-old Shirley Booth, who won a Tony for her performance. It was then made into the film *Summertime*, starring 46-year-old mega-mega star Katharine Hepburn. That kind of barnacled armorplating should have made the play immune from alteration for at least a couple of decades.

But now this upstart, this comparatively unknown director, was challenging the B'way Goliaths by interpreting the play differently and thinking he could make it better. In an off-B'way production down in the Village? Who the hell did Ragotzy think he was, anyway?

In Jack's interpretation of the play, Leona was not the stock Henry-James-lonely-American-spinster, saddled with middle-class morality that makes her reject a hot (albeit transitory) sexual relationship with a handsome, poor — and married — Italian merchant. Instead, she comes to accept Italy's motto: "We have no divorce, just discretion." Leona understands that this will not be the perfect love relationship of Hollywood films, but the love she will get is the best that life has to offer at the moment.

In short, the Ragotzy production foreshadowed a kind of feminist sexual revolution that would gain a head of steam in the sixties. The younger actress playing Leona would not be a star, and the production would not depend solely on her as a star, but would place its emphasis on the play and the ensemble work of all the characters to contribute to the play's meaning. And it would be done in a three-quarter round, rather than proscenium, venue.

Cuckoo was scheduled to open October 23, '58, but had to be postponed four days due to the B'way opening of *Make a Million*. Then another off-B'way show, in conflict with yet another B'way production, shifted its opening to the same night. Ragotzy dug in, although he knew by doing so, the first string critics such as Atkinson of the *NYTimes* would attend a new production instead of a revival.

Edward Ellis of the *NYWorld Telegram* reported that seeing the play "was like watching an American runner in the Olympics lose by a nose." He thought both Kathleen Maguire and Robert Pastene were "superb" and, with disappointment, concluded that the play "laid no egg. It just didn't

Jim Sikking — 1958

quite get off the ground — darn it!"

Frances Herridge of the *NYPost* suggested that Ragotzy's production made **Cuckoo** a "quite different play, less humorous in parts, but sharper, more substantial and more resolved." In describing the difference between Booth's and Maguire's Leona, she noted that on B'way, Booth made Leona "funnier," but after she found out the Italian was a married man, the affair "ended in tenuous despair." In the Ragotzy/Maguire interpretation, the character was "more attractive" and young enough so that she "might still expect her dream to materialize." Herridge ended her review by saying, "The cast, under Jack Ragotzy's sensitive direction, is excellent," and by praising Boyd Dumrose's setting as well as the costumes. "This is a first-rate production which should fare well in its off-B'way transplantation," she predicted.

Arthur Gelb of the *NYTimes* also wrote favorably: "In its first incarnation, the **Cuckoo** was a touching and rather rueful bird; reborn, it has become a little more than a lark. It is still a bit tenuous, but it has gained substance from the intimacy of its staging. In the current version," he observed, "as played by Kathleen Maguire, Leona is younger, more spirited, more venturesome and better equipped to compromise. Mr. Laurents has made Leona a more believable heroine and a more dramatic one, and Miss Maguire plays her eloquently. Jack Ragotzy, a young and untried director, has staged the play with great sensitivity and has chosen his cast with remarkable skill."

Jim O'Connor of the *NYJournal American* indicated that it took this "revived, revised version" to give Arthur Laurents "the kind of a production he felt his play merited." O'Connor ended with these words of praise: "This three-sided arena presentation downtown makes the play more

Craig Huebing and Margaret Draper in **The Time of the Cuckoo** — 1958

real; more meaningful. Now it's a drama of depth played deftly. You feel concerned with these people and their problems. If you ask me, I believe off-B'way showed B'way last night how to stage **The Time of the Cuckoo**. It's splendid!"

Variety maintained that those who saw **Cuckoo** on B'way "should be equally satisfied with the exceptionally good revival. Ragotzy has drawn about everything that could be wished from the play and his company by way of nostalgia, humor, delicacy, understanding and mood."

Jerry Tallmer of (the Village) *VOICE* declared: "Under the warm, almost caressing direction of Jack Ragotzy, a cast exquisitely headed by Kathleen Maguire takes **Time of the Cuckoo** and turns it into a better play than anyone saw with Shirley Booth on B'way and an infinitely deeper emotional experience than anyone obtained from the movie *Summertime*."

CUE magazine applauded it as "infinitely superior to the B'way production," and added, "If this keeps up, all the playwrights will be rewriting their scripts for off-B'way following their appearance in the B'way showcases."

In November, with such excellent reviews, the show was selling tickets through January 31, making a run of more than twice the show's originally scheduled six weeks. **Cuckoo's** success only whetted Ragotzy's resolve to make it to B'way.

Meanwhile, Betty Ebert reported to the press back home that, although she had to pack his bag and push him out the door, Jack had gone to Florida for a few days' rest and that Laurents had nominated him for a Ford Foundation grant. Unfortunately, the grant never materialized, but Laurents' nomination reveals the high esteem he held for Ragotzy. Later in **Cuckoo's** run, Lynn Fontanne, on her night off from B'way's *The Visit*, went to the Sheridan Square Playhouse with Noel Coward, and after the show, went backstage to congratulate Ragotzy and the cast.

Her contract up in January, Kathleen Maguire left **Cuckoo**, and Betty, who had done a *U.S. Steel Hour* show with Melvyn Douglas in November, took over the leading role for the remainder of the run. Three other **Cuckoo** actors, Craig Huebing, Reva Rose, and Grace Genteel, joined Noel Coward's *Look After Lulu*, which was being readied for B'way by director Cyril Ritchard. So, in addition to rehearsing **A Clearing in the Woods** — second in the Laurents cycle — Jack had to oversee rehearsals for **Cuckoo** replacements. **Clearing** was scheduled to open on Feb. 16, '59, but B'way's *A Majority of One* preempted the scheduled opening and **Clearing** was moved up to Feb. 12.

The play had opened on B'way only two seasons before, with Actors Studio icon Kim Stanley in the role of a 30-year-old career woman who, because of a failed love affair, attempts suicide. Failing, she goes home, where she relives relationships with three men plus her father. Eventually she comes to the conclusion that she should continue to strive for the ideal, while settling for the imperfect present.

Writing in the *NYTimes*, Louis Calta concluded, "**Clearing** was and is a pretentious work full of particles of philosophies that are not worth the trouble. Although Nancy Wickwire works valiantly, she cannot quite make a convincing person out of the character." He added, "Although Jack Ragotzy has generally done a good job of direction, he occasionally presses too hard for the emotional effect." Robert Coleman of the *NYMirror* stated, "Director Jack Ragotzy has done a great deal toward clearing away the muck in the script," and "Nancy Wickwire's acting has honesty and conviction and she makes a more sympathetic and understandable character than Kim Stanley did on the Main Stem." Frank Aston of *NYWorld Telegram/Sun* was also favorable. "Miss Wickwire proved again that she is an artist with power and perspicacity. The supporting players hardly could be better and were kept under nice control by their director, Jack Ragotzy."

Writing for the *NYHerald Tribune*, Judith Crist asserted, "Nancy Wickwire is giving a stunning, virtuoso performance." After praising other cast members she added, "Jack Ragotzy must share the kudos awarded the cast. He has made a fantasy come to life, with breath and pacing." John McClain of the *NYJournal/American* observed that the playwright "hadn't managed to get all the vines and brambles out of that clearing." He added, "The Ragotzy version has certain plus values, however," and noted that there were some "excellent performances."

Tallmer of the *VOICE* gave the production its best review declaring, "It is my feeling that the show has gained greatly in its rebirth and by way of those special virtues we like to think of as off-B'way's own: sincerity, focus, smaller scale. It is in the area of carefully controlled understatement that the present production, from Boyd Dumrose's uncluttered settings to Jack Ragotzy's well-paced direction, is superior to the attempt two years ago on B'way."

Although the Laurents' cycle closed with **Clearing**, Ragotzy was now closer than ever to attaining major recognition in NY's theatre arena. On April 2, '59, Herridge revealed in her *NYPost* column that four of the top NY talent agencies had asked Jack to sign. He went with Gilbert Parker of Music Corporation of America (MCA) and, with what Herridge termed "a discriminating eye," had already turned down the directing assignment for B'way's incoming *Masquerade*, which opened and closed the same night.

On Sunday, May 3, the *NYTimes* carried a story about Ragotzy taking over the direction of Frank Corsaro's **A Piece of Blue Sky**, starring Shelley Winters. Years later Jack described the situation. "Frank was directing his own play and Shelley was being difficult. The producers came to me and asked if I'd take over.

"In rehearsal, Shelley didn't throw the script at me, she threw it at Corsaro and I said, 'Frank may put up with this; I won't. We're accomplishing nothing.' And I went home. That night on *The Jack Paar Show*, she talked about this 'wonderful young director,' and I got about ten minutes of national coverage. So, I went back in the morning and weathered it out. Later, well-known agent, Audrey Wood, said Shelley was as disciplined as she had ever seen her."

The play opened May 5, '59, at the Fort Lee North Jersey Playhouse and was scheduled for follow-ups at Nyack's Tappan Zee and the Westport County Playhouses, to be followed in the fall by another out-of-town tour prior to B'way. Corsaro's choice of Ragotzy signaled the latter's growing NY reputation. This was Jack's third East Coast production since closing the Barn the previous fall, and he took it only on condition that he would be able to leave in time for the opening of the Barn's '59 season.

Variety's review of **Blue Sky** was modest. "As caught last week, the play seems promising — already improved by two weeks of performance and rewriting, but with further clarification and tightening required. Its prime asset is the central character, played with insight and skill by Miss Winters. Under Jack Ragotzy's workmanlike direction the cast is uneven but generally convincing."

Then came the glory. On Monday, May 25, '59, Obie Awards were handed out for the best of off-B'way. Judges for the event were Jerry Tallmer of *(the Village) VOICE*, Kenneth Tynan, who had been literary advisor for Sir Laurence Olivier at Britain's Old Vic and was now writing for *The New Yorker*, and Henry Hewes of *The Saturday Review*. Sponsored by the *VOICE*, Obies were presented by Kim Stanley.

Ragotzy received his award for "best direction of American plays"; Kathleen Maguire won "best actress" for her work in Ragotzy's production of **Cuckoo**; and Nancy Wickwire for a "distinguished performance" in Ragotzy's production of **Clearing**.

Not bad for a wrong-side-of-the-tracks kid from Kalamazoo!

> **1959**
> Third Best Sport
> Summer of the 17th Doll
> Tunnel of Love
> Bells Are Ringing
> Say, Darling
> Li'l Abner
> *Come Share My House
> The Girls in 509
> Auntie Mame
> Who Was That Lady?

At this point in his career, Jack was an established member of NY's theatre scene and, as such, had every right to crow. But he didn't have time for the obligatory swelled head. Back at the Barn, he had a world premiere coming up, on which he held the option, and fully expected it to open off-B'way in the fall. The play, Theodore Apstein's **Come Share My House**, was scheduled the week after the Barn's record-breaking two-week run of the musical, **Li'l Abner**. Apstein was no novice, his ill-fated *The Innkeepers* having made it to B'way a couple of years previously.

Come Share My House is a love story about an American architectural student studying in Mexico, who has an affair with a Mexican servant girl. When she becomes pregnant, he decides to do the "right thing," marries her, and takes her back to NY to live on the Upper West Side. There she encounters problems because of their "mixed marriage," and the student is forced to face his own prejudices.

Cast in the leading role was Ecuadorian

actress, Elisa Loti. After graduating from Vassar, she had made a name for herself in films and stage appearances in Europe and Mexico. Playwright Apstein had seen her work in a theatre in Mexico City and had written the play especially for her. The author came to Augusta for the production and remained through the week's run.

Bockstanz of the *Gazette* commented that, while the play "was a huge success on first night, it would be unfair to say that it was flawless." Of Elisa Loti he remarked, "The vivacious young actress is splendid in her interpretation, and she won a tremendous ovation at the end of the premiere performance."

F.J.S. (Frances Jane Sims, earlier signed "J.F.S.") of *The Enquirer* felt that, although the author had a sincere approach, the play was problematical and that Apstein had "failed to arouse" sympathy for the student. She went on to praise the actors: "The excellent acting by a hard-working cast helped to tighten up the rather loose, and too-long story. Elisa Loti was both tender and fiery as the Mexican girl, giving life and understanding to her part. Richard Armbruster gained in stature as the play progressed. Betty Ebert added humor and a touch of pathos."

The *Variety* critic remarked that the play "impresses as a sensitive, plausible exposition on an intermarriage theme," and that the drama "holds attention and shapes up as a strong off-B'way bet." He noted Ragotzy's direction positively, but advised, "Apstein's drama needs tightening and major last-scene revisions to give the story a more satisfying wrap-up."

The Barn's '59 season was big — with a total attendance that topped all others for a record high of nearly 33,000. When the season ended, the entire company headed back to the City. Now on a roll, Jack had departed early, just after the curtain came down on the opening night of **Who Was That Lady?** Once back in NY, he was negotiating fall productions. It was reported that he was committed for two B'way shows, one of which, **And So, Farewell**, would star the legendary Fay Bainter. He was also making plans for his off-B'way production of **Come Share My House** and had been invited to direct two productions at the Margo Jones Theatre in Dallas in the spring.

The differences between B'way and off-B'way was gaining some national press at this time. Two different kinds of producers were operating off-B'way — one group championed the *avant garde* and the other group undertook B'way-like productions, which they couldn't afford to produce on B'way. Charles McHarry of the *NYDaily News* disclosed that Richard Barr, one of the biggest producers of *avant garde* off-B'way, had produced *Krapp's Last Tape* and *The Zoo Story* at a cost of a mere $425, including set, costumes and props. The production of these two one-acts had been financed for $5,200 and grossed $4,800 a week as against $2,000 operating expenses.

According to Doris Kronenberger, writing in *Theatre Arts* magazine, off-B'way was booming. The number of playhouses expanded in the '50s from five to 29, 16 of them having 199 seats or less, and nine ranging from 200 to 299 seats. There were 76 off-B'way productions during the '58/'59 season. Ticket prices had jumped from $2 to $5. Increasing press attention and publicity were being given to off-B'way, and it had been attracting more audiences. Of course, this infuriated some of the B'way folks.

On B'way, tickets for a musical were up to $9.90 and the uptown folks felt, mistakenly perhaps, that some of their market was being siphoned off to the competition. In short, this was a defining moment in the NY theatre. What material was legitimately B'way's and what was off-B'way's? Could one serve both God and Mammon? It was in this climate that Jack started directing B'way-bound **A Distant Bell** — yet another major career step.

Katherine Morrill's play, set in mid-'30s New England, is the story of an eccentric gentlewoman who had been in a "rest home" for ten years. After her husband's death, she returns home to her three grown daughters. But the daughters are ashamed of her eccentricities. A young reporter comes calling on the middle sister, is charmed by the mother and seduced by the younger sister, who locks the middle sister in a closet. Her delicate, emotional balance snaps and she has to be removed to a rest home, just as her mother was years before. Escaping into the winter night, she freezes to death. The oldest daughter denounces the mother and suggests she should commit suicide. The mother is returned to the rest home, where she may find more compassion than in the outside world.

The story has Tennessee Williams overtones, i.e. those considered mad often have more understanding than those considered sane. Ragotzy had directed **Streetcar** ('51 and '56), **Rose Tattoo**, **Cat on a Hot Tin Roof** and produced **Summer and Smoke**. One would suppose he was hired as director, not only because he was B'way's new boy on the block and had made an impression at the Actors Studio, but also because he was that unusual triple-threat combination — director/writer/ actor — who could help the first-time playwright turn her show into a success. The cast consisted of eight women and six men, and only one of the men's roles was considered even a supporting part. So it was a woman's play, written by a woman. And this may or may not have had something to do with what happened during the tryout in Philadelphia.

In the cast were two Barnies: Louis Girard, who had a very small role, and Michael Gleason, who played the paperboy as well as being assistant stage manager. A young Texas actor named Dale Helward was also cast.

The play opened at the Eugene O'Neill Theatre in NY on Jan. 13, '60. Martha Scott, the play's star, received excellent notices from all the critics, but reviews of the play were decidedly mixed. "It is a touching creation that works its way honestly to a conclusion" (Aston, *NYWorld Telegram/Sun*); "The play is consistently drab and disappointing," (Rowland Field, *The* [Newark] *Evening News*); "There may have been worse plays produced on B'way in recent seasons, but surely none of them has seemed quite so fatuous and pointless"(Watts, *NYPost*); "It is a fascinating play. I recommend it. This is good, individual theatre, and I admire it" (Chapman, *NYDaily News*); "Despite its muddled dramaturgy, its incomplete motivations and its absence of a clear point of view, it should not be dismissed lightly, for Miss Morrill has both style and originality" (*Newsday*); "It is a play to respect" (Coleman, *NYMirror*); "The drama is uneven, reasonably absorbing and occasionally touching, but elusive and unsatisfying" (*Variety*); "It is only a drama of sensation. The characters are storybook people; the situations are fiction. The sensations are more polite than most. But they do not come out of life" (Atkinson, *NYTimes*); "Some of it created theatre magic, but much of it was mere muddy writing. Miss Morrill can create scenes of dramatic freshness and I look forward to her next play" (*NYTelegraph*); "The author has written a haunting and absorbing play. One of the best new plays of the current season" (*Women's Wear Daily*); "There are moments of good writing in it, but I found the sum-total disappointing (McClain, *NY Journal/American*); and "It would be easy to brush it away as a confusing play. But the most confusing thing about it is its erratic flashes of quality. It will be interesting to see what Miss Morrill comes up with the next time out" (Walter Kerr, *NYHerald Tribune*).

Directing credit was given to producer Norman Twain, with critics commenting: His "staging assures the power of understatement," "never gives the effect of being static," "a thoughtful production" and "Twain directed with taste and a lack of obtrusiveness."

Only two of the critics came right out with the facts: "Norman Twain took over the staging after the recent sudden departure of director Jack Ragotzy during the Philadelphia tryout." Another reported, "No one is credited with the staging, Jack Ragotzy having withdrawn during the

Dale Helward — 1960

Philadelphia tryout and producer Norman Twain giving himself program billing for 'production supervisor.'"

Why did Ragotzy withdraw as director on this, his first B'way play? The reported reason at the time was "a basic disagreement with the author over the play's interpretation." Jack said that he withdrew when "the author failed to provide rewrites."

The reasons given by Jack nearly 40 years later are the same. "Katherine refused to change the third act as per our arrangement with the agency," Jack said. "It was my first B'way show and MCA was very protective of my name. Agent Gilbert Parker (now Senior VP of William Morris Agency, Inc.) had negotiated a contractual 'out' clause for me because MCA felt I was too hot a property to come in with a failure in my first big B'way venture. I really didn't want to leave the show, but I couldn't stay with my name off the playbill. We probably shouldn't have gone into rehearsals without the third act fixed. I had a solution for the problem, but Katherine wouldn't, or couldn't, write it and she wouldn't let me write it. Norman wasn't as desirous of change as I was. He thought the actors could make up for the script's deficiency by their acting. The actors were already working their asses off trying to play what wasn't there. It just wasn't there. Too bad, because it was a very intriguing play."

A Distant Bell fizzled just four days after it opened in NY, but it had a great deal of potential, as one can conclude from the mixed notices.

Jack continued, "Katherine went back to Westinghouse. Her fame rested solely in the famous slogan she wrote, 'You can be sure if it's Westinghouse.' To my knowledge, she never wrote another play."

Although this failure was a definite set-

Louis Freedman, Ann Harding, Jack Ragotzy, and Beulah Bondi on the set of *Play of the Week's* **"Morning's at Seven"** – April, 1960

** 1960 SCHEDULE OF HITS **

GOLDEN FLEECING — JUNE 14-19
New comedy full of madness & hilarity!

TWO FOR THE SEESAW — JUNE 21-27
The smash comedy you're all waiting for!

THE WARM PENINSULA — JUNE 28 - JULY 3
Light-hearted romantic comedy!

✱ CAN-CAN — JULY 5-11
Joyously naughty musical hit!

MAKE A MILLION — JULY 12-17
Unabashed hokum! A laff riot!

TEAHOUSE OF THE AUGUST MOON — JULY 19-24
A complete joy! Enchanting hit!

DARK AT THE TOP OF THE STAIRS — JULY 26-30
William Inge's best & newest comedy!

✱ CALL ME MADAM — AUGUST 2-8
Irving Berlin's happy hit musical!

GOODBYE, CHARLIE — AUGUST 9-14
Dizzy new comedy by "7 Year Itch" author!

LOOK HOMEWARD ANGEL — AUGUST 16-21
Pulitzer Prize winner! Magnificent!

MARRIAGE-GO-ROUND ✱✱ — AUGUST 23-28
Brand new smash! Full of laughs & sin!

SWEETBIRD OF YOUTH — AUG. 30 - SEPT. 4
Tennessee Williams' latest blockbuster!

✱ MUSICAL. NOTE EXTRA ADDED MONDAY PERFORMANCE.
✱✱ This schedule subject to change.
"Marriage-Go-Round" is still pending release.

1960 PRICE SCHEDULE

REGULAR PRICES:
Tues. Wed. Thurs.	$1.75 - $2.25
Fri. Sun.	$2.25 - $2.75
Saturday	$2.50 - $3.00 2.75

MUSICAL PRICES:
Tues. Wed. Thurs. Mon.	2.75 $2.50 - $3.00
Fri. Sun.	$3.00 - $3.50
Saturday	$3.25 - $3.75

CURTAIN TIME — 8:30 every night except Sunday
On Sundays we feature our special
"Earlybird" show with curtain at 7:30

FOR RESERVATIONS —
Phone Augusta REDWOOD 1-3342

It's Summer Theater Time Again

On June 14th there'll be something to CROW ABOUT

the Barn Theatre
Augusta, Michigan
begins its 15th GALA SEASON of the Greatest BROADWAY HITS

FINEST PROFESSIONAL ACTORS

12 LAUGH-PACKED FUN-FILLED WEEKS

that mad, hilarious hit comedy
"GOLDEN FLEECING"
OPENS TUESDAY JUNE 14th

MICHIGAN'S LEADING SUMMER STOCK COMPANY

back for Ragotzy's NY career, it only increased his determination to succeed. He was now counting on **Come Share My House**, and it consumed all of his testosterone-driven energy.

*****

The premiere of **Come Share** was postponed from Feb.10 to Feb.18 to avoid two B'way and four off-B'way openings. Elisa Loti received rave reviews, but the play did not. Aston of the *NYWorld Telegram/Sun* proposed that the author "apparently tried to brew a bit of explosives with his play, but when the director, Jack Ragotzy, tossed it onto the stage last night it hardly did so much as phfft." Watts of the *NYPost* noted that the play was "a rather placid little sentimental narrative. Jack Ragotzy's staging is helpful. But the play's chief value is a vehicle for an appealing new actress." Field of *The* (Newark) *Evening News* thought that the play was "a moderately effective little marital exercise," and, "as staged by Jack Ragotzy, received a creditable performance." *Variety* called it "banal, never rising above soap opera, but Jack Ragotzy's staging is dependable." The *NY Telegraph* theorized, "What happens is that an entrancing bit of casting threw the play's values out of kilter. Instead of feeling sorry for poor Tom, you want to walk up onto the stage and shake him hard and say: 'You silly jerk, she's the best thing that could have happened to you.' The cast abounds in excellent performances. Jack Ragotzy has directed becomingly and with fond attention to useful detail." Atkinson of the *NYTimes*, writing in a style most unusual for him, ridiculed plot, characters and theme. Kerr of the

Susan Willis and Dale Helward with dancers Barbara Reser, Bobbie Byers and Johanna DeSalvo in **Can-Can** — 1960

NYHerald Tribune was equally derisive, but added, "I don't see how the acting, or Jack Ragotzy's direction, could be better."

However, in his review in the *VOICE*, Tallmer took a swipe at both Atkinson and Kerr's reviews and, after reiterating the plot, wrote: "Sounds like a movie, a television play, and a few other things? Yes, of course it does, and a number of the daily critics took great sardonic joy in underscoring the point. What they did not go on to say is that everything depends on what's *inside* the cliché, and that inside Mr. Apstein's effort there is a great deal of simple truth about masculine self-illusion and female reality, and what seemed to be an extraordinary amount of sophistication about the interracial social structure of much of Manhattan. There is also a lot of swift and touching humor.

"Much of my appreciation stems from the excellent understanding of all the play's shades and values by director Jack Ragotzy; he has cast without a flaw and encouraged many beautiful nuances."

Coming so close upon the failure of **A Distant Ball**, the lack of unified critical acceptance of **Come Share** rocked Ragotzy to the core. But he wasn't ready to give up. Instead, he would go in another direction and focus on TV — the nation's major entertainment.

Within weeks, he was directing Morton Wishengard's drama, "The Rope Dancers," for TV's prestigiou*s Play of the Week* series produced by Lewis Freedman. The production starred Siobhan McKenna, who had played the role on B'way, and Walter Matthau. In lesser roles were Audrey Christie and Jacob Ben Ami.

Sid Bakal, TV reviewer for the NY*Herald Tribune,* exclaimed, "Recommended? Yes indeed!" *Variety* gave the acting raves and noted

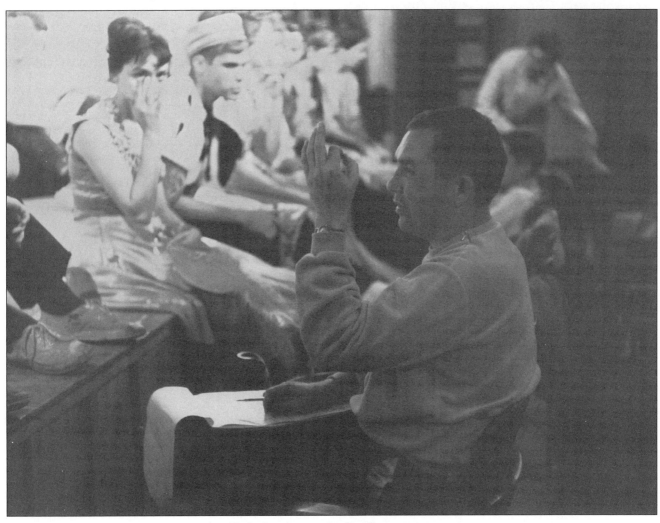

Jack gives notes to the **Can-Can** company

that "the direction by Jack Ragotzy is also of top caliber."

In April, Jack followed with Paul Osborn's **"Morning's at Seven,"** featuring an all-star cast that included: Ann Harding, Beulah Bondi, Dorothy Gish, Chester Morris, Eileen Heckert, Hiram Sherman and Frank Conroy. The work garnered rave reviews from TV critics at about the time **Come Share My House** ended its run. Perhaps Jack's luck was changing.

The '60 Barn season opened with **Golden Fleecing**, followed by William Gibson's **Two for the Seesaw,** directed by Lewis Freedman, producer of TV's *Play of the Week* ("You scratch my back; I scratch yours.")

Bockstanz of the *Gazette* claimed it starred "two of the finest actors ever seen on the Barn Stage," James Pritchett, who had replaced Hal March in the B'way production, and Susan Willis. "Miss Willis is devastating as Gittel Mosca. She captures the hearts of the first-nighters."

After **Can-Can,** which broke all Barn records for a two-week run, Jack opened **Teahouse of the August Moon**, with apprentice Norman Ornellas playing the role of Sakini, James Pritchett as Fisby, Al Hinckley as Purdy, and Natalie Ross as Lotus Blossom. Hugh Humphrey ("HH") of *The Enquirer* reported that Norman Ornellas played Sakini "as if the part had been written for him." Bell of the *Gazette* gave the show by John Patrick, whose script was based on Monroe, MI Vern Sneider's novel, an excellent review and pointed out that, with the role of Sakini, Ornellas achieved Equity status.

Ragotzy's choice for discussion from the '60 season is Kette Frings' adaptation of Thomas

1960
Golden Fleecing
Two for the Seesaw
Can-Can
The Teahouse of the August Moon
Kiss Me, Kate
Call Me Madam
*Look Homeward, Angel
The Dark at the Top of the Stairs
Ladies' Night in a Turkish Bath
Something Wild in the Country
Fall Season - 1960
Make a Million
The Marriage-Go-Round
The Gazebo
Three on a Honeymoon

Betty Ebert and Jim Pritchett in **Kiss Me, Kate** — 1960

Wolfe's **Look Homeward, Angel**. Bockstanz of the *Gazette* announced that the production "thrilled and pleased a sellout audience of first nighters and earned loud and continued applause for director Joe Stockdale in a homecoming triumph. Stockdale guided the cast into a nearly perfect production. Making the role of Eugene Gant come to life is Dale Helward, a young actor in his first summer at the Barn. His is, without doubt, the finest dramatic role seen this season." Humphrey of *The Enquirer* added, "Helward left no doubt that he is a true B'way star of the future."

As for my relationship with Ragotzy on this production, Jack knew I was an ardent devotee of the writing of Thomas Wolfe, able to recite from memory passages from his novels. Up to this point I had directed only 30 shows — all in University theatre. Yet, Jack signed me to an Equity contract. In addition to directing **Angel**, I was "coordinator" on **Teahouse** — easy enough because I had directed it previously — and assistant director on **Call Me Madam,** which ran two weeks and gave me two weeks of rehearsal for **Angel**.

During the rehearsal period, Jack was directing **Happy Ending** at Bucks County Playhouse in Pennsylvania. When he returned, he

Dale Helward, Francis Satter and Emmett Jacobs in **Look Homeward, Angel** — 1960

came to the final Sunday rehearsal — as he does to this day. Before we had even begun, Jack announced to the company that the play was not about what I had told the cast the show was about. Since Betty was playing Madam Elizabeth, I could only assume she had talked to him when he got home the night before.

As the run-through progressed, Ragotzy stopped it to make changes, which mostly had to do with a lighter interpretation. I was not used to having my work changed, but was confident that, during the two weeks of rehearsal, I had laid a solid foundation that could not easily be shaken. Ultimately, the show was a great success.

At the end of the opening night party, Jack asked me to block the first act of **The Dark at the Top of the Stairs** the next day. I had no idea he was going to have me direct that play, so I hadn't even read the script. Borrowing a copy, I gave it a go-through that night, met the cast at 11 a.m. and got through the first act in the five-hour rehearsal. Thursday was easier because, by then, I had read the play several times. By mid-afternoon Friday the play was blocked and we did a run-through. Saturday we ran through it again. Sunday was the big run-through and Jack was going to attend rehearsal, so I was nervous as I drove toward the Barn. Before I even got out of the car, Betty came running up and told me I was no longer needed.

I reminded her that unless I was given two weeks' notice in writing, I was to be paid two weeks' salary. This was more than a little cheeky of me, since Jack had done me the favor of signing me to an Equity contract. But Betty went into the house and reappeared with a check which had Jack's name signed to it. I drove back home to West Lafayette, Indiana. At the time, I had no idea why he didn't want me around any longer. **Dark** opened Tuesday evening on schedule, with Jack being credited as director and me as "assistant director."

The '60 season ended with a one-time experiment — adding a fall season from September 27 through October 30. Not only was there a profit motive, it also provided a total of 20 weeks' employment so that if actors could not get jobs in the theatre when they returned to NY, they would be eligible for unemployment.

Although moderately successful, the fall season was never again attempted. Why? "Michigan is just too damn cold!" Ragotzy declared.

Back in NY that fall, Jack was signed to direct a play titled *Candles in the Rain*, written by novelist Jean Arnaldi. Whether the production would be on B'way or off was to be decided. There was never any follow-up to this announcement. But in January, '61, Jack did sign a contract to direct Arthur Carter's **Hip, Hip, Hooray!**, to be produced by Lynn Loesser on B'way in the fall.

In March, Ragotzy was assigned his third show for TV's *Play of the Week* — Edwin Morris' **"The Wooden Dish,"** starring Martha Scott and Henry Hull, which played to good reviews. Following this success, Jack was signed on as script

Sunrise at Campobello Robin Reeds (in his first speaking role at the Barn) with his father, John Newton, and his mother, Dusty Reeds — 1961

editor for *Play of the Week*. The week of April 17, he directed his fourth show, **"Close Quarters,"** a two-character psychological melodrama starring Patricia Jessel and Richard Kiley, which was also favorably received.

1961
The Marriage-Go-Round
A Period of Adjustment
Under the Yum-Yum Tree
Destry Rides Again
*Sunrise at Campobello
Champagne Complex
The Pleasure of His Company
The World of Suzie Wong
West Side Story
A Majority of One

In April, '61, Ragotzy issued a news release saying John Newton, "the most popular actor ever to appear on the stage of the Augusta Barn Theatre," would return that summer. This was just after Newton had completed shooting an episode for the new, hour-long *Gunsmoke* and was playing the lead in *Send Me No Flowers* at the Hollywood Players Ring. For that performance the *LATimes* said he was "wonderful," and the *LAExaminer* called him an "excellent farceur." *The Hollywood Reporter* offered, "He is a plastic-faced comedian with a talent for punctuating his acting with spots of pathos." Enough good publicity was generated to induce master comedian Bob Hope to see the show.

But the summer season would prove to be, financially, the worst in the Barn's history. The problem? Highway M-96 road improvements made it virtually impossible for patrons to get to the theatre without taking circuitous and dusty back roads. It wasn't until August that a flyer could be printed announcing, "Good News, the way is clear!" — although, even in that essential month for theatre attendance, some roads remained in poor condition.

While playing the title role in **Destry Rides Again** and rehearsing the role of FDR in **Sunrise at Campobello**, John Newton auditioned for NY Producer Lynn Loesser (ex-Mrs. Frank Loesser) and playwright Arthur Carter, whose coming to the Barn had been instigated by Ragotzy. Newton read for the leading role in Carter and Loesser's B'way-bound show, **High Fidelity** (formerly *Hip, Hip, Hooray!*), which Jack was to direct. While visiting, the producer and playwright then got to see B'way-unknown Newton act in two shows. Although it was ballyhooed in the "trades" that producer and author were interested in such stars as Jack Carson and Robert Preston for the leading role, Newton got the part.

Dore Schary's **Sunrise at Campobello** was a Ragotzy kind of show and one of the season's best. It takes place during the three-month period in which Roosevelt triumphs against "infantile paralysis" to stand, with the aid of crutches, and nominate NY Governor Al Smith for president of the United States. Bockstanz of the *Gazette* declared: "Newton's performance is enhanced by an inspired cast. Dusty Reeds is tremendous. She creates a believable picture of a

The Jets and The Sharks duke it out in **West Side Story** — 1961

young Eleanor and stirs her audience to tears. [Eight-year-old] Robin Reeds [later Robin Haynes], son of John Newton and Dusty Reeds, is cast as John Roosevelt and carries off well his first major stage role. Credit, in fact, goes to the entire cast, none of which missed the inspiration of the occasion."

H.B. (H. Batchelder) of *The Enquirer* hailed the production. "John Newton's versatility seems boundless, a real *tour de force* for this splendid actor. Jack Ragotzy has directed a genuine picture of family life that mixes its tears with chuckles without the usual clichés. Dusty Reeds makes the difficult role of Eleanor Roosevelt take on depth and meaning."

Those were excellent reviews, to be sure. But not only were the roads being repaired, the area was a hotbed of Republicanism, while the show was sympathetic to FDR. To say it was not a hit is an understatement. But one would be coming.

Of **West Side Story**, H.B. of *The Enquirer* raved: "An ovation that carried through the raised house lights after countless curtain calls proved that the Barn Theatre had met its greatest challenge of many seasons. Wayne Lamb's exceptional choreography and the excellence of all the dancers swept it along at a breathtaking pace. Under the superb and adroit musical direction of Maurice Lewis, the Barn Theatre production is great theatre."

Bockstanz of the *Gazette* was more tempered, saying, "Members of the Barn Theatre, taking on what probably is the toughest assignment of their 16 years, came up with a pleasing, if slightly rough, premiere of **West Side Story**."

One interesting show that summer was **The World of Suzie Wong**, an unusual choice for the Barn. This show was directed by Clint Atkinson, who would also direct the final show of the season, **A Majority of One**, with imported NY actress Justine Johnson. Although Clint spent only one year at the Barn, mostly stage-managing, he was later to become artistic director of Long Island Stage.

Ragotzy had directed the two opening shows of the season, **The Marriage Go-Round** and **Period of Adjustment**; Louis Girard directed **Under the Yum-Yum Tree** and Jack followed with **Destry Rides Again**, **Campobello**, **Champagne Complex** and **The Pleasure of His Company**. After the last show opened July 18, Ragotzy was off to NY to prepare for his second B'way production, **High Fidelity**, slated to open at the Ambassador Theatre, October 9. Also scheduled was a two-week break-in at Philadelphia's famed Walnut Street Theatre, plus a third week yet to be booked. In addition to Newton playing the lead, Louis Girard (another Barnie) was an understudy. And if that wasn't enough to assure local interest, much of the show's nut — $135,000 — was financed by Kalamazoo and Battle Creek angels.

In summing up the Barn's '61 season, H.B. of *The Enquirer* commented, "Let us hope that **High Fidelity**, directed by Jack Ragotzy and starring John Newton, will some day break local

Jin Jin Mai and Dale Helward in **The World of Suzie Wong** — 1961

box office records after a long, successful run on B'way."

It didn't happen. *Variety*'s review tells the show-biz saga:

"**High Fidelity**, which relighted the non-air-conditioned Walnut on one of the hottest nights of the year, had two strikes against it with the weather. However it was highly doubtful that most of the audience would have remained if the show had been presented in a refrigerator. It is one of those entries in which the most interesting person in the play remains offstage throughout.

"The plot concerns a producer who is sore about the patronizing attitude and skirt-chasing habits of his star and director. The major plot gambit finds the producer in drunken enthusiasm making love to his wife in mistake for the siren who lives next door. That gives John Newton, as the producer-hero, a chance to wrestle around with Julie Wilson. Miss Wilson is visually fetching, but the playwright hasn't provided her with much in the way of dialogue except expletives.

"A bad situation was worsened opening night when a sheep dog, whose entrance is steadily built up during the first act, made an unscheduled appearance on stage 15 minutes before his cue and had to be hauled off."

Ragotzy's second B'way attempt closed in Philadelphia on Saturday, September 16, after four performances. Others would probably have tossed in the towel at this juncture. But ever the survivor, Jack would soon find another project — this one off-B'way.

King of the Whole Damn World was a musical version of George Panetta's Obie award-winning play, *Comic Strip*, which had an off-B'way run of 156 performances in '58. Tom Pedi starred in the play version and repeated his role as the rather dim-witted policeman in the musical version directed by Ragotzy.

The *Saturday Review* critic called the musical "a lightly comic *Street Scene*," and went on to say, "Director Jack Ragotzy has staged the show with care and a regard for its peculiar charm, and the performance is excellent." After pointing out some minor flaws, the critic ended, "Nevertheless, this poor man's *Fiorello* is certainly the best new musical comedy in an inordinate number of attempts in this off-B'way season."

The musical was one of 24 presented off-B'way that season, of which only four were still running when **King** opened on April 3, '62, at the Jan Hus Playhouse on 74th Street. Ragotzy felt the venue was wrong. "The show should have been done at the Sheridan Square Playhouse. It was a Bleeker Street kind of comedy."

CUE magazine called it "utterly beguiling, simple, good-natured, happy, and ingratiating." The critic for *The New Yorker* remarked, "The show has pleasant songs and dances, some amusing lines and some ideas that work, attractive scenery, a number of attractive performances and the always droll, rasp-voiced Tom Pedi, as a paternal cop. A fetching unactor of seven, Sheldon Golomb, almost

Louis Girard, Justine Johnson and Kathryn Crawford in **A Majority of One** — 1961

steals the show."

To Ragotzy's delight, the show ran for six months, which was substantial for off-B'way. It was also co-winner of an Obie Award for best original musical of the season. Ragotzy now had every reason to believe that his future in NY show biz was on the upswing again.

The following summer saw a major change in Barn policy. There would be seven performances a week — Tuesday through Sunday nights — with two performances on Saturday, one at 7:00, the other at 9:45. In addition, the two musicals, **The Music Man** and **Gypsy**, would play eight performances a week, with Monday nights being added. Curtain time was 8:30, except for the Sunday "early bird" show, which was at 7:30.

> **1962**
> Critic's Choice
> Pajama Tops
> The Music Man
> The Miracle Worker
> *Gypsy
> *A Hundred Percent Annie
> A Taste of Honey
> Send Me No Flowers

Announced with considerable hype was a new leading lady, Janet Hayes. A graduate of the New England Conservatory of Music and a brilliant concert singer who had performed in post-WWII Paris, Hayes, who was touring Europe, started her show-biz career when she returned to the States in the summer of '53. "I sang 'Over the Rainbow' for Richard Rodgers," she recalled, "who said my voice and looks were fine, but he wanted to see my legs." She got the job — an out-of-town engagement in the singing chorus of the national company of *South Pacific* playing in Detroit. From that point onward, she worked almost steadily in the singing chorus of B'way's *The Golden Apple*, *Plain and Fancy*, *Damn Yankees* (for 1,019 performances) and *The Music Man* (for 1,375 performances). In *Music Man*, as understudy, she played the role of Marian for two weeks opposite Bert Parks.

"Was that a thrill?" I once asked her.

"He never looked at me," she responded with a smile. "He was always facing front."

It was during this decade that she came to believe that B'way was interested only in a good set of, ah, vocal cords and her blonde good looks. But Hayes was determined to act. How to do this? — out-of-town engagements including one-a-week plays in summer stock. She had heard of the Barn, auditioned for Ragotzy, was hired, gave B'way's *Camelot* (in which she had appeared a year) two weeks' notice and was soon on her way to Augusta.

Hayes spoke for many other musical theatre performers when she said that appearing at Ragotzys' Barn was a "real joy because of the good acting company, spontaneity, audience intimacy and enthusiastic response." The work was "excellent training and allowed for versatility. I wanted to avoid being stereotyped as only a musical performer and jumped at the chance to intersperse acting and musical roles. Producers get the idea that musical performers can't act their way out of a paper bag. They may be right, but I wanted the chance to prove otherwise."

For the '62 season, there was also a new leading man, John Varnum, who had been in Jack's ill-fated **High Fidelity**, and a character actress, Ruth Gregory, whom he hired to play Kate Keller in **The Miracle Worker.** Jack had met Gregory the season before at Bucks County Playhouse when, on 48 hours' notice, she took over Ruth Chatterton's role in **Happy Ending**.

Ragotzy had also scheduled two pre-B'way premieres — George Penetta's **Kiss Mama** and Susan Slade's **A Hundred Percent Annie**. Option on the former was held by the producer of **King of the Whole Damn World,** but Jack held the option on the latter and was hoping for a hit that would eventually see Manhattan.

Janet Hayes — 1962

The season also saw extensive physical improvement to the Barn's property. Betty and Jack's home was enlarged. The theatre got a new speaker system, sound proofing and the stage was expanded from 26 to 30 feet. The size of the rehearsal hall was doubled.

The enlarged stage helped accommodate the 46-member cast of **The Music Man**, largest in the Barn's history. The show broke all box office records, was held over for an unprecedented third week, and Producer Ragotzy found himself in the producer's nightmare from hell — having to turn people away "by the hundreds." Eight thousand people saw the show in its first 14 performances! The musical was so popular that, in a reversal of the usual practice of a play benefitting from film publicity, Kalamazoo's Michigan Theatre booked a rerun of the film.

Bockstanz of the *Gazette* declared that the show was "nothing less than a spectacular triumph for director Ragotzy and his company." Top acting and singing honors went to John Varnum for a "brilliantly acted Harold Hill. But the musical thrill of the production is contributed by Janet Hayes, who easily has the finest singing voice ever heard on the Barn stage."

H.B. of *The Enquirer* wrote this glowing tribute: "With its rollicking production, the theatre has achieved its greatest triumph of many seasons. Jack Ragotzy has done a masterful job that, for sheer fun and bounce, surpasses the three B'way versions we have seen." Accounting for the musical's impact, the critic, in an obvious reference to the launching of Soviet cosmonaut Yuri Gagarin in '61 and our own Telstar in '62, continued: "America has taken such gigantic leaps into science and space that all of us feel a nostalgic yearning for the values and traditions of a simpler age. Herein lies the magic of River City, Iowa, in that wonderful year 1912. **Music Man** will take you back to that happy golden time when the only foreign objects in the heavens on the Fourth of July were skyrockets and Roman candles."

Gypsy was announced for one week and, due to demand, extended to two. These two musicals were a couple of hard acts to follow. But next on the Barn's bill was another world premiere — **A Hundred Percent Annie** by Susan Slade, former secretary to Marlon Brando and casting director for Dore Schary. The plot concerns an actor who has run out on a film and holes up in a NY apartment. He hires an attractive young actress, Annie, to be his general factotum. After the apartment door closes, complications arise and eventually lead to a striptease poker game.

The production starred Molly McCarthy, a TV actress Ragotzy jobbed in from NY for the assignment. The author, who had worked on the play three years, came to Kalamazoo for rehearsals and the premiere.

Bockstanz of the *Gazette* called it "a thin story featuring weak jokes and warmed-over clichés, played by an uninspired cast. It premiered before a large first-night audience and earned

Ruth Gregory and Georgia Brown in **The Miracle Worker** — 1962

little more than mild reaction from its viewers. The presentation appears doubtful for B'way without first undergoing major surgery." H.B. of *The Enquirer* agreed. "A feeling of excited anticipation prevailed last night at the Barn and lasted only until shortly after the curtain opened, despite a desperate attempt by the actors to salvage some comedy from the aimless quagmire of clichés and vulgarities. After a sparklingly successful season, the Barn has come up with a clinker."

Not surprisingly, Jack did not renew his option on the property. Yet, **A Hundred Percent Annie**, ironically, was one of the Barn's tryouts that eventually *did* reach B'way — albeit not under Ragotzy's direction. Renamed *Ready When You Are, C.B.!*, it starred Julie Harris and played for a moderate 80-performance run, opening on December 7, '64. Go figure!

When the '62 Barn season was over, Ragotzy reported that attendance achieved an all-time high. Many long-standing records fell, including biggest attendance for a single show and biggest attendance for a single week (**The Music Man**); biggest attendance for a single day (**Gypsy**, with two Saturday performances); and biggest attendance for the season — nearly 34,000.

However, at season's end, neither Jack nor Betty rushed back to NY, their usual practice. Why should they? They had their expanded living quarters; the fall leaves were coming on; and, with

(L to R) Arlene Mazure as Electra, Betty Ebert as Tessie Tura and Betty Vernan as Mazeppa in **Gypsy** — 1962

Merle Louise Letowt — 1963

the failure of not one but two premieres, there wouldn't be much happening in the City to hurry back to. What fields were greener than those around the Barn? Jack had been through the B'way crucible. Not only was he his own boss at the Barn, he was raking in the bucks.

Moreover, at the end of September, Jack was seen on TV as a narc in a brief segment of the season premiere of *The Nurses*. He had another role as a district attorney in a show dealing with birth control, and yet another spot on *The Nurses* in a to-be-released episode. He also had parts in two episodes of *The Defenders*, which were released that fall, and later did four more roles for the series. No wonder he was beginning to think maybe he should go back to acting.

The '63 Barn season would, for the first time, include three musicals. The first, **Carnival**, was memorable for introducing two actress/singers who made a lasting impression: Merle Louise Letowt (later she wisely dropped Letowt) and Karen Jensen (later, filmmaker Karen Arthur). Merle had played a long NY and nation-

Dale Helward, Farrar M. Cobb II, Steve Vickers and two onlookers watch as Merle Louise Letowt makes her entrance in **The Beauty Part** — 1963

al company run as Dainty June in Ethel Merman's *Gypsy*, and Jensen had played *Carnival*'s Rosalie in a national tour.

> **1963**
> Sunday in New York
> Carnival
> The Beauty Part
> A Shot in the Dark
> *The Unsinkable Molly Brown
> *The Hostage
> Come Blow Your Horn
> Bye Bye Birdie
> In One Bed... And Out the Other

Of Merle Louise, the *Gazette* critic announced, "She played to perfection," and of Jensen he said simply, "She is a smash." In addition to Dale Helward and Louis Girard, there were two new men in the company: Jim Kason, who did the male lead, and Mike Walsh, who played the role of Jacquot. All received special notices.

Next came **The Beauty Part**, played in NY by master comedian Bert Lahr. It was not exactly your typical summer stock vehicle, since the show has a cast of 32 men and 12 women. At the Barn, ten men and five women played the roles, all doubling in brass. But local theatregoers didn't cotton to the S. J. Perelman farce. However, they did take to Merle Louise in **The Unsinkable Molly Brown**, so much so that it proved to be "the Barn's all-time best seller" up to this point, seen by nearly 8,000 patrons, 3,450 of them (98.2 percent capacity) during the show's first seven-performance week.

Next was Brendan Behan's "bawdy, blasphemous and outrageously funny" **The Hostage**, which had just completed its two-year run off-B'way. Dave Nicolette of *The Press* declared, "**The Hostage** is quite a theatre experience. You may be offended. You may be entertained. You may even be enlightened. But you won't be bored."

Then, following the one-weeker came **Bye Bye Birdie**, in which Peter Simon (a future TV soap star) in the

Peter Simon — 1963

Mike Walsh, Betty Ebert and Louis Girard in Brendan Behan's **The Hostage** — 1963

title role changed from apprentice status to Equity member. I had recommended Simon to Ragotzy while I was a visiting professor and headed the Adams' Memorial Theatre at Williams College in '61-'2. As Humphrey of *The Enquirer* remarked, "There were many times when it became exceedingly tedious to remember that this young man is actually a most serious-minded individual, majoring in French literature and philosophy." William J. Swank of *The Citizen Patriot* concluded, "Simon was convincing as the rock 'n' roll singer and could easily land a contract with a recording company any time he wants to give up acting."

Director Louis Girard, choreographer Wayne Lamb and musical director Larry Wolfe were credited with the fine production. There were raves for actors Dale Helward, Ralph Strait (who was a stage manager making his first major onstage appearance) and Mike Walsh. But H.H. of *The Enquirer* countered, "The *piece de resistance* is Merle Louise Letowt. As Rose Alverez, she steals the show from start to finish."

Next came the English language premiere of **In One Bed. . . And Out the Other**, featuring Louis Girard — in drag. And what was the story Jack gave the newspapers about this off-beat casting? "A scarcity of gruff, competent, spinster types in the resident company had me stumped until I gazed at Girard and visualized his balding head bewigged." In '63 no one remembered, but drag was not unknown to Ragotzy. Not that he worked at the Jewel Box Review, but he did cut quite a caper, albeit Victorian, in the theatre's first production, **Charley's Aunt**.

In One Bed was a "French farce" — which basically means a little smut via circumlocuted *double entendres*, as opposed to British farce, which depends on an eight-door set for quick entrances, exits, and near misses. The authors, Mawby Green and Ed Feilbert, had made a killing by translating **Pajama Tops** from de Letraz's *Magma*, which played Paris for three years, Hollywood five years, London six years and B'way for only 38 days, but followed with ten years of coast-to-coast touring (Are Fran and Barry Weissler reading this?). Because of these successes, the translators felt there was more gold in "them thar" French farces and secured rights to *Une Nuit Avec Vous . . . Madame* from the widow of the so-called "well-known" playwright. Touted

Peter Simon as rock star Conrad Birdie in **Bye Bye Birdie** — 1963

in the tradition of P.T. Barnum's "They played before the Crowned Heads of Europe," the show was said to have had "great success in leading European capitals, plus North Africa and Turkey." (I'll let that pass!)

In the cast were Merle Louise, Ebert, Girard, Helward, Kason and Strait, along with special guest star, Sigrid Nelsson "from Uppsala Sweden." Jack spent a couple of weeks working on the script before Green and Feilbert showed up for the two-week rehearsal period. They were pictured in the newspaper with Nelsson, the Swedish bombshell, in a relaxed pose.

However relaxed at the photo-op session in front of the Barn, in rehearsals the authors were nothing if not uptight, insisting that every precious word of their dialogue be spoken verbatim. They followed the script religiously to make sure every "i" was dotted and "t" crossed, driving the actors up the wall.

The complicated plot concerns a young writer who decides he needs real-life experience to write a love story, the happily-married woman he chooses to have the experience with, her husband who is attempting to have an affair of his own, the girl with whom he hopes to have it and a visiting viscount disguised as a butler (Don't ask!).

And then there was "Aunt Alice."

Humphrey of *The Enquirer* enthusiastically wrote: "The vehicle definitely scored in its U.S. premiere. It is loaded with neatly timed racy dialogue and repartee. Director Ragotzy has an all-star cast. Louis Girard steals the show as the frumpish Aunt Alice. At one point, his stage foil 'cracked up' with laughter that infected the audience with near hysterics. Without question the show's hilarious."

Bockstanz of the *Gazette* maintained that it was "the funniest play since *Ladies Night in a Turkish Bath*. Playing to a sold-out audience," he continued, "the comedy sent its first nighters into convulsions of laughter, starting almost from the opening scene and continuing to the conclusion more than three hours later. This sparkling farce has a happy future, but we doubt that it will find it on B'way."

Nicolette of *The Press* suggested, "A tighter version with a more elaborate setting could easily turn out to be a comedy of the type acceptable to the sophisticated B'way theatregoer."

—From his lips to God's ear!

The 18th season, with a holdover week for the final show, ended up the best in the Barn's history with over 35,000 attendees in 15 weeks. **In One Bed** set a record of 3,186 attendance for a "straight" play.

Despite its negative reviews, **The Hostage** had done extremely well. The only show that lost money was **The Beauty Part**, which fell flat both as a production and as a box-office draw. Jack was glad for the season's success because he had put $10,000 worth of improvements in the property, including blacktopped roads, new underground wiring, new outdoor lighting fixtures and expanded dressing rooms. Life was good.

*****

World premiere! Jack Ragotzy with translators Ed Feilbert and Mawby Green – 1963

Pictured in *The Press* on October 27, '63, was Betty holding a baby, as a grinning Jack looked on. On the theatre's marquee directly behind them, as though advertising the next show, was the announcement, "And Introducing Brendan Jack Ragotzy." The article accompanying the picture said, "Mrs. Jack (Betty Ebert) Ragotzy sends a picture of the most recent addition to the Augusta Barn Theatre resident company. Little Brendan Jack was adopted by the Ragotzys last summer — or to report it in the proper theatrical manner, they signed Brendan late in the summer season. He is reported to have a long-term contract."

This was an especially difficult time in the private lives of Jack and Betty.

Brendan's (named for Irish playwright Brendan Behan) birth mother acted during two of the Richland years and helped backstage the first year at the Barn. According to Jack, she fell in love that summer with actor Stan Levitt. "They were very close. It was a serious relationship. Stan was killed that winter when he crashed his car on Hollywood's Sunset Boulevard."

At age 33, she made another appearance at the Barn when Jack was 41 and Betty 39.

"She came to see me in late June/early July of '62," Jack said. "She wanted to become a second-year apprentice and get her Equity card and was all set to come back the following year. During her visit, the company had a party away from the Barn, and after everyone left, the two of us were together. I was in a neck brace and I thought I couldn't do much sexually. She said, 'Sure you can. You can do it this way.' And we got to kidding around and it happened.

"Sometime in January, Betty got a call from her but she didn't say much. Thinking back on it, she probably didn't want to talk to Betty; she wanted to talk to me. I called her in April to tell her I didn't think she should come back because

Louis Girard as "Aunt Alice" in **In One Bed...And Out the Other** — 1963

she had two children — her husband had taken the other two when they divorced — and she said it wasn't two, but three. I asked, 'Who's the third and when was it born?' And she said March 12 — which was my mother's birthday.

"And then I really got angry with her because she had gone to NY, and I started to scold her. I got nothing from the other end. As I was talking, I began to think, to count back, and I said, 'You're not telling me I'm the father,' and she said 'No.' And I asked again, 'Am I the father?' And she said, 'It doesn't make any difference.' And we just kept going on and on, and finally she said that I was.

"I didn't know what the hell to do because I was going with a girl named Diana Walker. [Diana would eventually act in Woody Allen's *Play It Again, Sam* on B'way.] We — Betty and I — were on the breaking point, and I was kind of committed to Diana in terms of marriage. Later, when I mentioned the baby, Diana was all for it because then she could have a baby and not have to go through the problem of childbirth. I told Diana I would like to adopt it, and she thought that would be marvelous. But she was only 21 — and it was a terribly confusing time. I had hired Diana that summer for the Equity company, and Brendan's mother was there, and of course there was Betty.

"Betty and I resolved some of our problems, and I made no effort to keep up with Brendan's mother. But she contacted Betty every couple of years. She called me just before the 50th anniversary season; she was working in Beverly Hills for a very wealthy family. She was grateful to Betty for raising Brendan. And Betty *did* raise Brendan. I had fun with Brendan, but Betty raised him.

"You know, Betty and Brendan's mother looked an awful lot alike. She changed her hair color. I guess when she started getting a little gray, she went lighter. She used to take tickets at the door, and people often mistook her for Betty. It was really incredible.

"Brendan wanted — asked one time — I don't know if he *really* wanted to meet her, but one time I arranged a meeting. But there was a baseball game and Brendan didn't make the meeting. We waited around, but he didn't make a great effort to get back. So maybe he *didn't* want to meet her."

Jack and Betty were always absolutely open and honest with Brendan about the fact that he was adopted. Why didn't Betty have children? "She had an abortion — which was induced by a drug, when we did our first **Streetcar**," Jack said. "And I think whatever the guy gave her prohibited her from having children. Of course, we don't know that for sure. I obviously could manage. We never used any protection at all — ever. We kept trying, and then we just began to believe that it would never happen. I think that's one reason Betty wanted to adopt Brendan. Earlier I had wanted to adopt, and then I kind of cooled on the idea."

But then there appeared in the newspaper that wonderful smiling picture right out of Sam Shepard's *Buried Child*. Betty's holding the baby, Jack's smiling over her shoulder, and in the

Announcing the adoption of Brendan Jack Ragotzy!

background the marquee announces the new member of the family — heir apparent, apprentice to the Barn Theatre.

*****

There *was* life after the Barn for **In One Bed. . . And Out the Other**. The touring package was billed as "pre-B'way," even though it kept traveling *west*. It opened at the Coconut Grove Playhouse in Miami with Ava Six, "the Hollywood physique" from a D-cup pix *Bikini Holiday*, as the Swedish bombshell. After two weeks of trimming the original by 30 minutes and sending Miss Six back to La La Land, Jack imported Greta Thyssen (ex-Miss Denmark) for name lure and looks. The show moved on to Pittsburgh for three weeks to play the theatre where Duse died of a severe chill; then to Detroit's Shubert as that historic old theatre's last tenant — the wrecker's ball hanging from the crane just outside the stage door — then two weeks in Toronto.

In addition to director Ragotzy, Barnies included Ralph Strait and Merle Louise. Offstage, Merle was now Mrs. Peter Simon — the two getting married that winter having decided they couldn't live without each other, even though he was still a student at Williams College. Betty understudied at star's salary until the end of the run in Toronto. The new star of the show was B'way actor Jules Munshin, who ruled, fatally, against Aunt Alice being played by a man. Reviews in Miami were cool, but improved as the tour progressed west and the cast dropped the French accent. After the show folded, Betty and 11-month-old, two-toothed Brendan took a vacation to Nassau to visit Kalamazoo friends. It had been a busy, productive year.

The opening show for the '64 season was **Take Her, She's Mine**, starring John Newton. During opening night, a situation occurred that makes theatregoing so much more interesting than TV or films.

1964
Take Her, She's Mine
*My Fair Lady
*Here Come the Butterflies
*The Sound of Music
Rattle of a Simple Man
Irma La Douce
Oh Dad, Poor Dad...
The Fantasticks

At intermission, due to a thunderstorm, the theatre's lighting system failed. The interval stretched out for nearly half an hour, while Jack solicited flashlights from patrons' glove compartments and a boat light from a customer's truck. A couple of patrons drove their cars to the side of the theatre, aiming their headlights through the open double doors. Then, in the best tradition of "the show must go on," the second act got underway, with Jack occasionally explaining some physical action that wasn't illuminated. By the time the play finished, the audience had kicked back into a party mood.

And so did first-year apprentice George McDaniel (in the LA company of *Ragtime* at the time of this writing), who later called it "The Merciful Electrical Storm of Providence," even though he was not especially religious. Barnlore has it that when McDaniel came up from the University of Missouri, he was called in to meet the Great Oz. "Have you ever worked lights?" Ragotzy asked.

Determined to please and impress, McDaniel replied, "No, but I can handle a mean crescent wrench."

"Good," Ragotzy deadpanned, "You're my lighting designer."

Under the master's tutelage, McDaniel was going to light his very first show — **Take Her, She's Mine** — which wasn't a simple one-

George McDaniel — 1964

set couch-and-ottoman job. Oh no! Instead, it was a lumbering multi-set, indoor-outdoor monster that even challenged master set designer, Lee Fischer.

During the final dress rehearsals, McDaniel lit the show at least three times. Jack would come in, look, shake his head, give McDaniel pointers, and leave him hanging from the "A" ladder — in the grip of severe vertigo — to plow onward and upward. During Tuesday afternoon dress rehearsal, Jack was still "fine tuning" the lighting, and McDaniel had only enough time to write cues for the first act. Jack's words were not reassuring, "If worse comes to worse, I'll call cues on the squawker from the lobby for the second act."

Then came "The Merciful Electrical Storm of Providence."

By the following afternoon, McDaniel had gained enough time to write the cues for the entire show. He went on to light shows for the next three years. The production, incidentally, proved so popular it was held over a second week, which gave additional rehearsal time for readying another standout Barn show, **My Fair Lady**.

Janet Hayes, who would play Eliza Doolittle, arrived in time for opening night of **Take Her**. She was returning to the Barn after a hiatus of one year, during which time she was elevated from the B'way singing chorus to a small speaking role in Steven Sondheim's short-lived *Anyone Can Whistle*. She would meet the cast and her co-star, John Newton, the next morning at rehearsal, and this meeting would inaugurate a lifetime partnership for the couple.

After a 2,717 performance run on the Main Stem, **Lady** had been released for stock presentation. Some 80 productions were announced in summer theatres around the country; but since the show was scheduled as the Barn's second of the season, Jack was one of the first to produce it. In addition to Hayes and Newton, the cast included Alfred Hinckley as Doolittle, Louis Girard as Pickering, Dusty Reeds as Mrs. Higgins and newcomer Frank Coleman as Freddy. The show was directed by Ragotzy, choreographed by Wayne Lamb, with musical direction by John White, scenery by Lee Fischer and stage managed by Mike Gleason, who would eventually become a successful TV producer with such shows as *McCloud* and *Remington Steele*.

Bockstanz of the *Gazette* raved: "Assembling probably the strongest cast in the theatre's 19 years' history, producer-director Jack Ragotzy presented the musical before a capacity audience of first-nighters and was rewarded by wave after wave of applause and repeated demands for curtain calls. The production easily takes its place as one of the all-time greats in the annals of the Augusta playhouse.

"John Newton, who holds more acting laurels at the Barn than any other performer, moved like a stage genius into the central role of the phonetics expert who takes Eliza in hand and turns her into a lovely young lady, losing his heart in the process. Janet Hayes, who captured the hearts of the audience as Marian the Librarian in the '62 **Music Man**, did it again last night with a voice

John Newton and Janet Hayes in **My Fair Lady** — 1964

even more beautiful than before. Miss Hayes once again proves herself an excellent actress."

Hugh Humphrey (name, not initials, new policy) of *The Enquirer* concurred: "**My Fair Lady** made her debut at the Barn and got precisely what she deserved — a capacity audience and a tumultuous reception. Talented Janet Hayes has matured both in her singing voice and acting ability, and there were many moments when her effort provided fine competition to Miss Julie Andrews' performance. Newton fitted well into the role and looked, played and sang the part with aplomb. The final scene, when he sings 'I've Grown Accustomed to Her Face,' is unquestionably the highlight of the evening."

The show was accorded a record-breaking four weeks — the first in the Barn's history — closing after 32 performances — and we're talkin' Augusta, Michigan!

Next came another world premiere, which Jack hoped would go to B'way and revive his NY career, of Allen Boretz's **Here Come the Butterflies** (originally called *Artist in Residence*). The playwright described the play as "a criticism of the unthinking desire for success, and of how society insists upon a man conforming to preconceived patterns of success."

Boretz's had written Danny Kaye's first film, *Up In Arms*, Bob Hope's *Where There's Life . . .*, Esther Williams' *Bathing Beauty*, along with such potboilers as, *Two Guns from Texas*, *It Had to Be You* and *Copacabana*. He had written song lyrics and music routines for Bob Hope and Red Skelton. However, he was best known as co-author (with John Murray) of **Room Service**, which had a substantial run on B'way and was, incidentally, produced at the Barn during its first season.

Boretz said he chose to open **Butterflies** outside NY because he wanted to work on it further, and a play produced on B'way is either an immediate hit or a flop. He had met Ragotzy only six months before, but said Jack had read and understood the play and would be able to help him improve it. It was anticipated that representatives from the NY stage and Hollywood film producers would be at the preview.

Butterflies concerns a divorced husband who comes home to Monarch City, CA, to study the annual migration of butterflies. His ex-wife, a somewhat scatter-brained do-gooder, is about to re-marry. A lecherous neighbor living across the street is interested in the wife. There are two children, and there is a Rumanian beauty (ala Zsa Zsa Gabor) pursuing the wife's fiancé.

Swank of *The Citizen Patriot* noted that if the "reaction of the audience is any criterion, **Butterflies** has a bright future." He judged that the author had "put together a tightly written, fast-paced comedy, well stocked with laughs. It is first-rate entertainment and should enjoy a successful run." Bockstanz of the *Gazette* announced the author "came up with another winner, which is easily the best written and best received in a series of originals staged by the Barn in recent years."

The *Variety* critic gave some qualifications. "The play is generally tight, but with weaknesses apparent in character exposition and plot-line buildup. With further polishing, prospects for B'way would appear bright, for it's primarily an enjoyable narrative with emphasis on family foibles, salted with enough sex for popular appeal." Perhaps there was still hope of a B'way success for Jack after the Barn's summer season.

Next came **The Sound of Music**, starring Hayes and Newton, whom Jack knew were perfect for the leads — money being unable to buy the kind of chemistry the two radiated both on and off the stage. Bockstanz of the *Gazette* declared that it "was staged to near perfection before a sell-out audience. Directed by Louis Girard, it won for its company one of the loudest and longest ovations of the season. Janet Hayes is splendid and sings beautifully. And the Barn's all-time favorite, John Newton, master of comedy and drama alike, settles easily and comfortably into the dramatic role of the Baron." Swank of *The Citizen Patriot* noted, "Janet Hayes was accorded a noisy ovation. The old pro, John Newton, can sing and his ability as an actor is well-known."

Irma La Douce was the third big musical of the season and was important for two reasons. It starred Karen Jensen in the title role, and Angelo Mango, who had worked on the B'way production of **Irma**, returned to help Wayne Lamb and Jack Ragotzy stage it. Bell of the *Gazette* declared, "Vivacious Karen Jensen gives a dazzling performance both as a singer and dancer."

Humphrey of *The Enquirer* raved: "Karen Jensen is a diminutive ball of fire. Working under the severe handicap of a temperature and a

Karen Jensen Arthur in **Irma La Douce** — 1964

cold that bordered upon laryngitis, Miss Jensen figuratively knocked herself — and her audience — out with her performance." Swank of *The Citizen Patriot* added that tiny, red-haired Karen Jensen "scorched the stage of the Barn giving a dazzling performance."

The season ended with Wayne Lamb's production of **The Fantasticks**, starring Frank Coleman, Dulcie Creasy and George McDaniel. Although small, it was still a musical and the fourth one that summer. With it, Ragotzy brought his most successful season to a close. Prior to its end, he happily announced that he was scheduled to direct a B'way production the following spring of **Here Come the Butterflies**, for which he held the option. The play would be produced by Phil Rose, who produced B'way's *A Raisin in the Sun*, and Jack was hoping to once again re-establish himself as a NY contender.

An innovation in '65 was an arrangement with a local restaurant, Inmans, who offered a First Nighter Special that included "Your selection from our famous CONTINENTAL APPETIZER BUFFET, and choice of several dinners" all for $4.75 per person, including their "famous RAIN CHECK" so you could come back after the play for dessert and coffee. This arrangement — a new kind of spin on the dinner theatre idea — lasted for 17 years.

First thing of note in the 20th anniversary season is that lovely, red-haired actress Dulcie Creasy was hired, after only one year of apprenticeship, as a full-fledged Equity member because she was such a hit with audiences her first year. After graduating from the University of Missouri, where she and a TV student, Ron Camp, had fallen in love, Dulcie went to NY and then to the Barn, while Ron returned to his home town of Joplin. As Swank of *The Citizen Patriot* assessed the situation: "Being so far away from Dulcie was too much for Ron, so he packed all his hopes and a change or two into his knapsack and lit out for Michigan's Barn Theatre. There he talked himself into a job on the technical staff as an assistant in stage lighting." Now that they were together again, both wanted to get married and decided to do so in a simple ceremony on a Monday-off in late June.

Ever alert to the happenings of her apprentices, mother-hen Betty thought the occasion demanded more. Theatre folks might not be rich, but they often have a wealth of resources. Betty knew of several bridal gowns and veils in wardrobe, along with dresses that would do very well (after costumer Ora Crofoot's adjustments) for bridesmaids. Tuxes could be

rented at reduced rates from Clair's Tux Shop, where the Barn rented all such items. Del Lewis could sing Malotte's "The Lord's Prayer," while George McDaniel, another Missourian, could be best man and Betty, matron of honor.

The June ceremony was held in the Augusta Community Methodist Church on the company's last Monday-off. Both families came in from Missouri. Charles Dodsley Walker (husband of Janet Hayes as well as choir director and organist at the prestigious Fifth Avenue Church of the Heavenly Rest in NY and organist for the upcoming **Camelot**) played the wedding music for the double ring ceremony. A reception followed at Gary's Restaurant in Augusta, and then the couple had the rest of the day and night for the honeymoon, prior to reporting promptly to the theatre for work at ten o'clock the next morning.

The second show of the season, **Camelot**, brought Janet Hayes and John Newton together again. After a busy seven years in NY, Angelo Mango returned as a performer. Indeed, there was so much talent around the Barn that Dale Helward, Louis Girard, Del Lewis, Dulcie Creasy and George McDaniel all played supporting roles in **Camelot**. Equity newcomer Joan Dunham played Morgan Le Fey and first year apprentice, Adrienne Barbeau, was assigned a walk-on.

1965
Never Too Late
*Camelot
*Sell Me Down the River Darling
*Stop the World – I Want to Get Off
Mary, Mary
*Baby Talk
A Funny Thing Happened on the Way to the Forum
The Threepenny Opera
In One Bed... And Out the Other

The fact that **Camelot** had not received very good NY reviews but had became a lumbering-costumed-pageant-hit with star power (Julie Andrews, Richard Burton and Robert Goulet) and boasted a gorgeous *mise en scene* (the joke around NY was that people came away from the show humming the scenery) only served to challenge our feisty, theatrical contender. Ragotzy was determined he could, by clarifying the story line, make the production better than it had been on B'way.

Bockstanz of the *Gazette* obviously agreed: "It would indeed be presumptuous to claim that our nearby summer theatre has improved on B'way, but presumptuous we will be.

Joan Dunham — 1965

Adrienne Barbeau — 1965

The Barn crew, using its professional talent to the fullest, has taken the big musical, added sparkle here, subtracted turgidity there, and turned the pageant into a musical play — possibly for the first time anywhere. In short, the Barn's production is excellent — and it is fun."

Other critics were equally laudatory. *The Enquirer* called the show "another fine hit and Janet Hayes, the lovely blonde, a charming and talented Guenevere." Swank of *The Citizen Patriot* said, "The tune-packed show was an instant hit with the standing-room-only crowd and is a tribute to director-producer Jack Ragotzy and his highly efficient staff."

But the critics were unaware that, just before curtain on opening night, Janet Hayes suffered a severe asthma attack. Trouper that she was, she went on and her voice did not reveal her condition.

The show ran for three weeks to huge audiences — a stellar success.

Theodore Apstein's **Sell Me Down the River, Darling** provided yet another world premiere that season. Why was Jack continuously so intent on doing new plays when they usually did not make money? Obviously he was still looking for a show he could produce and direct either on or off-B'way. A director who held the option on a show and who could help the playwright get it on the boards would not only make a directing fee — plus a weekly percentage of the gross — but might share in future royalties. Big bucks as well

Janet Hayes as Guenevere, John Newton as Arthur, George McDaniel as Sir Dinadan and Angelo Mango (kneeling) as Lancelot in **Camelot** — 1965

as prestige would be gained if the play had a shelf life after the Barn, especially if it hit the jackpot — the Main Stem.

Ragotzy never produced an original show at the Barn on which he did not hold some kind of option — usually for six months with a six-month renewal clause. The Barn was a good place for a tryout, there being a knowledgeable audience, lots of apprentice labor, talented actors and first-rate set, lighting and costume designers. Authors saw the advantage of having their work tried out well away from NY and were willing to waive royalty payment. After the show opened, they could find out where the laughs were and what did or did not work.

Furthermore, by this time there were four newspapers in the area with solid critics. The producer and playwright could learn something from their criticism. Jack had been successful in producing Apstein's **Come Share My House**, which *did* have an off-B'way run in the Big Apple, and had advanced his ever-growing NY reputation as a hot, young director.

When your second stringers are as good as your star pitcher, you expect to win the ballgame. And Jack did expect to win with **Sell Me**. He imported NY black actor Phillip Lindsay, who had gotten such good reviews the year before in **Here Come the Butterflies**. Dusty Reeds flew in from California, and from his resident company Ragotzy cast an incredible supporting cast: Joan Dunham, John Newton, Betty Ebert, Janet Hayes, Dulcie Creasy, George McDaniel, Dale Helward, Louis Girard and newcomer, Adrienne Barbeau, among others.

But there was a problem.

The plot concerns a wife of 12 years, who begins to feel (as one of the critics so aptly put it) like a "pre-sleep habit." She suggests to her husband that they discard their Victorian morality and she have an affair. He reluctantly agrees, but wants final approval on her choice of partner.

It's a good premise for a comedy or sex farce, but the author also brings in a family with a mother — a real estate agent who benefits financially from marital splits in this closed community.

Philip Lindsay, Betty Ebert and John Newton in **Sell Me Down the River, Darling** — 1965

This social commentary on greedy real estate developers, plus ethnic tokenism in the form of one Jewish family and one black family living in the community, *vis a vis* the domestic problem of a failing marriage that could either be funny or serious, muddies the play's focus.

Bockstanz of the *Gazette* deplored the new comedy, saying that it "just laid there and fizzed like a damp fire cracker. It might have exploded at any moment but the blast never occurred. The new script wobbles back and forth on a wide roadway. There are 13 major characters surrounding a half dozen or more angles ranging from the plight of a bored housewife to the chance of a modern community graciously accepting a black family."

Variety added, "Sex — marital, extra-marital and pre-marital — provides the prime motivation for **Sell Me Down the River, Darling**. There's more, of course, such as racial integration in suburban NY, but Apstein has presumably aimed the play for the topical sex-and-spice sweepstakes. As unveiled on opening night, the comedy aspects of the play are subjugated by involved plot and interplot development."

Any Barn Theatre attendee reading the truncated plot synopsis of **Sell Me** in the newspapers knew in advance that it was a sex farce and expected to laugh a lot. But Apstein's story just didn't play that way. Serious social issues were involved and not just as satire. The audience and critics became confused, not knowing how to take the show.

As Nicolette of *The Press* described it, "The writing is tight, plot well thought out, direction excellent, setting refreshingly different and performances worthy. All that talent, however, appeared overspent on a play that can't make up its mind whether to be a hilarious situation comedy or dramatic commentary on society."

When one reads all the critics, it is possible to surmise that, with Jack's predilection for squeezing entertainment value out of even serious subjects, he inadvertently heightened the built-in incompatibility of the serious and comic genres that were already inherent in Apstein's text. The result was inevitably fatal.

Although one other small musical, **The Fantasticks**, had some success the season before, **Stop the World — I Want to Get Off** was a relatively small, one-set musical that made history for the Barn. Bockstanz of the *Gazette* enthusiastically wrote that it was "a stirring performance which surely must be judged the greatest we have ever seen on the stage of the Barn. Angelo Mango reached the actors' pinnacle at the summer playhouse. He reached across the footlights into the hearts of his first-night auditors, tickled their funny bones, set their imagination awhirling, drew forth a plentiful supply of tears and won the first standing ovation in the history of the big red showplace."

Humphrey of *The Enquirer* concurred, saying, "For the first time in twenty seasons, a capacity audience last evening stood at curtain call and roared out its approval of a performance. The Barn never has delivered a more superb production than it did in **Stop the World**. As Mr. Mango's silvery tenor soared through

Angelo Mango as Littlechap in **Stop the World — I Want to Get Off** — 1965

the emotional conclusion the audience simply went wild."

Swank of *The Citizen Patriot* added, "In the 20 year history of the Barn, producer Ragotzy has brought to this area many hit shows and musicals. It is safe to say, however, that none could match the over-all excellence of **Stop the World**. An orchid is due Wayne Lamb for his deft direction and his choreography. **Stop the World** is an absolute 'must.'"

In an unprecedented move, after playing **Mary, Mary** for a week, Ragotzy brought back **Stop the World** for another week, followed by such Herculean efforts for summer stock as the world premiere of **Baby Talk, A Funny Thing Happened on the Way to the Forum** and **The Threepenny Opera.**

The English language premiere and pre-B'way tryout of Feilbert and Green's farce, **Baby Talk**, adapted from French playwright Jean de Latraz's *Bichon* pleased the critics. Humphrey of *The Enquirer* was the only dissenting voice. "**Baby** talked entirely too much and too long at the Barn last evening," he chided. "Director Ragotzy threw his entire cast of top stars into this vehicle and it seems safe to say that any lesser talent would have failed to get the thing rolling at all."

However, headlines for Nicolette's review in *The Press* sang out, "Every Line Scores in Barn's Gay New Comedy." This, of course, was in more innocent days when "gay" meant merry, bright or lively and "score" had something to do with keeping a tally. Nicolette continued, "Almost every line, every situation has to be credited with scoring. Ragotzy directs and the laughs roll on in waves."

Swank of *The Citizen Patriot* agreed, calling it "one of the funniest plays to be seen here in years. The show has the best possibilities for a B'way run of any of the new plays premiered at the Barn in the last few years. Ragotzy's direction was deft and knowledgeable and the setting by Lee Fischer drew applause."

The season ended with a revised version of **In One Bed**. *Gazette's* Bockstanz remarked that although the farce "has all the depth of a dime store bowl of soup," it still is "guaranteed to inflict aching ribs and gasping breath." Nicolette of *The Press* was the only dissenter. Remembering the original production, he said, "It seems that whatever changes were effected don't make a great deal of difference."

*****

Back in NY in the fall, Betty was keeping an eye on Brendan playing in Central Park, while she penned publicity letters. She wrote that Ragotzy was doing a pilot TV film called "The Happeners," which was being made by the producers of *The Defenders*. No mention was made of the failure to interest NY money in a production of **Sell Me Down the River** or **Baby Talk**.

Then, during Christmas vacation while planning the beginning of their third decade at the Barn, the Ragotzys visited California. Jack sur-

Janet Hayes and Dale Helward in **Mary, Mary** — 1965

veyed the work situation and at the end of February, after living in NY for 17 years, he and Betty decided to move to the West Coast. Brendan stayed with Betty's mother, while Jack looked for a house to rent. Betty packed up the NY apartment, drove back across country, and they moved into a house in the Hollywood Hills on March 1.

The explanation for the move was obvious. The NY theatre, as they had known it, was drying up. In spite of all his efforts, Jack had not made it on B'way. The thrill was gone. Time to move on. Many of their old friends and contacts lived in California, the site of major television work. As if it confirmed his decision, Jack was immediately signed for an episode on the new *Dragnet* and one for *The Virginian*.

1966 – 1975

1966
Don Juan in Hell
Tobacco Road
Funny Girl
The Roar of the Greasepaint
*Who's Afraid of Virginia Woolf
How to Succeed in Business Without Really Trying
*Oliver!
Any Wednesday
The Owl and the Pussycat

In May, Jack and Betty migrated back to the Barn. Other returnees to the Equity Company included Louis Girard, Angelo Mango, Del Lewis, Dusty Reeds, Dulcie Creasy and George McDaniel. Karen Jensen was back to star in **Funny Girl**.

Meanwhile at Purdue's Professional Theatre — "Barn South" as it was often called — Barnies Janet Hayes, John Newton, Merle Louise, Peter Simon and Dale Helward formed the nucleus of that acting company under my direction. After seven grueling, eight-hour, six-day weeks of rehearsal — followed by a two week break-in of two plays a week — they would perform Pinter's *The Birthday Party*, Ibsen's *A Doll's House*, Anouilh's *Ardele* and the world premiere of Richard Bush's *Talk of Another Day* for six weeks. Often talked about but rarely done, this experiment in European style rotating repertory, where the play changes every day, gave these actors a unique experience.

At the Barn, the official opener was a third staging of **Tobacco Road**; but prior to this, an interesting innovation occurred. In '51, producer Paul Gregory had made a bit of theatrical history by sending on the road the First Drama Quartet, starring Charles Laughton, Sir Cedric Hardwicke, Charles Boyer and Agnes Moorehead in a staged reading — i.e. bare stage, music stands, lights, and formal dress — of George Bernard Shaw's rarely-performed second act of *Man and Superman*.

The long act, titled **Don Juan in Hell,** lay in the public domain — the play having been written in '03 and therefore royalty free. Ragotzy decided to present it for one week with Dulcie Creasy as Dona Ana de Ulloa, George McDaniel as Don Juan Tenorio, and Louis Girard as The Statue Don Gonzalo. Jack Ragotzy and Del Lewis alternated as the Devil. In addition to the reading, there was to be an informal discussion after each performance. Admission would be on twofers (two for the price of one).

This was a radical departure for the Barn and, as one might suspect, it was motivated not by art with a capital "A," but by the rules of Actors' Equity Association. What the season needed was an extra week of drama to balance out the production of four musicals, and the reading was an easy solution to the requirement. I should also note that this production was not one of Jack's choices for discussion in this book, and he has never included it in the listing of the Barn's productions on the final two pages of its programs.

Don Carlson of the *Gazette* pointed out that the Barn "was doing something different from anything it had ever done in its 20 years," and that Jack had made use of the theatre's new orchestra pit "to create an approximation of the drama's locale." He went on to describe the audience as small, "almost intimate."

"The reading provided a pleasurable, entertaining and mentally stimulating evening for those persons who appreciate the beauty of the English language. All the actors handled their tasks exceptionally well even though some rough edges were evident." Carlson further commented, "An unexpected dividend of the production was the discovery that Ragotzy's amplified voice is uncannily similar to that of Sir Cedric Hardwicke."

Perhaps one of the most controversial productions — and Ragotzy was well aware of the value of controversy — ever to take place at the Barn was Edward Albee's **Who's Afraid of Virginia Woolf?** Benefitting from national publicity after the drama was announced in May, it played from July 19 through 31 and preceded the showing of the film adaptation starring Richard Burton and Elizabeth Taylor in Kalamazoo by one week. On July 25, a local resident, noting the Barn was offering the stage version of the play, told the Kalamazoo City Commission that many were fearful the movie "would add to moral decay" and urged the commissioners to take action by enforcing "on-the-books obscenity laws" and halting the film's showing.

The complainant admitted she had not seen the film, nor had she read or seen the play, but based her objections on reviews of the film and articles in national magazines.

To his credit, the city attorney responded, "I think it's significant that the play was on B'way for two years, published, and is now in summer stock. If it were obscene enough to shock the American public, it would have been successfully condemned before now."

Nevertheless, Kalamazoo Youth for Christ took out a large newspaper ad that asked, "Who's Afraid of Virginia Woolf?" and answered its own

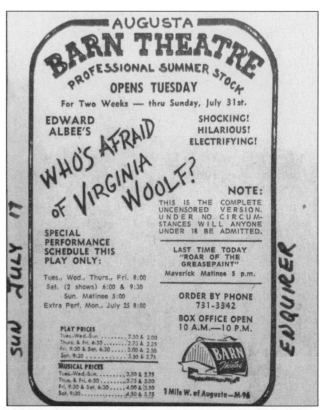

(L to R) George McDaniel, Louis Girard, Dale Hopkins and Betty Ebert — **Who's Afraid of Virginia Woolf?** — 1966

The final scene: George: (Louis Girard) "Who's afraid of Virginia Woolf..." Martha: (Betty) "I...am...George...I...am..."

question in large bold face type, "WE ARE!"

What were they afraid of? They continued by explaining:

"Afraid of The Effect That This Film & OTHERS SIMILAR WILL HAVE UPON Society When profane cursing & extreme sensuality are allowed to run rampant on today's motion picture screen.

"We ask that all Civic minded people in Kalamazoo interested in preserving common decency & morality irregardless of Race, Color, or Faith will join us in protesting this & other such films which so Flagrantly undermine the morality of our Country.

"REALISM IS NOT AN EXCUSE FOR OBSCENITY!" the ad concluded.

By contrast, a spirited defense of **Woolf** appeared in the *Gazette* in a letter to the editor from a reader who pointed out that she was most grateful to those who so loudly objected to the film and play because it broadened their audiences. She ended her letter by chastising those who would ban the film and by urging them to get rid of shows that "glorify war and teach violence" as a means of solving problems.

The show went on.

Of the Barn's production, Kenneth L. Peck of *The Enquirer* wrote: "Albee's play is most certainly veiled in what might be labeled 'shocking language.' However, he uses this as a vehicle for his 'message.' At no time does he use obscenity for the sake of obscenity. The play is one of the greatest of our time, and the prevailing truths revealed in it far outweigh any cry of 'obscenity.' The production is theatre at its finest. Director Ragotzy has assembled a talented foursome to handle the very demanding roles. The result is a production which is both exciting and terrifying."

Nicolette of *The Press* agreed: "The Albee drama is too well written to be called obscene. As performed at the Barn, it is forceful, stirring entertainment. Ragotzy, directing with a masterful

Brendan Ragotzy sits under the table and makes his debut in **Oliver!** — 1966

George McDaniel and Karen (Jensen) Arthur in **Sweet Charity** — 1967

feel for the playwright's efforts, guides the action with relentless purpose. Betty Ebert, in one of her finest efforts, moves impressively from mood to mood, alcoholically gay, harshly cutting, coy, crushed, sympathetic — all with control. Louis Girard is completely believable as the professor. Probably the best performance is offered by George McDaniel as Nick."

Swank of *The Citizen Patriot* added, "Any obscenity ascribed to it has to be in the mind of the viewer. I doubt that Albee ever has been accused of writing a morality play, but **Virginia Woolf** is probably as close to it as he will ever come. The cast was brilliant as was the direction by Ragotzy. This was the finest theatre the Barn has produced in its more than 20 year history. The setting drew a burst of applause as the curtain was drawn on the opening scene."

Carlson of the *Gazette*, while praising the production, did not so much defend the play against the obscenity charge as denounce it as a work of art: "There is some question whether it is a play or a reverse form of group psychotherapy, theatrically contrived and totally lacking in compassion. It's a great *one*-act play; but it's performed in *three*. It gets off to a roaring start and quickly establishes itself as an ivy-covered version of the studied insult. It falters in the second act as its wellspring of vulgarities begins to run dry or become monotonous. In the third act it comes flying apart like barrel staves with the girdling ring removed. The result is speciality entertainment for those persons who take a sadistic pleasure in seeing the soul not only bared but speared."

Lighter fare the rest of the season soothed the controversy. **Oliver!**, which Ragotzy got released for the first time in the area, was directed and choreographed by Lamb, with musical direction by Tom Kasdorf. Set on an ingenious turntable setting by designer Alan Hedges and costumed by Ora Crofoot, it received rave reviews. Calling it "a winner!" "filled with warmth and charm" and "a success," the critics had great praise for 13-year-old Jack Houston, a Kalamazoo lad in the title role. Also singled out for praise were Louis Girard as Fagin, Dulcie Creasy as Nancy, George McDaniel as Bill Sykes, Del Louis as Mr. Brumble and Angelo Mango as the Artful Dodger. Historically, the production is of interest for the fact that it "featured a three-year-old charmer who's so cute you'd like to wrap him up and take him home" — Brendan Ragotzy had made his stage debut as a workhouse boy and one of Fagin's gang.

> **1967**
> Barefoot in the Park
> Sweet Charity
> *On a Clear Day You Can See Forever
> The Odd Couple
> Half a Sixpence
> *Marat/Sade
> Luv

Of the six productions during the '67 season, **Sweet Charity,** starring Karen (Jensen) Arthur, was a two-week musical hit. But **On a Clear Day You Can See Forever** and **Marat/Sade** clearly stood out.

The Lerner and Lane musical, **Clear Day,** received mixed reviews on its initial showing in NY, but a revised version was sent on the road about six months prior to the Barn's presentation. Although an unusual practice at that time, today's shows (such as *Big* and *State Fair*) which fail on the Main Stem are often revised, simplified, clarified and sent out on tour. It was the revised script for **Clear Day** which Jack used as the basis for his production and to which he added his own fine tuning.

The show garnered good reviews for Joan Dunham and raised George McDaniel to star status. Barn newcomer, Joseph Cardinale, old-timer Louis Girard and, what one reviewer called "the precious littlest scout," Brendan Ragotzy received special mention. Jack and Wayne Lamb co-directed and the show also brought the return, albeit in a fairly small role, of Angelo Mango.

Carlson of the *Gazette* declared that the production was a "personal triumph. Many, if not all, of the show's shortcomings have been remedied by directors Ragotzy and Lamb. Their revisions were fairly extensive and all for the good. They have streamlined **Clear Day**, cleared away much of the musical debris and fashioned a show that may be more accurately described as a play with music."

When the road company starring John Raitt and Linda Michele hit Detroit the following March, critic Swank wrote this tribute: "Comparisons are odious, but I can't help but recall the superb performance of the role of Daisy at the Barn Theatre last July when it was played to perfection by Joan Dunham."

Perhaps the most unusual choice of play in the Barn's history — or for any summer stock theatre — was Peter Weiss' **The Persecution and Assassination of Jean-Paul Marat as Performed by the Inmates of the Asylum of Charenton under the Direction of the Marquis de Sade.** Nevertheless, Swank of *The Citizen Patriot* said it "was given a brilliant and spectacular performance." He also noted, "It took courage for producer Ragotzy to mount this vehicle, which is likely to be shunned by most summer theatres."

Dale Helward had again spent the summer acting at the Purdue Professional Theatre and when it closed at the end of summer school in early August, he returned to the Barn to play Marat. "He was superb throughout," Swank announced. "The highlight of his performance was the scene in which he is dumped into the pit by his erstwhile

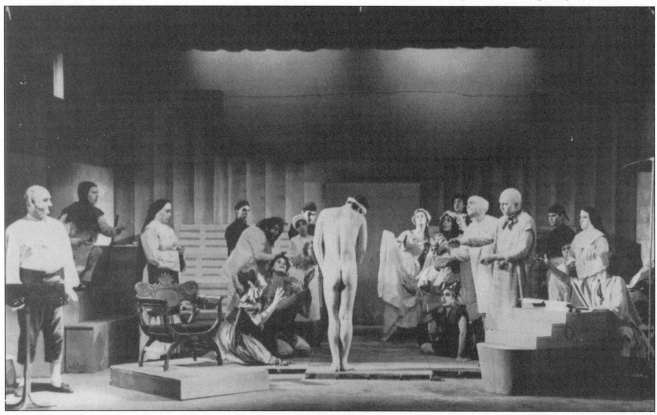

Marat/Sade — 1967

Sally Shockley and Angelo Mango in **Walking Happy** — 1968

followers and stripped, after which he climbs out naked and walks to the rear of the stage to be wrapped in a robe. It was a scene which could have been obscene, but Helward made it one of grace and beauty. The lighting of this action was masterful and one detects the fine hand of Producer Ragotzy."

Robert Alt of *The Press* quoted from Ragotzy's curtain speech: "We don't want to do the stock thing. I expect some of you will disapprove." Mary S. Oates of *The Enquirer* pointed out, "The advance billing warned that the show was an adult shocker, and it certainly lived up to its billing. Apparently the 'guests' at the asylum took it all in stride. There didn't seem to be any empty seats after intermission."

Carlson of the *Gazette* made these observations: "It's a welcome change if for no other reason than the fact that theater-goers need to be reminded occasionally that the world of theatrical imagination is not all lollipops, dancing girls and sugar plum fairies. The new ending, written by Ragotzy, gives a much-needed summing up. It's a distinct improvement over other versions in which **Marat/Sade** drifts into an indifferent conclusion. We have no doubt that many persons will dislike the play. Like it or not, it's a drama you won't forget."

In March, '68, Ragotzy announced from Hollywood a 12-week Barn season beginning June 11, with prices ranging from $3 to $4.35. Carlson of the *Gazette* remarked, "Ragotzy seems to have an inside track on obtaining production rights to current or recent B'way hits." He went on to suggest, "We would like to see Ragotzy's company try its hand at one of those folk rock musicals such as *Your Own Thing* or *Hair* which are exploring badly-needed new frontiers in musical theatre."

1968
The Impossible Years
Walking Happy
The Boys From Syracuse
The Killing of Sister George
Fiorello!
*Angela

The first musical of '68, **Walking Happy**, was a big hit with Joan Dunham and Angelo Mango playing the leads. On opening night, torrents of rain swamped the Barn's environs, but failed to dampen the enthusiasm of the capacity

113

Angelo Mango, Johnnie Reeds and Brendan Ragotzy in **Walking Happy** — 1968

audience. According to one reviewer, Ragotzy managed "to tighten the book and work out some good comedy touches to enhance the show."

Another most unusual show for summer stock, and seen for the first time in the area, was **The Killing of Sister George**. With an in-your-face lesbian theme, the story concerns a "butch" BBC radio star whose ratings have dropped, necessitating the killing off of her character. Bockstanz of the *Gazette* seemed pleased. "The play adds up to interesting fare, not objectionable for those who find theatrical excitement in a story that's off-beat." Of Betty Ebert he declared, "She, triumphant in countless difficult roles in the 22 years at the Barn, succeeds again as the cigar-smoking, gin-drinking, foul-mouthed Sister George. She never has been better."

It began to look as though Ragotzy's concentration was now exclusively on productions at the Barn and that he had abandoned his dream of making it to B'way. He produced no new plays in the first two years of the third decade and then, suddenly, there came the **Angela** premiere at the end of the '68 season. This time Ragotzy held one week of previews, to which the press was cordially *not* invited, and then officially opened the play on the second Tuesday of its run, giving himself, the playwright and actors time to make changes based on audience reaction. It was, in short, an in-town, out-of-town tryout tour, right at the Barn, followed by an opening night.

Angela, by Sumner Arthur Long (whose first play, *Never Too Late*, was a big B'way and film success), concerns a 48-year-old woman whose philandering husband, a Navy officer, has not been home for years. Having chosen TV as her nightly Sominex, she calls for a repair person when it goes kaput. He turns out to be a 24-year-

Jayne Bentzen, Dale Helward as Antipholus, and Betty Ebert as a courtesan in **The Boys From Syracuse** — 1968

old charmer who can't fix the TV and whom, after a few slugs of brandy, she beds. The next morning she hides his clothing, loans him her husband's pajamas and, finding he has an interest in inventions, sets up a basement workshop for him. It is the wife/husband/ young lover relationship that provides the comedy's complications.

Carlson of the *Gazette* announced, "There's reason to believe that this pre-B'way tryout may actually *be* a pre-B'way tryout, as it is the most promising of a number of new plays staged over the years. The opening was a triumph." He went on to bring up an "inescapable" comparison, that of the play's central situation — an older woman taking a young lover — being the same as the film, *The Graduate*. However, he points out that Angela and Mrs. Robinson are different, both in character and circumstances.

"The weakness of the comedy," he continued, "although it's a perilous business to suggest there's any such thing in a play that produces as many howls at this one, is the exposition of Angela's fundamental character. The 'Little Mary Sunshine' aspects do not always square solidly with the emotional bruises she has suffered from a husband who has assuaged his anxieties with a series of Lolitas. But this is the only serious complaint that can be entered and even it may be lint-picking when a show is as much fun as **Angela**."

Of the acting he noted, "Betty Ebert gives a keenly perceptive portrayal to the title role and Dale Helward is outstanding as the repairman. He gives quite probably the best performance of his Barn career. Since the humor is almost as much visual as it is verbal, credit must go to Ragotzy's direction. The stage setting designed by Dusty Reeds and John Figola is stunning. It's a great little comedy that holds considerable promise of achieving success in the canyons of Manhattan's theatrical district."

Helen Rambow of *The Enquirer* predicted that the author, "master builder of situation comedy, has another hit on his hands" and that the show would get to B'way. She noted that producers Elliott Martin and Michael Ellis (former manager of Bucks County Playhouse, now heading the LA Center Theatre Group) attended the opening.

Swank of *The Citizen Patriot* felt the new play surpassed the achievements of *Never Too Late* because it is "subtler, has greater depth and the hilarious situations are sustained at greater length." The play "was an instant success with the first-night audience which accorded the cast, director Ragotzy and Mr. Long a rousing ovation." He concluded that the play would be successful

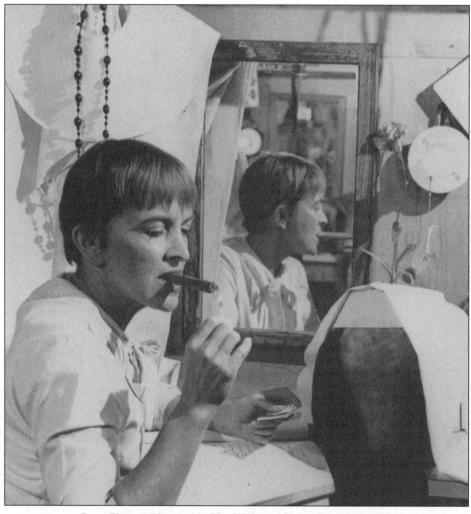

Betty Ebert as "George" in **The Killing of Sister George** — 1968

with sophisticated New Yorkers and reported that Elliott Martin and Michael Ellis were "both highly pleased with the Barn's production and had strong words of praise for Ragotzy and cast. Mr. Martin said that a number of stars were under consideration for the leading role. When asked who would direct the NY production he replied, 'We would like to have Ragotzy.'"

Nicolette of *The Press* suggested that Ragotzy "may very well have supplied the springboard for direct B'way exposure" for the new play. "The production is certainly the best of the season and it is not difficult at all to imagine the show just being bundled off to NY intact. But that isn't the way of B'way theatre. It was indicated by Ragotzy that a 'star' — probably Geraldine Page — is being sought for the title role. Anyone will have a tough time topping the character created by Betty Ebert."

He further recommended: "Anyone in the area would do well to catch **Angela**. It isn't often that the hinterlands has an opportunity to see a hit before NY declares it so. Anyway, it isn't likely that the show will come off any better if it does reach B'way, even with all the Manhattan trappings and a 'star.'"

Variety also reported that the play got "a successful initial showing and there are early indications it will get a B'way presentation. **Angela** is the most promising new script Ragotzy has presented in his 23 summers. It shapes up as a good bet for B'way. Ragotzy's staging is first-rate, as are the performances."

There was no doubt that **Angela** was the top-drawing attraction during the season.

No wonder that in late October, Jack was confident the play would receive a B'way production. With the glowing local reception, he had every right to be confident. Betty may have been slighted disappointed not to be considered for the title role, especially after the unanimous raves she had received for creating it. But she was nothing if not practical and not only accepted the producer's decision but agreed that for NY success the

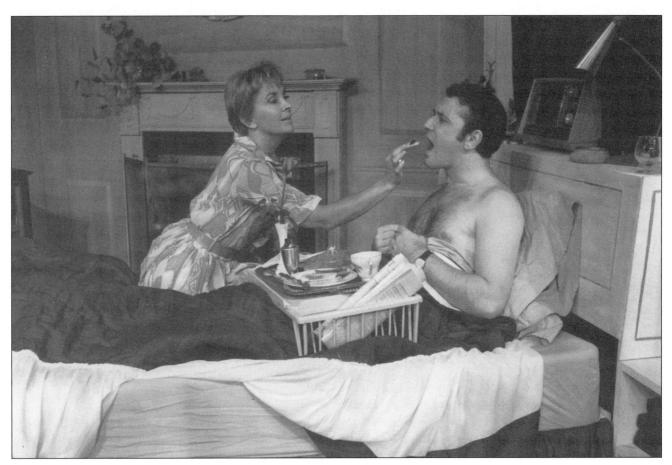

Betty Ebert and Dale Helward in **Angela** — 1968

show needed a star. She would be supportive without letting her personal ambitions get in the way. After all, Jack's success would be hers and Brendan's, too.

On November 3, '68, word finally came that **Angela** would open on B'way in the fall of '69 with Ragotzy directing. Although first choice for the title role was Maureen O'Sullivan, who had starred in Long's *Never Too Late*, Geraldine Page, who had recently been seen in Truman Capote's television drama, *The Thanksgiving Visitor,* was signed. This news first broke in the *NYTimes* in theatre editor Funke's "News of the Rialto" column. He also reported that Dale Helward was being considered for the role he created at the Barn.

In another column on December 22, Funke gave one of those panegyrics that critics sometimes indulge in, extolling Page's "versatility" and saying both critics and public never know what type of role will bring her back to the stage. He also noted that she had recently starred on the road in *The Little Foxes*. Funke said he had written about **Angela** in the fall of '66 and commented that the show might have gotten on the boards sooner had Miss Page, then appearing on B'way in *Black Comedy*, consented. But she "was unwilling to commit herself to playing again in comedy." Funke went on to report, "There was a problem of finding a suitable actress willing to play a 48-year-old wife having an affair with a 24-year-old television repairman. Such liaisons didn't assume respectability until Anne Bancroft created Mrs. Robinson in *The Graduate* without wrecking her career. Playwright Sumner Arthur Long," he added, "will quickly remind you that he wrote **Angela** before *The Graduate* turned up."

Funke gave the following footnote: "Curiously, the producers, Elliott Martin and Michael Ellis, gave the play separate tests last summer. Martin had it tested in Augusta, Michigan, under the direction of Jack Ragotzy. Ellis' venture, masquerading under the title *The Toy Boy* and credited to the authorship of 'Clermont Stanton,' was put on at Adelphi College."

That fall, while awaiting **Angela** negotiations, Ragotzy was seen in a substantial role in a feature TV film, *Dragnet,* that had been made in '66. He also found time to teach acting at the United States International University in San Diego. Finally, in March '69 came the long-awaited announcement that he would go to NYC for a couple of weeks in May to firm up casting and design assignments for **Angela**. Reportedly, he was hoping to sign set designer Tom Jones and would "launch negotiations for a performer for the other major role, the TV repairman" — which meant that Dale Helward was out of the picture, at least as the prime candidate. On June 25 the *NYTimes* announced that Rob Anthony was signed for the role.

Meanwhile, in promoting the Barn's coming season, Ragotzy said some better plays would be available, though top musicals remained a problem. First dibs on those he wanted were being given to touring companies that would play Kalamazoo.

1969
You Know I Can't Hear You When the Water's Running
Don't Drink the Water
*George M!
The Apple Tree
Cactus Flower
*The Most Happy Fella
The Star-Spangled Girl

The first musical of the season, **George M!**, starred Angelo Mango. Rambow of *The Enquirer* reported "a standing ovation, bravos, and highly enthusiastic applause for star Mango at the finale. His dancing prowess is beginning to match his constant growth as a singer. In the demanding role, he gave his finest performance in several seasons."

Carlson of the *Gazette* remarked that the musical, about America's most famous song and dance man, was "made-to-order for Mango who has virtually turned it into a one-man show. That was the verdict of an opening night audience who gave Mango a standing ovation." However, the critic went on to observe that there was an "abrasive quality" in the character of Cohan, but that in Mango's performance it was "less prevailing" than when Joel Grey played it in the initial tryout at Detroit's Fisher Theatre.

Of note is that the production took place at the height of the Vietnam War, a year after the assassinations of Martin Luther King and Robert Kennedy, the launching of the Vietcong's Tet Offensive and massive student moratoriums against the war — hardly a time to wave flags and sing "Over There."

Carlson added that **George M!** was a "family affair" for the Ragotzys, with "little Brendan appearing briefly as the very young George M. Cohan; his mother, Betty Ebert, portraying the

Joan Dunham and Angelo Mango in
The Most Happy Fella — 1969

actress Fay Templeton and even Papa Ragotzy getting into the act as one of the party guests."

In August, Frank Loesser's very difficult, almost operatic (35 songs and recitative)**The Most Happy Fella** was produced, constituting a major departure for Ragotzy. Rambow of *The Enquirer* called Angelo Mango, as Tony, and Joan Dunham, as his mail order bride, Rosebella, "Spellbinders! A splendid duo."

Carlson of the *Gazette* remarked with some surprise, "One hardly expected a musical that verges on opera to elicit thunderous applause from theatregoers accustomed to much lighter fare. People who have attended Barn attractions for 24 years tell us **Fella** is the Barn's crowning achievement.

"The performances by Angelo Mango and Joan Dunham seem destined to be remembered by Barn patrons for years to come. The production is a triumph, too, for director-choreographer Wayne Lamb, musical director Richard Hintz and producer Jack Ragotzy who have retained the integrity of the late [Loesser died two weeks prior to the production], great composer-lyricist's original."

Swank of *The Citizen Patriot* reported that the packed house was "delighted" opening night and that "Angelo Mango is cast perfectly as Tony. He gives one of his finest performances. His acting is flawless and his singing voice assumed almost an operatic quality rather than the musical comedy voice to which the Barn audience has been accustomed."

After these raves came the dissenting voice of a piqued Gerald Elliott, music critic for *The Press*. "The show needs excellent singers throughout," he lamented. "It didn't have them. In his curtain speech, Ragotzy explained that several of his singers had come down with laryngitis. But several of those who sang poorly were afflicted with nothing more virulent than tin ears." However, Elliott did offer some praise, saying, "Joan Dunham and Angelo Mango are first-rate. Both have excellent voices, both sing on pitch, and both handle a tune with assurance. In truth, they are the only two principals who seemed to me to be comfortable in their roles."

Meanwhile, of course, Jack had **Angela** on his mind. Because of its extremely positive reception at the Barn during the previous summer, he was sure he finally had a show that would make it on B'way. It was three years ago that he had left NY for Hollywood, discouraged that his dream of a B'way success hadn't materialized during his 17 years of struggling. But he had never really given up hope of having a B'way hit someday. He was beginning to think that if **Angela** succeeded, he might just move the family back to the City.

Then came the casting fiasco, the all night rewrites, Jim Hammerstein's putting in the changes during the day, the first NY preview, and finally Jim Hammerstein's words – "It's too bad but you were right; it's the boy's show. We should never have made the changes."

Ever since he had made his entrance on the NY Theatre scene with **Mamba's Daughters**, Jack had worked feverishly to bring in a successful production. He had told himself over and over that the difference between success and failure was hanging in, that most people gave up just shy of success. If they had stayed the course, he believed, they would have made it.

Three different Barnies have told me that they phoned Jack when he returned to California after the **Angela** debacle. All said he was experiencing a difficult depression, saying, "I just can't do this any longer."

Years later, when interviewed for this book, Jack explained, "Although it didn't happen all at once — because I was so depressed — eventually I began to wonder if directing on or off-B'way was really all that important. And then in early spring, Betty got me going on the summer season. There was a play that I respected and wanted desperately to direct, and I suddenly realized that none of the **Angela** angst stopped me from wanting to produce and direct at the Barn. So, at midpoint in my theatre career, I chose to continue to live in Hollywood. Betty and I would raise Brendan and focus our energy on the work at the Barn."

Every season there was a Ford ad on the back cover of the Barn programs.
(Don Seelye Ford dealership, Kalamazoo)

Part II

In the first 23 years of the Barn, Jack had directed 128 productions. Now he would concentrate on producing — and direct only those shows he felt needed his special touch. In some odd way, he felt the '70 season was like starting all over again. He assigned the first show, the two-character musical **I Do! I Do!**, to Lamb. The two of them would co-direct the second, **Mame**, and then Jack would direct the show he was excited about working on, **The Boys in the Band**.

1970
I Do! I Do!
Mame
*The Boys in the Band
*Man of La Mancha
Cabaret
A Flea in Her Ear

Two years after it first opened, Mort Crowley's play was still running strong in NY, but with dogged determination Jack had secured the first Michigan stock rights.

Rambow, the female critic from *The Enquirer*, wrote that the play is "a penetrating study of the plight of the homophile whose hang-ups are both similar to and different from those of all humanity."

By contrast, all of the male critics who gave rave reviews managed to include a subtle disclaimer, distancing themselves from the play's subject matter.

Nicolette of *The Press* called the production "stunning" and wrote, "It is fascinating to watch the portrayals of characters who seem to be from another world. At times the authenticity is questionable. Are there really such emotionally troubled individuals? Perhaps a deviate or a psychiatrist could best report on that. Crowley's greatest contribution is bringing the whispered subject into the open in a vehicle that is strong, thought-provoking and entertaining.

"The strong directorial hand of Jack Ragotzy is at the base of the production's success. The cast is exceptional, with Angelo Mango creating one of his most memorable characters as the pressured Michael. Dick Fuchs' Emory appears almost a caricature of the over-effeminate male, until his great scene in the second act when he

Dick Fuchs — 1970

tells Emory's touching story of rejection and ridicule as a youth. All the swishing and femininity suddenly unfold as a sad defensive ploy. George McDaniel is powerful in the role of Alan."

Swank of *The Citizen Patriot* said the drama "swings wide the doors so that the audience can get an intimate view of the homosexual's fears, loves, loneliness and self-recrimination. It is one of the most powerful plays to come to the American stage. It was so perfectly performed and directed that it very well could be the biggest hit of the Barn's season."

Carlson of the *Gazette* alleged, "**The Boys in the Band** is a play of substance and Jack Ragotzy's staging results in the best performed play seen at the Barn in years." He ends: "The play offers a new, highly entertaining and sometimes shocking view of contemporary Western society."

After its enormous success and controversy — Angelo Mango thought it was "the most controversial show at the Barn during his tenure there" — Ragotzy eventually slumped back into a state of ennui. He had no long range goal to substitute for his years of wanting to make it as a B'way director. He was burnt out and Betty knew he could not keep up the demands of the Barn's rehearsal schedule: 11 to 1 with an hour break for lunch, back at 2 and rehearse till 5, greet the audience, watch the show and then paper block the next act of the coming week's show to get ready for the morning rehearsal. No, he could not do that and, at the same time, act as producer.

It was then that a pattern began to emerge. In '70 Jack allowed Lamb to direct **La Mancha** and **Cabaret** (with co-director John Weeks) along with **A Flea in Her Ear** which ended the season. In '71 Jack would direct a non-demanding **Plaza Suite** and Wayne Lamb and Louis Girard would do all the shows for the rest of the season. In '72 Jack directed only two farces, a genre he was fond of, and left the rest of the season to Lamb.

And why not?

It has been said that as soon as a show is cast, it is about 70 percent completed. NY casting director Stuart Howard agrees, but with a caveat. The show is 70 percent finished if the director knows what he's doing; but if he doesn't, the production may flounder. As producer, Ragotzy always had input on the shows, even if someone else was directing. He could watch rehearsals during the week or he could make changes during the

The Boys in the Band (L to R in front) James D. Smith, Dick Fuchs (seated on floor), Louis Girard (wearing sunglasses), William Olen, George McDaniel; (L to R in back) Bob Shephard, Angelo Mango, Michael Reno and Wes Finley — 1970

traditional Sunday shop run-through before the opening.

A substitute for his all-consuming objective to make it on B'way took some years to develop, but it eventually came in the form of wanting to do the special play — like **Boys in the Band** which he believed in and felt strongly about — along with a proprietary interest in the Barn's apprentice alumni. Jack began to see and take pride in the fact that he was actually training talented young people for the profession. And after the **Angela** casting he knew that a first rate production did not depend on so-called star power. He could see the results of his training and effort when his kids would make it on B'way or in Hollywood. He remembered that once he actually thought he might be a teacher.

One apprentice he had a great deal of faith in was George McDaniel, who had been a good lighting designer and actor but hadn't yet received the role that would make him a Barn star. Jack took a risk when — in that transitional season in his own life, the summer of '71 — he cast young George as Cervantes in **Man of La Mancha**. He was rewarded enormously with the result that McDaniel became a Barn star and his opportunities in the larger world of show biz outside the Barn began to grow. Such victories would accumulate and give Ragotzy a new *raison d'etre*.

Jack had obtained the first stock company release in Michigan for **Man of La Mancha,** and it proved a money-making three-week hit, elevating George McDaniel into full-fledged Barn stardom. It also provided Jack an opportunity to have a creative outlet not by directing but by clarifying the story line. Nicolette of *The Press* observed, "In previous viewing of productions by touring companies, the story line was slightly confusing to those not familiar with Cervantes' writings. In the Barn production, the tale is clear as crystal and should absorb even those who never heard of Quixote or his tilting at windmills.

"McDaniel creates the two roles of Cervantes and Quixote, making the transition from vigorous and confident intellectual to aging and somewhat foolish idealist with great acting skill. He is also in peak singing form, delivering all the songs in a strong and steady baritone. Joan Dunham is a beautiful angel with a dirty face in the roles of the prostitute, Aldonza, and the spiritual lady of purity, Dulcinea. Her portrayal is touching, and she has an opportunity to make full use of her considerable range of singing voice. Howard McBride is a wonderful Sancho."

Swank of *The Citizen Patriot* said simply, "This is the finest show that producer Ragotzy has staged in many years."

La Mancha was a hard act to follow.

When Joan Dunham was unexpectedly called away, the leading role in the next show, **Cabaret**, was taken over by apprentice Cynthia Crumlish, who had appeared briefly in **Mame** and **La Mancha**. This was derring-do casting on Ragotzy's part. Swank of *The Citizen Patriot* remarked, "One of the surprises was the scintillating performance of Cynthia Crumlish, a first-year apprentice. Cast in the role of Sally, major attraction of the Kit Kat Klub, she was splendid in every way."

George McDaniel as Don Quixote in
Man of La Mancha — 1970

Carlson of the *Gazette* gave this appraisal: "The Augusta company has turned out a big, brassy, scenically imaginative, fast-moving show that seems to succeed in everything but being genuine. The result is a **Cabaret** that's good without being great. The show does have something, however, that not even the B'way original had. It's a song entitled 'I Don't Care Much.' We'll never understand why it was dropped from the NY staging."

In '71 Joan Dunham returned for two shows that would prove to be her last at the Barn. The first was **Hello Dolly!** Swank of *The Citizen Patriot* lauded Dunham, calling her "a brilliant star, who dazzled a capacity audience in a scintillating performance. She has been a star at the Barn for several years but her performance in this musical must be her finest."

Roger Leavenworth of *The Enquirer* agreed: "In spite of the heat, in spite of the bugs, in spite of tired voices and a ragged orchestra and in spite of the show's ponderous banality, opening night at the Barn turned out to be a considerable personal triumph for Joan Dunham."

Next came the first Michigan summer stock presentation of **Forty Carats**, which starred Dunham in her last appearance at the Barn. Tragically, several years later when she was playing at a dinner theatre in Chicago, she was killed in an automobile accident.

Next — something very special — the Barn's first production of **Fiddler on the Roof**. Nicolette of *The News* called it "beautiful" and noted, "The show is accompanied by one of the best orchestras — under the direction of Larry Wolfe — the Barn has had for any of its many musical presentations. Lamb and his cast have settled for nothing less than the very best in all the roles from Angelo Mango as a marvelous Tevye to villagers with no lines but completely involved reactions."

1971
Plaza Suite
Hello, Dolly!
Forty Carats
*Fiddler on the Roof
Play it Again, Sam

Swank of *The Citizen Patriot* declared, "**Fiddler** could undoubtedly be the Barn's longest running musical. The role is tailor-made for Mango. He long will be remembered for his superb performance." Leavenworth of *The Enquirer* gave this high praise: "Seems a shame that the Barn Theatre didn't open their sea-

Angelo Mango and Betty Ebert in **Fiddler on the Roof** — 1971

son this year with **Fiddler**. Had this been the case, no other production would have been necessary for the entire summer, or next summer or maybe even the summer after that. Yes, the show is that good — both as a play and production. Paul Abe, the lighting designer, and David Potts, who designed the scenery [both graduate students from Purdue], have done their best work of the season."

Fiddler was the second show in the Barn's history to play a four-week run. Jack announced during its third week that it had already played to more people than any other three-week production and would surpass all records after completing its fourth week. As Frankie would croon — "It was a very good year."

The outstanding show of the '72 season was **1776**. Elliott, the critic from *The Press* who had so disliked **The Most Happy Fella**, was back. This time he wrote, "Midway in the musical, John Adams looks perturbed following a ribald exchange with Benjamin Franklin. Whereupon Franklin says, 'Don't worry, John — the history books will clean it up.' It's doubtful Franklin ever said any such thing, but he was capable of it, and it was in character.

1972
Last of the Red Hot Lovers
*1776
Promises, Promises
A Funny Thing Happened on the Way to the Forum
Company
Norman, Is That You?

"In fact, one of the strong points of **1776** is that it's all in character. The historic figures, comprising the Continental Congress, are depicted as they really were — lusty, sometimes rude and often crude men;

(L to R in front) John Newton as Franklin, Howard McBride, (standing in back), Michael Reno, Larry E. Burash, Joe Boles, Michael McEowen, John Eldridge (on table). (Rear) Dale Helward, John Beilock and Ken Andrews in **1776** — 1972

earthy and tough-minded. For more than a century historians and biographers sanitized, dry-cleaned and ironed out the men who made the decision in the name of the 13 colonies to cut loose from England. And generations of Americans lived with these starched, overstuffed characters who were better fitted for Madame Tussaud's wax museum than for history books.

"So now, thanks to a really superb play, they are restored to us as they were. Peter Stone has taken only slight liberties with history, and his version is much nearer the facts than were those 19th century history books. And as always happens when history is told truthfully and the play of human emotions is given full sway, **1776** emerges as one of the finest, most satisfying and tensest dramas of the decade.

"At the center is John Adams, played magnificently by Angelo Mango. His performance is matched by John Newton's as Franklin. Although many other members of the cast have their brilliant moments on stage, it is these two who really carry the drama. What a glorious way to celebrate the Fourth of July, in the company of such extraordinary people — the originals and the actors who play them," Elliott concluded.

Art Sills, *Gazette* staff writer, had an opposite view. "As history, **1776** is a great gob of cotton candy. It is Edwards' and Stone's version of what went on in Philadelphia's Continental Congress as it prepared to adopt the Declaration of Independence. As entertainment, it is a perfect fable for a summer night. But it should carry a precautionary warning: it is a pure parody of patriotism. It's a vaudeville version of those historic months in Philadelphia, complete with clean blue jokes and skits that seriously distort the philosophical issues at stake."

Christopher Hughes of *The Citizen Patriot* pointed out that the sets by David Potts "are magnificent" and went on to say, "Potts, who designed and built the **Fiddler** set, returned from England

Judith Ann Williams as Amy and John Eldridge as Paul in **Company** — 1972

to be at the Barn this summer, and his presence is obvious." It's worth noting that Potts went on to design B'way's *As Is*, *The Musical Comedy Murders of 1940* and *Born Yesterday* with Madeline Kahn, as well as designing for national tours and the major regional theatres.

The following May, Betty had a late dinner with four apprentices. They had arrived at the Barn the previous week to help set up and get ready for the June 12 opening of **The Convertible Girl**. The four were Barbara McKay, 22, of St. Charles, Illinois; Michele Frierson, 20, of Los Angeles; her friend, Janette E. LaLanne, 21, of Hollywood; and Mark Schwamberger, 20, of Louisville, Kentucky.

Janette, the daughter of the well-known TV exercise program personality, Jack LaLanne, had driven across country from Hollywood after spending the winter completing an acting course with Lee Strasberg. The previous season — her first year of apprenticeship — she appeared in a small role in **Promises, Promises** and as Panacea in **A Funny Thing Happened on the Way to the Forum**. The experience had whetted her theatrical appetite, and she was hoping to win her Equity card and then head to NY after the season.

Around 9:45 p.m. the four decided to go to Kalamazoo. Janette was driving west toward Galesburg on M-96 when she lost control and struck a mailbox. The car rolled three and a half times and came to rest on its top. LaLanne and McKay, who was sitting in the seat behind her, were thrown from the vehicle. Both suffered chest and abdominal injuries. The four were transported to Borgess Hospital by the Galesburg Ambulance Service where LaLanne died at 1:10 a.m. McKay remained at the hospital in "satisfactory condition," while both Frierson and Schwamberger, who suffered only minor injuries, were released.

LaLanne's body was taken to the Farley-Schlueter Funeral Home in Augusta to await final arrangements by her parents, who could not immediately be reached since they were on their way home from Europe. Later, a funeral home spokesman said that cremation services

Megan Messing and Dick Fuchs in **Butterflies Are Free** — 1973

had been scheduled at Forest Lawn Memorial Gardens, Hollywood Hills, Glendale. It was one more tragedy for the Barn family to endure. In her memory, the Barn carried LaLanne's name in the company listing and displayed her photo in the lobby throughout the season.

1973
The Convertible Girl
Butterflies Are Free
Applause
How the Other Half Loves
Stop the World – I Want to Get Off
Pajama Tops
*Hair

The other three apprentices stayed for the Barn's season. Michele Frierson was in **Applause**, **Stop the World,** and **Hair**; Barbara McKay returned to play the role of Eve Harrington in **Applause**, Jane in **Stop the Word**, and Jeanie in **Hair**. Mark Schwamberger appeared in **Applause** and **Hair** and, in the extended production of that musical in September, replaced Jeff Lee as the character, Woof.

After an absence of ten years, Natalie Ross was welcomed back to star as Margo Channing in **Applause**. Following her '60 season at Augusta, she had gone to NY and within a year was cast as Connie, the leading female role in Neil Simon's *Come Blow Your Horn*, opposite Hal March. She did two more NY shows and appeared in television on *The Patty Duke Show*, *The Doctors* (with Jim Pritchett) and *The Ed Sullivan Show*.

A newcomer to the Equity company in '73 was Tim Landfield, who had made such a hit as Lee in **1776** and David in **Company** the previous season. Tim had completed a year of independent study in the performing arts at Hampshire College where he taught dance and acting.

In addition, one of my Purdue students,

Wayne Lamb directs rehearsal of **Stop the World — I Want to Get Off** (revival) starring Angelo Mango — 1973
(Michael Reno at the organ; Angelo Mango second from right)

Peter Schneider, who had apprenticed for two seasons, was hired as stage manager — a good job for acquiring the organizational skills he would use as the future President of Animation and Theatrical Productions in such shows as B'way's *Lion King* for Walt Disney Studios.

This was the summer of love and peace at the Barn — in short, the summer of **Hair**. Jack had worked for four months to get the release — the first for a stock company — of this hugely successful B'way musical. "I couldn't be happier," Ragotzy chortled. "We have a great company for the show and the decision wasn't just to do **Hair**, but to get a show that would exercise the talents of our company. The cast is so bloody enthused — and we'll be able to give our audiences a full production, complete and uncut."

The show was originally scheduled for only one week, but a second was added prior to the opening because "ticket sales exceeded every other show in the theatre's 28-year history." Since it didn't open until August 14 and apprentices had to get back to college for the fall term, there wasn't a possibility of more than a three-week run, however popular the show would be.

How was this highly controversial, uncut, '60s musical accepted in the environs of the small community of Augusta?

The critic for *The Citizen Patriot* found it an inter-generational experience. "**Hair** is probably the most ambitious ever staged in the 28-year history of the theatre. For 2-1/2 hours, the 34-member cast held the complete attention of the sell-out audience. The opening night acclaim is a tribute to the professionalism of the company and director and choreographer, Wayne Lamb.

"Is **Hair** just for the younger generation? I wouldn't bet on it. As the performance ended, a white-haired woman in her 70s in the sixth row was on her feet clapping and singing."

In a reference to the OPEC crisis which gripped the nation that year and resulted in shortages, price hikes and long lines at the gas pumps, Nicolette of *The Press* wrote, "Where is this energy crisis? Certainly not on the stage of the Barn Theatre. A very large cast of full-voiced, uninhibited and swinging young people have taken over the stage, nay, the whole theatre, for the production of **Hair**. Performances are generally very good, with Timothy Land-

Natalie Ross with her name on a B'way marquee — 1961

field and Dick Fuchs as Claude and Berger leading the Tribe in free and happy fashion.

"Yes, the Barn production includes nudity. First in the traditional scene in which some members elect to stand unclothed as Claude (Timothy Landfield) sings the plaintive 'Where Do I Go?' In another scene, Claude is presented without clothes as the group sings of 'What a Piece of Work Is Man.' Is this one necessary? Well, perhaps not, but there's nothing wrong or obscene about the human body. So, nudity is included in two brief scenes. Other songs or scenes may be more offensive to some. Sex is flaunted quite a bit, which is part of the protest against prudery."

(L to R in front) David L. Clow III, Peter Schneider, Earl Hughes and Michael Reno (in back with sunglasses) behind the scenes in **Hair** — 1973

Eric Riley — 1973

Tim Landfield — 1973

Carlson of the *Gazette* raised this point: "If **Hair** is here, can *Oh! Calcutta!* be far behind? Don't pooh-pooh the question. Four years ago **Hair** was shocking even by NY standards, and there were predictions it would never get west of the Hudson. But this production is not the laundered version presented by a touring company here in '71. It turned up last night at the Barn and a capacity audience appeared to take it in stride.

"The 'tribal love-rock musical' originally intended to be a putdown of the Establishment got embraced by it last night. Any show that has middle-aged squares dancing in the aisles when it was supposed to have outraged them, may be said to have been a success that died by its own hand."

Peggy Nelson of *The Enquirer* was impressed. "Bravo Mike Reno, Wayne Lamb, Dick Fuchs, Tim Landfield and producer Jack Ragotzy. Bravo for doing the rock musical **Hair** and doing it well." She called the production "an experience, rather than just a play" and repeated all the acclaim other critics gave the show with special emphasis: "The highlight of the show is the talented area black performers, including Eric Riley, who does the solo in 'Aquarius,' and Ron Wyatt, who leads 'Great God of Power.' Both are from Battle Creek. And Kalamazoo's James Peddy Hud and Edwina Lewis are particularly outstanding."

With the Barn's success that season, Jack decided to make two major additions to the physical plant. He'd had enough of spraying water over the Barn's roof to cool the auditorium down and decided to install real air-conditioning. He also turned the rehearsal shed into a bar that would

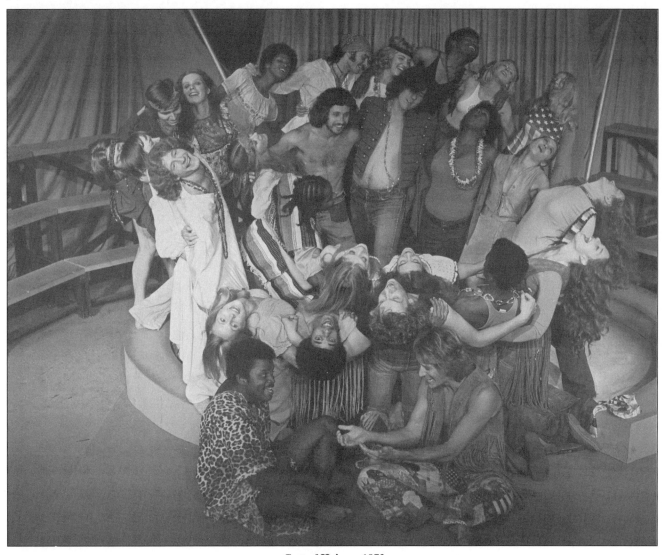

Cast of **Hair** — 1973

feature after-show entertainment. "This is an exciting concept," he announced, "and it will give us the opportunity to provide our audiences with a really full evening's entertainment." The Rehearsal Shed shows would be directed by Michael Reno, actor, dancer, choreographer and musical director.

Ragotzy found a "bar with character," only to learn it had already been purchased the day he went to make the down payment. With a lot of sweet talk and a little negotiating on the part of the store manager, the company arranged for the buyer to get a good deal on a new bar and then sold the used one to the ever-persistent Ragotzy.

That Championship Season with (L to R) Angelo Mango, Dick Fuchs, Jim R. Sprague, Tim Landfield and Louis Girard – 1974

Betty decorated the Rehearsal Shed with memorabilia from B'way shows that the Barn had produced, making the bar yet another reason for patrons to attend the main stage productions. It remains a money-maker to this day, a place where apprentices get experience not only in bartending but in entertaining an audience. Above all it's a place for customer enjoyment.

1974
6 Rms Riv Vu
No, No, Nanette
*That Championship Season
Sugar
The Prisoner of Second Avenue
*Jesus Christ, Superstar

During the '74 season, Ragotzy announced that he would produce Sumner Arthur Long's new play, *The Javelin Catcher*. The production never materialized, but the announcement revealed that Jack, who had even stopped visiting NYC, had not totally abandoned his interest in the production of new scripts.

Ragotzy's direction of **That Championship Season**, winner of a Pulitzer Prize, Tony, and the NY Drama Critics Circle Award, inspired James Shamp of the *Gazette* to write: "This is a play where the dialogue sizzles. And if you're the

Edwina Lewis — 1973

type whose ears can't stand the heat, get out of the Barn because the play is not your cup of tea. Director Ragotzy has taken a bold step in offering this production, replete with its locker-room lingo, for the first time in this area's straw hat circuit, where cotton candy often attracts more customers than does a heartier fare.

"Angelo Mango is outstanding and Jim R. Sprague, Dick Fuchs, Timothy Landfield and Louis Girard all log winning performances. **Season** is one of those rare productions you may want to see more than once."

Nicolette of *The Press* concurred: "Strong portrayals and excellent interpretation of the playwright's theme gave Jason Miller's drama the stature of one of the finest in American theatre. The strong guidance of director Jack Ragotzy keeps the play well in the field of powerful drama. The play offers plenty of humor, but the laughter becomes less pure enjoyment and more a nervous realization of emotional truths as the moral decay of the 'winning is everything' philosophy becomes evident.

"It is a rugged play, with popular expletives used freely and sexual escapades discussed with abandon. But it is not a dirty nor titillating play. Ragotzy apparently knew he had a good one going, because even before opening night, he extended the show's scheduled run from one week to two."

In mid-July an article in *The Citizen Patriot* about the Ragotzys headlined, "Team a hit — in marriage, theatre," and noted that Jack and Betty "had been married 28 years in spite of disapproving friends who said the marriage would never last." Betty is quoted as saying, 'In summer stock you have to work very hard and very fast. It's a seven-day work week from 10 a.m. each day to midnight. And what we've made always goes back into the theatre.'"

She went on to note that winters were easier than the long summers for her, but not for Jack. "He travels, working on theatrical negotiations while I'm at home, being a den mother for our 11-year-old son's Scout troop." Although Hollywood was their winter habitat, Betty said the family "considers Michigan their home and they are planning a permanent move here."

The final show of the season was **Jesus Christ, Superstar**. Nelson of *The Enquirer* wrote in Harlequin Romance cover-blurb style, "Jesus Christ is a dim star next to the dazzling Judas of Eric Riley, a first-year apprentice from Battle Creek, who mesmerizes the audience with his moving, intense portrayal. He uses all of his gorgeously gracefully limber body from his tight throbbing belly and sinewy arms, to his deep, hotly expressive eyes, strong emotions and great voice. His dancing, singing and acting brought goose bumps and near tears to the audience, particularly in his wrenching portrayal of a man's unbearable horror at having betrayed a friend in the song 'Judas' Death.'"

Ray Dennis of *The Citizen Patriot* extolled: "A brilliant production of the rock opera was rewarded with a standing ovation. The sellout audience was completely turned on by the beat and music for the musical superhit. The Barn personnel went all out on this production, and sur-

Tim Landfield in **Jesus Christ, Superstar** with Eric Riley as Judas — 1974

Tim Landfield in **Jesus Christ, Superstar** — 1974

passed the performance of last season's hit, **Hair**. Major credit for the smash success must go to Michael Reno, the Barn's musical director.

"Turning in his finest performance since joining the Barn company in 1972, was Timothy Landfield in the title role. But almost stealing the show was the performance of Eric Riley, who came into his own as the surly Judas, his gospel-like singing winning the acclaim of the audience. The Barn's presentation was the first authorized summer stock showing anywhere in the world, and is a cinch for a smash success during the two-week run. And it won't be surprising if it is held over for a third week."

Barbara Marineau — 1975

1975
An Evening with Angelo Mango
*The Sunshine Boys
Seesaw
*Move Over, Mrs. Markham
Godspell
Fiddler on the Roof
Hair
Not Now, Darling
An Evening with Angelo Mango

In '47, Ed Marineau of Battle Creek had played in **Kiss and Tell** and **Green Grow the Lilacs**. Now 28 years later his daughter, Barbara, who graduated from Western Michigan University and had studied at the Commonstock Theatre Workshop in White Chapel, London, was one of the few actors in Barn history to be signed to an Equity contract in her first summer of stock. Locally she had received accolades for her performances as Sally Bowles in *Cabaret* for the Battle Creek Civic and Reno Sweeney in *Anything Goes* for the Kalamazoo Civic.

Patricia Wettig returned for her second summer of apprenticeship and again played only small roles. Later, however, she would appear in the hit TV series *Thirty Something* and in both *City Slicker* films with Billy Crystal.

Eric Riley was also back, this time as an Equity member. Jack announced that Merle Louise would return to star in **Seesaw**, after having created the role of Susan on B'way in Sondheim's *Company*.

And there was the first edition of **An Evening with Angelo Mango**, which would precede the first main stage show and in which Mango would recap, for a two-week run, memorable musical moments from his twenty seasons at the theatre.

Dennis of *The Citizen Patriot* called this

Patricia Wettig — 1974/5 apprentice

first Rehearsal Shed show "an enjoyable evening of musical memories. With the combination of hit melodies and Mango's talents, the Barn's innovative effort seems assured of a hit run. Mango receives help from two talented young singers and dancers, Barbara Marineau and Patricia Wettig. It's an evening that should bring back pleasant memories for regular Barn Theatre patrons, and one that introduces an outstanding performer to those seeing him for the first time."

Bob Sinclair, who must have moved up from the sports page of *The Enquirer*, jock-talked, "Ragotzy-to-Mango-to-Marineau, the only triple-play in history that resulted in a hit, opened at the Rehearsal Shed lounge and got a standing ovation for fans of the Barn's most popular performer. Ragotzy provided the cozy facility, seating 75 at round tables, with genuine theatrical lighting, while his star, Angelo Mango, recreated songs and dances from many of his 48 shows at the Barn.

"Another star, Barbara Marineau, appeared and displayed beauty, talent and professional showmanship that enthralled the audience. The second she stepped on stage, everyone there knew it and is not apt to forget it. But the evening was devoted to Mango, a loveable, charming, effervescent triple-threat actor-singer-dancer."

In the season's opener, Neil Simon's **The Sunshine Boys,** Ragotzy cast himself as Al Lewis, a kindly, soft-spoken, retired comedian (obviously a stretch role!). Louis Girard played Willie Clark, the other half of the vaudeville team of Lewis & Clark, while Dale Helward was cast as Ben Silverman, Clark's nephew, a theatrical agent who attempts to reunite the two stubborn, former colleagues.

Sinclair of *The Enquirer* called Girard's performance "the finest of his career," saying he "wooed and easily won a sell-out audience with his portrayal of a stormy, stubborn, reluctantly retired vaudevillian in Simon's over-long but charming two-act character study. Providing perfect contrast to Girard's blustery role was Producer Jack Ragotzy as his former partner, in an all-too-infrequent appearance on stage. Ragotzy, a pro in every sense of the word, beautifully underplayed the part of the sincere and unhappily misunderstood member of a once-famous comedy team. He evoked sympathy and laughter as the foil for his overbearing ex-comrade-in-hilarity. His was a warm, sensitive portrayal with quiet power, a role masterfully played by a master."

Carlson of the *Gazette* commented that "Girard and Ragotzy make **The Sunshine Boys** a considerably better show than was evident in the touring company production seen here a couple of months ago." Nicolette of *The News* was off to Stratford, Canada, to cover the Shakespearean Festival; but in a naughty guys-will-be-guys column, inconceivable in today's climate of political correctness, his substitute, Frank Hill, lasciviously wrote, "This year the Barn is balancing things for the men. For several seasons now the ladies have had Dick Fuchs to ogle. Now the guys get some *quid pro quo* in the form of Barbara Marineau. Wow, what a form! The Marshall Rotary Club was in the audience, and what a lot of sunshine boys there are in that group. I will admit that all the bifocals got put to good use when Barbara Marineau bowed for the curtain call. Our hands were raw from applauding in hopes she would bow some more. I bet Ragotzy thought all that clapping was for him."

The opening musical was **Seesaw,** a second-rate musical which, very unlike producer Ragotzy, was badly miscast. Carlson of the *Gazette* pointed out that "Merle Louise looks and sounds like a gal from Omaha and Angelo Mango looks and sounds like a chap from NY. And that casts a visual and phonetic variation on the story about the slightly square, WASP lawyer from Nebraska who flees a suffocating marriage and turns up in NY to play roomy with a kooky, sleep-around, would-be dancer with an accent about six times as rich as lox."

As for **Move Over, Mrs. Markham**, one of Jack's favorite farces, Carlson of the *Gazette* (also printed in *The Citizen Patriot*) wrote this scathing critique: "**Markham** is a lower order of comedy with hoary jokes, tired situations and a suggestiveness that always nearly falls short of being out-and-out dirty. Detailing the plot would be only slightly less arduous than preparing instructions on how to build a thermonuclear reactor. All the performers carry off their assignments admirably, although courageously might be a better way to put it."

Sinclair of *The Enquirer* had an opposite opinion: "The Barn's production is directed with incredibly effective comic timing by Jack

Ragotzy. Much of the hilarity springs from sight gags, and thanks to Ragotzy's superior direction, the cast was a joy as it romped into and out of hiding, bed, and one another's identities."

Is it any wonder producers go crazy?

1976 – 1985

1976
Corn Crib Revue
Habeas Corpus
Not Now, Darling
1776
The Ritz
You Can't Take it With You
*Candide
Guys and Dolls
*Revelation
You Can't Take It With You (reprise)

The fourth decade opened with another evening show with Barn favorite, Angelo Mango, directed by Wayne Lamb with some narrative and skit material by Jack Ragotzy.

Sinclair of *The News* happily remarked, "Mango delights in what is quaintly billed as the **Corn Crib Revue**. This bubbly, little prancing dynamo may not be a great singer, he may not be a great dancer, but he can croon a ballad or belt a novelty number with the best of them. Lisby Lar-

Robin Haynes — 1976

son, one of the most attractive women ever to grace the Barn stage, along with Becky Gelke [formerly Becky Gilbert, and at the time of this writing, Becky Ann Baker] and Margo Smith are a most enjoyable presence, particularly when they ripple through a skit originally written by producer Jack Ragotzy [from Jack's Co-Star project] for none other than Tallulah Bankhead."

Bell of the *Gazette* (also published in *The Citizen Patriot*) called the revue "a pleasing and generous helping of informal cabaret entertainment. Mango is aided and abetted by a group of young performers getting in some spotlight licks before the regular season bows. Barn newcomer Lisby Larson is impressive along with Becky Gelke, Robin Haynes, and Barbara Whinnery."

The opening main stage production was yet another sex farce, **Habeas Corpus**, and Sinclair of *The News* saw a trend. "If Barn Theatre audiences ever get tired of silly, sexy English farces, Jack Ragotzy would have to cancel a third of each season, or, horrors, come up with something else. Two of the offerings last year were of this ilk, his regular theatre season opened with another, and next Tuesday he plans to present once

Lisby Larson — 1976

Barbara Whinnery — 1976

again the one with which he closed his season last year. Enough just may be enough. Either Ragotzy loves these pointlessly entertaining exercises in British sexual self-consciousness, or he figures his audiences do. One is led to venture a guess that they do — up to a point. That point may well have been reached. After seeing a few of these 'Hee, hee, we're talking about sex' episodes, one begins to feel one has seen them all."

Bockstanz of the *Gazette* added, "It's difficult to understand how playwright Bennett had the audacity — or the imagination — to ever think he could turn a pair of 'falsies' into a full blown evening of entertainment. But write it he did, and Ragotzy, knowing intimately the tastes of his rural audiences at the Barn, latched onto it and came up with a smash hit. It is a slapstick sort of evening, but what else did you expect on opening night?"

Both critics had high praise for the actors. But in light of the critical comments, one wonders why Ragotzy would, in this fourth decade, continue to present sex farces? One can only assume he was making money because of the inexpensive royalties and because of their appeal to Barn audiences. Since he continued to present them even in the fifth decade and beyond and has, for the most part, directed them himself, one can also conclude that he is fond of farce — a genre rarely seen on B'way since mid century, although hardly a season passes in London's West End when one is not played.

Habeas Corpus and **Not Now, Darling** were soon followed by a Terrence McNally farce, **The Ritz**, set in a pre-AIDS, gay men's bath house in NY City. Sinclair of *The News* was not amused. "Vulgarity is not necessarily funny, nor does frenetic stage activity necessarily constitute good theatre," he argued. "The Barn's newest offering abounds in both and is neither funny nor very good."

However, he did find some things to praise. "The only elements of the show worthy of applause are three musical numbers and a delightful, if somewhat over-exuberant, performance by Becky Gelke as a would-be singer who can barely speak the language. One of her musical numbers is sung in fractured English while two nearly nude males bump and grind. In another number, Louis Girard is marvelous pantomiming an old Andrews Sisters record in an ill-fitting WAC uni-

Becky Gelke — 1976

Tom Wopat — 1976

form. He brings down the house."

Becky Gelke also received kudos from Carlson of the *Gazette*: "She is absolutely terrific as Goodie Gomez, a chanteuse of virtually no talent whatsoever, who stalks a 'gay' NY steambath in search of a producer who will turn her into a second Bette Midler."

The next production was a real change of pace. Sinclair of *The Enquirer* remarked, "If **You Can't Take It With You**, directed by Ragotzy, isn't his biggest comedy hit in years, it'll be because area theatergoers just don't care for really good theatre. There isn't an off-color line in it, let alone a four-letter word and the near-sellout opening night audience loved every minute of it." Kit Lane of *The* (Glenn Shores) *Commercial Record* agreed, "After a summer season of sex farces, broken only by a two week Bicentennial run of **1776**, the Augusta Barn Theatre has tried a real old fashioned

(L to R foreground) Tom Wopat, Richard Pahl, Bradley James (a.k.a. James Knox), Brian Lewis and Ted Birke. (L back) John Reeds, Richard T. Alpers and Eric J. Schussler (standing); (R back) Lang Bethea and Louis Girard in **1776** — 1976

comedy — and the crowd loved it. **You Can't Take It With You** packed them in last week."

The play was so popular that Jack brought it back for another week's run at the end of the season. It would seem that the critics were trying to persuade Ragotzy that he should balance his seasons with a few American classics and not depend so much on the frivolous sex farces.

At one time, classic American plays of the '20s and '30s had been very important to Ragotzy. In the Barn's first decade, he produced 11 of them. Then there was a hiatus of 24 years before he did **You Can't Take It With You**. In the four decades, '56 through '95, he did only six. APA (Association of Producing Artists), under the general management of Barnie Norman Kean and artistic director Ellis Rabb in their seasons at the Lyceum Theatre in NY, had considerable success reviving American classics, including *The Show-Off* with Helen Hayes, *You Can't Take It With You* and *The Royal Family*. Since other theatres have also found these and similar shows equally popular, it seems counterproductive for Ragotzy to have abandoned this genre.

Next was a show that introduced the actor who would become the Barn's biggest star in his first leading role. First year apprentice, Tom Wopat, had come to Augusta on the recommendation of Barnie Del Lewis, then head of the Madison (WI) Civic Theatre. Wopat had been highly praised by critics for his appearance earlier in the season as Edward Rutledge in **1776.** Carlson of the *Gazette* had commented that some songs were sung by company members who had not been recognized as singers, "One in particular is Thomas Wopat, who turns 'Molasses to Rum' into the musical highlight of the entire evening." Nicolette of *The Press* concurred, calling "Molasses to Rum" as sung by Wopat a stand-out scene. Sinclair of the *Enquirer* agreed: "One number stands out above all the rest, thanks to Thomas Wopat. He stops the show with 'Molasses to Rum.' It's a great piece, but Wopat makes it even greater. He has a stunning voice and superlative ability as an actor." Lane of the *Commercial Record* added, "Thomas Wopat created one of the most emotional-packed moments of the evening."

But for all his critical acclaim in **1776**, Rutledge is a one-song role, and it is to Ragotzy's credit that he then matched Wopat's talent with a show that was said to be the first stock production in the country — Leonard Bernstein's **Candide**.

When first presented on B'way in '56, **Candide** ran for only 78 performances. Revived by Harold Prince 17 years later, the production jettisoned the book by Lillian Hellman and engaged playwright Hugh Wheeler to write a new one. Steven Sondheim was brought in to write new lyrics and add songs.

Sinclair of *The Enquirer* raved: "It's one of the finest productions the Augusta theatre has ever staged and the opening night audience was spellbound. Directed extraordinarily well by Wayne Lamb, with an absolutely marvelous cast, a theatregoer can't ask for a whole lot more. Almost nobody does a musical as well as the Barn, and this one just has to be one of the best Jack Ragotzy has ever produced."

Also celebrating a winner, Carlson of the *Gazette* wrote: "A bawdy comic book, an intellectual Flying Circus, more trials and tribulations than you'll find in a month of soap opera, and one

Thomas Wopat in the title role of **Candide** with Lisby Larson as Cunegonde — 1976

(L to R) Thomas Wopat, Robin Haynes, Michael Reno, Roslyn Roseman, and sound technician Roger Gans rehearsing Reno's world premiere of **Revelation** — 1776

of the best scores ever written for the American musical stage — that's **Candide**. There's never been a show approaching this one in all 31 seasons at the summer playhouse. Ragotzy has opened up and extended the stage and even put some spectators behind the performers along with the orchestra. The result is an 'open show' that often spills over into the audience.

"Wayne Lamb has given **Candide** one of the best stagings we've seen in a decade of Augusta show-going, thanks largely to a gifted young musical director, Michael Reno, and two beautiful fledgling performers, Thomas Wopat and Lisby Larson. Wopat is ideal as the young Candide. He handles the demanding singing chores with the ease of a hillbilly ditty. His rugged face and physique also accentuates the beauty and vulnerability of Miss Larson as Candide's lady love."

Then came a review which justifies the occasional acts of violence by theatre folk such as Maria Powers, star of Menotti's *The Medium,* who reportedly went to Chicago's *Tribune* Tower carrying a large purse containing a hatchet after reading critic Claudia Cassidy's review of her. A piqued Sylvia Miles unloaded a plate of spaghetti on the head of critic John Simon of *NY* magazine. And it was once said that if *The New Yorker* critic Alexander Wolcott were found dead along B'way, two thousand actors would have been rounded up as immediate suspects.

The new "critic" from *The Press* — one Mike Lloyd — scathingly wrote: "The best of all possible actors were trapped in the worst of all possible plays Tuesday when **Candide** opened at the Barn. The show has been successful, but that's in sophisticated, droll NY, not summer stock. A seven-man band, especially when everybody isn't playing the same notes, cannot be expected to reflect, even slightly, what the composer had in mind or ear. And Sondheim's word-game lyrics become tiring because they dangle from a storyline that cannot support them. After a while they sag from being cute just for the sake of cuteness."

To be fair, critic Lloyd went on to praise the cast: "Thomas Wopat, who plays Candide, has a fine voice and is a convincing actor in a not-to-be-believed role. Lisby Larson is a delight from her first entrance to the final curtain. Her voice is easily the best in the show. Both Robin Haynes and Becky Gelke are as delightful and Angelo Mango is amazing. But the real show stopper is Mary Conetto playing The Old Lady. She gives the role a rich flavoring of the Jewish mother, Hungarian style."

The '76 season cannot pass without mention of the only world premiere of the fourth decade, Michael Reno's **Revelation**, a soft-rock musical based on the prophecies of the Book of Revelations. Reno first came to the Barn in '70 as an apprentice, and by '72 was musical director as well as a member of the Equity company. In addition to his Barn work, he headed a rock group in the San Francisco Bay area and was the conductor and arranger for the San Francisco production of *The Rocky Horror Show*.

Reno composed 27 songs in styles ranging from jazz through rock to lullaby. Wayne Lamb staged the show with a cast of 27 acting more than 100 roles. Featured were Tom Wopat, Robin Haynes and Roslyn Roseman (Mrs. Michael Reno.)

Sinclair of *The Enquirer*, in praising Ragotzy for producing a world premiere — his first in six seasons — called it "a free-wheeling musical version of the Book of Revelations." He concluded that the show wasn't great in its present state and that it needed work, "but it's a brilliant attempt by a very talented young man to write a meaningful commentary on our times, with some of the finest music this critic has ever heard in the theatre. Some of his lyrics are very good, some not so good, his dialogue is pretty much the same. His action sequences tend to be ineffectively melodramatic and his theme obfuscated, but oh, that music!"

Nicolette of *The Press* also praised the Barn for doing a new work but observed, "It is the book or the body of the work on which the music must find reason for being that is shaky. Even with St. John as co-author, the mixture of ancient writing and modern interpretation fails to hold interest. It is a fine try and the makings of a mind-stir-

Tornado! — 1977

ring entertainment is evident in Reno's imaginative attempt."

Carlson of the *Gazette* added, "The production plainly suggests there is more than a spark of genius in its 26-year-old creator, and being on board for this shakedown cruise provides theatrical excitement. Reno's forte is composing and arranging. It all sounds exceptionally good on the elaborate amplification system [created by Roger Gans]. Better amplified rock music than this you've probably never heard, but some of the dialogue is not far from soap opera."

Then, just when events at the big red barn get to be too regular, something comes along to break the monotony.

On Saturday evening, April 2, '77, a tornado swept a six-mile trail across the theatre's 77 acres, struck the Barn and then devastated the village of Augusta, causing millions of dollars in damage. A dozen people were injured and 136 were left homeless. The wind was so ferocious that one of the houses in Augusta was left resting on its side.

Although the Barn's cement-block lobby, added in '56, was destroyed — roof caved in and walls blown out — the Barn survived and remained structurally intact. Betty said the only damage caused was to the Barn doors in the back of the theatre which blew off, miraculously allowing the release of pressures accompanying the twisting tornado. Phenomenally, the setting for the final production of the previous season, **You Can't Take It With You**, was still standing exactly as it was when the curtain rang down. Fortunately, 75 percent of the damage to "Big Red" was covered by insurance. Reconstruction of the lobby commenced almost immediately, and Ragotzy announced the season would open on schedule.

At the end of April came news that Barnie Karen (Jensen) Arthur had a film, *The Mafu Cage* (later retitled *My Sister, My Love* and *The Cage*), shown at the Cannes International Film Festival. The film, her second (she had previously made

Equus with Robin Haynes as Alan Strang, Tom Wopat as Horseman/Nugget and Dale Helward as Martin Dysart — 1977

Legacy), had cost one million dollars, starred Carol Kane and Lee Grant, and was the last screen appearance of actor Will Geer. Karen, who had started her film career by taking a six-week crash course at UCLA, had signed a three picture deal with Universal, important because by so doing, her work was assured distribution — the bottom line for film makers. In the same news report was a picture of Dick Fuchs appearing in Disney's *The North Avenue Irregulars*, which was to be released at Christmas time.

1977
Mango, Center Stage
The Bed Before Yesterday
One Night With You Madame
Something's Afoot
*Equus
Annie Get Your Gun
The Pajama Game

Knowing what the critics felt about sex farces, was it simple pigheadedness on Jack's part to open the '77 season with two? The second, **One Night With You, Madame**, was a new title, but it was the same old show which had premiered at the Barn in '63, toured and was reprised two years later as **In One Bed. . . And Out the Other**. Wouldn't the critical comments be predictable?

Sinclair of *The Enquirer* lamented, "The whole thing is virtually without wit. Why the show is deemed worthy of three presentations in 14 years in anybody's guess." Carlson of the *Gazette* simply acquiesced, "It's silly, interminably long and it would take a Philadelphia lawyer to detail the plot, providing there really is one. But it is also apparently popular with summer theatre audiences, especially at the Barn, so there will be no further deploring **One Night With You, Madame**. We're throwing in the towel, and will suppress the distress this play seems to generate in reviewers."

A highlight of the '77 season was Jack's production of Peter Shaffer's **Equus**, which was still playing on B'way when Ragotzy received the Michigan stock rights, although it had been seen in a touring edition at Miller Auditorium. Carlson of the *Gazette* wrote this glowing account: "It's unlikely that Dale Helward has ever given a better performance than his portrayal of the psychiatrist in **Equus** or that he'll ever get the opportunity to top it. Roles like this do not come along very often. Neither do literate, intelligent and worthy plays. Helward makes the most of his opportunity, but then so does every one else connected with Ragotzy's brilliant staging.

"'Everyone else' most certainly includes young Robin Haynes [a.k.a. Robin Newton, Robin Reeds], the second generation of a family long prominent at the summer playhouse. Haynes comes exceedingly close to perfection in his delineation of the challenging part of the young chap. But Dysart is the pivotal role. From three previous viewings — ranging from London's National Theatre to Western's Miller Auditorium — we're convinced that **Equus** succeeds in direct proportion to the capabilities of the man who searches for the key in this psychiatric detective story. It isn't often that we come away from any theatre totally satisfied with what we have viewed and completely divested of any complaint. That's exactly what happened last night, and this attraction alone makes the theatre's current season a memorable one.

"Among the supporting roles, the individual who makes the greatest difference is Dana Delany as Jill Mason, whose sexual liaison with the

Dana Delany — 1977

young man proves traumatic. It is obviously not a role every young actress would eagerly assume, considering the nature of the nude scene, but Ms. Delany handles it with aplomb and professional ease. We once referred to her as a pretty face. To that we can now add she's also an actress."

John Sherwood of *The Enquirer* echoed, "Rising to their feet in enthusiastic applause, theatre-goers at the Barn proved at the opening-night of **Equus** that cerebral drama can captivate and move audiences who often seem content to sit and feed on much baser fare." Nicolette of *The Press* noted, "Tom Wopat is particularly impressive as the horse, Nugget, to which the boy is most attracted."

After the '78 season's end, many Barnies were involved in theatre far from the Barn. Timothy Landfield was on B'way in Paul Giovanni's version of Sir Arthur Conan Doyle's *The Crucifer of Blood*, playing Dr. Watson to Paxton Whitehead's Sherlock Holmes. Barbara Marineau, who had been in the B'way company of *The Best Little Whorehouse in Texas*, *The Robber Bridegroom*, *Shenandoah* and its national touring package, was off to upstate NY's Artpark to play Ado Annie in *Oklahoma!*

Dick Fuchs was going on tour in *Dracula* with the Kenley Players of Ohio and his Disney film, *The North Avenue Irregulars*, was yet to be released. Becky Gelke received rave reviews in *The Best Little Whorehouse in Texas* at NY's off-B'way Intermedia Theatre, which was soon to transfer to the Main Stem. *Newsweek* magazine's critic called her "an appealing redhead who looks exactly like a double strawberry soda."

Tom Wopat was in the hit B'way musical, *I Love My Wife*, and Lisby Larson was understudying the leading lady in the same show. Later it was reported by Aaron Gold of the *Chicago Tribune* that for the Windy City's Drury Lane's production of *I Love My Wife* the producers decided to bring in Joanna Gleason and Tom Wopat from the B'way cast, predicting, "Wopat will be a matinee idol."

Janie Allen, who had been an apprentice in '75 appearing in three shows (**Seesaw**, **Godspell** [general understudy] and **Fiddler**) and Eric Riley were in the national touring company of *A Chorus Line*, and Jim Pritchett had just won his Emmy Award.

Sal (Joe) Aiello — 1978

In May, Jack announced two new arrivals to the Barn for the '78 season. New leading lady, Susan Gordon, graduated from Purdue in '72 and had gone on to perform at the Goodman Theatre and in dinner and stock theatres in the Chicago area. She would appear at the Barn in five shows during the summer, her most important role being Aldonza/Dulcinea in **La Mancha**. Another newcomer was Sal Aiello, a student of Dusty Reeds from San Jose State University. And Brendan Ragotzy, now 15 years old, was listed as a member of the Equity Company for the first time.

1978
Angelo Mango Sings
Light Up the Sky
13 Rue De L'Amour
Man of La Mancha
Count Dracula
Vanities
*Pippin
Anything Goes
Same Time Next Year
An Evening with Angelo Mango, VI

As usual, the season opened with an Angelo Mango show in the Rehearsal Shed. He was backed by a chorus of young apprentices, along with Wayne and Betty, who joined Angelo in the "Steam Heat" number they had done in **Pajama Game** some 20 years previously.

Vanities with Dana Delany (foreground), Jen Wolfe and Susan Gordon (lying down) — 1978

Although **Count Dracula** was not a highlight of the season, it was an important stepping stone in Sal Aiello's Barn career. *Dracula,* adapted from the novel by Hamilton Dean and John L. Balderston, had been given a 50th anniversary production on the Main Stem in '77 with Frank Langella in the title role. The immense popularity of this revival persuaded Ragotzy to include the old warhorse in his season. But the original was not yet released, so he used the available Ted Tiller version and spent less for royalties. **Count Dracula** was directed by Wayne Lamb, who combined scripts and used some of designer Edwin Gory's visual effects from the B'way production.

Sinclair of *The Enquirer* remarked, "Dracula is played by Sal Aiello, a newcomer at the Barn. And he is good." Elliott of *The Press* agreed, "Sal Aiello is a convincing Count Dracula, both visually and aurally." Carlson of the *Gazette* and *The Citizen Patriot* noted, "Sal Aiello excels in the title role, adding still another dimension to his apparent ability to play all kinds of characters."

Barbara Marineau was hired as a guest star to play Reno Sweeney in **Anything Goes**, a role she had previously played at the Kalamazoo Civic. She also played Catherine in **Pippin**, a production that cemented the popularity of Sal Aiello with both critics and audience alike. The Barn's production was one of the first summer stock presentations in the country — certainly the first in the Midwest.

Nicolette of *The Press* observed, "Cleverness and color, plus some lively tunes, are the big attractions of the Barn's **Pippin**. Aiello gives the Pippin character a nicely sympathetic doltishness in the early scenes, which creates fine humor. He also develops the character well as experience matures Pippin. He has a fairly pleasant voice. It's lacking a bit in range at times, but that's made up in expressive delivery. The production brightens noticeably in the second act with the appearance of Barbara Marineau, an attractive Catherine. Miss Marineau has a good show tune singing voice and, aside from Mango, is probably the most effective among the principals in solo work."

Carlson of the *Gazette* and *The Citizen Patriot* extolled, "Since the start of the current season, newcomer Sal Aiello has repeatedly shown promise of becoming one of the summer theatre's most talented performing discoveries. Confirmation seemed to simply wait the arrival of the proper role. The right one came along in the title character of Pippin. Aiello's barefoot (literally) boy with charm portrayal of an Eighth Century flower child is the distinguishing feature of the production. Director Wayne Lamb's zestful and innovating staging, combined with Aiello's performance, is a triumph over material. Producer Jack Ragotzy has elected to turn what was one long, one-act musical into a two-act show, and it seems to be an improvement."

Sherwood of *The Enquirer* concluded, "Tuesday night's audience fell in love with Sal Aiello, hanging on his every grimace and move. Aiello plays his role with consummate, skillful artistry, self-effacement and seeming ease."

*****

In November '78, Robin Haynes, who was committed to going to LA the first of the year, was given a two-week contract to replace an actor who had dropped out of the B'way cast of *The Best Little Whorehouse in Texas*. The management kept renewing Haynes' contract until he finally had to leave, which gave him several weeks on B'way with his good friend Becky Gelke as well as his dad, John Newton, both of whom were also in the cast. As he later observed, if he had stayed with the show instead of moving to California to get into TV (which didn't happen), he would have had four years of work on B'way, an enviable credit for any actor's resume.

On Friday, January 24, '79, *The Dukes of Hazzard*, a new comedy adventure series about three cousins who fight corruption in the rural South, premiered on CBS TV with Tom Wopat playing Luke Duke. The series became a hit and skyrocketed Wopat into stardom.

Other wintertime Barnie news: Merle Louise was in B'way's *Sweeney Todd* as The Beggar Woman, for which she received a Drama Desk Award.

In early February, word was received that actor Alfred Hinckley had died in his apartment on West 43rd Street in NYC. The actor and his wife, Gayle Hinckley (nee Beesey), had been divorced the previous year. His sister, Mrs. Sally Murray, said Al had completed a role in a forthcoming network TV production of Thomas Wolfe's *You Can't Go Home Again*. His last appearance in Kalamazoo had been in May of '77 when he and former Western Michigan University

Barbara Marineau as Catherine and Sal (Joe) Aiello (being restrained by Meg Curry and Doreen Remo) in the title role of **Pippin** — 1978

Theatre alumni David Wayne, Barbara Marineau, Sherman Lloyd, Jack Zaremba and others returned to campus for a Diamond Jubilee "celebrity production" of *The Ponder Heart* directed by Professor Zack York.

Then, on a freezing Friday night, February 9, Barnie Dick Fuchs pulled up in a chauffeured Mercedes-Benz in front of the Maple Hill Cinema in Kalamazoo for a special showing of the Disney film, *The North Avenue Irregulars*, his screen debut. More than a hundred fans showed up in spite of the bitter cold to greet him, get autographs and cheer his name when it appeared on the screen. Carlson of the *Gazette* suggested that the film "should give Fuchs's bid for a major performing career a definite assist. He has a surprising amount of time on screen for an unknown in his first film role, and he gives a polished, professional performance."

In early April, Ragotzy received a Michigan Foundation for the Arts award at a ceremony at the Detroit Institute of Arts. The Foundation, a privately funded organization, gave $2,500 checks to five Michigan artists who had made substantial contributions in their fields. Ragotzy was the first awardee in the field of theatre.

At the same time, Jack was supervising repair work caused by a heavy snow storm that collapsed the roof of "the Growth," an addition to the theatre auditorium made in '54. This was the second time nature inflicted serious damage to the Barn.

On April 28, Jack gave the commencement address to the graduating class at Nazareth College in Kalamazoo; and in early May, he was honored for his support of cultural activities in the area and awarded an honorary doctorate in humane letters by Nazareth. Also honored were arts philanthropist Dorothy Upjohn Dalton and the Most Rev. Paul V. Donovan, Bishop of the Catholic Diocese of Kalamazoo.

On May 13, *The Enquirer* ran an article announcing, "A world premiere, a recent B'way hit and some old favorites will make up the 17-week season of the Barn this summer — the longest schedule ever announced by producer Ragotzy." Jack was attempting to get a release on **Ballroom** but said if he couldn't get it, he was going to produce *Follies*. He was also going to reprise the farce, **Move Over, Mrs. Markham**,

Peter Strong — 1979

Brendan Ragotzy at 16

(L to R) Randi Rae Arnold, Nancy Coker, Mollie Collinson, Kani Seifert, Sherra Schick and Betsy Turner in **Chicago** — 1979

since it was being staged with great success at the Union Plaza Hotel in Las Vegas under the title *Too Many in the Bed*, featuring old-time movie star Virginia Mayo. In addition, Mawby Green and Ed Feilbert had given him the rights to their latest adaptation, a French comedy-mystery called *Ding, Dong, Dead*, for its world premiere, scheduled at the end of August.

Before the opening show of the '79 season, an article in the *Lansing State Journal* by Mike Hughes featured Jen Wolfe and Sal Aiello as young actors facing their first year in the Big Apple. Since there was another Sal Aiello registered with Actors' Equity, Sal had to change his name; he chose "Joe." He did love NY, but with nothing breaking for him, he was glad to be back at the Barn where he could be a star.

On June 21 another Hughes article mentioned that apprentice Peter Strong "happens to look like a young Paul Newman." He would later become a soap opera star. Hughes also reported that Brendan, then 16, "would be a natural for theatre some day being an immensely handsome young man who looks like movie star Robby Benson. He works as an assistant stage manager, but his heart is really in baseball."

It was Brendan who suggested that the Ragotzy family try staying in Michigan for a

1979
An Evening with Angelo Mango, VII
California Suite
*Chicago
No Sex Please, We're British
Ballroom
Move Over, Mrs. Markham
Sugar
Side by Side by Sondheim

winter. So Jack bought a beautiful Gull Lake cottage, but the experiment didn't work out. "It gets awful boring during the winter," Jack explained. Hughes then noted that "Ragotzy — troubled by an arthritis that he figures goes back to his old baseball catching days — couldn't find much exercise and put on weight. Betty, meanwhile, has taken up jogging and looks considerably younger than a woman in her fifties."

After the Angelo Mango Rehearsal Shed show, the '79 main stage season opened with **California Suite**, the first release of the show in the area. But perhaps the best of the season was Kander and Ebb's **Chicago** which had opened on B'way in June of '75 with Chita Rivera, Jerry Orbach and Gwen Verdon. Set in the '20s, the musical is based on the play of the same name by Maurine Dallas Watkins, who was a young reporter during the time when there were several murder trials in Chicago in which all the killers were women. The Ragotzy production would be the first in the Midwest, other than the touring company that had played Detroit and Chicago.

Marin Mazzie — 1980

Wayne Lamb was both director and choreographer for **Chicago**, the story of Roxie Hart, a honky-tonk entertainer who murders her lover and is thrown into the Cook County jail where she meets another murderess, Velma Kelly. The two get Billy Flynn, an ambulance-chasing lawyer who specializes in springing guilty floozies — jury nullification before there was such a thing as jury nullification — by stacking the juries with horny bachelors.

Ragotzy and Lamb changed the B'way concept by using a chorus of dancers who did not double in speaking parts, thus enlarging the cast and giving more opportunities to apprentices. Bockstanz of the *Gazette* declared the show was "loaded with stars. There is Jen Wolfe as Velma Kelly and Dusty Reeds as the Matron, who together make a tremendous team when they sing 'Class' — one of the real blockbuster numbers. Enter Roxie Hart, played by newcomer Krista Neumann. Her performance is nothing short of sensational. Angelo Mango does a tremendous job as Billy Flynn. A show stopper is contributed by Joe Aiello, who delights his audience with his 'Mister Cellophane.' As usual, his performance is flawless."

Dan Cooreman of *The South Bend Tribune* was equally laudatory. "It's a musical machine-gun filled with merry murderesses, fast-talking lawyers and other trademarks of the gangster era. As usual, the Barn's Equity company is the first area theatre group to acquire rights to this hit. Central to the Barn's **Chicago** success is Krista Neumann, who makes a dazzling debut as Roxie Hart. She is a gutsy yet graceful performer and totally in command. Her rendition of 'Roxie,' a hymn to herself, is worth a wait in a gasoline station line to get to Augusta."

*****

Grease, a musical that had originated in a basement of a community theatre in Chicago, was written by two out-of-work actors, Jim Jacobs and Warren Casey. Directed by Tom Moore (another Purdue student), it slid onto off-B'way at the 1,100 seat Eden Theatre in NY's Lower East Side, and within three months was transferred to the Royale on the Main Stem after some pretty awful reviews. Yet, it became one of the longest-running shows in the history of the American theatre with 3,888 performances. At the Barn it would be a three weeker, with an extra-added performance on Sundays — the hit of the '80 season.

1980
An Evening with Angelo Mango, VIII
Bedroom Farce
On the Twentieth Century
Do It for Your Country
*Grease
Chapter Two
Oklahoma!

The Barn's production would be the first in the area, outside of the national touring packages, and Ragotzy had worked years for its release. The show would require an unusual number of young people. But Jack had the perfect Danny Zuko in Equity member Joe Aiello. In Hollywood he signed Pamela Cordova to play Sandy Dumbrowski. Other Equity members in the cast were Betsy Turner as Patty, Peter Strong as Kenickie and Lonnie Vick as Teen Angel. He selected first-year apprentice Marin Mazzie knowing she could play Betty Rizzo, the role created on B'way by '65 Barnie Adrienne Barbeau. Another first-year apprentice was Scott Burkel (note the single "L" until 1989 when Betty suggested he add an extra "L" for clarity of pronunciation), who would play Roger. Staff members Susan Spindel would play Marty; John Reeds, Eugene, and Gordon Allen would be Johnny Casino. These kids would be perfect to play this salute to the rock-and-roll era of wild-cruisin,' hot-rodder, leather-jacketed, duck-tailed, bubble gum-chewin,' teased-hair, bobby-soxer, pedal pusher, professional virgins and horny male teens from Rydell High School's class of '59, with songs recalling what has been described as Buddy Holly hiccups, Little Richard yodels, Elvis gyrations, yackety-yacks and sha-na-nas.

Although Ragotzy hired Jonathan Larson this same season for Rehearsal Shed entertainment, he did not cast him in **Grease**. Larson

Jonathan Larson — 1980

Joe Aiello as Danny Zuko in **Grease** — 1980

(L to R) Julie Mote, Betsy Turner, Marin Mazzie, Susan Spindel and Cynthia Hatcher in back, Pamela Cordova, Joe Aiello, David Burgess, Peter Strong, Scott Burkel and Richard Marlatt - **Grease** – 1980

(L to R) Joe Aiello embraces Marin Mazzie; Dusty Reeds chaperones; Betsy Turner is surprised that Johnny Reeds is asking her to dance; and Scott Burkel dances with Cynthia Hatcher in the prom scene from **Grease** – 1980

would later write the B'way smash, *Rent*, and die tragically of an aortic aneurysm the night before it opened.

Opening night was sold out, extra performances added, and the demand for tickets was the biggest Ragotzy could remember. It was a producer's daydream, with director Lamb setting up folding chairs in the aisles for the overflow crowd. Cooreman of *The South Bend Tribune* opened his review by warning: "**Grease** may be the best show of the Michigan/Indiana summer- theatre season. But don't let it get to you. It got to me, at least subconsciously, en route home from the theatre, when I found myself pressing the gas pedal a little too hard on an open stretch on M-60. Maybe I had a secret desire to drive the 'Greased Lightin'' hot rod that's so prominent in the show. Unfortunately, I wasn't the only witness to my '50s fantasy. A Michigan state trooper saw its enactment, too, and was not pleased.

"And they say *theatre* tickets are expensive!

"That caution aside, the Barn's **Grease** is a fabulous night of summer theatre — a first-class, high-powered replica of the new granddaddy of B'way musicals. Put on your bobby sox (or 20 dabs of Brylcreem) and go.

"But drive carefully.

"Joe Aiello as Danny Zuko looks like he's been waiting for the role — and he makes the most of it. Pamela Cordova is delightful as Sandy, Julie Mote is a wacky Frenchy, the beauty-school dropout and Marin Mazzie effectively erases the abrasive Stockard Channing edge from the role of Rizzo, leader of the Pink Ladies.

"Among the 'Burger Palace' boys, David Burgess adds a Leave-it-to-Beaver touch to the character of Doody. Other laughs are provided by John Reeds as the lanky class valedictorian ('See you 'round the bookmobile,' Rizzo tells him) and Dusty Reeds as Miss Lynch, who looks like everyone's English teacher."

Sherwood of *The Enquirer* added, "It's vibrant, energetic and lots of good, unclean fun. Sure, it's stupid and gross. But, c'mon, if you remember white socks, Twinkies, slumber parties, hot rods and all the era's secret sexual hangups and perversions, you know it was all pretty stupid — and pretty gross. That's why **Grease** beat out **Fiddler on the Roof** (a more artistically satisfying musical) for the longest-running B'way show:

It was more real, more a social document to more Americans than paternity and pogroms in pre-Bolshevik Russia."

1981
An Evening with Angelo Mango, IX
On Golden Pond
*Carousel
Deathtrap
My Fair Lady
Whose Life Is It Anyway?
Damn Yankees
*The Elephant Man

For the '81 season, the sixth edition of **An Evening with Angelo Mango** included a supporting cast of Scott Burkel, Jon Larson, Marin Mazzie and Steve Owsley, with James Douglas Kent at the piano. The evening had by now settled into a routine, playing two weeks and featuring songs from favorite past shows plus advertising the upcoming season of musicals.

Dusty Reeds and Lou Girard kicked off the main stage season acting in **On Golden Pond**. It was an excellent show that won applause from the critics but was overshadowed by a major event to come.

In '81, the TV show with the second-highest ratings in the nation was *The Dukes of Hazzard*, in which Tom Wopat starred with John

Scott Burkel — 1981

153

Schneider. It had been four years since Wopat, then 25, left the Barn, Equity card in hand, and headed to NY. When Ragotzy asked him to come back to do **Carousel**, he was eager to do so, not only as an expression of gratitude to Jack and Betty, but as with most actors, including Laurence Olivier (who played Archy Rice in *The Entertainer* for Equity minimum at London's Royal Court Theatre), Tom desperately needed a live theatre fix so he could flex his creativity. He was willing to take minimum, but Ragotzy convinced him otherwise. They agreed on a percentage, "to keep his agent from ever interfering — then or now — and even with a percentage, he was still a real 'buy!'" Ragotzy admitted.

Facilitation, however, would be difficult. Even though Wopat knew many of the songs, a seven-day rehearsal for one of the most demanding roles in musical comedy was cutting it pretty short. Director Wayne Lamb would have to rehearse the cast and use an apprentice stand-in for Wopat.

On the evening of Friday, June 19, Wopat left LA on the red-eye to Chicago so he could make a 10 a.m. rehearsal at the Barn on Saturday. In Chicago, he hired a limousine, curled up in the back seat and slept. It was on I-94 that the '72 Cadillac broke down. Wopat thumbed to the nearest gas station. When he returned with the mechanic, the limousine was there, but mysteriously the keys and the driver had disappeared. Figuring the guy had gone off for help, he waited. But after a while, he gave up and hired the fellow from the gas station to drive him to Augusta, arriving an hour late for rehearsal.

After a hectic two days devoted to working him in the pre-blocked scenes which stand-in apprentice Robin Nuyen had rehearsed, Wopat flew back to LA on Sunday night for an early Monday morning shoot. The reason for the urgency of the summer filming was the threat of an impending directors' strike that would knock out all work. The producers wanted half a year's series in the can just in case. They'd wrapped nine hour-long episodes and needed this tenth to carry them through Christmas. If no directors' strike took place, filming on 12 more episodes was to resume in September.

Carousel opened on Wednesday, July 1. The production would play without break through July 12 — with 16 performances that included double performances on Saturdays and Sundays. "I was a little nervous at first," Wopat is reported to have said. "I haven't had to say many lines since I've been in the TV show."

But the great night came.

The show had the biggest advance sales in the Barn's 36-year history. Ticket prices ranged from $8 to $9.50. "It would have been remarkable," Ragotzy noted, "if we just broke even but it was our biggest hit. Tom's appearance was great

Tom Wopat as Billy and Joe Aiello as Jigger in **Carousel** — 1981

for us because it brought in people who had never been to the Barn before. We got many families because the kids watch Tom on TV and wanted to see him in person."

Lawrence DeVine, theatre editor of the *Detroit Free Press,* extolled, "Amid towns such as Oshtemo, Hickory Corners, Prairieville and Schultz, you have to know where to look in Michigan to find Shangri-la. On a rise above a new-mown green clearing three miles outside Augusta is a spot that comes close, the Augusta Barn Theatre. Their **Carousel** is marvelous, and the production is too exuberant, too professional, to be a once-in-a-lifetime happy accident.

"**Carousel** stars a magnetic young musical actor named Tom Wopat. The show closes in right around him in an exceptional example of ensemble playing. No one is going to take the pinnacles away from Wopat, but the supporting cast is also a star, notably an actress named Marin Mazzie as Julie's comic best friend, who has the expertise of decades in the theatre but who, it turns out, is an apprentice no more than 20 years old."

Carlson of the *Gazette* echoed the praise: "There's never been an opening night quite like this one at the Barn. For all of its 35 seasons, Michigan's oldest Equity summer playhouse shunned the big name performers who annually venture forth to ply their trade on the straw hat circuit. The Barn was content, as well as exceedingly successful, with a mixture of seasoned but less well-known professionals in a resident company combined with young hopefuls.

"The theatre was packed to the rafters, all of the 15 remaining performances and 8,000 seats are virtually sold out and negotiations are in progress for a third week of the now classic musical with Wopat as its star and in full voice and greeted by an enthusiastic and appreciative audience.

"This **Carousel** certainly worked to the total satisfaction of the opening night audience. Wopat plays the thick-headed but likeable merry-go-round barker as a virile and handsome young man with a perpetually pleasant smile, and he carries off his singing assignments effortlessly, bringing down the house, as might be expected, with

Opening night curtain call for **Carousel** (L to R) Marin Mazzie, Angelo Mango, Tom Wopat, Mariana Rence, Joe Aiello, Betty Ebert, Louis Girard — 1981

Publicity photo of Jack Ragotzy as the Heavenly Friend, Tom Wopat as Billy Bigelow and Betty Ebert as Nettie Fowler in **Carousel** — 1981

his 'Soliloquy.'"

Hughes of the *Lansing State Journal* added, "In case you're wondering, all the reports are true: Tom Wopat really does have a terrific singing voice. That's right, the same Wopat who spends most of his time zooming around TV's sillyland in 'Dukes of Hazzard.' As it turns out, that show uses roughly 2.5 percent of his talent."

While all the Wopat/**Carousel** hoopla was going on, George McDaniel was cooling his heels in the wings and getting an extra week of rehearsals. George, who played Dr. Jordan Baar on TV's *Days of Our Lives* for more than a year, was a regular on the short-lived *Nichols and Dymes*, appeared in *Little House on the Prairie*, *Rich Man Poor Man Book II*, *Hill Street Blues* and *Lobo* in addition to the national company of *Applause*, had returned to the Barn for two shows. Even so, Wopat would be a hard act to follow.

But McDaniel was terrific in both **Deathtrap** and **My Fair Lady**.

At the end of the season came **The Elephant Man**, directed by Ragotzy. Nicolette of *The News* announced, "This is an impressive production to bring to a close the Barn's 36th season. It is an artistic success. A three-quarters house opening night indicates it does not follow that good theatre is good box office — especially in summer stock."

Jim Dean of *The Enquirer* concurred. "It is far the best show to be produced this season at the Barn and certainly could hold its own against the London, off-B'way, B'way or touring company productions. Producer-Director Ragotzy's staging is top-notch, and he has put together a superb cast that is equal to the task of meeting the challenges of the show. The extremely versatile Joe Aiello turned in his finest performance of the season — perhaps of his career — as Merrick."

It is interesting to note that Robert Newman, a second-year apprentice during the '81 season, appeared briefly in **Carousel**, played Freddy Eynsford Hill in **My Fair Lady**, Harry in **Damn Yankees** and Lord Jim in **The Elephant Man**. Jonathan Larson, also a second-year apprentice, appeared in **An Evening with Angelo Mango**, briefly in **Carousel**, as the third Cockney in **My Fair Lady**, Dr. Barr in **Whose Life Is It Anyway?**, Schovik in **Damn Yankees** and as an extra in **The Elephant Man**.

Marin Mazzie, another second-year apprentice, appeared in **An Evening with Angelo Mango**, played Carrie Pipperidge in **Carousel**, Mrs. Eynesford Hill in **My Fair Lady** (for which she earned Equity status), Kay Sadler in **Whose Life Is It Anyway?** and Gloria in **Damn Yankees**.

Encore, a local magazine of the arts, pictured Jack and Betty on its November '81 cover. Although the focus of the article was a brief history of the Barn, it opened with a description of what was to be the biggest fight the Ragotzys ever undertook for the Barn's survival. A national company was planning to locate a landfill just over the hill from the theatre along M-96 between Augusta and Galesburg.

"Between the artistic end and the business end," Betty told the reporter, "summer theatre is a very delicately balanced thing. We have survived because of our patrons, the dedication of our staff, because of the quality of productions and because of our location in a country setting with plenty of wildlife nearby. Anything that upsets one of these ingredients throws the whole equation out of whack. For 36 years, we have maintained the balance, so the prospects of a landfill in our backyard

Tom Wopat entertained every night in the Rehearsal Shed bar show after each performance of **Carousel** and throughout the season —1981

is scary to us. People come out here to enjoy the environment, to get out in the country and maybe see a rabbit or a squirrel. In the future, maybe a few rodents, hordes of insects and lots of dust will be part of what we'll be offering them."

Jack added, "We don't want a landfill next door. The firm that wants to locate it here says there will be no problem with odors or noises or dust or rodents. They say that we won't even know they are there. But Betty and I have the feeling that the company is so big, that it doesn't really care about us or the surrounding area. We don't think it is fair to sacrifice the quality of life around here just for economic and geological conveniences."

The reporter then asked about their future.

"We intend to survive," Betty answered.

And survive they would! But this was the beginning of a war — The Battle of the Big Landfill — that would last an incredible five years.

In April '82, Jack and Betty took a trip to NY — their first trip back since the ill-fated **Angela** production closed in '69. Brendan, a freshman at Western Michigan University, joined them. In a chatty and informative letter sent to *The Enquirer*, Betty told about the "exhausting and exhilarating" week. "Visited the Jim Pritchetts Sunday evening and on Monday we joined the various members of Actors' Equity at the rally in front of the Morosco Theatre. This was a part of the effort of several theatre groups to try to save the Morosco and adjacent Helen Hayes Theatre from demolition. These two historic 'small' theatres are threatened by the wrecking ball — to be cleared away to make room for a 50-story, 2,000-room hotel.

"The rally was staged to coordinate with an anticipated decision by the State Court of Appeals on whether to continue a temporary stay barring the demolition. (The court did issue that temporary injunction a day later.) We, of course, felt a double kinship with everyone there. We have our

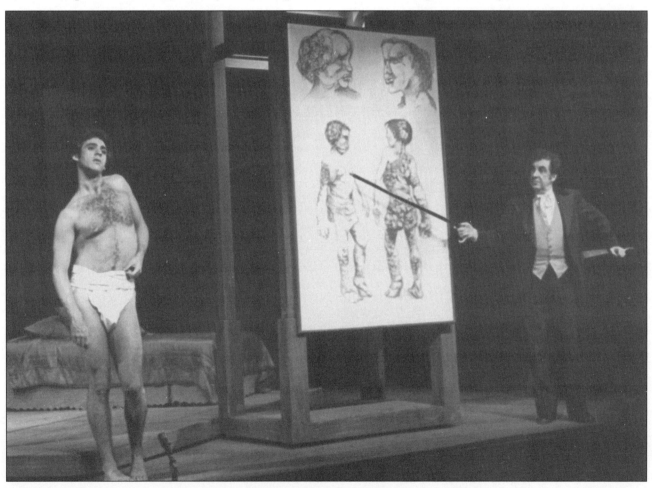

Joe Aiello and Angelo Mango in **The Elephant Man** — 1981

Robert Newman — 1981

own 'save the theatre' battle with Waste Management, Inc. still pressing plans to turn the property adjacent to the Barn into a major industrial dump."

Once her message had been delivered, Betty went on to report Barnie news: They saw *The Best Little Whorehouse in Texas*, noting that John Newton had left the company to do *Strider* at The Virginia Stage Company in Norfolk. After the show they met Becky Gelke (who was still in the show), Dale Helward and Eric Schussler at Becky's apartment in the Manhattan Plaza complex. Betty mentioned that Helward had just finished a short run in B'way's *The Curse of an Aching Heart* with Faye Dunaway.

Tuesday they saw *Amadeus*. After the show they spent time with Jen Wolfe and Dana Delaney. Delaney had been on *As the World Turns* and was to read the next day for a major motion picture — the role of the wife of John Schneider of *The Dukes of Hazzard* fame. During Dana's time at the Barn, she and Tom Wopat were a steady couple, Betty added.

Wednesday they saw *Crimes of the Heart* and at Sardi's afterward met with Barnies Robin Nuyen, Marta Hedges and Robert Newman, a regular on *The Guiding Light*. Since the Ragotzys had moved from NY when Brendan was only three and had taken him back only once, when he was seven, they spent Friday being "tourists." Then they all went to see *Oh! Calcutta!*, produced by Barnie Norman Kean. On Saturday they saw both *The Dresser* and *Barnum*, "and by that time we were exhausted."

Betty then warned everyone who might be going to NY: "Unless you are on an expense account, ticket prices are out of sight! Plays are $35 — musicals even more. Everyone we know gets into the half-price ticket line in Times Square. We could get tickets to any show in town at that booth!"

She added that two days before they left for NY, Jack had read for a small part in a pilot of a new TV series, *Remington Steele*. The studio called him in NY to tell him they wanted him to do it.

1982
An Evening with Angelo Mango, X
Morning's at Seven
Funny Girl
Tobacco Road
The Unsinkable Molly Brown
Pajama Tops
*Nuts

The '82 season was hyped as 14 weeks of musicals and plays and the return of three special guest stars. Barbara Marineau, who was starring at the Burt Reynolds Dinner Theatre in Florida, would return to star in **Funny Girl**; Becky Gelke in **The Unsinkable Molly Brown** and **Nuts**; and Dick Fuchs in **Morning's at Seven**, the first main stage show of the season.

Marin Mazzie would return as part of the Equity Company, playing Myrtle Brown in **Morning's at Seven**, Emma in **Funny Girl** and Pearl in **Tobacco Road**. She also would appear in **The Unsinkable Molly Brown** and **Pajama Tops** and play Hodel in **Fiddler on the Roof**.

Joe Aiello did not return for the season, nor did Scott Burkel.

An announcement of a more mundane sort was that the new curtain time for Saturdays was six o'clock and nine o'clock and that a new policy required telephone reservations to be picked up the night of the performance 30 minutes, rather than 15, prior to curtain time.

Carlson of the *Gazette* noted that times

were tough economically and wondered if that accounted for the "tried and true big hits of the past" schedule of shows Ragotzy announced. "There is some question how well such a selection will serve area theatergoers. Does the Kalamazoo area need another production of **Tobacco Road** which was a museum piece when last revived here back in 1966?" he queried.

He noted that the summer's line up consisted of five attractions culled from past seasons. The lone "new" production was **Nuts**, "an off-off-B'way hit that made it to B'way and subsequently became a big hit on the West Coast, where it captured the fancy of the Ragotzys. Aside from **Nuts**, theatergoers looking for something truly new apparently are going to have to go elsewhere," Carlson concluded.

The opener, Paul Osborn's **Morning's at Seven**, brought back Sue DeLano Parish, who had played the same role in the Village Players' production back in '46. But reviving the show was not just a sentimental journey on Ragotzy's part. When **Morning's** opened back in '39, it ran for only 44 performances; but in '79-'80, it was one of B'way's biggest hits. The production was touched off not by a savvy NY producer, but because of the critically-acclaimed '78 Chicago revival directed by Vivian Matalon.

Nicolette of *The Press* observed, "The play is a generation away from the raucous humor and randy characters of today's slick, quick-hitting, one-liner comedies. Director Ragotzy sets an easy pace, avoiding any attempt at excessive drama and keeping all the characters wonderfully muted. The result is entertainment that raises steady chuckles and only occasionally lifts to hilarity, then only as a character's eccentricity prompts such a response. The enjoyment of the play is in the character studies and Ragotzy has

Nuts with Becky Gelke and James Werner — 1982

gathered a wonderful group of performers who fit as smoothly into their roles as would natural family members."

Calling it "a gentle drama-tragedy-comedy," Bockstanz of the *Gazette* noted that the presentation "was a homecoming for both the play and for one of the main characters. Sue Parish plays the part of Cora with all the skill of a lifelong theatre professional. Her interpretation of an elderly lady is excellent, making one wonder how she could possibly have been comfortable in the part some 37 years ago." He went on to declare that the play "is brilliantly staged and played under Jack Ragotzy's direction."

It is curious to note that Becky Gelke (Baker) would originate the role of Charlotte Cardoza in B'way's *Titanic*, but her first experience on that ship was playing the title role in **The Unsinkable Molly Brown** at the Barn in '82. Reviews were mixed. Dean of *The Enquirer*, however, was positive: "Opening night was rewarded with a standing ovation. Becky Gelke is robust and almost lusty in the lead role and James Werner, with his powerful singing voice, is dynamic as Leadville Johnny Brown. Werner, who comes to the Barn after playing in the national touring company of *Fiddler on the Roof*, is both a fine actor and a splendid vocalist. He's an invaluable asset to the Barn's summer acting company."

Midseason, Hughes of the *Lansing State Journal* wrote a feature on Gelke observing that she "doesn't seem to fit the B'way image, for a couple reasons. In a world full of perfect little bodies, she's a bit overweight. And in a world of make-believe, she's real. She's a natural redhead, complete with lovely green eyes and great gobs of freckles. Even the gentle drawl is natural."

Prior to the season's final production, a revival of **Fiddler**, Ragotzy directed the first West Michigan production of Tom Toper's **Nuts**, which was soon to be turned into a major movie by director Mark Rydell and starring Barbra Streisand.

Nicolette of *The Press* wrote, "**Nuts** is an excellent courtroom drama — terse, not easily forgotten, and with excellent dialogue.

"Director Ragotzy controls the action with an expert feel for the dramatic, keeping the fabric of legal proceedings deceivingly routine, with the occasional renting of that fabric carrying powerful dramatic impact. The cast is excellent. Most impressive is Becky Gelke. As Claudia, she allows the sympathy to flow away from her, then very gradually wins cheers as she scores against the great odds of the judicial system."

Dean of *The Enquirer* called the play "a gripping courtroom melodrama — the kind of production that Producer Ragotzy likes to call 'an actor's play' — one in which each actor shines forth as a star in his own right. **Nuts** is electrify-

Rehearsal Shed Show with apprentice Tia Speros singing (on stool at R) — 1982

ing. Before the evening was over, members of the audience began to openly show their emotions and to take up sides for and against the various characters."

> **1983**
> An Evening with Angelo Mango, XI
> Present Laughter
> *The Best Little Whorehouse in Texas
> Arsenic and Old Lace
> Annie
> They're Playing Our Song
> I'm Getting My Act Together and Taking It on the Road
> Our Town

Fourteen weeks of playing were scheduled for the summer of '83, and Ragotzy continued the policy of importing guest stars to feature with his resident professional company. All of the imports, of course, were former Barnies who had gone on to make names for themselves.

James Pritchett played in **Present Laughter**, which George C. Scott had made into a resounding hit at NY's Circle in the Square that very season. Pritchett arrived at the Barn from filming a TV movie, Mark Twain's *Puddin' Head Wilson*. Becky Gelke was back to share top billing with Pritchett in **Laughter** and then to do **The Best Little Whorehouse in Texas**. Barbara Marineau, who was playing at the Burt Reynolds Dinner Theatre in Florida in *The Apple Tree*, came back to star in **They're Playing Our Song** and **I'm Getting My Act Together and Taking It on the Road** (music by Kalamazoo-born Nancy Ford). In addition, Joe Aiello, who had made such a good start with the theatre and was absent the previous season, was back, as was Scott Burkel — this time as an Equity member.

Of **Laughter**, Nicolette of *The Press* wrote, "Pritchett brings a great deal of comedy skill to the role. Director Ragotzy manages to keep the action moving through a dull first act." He ended his review, "Ragotzy needs a speech-dialect coach, if he's going to try having his performers sound British, or anything else. Unfortunately, the characters are so shallow and uninteresting, except for Garry, nothing really matters." He added this caveat: "Those who enjoy seeing a TV personality in person won't be disappointed in Pritchett's appearance."

In case there is anyone out there who still doesn't know, **The Best Little Whorehouse in Texas** tells the story, based on an actual incident, of a local bordello which existed peacefully on the outskirts of a small Texas town until a crusading television reporter brought about pressure to close it. Bockstanz of the *Gazette* called it "a real howler, leaving the audience of first nighters literally in stitches. It's unlikely the script will ever be called great literature, but it handles, in a not too discreet way, a subject which would have been taboo until only recently.

"Ragotzy and director Wayne Lamb got a running start in staging **Whorehouse** when they engaged Becky Gelke to star as Mona Stangley, who worked her way up from just one of the girls to the position of proprietor of the place called 'The Chicken Ranch.' It soon becomes evident they sell something other than pullets there. Gelke is tremendous in the part, lending an excellent voice in several numbers, and especially in the show-closing 'Bus From Amarillo.'

"Gelke couldn't pull it off were it not for the assistance of her friend, Sheriff Ed Earl Dodd, handled beautifully by James Pritchett. Enter Melvin P. Thorpe, television crusader carrying a long flashlight with which to spotlight wrongdoing. Played to perfection by Joe Aiello, Thorpe captures a TV tape of the sheriff and his profanity, and then there really is trouble in what used to be paradise."

Carla Hoffman of *The South Bend Tribune* agreed: "It would be difficult to imagine a production of this romping, stomping, ribald social satire much better than the one currently running at the Barn. Gelke's voice, husky as corn silk, her complexion like milk and roses, her lush body costumed in everything from siren blue satin to skin-tight leopard to blue jeans, croons such numbers as 'A Lil' Old Pissant Country Place' in which she describes her house of, not ill repute, but 'good clean fun.' Pritchett is swaggering, gruff, yet suave, and the surprise is that he can sing, a talent lost on his daytime television role."

Arsenic and Old Lace, one of the few American comedy classics presented in the Barn's latter four decades, featured Sue DeLano Parish and Betty Ebert as the two kindly murderers. It was followed by Wayne Lamb's **Annie**, in which Temple Ann Schultz — with a limited list of stage productions to her credit — was "nothing less than phenomenal in the title role," claimed Bockstanz of the *Gazette*. "If you don't think **Annie** is just about the best thing you've seen at the Barn, must be you don't like kids — or dogs — or singing and dancing — or millionaires — or maybe even President Franklin D. Roosevelt. It thoroughly thrilled a first night audience containing more children than we have ever seen at the Barn. Louis Girard is outstanding as Warbucks. Dusty Reeds has never been funnier than in her role of Miss Hannigan, the alcoholic matron of the orphanage. Her brother, played by Joe Aiello, appears fresh from a term at Leavenworth, with his floozy girl friend, Lily, as portrayed by Becky Gelke. The trio has a splendid song and dance called 'Easy Street,' one of the best musical numbers of the evening."

The season closed with an anomaly — if anything could ever be said to be irregular in a Barn season. Jack had scheduled the quintessential American classic, **Our Town**, so he could play the role of the Stage Manager, but then he thought better of it and assigned the role to Angelo Mango. Nicolette of *The Press* noted regretfully that the show "is a sharp contrast from the season's successful musicals and probably won't add many more customers for its week's run. Not that many people go to summer stock to see 'serious' plays, which is rather too bad."

Becky Gelke as Mona in **The Best Little Whorehouse in Texas** — 1983

1984
An Evening with Angelo Mango, XII
A Bedfull of Foreigners
The Music Man
*Amadeus
The Best Little Whorehouse in Texas
Mass Appeal
Beyond Therapy
Camelot

The news of the '84 season was that Pritchett would be back for **The Music Man** and for a repeat of **Whorehouse**, plus three former Barnies, now big name show-biz ladies — Gelke, Marineau and Whinnery (*St. Elsewhere*) in **A Bedfull of Foreigners**.

Peter Shaffer's **Amadeus** originated in London and had taken B'way by storm, winning every major award including a Tony for Best Play of the '81 season.

Exploring and contrasting mediocrity and genius, as illustrated by the envious and ungifted Salieri, court composer to Joseph II, Emperor of Austria, and Wolfgang Amadeus Mozart, it was an unusual choice, but one that excited Ragotzy. Fighting for months for the release, his was the only summer stock production in the entire country to get the rights, albeit only for one week.

Ragotzy then took the unusual step of renting costumes for the principals from Eaves-Brooks in NY. "We felt we needed a richness of fabric, detail and line for the leading male characters. Costumer Kevin McGuire is designing and constructing over a dozen new gowns for the leading female characters, and these will become a welcome addition to our own collection," he reported.

Dale Helward was brought in from NY for the role of Salieri. "He was the only actor I considered for the pivotal role," Jack said. "Helward had read for the NY understudy/replacement and was called back no less than three times before the final choice was made." Yes, this is the same Helward whom Geraldine Page rejected for the ill-fated **Angela**.

Amadeus was given an extra week of rehearsal since **The Music Man,** which starred Jim Pritchett and Barbara Marineau, was held over a third week. Nicolette of *The Press* hailed the production: "Paced by Dale Helward and Joe Aiello in virtuoso performances, the Barn has created an artistic triumph. The two are exciting and completely convincing in the demanding roles. Director Ragotzy has orchestrated the presentation with the skill of a symphony conductor, guiding great performances in solo, duet and mass ensemble. The production has a beautiful rhythm, the movement and sounds almost as lovely as the bits and pieces of Mozart composition which are interspersed in the play.

"**Amadeus** is great theatre," he concluded.

Dean Knuth of the *Gazette* was not as positive: "Aiello's Mozart is initially shrill, silly and blunt. Even for a spoiled child it seems too much, too unbelievable — until one recalls the early antics of tennis star John McEnroe. Helward's Salieri is a near-perfect realization for the reflective narration comprising most of the play.

"The air of the royal court is created through luxuriant furnishings, dripping sweets and an exceptional male wardrobe. A brief, tastefully done moment of frontal nudity made little artistic sense. Included as part of Salieri's deliberate departure from his puritanical past, it overbalanced the other important steps in the progression without rendering the character any more or less wicked than if a more substantial wrap and additional acting had been used. The play's dramatic message is too intriguing and too well delivered to risk the loss of a teenage audience for a needless 30 seconds of skin."

Every time a fat Barn scrapbook surfaces — '85 for example, it means that Tom Wopat is

Photo-op session for **A Bedfull of Foreigners** with Jack Ragotzy surrounded by (L to R) Barbara Whinnery, Barbara Marineau and Becky Gelke — 1984

1985
An Evening with Angelo Mango, XIII
Squabbles
*The Robber Bridegroom
*Cat on a Hot Tin Roof
Evita
*A Chorus Line
E/R

back. The kickoff for the season began with a new sign — an historic marker in front of the Barn that was unveiled at the end of May. The Barn was now included in the Michigan State Register of Historic Sites.

Wopat was again the cash cow that season. Starting at the end of June, just before he opened in **The Robber Bridegroom,** more publicity was generated than ever before in the Barn's history. Wopat's seven years of stardom on *The Dukes of Hazzard* were over, but Tom Haroldson, the *Gazette*'s TV/radio writer, observed in his interview that Wopat's "feet are planted firmly on the ground." Haroldson described Wopat as "polite, articulate, funny, unpretentious" and "down-to-earth." In addition to his TV and stage credits, Wopat had cut one album and had formed a band, the North Hollywood All-Stars.

The big news was that Wopat had returned as a husband and was settled in at Gull Lake with his wife, the former Vickie Allen, whom he met in Lake City, Tennessee, while filming a TV movie, *The Burning Rage*, with Barbara Mandrell.

Of his performance in **The Robber Bridegroom**, Nicolette of *The News* maintained, "Wopat has an opportunity to make use of all his considerable talents as the dashing Lockhart; singing with vigor in a big baritone, leaping and climbing about the clever stage settings something like one of the three musketeers and giving broad interpretation to his role.

"He also has fellow performers who don't let the spotlight linger long on a single player, especially co-star Barbara Marineau, who has a great time playing the fresh bright-eyed country girl, smitten with the bandit. She grasps her share of musical glory, fitting neatly her clear vocal tones, which range from pops to mezzo, to the bluegrass and ballads

Dale Helward as Salieri and Becky Gelke as Contanze in **Amadeus** — 1984

Historic marker includes the Barn in the State Register of historic sites, May, 1985. Taking part in the ceremonies: Charleston Township Supervisor Jerry Vander Roest, former Michigan Historical Commission member Alexis Praus, Jack Ragotzy, Betty Ebert and Wayne Lamb.

which dominate the score."

Fred Peppel, reviewing for the *Gazette*, didn't much care for the material, saying, "If knee-slapping, down-home country corn — set to music and skillfully performed — is on your agenda, by all means don't miss **The Robber Bridegroom**. This is a musical in one of the palest definitions of the word, written by Alfred Uhry and Robert Waldman, based on Eudora Welty's novella."

Next came Wopat in **Cat on a Hot Tin Roof**. The opening was one of those nights that point up the difference between live theatre and TV or the movies, where the film just keeps rolling regardless of what happens. It was in the middle of the third act when a violent thunderstorm brought flashes of lightening, rolling thunder and heavy rain so intense that it was almost impossible to hear the onstage dialogue. The wind opened a hole in the Barn's roof, causing audience members to scurry to drier seating.

Just as the storm outside subsided, Wopat, as Brick, hearing an onstage clap of thunder (Kazan's version was being used rather than Williams'), looked up and said, "There's a hell of a storm coming." The audience, having already experienced the real thing, laughed uproariously. It was a moment when theatrical reality simply could not compete with the real thing.

Nicolette of *The Press* summarized: "Jack Ragotzy has guided full-bodied portrayals out of each of the characters. Tom Wopat gives a strong, nicely muted portrayal of Brick. Physically he fits easily into the role of the handsome former football hero and sports announcer. In the inner dramatics he is just as convincing, his performance

Tom Wopat and Barbara Marineau in
The Robber Bridegroom — 1985

controlled even in the moments of tense emotional expression.

"Kathryn Jaeck captures beautifully the character of Maggie. Ragotzy brought in Jaeck from Chicago especially for the role and he couldn't have made a better choice. She's a sensual 'cat' without being slinky. Louis Girard is a formidable Big Daddy giving a performance of great breadth. Dusty Reeds gives one of her most impressive performances as Big Mama. Joe Aiello and Sandy Mulvihill are excellent as the scheming Gooper and May."

Wally Metts, Jr., reviewing for the *Homer Index*, made these astute observations: "Well done. The cast is talented. The set is striking. The production is well paced and the actors are well cast. But the reason to see **Cat on a Hot Tin Roof** is not because of its star, Tom Wopat. Nor should you see it because Katherine Jaeck does a better Maggie than Elizabeth Taylor. The reason to see **Cat** is because it is about man's infinite capacity for deceit. There's a time for light hearted, upbeat musicals, but there's also a time to be provoked, even shocked, into the truth. 'Mendacity is the system we live with,' Brick says, and every character in the play proves that it is true. The play reminds us that integrity is rare, and it challenges us not to deceive ourselves or each other. It is a play that tempts us to be honest."

After **Cat** came **Evita** with guest star Marin Mazzie. Mazzie had just played Beth in a revised version of Sondheim's *Merrily We Roll Along* at La Jolla Playhouse. Scott Burkel was given the role of Che after much lobbying. Jack wasn't sure he could do it. He did, and extremely well.

Also in the cast was first year Battle Creek apprentice Doug LaBrecque as one of "the people of Argentina." The years '77 to '85 should be called the decade of discovered talent

Marin Mazzie in title role of **Evita** with Joe Aiello as Peron — 1985

at the Barn. Labrecque, along with many others who apprenticed during these ten years, would go on into mainstream professional theatre.

But it was **A Chorus Line** — winner of the NY Drama Critics Circle Award, the Tony Award and the Pulitzer Prize, which was entering its eleventh year on B'way and had toured Miller Auditorium three times prior to Ragotzy's first released Michigan production — that was to be the Barn's big hit. For it, Ragotzy hired Becky Gelke along with two dancers — Steve Owsley and Reginal Ray-Savage.

Owsley had apprenticed at the Barn in '81 and '82 before heading to NY. He had just completed a six-month engagement on B'way in Hal Prince's *Grind* and had spent five months working on the film of *A Chorus Line*. Ray-Savage was a Chicago dancer who began his career in a Katherine Dunham troupe and toured in *The Music Man*. Gelke had just completed a workshop production and tryout of *To Whom It May Concern* at The Williamstown Summer Theatre.

Peppel for the *Gazette* gave **A Chorus Line** this praise: "Last night's opening was a red-hot sizzler. It was the Barnies at their best in a production that was bursting with excitement and youthful exuberance. Becky Gelke's Cassie came close to being a showstopper. She is vibrant, vulnerable and strong, particularly in her pivotal scenes with Joe Aiello as Zach, the almost sadistic director, whose insistence on honesty provides the drama in the show. As Diana, Marin Mazzie seems in her element with the touching 'What I Did For Love.' Steve Owsley shines as Mike as does Sandy Mulvihill as Val. Also worthy of note is Helen Morrison's Sheila and Reginal Ray-Savage's Richie."

Suzanne Blaine Siegel of *The Kalamazoo News* agreed wholeheartedly, saying the show "is a smash hit at the Barn — by far the finest production all season. Joe Aiello is superb throughout. The choreography by Lamb is directed with precision and humor and deep feeling for the personal styles of the individual dancers."

Scott Burkel as Che in **Evita** — 1985

Doug LaBrecque — 1985

A Chorus Line — 1985

At the end of the hugely successful '85 season the Ragotzys decided to spend some of their profits on improvements to the Barn. They worked November and into December, this time building with a construction crew.

This first major change in the Barn's structure since "the Growth" in '54 resulted in a new west wing, measuring 15 by 55 feet, and extending the entire length of the auditorium from the backstage wing to the lobby. It included restrooms, a photography studio for publicity shots, a musical director's office, and improved, barrier-free access to the auditorium for the handicapped, the ramps of which would be protected by a roof.

In February, Betty reported from Los Angeles. It seems Eric Riley had landed a scene-stealing five minutes with theatrical legends Carol Channing and Mary Martin in James Kirkwood's new comedy, *Legends*, playing at the Ahmanson in LA. In the second act Eric made an entrance as a Chippendale-like strip-o-gram messenger, in top hat and tails, and then stripped down to a gold bugle-beaded G-string to show a sequined crescent moon and star on each buttocks. Backed by a musical number he recorded, he "bumps, grinds and gyrates with both the stars."

Variety said simply, "Eric Riley brings down the house."

When the Ragotzys returned in early March from California, Jack told the press, "You may report that the *mature* owners of the Barn [he and Betty] have been up there on that pitched roof nailing down the boards. We have a couple of skilled people doing the more demanding work — Don White, a master plumber, and Ed Forward, a skilled carpenter — and Jim Knox is also helping out.

In the previous season, all during the four-week run of **A Chorus Line**, Ragotzy had assured the pa-

Eric Riley in *Legends* — 1986

David Holliday from NY to play de Becque. Nicolette of *The Press* said of Holliday, "He gives one of the finest interpretations of the romantic French planter since Ezio Pinza created the role on B'way. Holliday has the bearing, slight accent and excellent baritone necessary to make de Becque not only sympathetic but a convincing hero. Marineau brings to the role of Nellie the special charm of an attractive woman not quite sure of herself."

1986
An Evening with Angelo Mango, XIV
Brighton Beach Memoirs
South Pacific
Picnic
Little Shop of Horrors
*Sugar Babies
The Foreigner
Greater Tuna

Pacific was followed by **Picnic** starring Barnie Robert Newman who, in his first and only year at the Barn in '81, had been a second-year apprentice. Newman had not only played Josh Lewis on *The Guiding Light* for over three years, but was also in

trons he planned to build inside "facilities" to replace the traditional pair of prettily painted outhouses. Now Jack revealed to the press another reason for the improvements. "Additional restrooms will mean elimination of delays in second-act curtains. I think this will mean we won't have those intermission hangups. We've been known to have to delay the curtain ten to 15 minutes."

Prior to beginning the first season of the fifth decade, Ragotzy sprung for yet another major improvement. He paid over $50,000 for a Teatronics lighting control system and moved the old light board to the Rehearsal Shed. Both the main stage and the Rehearsal Shed shows would benefit.

1986 – 1995

After the opener, **Brighton Beach Memoirs,** in which Betty got excellent reviews as Kate, the Barn's first musical was the old warhorse, **South Pacific**. Wayne Lamb directed, with Scott Burkel as Lt. Cable, Joe Aiello as Luther Billis, Barbara Marineau as Nellie Forbush and Laura Collins as Bloody Mary. Ragotzy brought in

Robert Newman in **Picnic** — 1986

ABC's *General Hospital* and NBC's *Santa Barbara*. Starring with him was his fiancee of two months, Hollywood starlet Britt Helfer, who had been in half a dozen movies, including *Alley Cat*, *Making It* and *Young Warriors*. Area TV fans flocked to see Newman as the sexy Hal in **Picnic**.

Although many actors receive a kind of Barn stardom during their first season, this did not happen for Scott Burkel. He had plugged along for several seasons until he drew special attention for his work in **The Robber Bridegroom** and **Evita**. But it was the '86 season's **Little Shop of Horrors**, directed by Reeds, which made Burkel a Barn star. Peppel of the *Gazette* called it "the sleeper of the

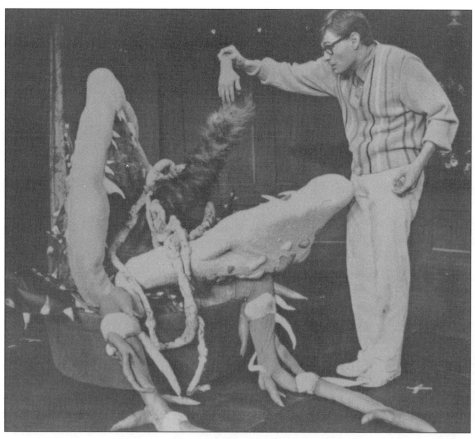
Scott Burkel in **Little Shop of Horrors** — 1986

Rudy Tronto and Angelo Mango in **Sugar Babies** — 1986

season this year" and said of Burkel, who played Seymour, "He makes nary a wrong move and can sing well to boot, with a clear and listenable voice. His range of ability has truly been showcased this season and this young man has got to be one of the best assets the Barn company has. He never overdoes and seems entirely different in each role he plays."

The show of the season, however, was **Sugar Babies** because it brought together old-time actor friends who had not worked together for 20 years. Angelo Mango played *Primo* Banana, while Rudy Tronto (whom Mango had worked with on B'way's *Irma La Duce* and in *The Boys From Syracuse* off-B'way), played Banana *Secundo*. Ann Hodges, who played Prima Donna, was their friend from *Syracuse*. She had been one of the original June Taylor dancers and had done *The Rothchilds* and *No Strings* on B'way and in the national companies.

The production, the nation's first summer stock version of the show that had run almost seven years on the Main Stem and in a national tour with Mickey Rooney and Ann Miller, was so successful that an extra week was added to its original two — making it one of a dozen or so three-weekers in Barn history. Tronto had directed the sketches for the original B'way production and understudied Rooney the first nine months of the run. "**Sugar Babies** is an entertainment confection," Ragotzy touted. "No story, no plot — just slightly naughty and very funny low-brow entertainment — with lots of dazzle and glitz!"

Peppel of the *Gazette* alliterated his kudos: "A big brassy, bawdy, baggy-pants bow to burlesque at its best and bluest burst onto the stage at the Barn with the opening of **Sugar Babies**. From the first rim shot to the last da-Da-dum, at the end of what seemed like a million punch lines, this production is fast, furious and, oh so funny. Mango is top banana and at his best, especially in the drag sequence as Madame 'Censored' reminiscing about her past, particularly sitting at the bar with a duck under her arm.

"Hodges has gorgeous gams, taps up a storm, and is all flash and pizzazz. She is one radiant red-head who sort of swings her way merrily through sketch or torch song, bearing the brunt of the comics' jokes. Tronto is an undeniable presence on the stage and did double duty by super-

Penelope Issichopoulos — 1986

vising the entire production. This man has a gleam in his eye that is absolutely wicked and timing that is superb."

Frances Franklin of *The Enquirer* called it "bawdy, titillating, raunchy, raucous, and hilarious, with corny, off-color skits and rim-shot one-liners filling the air like confetti. The show left the audience practically rolling in the aisles."

This season cannot pass without noting that Penelope Issichopoulos was a first-year apprentice who eventually changed her name — twice! More about that later.

And now some statistics on Barn apprentices and their pay. At the start of the fifth decade, the life of a Barn apprentice was one of performing at the Rehearsal Shed after a grueling ten- or 12-hour day. As for remuneration: Dick Fuchs was the first Barn apprentice to be paid. In '65 he received $15 a week as a second-year apprentice/staff assigned worker. By '86 all second-year apprentices were paid $40 a week; the following year all first-year apprentices were paid $50 and second-year apprentices $75 a week. By '95, first-year apprentices were paid $150 and second-year apprentices $175 a week. All apprentices paid their own transportation and expenses (food and lodging) but made some tip money waiting tables at the Rehearsal Shed show. Of course, they were gaining valuable professional as well as life experience. Undoubtedly, they all felt they needed the Actors' Equity card as an entree into professional theatre auditions.

This, of course, had been true at one time, but by the early '80s the law required that all productions, B'way, regional and summer stock, set aside a certain number of days for the auditioning of non-members. Or, an alternative was that any franchised Equity producer who felt an actor was professionally qualified could sign him/her to an Equity contract, as Ragotzy had done with Marineau in '75 and Aiello in '78. Or, students from professional training schools who got work in television and joined AFTRA (American Federation of Television and Radio Artists) could simply transfer to sister unions — Actors' Equity, AGVA (American Guild of Variety Artists) or SAG (Screen Actors Guild).

But in spite of these new rulings, apprentices continued to come to the Barn and other stock theatres since the experience of working in a variety of shows in such a short period of time was one that could not be duplicated anywhere else. And it certainly enhanced their resumes.

1987
An Evening with Angelo Mango
Move Over, Mrs. Markham
Brigadoon
Biloxi Blues
A Funny Thing Happened on the Way to the Forum
*42ⁿᵈ Street
Crimes of the Heart
*Nunsense

The '87 season got under way with the Rehearsal Shed show directed by Wayne Lamb which starred — who else? — Angelo Mango. What was special about this edition was that it marked Mango's 25th season at the Barn.

The season's main stage opener was third-time-produced **Move Over, Mrs. Markham**, featuring Dick Fuchs as special guest star. As for the season's "big" musical, Marcia L. Groat of *The Enquirer* called **42ⁿᵈ Street** "a slam bang, sock-it-to-'em show of stellar production numbers and glorified glitz, performed with the sort of professional ease that one has come to expect from the Barn's staff." She noted that at the show's conclusion "the audience leapt to its feet to give a standing ovation. The show has a terrific pace, lots of machine-gun footwork and plenty of action-packed song-and-dance routines — not to mention a well-handled storyline that would give you *deja vu* to relate here.

"Sandy Mulvihill does a great job in fulfilling all the demands placed on her shoulders as the chorus-gal-who'd-be-a-star. Her singing, dancing and acting are all first-rate. Jeff Lettiere steals several scenes as a grinning, happy hoofer, his rich tenor voice filling the theatre. Joe Aiello is vibrantly stoic as the cynical producer, and practically brought down the house with his closing number. Jen Wolfe is amusingly bright, commanding and multi-sided as the bitchy stage star whom Mulvihill supplants."

Nicolette of *The Press* reported that Ragotzy had extended the show's run prior to the opening, a move that knocked out the final announced show, *Bent*. He continued: "**42ⁿᵈ Street** has some of the best dance routines seen on the Barn stage since **A Chorus Line**, and Steve Owsley, who plays choreographer Andy Lee in the show, brings a great deal of the feel of **Chorus Line** to this show. Owsley is excellent both as the real and character choreographer, leading the ensemble with exceptional dance designs, his work made distinctive by the lovely flow of the body and the colorful and exciting use of the hands and arms."

42ⁿᵈ Street marked a beginning for 30-year-old Steve Owsley, who was from Michigan City, IN, and did undergraduate work at Western Michigan University. He had apprenticed at the Barn in '81 and '82 and played in four musicals each season. In '85 he returned as an Equity member specifically to assist Wayne Lamb on **A Chorus Line**. In '86 he was hired as assistant choreographer as well as an Equity company member and worked on Lamb's production of **South Pacific**. Then in '87, Ragotzy replaced Lamb with Owsley. During the season, he assisted Lamb on the Rehearsal Shed show but was choreographer on **Brigadoon**, did a role in **Biloxi Blues** and made his big splash with the critics as choreographer for **42nd Street**. He was a dancer/choreographer on the move.

Nunsense, written by Alma, MI, ex-seminarian Dan Goggin, closed the season. Katherine Doud of the *Gazette* remarked, "It is a wacky, wonderful night out, a delightful production, carried swiftly along by Betty Ebert, as the irascible

Mother Superior, who is at her best when paired with Edwina Lewis, as Sister Hubert."

Sherwood of *The Enquirer* added, "Going on sheer energy alone, the Barn production could light up New Jersey for a week. In fact, energy and talent allowed the show to deserve the raucously enthusiastic standing ovation it received. Credit Edwina Lewis for a lot of the fun. Not only is she one-fifth of the cast, but she directed the show with what they call pizzazz, instilling the author's slapdash script with pace, sight gags and frenzy.

However, Sherwood ended with this lament: "The show is the last of the Barn's current season, replacing the recent homosexual drama *Bent*, which unfortunately may never see the light of day in this area; more's the pity since drama was sadly lacking in this year's Barn season."

In November, Tom Wopat, who had lived in Nashville for a year, was reinventing himself as an emerging country singing star ("Susannah" and a video, "A Little Bit Closer," reached Country's top 20), was back in the news. He and his co-star from *Hazzard* were in a TV movie called "Christmas Comes to Willow Creek" — shot in Vancouver and the Yukon. It was their first appearance together since their hit TV series. Immediately afterwards Wopat was filming *Blue Skies* for a CBS summer series, which provided a role that he felt might help him break away from his "Hazzard" image and build his credibility as an actor. In addition, he had done *Carousel* at the Kennedy Center in Washington D.C. where a critic questioned his voice qualifications for playing the role. Tom snapped back three months later in off-B'way's *Olympus on My Mind*.

January 15, '88, brought tragic news about Barnie Norman Kean, who apprenticed in '54 and got very good reviews as a young Cherokee Indian in my play **Desire Is a Season.** Rather than being taken captive by local North Carolina police after a murder, the Indian runs to the cliff near the swimming hole and dives to his death.

"Did you see it . . .?" his sister says. "He was tall on the rock. His shirt off. He dove . . . . beautifully. . . to the point on the rock. It was only that split second — the time between — now it's ended. Ended. There'll be no more waiting."

In '56 Norman Kean moved to NY City. Two years later he married actress Gwyda DonHouwe. On B'way he stage-managed *Orpheus Descending* with Maureen Stapleton and *A Touch of*

Edwina Lewis and Betty Ebert in **Nunsense** — 1987

the Poet with Helen Hayes, became general manager for Ellis Rabb's APA Company, then a producer. Among his productions was the long-running *Oh! Calcutta!* at NY's Hotel Edison Theatre.

In the early morning of January 15, Norman stabbed his wife to death and, after writing three notes — one to the police and two to his 14-year-old son — climbed to the roof of his building at 280 Riverside Drive, removed his glasses and leapt to his death onto the rocks of the stone courtyard below.

I have often wondered about the similarity of Norm's means of suicide and the same means of suicide for the character in my play. Norm was an actor who worked from the inside out — in short, to understand a character's action, he dug deeply into his own psyche to find motivation. And he did such a realistic job in the role of a young Indian that he received special recognition from all the critics. There is no explanation, of course, but the similarity of art and real life in this instance haunts me still.

In early March of '88, Barnie Becky Gelke opened in B'way's Circle in the Square, playing Eunice in *A Streetcar Named Desire*. Star of the production was Blythe Danner as Blanche. Becky had been scheduled to return to the Barn the summer before and star in **Sweet Charity**, but stayed in the city for the role of Lucetta in Joe Papp's Central Park production of *Two Gentlemen of Verona*. In September she married actor Dylan Baker, whom she met while they were both appearing in off-B'way's *To Whom It May Concern*, directed by Geraldine Fitzgerald. Becky also went to Texas to film *Full Moon in Blue Water*, playing Gene Hackman's wife. The movie, directed by Peter Masterson of *Best Little Whorehouse* fame, starred Teri Garr and featured old-timer, Burgess Meredith.

1988
An Evening with Angelo Mango
The Nerd
Nunsense
*Oklahoma!
The Musical Comedy Murders of 1940
*The Most Happy Fella
*La Cage aux Folles
Some Enchanted Evening

The '88 season featured three shows Ragotzy was especially fond of. Tom Wopat's return to the Barn to do Curley in **Oklahoma!** (this time without a wife) was greeted with full houses. He had played the show at the Equity Library production ten years previously in NY when he was 26, so he was anxious to do it again. It was a down time while he was waiting to hear if the summer TV series *Blue Skies* would be picked up for the fall lineup. *Hazzard* had gone into syndication, Capitol Records had recently released several singles from his "Tom Wopat: A Little Bit Closer" LP and he had a new album, "Don't Look Back" — some rockabilly and blues — which was being released during the weeks he played Curley.

Peppel of the *Gazette* described his interview with Wopat. "With a grin on his ruggedly handsome face and a friendly twinkle in his blue eyes, Tom Wopat sits down at a large oak table and says, 'I'll talk about anything you like except my personal life.'" When Peppel asked him about the criticism he received in Washington D.C. for his *Carousel* performance, Wopat replied philosophically, "I had vocal problems. They wore me out before we opened. I take criticism with a grain of salt. *Carousel* was a humbling experience in a way, but I grew from it personally and professionally."

Coming up was a reprise of **The Most Happy Fella,** which Angelo Mango had played 18 years earlier under Wayne Lamb's direction, and which Ragotzy wanted him to play again. However, according to Mango, Ragotzy did not give him enough advance notice so that he could build his voice from its natural light baritone to a more operatic sound. On the other hand, according to Jack, Mango suddenly, and at the last moment, withdrew "for personal reasons."

Both Mango and Lamb had given enormous service to the Barn throughout the years and their hard work and loyalty were genuinely appreciated by the Ragotzys. But as producer, Jack felt it was time to retire Lamb (who had suffered a mild stroke earlier) from the more strenuous activities of being choreographer, and he had gone about this in a systematic way by hiring Steve Oswley as Lamb's assistant on several productions.

Furthermore, Ragotzy had decided to cast Joe Aiello in the role of Albin in **La Cage aux Folles**, a part that certainly would have been assigned to a younger Mango and one Mango thought should be his. Lamb entered the argument by contending that Mango had sung **La Cage's** signature song, "I Am What I Am" in the Rehearsal Shed show a year before and, traditionally, no one had sung a song in that venue who did

175

not sing it in the main stage production. Jack confided later that he would have assigned the role to Mango if Lou Girard, who was then in his late 60s, had been able to sing the role of George.

So there were some hard feelings. But for business' sake — and that is what the Barn was and is, a business — management had to do what management had to do. There is no question that Ragotzy had personal loyalties that made for a terrible internal struggle — underneath the often brusque exterior he is, in fact, a softie — but with Betty's less sentimental approach and support, he did what he felt was best. Mango's "personal reasons" were highly complex and he withdrew not only from **Fella**, but from all activity at the theatre from then on.

Ragotzy, always challenged by adversity, launched a last-minute search for an actor to play the role of Tony and this time he had to go outside the alumni of Barnies. "I was determined to start at the top and that person was someone who had played the role in the '79/'80 B'way revival. So I called Giorgio Tozzi's home in Scottsdale, Arizona, only to learn he was in San Francisco. His wife said she would have him call me at 5:30 that evening. I never dreamed he would actually do it — but he did, exactly at 5:30. He was not only interested, he was available. He returned to Arizona the following Sunday and flew to Detroit the next night. On Monday, he joined us in Augusta for rehearsals. To say the entire staff and company are thrilled is the understatement of the year."

The casting of Tozzi — a Metropolitan Opera star, four-time winner of the Grammy and a Tony nominee — was indeed a coup. Not only had he played Tony in the smash B'way '82 revival, but his *bona fides* included having been the first singer to receive screen credit for dubbing for a

Giorgio Tozzi in **The Most Happy Fella** — 1988

star. This was for Rossano Brazzi's Emile de Becque in the film version of *South Pacific*. Tozzi also received a Gold Record for the soundtrack album. Seems that when the film's musical directors heard Brazzi sing, they hired Tozzi, who at the time was playing the role of de Becque opposite Mary Martin in Los Angeles.

Edward Hayman, *The Detroit News* drama critic, wrote this glowing tribute: "They don't write musicals like **Most Happy Fella** any more. And there aren't many theatres like the Barn, that could produce them properly, anyway. The Barn is a classic old-time summer stock theatre, one of the best of its kind, and, sadly, one of the last. It's the sort of thoroughly professional summer theatre that proliferated in the '40s and '50s — one of those places where youngsters learn old-fashioned B'way values from a few old-timers who have been there. Tozzi is magnificent as Tony. His performance is as big and warm as his voice, operatic in its force and directness. And, as staged so carefully by Joe Aiello, his young colleagues achieve the same clarity and intensity. It's terrific ensemble work. This is a magic production, a rare treat, a kind of summer theatre experience that isn't often available any more. The drive to Augusta is well-rewarded."

C.J. Gianakaris, reviewing for the *Gazette*, added his praise, "Tozzi's commanding presence helped ignite one of the most energetic and professional musical productions seen in the Kalamazoo area this season. But no account of this production is complete without acknowledging the splendid singing and dancing of the company as a whole. Over three dozen performers take the stage and the large choruses are marvelously well sung. Music Director James Douglas Kent clearly has rehearsed his charges well. For an evening of great vitality fused with musicality of high professionalism, the Barn's **The Most Happy Fella** is the show to see."

It's hard to think of topping **Fella**, especially in summer stock, but then the Barn isn't your regular summer stock company. Immediately following came the Tony award-winning **La Cage aux Folles**, directed by Ragotzy with Charlie Misovye as choreographer and Dusty Reeds as set designer. The production starred Joe Aiello as Albin, the slightly over-the-hill drag queen, along with guest star George McDaniel as his partner, Georges. Jack imported Gordon McClure, who had performed the role of Jacob the "maid" at the Candlelight Dinner Theatre in Chicago, to reprise his role. Ragotzy rented the costumes for the 'Cagelles' from the Grand Dinner Theatre in LA, claiming, "The Cagelles at the Barn will rival any Las Vegas chorus line!"

Peppel of the *Gazette* applauded the production enthusiastically: "The show makes demands of production values and performances that seem almost impossible outside of B'way. These demands certainly weren't met in the limping touring-company that played Kalamazoo last November. They were, however, exceeded Tuesday night as performance after performance, costume after costume, musical

Joe Aiello and George McDaniel in **La Cage aux Folles** — 1988

number after musical number, and set after set paraded by in a fast, absorbing two hours and 15 minutes of entertainment.

"**La Cage** is a delight to the eye, ear, and sensibilities, laced with humor, tenderness, pathos, and some of the most delightful songs to be heard in a long time. It is probably the most elaborate show ever staged at the Barn. The 'Cagelles' rival any Las Vegas or Folies-Bergere production, aided in no small measure by Garrylee McCormick's astonishing array of nearly 50 elaborate and convincing wigs and Mela Hoyt-Heydon's original costumes, which the Barn brought from California.

"Joe Aiello and George McDaniel are superb. Aiello's Albin is funny, ultra-feminine, giving, loving, and flamboyant. He doesn't overdo it or go for the obvious or the leer. Aiello *is* Albin. You root for him, cry for him, laugh at him and with him. His signature song, 'I Am What I Am,' a furious, pleading cry for acceptance, brought the first act to a close with the audience roaring its approval.

"McDaniel's Georges sings extremely well, is suave, and totally convincing. You must believe his relationship with Albin as well as believe the fact that he could sire a son. McDaniel never wavers, is never snide, and brings a warmth and compassion to the role not seen so far in any production of the show.

"Gordon McClure as Jacob the 'maid' is hysterical, professional, and a welcome addition to the roster of performers in this area. There is an infectious magic about this **La Cage** that happens once in a blue moon. You can feel it in this production from the first note of the overture to the last note of the finale. Producer-director Ragotzy is wondering what to do for the last week of his season. Not to worry — when word gets out about this **La Cage**, it could run until November," Peppel concluded.

In the fall, Jack and Betty were in London and saw a farce, *Run for Your Wife*, which would be on the coming summer season's schedule. In late October, Barnie Dana Delany was filming ABC's *China Beach*, in which she played Army nurse Colleen McMurphy. The series about the Vietnam War, seen through the eyes of the women who served there, aired to excellent critical notices. Delany would receive an Emmy in '90 for her role. In the two years previous, Delany had played the love interest to Tom Selleck in *Magnum, PI*, Bruce Willis in *Moonlighting* and Peter Horton in *thirtysomething*. She had also appeared in three films, *Moon Over Parador*, *Patty Hearst* and *Masquerade*.

In October, Barnie Marin Mazzie, who had been understudying several roles in Sondheim's *Into the Woods* on B'way, was given the role of Rapunzel. She also understudied Cinderella and The Witch, the latter role originated by Bernadette Peters. But she wanted more. "I want to *originate* a B'way role," she told Nicolette of *The Press*. "I think it's a goal that's attainable." She eventually got her wish, originating the roles of Clara in Sondheim's *Passion* and, at the time of this writing, Mother in *Ragtime,* receiving Tony Award nominations for both.

As to other news — in November, Penelope Issichopoulos changed her name to Mrs. Brendan Ragotzy. In March, Tom Wopat gave a concert at the 1,800 seat Frauenthal Theatre in Muskegon, MI. In May, Doud of the *Gazette* announced that, for the first time in 16 years, singer-actor Angelo Mango would not be the featured performer in the Rehearsal Shed show. "Ragotzy said family matters will keep Mango in NY until June. But he'll be seen later in the season in regular Barn productions" — which, of course, he was not.

1989
Music! Music! Music!
Barefoot in the Park
The 1940's Radio Hour
Run for Your Wife
Hair
*Steel Magnolias
*Hello, Dolly!
Les Liasons Dangereuses

The Rehearsal Shed production was titled **Music! Music! Music!** and featured some younger, favorite performers of recent seasons — Scott Burkell (note the new spelling of his last name), Sandy Mulvihill, Jeff Lettiere and Penelope Alex (formerly Issichopoulos Ragotzy — Alex being her mother's maiden name). The show was directed by Joe Aiello.

Ticket prices for main stage productions were up to $14 on weekdays and $16.50 on weekends, compared with $12.50 and $15 the year before. The season's opener was **Barefoot in the Park**, starring Robert Newman and Britt Helfer, both of whom had played in **Picnic** in '86, two months prior to their marriage. Newman was still Josh on CBS's *The Guiding Light*. Helfer had taken time off her ABC soap, *Loving*, and on April 3 gave birth to their son, Connor. The couple told reporters how having the baby had changed their lives. They were coping with fatigue and had moved from Manhattan to Yonkers where they bought a four-bedroom Tudor home for what they were spending on the one bedroom apartment in the City.

Midsummer, there appeared three long articles in various local newspapers. The first featured Paul Robbins of 301 Chestnut Street in Augusta, who rented rooms to Barn actors in his restored 127-year-old house, filled with antiques. Jim Knox, who was in charge of locating housing for some 50 Barnies per summer, was grateful to him. The Augusta view of Barnies had changed since the '50s and '60s, Knox and Robbins concluded. "The village has gotten used to them."

It may have helped that Barnies were pumping more than $100,000 annually into the coffers of the village's businesses, while also providing the local people with a feeling of being on the cutting edge of show biz. One of their biggest fans, Shirley Greek, was the cook at The Spinning Wheel. "I don't know all their names," she confessed, "but I know how they want their eggs cooked, the dressings for their salads and if they eat onions." She didn't know Louis Girard by name, but she knew he liked "two egg-salad sandwiches on wholewheat bread without lettuce."

Wopat?

"He likes two eggs over easy."

A Gazette article reported that years earlier — perhaps in the mid '50s — Augusta milling executive Charles B. Knappen, Jr. told the Ragotzys the Barn would put the village on the map. It took time — and Betty's lobbying — but the State Department of Transportation finally threw in the towel in '89 and agreed to add Augusta exit signs on eastbound and westbound I-94.

Betty, who was 66 at the time, was in a very realistic mood when she told reporters, "We'd like to do what we're doing forever, but we can't. But we have the framework in place for the Barn to carry on without us." Son Brendan and daughter-in-law Penelope were the major part of that framework. Having been carried on stage before his first birthday, Brendan had been a "special assistant" at the theatre in '73 (working a follow spot on **Hair**), had stage managed since '86 and was now ready to direct his first show. "I hope," Betty said, "the Barn is one of their long-term goals."

Brendan's revival of **Hair** turned out to be so successful that it became a three-weeker. It was followed by **Steel Magnolias**, directed by Joe Aiello, which played for one week and was the major "sleeper" of the season. Groat of *The Enquirer* called it an "exemplary production. Aiello directed with a keen eye for detail, seeing that beauty parlor realism is abundant, but not letting it detract from the play." Ruth Butler of *The Press* added, "The production offers plenty of laughs as well as a good cry. Betty Ebert is a standout as M'Lynn. Her gripping scene late in the play keeps the audience entranced."

The first color-blind casting for a show at the Barn came with the production of **Hello, Dolly!** Sure, Pearl Bailey had done **Dolly** — but with an all black cast. The Barn's production, casting Edwina Lewis as Dolly and Louis Girard as Horace, received unanimous acclaim.

Hayman of *The Detroit News* applauded: "After all these years and hundreds of productions, large and small, the great temptation would be to play **Hello, Dolly!** with an elbow in the ribs, winking and kidding the corny, sentimental, overly-familiar material. What else is there to do with it? Well, start by substituting innocent for corny. Then look for genuine good-heartedness instead of predictable sentimentality. And what happens? The overly-familiar becomes fresh again — and we're reminded why we love it so much in the first place.

"That's how they're doing **Hello, Dolly!** at the Barn — playing to sold-out houses, and holding over a third week. Indeed, that's how they do everything at the Barn — everything I've seen, anyway.

"The 'they' this time is a buoyant and thoroughly professional young cast led by former Detroiter Edwina Lewis in the title role, a young director named Joe Aiello who knows what B'way magic feels like, and a young choreographer named Charles Misovye who has embellished every step in his simple dance numbers with just the right touch of B'way aplomb.

"Lewis is a dimpled, cherubic actress who makes us think of a kewpie doll until she opens her mouth and out comes a silken boom that would give Carol Channing a run for her money.

Hers is a deceptively demanding role, and the dynamic Lewis glides through its many moods, comically, wistfully, gracefully with a contagious sunny magnetism.

"Like all Barn musicals, this **Dolly** is produced with a fullness that is as refreshing as it is rare. Nowadays, the economics of the theatre being what they are, summer and dinner theatre operators tend to be ardent minimalists, searching for every possible way to cut corners. But Barn producers Jack and Betty Ragotzy, who are from the old school, have the opposite goal. They're out

Marin Mazzie in **Born Yesterday** — 1990

to pack their productions with everything they can get for their dollars, and it shows in the production values — in the fullness of the pit orchestra, the richness of the costumes and the sets. This kind of professional summer theater was the norm 30 years ago. Now there's not much of it left."

Terry Pow of *The Citizen Patriot* concurred. "The hardest part about experiencing the Barn's production of **Dolly** is saying goodbye to actress Edwina Lewis at the final curtain. Lewis pours her all into the part and that adds up to a potent mixture of vivacious personality, natural comic timing, and a voice that can shake the beetles out of the Barn's rafters. She carries the show, and the audience, in the warmth of her cheeky smile."

The season ended with the extremely difficult **Les Liaisons Dangereuses**, not one of Jack's or the critics' favorites. But it should be noted that this was Scott Burkell's first directing assignment at the Barn.

In January '90, Jack and Betty went to London to see shows — 14 of 'em — and then went on to Paris. John Newton and Edwina Lewis were in Washington, D.C., in *Cat on a Hot Tin Roof* starring Kathleen Turner, Newton as an understudy. The show was headed to NY after the Washington run. In early February, Jack was acting in an episode of *Hunter* for TV. Barnies Marin Mazzie and Becky Gelke (now using her married name, Becky Ann Baker) were in Washington, D.C., in a production of Sondheim's *Merrily We Roll Along*.

On May 24, the Hon. Howard Wolpe of Michigan read a statement entered into *The Congressional Record*: "Mr. Speaker, I rise to pay tribute to a very special theatrical institution in my district, the Barn Theatre, which is celebrating its 45th anniversary. The Barn Theatre is the oldest Equity playhouse in Michigan and one of the oldest in the United States. In its 44 years of stock performance, the Barn has entertained more than one million patrons and has produced more than 300 shows. It is well known for the extraordinary quality of its actors, directors, and stage managers, and for the inspiring management team of Jack and Betty Ragotzy."

The Congressman ended by saying, "In 1981 - '85, the Barn Theatre faced the threat of a landfill being placed less than 2,000 feet from the site. The theatre fought the landfill and simultaneously helped estab-

Joe Aiello as scientist Dr. Frank N. Furter in **The Rocky Horror Show** — 1990

lish new air quality standards for all Michigan landfills. Mr. Speaker, the people of Augusta take tremendous pride in the historic Barn Theatre. It has been my privilege to represent two remarkably talented and dedicated individuals, Jack and Betty Ragotzy, and I know my colleagues will want to join me in paying tribute to them and to the Barn Theatre on the occasion of the theatre's 45th anniversary."

In '90, Marin Mazzie came back for the first three shows of the season. She was Josefine in **Romance Romance** with Scott Burkell, Babe Williams in **Pajama Game** with Tom Wopat, and Billy Dawn in **Born Yesterday** with Joe Aiello.

```
1990
Romance Romance
The Pajama Game
Born Yesterday
*The Rocky Horror Show
The Man Who Came to Dinner
Me and My Girl
*Driving Miss Daisy
```

These shows were followed by a cult classic, **The Rocky Horror Show,** which Brendan directed. Jack at first would have none of it, but finally consented, and the show was so popular with the audience that it was held over for a third week. Hayman of *The Detroit News* declared, "The Barn has tackled **The Rocky Horror Show** with its customary zeal, and, under the direction of Brendan Ragotzy, has the tone and tongue-in-cheek style just right. These people don't stint on anything, and the stage is constantly full of writhing freaks in stunningly weird costumes, smoke, explosions, organ music and, along the way, first-rate vocal and instrumental arrangements by Mark Elliott."

Pow of *The Citizen Patriot* was more than delighted. "Maybe I've lived a sheltered life, or my fishnets were always in the wash, but somehow I've never gotten around — not on stage or on the screen — to seeing that ultimate camp classic, **The Rocky Horror Show**. Well, thanks to the Barn, I'm no longer a 'virgin' — and it feels wonderful. An exuberant cast of Barnies disposed of my innocence during a boisterous performance here the other night.

Louis Girard and Kelly McAllister in **The Man Who Came To Dinner** — 1990

"I can't recall the precise moment the earth moved for me during **Rocky Horror**, but it could well have been when actor Joe Aiello rose through a stage trap door looking like the queen bug from 'Aliens,' only in drag. As the transsexual Dr. Frank N. Furter, Aiello presents an image of pouting provocativeness that's forever lodged in some dark ambivalent corner of my psyche for psychiatrists to feast upon for years to come.

"Corrupted?" Pow continued. "Yes, by laughter. This is an irresistible show. As the hunchback servant, Riff-Raff, Scott Burkell comes within an inch of upstaging Aiello — no mean feat. I had to look twice to see if it really was that nice Mr. Burkell beneath the wig and paint."

The season ended with Alfred Uhry's **Driving Miss Daisy**, directed by Joe Aiello, with Betty Ebert in the title role and newcomer Kent Martin playing Hoke, the chauffeur. Martin had performed off-B'way and had gone to Hollywood to make a film, *Black Girl*, with Brock Peters, Ruby Dee, Leslie Uggams and Claudia McNeil. He also had credits for national tours and at various regional and summer theatres, had done commercials and had been featured in a Disney NBC-TV movie, "A Mother's Courage: The Mary Thomas Story."

Pow of *The Citizen Patriot* was charmed. "As the peppery, constitutionally suspicious Miss Daisy ('They steal things, you know,' she says in general reference to servants everywhere), Betty Ebert is a delight to watch. From the first explosive outing with Hoke in the Piggly Wiggly grocery to the final loving look as she accepts a spoonful of cake from him in the retirement home, Ebert builds and shades her performance with skill and restraint. Kent Martin's Hoke is a delicious foil. Wise to the ways of a white man's world, Hoke balances

Kent Martin and Betty Ebert in **Driving Miss Daisy** — 1990

a sense of survival with a sly opportunism and a natural generosity of spirit. Martin captures it all. Scott Burkell is the son — a good performance, though I was not entirely convinced that he'd aged to 65 in the last scenes. Joe Aiello directs with a feather-light touch." Groat of *The Enquirer* added of Ebert, "She's terrific. She has just the right touch with the humorous and dramatic demands of the part."

Tom Wopat was back in the news that winter with an excellent personal notice in the *NY-Times* as the six-month, New Year's Eve replacement for James Naughton in the leading role of gumshoe Stone in the Tony Award-winning musical, *City of Angels*. Critic Frank Rich remarked, "Tom Wopat's rumpled, battered masculinity proves ideal for Stone, the fictional, hard-boiled private eye."

Eric Riley was also back on B'way — this time in *Once on this Island*, playing Papa Ge, a role he originated off-B'way and in the workshop production.

In February, Jack was seen in a bit part on *Knots Landing* in an episode titled "Call Me Dimitri," in which he played a Lithuanian relative at a funeral. He also played a small role as a World War II veteran in an episode of *China Beach* in a segment titled "Through and Through."

Mid-April, Michigan-born Todd Zamarripa opened on B'way in *Miss Saigon*. After his graduation from Western Michigan University in '87, he spent the summer apprenticing at the Barn. "That was an intense experience and it opened a lot of doors in my mind about what I would have to do and where to go to make this business a career," he said.

At the end of March a news item reported that not only had Jack and Betty made a quick trip to NY where they saw nine shows, but that Betty was appearing briefly in a segment of NBC's daytime serial *Days of Our Lives*, and Jack had been cast as a train conductor in the new Chevy Chase film called, *Memories of an Invisible Man*.

The '91 season opened with a second edition of **Music! Music! Music!** in the Rehearsal

Scott Burkell and Jack Ragotzy in **How to Succeed in Business Without Really Trying** — 1991

1991
Music! Music! Music! II
Romantic Comedy
How to Succeed in Busines Without Really Trying
Lend Me a Tenor
Jesus Christ, Superstar
Anything Goes
*Bay House

Shed lounge; **Romantic Comedy**, starring Robert Newman and his wife, Britt Helfer, opened the main stage. Returning Marin Mazzie said she felt fortunate to have two summer jobs in Michigan — one in Birmingham Theatre's production of *South Pacific* and the other at the Barn. "It's the worst fall and winter I've had in my nine years in NY City," she said. "I go to auditions and everybody is there. Nobody has a job. The dearth of shows makes the Tony Awards almost a joke. But they have to nominate *somebody*. It's very frustrating. A lot of NY actors went to LA hoping to land jobs in pilots being made for the fall TV season, but there were 55 percent fewer pilots made this year than last. Those actors are now out there with no work."

If there was a solidifying role into continued Barn stardom for actor Scott Burkell, it was Finch in **How to Succeed in Business Without Really Trying**, directed by Joe Aiello. Peppel of the *Gazette* affirmed, "Scott Burkell, charm and voice down pat, is particularly good and Marin Mazzie as Hedy LaRue is a slinky stitch and brings the rafters down with her rendition of 'Love From a Heart of Gold' done like nails on a blackboard."

Mark Stryker of *The South Bend Tribune* added, "As Finch, Scott Burkell combines just the right amount of boyish charm and rattlesnake ven-

Melissa Gilbert in the world premiere of **Bay House** — 1991

om so that his barracuda-like tactics never turn him into a villain. As each of his plots comes to fruition and he stomps on yet another co-worker in his climb up the corporate ladder, Burkell turns to the audience and grins, so completely delighted with his devilishness that we can't help but be so too. There's nothing subtle about Marin Mazzie as the luscious redheaded busty bombshell whose wiggle and jiggle endear her to a whole pack of office wolves. She vamps and whines her way through her numbers, wearing skin-tight dresses and a fox stole that looked freshly trapped. The rest of the cast, as is usually the case in Barn productions, is throughly professional."

Ragotzy had managed to obtain the first area rights to Ken Ludwig's '89 B'way hit, **Lend Me a Tenor,** which, under the direction of Steven Hauck and featuring Marin Mazzie, turned out to be one of the top hits of the Barn's '91 season. Mazzie was also featured in **Jesus Christ, Superstar** and played a lead role in **Anything Goes**.

At the end of the season was a world premiere, **Bay House**. It was one of two premieres presented by the Barn in its fifth decade — a far cry from what Ragotzy did in the first three. **House** was written by Texas-born Bo Brinkman, 34, a member of the playwright/directors unit of the Actors Studio and the husband of one of Brendan Ragotzy's childhood schoolmates, Melissa Gilbert.

Gilbert had appeared in *Little House on the Prairie* for ten years as Laura Ingalls, TV daughter of Michael Landon who, only weeks before, had died of cancer at the age of 54. *Little House* and Michael Landon were very much in the news, including a special tribute to his television career as part of the Emmy Awards on August 25 — just three days prior to the opening of **Bay House**. A chartered plane was sent to Kalamazoo for Gilbert so she could present the posthumous Emmy. *Entertainment Tonight* sent television representatives

Penelope Alex (on floor), Betty Ebert, Louis Girard and Joellyn Cox Young (seated),
Bo Brinkman, Joe Aiello and Melissa Gilbert (last row)
in world premiere of **Bay House** — 1991

to Augusta to interview her about appearing at the awards ceremony, and of course she mentioned that she was appearing in her husband's play at the Barn.

Because of the amount of publicity generated by Gilbert, there was a heavy advance ticket sale and Ragotzy had to schedule a second week of **Bay House** before it opened on August 28.

Hayman of *The Detroit News,* with the caveat that the play was getting its first public exposure, was not impressed. "Unhappily, this exposure is painfully premature. **Bay House** is light years away from being ready for an audience. And, unless its freshman author, Bo Brinkman, goes back to his creative well and comes up with something more believable — not to mention original — this sputteringly histrionic and derivative melodrama never will be ready. If there's a worthwhile new voice here, it's too soon to tell."

After reiterating the plot, Pow of *The Citizen Patriot* asked, "Is it entertaining? Up to a point — which, for me, arrived about a half-hour into the play when I realized I'd been over this ground too many times before, and that **Bay House** didn't have anything fresh or insightful to tell me about unhappy families. From that point on, boredom began to set like concrete in my brain as the family talked and talked and yelled and yelled at each other."

Leading with a justification, Peppel of the *Gazette* concurred. "It would be so simple to tear the production to shreds. But, what must be borne in mind is that this is a new play, a work in progress. Albeit, the feeling is strong that much of the progress must be put into more work on the script. In other words, the Barnies probably did the very best they could with what they had to work with.

"Inevitably, comparisons will be drawn between the play and Tennessee Williams' *Cat on a Hot Tin Roof.* Many of the characters seem drawn from the same pages, though in a different plot. We have the strong father, the crippled son at odds with his wife over a personal tragedy, family conflicts, and the velvety southern women with steel for guts. However, any further comparisons to "Cat" would be a disservice to Williams and give entirely too much credence to Brinkman's effort.

"Other than stock weird family with a lot of hang ups, which can be seen on any soap opera, the drama doesn't occur in act one. We merely have shouts and stompings on chicken bones, bratty siblings, and dark hints, which only left this reviewer in the dark with more questions than answers," he commented.

March '92 was a busy month for the Ragotzys. Betty reported that she and Jack had been to NY for a whirlwind, six-day, eight-show trip and that their favorites were *The World Goes Round, Crazy for You* and *The Will Rogers Follies.* She also said that at a recent screening of Chevy Chase's *Memories of an Invisible Man,* only by looking intently could they make out the figure of the train conductor which Jack had played and thought would be an important scene in this, his first feature film.

Ragotzy had even researched the role, interviewing an Amtrak conductor and taking a short trip on the train. However, everything but the hazy figure ended up on the cutting room floor. Jack had just done a small role in the latest Mel Gibson picture, *The Rest of Daniel,* released under the title, *Forever Young,* in which he played the man at the air show and hoped his efforts wouldn't be cut this time.

In April came news that Steven Hauck, actor-director at the Barn, debuted in the lead role of Erick in the Ken Hill version of *Phantom of the Opera* at Paris' *Opera Comique.* Steven was one of a company of fourteen based in Germany and started touring in December, first to Berlin and later to Switzerland and the Netherlands. Actors in the company rotated in major and minor roles during a ten-week run.

In April, Nicolette of *The Press* did a feature on Robin Haynes, who was in Grand Rapids in his first national tour playing the role of Norman Petty in *Buddy: The Buddy Holly Story* at DeVos Hall. Haynes said he liked being on the road and that if it weren't for his family back in New Jersey — wife Suzanne, daughter Morgan and son Whitney — he'd be very happy traveling.

The big news was that the Barn had a renovation that winter. Ragotzy reported, "We have recognized for quite a while that the Barn would require structural strengthening if we were to continue adding heavy theatrical equipment. We didn't know what specific steps needed to be taken, but we did know that we didn't want to put that magnificent wooden building in jeopardy.

"Last fall we called Stuart Eddy of the Miller-Davis building company — a structural engineer who is known for his work with historic wooden buildings. What followed was an intense and unconventional seven-month renovation. The first order of business was to secure the building. The sides of the structure were trussed with steel cables, which were held in place by iron bars on the outside. Slowly, the cables were tightened to 'take up' the sides of the auditorium and restore the Barn to its original shape. So remarkable was the difference that the cupola on the top of the roof was actually five inches higher when the work was completed.

"After that, 22-foot steel ribs were placed on each side of the Barn's crucial curved beams as reinforcement. We added a new proscenium arch, the base of which rests in the basement which makes the stage 15 inches higher. Now we'll be able to have a real two-story set and the audience will be able to see the actors from toe to head. The auditorium looks essentially the same, but the audience will notice the proscenium arch has a little different shape. The renovation cost about $60,000. But what is more important than the cost is what has been accomplished. The Barn now truly has a future."

On Friday, prior to the opening of the '92 Rehearsal Shed show, second-year apprentice Bruce Hammond took off at 5 p.m. to have a dinner at his home in Richland. Another car filled with first-year apprentices Amy Francis, Don Berry and Paul Loesel (who would become musical director at the Barn and, still later, play keyboard for B'way's *Ragtime* and *The Lion King*) also left for a dinner break. There was a heavy rainstorm and Hammond failed to stop at the intersection of G Avenue and 36th Street, hitting an eastbound car. He was then struck by another car — the one filled with the Barn apprentices. Wearing no seat belt, Hammond flew through the rear window of his car, skidding 60 feet along the pavement. The driver of the car Hammond hit sustained only minor injuries and the same was true of the apprentices.

Hammond was rushed by ambulance to Bronson Hospital where he received more than twenty staples to close the wound in his scalp and on his left arm. When the police officer came to the Barn several days later to inquire if Hammond was still alive, he found that the young man was back in rehearsals on Sunday. Hammond, quoted by Peppel of the *Gazette*, lamented, "But all I could do was sit and watch. Monday I got up and moved around. After all, I didn't want anyone else taking my place." On opening night he performed in all three acts and the day afterwards said, "I feel great!"

The Rehearsal Shed show was a departure from the usual practice, inasmuch as it was a review — **Perfectly Frank** by Frank Loesser — for which royalties had to be paid. Previously the

Tom Wopat and Kathy Taylor in **Kiss Me, Kate** — 1992

1992
Perfectly Frank
Rumors
Kiss Me, Kate
*M. Butterfly
*Phantom
Social Security
Man of La Mancha
The Rocky Horror Show

shows were put together by Barn staff. Peppel of the *Gazette* remarked, "The evening belonged to the apprentices. We haven't seen quite as attractive or talented a group of aspiring actors to hit the Barn in many a season."

Wopat was back in Cole Porter's **Kiss Me, Kate**, co-directed by Ragotzy. The show was such a hit that Ragotzy held **Kate** over for a third week. Mark Glubke of *The Enquirer* proclaimed, "Tom Wopat is the big drawing card here. With his rugged good looks, booming voice and abiding machismo, Wopat doesn't disappoint. And while he may be the show's big name, guest star Kathy Taylor, as the mercurial Lilli, is its star. Boasting a bell-like voice, the Chicago actress offers several of the evening's highlights."

For the role of Song Liling in David Henry Hwang's **M. Butterfly**, Jack hired California actor Dexter Echiverri, who had been in the chorus of the first national touring company of *Miss Saigon*.

Hayman, critic for *The Detroit News,* was obviously impressed. "Good summer theatre has an exhilarating slam-dunk quality. There's no time, when seven or eight plays are being done in the same short summer, to pussy-foot around. You get together a team of good players, you get your hands on the ball and you go for it. Slam-dunks are routine here at the venerable Barn Theatre, and its latest is the difficult **M. Butterfly** about the French diplomat who fell in love with a Chinese opera star and lived with 'her' for 20 years before finding out that she was really a man and a Communist spy.

"The Barn's odd couple are Joe Aiello, the diplomat, and Dexter Echiverri as Song Liling, the modern Madame Butterfly of the piece. Theirs is

Facing front are Joe Aiello and Dexter Echiverri (as Song Liling) in **M. Butterfly** — 1992

a delicate, complex relationship, not easy to delineate in a few scant weeks of rehearsal. Under the direction of Jack Ragotzy, Aiello and Echiverri capture neatly both the fantasy and the heartsick reality the two must face when 'she' finally takes off 'her' clothes and he winds up in prison, still clinging to the illusion that this angry young man really is Butterfly.

"Echiverri impersonates beautifully the soft, gliding geisha doll with the passionate inner core. This adroit actor is a real find, a worthy successor to B.D. Wong and Alex Mapa, who played the role on B'way and the national company, respectively. But the story is really Gallimard's, and it is Aiello who must keep us interested and sympathetic, and he does, as this funny but pathetically lovelorn fool who knows he's the victim of his own delusions."

Stryker of *The South Bend Tribune* declared that Aiello and Echiverri were "outstanding" and called the production "the company's strongest effort in recent memory. Superb acting, clear direction by Jack Ragotzy, a spare yet striking set, stunning visuals, costumes and movement combine into a seamless, mesmerizing whole, bringing to life a most intriguing play by one of America's most important young playwrights."

Brendan's fourth directing stint, co-directed with Charlie Misovye, was **Phantom**. This was not the hit B'way musical *Phantom of the Opera* by Andrew Lloyd Webber, but rather one written by Arthur Kopit and Maury Yeston. It had been in progress since '83, before the Webber version was started, and had its premiere in '91 in Houston's Theatre Under The Stars. The Barn's production was the first for Michigan.

The Kopit/Yeston version had been playing with "incredible success" at Chicago's Candlelight Dinner Theatre, drawing nearly 100,000 patrons. However, length of a Chicago run is not necessarily proof of quality. If it were, *Ladies Night in a Turkish Bath* with Skeets Gallager and Buddy Ebsen would be considered a classic. The Kopit/Yeston version was selected because it was

Joe Aiello as Gallimard and Dexter Echiverri as Song Liling in **M. Butterfly** — 1992

the only one released and patrons could conclude that it was the same as the B'way production, even though the Barn advertised otherwise.

Nevertheless, Marcie Fulmer of *The Elkhart Truth* was captivated: "This **Phantom** could run for the rest of the season. It's not easy to put your own stamp on a role as closely identified with another actor as that of the Phantom is with Michael Crawford, but Scott Burkell is more than equal to the challenge. You never see his face, but through Burkell's sensitive, intelligent portrayal, you know his heart. Director Brendan Ragotzy and co-director/choreographer Charlie Misovye have put together an outstanding cast and the Barn's always fine production staff has risen to the challenge."

Nicolette of *The News* was less enthusiastic. "The Barn has a production that is expected to trade on the name value of Webber's *Phantom*, without giving the impression that it is. As to the script and most of the melodies, it is doubtful that this musical would have been done by the shrewd Ragotzy without that aforementioned name association.

"Scott Burkell is a convincing Phantom, and the beautiful Jill Walmsley a lovely light and lilting soprano. Musical director David S. Young leads a fine group of instrumentalists who handle the score well and support rather than overpower the singers."

During the year, Barnie Doug LaBrecque, an '82 graduate of Lakeview High School in Battle Creek and music theatre graduate of the University of Michigan, who had apprenticed with the

(L to R) Bruce Hammond, Penelope Alex as Aldonza/Dulcinea and Eric Parker
(Charlie King playing guitar) in **Man of La Mancha** — 1992

Barn in '86/'87, appearing in **Evita**, **A Chorus Line**, and **Sugar Babies**, was on the road in Andrew Lloyd Webber's *The Phantom of the Opera*. In Toronto he went on as Raoul. He had joined the *Phantom* company after appearing in San Francisco in the first national company of *Les Miserables*.

In August of '92, Marin Mazzie was in the national tour of Kander and Ebb's musical review, *The World Goes 'Round*, but before it started, she managed to create a role in John Logan's *Riverview* at Chicago's Goodman Theatre. *World* opened in Cincinnati, then moved on to Los Angeles where it was hugely successful and won all of the Dramalogue awards. In February the show was playing the Shubert Theatre in Chicago. Mazzie remained on tour until the following summer.

At the end of March '93, Robin Haynes was cast in *Blood Brothers*, which was rehearsed in Toronto. He went to NY with the show for previews April 16. Although it opened on April 30 to some pretty bad reviews, it managed to run until the end of May '95 and gave Haynes two years on B'way.

Kim Zimmer and Tom Wopat in **The Rainmaker** — 1993

```
1993
Music! Music! Music!
*The Rainmaker
*City of Angels
A Few Good Men
Nunsense II
L'il Abner
The Best Little Whore-
  house in Texas
Jake's Women
```

The opening main stage show in '93 was N. Richard Nash's 40-year-old comedy, **The Rainmaker**, starring Tom Wopat and newcomer to the Barn, Kim Zimmer. Ragotzy reported, "Robert Newman had told Zimmer — both being *Guiding Light* stars — about the Barn and they had talked about doing a show here. The three of us met and considered several possibilities but couldn't seem to find the right show. But as we talked I realized Kim would be a perfect Lizzie for **The Rainmaker**. I suggested the possibility to her and not only was she interested, but she told me she was a native of Grand Rapids which would make the show something of a homecoming for her!"

The '93 Barn season was full of great offerings. Wopat was staying on after **The Rainmaker**, directing and starring in **City of Angels**, a first release that Ragotzy obtained while the show was still touring. In addition, there was **A Few Good Men**, which had just been made into a film with Jack Nicholson, Tom Cruise and Demi Moore. Plus — Edwina Lewis was returning to do **Nunsense II: the Second Coming** and direct a revival of **The Best Little Whorehouse in Texas**.

Fulmer of *The Elkhart Truth* reported that **The Rainmaker** was playing to capacity audiences. "At first glance it would seem that star power has a lot to do with the SRO signs being posted by producer Jack Ragotzy, who also directed the tightly-paced production. Well, starpower may fill the Barn's seats initially, but strong performances by an excellent ensemble in a touchingly humorous and solid play keep them that way."

With the caveat that the play was written in a "pre-woman's lib era," she went on to say, "Wopat takes the stage from his first impressive entrance and creates a brashly virile and arrogant persona which is eventually revealed (as every woman in the audience knows from the start) as a facade hiding a sensitive romantic who finally declares, 'I just want things to be as pretty in my hand as they are in my head.'

"Zimmer's Lizzie is a wonderfully multi-faceted woman. Full of bravado when facing down her marriage-minded siblings, she is at once poignant and agonizingly humorous in revealing to her sympathetic father, 'I'm afraid to think I'm beautiful when I know I'm not.'"

There was only one review found in this 50-year study that compared *two* productions of a play running simultaneously. Reed Johnson of *The Detroit News* reported that "two West Michigan companies — one professional and one not, an hour apart by car and nearly a half-century removed in longevity — opened with dueling versions of N. Richard Nash's pastoral yarn, **The Rainmaker**. Ragotzy has hammered together a **Rainmaker** that's everything most people ask of summer drama: a laugh every 45 seconds, recognizable faces in the lead roles and mental stimulation that doesn't require breaking a sweat. Up the road in Grand Rapids, The [first year] Heritage Group, presents a darker **Rainmaker**, with storm clouds circling and revelations flashing across the prairie landscape.

"You pays your money and takes your choice, but with these two productions you can't choose badly. The Heritage offers emotional conviction, the Barn counters with terrific escapism. Ragotzy picks up the play's tempo by hitting the comic marks and sweeping through the scenes with the speed of a B'way musical. On opening night The Heritage Theatre Group was about half full, meaning roughly 300 people missed out on a fine evening that promises even better things ahead. Fully half an hour longer than the Barn production, HTG's **Rainmaker** probes the dialogue as if searching for meaning with a divining rod. Artistic director Don Rice's approach pays off. More naturalistic and internalized than the Barn version, this **Rainmaker** emphasizes subtle emotional colorations."

Next was Wopat's **City of Angels**.

Dave Hoger of *The Citizen Patriot* was enthusiastic. "To get to B'way, you hit the highway, hang a left or two, and set the cruise control for 600 miles. Or, you could drive to Augusta, where theatre doesn't get much better than what the Barn unveiled Tuesday night. Because not only has the Barn pulled off the technically improbable — staging the hit B'way musical **City of Angels** with its zillions of set changes — it has done so with such flair, such style, such brilliance, this production is easily *the* theatrical event of the season. The show sizzles from the opening curtain and doesn't take a breath.

"It has a lot to do with Tom Wopat, who recreates Stone, the fictional hard-boiled detective he won critical acclaim for on B'way. Wopat is also making his stage directorial debut with the Barn production and its success has a lot to do with David S. Young and a marvelous pit orchestra; with Michael E. Baggesi, the mastermind behind the sets that transform like a dream on two 16-foot turntables.

"Jammed with the wit and charm of a farce, plenty of music and enough snappy one-liners for an entire season, **City of Angels** is further energized by what has become regarded as the premier summer stock company in the Midwest. It's the marvelous acting that steals this show. Forget that hayseed Luke Duke. Wopat is brilliant — make that perfect — as Stone, the rumpled private eye with the quick tongue and the dynamic singing voice. He's not alone, either. Barn regu-

Tom Wopat recreates the role of Stone in **City of Angels** with Penelope Alex as Oolie — 1993

lars Scott Burkell, Joe Aiello and Penelope Alex will knock your socks off with the way they master their roles. Barn newcomer Christine Hunter sparkles and Rachel Fisher is no less spectacular in her dual roles," Hoger concluded.

Doud of the *Gazette* agreed. "If you're hot on the trail of a good musical, flatfoot it over to the Barn where **City of Angels**, a hilarious parody of 1940s detective movies, opened with huge success last night. With its dizzying array of sets, and cast of over 40 characters, this Tony Award-winning musical is a delightful escapade into the glitz and glamour of old Hollywood, complete with the Big Band music and torch songs which embroidered that bygone era. Tom Wopat proves absolutely riveting as a gumshoe detective in a rumpled trench coat who stalks the underbelly of Los Angeles mumbling one-liners about thugs and dames."

Then came a two week run of **Nunsense II** starring Edwina Lewis. Her next assignment was to direct **The Best Little Whorehouse in Texas** and to play the role of Jewel in that production which would star Kim Zimmer. Kim was originally scheduled to return to the Barn as Maggie in **Jake's Women** at the end of the season, but Ragotzy and Lewis thought she would make a helluva of a great Miss Mona in **Whorehouse**.

Edwina Lewis welcomed the chance to perform almost anytime and anywhere. As she once said, "If you called me to sing the 'Star-Spangled Banner' at a dogfight, I'd do it." She was a no-BS kind of actor's actor, and everyone at the Barn loved her. Jack and Betty had known her since '73 when she was a jobber for the first production of **Hair**. When they went to NY, they always saw her. She was family. And Lewis and Zimmer got along together like gangbusters. When asked if they were bothered by the portrayal of the women as prostitutes in **Whorehouse**, they both said no. "No one is forcing them into this house," Edwina said. "They're a lot safer here than on the street," Zimmer added.

Jack's curtain speech on the Tuesday night of the opening of **The Best Little Whorehouse in Texas** was the toughest pre-show talk of his life. In a *Gazette* photo of him giving the speech, his face is a mask of grief; one can see him trying to hold back the tears. But the speech had to be given to inform the audience that a member of the Barn family was gone. During the dress rehearsal the night before, Edwina had finished the first act sweating profusely. Complaining of chest pains, she went to her dressing room to prepare for the second act when she suddenly bent over in agony. She asked to have her friend, Howard McBride, come to the dressing room while Betty called 911 for an ambulance. As it sped toward Borgess Medical Center, McBride at her side, the 42-year-old actress/singer went into cardiac arrest dying at 11:37 p.m., minutes after the ambulance arrived.

Back at the Barn the rehearsal continued. At its end, Jack was giving notes to the actors when Howard called from the hospital. The anguish of the shocked company was palpable. But,

Tom Wopat as Stone and Christine Hunter as Bobbi and Gabby in **City of Angels** — 1993

Edwina Lewis directing **The Best Little Whorehouse in Texas** — 1993

1994
Music! Music! Music!
Don't Dress for Dinner
Guys and Dolls
The Odd Couple
*Billy the Kid
Damn Yankees
Lost in Yonkers
The Rocky Horror Show

As if the '94 season weren't blessed enough to have Wopat back doing **Guys and Dolls**, Jack hired Kim Zimmer to star in **Damn Yankees** and **Lost in Yonkers.** However, the show chosen by Jack for discussion in this book is Brendan Ragotzy's **Billy the Kid.** This was a world premiere and only the second in the fifth decade. Brendan, 31, not only wrote the book and lyrics, but directed the show as well.

A great deal of publicity was generated by the production and some of it lends insight into young Ragotzy, the heir apparent of the Barn. Why, for example, did the subject interest him? As a kid during the long trips back to California after the Barn seasons, and at nearly every restaurant and gas station through New Mexico and Arizona, Brendan found illustrated pamphlets and folders on the outlaws of the Old West. He became fascinated with Billy the Kid. "I read more books about

numbed with disbelief, they had to make a decision about the opening. It was unanimous. If Edwina were alive, she, above all, would want the show to open, to open *on time* and for the audience to enjoy themselves. Her understudy, first-year apprentice Holly Walker, 26, of Battle Creek, whom Edwina had taken under her nurturing wing, had to get up in the part.

Opening night, in a choked voice, Ragotzy told the stunned audience exactly that. "This evening's performance is a tribute to Edwina. All of us agree there's no greater way we can show our love and admiration than by getting her show off and *on time*. We hope you enjoy her version of **The Best Little Whorehouse in Texas**." With that, the audience gave a standing ovation to her memory and a weeping Ragotzy stepped back through the green velvet curtain to a cast who could hardly contain their grief. The stage manager called the first cue.

It was one helluva show.

*****

Joe Aiello, Penelope Alex and Scott Burkell in
Music IV — 1994

him than I read in all my years at college," he said.

Brendan visited Billy's grave and the town of Lincoln, which he said was "much the same as when the Kid was alive — the hotel, the store, the houses are still there." In addition to having "Billy on the Brain," he said he had a need to create and had been encouraged by college instructors to nurture his writing skills.

An aspect of the story that particularly fascinated him was that in '49 a man named Brushy Bill Roberts claimed to be Billy the Kid. Brendan would incorporate this character as a framing device for his play — Brushy telling the story and having it play in flashback. Brushy claimed another outlaw was shot and passed off as the Kid. So — did Billy really die at Fort Sumner? Brendan deliberately left this an open question at the end of his show.

Spending two and a half years of research on the subject, Brendan hoped his play would give audiences "a little bit of history and allow them to get into the heads and hearts of people who lived tough and died young on the American frontier." He felt the Lincoln County War factions were somewhat comparable to what today would be called gangs. "Billy's legacy was violence and cold-blooded killing," Brendan said, "but there was another side to him — his justice-seeking side. He believed in justice — though a little on the vigilante side."

Visually, Brendan wanted the production to replicate the Old West "right-down-to-bone-historical-accuracy, rather than the Hollywood glamour approach." To this end, his design collab-

Steve Owsley, Ken Rosen, Marvin Graham Lewis, Tom Wopat, Charlie King and Richard Hawkins in the crap game scene from **Guys and Dolls** — 1994

orators gave the production the still photography sepia look of a small western town in the latter part of the 19th century. Brendan summed up his feelings about the show by saying, "I think people will enjoy **Billy** because it says something about the history of our country and how it was born. I think that's important to say."

The show's musical numbers had been tested for a couple of years as part of the Rehearsal Shed shows. Brendan described the music as "soft rock, in which there's a lot of passion and emotion. I'm of that generation and so is David [S. Young] who composed the music. That's the music I really understand." The score consisted of 18 pop/rock songs. Even though it was a musical set in the Old West, there would be no strummin' guitar and singing cowboys *ala* Gene Autry. For his lead he cast third-year apprentice Bruce Hammond, who actually looked like the historic Billy. There were more than 45 actors who covered some 80 roles.

Nicolette of *The Press* observed, "**Billy** is surprisingly complete. Long, but complete. But Brendan Ragotzy and composer David S. Young would best approach with care any effort to eliminate songs. They are wonderfully entertaining, even after interest has waned in the legend's story." Nicolette went on to say that both the frame characters Brushy Bill and Attorney Morrison "are real, but the writer's use of them is not convincing. They might easily be dropped and another device used to fill in the details. Brendan Ragotzy is obviously a stickler for details, his script is loaded with times, places and actions in an attempt to capture the true personality of Billy the Kid. Undoubtedly his research has served him well in the story telling, but trying to cover the man from birth to death, with full scenes and songs, is rather trying.

"He and the artistic staff certainly have done wonders in creating the proper atmosphere. The gunfights are great, as are the stagings of many of the narrative songs. As they are sung, a general picture of Billy's early life and his introduction to violence unfolds. But the musical doesn't really make Billy very interesting or sympathetic, although Bruce Hammond does well in the title role. Perhaps the character is just too cleancut to have been so quick to kill, no matter what excuses are made."

Carla Johnson of *The South Bend Tribune* gave this analysis: "Without benefit of a preview or tryout phase, **Billy the Kid** needs work, but writer/director Brendan Ragotzy has launched a strong production of his own fascinating book and Barn music director David S. Young's energetic score. The songs' lyrics aren't just mood-setters; they advance the action and require close listening. There are so many of them that they begin to bear a sameness. For long-term success, painful cutting would rectify the play's cumbersome

Bruce Hammond in the title role of Brendan Ragotzy's **Billy the Kid** (world premiere) — 1994

length [nearly three hours] and help the stronger songs emerge as memorable, a necessary component in a musical's success. [Brendan] Ragotzy and Young certainly know **Billy** needs work, but they're off like the opening song: 'Train A Runnin'."

Pow of *The Citizen Patriot* added gentle humor to his account: "Pursuing **Billy the Kid** across New Mexico is a long, dry ride. Easing myself from the saddle at the intermission, I faced a melancholy prospect. We'd been on the trail for more than 90 minutes. The show was only half-done.

"Not that the first half had been without incident. We'd seen four or five gunfights between rival clans. One gunfight, however, is much like another, even when enhanced by digital sound, strobe lights and people dying in slow motion like extras in a Sam Peckinpah movie. But my most desperate thought was that we hadn't yet seen a horse's whisker of Pat Garrett — the Kid's cattle-rustling friend-turned-nemesis — who, with one well-placed bullet, was the only person who could get the audience home before midnight.

"The show needs radical surgery, the framing device of having the Kid survive to old age and recount his story to a lawyer is not too original, and David S. Young's music is adequate but only occasionally memorable. And yet I found myself beginning to admire writer-director Brendan Ragotzy's determination to tell us a story with some period texture rather than just another pulp-fiction version of the legend.

"The staging also is often effective, like old photos of flinty-eyed frontier folk staring into the middle distance that suddenly come to life. John Kristiansen's fine costume designs make a big contribution to this. We also get a sense of the brute political power and expedient law, or lawlessness, that shaped the West. And clearly Ragotzy feels there's more to Billy the Kid than just another young punk on the lam."

*****

Although the summer was successful and without incident, Betty Ragotzy now 71 and always immensely vigorous, was having some minor health problems. Still, she successfully played Grandma Kurnitz in Neil Simon's **Lost in Yonkers** and planned for the 50th anniversary of the Barn the following summer. This was a winter the Ragotzy's were staying in Michigan since they had rented their California property. Betty was taking arthritis medicine that reportedly led to side effects and expanded a cold into pneumonia-like symptoms of internal rheumatoid arthritis.

Taken to Borgess Medical Center January 17, '95, she developed severe breathing problems and had to have a tracheotomy, which meant she could not speak. On January 22, she was put into the intensive care unit and eventually on a ventilator. In the same hospital, her first grandchild, Luke Ragotzy, was born on January 23. Betty remained sedated in intensive care for about two months, her lungs eventually not functioning.

At one point early on, hooked to a respirator with no hope of recovery, she mouthed something to Jack. "I know, I love you too," he responded. Betty shook her head vigorously and again mouthed the three words, "Let me go." Sometime later she reminded him of her "living will." This act was quintessential Betty Ebert Ragotzy — clear thinking, practical, accepting the inevitable, and above all, leading and helping Jack in what she knew he could never do on his own.

Finally, and with Jack's permission, doctors disconnected the life supports in accordance with her wishes. Jack explained, "sshe accepted the fact that her lungs were hopelessly damaged. I'm sure it wasn't easy for her to recognize this fact. I refused to recognize it. I kept hoping something could be done, but we had all kinds of people working on the problem and there seemed to be nothing that anyone could do."

Betty Ebert Ragotzy died on Sunday, March 19, 1995.

"When she was a little girl," Betty's mother, Pearl Burr of San Bernardino, told Jack, "she always said she wanted a big funeral. She sought the dramatic way."

And that, of course, is exactly what she got — a big one. Jack and Brendan saw to that. It was held the following Thursday at the Gull Lake Area Community Church in Richland with Rev. James D. Hill officiating.

After the service, various Barnies spoke.

Tom Wopat flew in from California "to represent the hundreds of other Barn apprentices." Wopat, a notoriously private person, revealed to the assembled crowd that he had lost his mother at the age of seven, adding, "Betty was the closest I had to that kind of relationship. She had amazing strength. She was the mother hen, very nurturing and a disciplinarian. Yet when she kicked back and had a good time, she had a *great* time."

Dusty Reeds said her "fondest memory of Betty was when they were on stage together in **Steel Magnolias**. Betty had a long speech talking about the death of her daughter. Penelope was also on stage and we both cried. Betty was such an honest actor; she played from the heart. She could make you laugh as well as make you cry."

Hairdresser Garrylee McCormick told how Betty always came to him five minutes before curtain time with wet hair. "Work your magic," she would say. Gary remembered standing offstage, tears in his eyes, when she did **Miss Daisy**. "She was so believable and so wonderful."

Katie Hunter talked about how, as the first apprentice to arrive in '89, Betty gave her an early lesson in Barn apprenticeship by handing her a rake, and with a nod toward the five acres of grass in front of the Barn said, "Tidy up the lawn." Then out of the blue one day while working in the box office, Betty asked Hunter what she wanted to do with her life. Hunter said, "I want to be you."

Dick Fuchs remembered that "Betty was notorious for making late entrances. Usually it was five seconds at most; but one time while I was performing **Cabaret**, she was downstairs writing a press release for next week's show when I gave the cue. I had to ad-lib in a play about 1930s Nazi Germany, without giving away what happened in WWII, for what seemed like a very long time. But when she arrived on stage, she stepped from publicist to actress without missing a beat, giving a performance that had me in tears.

"Some people asked why Betty had such energy," Fuchs continued. "It's because she gave birth to 20 people each year. And she's been doing this for 49 years."

Howard McBride, who served as a pallbearer at her funeral, remembered when he met her. "I'm Howard McBride," he said, introducing himself and holding out his hand. "I'm Betty Ragotzy," she responded, shaking his hand. "Let's get to work."

"Though she would take young, aspiring actors under her wing, she wasn't a pushover. She was tough, and you had to earn her respect," McBride added. "Betty was ahead of her time. She was a liberated woman before being liberated was in fashion. On stage and off, no one could equal her accomplishments. She knew about everything related to the Barn, and if she didn't, she'd find out. Jack was the brains and the creative impulse behind the theatre. But Betty was the muscle. Betty got it done. Together they became the heart of the Barn Theatre."

Jack said at the time, "She was one of the best actresses I've ever directed. Once I directed Betty and Geraldine Page in the same role. Betty was much better. We had a great personal relationship. We loved each other. We argued and fought and did things everybody does and we had 49 years of that, for which I am eternally grateful."

After those who wanted to speak, spoke, and cried and laughed and hugged, the funeral procession of 150 cars drove back toward Augusta. Veering from a direct route to the cemetery, the procession wound its way up the Barn's long horseshoe driveway. People got out of their cars. It was an overclouded day, slightly cold, but with a feel of Michigan spring in the air. Then someone started applauding. And the little ripple of applause spread into a wave — an ovation. It was the only way they knew to pay tribute to Betty Ebert Ragotzy, a woman who, by her strength and fortitude, showed her belief in the theatre. She worked and acted at the Barn for almost 50 years, in plays and musicals, and through the laughter and sometimes the tears she shared of herself and touched the lives of the audience as only the live theatre can. When they had finished applauding her, these fellow workers and neighbors got back in their cars and the procession slowly wound its way through the tiny village of Augusta and into its cemetery.

After the interment, Jack and Brendan held a reception at the Gull Lake Cafe in Betty's honor.

*****

1995
Music! Music! Music!
Pure as the Driven Snow
The Music Man
*Sweeney Todd
Love Letters
Fiddler on the Roof
Hair
Out of Order

As Dusty Reeds pointed out at the time, "Theatre people have a way of coping with tragedy. This coming season will be a tribute to Betty's memory. We'll do the 50th without her, but we'll do it *for* her." And using a kind of dark hu-

Tom Wopat and Barbara Marineau in **Sweeney Todd** — 1995

mor to get through his grief, Jack added, "It had better be *damn good*, because if it isn't, Betty will haunt the hell out of me." So they did what theatre people have always done — they went back to work.

The season opened with **Pure as the Driven Snow** in which my wife, Robin, and I had played the heroine and hero that first season in Richland in '46. In '49, the first season at Augusta's Barn, the show was reprised with Betty and Drew Handley in the same roles.

Next came Tom Wopat as Harold Hill in **The Music Man**, directed by Jack, which sold out its two-week run prior to opening. **Sweeney Todd** was followed by **Love Letters** with Dick Fuchs and Adrienne Barbeau and directed by Jack; **Fiddler** was directed by Dusty Reeds; **Hair** by Brendan and finally, **Out of Order,** directed by Jack.

The reuniting of Wopat and Marineau in **Sweeney Todd** was a stroke of casting genius. But Wopat had been suggesting the idea to Jack for some time. Marineau took a leave of absence from B'way's *Beauty and the Beast* to come to Michigan, but before leaving the city, spent three weeks with vocal coaches learning the difficult music. When she finished, she said she felt she had learned an opera. About being selected by Ragotzy and Wopat for the role of Mrs. Lovett, she said, "I was incredibly flattered. Let's face it, after you hit 40, there are not a lot of great roles for women. And even if you're not over 40, this has to be one of the greatest musical comedy roles ever written."

If the almost operatic role of Sweeney seemed to be odd casting for Wopat — who was singing **The Music Man** evenings, strumming his guitar and singing country-western at the Rehearsal Shed bar at night, and rehearsing **Sweeney** during the day — he justified it by saying, "It's a return to the type of thing I did a long time ago when I studied opera at the University of Wisconsin. One of the things that amazed me when we started rehearsals was how well it lay in my voice. I think Betty knew that side of my voice was there, and enjoyed seeing me stretch acting-wise. She was always kind of my champion here in making me try to stretch and try to accomplish those things that were maybe a little bit beyond the pale for me."

In comparing Harold Hill and Sweeney, Wopat observed, "The two characters are the extreme sides of my personality — Hill is more of an extrovert while Todd is soooo dark and demented. Hill's lyrics are like a stream of consciousness. With Sondheim, it's easy when you understand the character. His lyrics are more cohesive and sequential."

Nicolette of *The Press* called **Sweeney** "a wonderful production. Wopat is a rugged Todd, his voice well suited to the Sondheim songs and his diction deft with the lyrics. He has an excellent companion in Marineau, who also has all the vocal dexterity needed for the melodies and lyrics."

Pow of *The Citizen Patriot* applauded: "You have to credit the Barn for sticking its neck out. **Sweeney Todd, the Demon Barber of Fleet Street** is not 'Mary Poppins,' as actor Tom Wopat so correctly pointed out in post-performance comments on opening night. Forget the gooey melodies and soppy lyrics that made up most of the musicals you're likely to encounter during a summer stock season. This show has edge.

"You can almost cut yourself on the cleverness of Stephen Sondheim's music and lyrics as he tells his grisly tale of murder and cannibalism in the seamy back streets of Victorian London. In addition to its macabre subject matter, the show pushes to the limits the performance and technical resources of any company, and the Barn team pulls it off wonderfully. It's not even a close shave. In fact, it's quite the best piece of work I've seen on the Augusta stage.

"Directors Joe Aiello and Scott Burkell — who also turn in a couple of nice performances — keep the humor front stage. In this they're aided by a superb performance from Barbara Marineau as Mrs. Lovett, Sweeney's partner in crime. With her pert smile, she looks as if she's just stepped off a Punch and Judy stage. Not to stint the other performers, but she holds the whole production in her ample embrace," Pow asserted.

And on that note of triumph the curtain rang down on the first 50 years of the Ragotzys' Barn Theatre.

Part III

In today's 'reinventing itself' society it's hard to think of anything that's lasted 50 years, let alone made a profit — especially in the arts. In '95, more than half the membership theatres of Theatre Communication Group (TCG), which comprises the major professional regional theatres in the United States, registered year-end operation deficits.

The Barn Theatre, now the quintessential resident stock theatre in America, celebrated its 50th profit-making season in the summer of 1995. And the only subsidy it, or Jack, ever received during that time was $2,500 from the Michigan Foundation for the Arts, awarded to Ragotzy for "outstanding theatre work."

In an age of support from The National Endowment for the Arts, state and city arts council grants and hoped-for "trickle down" from big business, a theatre dependent for survival on box office, concessions and money from its bar is a dinosaur — or perhaps, more appropriately, a lion king making its way through another hot summer on the Serengeti's straw-hat circuit.

What are the figures? The Barn Theatre seats 484. There are seven performances a week. At the time of this writing, ticket prices for season book holders (about a third of the audience) average $14.91. Regular box office prices are $20 and $22.50. Ragotzy reports that operating expenses, including those for the two-week pre-season, average close to $50,000 a week, which means that during the 12-week season he must play to about 75 percent capacity. The concession stand and the show bar, where cast members and apprentices entertain after the regular main-stage shows, account for about 10 percent of the revenue. "The latter is really the margin which keeps the theatre in business," Ragotzy noted.

The original 14 investors worked for 70 cents a week the first season. And don't kid yourself that the work — regardless of what you may remember of Judy Garland and Micky Rooney in the movie, *Summer Stock* — wasn't damned hard.

Why did we do it?

We were a group of young people not so much interested in making money as in wanting to work in the theatre. We had been through the worst of times, the Depression and World War II, so the year '46 with its gutsy, post-war optimism looked like the best of times. There was faith in the nation, a belief in the system and a confidence in a deeply-ingrained ethic — that with hard work and perseverance we could make it to the top.

And many of us would-be actors figured what the hell? Why should we go out East, pay a thousand bucks to be an apprentice doing menial labor at the Cape Playhouse in Massachusetts, and work *backstage* on a package show starring Tallulah Bankhead and Estelle Winwood when we could start our own theatre at home and be *on-stage*?

From the start, the theatre was Ragotzy's; or to put it another way, he was first among equals. He denies it today, saying that when the group formed, "It was to be a democracy; but then around the third show, in a round-table discussion, they decided the theatre needed 'a director,' someone to be in charge and they voted me in." Since that time, as producer-director, Jack has sometimes delegated decision making, but the final decision on all matters — including delegating decision making — was always his.

The activity — the "learning by doing" of the Village Players' first decade — set the course for the next 50 years. Discovering the Barn in their fourth year and deciding to buy and improve the property in their ninth, signified the Ragotzys' intent to dig in. Additional purchases of land would amount to 77 acres. And they would make additions to the Barn, update the equipment, add shops and a house and continually improve the grounds until the physical plant was one of the — if not *the* — best summer theatre plants in the United States, with much of the labor being provided by apprentices.

After having 14 and 15 partners for the first and second seasons and eight in the third, Jack and Betty assumed full financial responsibility as well as profits by the fourth season. Jack became producer and remains so to this day. Virtually penniless at the time the theatre was formed, he now owns the Barn and 77 acres of land at an estimated value of God only knows, but his Hollywood home is valued at $1 million. He also owns three other properties in the Augusta vicinity. He certainly is not in the Andrew Carnegie or B.F. Goodrich class of millionaire; but, on the other hand, he has picked up a nice piece of change in the notoriously risky business of show biz.

And as for profit, let's start with a level playing field. Isn't profit the motivating force of our society and the envy of the world? If so, why should theatre be exempt? Is there anything wrong with the profit motive? Well, there are plenty of people who question it — people who want government-subsidized theatre so that the market place doesn't dictate the kind of plays produced. But they know that until we live in a perfect world, it ain't gonna happen. Ragotzy knew this the first year he ran his theatre.

His decision to go Equity toward the end of the sixth season destined a professional company with professional actors, operating under union demands. Or — when union demands became too tough — finding ways around rules and regulations.

Early productions of farces, comedies, and melodramas convinced Jack of the popularity of these genres, as did productions of **Tobacco Road**, **A Streetcar Named Desire** and his own, **Country Mile**, all of which included profanity and sexually-explicit material. It became obvious during the first years that many theatregoers were eager to be titillated, or, to put a more positive spin on it, to see life as it was being represented on the American stage in mid-20th century.

The transition from straight plays to the inclusion of the highly successful **Finian's Rainbow** in their seventh season, and **Guys and Dolls** in the tenth, led immediately to the production of one, then two, and eventually three or more musicals a season, along with the hiring of the necessary personnel.

Of his scheduling, Jack explains, "We try for a balance between shows that are fun, new shows that will appeal to younger people and those that will be liked by the older members of our audience. I try to give a variety — that's the main thing — and, at the same time, keep the scenic department and technical staff from going crazy. Musicals put our theatre on the map. Musical productions now far exceed the number of plays produced, because that's what people want to see. If we do straight plays, we need stars to sell them."

And how does his policy differ from what's happening in the greater American Theatre? As I write this there are 21 B'way productions on tour in the United States. This number includes four productions of *Phantom of the Opera*, three of *Show Boat*, two of *Rent* and two of *Beauty and the Beast*. All but one, *Master Class*, is a musical. On B'way there are also 21 productions of which only two, *The Last Night of Ballyhoo* and *Barrymore* (a one man show), are straight plays.

Consider the Barn's statistics over a half century. At the end of their 50th season there have been 407 productions. Of that number, 46 percent were comedies (13 by Neil Simon) and farces, 37 percent musicals and cabarets — all of which run about twice as long as the straight plays — and 13 percent dramas. The remaining four percent do not fit neatly into genre classification. Also included in the total number are 14 tryouts of new works.

Of the total 407 productions, 64 had won Pulitzers, Drama Critics, or Tony Awards. There are, of course, no early (Sophocles, Shakespeare, Sheridan) or modern (Chekhov, Ibsen) classics, but classics are also in short supply on B'way — except as an occasional star vehicle. I'm sure if Ragotzy could get Ralph Feinnes out to the Barn, he'd produce *King Lear* — the musical — nude.

In directing **Morning's at Seven** the first year, Jack solidified his belief that productions were done for an audience. A director should be true to a play's seriousness and its depth of characterization but not allow actors to indulge in excessive personal emotion that ignores the audience as a participant or subverts the play's text and entertainment value. This was to prove his major strength as a producer/director and a reason why audiences returned again and again to the Barn's shows.

Ragotzy provided entertainment, and for this he was rewarded by a core audience that stayed remarkably loyal throughout the years. The same was once true of the hard-core NY audience and their loyalty to B'way before critics, who often revealed little sense of theatre — let alone what an audience liked — wrote reviews that effectively killed show business. Today it is estimated that no more than 16 percent of the B'way audience is comprised of anyone who lives in the five boroughs of NY, nearby Connecticut or New Jersey.

Ragotzy also knew that highbrow, avant-garde theatre would not attract a large-paying audience. As OyamO, Associate Professor of Theatre and Resident Playwright at the University of Michigan observed in *The New Yorker* (Feb 3, '97), such theatre *"bores the shit out of people. . ."* and went on to ask, "If this stuff is so significant, why can't it touch ordinary people?"

Ragotzy knew in the first decade that audiences should enjoy a show that was different from other entertainment. Live theatre should provide an excitement that is missing from TV or films. On the tube, the spool is going to reel off regardless of what happens in the "rec room." In live theatre there is that edge which only an actual happening can provide!

Think of when Alicia Krug (in her closing number in the Barn's **Finian's Rainbow**) stepped on a tack, paused a moment, removed the tack and finished the number; or the time during **Take Her, She's Mine** when there was a power loss and the audience held flashlights to illuminate the stage; or, on opening night — a story not told earlier in this book — when the atmosphere of **The Teahouse of the August Moon** was unexpectedly enhanced by the sudden, unannounced arrival of a cluster of fireflies that flitted over the audience for a few enchanting minutes.

Did Ragotzy ever cancel a performance? No, but he came close. Once an actor got drunk, overslept and didn't show up till the middle of the second act. Ragotzy filled in, book in hand, until the actor finally arrived and went on. At other times, performances had to be interrupted and the audience sent outside to wait while the apprentices got rid of a visiting skunk. But these incidents prove the point — spontaneous, exciting things like that just don't happen while you're watching TV or a movie.

Jack's entrance into the NY theatre scene as a director in '53 provided him with contacts in talent's toughest town. Kander and Ebb were right when they wrote that if you could make it there, you could make it anywhere. Jack's concentration on the single focus of show biz meant he would drop work on his doctorate, thereby making impossible a retreat into the security of academia. When he received excellent NY reviews for his off-off-B'way production of **Mamba's Daughters**, he became a contender. He would not only direct off and on B'way and for TV, but he would act in major television shows. It was only because he ran the B'way gauntlet that, after the fiasco of **Angela,** he could conclude that directing in NY was not all that important.

Jack got the first stock production rights for **The Silver Whistle** in his fifth season and the following year the first rights in Michigan for **A Streetcar Named Desire.** He would secure first rights over and over again, including those for **Hair**, so that the Barn's programming would reflect the cutting edge of NY theatre. In addition, he would be keenly aware of national publicity generated by current Hollywood films or B'way shows and exploit it to the fullest in advertising his Barn productions.

As early as his second year of operation he advertised **Green Grow the Lilacs** as "that *Oklahoma* show" while the musical was still playing on B'way, as, forty years later, he would advertise the revival of **La Cage aux Folles** as "the play from which the recently released *The Birdcage* was made."

Jack's risk-taking during the early years in the production of new works indicated his interest in theatre's lifeblood — the new play. Unfortunately, the Barn's development of new plays was essentially halted when Actors' Equity passed a ruling that any actor who originated a role in a new play would have to be given first chance to play the role in a NY production, or, if not, be paid a certain number of weeks' salary. Even when he couldn't do new plays, Ragotzy's interest in playwriting never wavered. Sometimes this interest resulted in the reworking of standard B'way scripts. Once he was fined for doing so, but, as often as not, the matter passed, unnoticed.

He also changed titles — Tennessee Williams' *Orpheus Descending* became **Something Wild in the Country** — which is not only more commercial, but a better title and the one used for the film. He changed Harry Kurnitz's *Reclining Figure* — the title under which it played on B'way — back to the original, **Reclining Nude**, which was better box office. And he rewrote the B'way script of **Point of No Return**.

He would become a master promoter, learning to advertise a show not for the actual number of performances he thought it would run but "for one week only" and then extending the run "by popular demand" — and often extending it again or reviving it "by popular demand." The revamping of the advertised schedule — frowned upon by most theatre business managers — only resulted in enveloping Ragotzy in an aura of risk-taking spontaneity, along with increased box office revenues.

The fact that Jack and others in the original partnership were from colleges and universities resulted in his policy of recruiting talented apprentices from institutions of higher learning. A summer at the Barn was laughingly called "the short course." But former Barnies, like me, knew very well that serious students — if they would work their butts off — could probably learn more of what the commercial theatre was really about in a summer at the Barn than they could in all four years of most undergraduate institutions that advertise "professional training" but are taught by people who never worked professionally. In their first decade, both Jack and Betty came to recognize the importance of networking the academy. Both nurtured an active liaison between the Barn and former Barnies-turned-academicians.

During the first decade, leading men such as Drew Handley and Michael Capanna often doubled in brass as technical directors. Actors were required to participate in aspects of production other than acting. At the time of this writing some 50 years later, two members of the company criticized a potential member for not being able to "wear two or more hats." The hard-knuckled fist of reality that forced double- and triple-duty for members of the early companies forecast the same for future Barnies. There are those in the professional acting company today who design, direct and work the box office as well as act. And although Equity sets the parameters for all that can be required of an actor in both rehearsal and performance, the union has no jurisdiction over what an actor *chooses* to do in addition to acting.

My personal belief is that the wearing of two hats can lead to exploitation. I totally disagree with the myth that hard physical labor, such as putting in walls for the terrace behind the Barn, will make one a better actor. Does anyone think Helen Hayes, Katherine Cornell, Laurette Taylor or Laurence Olivier were less talented because they didn't park cars or mow acres of grass? But perpetuating the myth does help keep a theatre alive and operating, and only an operating theatre can provide career opportunities for young talent.

As Ragotzy's NY career progressed, the resulting contacts enhanced the Barn's reputation and prestige, provided new ideas and fostered professional linkage. However, Ragotzy never became "Big City." Both he and Betty were neighborly and had direct contact with the people of the surrounding community. Moreover, Jack's folksy and sometimes corny, but always heartfelt, curtain speeches welcoming his audience, as well as his sitting in the audience and chatting with them at intermission, made the "neighbors" feel a part of the Barn family.

Another factor in the Barn's success was the considerable support of area newspapers. At the beginning, both the Battle Creek and Kalamazoo papers were reluctant to review the shows. But with Betty's persistence — she did, in fact, write a couple of "reviews" herself — the editors of both papers finally came around. Now there are as many as ten newspapers, plus TV and radio stations, covering openings at the Barn. And the critics actually seem to like theatre and approach it from the point of view of the audience rather than imposing a look-down-the-nose academic attitude. In short, while some reviewers are better than others, there are few, if any, butchers of show business in this area.

This critical coverage is vital. One reason NY actors come to the Barn is because they hope to take back intelligent and well-written reviews for their portfolios and to show their agents. After the first two difficult years, a southwestern Michigan perk has been that knowledgeable area editors have assigned astute critics (there are certainly some exceptions) as Barn reviewers, and their well-written criticism has contributed to the theatre's success and prestige. When first-rate critics began to retire, a single critic's review was published in two or more area newspapers. Although editors save money and hassle from local theatregoers with vested interest in certain players by not having their own critic, Betty argued that diversity of opinion was lessened, which was not good for the theatre or the theatregoing public. And, of course, she prevailed.

Another success factor initiated that first decade was that the Ragotzys wanted local people to begin to know the actors and vice versa — so there could develop a kind of a family feeling. Jack and Betty realized how audiences appreciate seeing familiar actors perform a variety of roles, how they enjoy watching them grow season after season, and how they love welcoming them home after they've made it in the big time.

Thus what was experienced and learned through the rigors of doing during the first ten years would become the basis of the Barn's policies and its success for the next 40. In no way does this mean that everything would stay the same — far from it. The Rehearsal Shed shows were not inaugurated until the end of the third decade. In the fourth decade, Ragotzy shifted from Equity's NY office — which applies rules and regulations with a myopia so typical of that hysterical center of the universe — to the Chicago office. Not having so much theatre to oversee, Second City could give him better attention, more understanding and common sense application to the rules as they applied to the Barn, especially on the apprentice/Equity ratio. He knew he could find good Equity actors in the Chicago area and thus save expenses on transportation.

Equity membership has had its problems. In November '81 Ragotzy was quoted as saying, "The Theatre's a struggle, now more than ever. We have to dodge more economic bullets: union pensions, the state's unemployment compensation benefits which are much higher than those in California, health insurance, the actors' traveling expenses to get here and all costumes. The profit margin is slim and anything that takes a bite out of it jeopardizes our operations."

Increased competition also became a problem — not so much from the great number of summer theatres that sprouted up after the first season in '46 or the local community theatres, but with venues such as Western Michigan University's Miller Auditorium. Opened in January of '68, it seats 3500 and books touring shows each season.

In its beginning, the Village Players had welcomed competition, feeling it was good for business. Later, as an Equity company, it had priority over all other area theatres in the matter of first rights. But having those first rights being usurped by touring companies is a different matter. Sure, it's flattering to have the critics note that when the Barn is given the rights to produce a hit show that has already toured the area, its productions are often better than the touring packages. But it stands to reason that if potential theatregoers have seen the touring show, they would think twice about spending their hard-earned entertainment dollars to see it again at the Barn. In short, big local auditoriums provided a non-level playing field. Subsidized by city, county, state governments, and with capacities roughly six or seven times larger than the Barn, these tax- supported physical plants (both initial cost and upkeep) definitely stick a dagger into private enterprise.

But above all, a factor that did not, and could not, stay the same was that there would be exciting new personnel each season. The Barn would nurture new talent — some of whom would achieve stardom on B'way and TV.

In thumbing through the Barn programs in the Appendix to this book you might very well ask, "Hey, what ever happened to Whoozits? But if you look at the cast listings of the *Best Plays of the Year* or the various yearly volumes of *Theatre World*, you can't help but be struck by the fact that very few of the players who did make it to B'way are known or remembered — even by those who have spent a lifetime in the theatre. Either the actors chose not to continue in theatre or they simply were unsuccessful in finding work in a profession that employs approximately ten percent of the Equity membership at any given time. And the fact is that being "successful" in show business doesn't always have a hell of a lot to do with talent or lack of it — nor does longevity. In England, older actors keep working and some are even knighted. In the U.S. we prefer to chew-'em-up, spit-'em-out and get something new.

Some Barnies went into other careers. For example, Betsy Turner, '79 and '80 apprentice, is now a lawyer "of counsel" in the Armonk (NY) firm of Boies, Schiller & Flexner. Her senior colleague, David Boies, argued before the Florida and U.S. Supreme Court in the Bush v. Gore campaign. At the Barn, Betsy said she was "the overachieving witchy (spelled with a 'b') cheerleader, Patty, in **Grease** when Marin Mazzie played Rizzo in a big black wig. And there was absolutely no doubt in anyone's mind that Marin was going places."

Although no longer on stage, Betsy is a member of NYC's Drama League that supports aspiring directors and honors plays and performers. "It was a thrill to see Marin up there on the League's dais being honored for *Ragtime* and *Kiss Me Kate*," Betsy said.

What does she think of her Barn experience? "We worked really hard. We faced a lot of frustrations and derived a lot of gratification we were usually too tired to enjoy. We dealt with good and bad egos and lots of varied personalities. But I now compare my time at the Barn with working on a trial. It takes the same kind of over the top energy and focus to get a trial up and running and closed as it did to get one of those big musicals up and running and then struck."

Other Barnies, as readers know from this book, did go on to theatre careers. But the vast majority, like Betsy, did not; or possibly I just don't recognize their names. My apologies to any I might have overlooked. But all Barnies, regardless of whether they "made it" in the entertainment world or not, helped create what is known as Ragotzys' Barn Theatre.

Perhaps the major policy, established early on, that led to the Barn's success was the hiring and rehiring of talented, loyal and hard-working personnel — technicians, designers and actors. Also not to be overlooked are the business people

Some "Giants" of 5 decades: (seated L to R) Louis Girard, Betty and Jack Ragotzy, Dusty Reeds and Wayne Lamb; (standing L to R) Jim Knox, (Becky Gelke who happened by) and Angelo Mango

such as Earl Clason, who was the Barn's advertising representative ('51 - '77), corporative resident agent and general counsel Jack H. Fisher ('52 - '85) and Gayle Hinckley, who was both business manager/accountant and member of the acting company ('56 - '77).

Although they are not household names, they are, as Betty called them, "The Giants" — the workers who made a lifetime artistic commitment to the Barn. And Jack has always acknowledged their contribution to the success of this theatre.

So let us take some space to honor them now.

Arthur L. Crain ("Art"), Grant Baxter and Paxton Stratton ("Pax") have to be mentioned together since they started working in various technical aspects during the theatre's first season. They continued part-time for the rest of their lives, in addition to holding jobs in Kalamazoo, marrying and raising families. All of them had the distinction of liking both the theatre and actors. They were gentle men with a sense of humor, low-keyed, hard-working, loyal, curious, and above all, problem solvers.

Art was first credited as a "painter" (two years with Helen Hice, who the following year became Helen Crain), then "scenic artist," "technical consultant," "gadgets and gimmicks" (**Gypsy**) and "master technician." His last program credit was in '89. He died March 23, '90, having been connected with the Barn for 44 seasons. Grant Baxter was listed variously as a "stage electrician" "lighting and sound," "sound engineer" and "special technician." His last program credit was in '77. Grant died December 2, '77, having been with the theatre 31 years. Paxton Stratton started as a "stage electrician," then "follow spot operator," "lighting and sound" and finally "master mechanic." His last program credit was in '91. He died April 1, '94, having been associated with the group for 46 years.

Of these men Betty Ebert said: "We could not have gotten along without them. Their work helped set us apart scenically from other theatres in the area. With Jack's architectural and design sense, and their technical expertise and maturity, our productions were given a level of artistry and professionalism that went clear beyond that something-thrown-together look of the visual aspects in most summer stock companies. We never had that look. Never!" For several years, the three men had their group photo in all the programs as "Three Very Special People."

And think of having a permanent property master on your staff who knows every antique dealer in the area plus every prop in his own and every other theatre's prop shop. At the end of the 50th season, Jim Knox had worked 27 years, coming to the Barn in '68 from Purdue University where he had worked as property master for me when I was artistic director of the Purdue Professional Theatre Company. That fall at the Arena Stage in Washington, D.C., he designed and built Stacy Keach's horse for Arthur Kopit's *Indians*. The horse (without program credit) went on with Keach to B'way and Knox went back to the Barn and propped (and did set decoration) for every show since — 209 of 'em, plus acting in 30. In addition, he is the year-round resident manager of the Barn and liaison with the company's community landlords.

First show for Garrylee McCormick was **Under the Yum Yum Tree** in '61, which means he's been the Barn's hair and wig stylist for 34 years. "It's a luxury for us to have him," Betty

Property Master, Jim Knox.

said. "Few theatres have a hair specialist and he has made himself indispensable. He is also master of wigs. Garrylee's a shoulder to lean on and a long term friend. It means so much to an actor to have someone like him around the theatre because if your hair isn't right, your character isn't."

His most demanding show was **La Cage aux Folles**, for which he created 55 wigs. All had to be restyled after each performance. They also had to be kept in a specific order to facilitate the many quick changes the show called for. Special shelves were constructed backstage to hold each wig on its own wig stand.

"I have no wild hair stories," he said, "because I pin the hair too tightly to allow a wig to go flying off an actor's head." Betty agreed. "Your whole head will come off before one of Gary's wigs does. He really anchors them on."

Remembering fondly the many actresses he worked with, Garrylee said that Karen (Jensen) Arthur signed her picture, "Without you and your magic comb I never would have made it," and so he dubbed his hair salon in downtown Kalamazoo "The Magic Comb."

Yet another giant was Ora Crofoot, who was asked in '58 to cover a sofa to be used onstage and then to make a bathrobe for Big Daddy in **Cat on a Hot Tin Roof**. Her first program credit was not until the end of June '59 for **Bells Are Ringing**. That was the beginning for one of the best stitch-gypsy/costumer-designer any theatre ever had.

What was her background — Manhattan's Fashion Institute?

Get real!

When Ora's first husband died and left her, in today's lingo, "a single mother" with three kids, there were two choices — work or starve. The "safety net" of welfare being foreign to her character, and being good at sewing, she got a job working as a 4-H sewing teacher. At the same time, she took extension courses at Western, got

Hair and wig sylist, Garrylee McCormick

Costumer and "Housemother" Ora Crofoot

her teaching certificate and taught for 11 years in country schools. Then the state, goaded on by the big Education Department lobby, "raised standards" (meaning more methodology courses) and Ora was out of a job.

Her second husband was a retired administrator and teacher. Ora finished raising her three children (along with his five) on a small farm in Hastings and did not become traumatized by the "empty-nest syndrome" when they went off on their own. So when Mary Adams, who had developed a "School of the Dance" in Hastings, called to see if Ora could help with costumes for a student recital, she was ready.

In addition to costumes, Ora made herself valuable in other ways: as cook, baby sitter and housekeeper. When Miss Mary injured herself and went to Florida, turning the dance studio over to Wayne Lamb, she told him that Ora was "indispensable," and he soon found out that this was true. And so to complete the loop, it was Wayne's suggestion that Ora be hired to cover the sofa and to make "Big Daddy's" robe at the Barn.

And that's how this Michigan farm woman, already past retirement age according to present thinking, got into show biz in '59 and worked in some capacity on all shows until her retirement in '76 — a total of 17 years, during which time she designed 110 shows, often with Ken Andrews ('61 - '72), or listed herself modestly with two or more designers. For another 13 years, from '76 through '88, Jack listed her on the program as "Costume Consultant," even though she was inactive due to failing eyesight and a stroke.

In addition to wardrobe duties throughout the years, she made "Ora's soup" — hot lunches for hungry apprentices. Once when she was asked what her job was, Ora replied in strictly non-LORT *costumiere* terms, "'Housemother' pretty much covers it. I enjoy show people and I'm alive. Not many women are as lucky as I am, doing work I really like and meeting so many wonderful people."

Ora Crofoot died July 2, 1990.

Another "Giant" to appear in the first decade was Massachusetts-born Angelo Mango, whose career began at age nine when he was singing regularly on radio and later joined "The Rhythm Boys" song-and-dance team. After serving in the Army during WWII, he studied at NY's Alviene Academy of Dramatic Art, won first place in an Arthur Godfrey Radio talent competition, worked nightclubs, radio engagements, and recorded under both Abby and Rainbow labels.

He first came to the Barn in '56 and again in '57. Then he got hot in NY, being cast in the role of "Stubby" in off-B'way's *Leave It to Jane,* which opened at the end of May '58 at the Sheridan Square Playhouse and ran for almost two years. (Although it's now a collector's item, you can still hear him on the original Strand recording if you can find it, or the reissued LP by AEI, a new CD cut from the original master tapes.) Then came work on B'way's *Irma La Duce* and later off-B'way's *The Boys From Syracuse*. He returned to the Barn in '65 and remained for the next 24 seasons.

Angelo retired after the '88 season, having appeared in 125 productions. His **An Evening with Angelo Mango** in the Rehearsal Shed grew from a one-man cabaret in '75 into a mini-musical

Angelo Mango

and was presented with great critical — not to mention financial — success for 16 years.

Angelo was a great favorite with Barn audiences. There was an incredible vulnerability in his onstage *persona* — a kind of enigmatic uncertainty that made the audience want to "take him home in their pocket," as one critic put it. Think of a male Judy Garland and you get the picture. But Angelo added to this *persona* by projecting his love of performing with a ballsy touch of George M. Cohan song-and-dance-man spunkiness. When he was hoofing and singing and sweating and looking like he was giving more than was possible for a single performer, it was just two friends — the audience and "Ange" — in a not-so-quiet schmooz.

It was these qualities that made Angelo, who had never acted in a straight show before he came to work for Ragotzy, beloved — and not only by the theatre crowd but by farmers, clerks at the various thrift shops and supermarkets where he loved to shop and by blue-collar workers. They always called him Ange; and he was on a first-name basis with them, their wives and children. And if he couldn't think of their names, he called them "Babe." He recorded everybody's birth dates and anniversaries in a little book, and he kept the local greeting card people in business.

As a good Italian Catholic, he never missed Mass.

He might have clawed his way up the talent chain in NY, but he was probably better off in the long run building up his Equity pension while learning his craft by playing great roles and starring — and he *was* a star — at Ragotzys' Barn Theatre.

Another "Giant" who appeared during the first decade was Dusty Reeds. Coming to the Barn in '54 as wife of actor John Newton, her first program credit, "Rocks by Reeds," was for my play, **Desire Is a Season**. It was not until '55, as a member of the Equity Company, that she received full name credit as designer of both scenery and costumes for **Guys and Dolls**.

Dusty says that even though her name is not on the program in the creative credits under the plays' titles, she actually co-designed the last five shows of the '54 season and all of the shows in '55. With this correction of the record, we conclude she designed scenery for 138 productions, including 19 co-design credits, most of which she shared with her student designers from San Jose State University so they could enhance their resumes.

In addition, she acted in 112 productions and directed 17 — her favorites being **Camelot** and **The Robber Bridegroom**. In '86 Ragotzy appointed her "associate producer/director," a position she still holds.

As well as bringing many of her students from San Jose as apprentices, Dusty's contribution to the success and continuance of the Barn is enormous. She is multi-talented, intelligent and a workhorse with so much energy she accepted the jobs of director, actor, and designer for the opening production for the 50th anniversary season. She crawls up ladders and paints scenery in the summer heat under the hot tin roof of the scenery shed. Like Ado Annie Carnes, she seems to be "just a girl who can't say no," only in her case — to work.

Her strength as a designer — especially for the number of musicals Ragotzy produces — is her ability to suggest location and mood by us-

Dusty Reeds

ing minimalist scenic elements that are also inexpensive (she does a lot of recycling). Her expertise is as a scene painter, examples of which are the brilliant show curtain — a replica of the Constitution — for **1776**, the Will Rogers portrait for **The Will Rogers Follies** and the castle drop for **Camelot**. She creates scenery that facilitates the movement of the production as a whole, while being unselfish enough to leave plenty of creative opportunity for both costumer and lighting designer to aid in the total visual statement.

By late August '68, Dusty and John Newton had gone their separate ways. In her early 40s she had a mediocre glass ceiling job in LA. At the time, funds for two $300 a month, tuition-free assistantships became available at Purdue for master's degree candidates who would assist in the technical area of the Purdue Professional Theatre Company. I tracked Dusty down in Lincoln, NE, where she and the two boys were visiting her parents on their way back to LA after a season at the Barn. Was she interested in getting her degree? Her "yes" was immediate.

Driving to LA, she closed the apartment, drove back across country and moved into a small, two-bedroom house in Lafayette, enrolled the boys in school and registered for classes at Purdue one week late. Along with doing double duty in the technical area, she took 12 credit hours of graduate courses per semester, passed her written exams, the following summer wrote her thesis, passed her orals and graduated in August of '69 at which time we immediately hired her as a fulltime faculty member with the rank of assistant professor.

Three years later, after Purdue's Professional Theatre had folded, she joined our former technical director who was on the faculty of San Jose State University. Among her many students who were, or would be, connected to the Barn were Sal Aiello and a shy Brendan Ragotzy — whom she introduced to another student, Penelope Issichopoulos.

Rising to the rank of full professor, she retired after 19 years and came back to settle in a farmhouse near Richland where in addition to her duties at the Barn she became active in the animal rights movement.

No doubt about it, she has been, and is, an invaluable asset to Ragotzys' Barn. But Ragotzy and the Barn have also been an invaluable aid to Dusty, helping her to find and develop her uniqueness and individuality as well as helping her to buy a house. In short, she's 'come a long way, baby!'

Another Giant to appear during those first ten years was actor Louis Girard who was with the Players in '53 and returned in '57 to stay the next 38 seasons, acting in 228 productions. Additionally, Louis directed 24 productions, co-directed three with Ragotzy and was assistant director on four.

Because of the rapidity in which shows are mounted, actors are often advised to work no more than a few seasons in summer stock. A "stock actor" is considered one who memorizes lines and blocking and executes them mechanically, without any thought feeding through the actor's system to give life to the character and motivate his actions. Stock actors rely on cliches and stereotypes and they indicate reactions ("mugging") and fake emotions rather than feeling them. When they do so, the acting is predictable and boring.

Louis Girard

Louis was never this kind of an actor. I saw him in various productions through many Barn seasons, including his performance in **Pure as the Driven Snow** which opened the Barn's 50th season. In the role of the innkeeper, Louis trusted the script (admittedly a hard thing to do with that hoary chestnut), played his role simply, lived moment by moment and, above all, listened and responded in character. He made no attempt to make more of the character than was written. Instead, he believed in the situation and thought in character — even in scenes in which he did not speak — and in doing so, he was enormously effective.

Louis began his acting career with the famed Brattle Theatre in Cambridge. He toured with Gloria Swanson, Diana Barrymore and Charlie Ruggles. He was on B'way in Jack's production of **A Distant Bell** and in Chicago in *Laura*. Additionally, he acted at the Lakewood Theatre, Bucks County Playhouse and Drury Lane. Girard was many things, including at one point an incipient alcoholic, and although he may never have "made it big" in the theatre, he was a first-rate actor. Indeed, when one thinks of the roles he played at the Barn, he may have had a more satisfying career there than the vast majority of NY actors.

In his late 70s and looking forward to retirement after the 50th anniversary season, he planned to travel to his beloved London the following spring. Returning home to Guilderland, NY, where he lived with Arthur, his long time companion, Louis became ill that winter and died of cancer on April 17, '96.

Another giant who came to the theatre during its first ten years was Wayne Lamb. From Dodge City, KS, he danced prior to World War II in a touring *Earl Carroll's Vanities*, and when he came out of the Army in '45, he continued his professional career in NY. A featured dancer on B'way in *Make Mine Manhattan* and *Yours Is My Heart*, he also appeared in *Bloomer Girl* and *Day Before Spring,* as well as the national company of *Call Me Mister* (Wayne was the ballet dancer and Bob Fosse the tap dancer in that production). He was in the pre-B'way tryout of *Bonanza Bound!,* which was choreographed by Jack Cole and, in addition to Wayne, had Gwen Verdon in the chorus. He was also a dancer on TV's *Your Show of Shows*, *The Martha Raye Show*, *Colgate Comedy Hour* and *The Ed Sullivan Show*. As a young dancer he had an animal grace that was electric in its force and energy. How do I know? Village Player actress Robin Fastenrath and I saw him in Chicago in *Call Me Mister* on the fifth of July, 1947 — the day after we were married.

Wayne studied with three greats in the modern dance movement: Martha Graham, Hanya Holm and Doris Humphrey. He once choreographed a poem for Miss Humphrey. "After the piece was presented," he said, "she gave me the best advice of my life. 'Never work on anything unless you can add something of yourself to the work. If you can't add something of yourself, the work is already complete and there is no need for you to spend your time or energy on it.'"

After Lamb's first job at the Barn as choreographer for the '55 production of **Guys and Dolls**, Ragotzy asked him to return, promoting him quickly to "assistant to the producer" ('57 – '60), "associate producer" ('65 – '66), "associate producer-director" ('67 – '87), followed by "master choreographer" in '88 and "associate produc-

Wayne Lamb

er" in '89. In '90 he became "producer emeritus" after 34 years of service. He is listed in the theatre's program to this day and his picture is displayed prominently in the lobby.

During his tenure at the Barn, Lamb is credited with having directed or "staged" (which we define as both direction and choreography of the same musical) a total of 93 productions which include: eight plays, 16 Rehearsal Shed **Evenings with Angelo Mango** and nine co-directed credits. Further, he choreographed 107 productions which include 16 of the pre-and post-season Rehearsal Shed shows starring Mango. Still further, he acted and/or danced in 42 productions.

Wayne's major choreographic influences were Katherine Dunham and Jack Cole. His style, for the most part, was characterized by a centering that came straight from the pelvis. His strength as a choreographer was that he created dances for actors who, for the most part, were not trained dancers. He never choreographed a dance in his head and then required an actor to recreate it. Instead, he worked in rehearsals, listening to the music, assessing the actor's skills and creating the movement accordingly as he went along — movement that would sometimes make actors look like a young Nureyev!

What he created on the floor improvisationally often ended up in the show. Both at the Barn and at Purdue University, where he taught and directed for 27 years, he would stretch untrained dancers to the utmost of their abilities, but never beyond.

He was a gentle man. Although he occasionally got angry, I never heard him berate or make fun of an actor, however inept, for not being able to execute the movements. He didn't communicate very well with words. Instead, he would start talking and inevitably begin moving to demonstrate what he meant. Lamb's work was instinctive rather then cerebral.

There are also some Barn actors who do not yet qualify as "Giants" in Betty's definition of the term — not having devoted their lives to the Barn. But some of them hover on the edge. The reviews on these actors throughout this book speak eloquently of their talent.

Of this younger group, the company member with the longest continuous service at the end of the 50th season is Joe Aiello, who came to the Barn in '78, became a star in his first season and has remained a leading member of the company. A great talent, both for comedy and serious drama, Joe has 17 seasons under his belt. At the end of the 50th season, he had acted in 109 shows doing leading and supporting roles in both straight plays and musicals. In addition, he directed 14, co-directed two and has been assistant to the director on three.

Scott Burkell made Equity in his second season. He was not asked back the third year, but moved to NYC. Then in '83, "I campaigned hard, saying I thought I should be a part of the company, and I think the thing that got me back was I said I would be in charge of the Bar Show," he said.

Burkell has returned every season since. At the end of '95, he had worked 15 seasons, acted in 86 shows, directed three and co-directed two. Although he loves the Barn and has said, "Coming back became important to me very early and if something got in the way of that, such as a

Howard McBride

tour, I didn't want to do it." But acting on B'way isn't a tour and Burkell is, at the time of this writing, on B'way in the hit musical, *Titanic*.

Howard McBride has chalked up 15 seasons and appeared in 56 shows, in supporting roles, through the '95 season. His first onstage appearance was as a non-speaking "party guest" in **Don't Drink the Water** in '69. The following summer, he played in four shows and received special notice for his Sancho Panza in **Man of La Mancha**. He was not invited back for a third season, but in '72, Ragotzy offered him the box office position along with Equity membership. He returned again in '84, stayed and has become the Barn's indispensable general manager.

General manager is an all-encompassing title. As well as being a company manager who deals with problems involving actors, technicians and staff, Howard is a business manager who answers all letters, pays all bills, keeps the books and does the taxes. In addition, he manages the box office and accompanies Jack daily to lunch to keep him informed. Being a member of Equity, his name is needed for the required ratio between apprentices and professionals in most productions. This investment of an unusually large responsibility in a single person seems risky from a management point of view.

Obviously, at times the job is overwhelming. There are no set hours and no set vacation times. But like his colleague, Dusty Reeds, who doesn't seem to be able to say no to job demands, Howard seems to delight in the responsibility which includes, by its very nature, a great deal of power.

The youngest talent in this group — the one who will have the greatest access and influence on heir apparent Brendan Ragotzy — is Penelope Alex. At the end of '95 she had worked ten seasons and chalked up 57 acting/singing credits. She co-directs the Rehearsal Shed shows and heads the Equity Membership Candidate Program. Although not having received the same kind of critical acclaim as either Aiello or Burkell, she is in my view, technically the company's best singer. She and Brendan have two children, and if she chooses not to make a try for NY theatre, she will continue doing what she now does — being a solid company member with both talent and brains.

So these are the Barn's Giants and near Giants, and both Jack and Betty acknowledge their enormous contributions.

Jack's hiring and rehiring talented and loyal workers has resulted in a group of people who stayed with the Barn until they retired. He kept them by empowering each with the responsibility for their area of expertise. And they kept sharp because they developed a hot-wired, built-in, sibling-like rivalry as they competed each summer for their bosses' resources and attention. And Ragotzy usually had some talented younger workers waiting in the wings to keep the oldsters wondering which of the young lions would replace them in the survival race. This scheme spawns competition and occasionally results in the same dysfunctional behavior found in any family, but as a strategy, it is sure fire.

Sure, the Barn gained from their enormous work effort, but so did the Giants and near Giants. They held a kind of tenure and job security, not by union demand, but simply due to the fact that Jack and Betty both believed in rewarding their col-

Betty Ebert Ragotzy

Jack Ragotzy

leagues' contributions. Both also respected age and so did the theatregoing public — and they still do. Longtime actors at the Barn are accorded a hand on their first entrance — the same kind accorded Dame Edith Evans, who at 77, played 40-ish Judith Bliss in *Hay Fever* at London's Old Vic in the mid '60s.

Jack and Betty

And speaking of giants. . .

The biggest giants of them all are Jack and Betty. What are their statistics?

Betty worked at the Barn for 49 years and acted in 249 shows. Of these, 217 were real credits, with her greatest success being Blanche in the second production of **A Streetcar Named Desire**, Martha in **Who's Afraid of Virginia Woolf?** and Miss Daisy in **Driving Miss Daisy**. In her first decade she played 60 roles, second—67, third—40, fourth—44 and fifth—38 (32 of which were nonexistent, such as "lost people" in **Sweet Charity**, "stowaway" in **On a Clear Day**, "other prisoners" in **Man of La Mancha**, "citizen of the world" in **Candide**, "townsperson" in **Our Town** and "people of Argentina" in **Evita**).

In his 50 years at the Barn, Jack produced 407 productions, directed 199, co-directed 14, acted in 35, plus receiving program credit for appearing in 18 more. In addition, he designed or co-designed most of the shows during the first decade. In the theatre's first ten years he directed 67 productions, second—61, third—19, fourth—33 and fifth—19.

Tell me, who do you know in the theatre who ever did more?

*****

I first met Betty when I returned from the Navy after WWII in April of '46 and got a small role in *I Remember Mama* at the Civic where she was finishing her apprenticeship. In short, I met her just four months after Jack did, and although I certainly do not claim to have known her as well as her Giant colleagues, I knew both Jack and Betty for over a much longer period than anyone else who worked at the Barn. I believe I knew Betty well enough to know she would not want to be canonized posthumously, nor would she want a distorted view presented of her role at the Barn.

Some myths have evolved — possibly motivated by political agendas intent on revising history. "Betty *wa*s the Barn theatre" is one such statement which is not only divisive, but does a disservice. Betty would have hated being used to promote an agenda. Betty was a liberated woman long before woman's liberation was politically correct.

Howard McBride said that Betty was the energy behind the Barn, Jack the creativity. A successful theatre takes both, but this does not mean that either partner is devoid of the other quality. It means only that one exercises one quality to a greater degree than the other. Jack exercised artistry, Betty energetic detail-work, and the Barn needed both those qualities to succeed.

When a *Gazette* reporter interviewed various local theatre people after Betty's death, one said, "Frankly, I think a lot of the success came from Betty." If he was talking about the Barn's product — the shows — that opinion is not based on the record and Betty would be the first to say so. What is true, and Jack readily admits this, is that Betty was the glue that held the theatre together and who knew what buttons to push and how to push them every March to get Jack going — especially in later years — to plan the coming season. As one of the world's great procrastinators, he needed that nudge.

In the winter of '49, from an apartment at 161 West 74th Street in NYC, Betty ended a letter to me: "Whoops! the boss just came in!" For the Barn's 25th anniversary, Nicolette of *The Press* wrote that after the first production, Jack decided Betty should be the actor and he'd take care of the directing. "That's the way it has been," said Betty, "Jack's the boss." Jumping ahead some 19 years to July '89, Betty is quoted as saying, "Jack's the producer, casts the shows, is in charge of the finances — the one in the kitchen (and its heat) who makes the ultimate decisions."

Still later she said, "Jack is the boss. Make no mistake about that. He decides on what shows to select for a season, who should be a member of the acting company, how much money should be spent on what. He keeps the books and knows where every single penny goes and where it comes from. He casts each show and that's not an easy task when you are doing both musicals and drama with a relatively small company. For a season to be a financial success for us, Jack has to use the actors in the best, most economical manner. It all adds up to a lot of hard work."

To pass off these remarks as "she was just being a good wife of that time," is to lessen both Betty's intelligence and integrity.

Another myth is that Betty came to Kalamazoo "attempting to work her way to NY to become an actress." Betty came for exactly what the Civic Theatre's contract stipulated: to learn about all aspects of community theatre. And she did not "regularly appear" in shows at the Civic, as some have claimed. In her apprenticeship season she appeared in only one, and that was as the second ingenue.

That Betty "gave up a B'way career for the Barn" is another myth. According to Jack, Betty was offered a contract to play in the original B'way production of *Gypsy*. The author, Arthur Laurents, had been at the Barn that summer seeing his revised **The Time of the Cuckoo** produced and that winter was working with Jack on the off-B'way Laurents cycle. Because of Jack's Laurents connection, the two roles Betty was considered for in *Gypsy* were: a woman with "eight lines" at the show's beginning (lines which were later taken over by Ethel Merman when the role was cut) plus the role of Miss Cratchitt. Betty had much better sense than to think that these small roles in *Gypsy* would lead her to a B'way career at the age of 36.

In short, there was no martyr/nobility about "giving up a B'way career" for the sake of the Barn. Betty wasn't interested in a B'way career and she never "acted on B'way." She acted off-off B'way in the Equity Library Production of Jack's **Point of No Return** for four performances and off-B'way for three weeks as a replacement for Kathleen Maguire at the end of **The Time of the Cuckoo**'s run. But Betty made no attempt to crack the hard shell of NY theatre. She was not as driven as Jack. Betty loved to see the productions on B'way and in London, but she was essentially a California girl.

Listen to Betty talk about **Miss Daisy**:

"I had seen the play in London with Dame Wendy Hiller and wondered what all the fuss was about. I never wanted to play Miss Daisy. But then, I never feel that way about a part. Never! I always see myself as part of a company and whatever is best for the company and right for me is what I play. I don't know of a single part I've really wanted to do."

Does that sound like an actress who wanted a NY acting career?

The *Gazette* editorial after her death was only partially correct. "The long-term financial and artistic stability of this Midwestern theatre is rare and a tribute to the tenacity and leadership of the Ragotzys and the close associates they had attracted over the years. The two always worked hand-in-glove, but each in their own spheres, with Jack as executive producer and director and making artistic decisions. Betty handled the business and administrative end of things."

Betty never handled "the business and administrative end of things." Betty's great contribution to the Barn was her public relations work, which included news releases and contact with reporters and critics in newspapers, radio and television stations.

After Betty's death, Fulmer of *The Elkhart Truth* said that in public relations, "There was no one around who could top her. Not only did she supply everything you could possibly need, she did it *before* you asked and made sure that, from the first release to final review — good or bad —

no request went unanswered. Many do that capably but to Betty, it was much more than a job. It *was* the theatre; it was the Barn Theatre and, along with Jack and son Brendan — it was her life."

In addition, she also headed up the Equity Membership Candidate Program; she had knowledge of the Barn's costumes; she had skills in organization; she was an expert at detail work and had the tact to deal with bureaucratic organizations — work that would have driven a short-fused Ragotzy up the wall! And she was the person responsible for the Barn's history as preserved in scrapbooks and recorded in her notebook — the source of so much of this work. It is impossible to find anyone to replace her in these areas of contribution because the Barn was her life. These days it's rare to find that kind of devotion.

And, as the *Gazette* editorial said, "She could be a tiger when it came to protecting the Barn's well-being. Whether it was protesting an unfavorable review, refusing to submit passively to a box office robbery or successfully fighting a landfill, she could and sometimes did pull out all the stops."

Her stage roles were fairly rare in the later years. But her best role at the Barn was as organizer. "She knew about everything" — had a "fierce enthusiasm and mastered everything except the computer and directing." A primary interest during the last year of her life was to start a School of Advanced Theatre Training, which she hoped would open during the 50th season. Such a school, of course, would have had to be accredited and provided with a proper teaching staff. In fact, she did much of the preliminary work to make this possible. However, this was not pure altruism; Betty knew that such a school would also provide the Barn with at least partial tax-exempt status, which is not to say that she was not genuinely interested in education. She even started using such terms as "training" and referred to the apprentices as "graduates."

She was caring, a perfectionist, a hard worker and constantly enthusiastic. But she was not the producer or director of the Barn's product — the shows.

And now for Jack, since this book is about Jack — his actions, his producing, acting, directing, designing his choice of shows discussed and actors hired — the whole ball of theatrical wax.

Readers may have already come to their own conclusions, but there is a little more to say.

While researching this book, I learned that Jack did not know I was let go without two weeks' notice when I directed **Dark at the Top of the Stairs**. But like most family spats, the incident never severed our relationship. I came back to the Barn as a visitor year in and year out. I was always given "comps," always greeted by Jack from the stage as a founding member of the Barn and usually saw both Jack and Betty on their visits to NY after Robin and I moved there in '75 when I became Dean of Theatre and Film, School of the Arts, State University of NY at Purchase. In short, we remained good friends.

As I write this, I have the advantage of 37 years of hindsight. I'm grateful for the opportunity to revisit and re-evaluate what happened — to come to closure on an old wound.

When I directed at the Barn in '60, I was a tenured theatre professor and was therefore free to value art more than show biz and to respect the tragic more than the comic without any marketplace corrective. And, thanks to Jack, I took that all-important step of working in a theatre that was completely dependent on box office and dealt with professional actors — an experience that goes far beyond the rather limited relationship between an actor and a teacher in academic theatre. And I came out of the experience feeling good about myself — confident as a young director.

I went on to start my own summer theatre, albeit inside a university and therefore subsidized — and to found an Equity/LORT (League of Resident Theatres) company in which I directed such stars as Frances Farmer along with Tony and Academy Award winners Anne Revere and James Earl Jones. Some of the Barn's best actors — John Newton, Janet Hayes, Merle Louise, Peter Simon, Dale Helward, Louis Girard, and Angelo Mango — also acted at the Purdue Professional Theatre in plays by Moliere, Chekhov, Shaw, Miller, Williams, Ibsen, Anouilh, Wilde, Shakespeare, Steinbeck, Pinter, Brecht, and O'Neill. Much of my drive toward excellence may have been sparked by a kind of "Hey, big brother, look at me!" payback.

But eventually I came to realize that, as producer, Ragotzy had every right to see that the product representing his theatre was what he wanted it to be. And I do believe he tilted the balance of my directing of **Look Homeward, Angel** just a bit toward the comic — and was therefore partially responsible for the production's huge success.

I never saw **Dark at the Top of the Stairs**, but I understand he changed the play so that Sammy Goldenbaum did not die. That would be tilting the comedy balance a bit *too* far! And if I had stayed around, we would certainly have clashed over this point.

The experience of directing for Jack taught me that I was a bit one-sided. Thereafter, I began to be more conscious of the entertainment value of the theatre — "entertainment" meaning emotional and intellectual stimulation that includes both laugher and tears.

In short, I learned much from Ragotzy.

At the time of this writing there is an article in the *Gazette* on Barnie Todd Zamarripa (apprenticed in '87) of B'way's *Miss Saigon* and the touring *Les Miserables*. Describing his summer at the Barn, he says, "It sure was a good push-off experience for me. I was there three months and had two days off. We started our day about 10 a.m. riding a mower, or something like that, and ended around midnight or later doing the lounge [Rehearsal Shed] show. It was tough. It was a great experience. And on the last day it was, like, 'Hey, we survived.'"

The interviewer describes the apprenticeship as "no picnic," but what he does not say is that not only did Zamarripa do the Rehearsal Shed shows for the entire summer, he was on stage for two weeks in both **Brigadoon** and **A Funny Thing Happened on the Way to the Forum** and for three weeks in **42nd Street** — invaluable performance time before an audience, the most important learning experience for an actor.

Everyone who ever worked at the Barn knows that Ragotzy can be difficult. But if we are fair, we will admit that difficult is not all Jack is. Like all artists (and he will hate me calling him that), he is a complex individual. There is no one adjective that sums him up or any simple answers to what makes him tick. If we harbor any grudges, all we need to do is ask ourselves, "Why did we stick it out?" We stuck it out and came back for more because we gained something from Ragotzy and his Barn Theatre — for ourselves.

Betty was right when, being interviewed just after the 49th season she said, "All the people who worked at the Barn were here by choice." Jack interjected, "You know I could be pretty arrogant and ugly at times," to which Betty answered, "That's what was needed sometimes. Because any theatre is just as good as the son-of-a-bitch at the top!"

Jack wouldn't want to be whitewashed or lionized any more than Betty. He was, and is, like all of us, both good and bad. The good — his talent, intelligence, loyalty, his generosity (he's a *real* soft touch) — has been written about earlier in this book. But there was another side — the dark side, as many Barnies knew. He was sexually aggressive, an ardent womanizer (although Jack objects to this word, preferring "a lover of women") which, in the first half of the 20th century, was not so much frowned upon as taken as a plus in a man. So even today, when he goes to lunch, he can't help but flirt with middle-aged waitresses, shaking his head and muttering in his George Burns rasp, "If only you were a little older."

We were working late one night that first long-ago summer. He was married, I wasn't. We were talking about women, and he told me a story of a sexual experience he had in Virginia while he was in training to be a bombardier. He convinced a very beautiful woman from one of the First Families of Virginia, whose husband was overseas, to go to bed with him. Although she protested, he succeeded — and used a technique that was pretty unusual, or at least I thought so — in arousing her. The next morning she said, "I shouldn't have done that." Jack asked, "Are you sorry?" She thought a moment and said, "No." The thing that struck me most about the story was his conclusion of it. "First Family of Virginia or not," he said, "underneath, she was just an animal like everyone else."

Not to paint the man as a cloven-hoofed satyr, but there is no doubt he was highly active sexually and much of the activity may have been motivated by a leveling instinct — a combative reaffirmation — that regardless of social position or money or anything else, as far as the basics are concerned, we are all the same.

As our society is struggling to learn: The bottom line is that for a person in power — a producer, teacher, or armed services officer — to have sex with a person who stands to benefit, is a mistake. It can be interpreted as taking sexual advantage — from either party. If you can come up with a solution to this problem, send it to the commander-in-chief of the Armed Services!

Another dark side of Ragotzy is that, for a period of time, he slapped Betty in rehearsals. I know this happened and so do other Barnies. But we also know that Betty stayed with Jack, not out of fear or economic necessity (after all, she was co-owner of the Barn), but because she believed in their partnership – in the manner described above – as the heart of the Barn.

When interviewed about this matter, Jack was forthcoming and direct. "The slap happened about once a season when she played her first big role. She would tighten up, feeling she had to prove herself to the company so they wouldn't think she got the part because she was married to me. The slap was a method of getting her to relax and eliminate the debilitating tension that blocked her freedom of movement and prevented a relaxed vocal delivery. I stopped this practice at a rehearsal in the early 60s when I took her aside and told her she would have to find her own method of dealing with her tensions."

If you think Jack's explanation for getting a performance out of Betty sounds farfetched, you should know that physical, and more often psychological, abuse was often a practice in early and mid-twentieth century theatre, ballet, films and music. Slapping was used by the great acting teacher, Alvina Krause, of Northwestern University; Martha Graham used the slap technique to get emotion from her dancers. Nijinsky made dancers cry, and it is still customary in some countries for the ballet teacher to carry a riding crop and lay it across the thigh of a student who misses a step (much as teacher/nuns used to lay a ruler across the back of an academically errant student's hand). Toscanini's rants and rages at musicians were well-known. In films, stories are legion of directors who have gotten performances out of actors by a method that in real life came to be called psychological abuse. Jerome Robbins' treatment of Larry Kert as he prepared for the role of Tony in *West Side Story* is documented in Arthur Laurents' autobiography. In short, an essay could be written about this subject. Suffice it to say that I believe Jack's explanation for slapping Betty is, in context, credible.

In real life it would be nice to live by Hannah's philosophy in Tennessee Williams' *The Night of the Iguana*. Hannah tells of an incident in Singapore when she goes out in a sampan with an Australian salesman. He asks her to "take off some piece of your clothes and let me hold it, just hold it." She does, while he "gratifies himself." The defrocked minister, Shannon, asks, "It didn't disgust you?" And Hannah replies, "Nothing human disgusts me unless it's unkind, violent."

But the theatre is not real life.

Outside of the theatre Jack was, at times, both unkind and violent. His survival and leveling instincts were no doubt responses formed early in life. Which of us is to cast the first stone? Jack Ragotzy was a first-rate theatre artist and Betty knew it. In real life I think she saw him as a good man.

And I know they loved one another.

*****
The Future

All during the writing of this book, I have been wondering about the future of the Barn

Brendan Ragotzy

knowing that Jack is genuinely trying, but understandably unable, to give up all involvement while also trying to ease the burden onto Brendan's shoulders.

With Penelope's help, Brendan should do well. He is extraordinarily low-keyed, even-tempered and unflappable. When he directs, he listens to the actors and encourages them in their creative process; he appears to have no acting agendas and no destructive ego. He is conscientious and takes delight in doing apprentice-type jobs such as car parking and lawn mowing, perhaps as a role model to the apprentices or maybe just to get away from the grind of administration.

Since he seems to be a status-quo kind of guy, he may attempt to continue producing farces and "golden oldies" from the musical comedy theatre in an attempt to keep the Barn pretty much as it has been. Such a policy could be a plus as far as the business aspect is concerned. Or, he might decide to empower an artistic director like Joe Aiello, Scott Burkell or Robin Haynes, for example, who has the depth of experience in acting and professional theatre to operate such a company and who might schedule, as Jack always did, some cutting-edge plays as well as musicals.

In the meantime, while Brendan is waiting to take over completely, he should continue writing and systematically view the best of theatre in both NY and London so that he becomes acquainted with the plays and talent in the B'way and West End theatres.

Of course, Brendan is not Jack — doesn't look, think or act like him. Brendan is his own man. As a young producer/director, Jack was an actor; Brendan definitely is not. Jack's style was, and still is, totally different. Of course, directors' styles were different 50 years ago. Ragotzy had the flamboyance and the showmanship of a Jed Harris or David Merrick — both men a little larger than life with skittish egos and all-consuming drives. These are different times and Brendan's approach to producing and directing is totally different — but it can be valid.

Brendan has grown up at the Barn and has worked there each summer in some capacity since he was old enough to walk. In '86 he alternated between being stage manager and assistant stage manager. At the end of the 50th season he had directed only nine productions. Obviously he needs seasoning, but that may come in time. One thing is certain, he will not be tested until he is fully in command as producer.

One takes Brendan at his word, albeit low-keyed, when he says he will listen to the suggestions of such long-time Barnies as Tom Wopat, Marin Mazzie, Barbara Marineau, Eric Riley, Becky Ann Baker, Robin Haynes and others who have gone on to the big time and may wish to come back for a specific show. In addition, he will listen to his colleagues, who, at end of this first 50 years of Barn's history, are a new group of workers. They include choreographer Charlie Misovye who, at the end of '95, has been with the theatre for seven years; actor/singer Eric Parker—three years; stage manager, Gregg Rehrig—two years. Three extremely talented newcomers include: actor/musician John C. Brown, costumer Elaine Kauffman and technical director Fred Gillette.

After listening carefully to his staff, along with former stars, Brendan will make up his own mind. He may become mainly a producer and

Penelope Alex

manager and leave the everyday operation of the theatre to an artistic director of his choosing. Whatever happens, his decisions will determine the Barn's future only when, as Sondheim writes, there are. . .

"*No More. . . Giants.*"
*****

As a little kid, Jack P. Ragotzy watched fascinated as the tall figure dressed in a stovepipe hat, a blue swallow-tailed coat and spangled pants, pranced up Burdick Street from the train station so many years ago. And like that magical figure in spangled pants, Jack, too, became a leader of a band, or at least the circus of show folks – gypsies, roustabouts and jugglers who paraded through the Barn Theatre over a period of 50 years entertaining us. And the magic and joy that little kid created out of make-believe *was* better than what he saw all around him in everyday life. And all of us, audiences, critics and theatregoers alike, were the recipients of that magic. Ephemeral, yes! and as transitory and fleeting as a whiff of smoke in the air, but nonetheless real, if only as part of our memories. That's Jack's legacy to us, remembrances of magical moments past.

###

Intermission at a Sunday matinee, 1992

Appendix

Note:
- *Data for programs not on file have been taken from Betty Ebert's scrapbooks.*
- *Regrettably, space limitations prohibit the inclusion of staff, crews and orchestra members.*

1946 Season

#1
July 3 - 6, 1946
Charley's Aunt
by Brandon Thomas
Directed by Betty Ebert
CAST

Jack Chesney	Joseph G. Stockdale
Brassett	Lance Ferraro
Charley Wykeham	Frank Bradley, Jr.
Lord Fancourt Babberly	Jack P. Ragotzy
Kitty Verdun	Ellen Hitchcock
Amy Spettigue	Marjorie Taintor
Col. Sir Francis Chesney	Robert Finley
Stephen Spettigue	Robert Baker
Donna Lucia D'Alvadorez	Robin Fastenrath
Ela Delahay	Violet Kroeger

#2
July 17 - 20, 1946
The Bishop Misbehaves
by Frederick Jackson
Directed by Jack P. Ragotzy
CAST

Red Eagan	Frank Bradley, Jr.
Donald Meadows	Lloyd Kaechele
Hester Grantham	Sara Woolley
Guy Waller	Robert Finley
Mrs. Waller	Sue DeLano
The Bishop of Broadminister	Robert Baker
Lady Emily Lyons	Betty Ebert
Collins	Lance Ferraro
Frenchy	Joseph G. Stockdale
Mr. Brooke	Robert Cass

#3
July 31 - August 3, 1946
Pure as the Driven Snow or A Working Girl's Secret
by Paul Loomis
Directed by Madam Betty Ebert
CAST

Purity Dean	Robin Fastenrath
Jonathan Logan	Jack P. Ragotzy
Zamak Logan	Freda B. Winters
Leander Longfellow	Joseph G. Stockdale
Mortimer Frothingham	Robert Finley
Jed Lunn	Robert Wunderlin
E.Z. Pickens	Frank Bradley, Jr.
Imogene Pickens	Marjorie Taintor
Mrs. Hewlitt	Margaret Ann Curran
Alison Hewitt	Julia Stewart
Nellie Morris	George Spelvin
Mrs. Faith Vogue	Delphine Stratton

#4
August 14 - 17, 1946
Morning's at Seven
by Paul Osborn
Directed by Jack P. Ragotzy
CAST

Theodore Swanson	Frank Bradley, Jr.
Cora Swanson	Sue DeLano
Aaronetta Gibbs	Betty Ebert
Ida Bolton	Margaret Ann Curran
Carl Bolton	Walter Wagner
Homer Bolton	Joseph G. Stockdale
Myrtle Brown	Robin Fastenrath
Esther Crampton	Delphine Stratton
David Crampton	Robert Baker

#5
August 28 - 31, 1946
Goodbye Again
by Allan Scott and George Haight
Directed by Betty Ebert and Jack P. Ragotzy
"Who give a very special note of thanks to Howard Chenery for his help."
CAST

Anne Rogers	Betty Ebert
Kenneth Bixby	Jack P. Ragotzy
Bellboy	Robert Wunderlin
Maid	Margaret Ann Curran
Julia Wilson	Robin Fastenrath
Harry Archer	Don Griffith
Private Earhart	Don Keil
Arthur Westdale	Robert Dewey
Harvey Wilson	Robert Baker
Mr. Clayton	Joseph G. Stockdale
Theodore	David Field

1947 Season

#6
July 2 - 5, 1947
Kiss and Tell
by F. Hugh Herbert
Directed by Jack P. Ragotzy
CAST

Mr. Willard	Walter Wagner
Louis	Elise Stroud
Corliss Archer	Maryjane Schilling
Raymond Pringle	David Field
Mildred Pringle	Joan Wylie
Dexter Franklin	Robert Bonfoey
Janet Archer	Robin Fastenrath
Harry Archer	Don Griffith
Private Earhart	Don Keil
Lieut. Lenny Archer	Don Clark
Mary Franklin	Betty Ebert
Bill Franklin	Joseph G. Stockdale
Uncle George	Robert Baker
Robert Pringle	Ed Marineau

#7
July 16-19, 1947
Dirty Work at the Crossroads or Tempted, Tried, and True
by Bill Johnson
Directed by Monsieur J. Peyton Ragotzy
Scenic embellishments by Signor Arturo L. Crain
CAST

Nellie Lovelace	MME. Elizabeth Ebert
Adam Oakhart	MSSR. Donald Griffith
The Widow Lovelace	MME. Robin Fastenrath
Munro Murgatroyd	MSSR. Joseph Stockdale
Ida Rhinegold	MLLE. Margaret Ann Curran
Mookie Maguggins	MSSR. Robert Bonfoey
Mrs. Upson Asterbilt	MLLE. Helena Tift
Leonie Asterbilt	MILLE. Yvonne Moffett
Fleurette	MLLE Jeannine Beatty

#8
July 30 - August 2, 1947
Laburnum Grove
by J. B. Priestley
Directed by Jack P. Ragotzy
CAST

Elsie Radfern	Yvonne Moffett
Mrs. (Lucy) Baxley	Margaret Ann Curran
Bernard Baxley	Joseph G. Stockdale
George Radfern	Robert Baker
Harold Russ	Donald Kiel
Joe Fletten	Robert Bonfoey
Mrs. (Dorothy) Radfern	Betty Ebert
Inspector Stack	Donald Griffith
Sergeant Morris	Richard Snyder

#9
August 13 - 16, 1947
Green Grow the Lilacs
by Lynn Riggs
Directed by Jack P. Ragotzy
CAST

Curley McClain	Donald Griffith
Aunt Eller Murphy	Delphine Stratton
Laurey Williams	Betty Ebert
Jeeter Fry	Ned Turner
Ado Annie Carnes	Suzanne Delano
A Peddler	Joseph G. Stockdale
Old Man Peck	Robert Bonfoey
Cord Elam	Donald Clark
Shorty	Robert Wunderlin

Cowboys and Farmers:
Charles Daugherty, Edward Marineau, Donald Keil, Joe Gagen, Loy J. Norrix,
Girls:
Margaret Ann Curran, Robin Stockdale, Betty Bird, Jane Christy, Jean LaDella, Maryjane Shilling, Ann Butterfield.

#10
August 27 -30, 1947
Boy Meets Girl
by Bella and Samuel Spewack
Directed by Jack P. Ragotzy
CAST

Robert Law	Harry Travis
Larry Toms	Joseph G. Stockdale
J. Carlyle Benson	Walter Wagner
Rosetti	Robert Bonfoey
Mr. Friday (C.F.)	Jack P. Ragotzy
Peggy	Betty Ebert
Miss Crews	Margaret Ann Curran
Rodney Bevan	Donald Kiel
Green	Robert Wunderlin
Slade	Donald Clark
Susie	Robin Stockdale*
A Nurse	Jean La Della
Chauffeur	Loy J. Norrix
Young Man	Jim Norrix
Cutter	Richard Gregg
Major Thompson	Deo Kingsley

*name left off program

1948 Season

#11
July 7 - 10, 1948
See My Lawyer
by Richard Maibaum and Harry Clork
Directed by Jack P. Ragotzy
CAST

Fay Frankel	Betty Ebert
Arthur Lee	Jack P. Ragotzy
Joseph O'Rourke	Drew Handley
Peter Russo	Loy G. Norrix
Morris Schneerer	O.S. McQueen
Sydonia Tyler	Donna McQueen
Irving Frankel	David Field
Charlie	Gordon Smith
Mamie	Mary Jane Schilling
Telephone Linesman	Donald Brink
Robert Carlin	Jack Pickering
Emmanuel Kato	Edwin Phelps, Jr.
S. B. Jameson	Albert Grady
Blossom LeVerne	Ann Butterfield
A Stenographer	Pat Hanlon
Policeman	Richard Stroud

#12
July 21 - 24, 1948
**Love Rides the Rails or
Will the Mail-train Run Tonight?**
by Morland Cary
Directed by Monsieur J. Peyton Ragotzy
CAST

Mrs. Hopewell	MME Ruth Phelps
Prudence Hopewell	MME. Betty Ebert
Simon Darkway	MSSR. Drew Handley
Truhart Pendennis	MSSR. Joseph Stockdale
Harold Stanfast	MSSR. Donald Kiel
Dirk Sneath	MSSR. Edwin Phelps, Jr.
Carlotta Cortez	MLLE. Margaret Ann Curran
Fifi (her maid)	MME. Robin Stockdale
Fred Wheelwright	MSSR. Don Brink
Dan (a bartender)	MSSR. Cliff Stuart
Beulah Bell	MLLE. Ann Butterfield
Sheriff	MSSR. Tom Upham

Railroad Workers:
MSSE. James Norrix, George Spelvin

#13
August 4 - 7, 1948
Petticoat Fever
by Mark Reed
Directed by Jack P. Ragotzy
CAST

Dascom Dinsmore	Drew Handley
Kimo	Edwin Phelps, Jr.
Sir James Fenton	Joseph G. Stockdale
Ethel Campion	Robin Stockdale
Little Seal	Mary Jane Schilling
Snow Bird	Pat Hanlon
The Reverend Arthur Shapman	Bob Tazelaar
Captain John Landry	Don Brink
Scotty	Rick Stroud
Clara Wilson	Ann Butterfield

#14
August 18 - 21, 1948
Ah, Wilderness!
by Eugene O'Neill
Directed by Jack P. Ragotzy
CAST

Nat Miller	Howard Chenery
Essie	Delphine Stratton
Arthur	Loy Gene Norrix
Richard	Jack P. Ragotzy
Mildred	Mary Jane Schilling
Tommy	David Field
Sid Davis	Edwin Phelps, Jr.
Lily Miller	Margaret Ann Curran
David McComber	Drew Handley
Muriel McComber	Betty Ebert
Wint Selby	Richard Stroud
Belle	Jean Henderson
Nora	Charlene Page
Bartender	Don Brink
Salesman	Mr. Handley

#15
September 1 - 4, 1948
The Male Animal
by James Thurber and Elliott Nugent
Directed by Jack P. Ragotzy
CAST

Cleota	Margaret Ann Curran
Eileen Turner	Betty Ebert
Tommy Turner	Drew Handley
Patricia Stanley	Ann Butterfield
Wally Myers	Reed Badgley
Dean Frederick Damon	Charles T. Lynch
Michael Barnes	Loy Gene Norrix
Joe Ferguson	Jack Pickering
Mrs. Blanche Damon	Jean Henderson
Ed Keller	Edwin Phelps, Jr.
Myrtle Keller	Lorna Young
"Nutsy" Miller	Tom Upham
Newspaper Reporter	Don Brink

1949 Season

#16
July 19 - 23, 1949
Room Service
by John Murray and Allen Boretz
Directed by Jack P. Ragotzy
CAST

Sasha Smirnoff	Lazar Purigraski
Gordon Miller	Harry Travis
Joseph Gribble	Olin S. McQueen
Harry Binion	Drew Handley
Faker Englund	Stan Levitt
Christine Marlowe	Betty Ebert
Leo Davis	Robert Bonfoey
Hilda Manney	Loretta Leversee
Gregory Wagner	Paul Hahn
Simon Jenkins	Don Kiel
Timothy Hogarth	Bradley Taylor
Dr. Glass	Don Brink
Bank Messenger	George Ongley
Senator Blake	Edwin Phelps, Jr

#17
July 26 - 30, 1949
Night Must Fall
by Emlyn Williams
Directed by Jack P. Ragotzy
CAST

Mrs. Bramson	Jean Henderson
Olivia Grayne	Barbara Donahue
Hubert Laurie	Stan Levitt
Nurse Libby	Pat Hanlon
Mrs. Terence	Norma Platt
Dora Parkoe	Peggy Sparks
Inspector Belsize	Paul Hahn
Dan	Bradley Taylor

#18
August 2 - 6, 1949
**Pure as the Driven Snow or
A Working Girl's Secret**
by Paul Loomis
A thrilling and educational masterpiece demonstrating the triumph of Virtue over Evil. Entire production under the direction of that world-renowned impresario, J. Peyton Ragotzy.
Signor Arturo Crain and Mlle. Helena Hice, lately of the Beaux Arts, Paris, creators of scenic embellishments.
CAST

Purity Dean	MME. Betty Ebert
Jonathan Logan	MSSR. Don Brink
Zamah Logan	MME Queen Berwald
Leander Longfellow	MSSR. Drew Handley
Mortimer Frothingham	MSSR. Stan Levitt
Jed Luhn	MSSR. Fred Whited
E.Z. Pickens	MSSR. Bradley Taylor
Imogene Pickens	MLLE Norma Platt
Mrs. Hewlitt	MME. Peg Reeves
Alison Hewlitt	MLLE. Pat Hanlon
Nellie Morris	MLLE. Betsy Davis
Mrs. Faith Hogue	MME. Delphine Stratton

#19
August 9 - 13, 1949
The Milky Way
by Lynn Root and Harry Clork
Directed by Jack P. Ragotzy
CAST

Spider	Stan Levitt
Speed McFarland	Paul Hahn
Anne Westley	Betty Ebert
Gabby Sloan	Bradley Taylor
Burleigh Sullivan	Drew Handley
Mae Sullivan	Pat Hanlon
Eddie	Fred Whited
Willard	Don Brink
Wilbur Austin	Loy Gene Norrix

#20
August 16 - 20, 1949
[World Premiere]
Verily I Do
by Gladys Charles and George Savage
Directed by Jack P. Ragotzy
CAST

Verily Wilson	Loretta Leversee
Archie Barker	Robert Bonfoey
Tom Bolles	Drew Handley
Sooner Bolles	Fred Whited
Jason Hall	Loy Gene Norrix
Sarah Boggs	Norma Platt
Idy Welles	Ann Butterfield
Big Ed Bolles	Charles Daugherty
Lt. Charles S. Folsom	Paul Hahn
Sgt. Daniel O'Conner	Stan Levitt
Granny Fearsome	Betty Ebert
Billy Beefham Brer	Don Brink
Preacher Graham	Bradley Taylor

#21
August 23 - 27, 1949
[World Premiere]
Country Mile
by Jack P. Ragotzy
Directed by Jack P. Ragotzy
CAST

Alex	Jack P. Ragotzy
Slim	Loy Gene Norrix

Kansas	Drew Handley
Lowell	Paul Hahn
Jerry	Robert Bonfoey
Georgia	Stuart Main
Richard	Bradley Taylor
Pearl	Barbara Donahue
Tars Lampedo	Stan Levitt
Mr. Pifer	Chuck Daugherty
Myrtle	Peggy Sparks
Sally	Pat Hanlon
Peggy	Norma Platt

1950 Season

#22
June 26 - July 1, 1950
The Silver Whistle
by Robert E. McEnroe
Directed by Jack P. Ragotzy
CAST

Mr. Beebe	Herbert Lane
Mrs. Hanmer	Jean Henderson
Miss Hoadley	Monica Keating
Miss Tripp	Julia Miles
Reverend Watson	Richard Thrall
Mrs. Sampler	Betty Ebert
Mrs. Gross	Margaret Ann Curran
Mr. Cherry	Arvid Nelson
Oliver T. Erwenter	Paul Levitt
Emmett	Drew Handley
Bishop	William Miles
Father Shay	Robert Bonfoey
Mr. Beach	Loy Gene Norrix
Mr. Reddy	Gordon Evans
Policeman	Charles Daugherty

#23
July 3 - 8, 1950
Three's a Family
by Phoebe and Henry Ephron
Directed by Jack P. Ragotzy
CAST

Sam Whitaker	Herbert Lane
Irma Dalrymple	Margaret Ann Curran
Adelaide	Betty Ebert
Kitty Mitchell	Anne Butterfield
Archie Whitaker	Loy Gene Norrix
Hazel (his wife)	Patricia Hanlon
Frances Whitaker	Monica Keating
Delivery Man	Paul Levitt
Eugene Mitchell	Drew Handley
Two Moving Men:	
William Miles, Arvid Nelson	
Another Maid	C. Daugherty
A Girl	Porter Handley
Dr. Bartell	Robert Bonfoey
Joe Franklin	Richard Thrall
Marion Franklin	Julia Miles

#24
July 10 - 15, 1950
Apple of His Eye
by Kenyon Nicholson and Charles Robinson
Directed by Jack P. Ragotzy
CAST

Stella Springer	Monica Keating
Foss Springer	Charles Daugherty
Lily Tobin	Betty Ebert
Tude Bowers	Herbert Lane
Sam Stover	Howard Chenery
Nina Stover	Anne Butterfield
Ott Tobein	Arvid Nelson
Nettie Bowers	Margaret Ann Curran
Glen Stover	Richard Thrall
Carol Ann Stover	Sandra Taylor
Ott Tobein	Edwin Phelps, Jr.

#25
July 17 - 22, 1950
See How They Run
by Philip King
Directed by Jack P. Ragotzy
CAST

Ida (a maid)	Betty Ebert
Miss Skillon	Margaret Ann Curran
The Reverend Lionel Toop	Paul Levitt
Penelope Toop (his wife)	Monica Keating
Corporal Steve Winton	Drew Handley
The Intruder	Arvid Nelson
The Bishop of Lax	Herbert Lane
The Rev. Arthur Humphrey	Robert Bonfoey
Sergeant Towers	Charles Dougherty

#26
July 24 - 29, 1950
The Curse of an Aching Heart
by Herbert E. Swayne
Directed by J. Peyton Ragotzy
CAST

Hiram Abernathy	MSSR. Lane
Sarah Abernathy	MLLE. Curran
Sheriff Two Gun	MSSR. Bonfoey
Red Wing	MLLE. Hanlon
Windermere Hightower	MSSR. Levitt
Lucius Goodenough	MSSR. Handley
Aurelia Abernathy	MLLE. Miles
Melody Lane	MADAM Ebert
Nellie Blythe	MADAM Keating
Muriel Atkins	MADAM Butterfield
An Unexpected Male Arrival	MSSR. Thrall

#27
July 31 - August 4, 1950
But Not Goodbye
by George Seaton
Directed by Jack P. Ragotzy
CAST

Sam Griggs	Herbert Lane
Howard Baker	Richard Thrall
Amy Griggs	Margaret Ann Curran
Jennifer Griggs	Julia Miles
Tom Carter	Arvid Nelson
Ralph Humphrey	William Miles
Jimmie Griggs	Loy Gene Norrix
Dr. Wilson	Charles Daugherty
Benjamin Griggs	Paul Levitt
Rev. Pritchard	Robert Bonfoey

#28
August 7 - 12, 1950
Of Mice and Men
by John Steinbeck
Directed by Jack P. Ragotzy
CAST

George	Drew Handley
Lennie	William Miles
Candy	Herbert Lane
The Boss	Edwin Phelps, Jr.
Curley	Paul Levitt
Curley's Wife	Julia Miles
Slim	Arvid Nelson
Carlson	Charles Daugherty
Whit	Richard Thrall
Crooks	Robert Bonfoey

#29
August 14 - 19, 1950
Hooray for the Madam
by Samson Raphaelson
Directed by Jack P. Ragotzy
CAST

Miss Crane	Betty Ebert
Violet	Margaret Ann Curran
Mike Ambler	Paul Levitt
Jason Otis	Jack P. Ragotzy
Lisa Otis	Barbara Donahue
George Bronson	Richard Thrall
Bill Squibb	Arvid Nelson
Humphrey Crocker	Robert Bonfoey
Nick Wiggins	Charles Daugherty
Mr. Kennedy	Herbert Lane
Mrs. Kennedy	Monica Keating

#30
August 21 - 26, 1950
Harvey
by Mary Chase
Directed by Jack P. Ragotzy
CAST

Myrtle May Simmons	Margaret Ann Curran
Veta Louise Simmons	Jean Henderson
Elwood P. Dowd	Drew Handley
Harvey	Himself
Miss Johnson	Betsy Davis
Mrs. Ethel Chauvenet	Delphine Stratton
Ruth Kelly, R.N	Betty Ebert
Marvin Wilson	Charles Daugherty
Lyman Sanderson, MD	Richard Thrall
William R. Chumley, MD	Herbert Lane
Betty Chumley	Monica Keating
Judge Omar Gaffney	Paul Levitt
E.J. Lofgren	Robert Bonfoey

#31
August 28th - September 2, 1950
Light Up the Sky
by Moss Hart
Directed by Jack P. Ragotzy
CAST

Miss Lowell	Anne Butterfield
Carleton Fitzgerald	Herbert Lane
Frances Black	Betty Ebert
Owen Turner	Arvid Nelson
Stella Livingston	Margaret Ann Curran
Peter Sloan	Loy Gene Norrix
Sidney Black	Paul Levitt
Sven	Robert Brown
Irene Livingston	Monica Keating
Tyler Rayburn	Richard Thrall
Max (a Shriner)	Robert Bonfoey
Ed (a Shriner)	James Norrix
William H. Gallegher	Charles Daugherty
A Plain-clothes Man	Drew Handley

1951 Season

#32
June 26 - 30, 1951
Mr. Barry's Etchings
by Walter Bullock and Daniel Archer

Designed and Directed by Jack P. Ragotzy
CAST
Mildred . . . . Mary Jo Henderson
Mrs. Taylor . . . . Jean Henderson
Evelyn Taylor . . . . Joan Creears
Judson Barry . . . . Howard Chenery
Marvin Pritchard . . . . Burton Wold
Carrie Stanwich . . . . Ann Brignole
"Fifty" Ferris . . . . Betty Ebert
"Sawbuck" Sam . . . . Jerome Gardino
Mrs. Griswold . . . . Elsie Dalawrak
Sam Jordan . . . . Milton Hamerman
Tom Crosby . . . . John Mcalpine
Daisy . . . . Frances Price
Kenneth Plunkett . . . . Leon B. Stevens.

#33
July 3 - 7, 1951
Papa Is All
by Patterson Greene
Directed by Howard Chenery
CAST
Mama . . . . Helen Burdick
Jake . . . . Ralph Stein
State Trooper Brendle . . . . Milt Hamerman
Emma . . . . Joan Creears
Mrs. Yoder . . . . Charlotte Shoaff
Papa . . . . Howard Chenery

#34
July 10 - 14, 1951
**Dirty Work at the Crossroads
or Tempted, Tried and True**
by Bill Johnson
Directed by Monsieur J. Payton Ragotzy
Scenic embellishments by
Signor and Senora Crain
CAST
Nellie Lovelace . . . . MME Elizabeth Ebert
Adam Oakhart . . . . MSSR. Milt Hamerman
The Widow Lovelace . . . . . . MLLE. Beth Garde
Munro Murgatroyd . . . MSSR. Jerome Gardino
Ida Rhinegold . . . . MLLE. Charlotte Shoaff
Mookie Maguggins . . . MSSR. Robert Bonfoey
Mrs. Upson Asterbilt . . . . MLLE. Joan Hoey
Leonie Asterbilt . . . . MLLE. Frances Price
Fleurette . . . . MLLE. Ann Brignole

#35
July 17 - 21, 1951
The Voice of the Turtle
by John Van Druten
Directed by Howard Chenery
CAST
Sally Middleton . . . . Joan Creears
Olive Lashbrook . . . . Miriam Oakes
Bill Page . . . . Milt Hamerman

#36
July 31 - August 4, 1951
A Streetcar Named Desire
by Tennessee Williams
Directed by Jack P. Ragotzy
CAST
Negro Woman . . . . Beth Garde
Eunice Hubbel . . . . Delphine Stratton
Stanley Kowalski . . . . Jerome Gardino
Harold Mitchell ("Mitch") . . . . Leon B. Stevens
Stella Kowalski . . . . Charlotte Shoaff
Steve Hubbel . . . . Milt Hamerman
Blanche DuBois . . . . Betty Ebert
Pablo Gonzales . . . . John McAlpine
A Young Collector . . . . Burton Spiller
Mexican Woman . . . . Ann Brignole
A Strange Woman . . . . Joan Hoey
A Strange Man . . . . Burton Wold
And other habitues of the Quarter

#37
August 7 - 11, 1951
The Curious Savage
by John Patrick
Directed by Jack P. Ragotzy
CAST
The Guests
Florence . . . . Frances Price
Hannibal . . . . Leon B. Stevens
Fairy May . . . . Joan Creears
Jeffrey . . . . John McAlpine
Mrs. Paddy . . . . Beth Garde
The Family:
Titus . . . . Milt Hamerman
Samuel . . . . Jerome Gardino
Lily Bell . . . . Charlotte Shoaff
Ethel . . . . Helen Burdick
The Staff:
Miss Wilhelmina . . . . Ann Brignole
Dr. Emmett . . . . Ralph Stein

#38
August 14 - 18, 1951
The Show-Off
by George Kelley
Directed by Howard Chenery
CAST
Clara . . . . Barbara Donahue
Mrs. Fisher . . . . Charlotte Shoaff
Amy . . . . Joan Creears
Frank Holland . . . . Jerome Gardino
Mr. Fisher . . . . Leon B. Stevens
Joe . . . . Loy Norrix
Aubrey Piper . . . . Milt Hamerman
Mr. Gill . . . . Arvid Nelson
Mr. Rogers . . . . John McAlpine

#39
August 21 - September 1, 1951
Tobacco Road
by Erskine Caldwell
Directed by Jack P. Ragotzy
CAST
Dude Lester . . . . John McAlpine
Ada Lester . . . . Jean Henderson
Jeeter Lester . . . . Milt Hamerman
Ellie May . . . . Joan Creears
Grandma Lester . . . . Betty Ebert
Lov Bensey . . . . Leon B. Stevens
Henry Peabody . . . . Arvid Nelson
Sister Bessie Rice . . . . Charlotte Shoaff
Pearl . . . . Mary Jo Henderson
Captain Jim . . . . Loy G. Norrix
George Payne . . . . Jerome Gardino

#40
September 4 - 8, 1951
Come Back Little Sheba
by William Inge
Directed by Jack P. Ragotzy
CAST
Doc . . . . Leon B. Stevens
Marie . . . . Joan Creears
Lola . . . . Ruth Clason
Turk . . . . Jerome Gardino
Postman . . . . Jack Ragotzy
Mrs. Coffman . . . . Charlotte Shoaff
Milkman . . . . Arvid Nelson
Messenger . . . . John Scudder
Bruce . . . . Loy G. Norrix
Ed Anderson . . . . Milt Hamerman
Elmo Huston . . . . John McAlphine

#41
September 11 - 15, 1951
Springtime for Henry
by Benn W. Levy
Directed by Jack P. Ragotzy
CAST
Mr. Dewlip . . . . Milt Hamerman
Mr. Jelliwell . . . . Leon B. Stevens
Mrs. Jelliwell . . . . Betty Ebert
Miss Smith . . . . Barbara Donahue

1952 Season

#42
June 24 - 28, 1952
Twentieth Century
by Ben Hecht and Charles MacArthur
Directed by Jack P. Ragotzy
CAST
Dr. Johnson . . . . Margaret Curran
Train Secretary . . . . Irene Ryan
Porter . . . . Harry Arnold
Grover Lockwood . . . . Leon B. Stevens
Anita Highland . . . . Teri Robin
Owen O'Malley . . . . Michael Capanna
Conductor . . . . Ray Wegner
Oliver Webb . . . . William Flatley
Flannagan . . . . Verbel Orr-Veral
Matthew Clark . . . . Louis Cutelli
First Beard . . . . Arvid Nelson
Second Beard . . . . Don Keil
Oscar Jaffee . . . . Milt Hamerman
Sadie . . . . Jean Henderson
Lily Garland . . . . Betty Ebert
George Smith . . . . Joan McAlpine
Detective . . . . Byron Clark
Max Jacobs . . . . Jack P. Ragotzy
Reporter . . . . Mary Jo Henderson
plus Reporters, Passengers, Photographers, etc.

#43
July 1 - 5, 1952
Rain
by John Colton and Clemence Randolph
Directed by Howard Chenery
CAST
Ameena . . . . Ann Curran
Private Griggs . . . . John McAlpine
Corporal Hodgson . . . . Louis Cutelli
Sergeant O'Hara . . . . Michael Capanna
Trader Joe Horn . . . . Leon B. Stevens
Dr. MacPahel . . . . Milt Hamerman
Mrs. MacPahel . . . . Irene Ryan
Mrs. Davidson . . . . Jean Henderson
Quartermaster Bates . . . . William Flatley
Sadie Thompson . . . . Alicia Krug
Rev. Alfred Davidson . . . . Howard Chenery

#44
July 8 - 12, 1952
Season in the Sun
by Wolcott Gibbs
Directed by Jack P. Ragotzy
CAST

A Girl . . . . .Teri Robin	Sharon McLonergan . . . . .Betty Baisch	Estelle Hohengarten . . . . .Betty Ebert
A Boy . . . . .Jon Crain	Woody Mahoney . . . . .Arvid Nelson	The Strega . . . . .L. Cutelli
George Crane . . . . .Michael Capanna	Og (a leprechaun) . . . . .Louis Cutelli	Guiseppina . . . . .Nancy Connable
Emily Crane .Betty Ebert	Howard . . . . .Harry Arnold	Peppina . . . . .Delphine Stratton
Mae Jermyn .Ann Curran	Senator Billboard Rawkins . . . .Leon B. Stevens	Father DeLeo . . . . .Milt Hamerman
Charles Farber . . . . .John McAlpine	First Geologist . . . . .John McAlpine	A Doctor .Arvid Nelson
Michael Lindsay . . . . .Louis Cutelli	Second Geologist . . . . .Michael Wilsie	Miss Yorke . . . . .Irene Ryan
Paula Anderson . . . . .Irene Ryan	Jane . . . . .Sandra Taylor	Flora . . . . .Billie Sanders
Deedy Barton . . . . .Alicia Krug	John (the preacher) . . . . .Milt Hamerman	Bessie . . . . .Cynthia Arnold
John Colgate . . . . .Arvid Nelson	Necessity Singer . . . . .Ann Curran	Jack Hunter . . . . .John McAlpine
Molly Burden . . . . .Jean Henderson	City Lady . . . . .Betty Ebert	The Salesman . . . . .Leon B. Stevens
Will Quigley . . . . .William Flatley	Mr. Robust . . . . .Milt Hamerman	Alvaro Mangiacavallo . . . . . . .Michael Capanna
Horace William Dodd . . . . . . .Milt Hamerman	Mr. Shears . . . . .Veal Orr	
	First Gospeleer . . . . .Milt Hamerman	

#45
July 15 - 19, 1952
Burlesque
by George M. Watters and Arthur Hopkins
Directed by Jack P. Ragotzy
CAST

Bonny . . . . .Alicia Krug
Jimmy . . . . .Harry Arnold
Skid . . . . .Milt Hamerman
Lefty . . . . .Leon B. Stevens
A Fireman . . . . .Byron Clark
Mazie . . . . .Billie Sanders
Gussie . . . . .Ann Curran
Sylvia Marco . . . . .Betty Ebert
Bozo . . . . .Louis Cutelli
Harvey Howell . . . . .Michael Capanna
Jerry Evans . . . . .Ford Campbell
A Waiter . . . . .Michael Wilsie
Stage Carpenter . . . . .Arvid Nelson
Scotty . . . . .John McAlpine
Jack . . . . .Byron Clark
A Comic .William Flatley

Chorus Girls:
Teri Robin, Irene Ryan, Anne Hampton and
Sonia Valler

#46
July 22 - 26, 1952
Clutterbuck
by Benn W. Levy
Directed by Howard Chenery
CAST

Julian Pugh . . . . .Milt Hamerman
Arthur Pomfret . . . . .Leon B. Stevens
Deborah Pomfret . . . . .Barbara Donahue
Jane Pugh . . . . .Betty Ebert
Clutterbuck . . . . .Howard Chenery
Waiter . . . . .Michael Capanna
Melissa . . . . .Cindy Arnold

#47
July 29 - August 9, 1952
Finian's Rainbow
Music by Burton Lane,
Book by E.Y. Harburg and Fred Saidy,
Lyrics by E.Y. Harburg
Directed by William Flatley
Choreography by Alicia Krug
Conductor and Pianist, Mike Schacht
CAST

Buzz Collins . . . . .Michael Capanna
Sheriff . . . . .Jack Ragotzy
First Sharecropper . . . . .John McAlpine
Second Sharecropper . . . . .Byron Clark
Susan Mahoney . . . . .Alicia Krug
Henry . . . . .Joe Finn
Third Sharecropper . . . . .Ann Curran
Finian McLonergan . . . . .William Flatley

Second Gospeleer . . . . .Dale Smith
Third Gospeleer . . . . .Harry Arnold
Deputy . . . . .Veal Orr
Chorus:
Harry Arnold, Byron Clark, Ann Curran,
Richard Gould, Anne Hampton, Mary Jo
Henderson, John McAlpine, Teri Robin, Irene
Ryan, Billie Sanders, Dale Smith, Phyllis Smith,
Sonia Valler, Michael Wilsie

#48
August 12 - 16, 1952
The Great Big Doorstep
by Frances Goodrick and Albert Hackett
Directed by Jack P. Ragotzy
CAST

Evvie Crochet . . . . .Sonia Valler
Topal Crochet . . . . .Mary Jo Henderson
Mrs. Crochet . . . . .Jean Henderson
Gussie Crochet . . . . .Joe Finn
Paul Crochet . . . . .Robert Henderson
Arthur Crochet . . . . .John McAlpine
Mr. Tobin . . . . .Arvid Nelson
Commodore . . . . .Leon B. Stevens
Mr. Dupre . . . . .Louis Cutelli
Tayo Delacroix . . . . .Michael Capanna
Dewey Crochet . . . . .Milt Hamerman
Mrs. Beaumont Crochet . . . . .Ann Curran

#49
August 19 - 23, 1952
The Gorilla
by Ralph Spence
Directed by Howard Chenery
CAST

Jefferson Lee . . . . .Harry Arnold
Cyrus Stevens . . . . .Leon B. Stevens
Alice Denby . . . . .Irene Ryan
Arthur Marsden . . . . .Michael Capanna
Mr. Milligan . . . . .Milt Hamerman
Mr. Garrity . . . . .Louis Cutelli
Simmons . . . . .Betty Ebert
The Stranger . . . . .Arvid Nelson
A Sailor . . . . .John McAlpine
Poe . . . . .Byron Clark
Dr. Wilner . . . . .Michael Wilsie

#50
August 26 - September 6, 1952
The Rose Tattoo
by Tennessee Williams
Directed by Jack P. Ragotzy
CAST

Bruno . . . . .Joe Finn
Salvatore . . . . .Robert Henderson
Assunta . . . . .Jean Henderson
Rosa Della Rose . . . . .Teri Robin
Serafina Della Rose . . . . .Ann Curran

#51-A
September 9 - 13, 1952
The Orangutang
by Tom Tiler
Directed by Arvid Nelson
CAST

Lt. Larry Schwartz . . . . .Arvid Nelson
Lt. Glenn "Horse" Tiedeman . . . . .Michael Capanna
"Doc" Stollar, Lt., U.S.N . . . . .Leon B. Stevens
Lt. Sam Berry . . . . .Harry Dorman
Lt. Joe Santa-Marie . . . . .Milt Hamerman
Capt. Gerald Perkins . . . . .Veal Orr

#51-B
September 9 - 13, 1952
The Respectful Prostitute
by Jean-Paul Sartre
Directed by Jack P. Ragotzy
CAST

Lizzie . . . . .Betty Ebert
Negro . . . . .Milt Hamerman
Fred . . . . .Arvid Nelson
John . . . . .Michael Capanna
Senator . . . . .Leon B. Stevens
Man . . . . .Harry Dorman
Second Man . . . . .Veal Orr

1953 Season

#52
June 23 - July 5, 1953
Stalag 17
by Donald Bevan and Edmund Trzcinski
Directed by Jack P. Ragotzy
Lights - Patricia Sikes
Costumes - Mary Beth Moore, Marianne Ringe
CAST

1st Guard . . . . .Ed Phelps
Stosh .William Bramley
Harry Shapiro . . . . .Louis Cutelli
Price . . . . .John Dutra
Herb Gordon . . . . .Harry Dorman
Hoffman .Louis Girard
Sefton . . . . .Michael Capanna
Duke . . . . .Larry Simpson
McCarthy .Lee Swanson
Horney . . . . .Dirk Wales
Marko . . . . .Joel Hepner
Corporal Shultz . . . . .Charles Zeeman
Dunbar . . . . .William Sollner
Reed . . . . .Bob Hamilton
Red-Dog . . . . .John Scudder
German Captain . . . . .Jack Ragotzy
Geneva Man . . . . .Howard Chenery

#53
July 7 - 19, 1953
The Moon Is Blue
by F. Hugh Herbert
Directed by Jack P. Ragotzy
Lights - Lee Swanson
Special Art Work by Art Crain, Helen Crain
CAST
Patty O'Neill . . . . .Carole McCrory
Donald Gresham . . . . .John Dutra
David Slater . . . . .Louis Girard
Michael O'Neill . . . . .William Bramley

#54
July 21 - 26, 1953
Point of No Return
by Paul Osborn
(based on the novel by John P. Marquand)
Directed and Designed by Jack P. Ragotzy
Lighting by Dirk Wales
Costumes by Jerre Locke
CAST
Malcolm Bryant . . . . .Louis Girard
Evelyn Gray . . . . .Jo Ann Reed
Nancy Gray . . . . .Betty Ebert
Bill Gray . . . . .Joe Finn
Charles Gray . . . . .John Dutra
Joe . . . . .William Sollner
Miss Marble . . . . .Pat Sikes
Miss Dingle . . . . .Jerry Locke
First Teller . . . . .Irene Ryan
Second Teller . . . . .Mary Beth Moore
Hazel .Marianne Ringe
Miriam . . . . .Araxi Arabian
Robert Blakesley . . . . .Michael Capanna
Mr. Burton . . . . .William Bramley
Conductor . . . . .Harry Dorman
Jackie Mason . . . . .Jack P. Ragotzy
Jessica Lovell . . . . .Carole McCrory
Laurence Lovell . . . . .Howard Chenery
John Gray . . . . .Louis Cutelli
Tailor . . . . .Larry Simpson
Esther Gray . . . . .Nina Carroll
Man on Train . . . . .Dirk Wales
Mrs. Burton . . . . .Mary Van Fleet

#55
July 28 - August 2, 1953
Season in the Sun
by Wolcott Gibbs
Directed and Designed by Jack P. Ragotzy
Lighting by Jerre Locke
Costumes by Araxi Arabian
CAST
George Crane . . . . .Michael Capanna
Emily Crane . . . . .Betty Ebert
Billy Crane . . . . .Joe Finn
Marcia Crane . . . . .Jo Ann Reed
Mae Jermyn . . . . .Mary Beth Moore
Charles Farber . . . . .Dirk Wales
Michael Lindsay . . . . .Louis Cutelli
Paul Anderson . . . . .William Bramley
Virginia Anderson . . . . .Irene Ryan
Deedy Barton . . . . .Carole McCrory
John Colgate . . . . .John Dutra
Molly Burden . . . . .Mary Van Fleet
Horace William Dodd . . . . .Louis Girard
Will Quigley . . . . .Harry Dorman
Messenger Boy . . . . .Lee Swanson

#56
August 4 - 8, 1953
Summer and Smoke
by Tennessee Williams
Directed by Howard Chenery
Set Designed by Jack P. Ragotzy
Lighting by Dirk Wales
Costumes by Irene Ryan, Louis Cutelli
CAST
Rev. Winemiller . . . . .Louis Girard
Mrs. Winemiller . . . . .Mary Van Fleet
John Buchanan . . . . .Michael Capanna
Pearl .Araxi Arabian
Dusty .Lee Swanson
Dr. Buchanan . . . . .Howard Chenery
Alma Winemiller . . . . .Betty Ebert
Nellie Ewell . . . . .Carole McCrory
Rosa Gonzales . . . . .Mary Beth Moore
Roger Doremus . . . . .Louis Cutelli
Mrs. Bassett . . . . .Nina Carroll
Rosemary .Irene Ryan
Vernon .Larry Simpson
Papa Gonzales . . . . .William Bramley
Archie Kramer . . . . .Harry Dorman

#57
August 11 - 15, 1953
I Am a Camera
by John Van Druten
(adapted from *The Berlin Stories*
by Christopher Isherwood)
Directed and Scenic Design by Jack P. Ragotzy
Lighting by Dirk Wales
Costumes by Araxi Arabian
CAST
Christopher Isherwood . . . . .John Dutra
Fraulein Schneider . . . . .Nina Carroll
Fritz Wendel . . . . .Louis Girard
Sally Bowles . . . . .Carole McCrory
Natalia Landauer . . . . .Mary Van Fleet
Clive Mortimer . . . . .William Bramley
Mrs. Watson-Courtneidge . . . . .Betty Ebert

#58
August 18 - 29, 1953
The Member of the Wedding
by Carson McCullers
from her novel of the same name
Directed and Designed by Jack P. Ragotzy
Lighting by Dirk Wales
Costumes by Jo Ann Reed
CAST
Jarvis . . . . John Dutra
Frankie Addams . . . . .Carole McCrory
Janice . . . . .Mary Beth Moore
Berenice Sadie Brown . . . . .Mattie Willis
Royal Addams . . . . .Louis Girard
John Henry West . . . . .Joe Finn
Mrs. West . . . . .Mary Van Fleet
Helen Fletcher . . . . .Marianne Ringe
Doris . . . . .Jo Ann Reed
Sis Laura . . . . .Araxi Arabian
T.T. Williams . . . . .William Bramley
Honey Camden Brown . . . . .Harry Dorman
Barney McKean . . . . .Lee Swanson

#59
September 1 - 5, 1953
The Male Animal
by James Thurber and Elliott Nugent
Directed by Howard Chenery
Set Designed by Jack P. Ragotzy
Lighting by Dirk Wales
Costumes by Araxi Arabian
CAST
Cleota . . . . .Mary Beth Moore
Ellen Turner . . . . .Betty Ebert
Tommy Turner . . . . .Louis Girard
Patricia Stanley . . . . .Carole McCrory
Wally Myers . . . . .Dirk Wales
Dean Frederick Damon . . . . .Larry Simpson
Michael Barnes . . . . .Harry Dorman
Joe Ferguson . . . . .Michael Capanna
Blanche Damon . . . . .Mary Van Fleet
Ed Keller . . . . .William Bramley
Myrtle Keller . . . . .Nina Carroll
"Nutsy" Miller . . . . .Lee Swanson
Newspaper Reporter . . . . .John Dutra

#60
September 8 - 12, 1953
The Shrike
by Joseph Kramm
Directed and Designed by Jack P. Ragotzy
Lighting by Dirk Wales
Costumes by Jo Ann Endres
CAST
Miss Cardell . . . . .Jo Ann Reed
Fleming . . . . .William Sollner
Miss Hansen . . . . .Jo Ann Endres
Dr. Kramer . . . . .John Dutra
Perkins . . . . .Larry Simpson
Grosberg .Ed Phelps
Dr. Barrow . . . . .Mary Van Fleet
Patient . . . . .Dale Campbell
Ann Downs . . . . .Betty Ebert
Jim Downs . . . . .Louis Girard
Dr. Schlesinger . . . . .William Bramley
Miss Gregory . . . . .Mary Beth Moore
Sam Tager . . . . .Dirk Wales
George O'Brien . . . . .Harry Dorman
Joe Major . . . . .William Brambley
John Ankoritis . . . . .Michael Capanna
Frank Carlisle . . . . .Larry Simpson
William Schloss . . . . .Dale Campbell
Dr. Bellman . . . . .Jack P. Ragotzy
Miss Wingate . . . . .Nina Carroll
Harry Downs . . . . .Ed Phelps
Tom Blair . . . . .William Sollner
Mrs. Ankoritis . . . . .Araxi Arabin
Visitor . . . . .Jan Foley

#61
September 15 - 19, 1953
Separate Rooms
by Joseph Carole and Alan Dinehart
in collaboration with Alex Gottlieb
and Edmund Joseph
Directed by Louis Girard
Set Designed by Jack P. Ragotzy
Lighting by Dirk Wales
CAST
Gary Byrce . . . . .Harry Dorman
Taggart . . . . .Louis Girard
Don Stackhouse . . . . .Jack P. Ragotzy
Scoop Davis . . . . .Dirk Wales
Pamela Barry . . . . .Betty Ebert
Jim Stackhouse . . . . .William Bramley
Linda Roberts . . . . .Mary Beth Moore
Leona Sharpe . . . . .Jan Foley
Mr. Chito Montoya: Estrella's Wee Winkie
(Courtesy of P.U.P.S. Kennel)

1954 Season

#62
June 22 - July 3, 1954
Mister Roberts
by Thomas Heggen and Joshua Logan
Based on a novel by Thomas Heggen
Directed and Set Designed by Jack P. Ragotzy
Lighting by Mary Van Fleet and John Berke
Costumes - Anne Linden and Dawn Birch
CAST
Chief Johnson . . . . .Edwin Phelps
Lieutenant (JG) Roberts . . . . .James T. Pritchett
Doc .Leon B. Stevens
Dowdy . . . . .John Newton
The Captain . . . . .William Bramley
Insigna . . . . .Jack Ragotzy
Mannion . . . . .Larry Ward
Lindstrom . . . . .Harold Ballou
Stefanowski . . . . .Dirk Wales
Wiley .Norman Kean
Schlemmer . . . . .John Scudder
Ensign Pulver . . . . .Gordon Russell
Dolan .Harry Dorman
Lieutenant Ann Girard . . . . .April Kent
Shore Patrolman . . . . .John Berke
Military Policeman . . . . .Philip Lussier
Shore Patrol Officer . . . . .William Sollner

#63
July 6 - 10, 1954
[World Premiere]
Rhom
by Larry Ward and Gordon Russell
Directed by Jack P. Ragotzy
Set Designed by Dirk Wales
Lighting by John Berke
Costumes by Betty Bogan
CAST
Lieutenant Curtis . . . . .Norman Kean
Sergeant Bill Travers . . . . .William Sollner
PFC Arthur Grant . . . . .John Newton
Pat Linder . . . . .Jo Anna March
PFC Watkins . . . . .Harry Dorman
Sergeant Frank Morris . . . . . . .William Bramley
First Guard . . . . .Harold Ballou
Sergeant Major Karl Rhom . . James T. Pritchett
Staff Sergeant Duffy . . . . .Edwin Phelps
Major Tom Sekerik . . . . .Jack Ragotzy
Colonel John Blake . . . . .Leon B. Stevens
Laura Blake . . . . .Betty Ebert
Master Sergeant Ferris . . . . .Philip Lussier
The Inspector General . . . . .Al Hinckley
Second Guard . . . . .Dirk Wales

#64
July 13 - 17, 1954
My Three Angels
by Sam and Bella Spewack
(Based on *La Cuisine des Anges*
by Albert Husson)
Directed and Set Designed by Jack P. Ragotzy
Lighting by Dirk Wales and Harold Ballou
Costumes by Dawn Birch and Mary Patton
Scenic Artists - Art Crain and Helen Crain
CAST
Felix Ducotel . . . . .Al Hinckley
Emilie Ducotel . . . . .Mary Van Fleet
Marie Louise Ducotel . . . . .April Kent
Mme. Parole . . . . .Brian Moore
Joseph . . . . .Leon B. Stevens
Jules . . . . .John Newton
Alfred . . . . .James T. Pritchett
Henri Trochard . . . . .William Bramley

Paul . . . . .Harry Dorman
Lieutenant . . . . .Dirk Wales

#65
July 20 - 31, 1954
The Fourposter
by Jan de Hartog
Directed by Jack P. Ragotzy
Set Designed by Jack P. Ragotzy and Dirk Wales
Lighting by Dirk Wales and Ann Linden
Costumes Designed by Dusty Reeds
Scenic Artists: Art Crain and Helen Crain
CAST
Agnes . . . . .Betty Ebert
Michael .John Newton

#66
August 3 - 7, 1954
[World Premiere]
Desire Is a Season
by Joseph G. Stockdale, Jr.
Directed and Set Design by Jack P. Ragotzy
Lighting by Dirk Wales and Betty Bogan
Costumes by Phillip Lussier
CAST
Agnes Saunook . . . . .Ginger Russell
"Chief" Saunook . . . . .William Bramley
Jim Tagua . . . . .John Newton
Virgil Downs . . . . .Leon B. Stevens
Lee Saunook . . . . .Norman Kean
Woman Tourist . . . . .Mary Patton
2nd Woman Tourist . . . . .Jo Anna March
Ann Saunook . . . . .Betty Ebert
Male Tourist . . . . .Edwin Phelps, Jr.
Bus Driver . . . . .Gordon Russell
Miss Whiting . . . . .Mary Van Fleet
Mike Eaton . . . . .James T. Pritchett
Mr. Jennet . . . . .Al Hinckley
Walt . . . . .Dirk Wales
Slim . . . . .Harry Dorman
2nd Male Tourist . . . . .Philip Lussier
Indian Woman . . . . .Brian Moore
2nd Indian Woman . . . . .Anne Linden
Indian Man . . . . .Harold Ballou
2nd Indian Man . . . . .George Spelvin

#67
August 10 - 21, 1954
For Love or Money
by F. Hugh Herbert
Directed by Leon B. Stevens
Designed by Dirk Wales
Lighting by Dirk Wales and Patti Putt
Costumes by Jo Anna March
CAST
Mrs. Tremaine . . . . .Brian Moore
Bill Tremaine . . . . .Harry Dorman
Mr. Tremaine . . . . .William Bramley
Mrs. Early . . . . .Mary Van Fleet
Wilbur .John Newton
Nita Havemeyer . . . . .Betty Ebert
Preston Mitchell . . . . .James T. Pritchett
Janet Blake . . . . .Ginger Russell

#68
August 24 - September 4, 1954
Mrs. McThing
by Mary Chase
Directed by Jack P. Ragotzy
Designed by Dirk Wales, Dusty Reeds
and Jack P. Ragotzy
Lighting by Dirk Wales and Norman Kean

Scenic Artist - Dusty Reeds
Costumes by Brian Moore
CAST
Mrs. Howard V. Larue III . . . . .Mary Van Fleet
Carrie .Brian Moore
Sybil . . . . .Ginger Russell
Maude Lewis . . . . .Jo Anna March
Grace Lewis . . . . .Mary Patton
Eva Lewis . . . . .Dusty Reeds
Nelson . . . . .James T. Pritchett
Boy . . . . .Joe Finn
Ellsworth . . . . .Leon B. Stevens
Virgil . . . . .John Newton
Dirty Joe . . . . .Harry Dorman
The Stinker . . . . .Dirk Wales
Poison Eddie Schellenbach . . .William Bramley
Mrs. Schellenbach . . . . .Betty Bogan
Howay . . . . .Joe Finn
Mimi . . . . .Diane Ellis
Mrs. McThing (a witch) . . . . .Anne Linden
Mrs. McThing (a witch) . . . . . . .Miss Linden
Bert .Harold Bellou
Second Policeman . . . . .Norman Kean

#69
September 7 - 11, 1954
Anna Lucasta
by Philip Yordan
Directed by Leon B. Stevens
Designed by Jack P. Ragotzy
Lighting by Dirk Wales and Philip Lussier
Costumes by Mary Van Fleet
CAST
Katie . . . . .Anne Linden
Stella . . . . .Brian Moore
Theresa . . . . .Mary Van Fleet
Stanley . . . . .Harry Dorman
Frank . . . . .William Bramley
Joe . . . . .John Newton
Eddy . . . . .Dirk Wales
Noah . . . . .Leon B. Stevens
Blanche .Betty Ebert
Officer . . . . .Edwin Phelps, Jr.
Anna . . . . .Ginger Russell
Danny . . . . .James T. Pritchett
Lester .Harold Ballou
Rudolf . . . . .Norman Kean

#70
September 14 - 18, 1954
Petticoat Fever
by Mark Reed
Directed and Designed by Jack P. Ragotzy
Lighting by Dirk Wales
Scenic artists: Art Crain and Helen Crain
Costumes - Mary Van Fleet
CAST
Dascom Dinsmore . . . . .James T. Pritchett
Kimo .Harry Dorman
Sir James Fenton . . . . .William Bramley
Ethel Campion . . . . .Ginger Russell
Little Seal . . . . .Brian Moore
Snow Bird . . . . .Jo Anna March
The Reverend
Arthur Shapham . . . . .John Newton
Captain John Landry . . . . .Dirk Wales
Scotty . . . . .Philip Lussier
Clara Wilson . . . . .Betty Ebert

#71
September 21 - October 2, 1954
The Little Hut

by Andre Roussin
(Adapted from the French by Nancy Mitford)
Directed by Jack P. Ragotzy
Designed by Dirk Wales amd Dusty Reeds
Lights by Dirk Wales
CAST
Henry ....William Bramley
Susan ....Betty Ebert
Philip ....John Newton
Stranger ....James T. Pritchett

1955 Season

#72
June 14 - 26, 1955
Oh, Men! Oh, Women!
by Edward Choderov
Directed by Jack P. Ragotzy
Set Design by Dusty Reeds
Lighting by Arvid Nelson
and Rudy Chromchak
Costumes by Cathy Shaw
CAST
Alan Coles ....James T. Pritchett
Miss Tacher ....Jo Anna March
Grant Cobbler ....John Newton
Myra Hagerman ....Ellen Madison
Dr. Krauss ....Al Hinckley
Mildred Turner ....Betty Ebert
Arthur Turner ....William Trotman
Steward ....Harry Dorman

#73
June 28 - July 3, 1955
Dial "M" for Murder
by Frederick Knott
Directed by Jack P. Ragotzy
Set Designed by Dusty Reeds
Lighting by Arvid Nelson
CAST
Margot Wendice ....Betty Ebert
Max Halliday ....Arvid Nelson
Tony Wendice ....James T. Pritchett
Captain Lesgate ....Al Hinckley
Inspector Hubbard ....John Newton
Thompson ....William Trotman

#74
July 5 - 25, 1955
Guys and Dolls
Based on a story and characters
by Damon Runyon
Music and Lyrics by Frank Loesser
Book by Jo Swerling and Abe Burrows
Directed by Rinaldo Capillupo
Choreographed by Wayne Lamb
Sets and Costumes designed by Dusty Reeds
Lighting by Grant Baxter and Paxton Stratton
At the Piano: Monte Aubrey
On the Bass: Robert Sanders
CAST
Nicely-Nicely Johnson ....Otto Lohmann
Benny Southstreet ....Jack Ragotzy
Rusty Charlie ....Boyd Dumrose
Sarah Brown ....Cindy Arnold
Arvide Abernathy ....Harry Dorman
Mission Band:
Mary Patton, Gary Kloppenburg,
Rinaldo Capillupo
Harry the Horse ....William Trotman
Lt. Brannigan ....Al Hinckley
Nathan Detroit ....John Newton
Angie the Ox ....Avid Nelson
Miss Adelaide ....Carol Doughty
Sky Masterson ....James T. Pritchett
Joey Biltmore ....Jack Fisher
Mimi ....Dona Cauthen
Hot Box Girls:
Betty Ebert, Jo Anna March, Mary Patton,
Dona Cauthen
Scarecrow ....Wayne Lamb
Poodles ....Siren and Folly
General Matilda B.
Cartwright ....Dusty Reeds
Big Jule ....Ray Barbata
Crap Game Dancers:
Wayne Lamb, Rudy Chromchak, Boyd Dumrose,
Henry Edid, Gary Kloppenburg
The Ensemble:
Richard Bailey, Dona Cauthen, Rudy
Chromchak, Boyd Dumrose, Henry Edid, Jack
Fisher, Gary Kloppenburg, Marcia Laurence,
Ellen Madison, Jo Anna March, Arvid Nelson,
Mary Patton, Cathy Shaw, Vera Stough,
William Trotman

#75
July 26 - 31, 1955
The Caine Mutiny Court-Martial
by Herman Wouk
(Based on his novel *The Caine Mutiny*)
Directed by Jack P. Ragotzy
Lighting by Gary Kloppenburg
CAST
Lt. Stephen Marky ....Arvid Nelson
Lt. Barney Greenwald ......James T. Pritchett
Lt. Com. John Challee ......William Trotman
Captain Blakely ....Al Hinckley
Lt. Com. Philip Francis
Queeg ....John Newton
Lt. Thomas Keefer ....Monte Aubrey
Signalman 3rd Class
Junius Urban ....Harry Dorman
Lt. (J.G.) Willis Keith ......Gary Kloppenburg
Capt. Randolph Southard ....Ray Barbata
Dr. Forrest Lundeen ....Jack P. Ragotzy
Dr. Bird ....Rudy Chromchak
Stenographer-Orderly ....Henry Edid
Members of the Court:
Richard Bailey, Art Crain, Boyd Dumrose,
Jack Fisher

#76
August 2 - 7, 1955
The Remarkable Mr. Pennypacker
by Liam O'Brien
Directed by Jack P. Ragotzy
Designed by Dusty Reeds
Lights by Boyd Dumrose, Gary Kloppenburg
Costumes by Mary Patton
CAST
Laurie Pennypacker ....Vera Stough
1st Pupil ....Mary Patton
2nd Pupil ....Dona Cauthen
David Pennypacker ....Joe Finn
Edwina Pennypacker ....Diane Ellis
Elizabeth Pennypacker ......Marcia Laurence
Aunt Jane Pennypacker ....Dusty Reeds
Wilbur Fifield ....James Pritchett
Kate Pennypacker ....Jo Anna March
Ma Pennypacker ....Betty Ebert
Henry Pennypacker ....Gary Kloppenburg
Teddie Pennypacker ....Richard Bailey
Grampa Pennypacker ....Al Hinckley
Quinlan ....Rudy Chromchak
A Young Man ....Harry Dorman
Dr. Fifield ....Ray Barbata
Sheriff ....William Trotman
Pa Pennypacker ....John Newton
Policeman ....Henry Edid

#77
August 9 - 14, 1955
Gigi
by Anita Loos
adapted from the novel by Colette
Directed by Jack P. Ragotzy
Designed by Boyd Dumrose
Lighting by Arvid Nelson and Henry Edid
Costumes by Dusty Reeds, Jo Anna March and
Dona Cauthen
CAST
Gigi ....Ellen Madison
Mme. Alvarez ....Mary Patton
Andree ....Betty Ebert
Gaston LaChaille ....James T. Pritchett
Victor ....John Newton
Alicia De St. Ephlam ....Dusty Reeds
Sidonie ....Dona Cauthen

#78
August 16 - 21, 1955
Dear Charles
by Alan Melville
Directed by Jack P. Ragotzy
Set Designed by Dusty Reeds
Lighting by Arvid Nelson, Richard Bailey
Costumes by Marcia Laurence
CAST
Martha ....Mary Patton
Walter ....Rudy Chromchak
Bruno ....Harry Dorman
Edward ....Al Hinckley
Dolores ....Betty Ebert
Martine ....Jo Anna March
Sir Michael Anstruther ....John Newton
Jan Letzaresco ....James T. Pritchett
Jeffrey ....Arvid Nelson
Madame Bouchemin ....Dusty Reeds
Lucienne ....Vera Stough
Jean-Pierre ....Monte Aubrey

#79
August 23 - September 4, 1955
The Fifth Season
by Sylvia Regan
Directed by Jack P. Ragotzy
Set Designed by Arvid Nelson
and Boyd Dumrose
Lighting by Harold Ballou
CAST
Ruby D. Prince ....Monte Aubrey
Shelly ....Dona Cauthen
Lorraine McKay ....Jo Anna March
Ferelli ....Henry Edid
Max Pincus ....John Newton
Johnny Goodwin ....James Pritchett
Frances Goodwin ....Dusty Reeds
Marty Goodwin ....Harry Dorman
Miriam Oppenheim ....Betty Ebert
Dolores ....Mary Patton
Midge ....Cindy Arnold
Carol ....Vera Stough
Miles Lewis ....William Trotman

#80
September 6 - 11, 1955
The Rainmaker
by N. Richard Nash
Directed by Jack P. Ragotzy
CAST
H.C. Curry . . . . .John Newton
Noah Curry . . . . .William Trotman
Jim Curry . . . . .Harold Ballou
Lizzie Curry . . . . .Betty Ebert
File . . . . .Arvid Nelson
Sheriff Thomas . . . . .Monte Aubrey
Bill Starbuck . . . . .James T. Pritchett

#81
September 13 - 25, 1955
Tobacco Road
by Jack Kirkland
(adapted from the novel by Erskine Caldwell)
Directed by Jack P. Ragotzy
Set and Lighting by Arvid Nelson
Costumes by Betty Ebert
CAST
Dude Lester . . . . .Harry Dorman
Ada Lester . . . . .Dusty Reeds
Jeeter Lester . . . . .John Newton
Ellie May . . . . .Ruth Clason
Grandma Lester . . . . .Betty Ebert
Lov Bensey . . . . .James Pritchett
Henry Peabody . . . . .Arvid Nelson
Sister Bessie Rice . . . . .Dona Cauthen
Pearl . . . . .Jo Anna March
Captain Tim . . . . .Gary Kloppenburg
George Payne . . . . .William Trotman

#82
September 27 - October 2, 1955
The Tender Trap
by Max Shulman and Robert Paul Smith
Directed by Jack P. Ragotzy
Set Designed by Dusty Reeds
Lights by Arvid Nelson
CAST
Charlie Reader . . . . .John Newton
Poppy Matson . . . . .Dona Cauthen
Joe McCall . . . . .James Pritchett
Jessica Collins . . . . .Dusty Reeds
Sylvia Crewes . . . . .Betty Ebert
Julie Gillis . . . . .Jo Anna March
Earl Lindquist . . . . .Harry Dorman
Sol Schwartz . . . . .Arvid Nelson

[End of 1st 10 Years]
1956 Season

#83
June 12 - 17, 1956
Reclining Nude
by Harry Kurnitz
Directed by Jack P. Ragotzy
Set Designed by Dusty Reeds
Lighting by Robert Cadman
Costumes by Gay Kleimenhagen
and Donna Herr
CAST
Wilma . . . . .Gay Kleimenhagen
Samuel Ellis . . . . .Jon Cypher
Cass Edgerton . . . . .Jane McArthur
Lucas Edgerton . . . . .John Newton
Agramonte . . . . .Robert Turoff
Paul Weldon . . . . .Al Hinckley
Jonas Astorg . . . . .Edwin Barron
Denesco . . . . .Harry Dorman
Dr. Hickey . . . . .George Vafiadis
Professor Jumelle . . . . .Vito De Marzo

#84
June 19 - July 1, 1956
A Girl Can Tell
by F. Hugh Herbert
Directed by Jack P. Ragotzy
Sets by Dusty Reeds, Boyd Dumrose,
Robert Cadman and Jack Herr
Lighting by Richard Foose and Joseph Ritacco
Costumes by Gay Kleimenhagen
and Donna Herr
CAST
Hannah . . . . .Dusty Reeds
Nancy .Vera Stough
Vernon . . . . .Richard Foose
Jennifer Goodall . . . . .Jane McArthur
Artie .Harry Dorman
Mr. Benton . . . . .Al Hinckley
Mrs. Benton . . . . .Betty Ebert
Bill . . . . .Jon Cypher
Freddie . . . . .Robert Turoff
George . . . . .Edwin Barron
J.G. . . . . .John Newton
Nathasha . . . . .Karen Lauridsen
Emmett . . . . .George Vafiadis
Man (phone voice) . . . . .Vito De Marzo
David (phone voice) . . . . .Herbert Kline
D.F. (phone voice) . . . . .George Wasko

#85
July 3 - 8, 1956
Champagne Complex
by Leslie Stevens
Directed by Jack P. Ragotzy
Set by Boyd Dumrose and Jack Ragotzy
Lighting by Boyd Dumrose
CAST
Helms Fells Harper . . . . .Edwin Barron
Allyn Macy . . . . .Jane McArthur
Carter Brown . . . . .John Newton

#86
July 10 - 29, 1956
Annie Get Your Gun
Music and Lyrics by Irving Berlin
Book by Herbert and Dorothy Fields
Directed by Rinaldo Capillupo
Choreographed by Wayne Lamb
Set Design by Boyd Dumrose
Lighting by Art Crain and Boyd Dumrose
Costumes by Dusty Reeds
At the Piano: Rianaldo Capillupo
and Larry Wolfe
On the Bass, Robert Sanders
CAST
Charlie Davenport . . . . .Jack Ragotzy
Mac (Property Man) . . . . .George Wasco
Foster Wilson . . . . .Harry Dorman
Dolly Tate . . . . .Jean Thomas
Winnie Tate . . . . .Nancy Holt
Tommy Keeler . . . . .Angelo Mango
Frank Butler . . . . .Jon Cypher
Bad Bad Girls:
Betty Ebert, Anne Crowell, Ann Stinchcomb,
Jane McArthur, Lila Johnson
Bad Bad Dream Man . . . . .Wayne Lamb
Annie Oakley . . . . .Carol Doughty
Jessie . . . . .Vera Stough
Nellie . . . . .Diane Ellis
Little Jake . . . . .Joe Finn
Col. Wm. F. Cody
(Buffalo Bill) . . . . .John Newton
Mrs. Little Horse . . . . .Mimi MacBaisey
Conductor . . . . .Robert Turoff
Waiter . . . . .Robert Cadman
Trainman .Jack Herr
Maj. Gordon Lillie
(Pawnee Bill) . . . . .Edwin Barron
Sitting Bull . . . . .Alfred Hinckley
Delegation from Gun Club:
Boyd Dumrose, Robert Turoff, Robert Cadman,
Jack Herr
The Wild Horse . . . . .Wayne Lamb
Indian Chanter . . . . .Gay Kleimenhagen
Ceremonial Indians:
George Vafiadis, Joseph Ritacco, Herbert Kline,
Richard Foose, Vito De Marzo, Robert Turoff,
Lila Johnson, Ann Crowell, Ann Stinchcomb,
Jane McArthur
Pawnee's Messenger . . . . .Boyd Dumrose
Mrs. Sylvia Potter-Porter . . . . .Karen Lauridsen
Mr. Henderson . . . . .Richard Foose
Mrs. Henderson . . . . .Lila Johnson
A Gentleman . . . . .Vito De Marzo
A Cowboy . . . . .Herbert Kline
Mousey . . . . .George Vafiadis

#87
July 31 - August 5, 1956
[World Premiere]
The Painted Days
by John Byrne
Directed by Jack P. Ragotzy
Set Designed by Dusty Reeds
Lighting by Richard Foose and Jack Herr
Costumes by Karen Lauridsen and Vera Stough
CAST
Stacy . . . . .Betty Ebert
Tom Foley . . . . .Edwin Barron
Brigit . . . . .Dusty Reeds
Martin Laurey . . . . .John Newton
Julia .Jane McArthur
Tim . . . . .Jon Cypher
Giddap O'Dea . . . . .Al Hinckley
Dr. Mooney . . . . .Harry Dorman
Micko . . . . .Robert Turoff

#88
August 7 - 12, 1956
The Seven Year Itch
by George Axelrod
Directed by Jack P. Ragotzy
Set Design by Boyd Dumrose
Lighting by Richard Foose and Boyd Dumrose
Costumes by Karen Lauridsen and Nancy Holt
CAST
Richard Sherman . . . . .John Newton
Helen Sherman . . . . .Betty Ebert
Miss Morris . . . . .Anne Crowell
Elaine . . . . .Nancy Holt
Marie What-ever-her-
name-was . . . . .Karen Lauridsen
The Girl . . . . .Jane McArthur
Dr. Brubaker . . . . .Edwin Barron
Tom Mackenzie . . . . .Jon Cypher
The Voice of Richard's
Conscience . . . . .Jack Herr
The Voice of the Girl's
Conscience . . . . .Vera Stough

#89
August 14 - 26, 1956
Tea and Sympathy
by Robert Anderson
Directed by Jack P. Ragotzy
Set Designed by Boyd Dumrose
Lighting by Joseph Ritacco, and Jack Herr
Costumes by Mimi MacBaisey
CAST

Laura Reynolds	Betty Ebert
Lilly Sears	Dusty Reeds
Tom Lee	Harry Dorman
David Harris	Edwin Barron
Ralph	George Vafiadis
Al	Robert Cadman
Steve	Richard Foose
Bill Reynolds	John Newton
Phil	Herbert Kline
Herbert Lee	Al Hinckley
Paul	Joseph Ritacco

#90
August 28 - September 9, 1956
Where's Charley?
Music and Lyrics by Frank Loesser
Book by George Abbott
Based on Brandon Thomas' *Charley's Aunt*
Directed by Rinaldo Capillupo
Choreographed by Wayne Lamb
Set and Costumes Designed by Dusty Reeds
Lighting by Art Crain, Grant Baxter
and Paxton Stratton
Costumes by Gay Kleimenhagen and
Mimi MacBaisey
Assistant to the Director - Al Hinckley
At the Piano - Rinaldo Capillupo, Larry Wolfe
On the Bass - Robert Sanders
CAST

Brassett	Al Hinckley
Jack Chesney	Angelo Mango
Charley Wykeham	John Newton
Kitty Verdun	Nancy Holt
Amy Spettigue	Karen Lauridsen
Wilkinson	George Wasko
Sir Francis Chesney	Jon Cypher
Mr. Spettigue	Edwin Barron
Drum Majorette	Bobbie Waite
Donna Lucia D'Alvadorez	Gay Kleimenhagen
Lt. Frank Chesney (pas de deux)	Wayne Lamb
Lucy (pas de deux)	Lila Johnson
Photographer	Vito De Marzo

Quartet:
Robert Cadman, Boyd Dumrose, Richard Foose,
Robert Turoff
Gossips:
Anne Crowell, Betty Ebert, Lila Johnson,
Rena Leiter, Mimi MacBaisey, Bobbie Waite
Students and Ladies:
Anne Crowell, Vito De Marzo, Harry Dorman,
Betty Ebert, Richard Foose, Lila Johnson,
Herbert Kline, Rena Leiter, Dusty Reeds,
Joseph Ritacco, George Vafiadis, Bobbie Waite,
Boyd Dumrose

#91
September 11 -16, 1956
A Streetcar Named Desire
by Tennessee Williams
Directed by Jack P. Ragotzy
Set Designed by Boyd Dumrose
Lighting by Dick Foose and Joseph Ritacco
Costumes by Gay Kleimenhagen
and Mimi MacBalsey
CAST

Negro	George Vafiadis
Eunice Hubbel	Dusty Reeds
Stanley Kowalski	Jon Cypher
Harold Mitchell ("Mitch")	John Newton
Stella Kowalski	Karen Lauridsen
Steve Hubbel	Al Hinckley
Blanche DuBois	Betty Ebert
Pablo Gonzales	Vito De Marzo
A Young Collector	Harry Dorman
Mexican Woman	Mimi MacBaisey
A Strange Woman	Anne Crowell
A Strange Man	Edwin Barron

#92
September 18 - 23, 1956
Bus Stop
by William Inge
Directed by Jack P. Ragotzy
Set Designed by Dusty Reeds
Lights by Joseph Ritacco
Costumes by Anne Crowell
CAST

Elma Duckworth	Vera Stough
Grace	Betty Ebert
Will Masters	Edwin Barron
Cherie	Karen Lauridsen
Dr. Gerald Lyman	John Newton
Carl	Al Hinckley
Virgil Blessing	Robert Turoff
Bo Decker	Jon Cypher

#93
September 25 - October 7, 1956
Anniversary Waltz
by Jerome Chodorov and Joseph Fields
Directed by Jack P. Ragotzy
Set Designed by Dusty Reeds
Lights by Joseph Ritacco
CAST

Millie	Anne Crowell
Okkie Walters	Harry Dorman
Alice Walters	Betty Ebert
Debbie Walters	Vera Stough
Bud Walters	John Newton
Chris Steelman	Edwin Barron
Janice Revere	Karen Lauridsen
Harry	Jon Cypher
Sam	Joseph Ritacco
Mr. Gans	Al Hinckley
Mrs. Gans	Dusty Reeds
Handyman	Vito De Marzo
TV Announcer	George Wasko

1957 Season

#94
June 4 - 16, 1957
Will Success Spoil Rock Hunter?
by George Axelrod
Directed by Jack P. Ragotzy
Set Design by Royal Eckert
Lighting by Boyd Dumrose and Richard Foose
Costumes by Dusty Reeds
and Gay Kleimenhagen
Assistant to the director, Alfred Hinckley
CAST

Rita Marlowe	Diane Ladd
Masseur	George Wasko
George MacCauley	Stan Watt
Michael Freeman	John Newton
Irving LaSalle	Louis Girard
Harry Kaye	Alfred Hinckley
A Secretary	Sammy Cauthen
Bronx Brannigan	Gary Kanin
A Chauffeur	Andy Rasbury

#95
June 18 - 23, 1957
A Hatful of Rain
by Michael V. Gazzo
Directed by Jack P. Ragotzy
Lighting by Andy Rasbury and Emmett Jacobs
CAST

John Pope, Sr	Alfred Hinckley
Johnny Pope	Stan Watt
Celia Pope	Betty Ebert
Mother	Louis Girard
Apples	Royal Eckert
Chuch	Gary Kanin
Polo Pope	John Newton
Man	Emmett Jacobs
Putski	Norma Kessler

#96
June 25 - July 7, 1957
Inherit the Wind
by Jerome Lawrence and Robert E. Lee
Directed by Jack P. Ragotzy
Set Designed by Royal Eckert
Lighting by Dona Cauthen
Costumes by Mary Jo Davis
CAST

Howard	Richard Foose
Melinda	Flo Rasbury
Rachel Brown	Sue Jacobs
Meeker	Royal Eckert
Bertram Gates	Andy Rasbury
Mrs. Krebs	Gay Kleimenhagen
Storekeeper	Herbert Kline
Rev. Jeremiah Brown	Alfred Hinckley
Mr. Dunlap	Boyd Dumrose
Mrs. Blair	Jeannette Jung
Miss Cooper	Eleanor Yeager
Hot Dog Man	Wayne Lamb
Mrs. McClain	Dona Cauthen
Bible Man	Rinaldo Capillupo
E.K. Hornbeck	Stan Watt
Mr. Gurdy	Ralph Yelenich
Mayor	Monte Aubrey
Mathew Harrison Brady	Louis Girard
Mrs. Brady	Dusty Reeds
Tom Davenport	Gary Kanin
Photographer	Norma Kessler
Mrs. Foster	Mary Jo Davis
Mrs. Loomis	Betty Ebert
Master Loomis	Robin Reeds
Henry Drummond	John Newton
Judge	George Wasko
Mr. Bannister	James Malloy
Sillers	Emmett Jacobs
Reporter	Virginia Christopher
Miss Platt	Nomi Kluger
Harry Esterbrook	Angelo Mango

#97
July 9 - 28, 1957
The Pajama Game
(Based on the novel *7 1/2 Cents*
by Richard Bissell)
Book by George Abbott and Richard Bissell

Music and Lyrics by Richard Adler
and Jerry Ross
Directed by Rinaldo Capillupo
Choreographed by Wayne Lamb
Set Designed by Dusty Reeds
Lighting Designed by Emmett Jacobs
Costumes by Gay Kleimenhagen
CAST

Hines	John Newton
Prez	Jack Ragotzy
Joe	Gary Kanin
Hasler	Alfred Hinckley
Gladys	Betty Ebert
Sid Sorokin	Alan Ansara
Mabel	Dusty Reeds
1st Helper	Emmett Jacobs
2nd Helper	Herbert Kline
Charley	George Wasko
Babe Williams	Carol Doughty
Mae	Dona Cauthen
Brenda	Gay Kleimenhagen
Poopsie	Eleanor Yeager
Max	Stan Watt
Pop	Louis Girard
Poopsie's Pal	Richard Foose
3rd Helper	Andy Rasbury
4th Helper	Jim Malloy
Midget	Royal Eckert
Waiter	Ralph Yelenich
Apache Dancer	Boyd Dumrose
Steam Heat Boys	Angelo Mango, Wayne Lamb
Mara	Flo Rasbury
Pat	Sue Jacobs
Sandra	Norma Kessler
Sara	Virginia Christopher
Carmen	Jeannette Jung
Ann	Nomi Kluger
Rita	Mary Jo Davis

#98
July 30 - August 4, 1957
[World Premiere]
States with Pretty Names
by Elliott Baker
Directed by Jack P. Ragotzy
Set Designed by Royal Eckert
Lights by Emmett Jacobs
Costumes by Dona Cauthen
CAST

Blanche Merimee	Dona Cauthen
Dr. Oliver Wren	Louis Girard
Bernice Bueler	Sue Jacobs
Rhoda Shilling	Carol Doughty
Lydia Wren	Betty Ebert
Dr. Frederic Voegler	Alfred Hinckley
Dr. Susan Akers	Jeannette Jung
Dr. Andrew Holland	Royal Eckert
Simon Shilling	John Newton
Sergeant Percenti	Emmett Jacobs
Harry Merimee	Stan Watt

#99
August 6 - 18, 1957
South Pacific
Book by Oscar Hammerstein II
and Joshua Logan
Music by Richard Rogers,
Lyrics by Oscar Hammerstein II
Based on James A. Michener's
Tales of the South Pacific
Directed by Rinaldo Capillupo
Choreographed by Wayne Lamb
Sets Designed by Boyd Dumrose
Lights by Emmett Jacobs
Costumes by Norma Kessler
CAST

Ngana	Robin Barlock
Jarana	Wren Barlock
Henry	Herbert Kline
Ensign Nellie Forbush	Carol Doughty
Emile De Becque	John Newton
Bloody Mary	Gay Kleimenhagen
Abner	Boyd Dumrose
Bloody Mary's Assistant	Sue Jacobs
Stewpot	Andy Rasbury
Luther Billis	Alfred Hinckley
Professor	George Wasko
Lt. Joseph Cable, U.S.M.C.	Angelo Mango
Capt. George Brackett, U.S.N.	Royal Eckert
Cmdr. William Harbison, U.S.N	Louis Girard
Yeoman Herbert Quale	Richard Foose
Sgt. Kenneth Johnson	Gary Kanin
Seabee Richard West	James Malloy
Seabee Norton Wise Radio Operator	Herbert Kline
Bob McCaffrey Marine Cpt.	Ralph Yelenich
Hamilton Steeves	Emmett Jacobs
Seaman James Hayes	Wayne Lamb
Ensign Dinah Murphy	Norma Kessler
Ensign Janet MacGregor	Dona Cauthen
Ensign Cora MacRae	Virginia Christopher
Ensign Sue Yeagor	Eleanor Yeager
Ensign Lisa Minnelli	Jeannette Jung
Ensign Connie Walewaka	Mary Jo Davis
Ensign Bessie Noonan	Nomi Kluger
Liat	Flo Rasbury
Lt. Buzz Adams	Gary Kanin

#100
August 20 - 25, 1957
The Desk Set
by William Marchant
Directed by Jack P. Ragotzy
Assistant to the Director, Alfred Hinckley
Set Designed by Boyd Dumrose
Lights by Emmett Jacobs
Costumes by Eleanor Yeager
CAST

Sadel Meyer	Carol Doughty
Peg Costello	Muriel Turk
Ruthie Saylor	Dona Cauthen
Richard Sumner	John Newton
Bunny Watson	Betty Ebert
Abe Cutler	Louis Girard
The Man from Legal	Alfred Hinckley
The Mysterious Lady	Sue Jacobs
Kenny	Herbert Kline
Elsa	Norma Kessler
Elsa's Friend	Richard Foose
Party People	Members of the Barn Company
Pianist	Andy Rasbury
Miss Warriner	Jeannette Jung
A Reporter	Gary Kanin
Photographer	Ralph Yelenich

#101
August 27 - September 1, 1957
Twin Beds
by Margaret Mayo and Salisbury Field
Directed by Louis Girard
Lights by Emmett Jacobs
Costumes by Flo Rasbury
CAST

Harry Hawkins	John Newton
Signor Monti	Alfred Hinckley
Blanche Hawkins	Betty Ebert
Andrew Larkin	Gary Kanin
Amanda Larkin	Flo Rasbury
Signora Monti	Gay Kleimenhagen
Norah	Dona Cauthen

#102
September 3 - 14, 1957
Janus
by Carolyn Green
Directed by Jack P. Ragotzy
Lighting by Andrew Rasbury
Costumes by Nomi Kluger
CAST

Jessica	Betty Ebert
Denny	Louis Girard
Miss Addy	Muriel Turk
Gil	John Newton
Mr. Harper	Alfred Hinckley

1958 Season

#103
June 3 - 8, 1958
Visit to a Small Planet
by Gore Vidal
Directed by Jack P. Ragotzy
Set Designed by Robert Cadman
Lighting by Jack Herr
Costumes by Gay Klimenhagen
CAST

General Tom Powers	Alfred Hinckley
Roger Spelding	Louis Girard
Reba Spelding	Gay Kleimenhagen
Ellen Spelding	Natalie Ross
Conrad Mayberry	Craig Huebing
Kreton	John Newton
Aide	James Barrie
Rosemary	Marshmallow Puddy Tat
Television Technicians	Robert Cadman
	Michael Gleason
Delta 4	James Malloy

#104
June 10 - 15, 1958
The Waltz of the Toreadors
by Jean Anouilh
(English version by Lucienne Hill)
Directed by Jack P. Ragotzy
Set Designed by Dusty Reeds
Lighting by George Stokes
Costumes by Gay Kleimenhagen
CAST

General St. Pe	John Newton
His Wife	Dusty Reeds
Estelle	Natalie Ross
Sidonia	Sue Hopwood
Gaston (his secretary)	Craig Huebing
Mlle. De St. Euverte	Betty Ebert
Mme. Dupont-Fredaine	Gay Kleimenhagen
Doctor Bonfant	Louis Girard
Father Ambrose	Alfred Hinckley
Two Maids	Nanci Hall, Joan Lindstrom

#105
June 17 - 28, 1958
Cat on a Hot Tin Roof
by Tennessee Williams
Directed by Jack P. Ragotzy
Assistant Director - Alfred Hinckley
Set Designed by Robert Cadman
Lighting Design by Emmett Jacobs
Costumes by Peggy Plimmer Stockton
CAST

Lacey	James Barrie
Sookey	Gay Kleimenhagen
Margaret	Natalie Ross
Brick	Craig Huebing
Mae	Betty Ebert
Gooper	John Newton
Big Mama	Dusty Reeds
Dixie	Peggy Plimmer Stockton
Sonny	George Stokes
Buster	Robin Lee Reeds
Big Daddy	Louis Girard
Rev. Tooker	Monte Aubrey
Dr. Baugh	Alfred Hinckley
Brightie	Margaret Nerad
Small	Raphael Le Tourneaut

#106
July 1 - 13, 1958
Damn Yankees
Book by George Abbott and Douglass Wallop
Music & Lyrics by Richard Adler
and Jerry Ross
Based on the novel by Douglas Wallop,
The Year the Yankees Lost the Pennant
Directed by Rinaldo Capillupo
Choreographed by Wayne Lamb
Sets Designed by Dusty Reeds
Lighting by Emmett Jacobs
Costumes by Gay Kleimenhagen
CAST

Meg	Gay Kleimenhagen
Joe Boyd	Louis Girard
Applegate	John Newton
Sister	Harriet Olson
Doris	Sue Hopwood
Joe Hardy	James Barrie
Henry	James Malloy
Sohovik	Bill Montgomery
Linville	Emmett Jacobs
Smokey	Steve Strong
Van Buren	Alfred Hinckley
Rocky	Jack Herr
Gloria	Betty Ebert
Lynch	Doug Streff
Welch	Craig Huebing
Lola	Natalie Ross

Teenage Fan Club:
Nanci Hall, June Frye, George Stokes,
Arlene Avril

Miss Weston	Joan Lindstom
Wayne	Wayne Lamb
Commissioner	James Malloy
Postmaster	Bill Montgomery

Dancers:
Barbara Bassler, Ann Douglas, June Frye, Don
Gilleland, Cherie Graves, Nanci Hall, Raphael
Le Tourneaut, Joan Lindstrom, Margaret Nerad,
Peggy Plimmer Stockton, George Stokes,
Doug Streff, Arlene Avril

#107
July 15 - 27, 1958

Gentlemen Prefer Blondes
(No Program on File)
Music by Jule Styne, Lyrics by Leo Robin
Book by Anita Loos & Joseph Fields,
adapted from the novel by Anita Loos
Directed and Staged by Rinaldo Capillupo
Book directed by Jack P. Ragotzy
Choreographed by Wayne Lamb
Sets Designed by Dusty Reeds
and Robert Cadman
Lights by Emmett Jacobs
Costumes by Peggy Plimmer Stockton
Showgirl Costumes
by Natalie Ross and Wayne Lamb
CAST

Dorothy Shaw	Natalie Ross
A Steward	Doug Streff
Lorelei	Arlene Avril
Pierre (a steward)	Raphael Le Tourneout
Gus Esmond	John Newton
Frank (an Olympic boy)	Bill Montgomery
George (another Olympic boy)	Jack Herr
Sam (another Olympic boy)	Don Gilleland
Bill	Wayne Lamb
Sir Francis Beekman	Alfred Hinckley
Lady Phyllis Beekman	Gay Kleimenhagen
Mrs. Ella Spoffard	Sue Hopwood
Henry Spoffard	James Barrie
Josephus Gage	Robert Cadman
Olympic Man	James Malloy
A Steward	Francis Speed Sattler
Gloria Stark	June Frye
Leon (a valet)	Doug Streff
Robert Le Manteur	Louis Girard
Louis Le Manteur (his son)	Craig Huebing
Maitre D'	James Malloy
Zizi	Peggy Plimmer Stockton
Flower Girl	Carol Medusky
Lamb	Wayne Lamb
Capillupo	Rinaldo Capillupo
Michael	Francis Speed Sattler
Mr. Esmond, Sr	Craig Huebing

Show Girls:
Barbara Bassler, Ann Douglas, Betty Ebert,
Georgia Haag, Margaret Nerad, Joan Lindstrom
Singers:
Don Gilleland, Cherie Graves, Nanci Hall, Jack
Herr, Francis Speed Sattler, Peggy Plimmer
Stockton, George Stokes, Steve Strong

#108
July 29 - August 3, 1958
The Time of the Cuckoo
by Arthur Laurents
Directed by Jack P. Ragotzy
Set Design by Robert Cadman
Lights by Jack Herr
Costumes by Margaret Nerad
CAST

Signora Fioria	Betty Ebert
Eddie Yeager	Craig Huebing
June Yeager	Natalie Ross
Giovanna	Nanci Hall
Leona Samish	Margaret Draper
Mrs. McIlhenny	Gay Kleimenhagen
Mr. McIlhenny	Louis Girard
Mauro	Joe Racz
Renato Di Rossi	John Newton
Vito	George Stokes

#109
August 5 - 10, 1958

Picnic
by William Inge
Directed by Louis Girard
Set by Robert Cadman
Lighting by Emmett Jacobs
Costumes by June Frye
CAST

Mrs. Helen Potts	Gay Kleimenhagen
Hal Carter	Craig Huebing
Millie Owens	Peggy Plimmer Stockton
Bomber	Don Gilleland
Madge Owens	Natalie Ross
Flo Owens	Margaret Draper
Miss Rosemary Sydney	Betty Ebert
Alan Seymour	James Barrie
Irma Kronkite	Sue Hopwood
Christine Schoenwalder	Cherie Graves
Howard Bevans	John Newton

#110
August 12 - 24, 1958
No Time for Sergeants
(No Program on File)
by Ira Levin
Directed by Jack P. Ragotzy
Assistant Director - Alfred Hinckley
CAST

Preacher	Louis Girard
Will Stockdale	John Newton
Pa Stockdale	Monte Aubrey
Draft Man	James Malloy
Bus Driver	Jack Herr
Irvin Blanchard	James Barrie
Rosabella	Cherie Graves
Inductee No 1	Rafael Le Tourneout
Inductee No. 2	Don Gilleland
Inductee No. 3	George Stokes
Inductee No. 4	Doug Streff
Inductee No. 5	Steve Strong
Wiggins	Bill Montgomery
Zouder	Michael Gleason
Ben Whitledge	Craig Huebing
Sergeant King	Alfred Hinckley
A Captain	Doug Streff
A Nurse	Barbara Bassler
Corporal No. 1	George Stokes
Corporal No. 2	Rafael Le Tourneout
Woman Lieutenant	Natalie Ross
Psychiatrist	Emmett Jacobs
Cigarette Girl	Joan Lindstrom
Infantry Private	Robert Cadman
Air Force Policeman	Don Gilleland
A Colonel	Steve Strong
Lieutenant Bridges	Monte Aubrey
Lieutenant Gardella	Bill Montgomery
Lieutenant Kendall	George Stokes
Lieutenant Cover (navigator)	Jack Herr
General Bush	Louis Girard
General Pollard	Steve Strong
Senator	James Malloy
Aide to Gen. Pollard	Rafael Le Tourneout
Lieutenant Abel	Don Gilleland
Lieutenant Baker	George Stokes
Captain Charles	Doug Streff

#111
August 26 - 31, 1958
The Happiest Millionaire
(No Program on File)
by Kyle Chichton
Directed by Louis Girard

234

CAST

John Lawless	Alfred Hinckley
Emma	Cherie Graves
Livingston Biddle	George Stokes
Joe Nancuso	Bill Montgomery
Tony Biddle	Jack Herr
Charlie Taylor	James Malloy
Cordelia Biddle	Natalie Ross
Anthony J. Drexel Biddle	John Newton
Mrs. Anthony J. Drexel Biddle	Betty Ebert
Aunt Mary Drexel	Dusty Reeds
Cousin Lucy Rittenhouse	June Frye
Angier Duke	Craig Huebing
Spike O'Mally	Steve Strong
Mrs. Benjamin Duke	Sue Hopwood

#112
September 2 - 7, 1958
Fair Game
(No Program on File)
by Sam Locke
Directed by Jack P. Ragotzy
Set Designed by Dusty Reeds
Lights by James Malloy
Costumes by Peggy Plimmer Stockton

CAST

Lucille Bohlan	Sue Hopwood
Harry Bohlan	Craig Huebing
Susan Hammarlee	Natalie Ross
Lou Winkler	John Newton
A Waiter	Bill Montgomery
Arlene	Betty Ebert
Janet	Joan Lindstrom
Irene	Margaret Nerad
Speed Myers	Louis Girard
Maid	Barbara Bassler
Prof. Spencer Thornton	Alfred Hinckley
Marian Thornton	Cherie Graves
Rush Potter	James Malloy
Frank Salinder	Jack Herr

#113
September 9 - 14, 1958
Nothing But the Truth
(No Program on File)
by James Montgomery
Directed by Louis Girard

CAST

Bennett	John Newton
VanDusen	Craig Huebing
Ralston	Alfred Hinckley
Donnelly	Jack Herr
Bishop Doran	Louis Girard
Gwendolyn	Natalie Ross
Mrs. Ralston	Cherie Graves
Mabel	Betty Ebert
Sabel	Joan Lindstrom
Ethel	Margaret Nerad

1959 Season

#114
June 2 - 7, 1959
Third Best Sport
by Eleanor and Leo Bayer
Directed by Jack P. Ragotzy
Set Designed by Robert Cadman
Lights by Emmett Jacobs
Costumes by Charlotte Smith

CAST

Bellboy	Vito De Marzo
Helen Sayre	Betty Ebert
Douglas Sayre	Maurice Ottinger
Chuck Robbins	Hal Ballou
Arthur Underhill	Louis Girard
Amy Underhill	Gay Kleimenhagen
Marge Robbing	Joan Baker
John Wagner	Alfred Hinckley
Dr. Jonas Lockwood	Richard Armbruster
Myra McHenry	Sue Hopwood
Spencer McHenry	Monte Aubrey

#115
June 9 - 14, 1959
Summer of the 17th Doll
by Ray Lawler
Directed by Jack Ragotzy
Set Design by Richard Jackson
Lights by Vito De Marzo and Michael Birtwhistle
Costumes by Gay Kleimenhagen

CAST

Pearl Cunningham	Betty Ebert
Bubba Ryan	Joan Baker
Olive Leech	Sue Hopwood
Barney Ibbot	Alfred Hinckley
Emma Leech	Gay Kleimenhagen
Roo Webber	Louis Girard
Johnnie Dowd	Maurice Ottinger

#116
June 16 - 28, 1959
Tunnel of Love
by Joseph Fields and Peter De Vries
(Based on the novel by Peter DeVries)
Directed by Jack Ragotzy
Assistant Director - Louis Girard
Setting by Robert Cadman
Lights by Vito De Marzo and Bill Leonard
Costumes by Peggy Plimmer Stockton

CAST

Augie Poole	John Newton
Isolde Poole	Betty Ebert
Dick Pepper	Maurice Ottinger
Alice Pepper	Joan Baker
Estelle Novick	Barbara Reser
Miss McCracken	Sue Hopwood

#117
June 3 - July 12, 1959
Bells Are Ringing
Book and Lyrics by Betty Comden
and Adolph Green
Music by Jule Styne
Directed by Rinaldo Capillupo
Choreographed by Wayne Lamb
Sets by Robert Brand and Robert Cadman
Lights by Emmett Jacobs
Costumes by Florence Di Re, Ann Boyter, and Ora
[Note: "Ora" is all that is listed in program]

CAST

Sue	Gay Kleimenhagen
Gwynne	Betty Ebert
Ella Peterson	Joan Baker
Carl	Michael Birtwhistle
Inspector Barnes	Louis Girard
Francis	Vito De Marzo
Sandor	Alfred Hinckley
Jeff Moss	Richard Armbruster
Larry Hastings	Steve Strong
Telephone Man	Bill Leonard
Ludwig Smiley	Emmett Jacobs
Dr. Kitchell	Hal Ballou
Blake Barton	Maurice Ottinger
Actor	Norm Ornellas
Olga	Margaret Nerad
Man from Corvello Mob	Norm Ornellas
Second Mobster	Richard Marriott
Marno	Wayne Lamb
Paul Arnold	Richard Jackson
Michelle	Florence Di Re
Maid	Anne Boyter
Nightclub Singer	Richard Marriott

Adagio Dancers:
Florence Di Re, Robert Cadman
Singers:
Anne Boyter, Elaine Claire, Mary Ann Cottrell,
Ann Douglas, Cherie Graves, Carol Medusky,
Barbara Reser, Charlotte Smith,
Peggy Plimmer Stockton
Dancers:
Michael Birtwhistle, Elaine Claire, Ann Douglas,
Richard Jackson, Bill Leonard, Carol Medusky,
Norm Ornellas, Charlotte Smith

#118
July 14 - 26, 1959
Say, Darling
A Comedy About a Musical
Book by Richard Bissell,
Abe Burrows & Marian Bissell
Based on the novel by Richard Bissell
Songs by Betty Comden, Adolph Green
and Jule Styne
Directed by Jack Ragotzy
Musical Direction by Rinaldo Capillupo
Choreographed by Wayne Lamb
Sets by Robert Cadman and Jack Ragotzy
Lighting by Steve Strong and Richard Marriott
Costumes by Peggy Plimmer Stockton

CAST

Mr. Schneider	Monte Aubrey
Frankie Jordan	Betty Ebert
Jack Jordan	Maurice Ottinger
Photographer	Vito De Marzo
Pilot Roy Peters	Emmett Jacobs
Ted Snow	Hal Ballou
June (the secretary)	Sue Hopwood
Schatzie Harris	Alfred Hinckley
Richard Hackett	Louis Girard
Irene Lovelle	Joan Baker
Rudy Lorraine	Richard Armbruster

Sidemen:
Robert Sanders, Bill Leonard

Boris Reshevsky	Wayne Lamb
Charles Williams	Michael Gleason
Maurice	Monte Aubrey
Arlene McKee	Cherie Graves
Jennifer Stevenson	Elaine Claire
Earl Jorgenson	Richard Marriott
Cheryl Merrill	Gay Kleimenhagen
Sammy Miles	Vito De Marzo
Rex Dexter	Robert Cadman
Waiter	Michael Birtwhistle
Chorus Girls	Barbara Reser, Margaret Nerad
Ann	Ann Douglas
Carol	Carol Medusky
Charlotte	Charlotte Smith
Norman	Norm Ornellas
Dick	Richard Jackson

#119
July 28 - August 9, 1959
Li'l Abner
by Norman Panama and Melvin Frank
Based on Characters created by Al Capp
Music and Lyrics by Johnny Mercer
and Gene de Paul
Stage and Musical Directed
by Rinaldo Capillupo
Choreographed by Wayne Lamb
Sets Designed by Richard Jackson
Lighting by Robert Brand
Costumes by Gay Kleimenhagen and Flo Di Re
CAST
Dogpatch Girl . . . . .Mary Ann Cottrell
Lonesome Polecat . . . . .Wayne Lamb
Hairless Joe . . . . .Hal Ballou
Romeo Scragg . . . . .Richard Armbruster
Clem Scragg . . . . .Norm Ornellas
Alf Scragg . . . . .Richard Foose
Moonbeam McSwine . . . . .Betty Ebert
Marryin' Sam . . . . .Otto Lohmann
Earthquake McGoon . . . . .Steve Strong
Daisy Mae . . . . .Joan Baker
Pappy Yokum . . . . .F. Di Re
Mammy Yokum . . . . .Sue Hopwood
Li'l Abner . . . . .Robert Cadman
Cronies:
Richard Armbruster, Richard Foose,
Emmett Jacobs, Richard Marriott
Mayor Dawgmeat . . . . .Richard Marriott
Scarlet . . . . .Margaret Stratton
Tobacco Rhoda . . . . . . .Peggy Plimmer Stockton
Senator Jack S.
Phogbound . . . . .Alfred Hinckley
Dr. Rasmussen T.
Finsdale . . . . .Maurice Ottinger
Government Man . . . . .Vito De Marzo
Available Jones . . . . .Bill Leonard
Stupefyin' Jones . . . . .Margaret Nerad
Speedy McRabbit . . . . .Michael Birtwistle
Husbands:
Robert Brand, Rinaldo Capillupo,
Richard Jackson, Emmett Jacobs
Guinea Pig Husbands:
Pete Bess, Vern E. Gorham, Jim Gregoire,
Pando Nanis
General Bullmoose . . . . .Louis Girard
Secretaries:
Michael Birtwistle, Cherie Graves,
Gay Kleimenhagen, Richard Marriott
Appassionata
Von Climax . . . . .Barbara Reser
Evil Eye Fleagle . . . . .Vito De Marzo
Dr. Smithborn . . . . .Alfred Hinckley
Dr. Krogmeyer . . . . .Gay Kleimenhagen
Dr. Schleifitz . . . . .Richard Armbruster
Cedric Softwicke . . . . .Norm Ornellas
Wives:
Elaine Claire, Gay Kleimenhagen,
Charlotte Smith, Peggy Plimmer Stockton
Maid . . . . .Anne Boyter
Dogpatch Dancers:
Elaine Claire, Ann Douglas, Carol Medusky,
Charlotte Smith, Bobbi Waite, Michael
Birtwistle, Richard Foose, Bill Leonard,
Norm Ornellas, Maurice Ottinger

#120
August 11 - 16, 1959
[World Premiere]
Come Share My House
(No Program on File)
by Theodore Apstein
Directed by Jack Ragotzy
Stage Manager - Michael Gleason

CAST
Nellie . . . . .Gay Kleimenhagen
Tom Brooks . . . . .Richard Armbruster
Amparo . . . . .Elisa Loti
Concha Varela . . . . .Betty Ebert
Evie . . . . .Yvette Espy
Joe Sagredo . . . . .Vito De Marzo
Mrs. Ramirez . . . . .Cherie Graves
Ray . . . . .Maurice Ottinger
Charlotte Ogden . . . . .Joan Barker
Estelle Wilcox . . . . .Sue Hopwood
Mr. Brooks . . . . .Louis Girard
Mrs. Brooks . . . . .Delphine Stratton
Professor McKay . . . . .Alfred Hinckley
Judge .Monte Aubrey

#121
August 18 - 23, 1959
The Girls in 509
by Howard Teichmann
Directed by Emmett Jacobs
Assistant Director - Louis Girard
Sets and Lighting by Robert Brand
Costumes by Peggy Plimmer Stockton
CAST
Mimsy . . . . .Sue Hopwood
Aunt Hettie . . . . .Gay Kleimenhagen
Old Jim . . . . .Alfred Hinckley
Ryan (of the Daily News) . . . . . . .Monte Aubrey
Rusey . . . . .Maurice Ottinger
Miss Freud . . . . .Cherie Graves
Winthrop Allen . . . . .Louis Girard
Summers (of the
Herald Tribune) . . . . .Richard Marriott
Johnson (of the Daily
Mirror) . . . . .Hal Ballou
Rosenthal (of the Post) . . . . .Vito De Marzo
Francis X. Nella . . . . .Louis Girard
Aubrey McKittridge . . . . . . .Richard Armbruster

#122
August 25 - September 7, 1959
Auntie Mame
by Jerome Lawrence and Robert E. Lee
(Based on the novel by Patrick Dennis)
Directed by Jack Ragotzy
Sets Designed by Robert Cadman
Lighting by Andrew Smith and Bill Leonard
Costumes by Elaine Clare, Florence Di Re, and
Joan Baker
CAST
Norah Muldoon . . . . .Cherie Graves
Patrick Dennis (as a
boy) . . . . .Joey Racz
Ito . . . . .Norm Ornellas
Vera Charles . . . . .Joan Baker
Radcliffe . . . . .Mary Ann Cottrell
Osbert .Hal Ballou
Dr. Fuchtwanger . . . . .Richard Marriott
Ralph Devine . . . . .Robert Cadman
Monk Eleftharosees . . . . .Steve Strong
M. Lindsay Woolsey . . . . .Monte Aubrey
Auntie Mame . . . . .Betty Ebert
Mr. Waldo (a paper
hanger) . . . . .Vito De Marzo
Mr. Babcock . . . . .Louis Girard
Al Linden . . . . .Andrew Smith
A Theatre Manager . . . . .Steve Strong
Assistant Stage
Manager .Bill Leonard
A Maid . . . . .Margaret Nerad
A Butler . . . . .Richard Marriott
A Leading Man . . . . .Richard Armbruster
Lord Dudley . . . . .Alfred Hinckley
A Customer . . . . .Margaret Nerad
Mrs. Jennings . . . . .Barbara Reser
Beauregard Jackson
Pickett Burnside . . . . .Maurice Ottinger
Mr. Loomis (a floor
walker) . . . . .Hal Ballou
Cousin Jeff . . . . .Steve Strong
Cousin Jeff's Wife . . . . .Margaret Nerad
Cousin Fan . . . . .Mary Ann Cottrell
Cousin Moultrie . . . . .Bill Leonard
Sally Cato
MacDougal . . . . .Peggy Plimmer Stockton
Emory MacDougal . . . . .Elaine Claire
Mother Burnside . . . . .Sue Hopwood
Aunt Euphemia . . . . .Anne Boyter
Lizzie Beaufort . . . . .Charlotte Smith
Fred, a groom . . . . .Vito De Marzo
Dr. Shurr (a vet) . . . . .Richard Marriott
Patrick Dennis
(a young man) . . . . .Michael Birtwistle
Agnes Gooch . . . . .Florence Di Re
Brian O'Bannion . . . . .Richard Armbruster
Gloria Upson . . . . .Barbara Reser
Mrs. Upson . . . . .Gay Kleimenhagen
Mr. Upson . . . . .Alfred Hinckley
Pegeen Ryan . . . . .Elaine Claire
Michael Dennis . . . . .Joey Racz

#123
September 8 - 13, 1959
Who Was That Lady?
by Norman Krasna
Directed by Louis Girard
Set Designed by Robert Cadman
Lighting by Andrew Smith
Costumes by Gay Klimenhagen
CAST
David Williams . . . . .Maurice Ottinger
Michael Haney . . . . .Richard Armbruster
Schultz . . . . .Richard Marriott
Ann Williams . . . . .Betty Ebert
Robert Doyle . . . . .Emmett Jacobs
Harry Powell . . . . .Alfred Hinckley
Lee Wong . . . . .Norm Ornellas
Gloria Google . . . . .Barbara Reser
Florence Google . . . . .Peggy Plimmer Stockton
Joe Bendix . . . . .Bill Leonard
Secretary . . . . .Mary Ann Cottrell
Evans .Vito De Marzo
Parker . . . . .Hal Ballou
Orlov .Andrew Smith
Belka .Monte Aubrey
First Tenant . . . . .Mary Ann Cottrell
Second Tenant . . . . .Michael Birtwistle
Building Employee . . . . .Bill Leonard
Third Tenant . . . . .Cherie Graves
McCarthy . . . . .Richard Marriott

1960 Season

#124
June 14 - 19, 1960
Golden Fleecing
by Lorenzo Semple, Jr.

Directed by Jack Ragotzy
Setting Designed by Dean James
Lights by Emmett Jacobs
Costumes by Elaine Claire
CAST
Porter . . . . .Francis Sattler
Beau Gilliam . . . . .Dale Helward
Jackson Eldridge . . . . .Robert Horen
Waiter . . . . .George Stokes
Fergie Howard . . . . .James Pritchett
Pete Di Lucca . . . . .Norman Ornellas
Julie . . . . .Natalie Ross
Ann Knutsen . . . . .Betty Ebert
Benjamin Dane . . . . .Emmett Jacobs
Admiral Fitch . . . . .Alfred Hinckley
Taylor . . . . .Richard Higgs
1st Shore Patrol Sailor . . . . .Bill Leonard
2nd Patrol Sailor . . . . .Don Westbrook

#125
June 21 - July 3, 1960
Two for the Seesaw
(No Program on File)
by William Gibson
Directed by Lewis Freedman
CAST
Jerry Ryan . . . . .James Pritchett
Gittle Mosca . . . . .Susan Willis

#126
July 5 - 17, 1960
Can-Can
Music and Lyrics by Cole Porter
Book by Abe Burrows
Stage and Musical Director - Rinaldo Capillupo
Choreography by Wayne Lamb
Scenery Designed by Jack H. Cornwell
Lights Designed by Emmett Smith
Costumes by Ora Crofoot
CAST
Bailiff . . . . .Don Westbrook
President . . . . .Dean James
Paul Barriere . . . . .Richard Higgs
Aristide Forestier . . . . .James Pritchett
Claudine . . . . .Natalie Ross
Celestine . . . . .Elaine Claire
Gabrielle . . . . .Johanna DeSalvo
Marie . . . . .Brenda Berlin
Michele .Florence Di Re
Suzanne . . . . .Leonora Eden
1st Policeman . . . . .Bill Leonard
2nd Policeman . . . . .Christopher Jones
Hilaire Jussac . . . . .Alfred Hinckley
Boris Adzinidzinadze . . . . .Dale Helward
Waiter . . . . .George Stokes
Pistache .Susan Willis
Hercule .Francis Sattler
Etienne .Dan Wilcox
Theophile . . . . .Emmett Jacobs
Tabac Waiter . . . . .Norman Ornellas
Monarchist . . . . .Don Westbrook
Matron .Suzanne Mills
Model . . . . .Mary Ann Cottrell
Chocolat . . . . .Wayne Lamb
Litte Egypt . . . . .Florence Di Re
Blackbird . . . . .Barbara Reser
Streetwalker . . . . .Margaret Nerad
Woman Swell . . . . .Bobbie Byers
Man Swell . . . . .Dean James
Doctor . . . . .Don Westbrook
Second .Christopher Jones
Turnkey .Norman Ornellas

Prosecutor . . . . .Bill Leonard
Singers:
Bobbie Byers, Mary Ann Cottrell, Richard
Higgs, Suzanne Mills, Margaret Nerad,
Barbara Reser, George Stokes
Dancers:
Brenda Berlin, Elaine Claire, Leonora Eden,
Johanna DeSalvo, Jack Howard, Christopher
Jones, Bill Leonard, Margaret Nerad, Norman
Ornellas, Barbara Reser, George Stokes,
Don Westbrook

#127
July 19 - 24, 1960
The Teahouse of the August Moon
by John Patrick (based on the novel
of the same name by Vern Sneider)
Directed by Jack Ragotzy
Set Designed by Jack Cornwell
Light Design by Emmett Jacobs
Costumes by Leonora Eden
CAST
Sakini . . . . .Norman Ornellas
Sergeant Gregovich . . . . .Emmett Jacobs
Col. Wainwright III . . . . .Alfred Hinckley
Captain Fisby . . . . .James Pritchett
Old Woman . . . . .Susan Willis
Old Woman's Daughter . . . . .Florence Di Re
The Daughter's Children . . . . . . .Bobbie Byers,
 . . . . .George Stokes
Lady Astor . . . . .Mary Ann Cottrell
Ancient Man . . . . .Dan Wilcox
Mr. Hokaida . . . . .Robert Cadman
Mr. Omura . . . . .Bill Leonard
Mr. Sumata . . . . .Francis Sattler
Mr. Sumata's Father . . . . .Dan Wilcox
Mr. Seiko . . . . .Dale Helward
Miss Higa Jiga . . . . .Sue Hopwood
Mr. Keora . . . . .Don Westbrook
Mr. Oshira . . . . .Christopher Jones
Villagers:
Jack Howard, Barbara Reser, Johanna De Salvo
Ladies League for Democratic Action:
Susan Willis, Florence Di Re, Johanna De Salvo,
Barbara Reser
Lotus Blossom . . . . .Natalie RossCaptain
McLean . . . . .Monte Aubrey

#128
July 26 - August 7, 1960
Kiss Me, Kate
Music and Lyrics by Cole Porter
Book by Sam and Bela Spewak
Book staged by Jack Ragotzy
Music and Musical Numbers Staged
by Rinaldo Capillupo
Choreography by Wayne Lamb
Setting Designed by Corwin Rife
Lights by Emmett Jacobs
Costumes by
Elaine Claire, Ora Crofoot, Jane Fisher,
Helen Crain and Jane Groscost
CAST
Fred . . . . .James Pritchett
Harry . . . . .Emmett Jacobs
Lois . . . . .Natalie Ross
Ralph . . . . .Norman Ornellas
Lilli . . . . .Betty Ebert
Hattie . . . . .Susan Willis
Doorman . . . . .Dan Wilcox
Paul . . . . .Wayne Lamb
Bill . . . . .Dale Helward

1st Man .Alfred Hinckley
2nd Man . . . . .Robert Cadman
Harrison Howell . . . . .John Richards
Cab Driver . . . . .Andy Rasbury
Doctor . . . . .Bill Leonard
2 Nurses:
Suzanne Mills, Bobbie Byers
"Taming of the Shrew" players:
Bianca . . . . .Natalie Ross
Baptista .Emmett Jacobs
Gremio .George Stokes
Hortensio . . . . .Francis Sattler
Lucentio . . . . .Dale Helward
Katharine . . . . .Betty Ebert
Petruchio . . . . .James Pritchett
Nathaniel . . . . .Norman Ornellas
Gregory . . . . .Christopher Jones
Phillip . . . . .Dan Wilcox
Habadasher . . . . .Don Westbrook
Dancers:
Barbara Reser, Don Westbrook, Johanna
DeSalvo, Christopher Jones, Margaret Nerad,
Jack Howard, Elaine Claire, Bill Leonard
Singers:
Bobbie Byers, Suzanne Mills, Mary Ann
Cottrell, Leonora Eden, Florence Di Re,
Margaret Nerad, Barbara Reser, Johanna De
Salvo, Don Westbrook, Dan Wilcox, Jack
Howard, Bill Leonard, Christopher Jones, John
Richards, Francis Sattler, Norman Ornellas

#129
August 9 - 23, 1960
Call Me Madam
Music and Lyrics by Irving Berlin
Book by Howard Lindsay and Russel L. Crouse
Stage and Musical Directed
by Rinaldo Capillupo
Choreography by Wayne Lamb
Settings designed by Dusty Reeds
Lighting by Emmett Jacobs
Costumes by Florence Di Re, Ora Crofoot
CAST
Mrs. Sally Adams . . . . .Susan Willis
The Secretary of State . . . . .Wayne Lamb
Supreme Court Justice . . . . . . .Christopher Jones
Congressman Wilkins . . . . .Emmett Jacobs
Henry Gibson . . . . .Dan Wilcox
Kenneth Gibson . . . . .Dale Helward
Miss Phillips . . . . .Florence Di Re
Maid . . . . .Bobbie Byers
Senator Brockbank . . . . .Steve Strong
Senator Gallagher . . . . .Alfred Hinckley
Cosmo Constantine . . . . .Richard Higgs
Pemberton Maxwell . . . . .John Richards
Clerk . . . . .Jack Howard
Hugo Tantinnin . . . . .Francis Sattler
Sebastian Sebastian . . . . .Norman Ornellas
Princess Maria . . . . .Natalie Ross
Court Chamberlain . . . . .George Stokes
Grand Duchess Sophie . . . . .Sue Hopwood
Grand Duke Otto . . . . .Dean James
Dancers:
Elaine Claire, Johanna DeSalvo, Jack Howard,
Christopher Jones, Bill Leonard, Margaret Nerad,
Barbara Reser, Don Westbrook
Singers:
Bobbie Byers, Mary Ann Cottrell, Leonora Eden,
Suzanne Mills, Norman Ornellas, Francis Sattler,
George Stokes, Margaret Stratton, Dan Wilcox
Ocarina Players:
Bill Leonard, George Stokes, Dan Wilcox

#130
August 23 - 28, 1960
Look Homeward, Angel
by Ketti Frings
(from the novel by Thomas Wolfe)
Directed by Joe Stockdale
Scenery Designed by Robert Cadman
and Dusty Reeds
Lighting by Emmett Jacobs and Bill Leonard
Costumes by Lynn Eden and Ora Crofoot
CAST

Eugene Gant	Dale Helward
Ben Gant	Emmett Jacobs
Marie "Fattie" Pert	Bobbie Byers
Helen Gant Barton	Sue Hopwood
Hugh Barton	Monte Aubrey
Eliza Gant	Susan Willis
Will Pentland	Robert Cadman
Jake Clatt	Bill Leonard
Mrs. Clatt	Mary Ann Cottrell
Florry Mangle	Elaine Claire
Mrs. Snowden	Johanna De Salvo
Miss Brown	Barbara Reser
Mr. Farrel	Dan Wilcox
Laura James	Florence Di Re
W.O. Gant	Alfred Hinckley
Dr. Maguire	Francis Sattler
Tarkington	Christopher Jones
Madame Elizabeth	Betty Ebert
Luke Gant	Dean James
Newsboy	Norman Ornellas

#131
August 30 - September 4, 1960
The Dark at the Top of the Stairs
by William Inge
Directed by Jack Ragotzy
Assistant Director - Joe Stockdale
Setting Designed by Robert Cadman
Lighting by Bill Leonard
Costumes by Florence Di Re
CAST

Cora Flood	Betty Ebert
Rubin Flood	Emmett Jacobs
Sonny Flood	George Stokes
Jonathan	Norman Ornellas
Reenie Flood	Bobbie Byers
Flirt Conroy	Barbara Reser
Morris Lacey	Alfred Hinckley
Lotty Lacey	Susan Willis
Punky Givens	Dan Wilcox
Sammy Goldenbaum	Dale Helward
Chauffeur	Bill Leonard

#132
September 6 - 18, 1960
Ladies' Night in a Turkish Bath
by Cyrus Wood
(based on a farce by Avery Hopwood
and Charlton Andrews)
Directed by Jack Ragotzy
Special Choreography by Wayne Lamb
(No Program on File)
CAST

Dodie	Natalie Ross
Marie	Florence Di Re
Kittie	Betty Ebert
Mike	Alfred Hinckley
Mrs. Tarleton	Sue Hopwood
Alicia	Barbara Reser
Fred	Emmett Jacobs
Professor Matthews	Dale Helward
Mrs. O'Brien	Mary Ann Cottrell
Myrtle	Elaine Claire
Anna	Bobbie Byers
La Bouche	Johanna De Salvo
Policeman	Monte Aubrey
Fireman	Dan Wilcox

#133
September 20 - 25. 1960
Something Wild in the Country
(*Orpheus Descending*)
by Tennessee Williams
Directed by Emmett Jacobs and Jack Ragotzy
Setting Designed by Robert Cadman
Lights by Emmett Jacobs
Costumes by Florence Di Re

CAST

Dolly Hanna	Mary Ann Cottrell
Beulah Binnings	Barbara Reser
Pee Wee Binnings	Monte Aubrey
Dog Hanna	Robert Cadman
Carol Cutrere	Natalie Ross
Eve Temple	Florence Di Re
Sister Temple	Elaine Claire
Val Xavier	Dale Helward
Vee Talbot	Sue Hopwood
Lady Torrance	Betty Ebert
Jebe Torrance	Alfred Hinckley
Sheriff Talbot	Emmett Jacobs
David Cutrere	Andy Rasbury
Nurse Porter	Bobbie Byers
lst Man	David Masson

Fall Comedy of 1960

#134
September 27 - October 2, 1960
Make a Million
by Norman Barasch and Carroll Moore
Directed by Jack Ragotzy
Setting Designed by Robert Cadman
Lights by Emmett Jacobs
Costumes by Ora Crofoot and Florence Di Re
CAST

Betty Phillips	Barbara Reser
Mrs. Winters	Florence Di Re
Claire Manning	Betty Ebert
Sid Gray	Alfred Hinckley
Howard Conklin	Art Middleton
Bernie Leeds	Andy Rasbury
Harold Fairbanks	Emmett Jacobs
Julie Martin	Natalie Ross
Mr. Merganthaler	Louis Girard
General Potter	Monte Aubrey
Lt. Friedlander	Sue Hopwood
Ferris	Art Middleton
King	Dale Helward
Reeves	Donald Kantner
Bradford	Fred Tupper
Juliano	Arthur Smith
Henry Whipple	Robert Cadman
Manicurist	Elaine Claire
Reardon	Art Middleton

#135
October 4 - 16, 1960
The Marriage-Go-Round
by Leslie Stevens
Directed by Jack Ragotzy
Designed by Robert Cadman
Lighting by Emmett Jacobs
Costumes by Ora Crofoot and Florence Di Re
CAST

Paul Delville, Ph.D. M.Sc., D. Litt., M..F.A., F.R.S. Professor of Anthropology	Louis Girard
Content Lowell, Ph.D., D.Litt., M.F.A., Soc. Sc., Dean of Women, Mrs. Paul Deville	Betty Ebert
Katrin Sveg	Barbara Reser
Ross Barnett, Ph.D., M.Sc., LI. D, M.F.A., Maitland Chair	Emmett Jacobs

#136
October 18 - 23, 1960
The Gazebo
(No Program on File)
by Alec Coppel
Directed by Jack Ragotzy
Setting Designed by Robert Cadman
Lights by Emmett Jacobs
Costumes by Ora Crofoot and Florence Di Re
CAST

Elliott Nash	Louis Girard
Harlow Edison	Emmett Jacobs
Matilda	Florence Di Re
Nell Nash	Betty Ebert
Mrs. Chandler	Sue Hopwood
Mrs. Thrope	Barbara Reser
The Cook	Monte Aubrey
Louie	Robert Cadman
Jenkins	Andy Rasbury
Dr. Wyner	Wayne Lamb
Miss Druker	Elaine Claire
A Cop	Monte Aubrey

#137
October 25 - 30, 1960
Three on a Honeymoon
by Don Appell
Directed by Louis Girard and Jack Ragotzy
Set Designed by Robert Cadman
Lighting by Emmett Jacobs
Costumes by Ora Crofoot and Florence Di Re
CAST

A Bellhop	Jack Ragotzy
Johnny	Emmett Jacobs
Eadie	Betty Ebert
The Mother	Sue Hopwood

1961 Season

#138
May 26 - June 4, 1961
The Marriage-Go-Round
by Leslie Stevens
Directed by Jack Ragotzy
Lighting Designer by Emmet Jacobs
Costumer by Ora Crofoot
CAST

Paul Delville, Ph.D. M.Sc., D. Litt., M.F.A., F.R.S. Professor of Anthropology	Louis Girard
Content Lowell, Ph.D., D.Litt., M.F.A., Soc. Sc., Dean of Women, (Mrs. Paul Deville)	Betty Ebert
Katrin Sveg	Dolores Vaage

Ross Barnett, Ph.D.,
M.Sc., Ll.D., M.F.A.,
Maitland Chair . . . . .Emmett Jacobs

#139
June 6 - 11, 1961
A Period of Adjustment
by Tennessee Williams
Directed by Jack Ragotzy
Set Designed by Orison Bedell
and Dusty Reeds
Lighting by Bill Leonard
Costumes by Ora Crofoot
CAST

Ralph Bates . . . . .John Newton
Josephine .Little Jo
Isabel Haverstick . . . . .Myra Mailloux
George Haverstick . . . . .Emmett Jacobs
Susie . . . . .Linda McAllister
Mrs. McGillicuddy . . . . .Betty Ebert
Mr. McGillicuddy . . . . .Louis Girard
Police Officer . . . . .Mike Barton
Dorothea Bates . . . . .Sue Hopwood

#140
June 13 - 24, 1961
Under the Yum-Yum Tree
by Lawrence Roman
Directed by Louis Girard
Set Designed by Dusty Reeds
Lighting Design by Bill Leonard
Costumes by Ora Crofoot, Patricia Pronz
CAST

Irene Wilson . . . . .Betty Ebert
Robin Austin . . . . .Dolores Vaage
Milkman . . . . .Donald Tull
Dave Manning . . . . .Dale Helward
Hogan . . . . .John Newton
Cab Driver . . . . .Richard Silberg

#141
June 27 - July 9, 1961
Destry Rides Again
Music & Lyrics by Howard Rome
Book by Leonard Gershe
Based on the story by Max Brand
Directed by Jack Ragotzy
Musical Direction - Maurice Lewis
Choreography - Wayne Lamb
Set Designed by Boyd Dumrose
Lighting Design by Bill Leonard
Costumes by Ora Crofoot and Patricia Pronz
CAST
Prologue:
Dale Helward, Mike Barton, Mark Tinson,
Joseph Gauthier

Bar Pianist . . . . .Leon Odenz
Bartender . . . . .John Ovens
Man . . . . .Richard Silberg
Frenchy .Betty Ebert
Claggett .Dan Wilcox
Sheriff Keogh . . . . .Clint Atkinson
Bugs . . . . .Mark Tinson
Gyp . . . . .Mike Barton
Rockwell . . . . .Joseph Gauthier
Kent . . . . .Dale Helward
Slade . . . . .Winston Gould
Wash . . . . .Louis Girard
Rose Lovejoy . . . . .Dusty Reeds
Men:
Pat Hardy, Dave Parker, Kenneth Andrews
Tyndall .Donald Tull
Stage Driver . . . . .Kenneth Solms
Ming Li . . . . .Beverly Long
Tom Destry . . . . .John Newton
Clara . . . . .Linda McAlister
1st girl .Patricia Pronz
2nd girl . . . . .Dolores Vaage
Mrs. Claggett . . . . .Betty Ladd
Boy . . . . .Robin Reeds
1st Man .Donald Tull
2nd Man . . . . .Richard Silberg
Bailey . . . . .Kenneth Solms
Chloe . . . . .Johnnie Sibold
Dimples . . . . .Nancy Barrett
Frenchy's Girls:
Myra Mailloux, Johnnie Sibold,
Kathryn Crawford, Jeanne Morrice
Rose Lovejoy's Girls:
Judy O'Dea, Dolores Vaage, Beverly Long,
Mary Hartman

#142
July 11 - 16, 1961
Sunrise at Campobello
by Dore Schary
Directed by Jack Ragotzy
Set Designed by Boyd Dumrose
Lighting Design by Bill Leonard
Costumes by Ora Crofoot and Betty Ladd
CAST

Anna Roosevelt . . . . .Margaret Ladd
Eleanor Roosevelt . . . . .Dusty Reeds
Franklin D. Roosevelt, Jr . . . . . . .Ken Andrews
James Roosevelt . . . . .Dale Helward
Elliott Roosevelt . . . . .Bill Leonard
Edward . . . . .Richard Silberg
Franklin Delano
Roosevelt . . . . .John Newton
John Roosevelt . . . . .Robin Reeds
Marie . . . . .Linda McAlister
Louis McHenry Howe . . . . .Louis Girard
Mrs. Sara Delano
Roosevelt . . . . .Jean Henderson
Miss Marguerite
(Missy) Le Hand . . . . .Dolores Vaageet
Doctor Bennet . . . . .Dan Wilcox
Franklin Calder . . . . .Mike Barton
Stretcher Bearers:
John Ovens, Donald Tull, Clint Atkinson
Duffy Champion . . . . .Anstamm Hi-Jinker
Miss Jenkins . . . . .Kathryn Crawford
Mr. Lassiter . . . . .Donald Tull
Governor Alfred E. Smith . . . . . .Winston Gould
Daly . . . . .Mike Barton
Policeman . . . . .John Ovens
Senator Walsh . . . . .Dan Wilcox
A Speaker . . . . .Clint Atkinson

#143
July 18 - 23, 1961
Champagne Complex
by Leslie Stevens
Directed by Jack Ragotzy
Assistant Director - Louis Girard
Set Designed by Boyd Dumrose
Lighting Designed by Bill Leonard
Costumes Designed by Ora Crofoot
and Margaret Ladd
CAST

Helms Fell Harper . . . . .Dale Helward
Allyn Macy . . . . .Rosalyn Newport
Carter Bowen . . . . .John Newton

#144
July 25 - August 6, 1961
The Pleasure of His Company
by Samuel Taylor with Cornelia Otis Skinner
Directed by Jack Ragotzy
Set Designed by Boyd Dumrose
Lighting Designed by Bill Leonard
Costumes by Ora Crofoot and Johnnie Sibold
CAST

Toy . . . . .Leon Odenz
Biddeford Poole . . . . .John Newton
Jessica Poole . . . . .Rosalyn Newport
Katharine Dougherty . . . . .Betty Ebert
Jim Dougherty . . . . .Alfred Hinckley
Mackenzie Savage . . . . .Louis Girard
Roger Henderson . . . . .Dale Helward

#145
August 8 - 19, 1961
Jin Jin Mai
in
The World of Suzie Wong
by Paul Osborn,
based on the novel by Richard Mason
Directed by Clint Atkinson
Special Choreography by Wayne Lamb
Set Designed by Boyd Dumrose
Lighting Designed by Bill Leonard
Costumes by
Ora Crofoot, Patricia Pronz, Kathryn Crawford,
Lora Babcock
CAST

Robert Lomax . . . . .Dale Helward
Suzie Wong . . . . .Jin Jin Mai
Chinese Officer . . . . .Leon Odenz
Ah Tong . . . . .Don Wilson
Typhoo . . . . .Judy O'Dea
Gwenny . . . . .Patricia Pronz
Wednesday Lulu . . . . .Beverly Long
Minnie Ho . . . . .Margaret Ladd
Fifi . . . . .Kathryn Crawford
George O'Neill . . . . .Winston Gould
Kay Fletcher . . . . .Betty Ebert
British Sailor . . . . .Donald Tull
Ben Jeffcoat . . . . .Louis Girard
Drunken Sailor . . . . .Mike Barton
Lily .Johnnie Sibold
Vendors, Coolies, Sailors and Tourists
Ken Andrews, Bill Leonard, Joseph Gauthier,
John Oven, Kenneth Solms, Richard Silberg,
Donald Tull, Mark Tinson, Kathryn Crawford.

#146
August 22 - September 3, 1961
West Side Story
Book by Arthur Laurents
Music by Leonard Bernstein
Lyrics by Stephen Sondheim
Directed by Louis Girard
Musical Direction - Maurice Lewis
Choreography - Wayne Lamb
Set Designed by Boyd Dumrose
Lighting Designed by Bill Leonard
Costumes: Ora Crofoot, Mark Tinson,
Ken Andrews, Patricia Pronz, Kathryn Crawford
CAST
The Jets:

Riff . . . . .Bill Leonard
Tony .Dale Helward
Action .Wayne Lamb
A-Rab . . . . .Kenneth Solms
Baby John . . . . .Ken Andrews

Diesel . . . . .Dan Wilcox
Big Deal .John Oven
           Their Girls:
Velma . . . . .Beverly Long
Winnie . . . . .Bobbi Waite
Anybody's . . . . .Patricia Pronz
           The Sharks:
Bernardo . . . . .Mike Barton
Chino . . . . .Leon Odenz
Pepe .Joseph Gauthier
Indio . . . . .Mark Tinson
Luis . . . . .Richard Silberg
Anxious . . . . .Pat Hardy
           Their Girls:
Maria . . . . .Stephanie Winters
Anita . . . . .Judy Granite
Rosalia . . . . .Johnnie Sibold
Consuelo . . . . .Kathryn Crawford
Teresita .Sheran Meyer
           The Adults:
Doc . . . . .Louis Girard
Schrank . . . . .Winston Gould
Krupke .Donald Tull
Gladhand . . . . .Clint Atkinson

#147
September 5 - 10, 1961
A Majority of One
by Leonard Spigelgass
Directed by Clint Atkinson
Set Designed by Boyd Dumrose
Lights Designed by Bill Leonard
Costumes by Ora Crofoot
CAST
Mrs. Rubin . . . . .Alice Bulter
Mrs. Jacoby . . . . .Justine Johnston
Alice Black . . . . .Judy Granite
Jerome Black . . . . .Dale Helward
Koichi Asano . . . . .Louis Girard
Dick Steward . . . . .Ken Andrews
Eddie . . . . .Leon Odenz
House Boy . . . . .John Oven
Noketi .Pamela Smith
Ayako Asano . . . . .Kathryn Crawford
Chauffeur .John Oven
Captain Norcross . . . . .Don Wilson

1962 Season

#148
June 12 - 17, 1962
Critic's Choice
by Ira Levin
Directed by Jack Ragotzy
Assistant Director, Louis Girard
Set Designed by Lee Fischer
Costumier - Ora Crofoot
Lighting by Bill Leonard
CAST
Parker Ballantine . . . . .John Varnum
Angela Ballantine . . . . .Janet Hayes
John Ballantine . . . . .Nick Rock
Dion Kapakos . . . . .Dale Helward
The Maid . . . . .Kathryn Sable
Charlotte Orr . . . . .Ruth Gregory
Ivy London . . . . .Betty Ebert

#149
June 19 - 30, 1962
Pajama Tops
by Mawby Green and Ed Feilbert
(from *Moumou* by Jean de Letraz)
Directed by Jack Ragotzy
Set Designed by Lee Fischer
Lighting Design by Bill Leonard
Costumiers - Ora Crofoot and Ellen O'Brien
CAST
Claudine . . . . .Patti Madden
Inspector LeGrand . . . . .Arnie Stenseth
Yvonne Chauvinet . . . . .Janet Hayes
Georges Chauvinet . . . . .Louis Girard
Leonard Jolijoli . . . . .Dale Helward
Babette LaTouche . . . . .Arlene Mazure
Jacques .John Varnum

#150
July 3 - 22, 1962
The Music Man
Book, Music and Lyrics by Meredith Willson
Based on a story by Meredith Willson
and Franklin Lacey
Directed by Jack Ragotzy and Louis Girard
Choreography by Wayne Lamb
Musical Direction by Maurice Lewis
Set Designed by Lee Fischer
Lighting Designed by Bill Leonard
Costumiers - Ora Crofoot, Fred Jackson,
Betty Vernan
CAST
Conductor . . . . .Leon Odenz
Traveling Salesman #1 . . . . . . .Ivars Rushevics
Traveling Salesman #2 . . . . . . .David Hatfield
Charlie Cowell . . . . .Louis Girard
Traveling Salesman #3 . . . . . . .Arnie Stenseth
Traveling Salesman #4 . . . . . .Richard Marriott
Traveling Salesman #5 . . . . .Fred Jackson
Newsman #1 . . . . .Steven Vickers
Newsman #2 . . . . .Joe Racz
Newsman #3 . . . . .David Smith
Harold Hill . . . . .John Varnum
Alma Hix . . . . .Katherine Sable
Ethel Toffelmier . . . . .Rita Strang
Mayer Shinn . . . . .Alfred Hinckley
1st Workman . . . . .Fred Jackson
2nd Workman . . . . .Steven Vickers
Farmer's Wife . . . . .Patti Madden
Farmer .Leon Odenz
Jacey Squires . . . . .Richard Marriott
Ewert Dunlop . . . . .David Hatfield
Oliver Hix . . . . Bill Leonard
Olin Brett . . . . .Arnie Stenseth
Marcellus Washburn . . . . .Dale Helward
Eulalie MacKecknie Shinn . . . . .Ruth Gregory
Zaneeta Shinn . . . . .Ellen O'Brien
Gracie Shinn . . . . .Carol Medusky
Tommy Djilas . . . . .Peter Simon
Constable Locke . . . . .Ivars Rushevics
Mrs. Squires . . . . .Betty Vernan
Maud Dunlop . . . . .Arlene Mazure
           Townsladies:
Pat Souza, Patti Madden, Bev Leonard, Diane
Ellis, Diane Newton, Rucy Jason, Bobbi Waite
           Townsmen:
David Smith, Fred Jackson,
Steven Vickers, Wayne Lamb
           Townchildren:
"Joey" . . . . .Joe Racz
"Joy" . . . . .Joy Glasheen
"Jimmy" . . . . .James Marion
"Jan" . . . . .Jan English
"Ronnie" . . . . .Ron Dundon
Marian Paroo . . . . .Janet Hayes
Amaryllis . . . . .Andrea Perejda

Mrs. Paroo . . . . .Margaret Cheeseman
Winthrop Paroo . . . . .Jack Houston

#151
July 24 - August 4, 1962
The Miracle Worker
by William Gibson
Directed by Louis Girard
Set Designed by Lee Fischer
Lighting Designed by Bill Leonard and Peter Simon
Costumiers - Betty Vernan, Rucy Jason
CAST
Doctor . . . . .Arnie Stenseth
Kate Keller . . . . .Ruth Gregory
Captain Keller . . . . .John Varnum
Martha .Rucy Jason
Helen Keller . . . . .Georgia Brown
Viney . . . . .Diane Ellis
James Keller . . . . .Peter Simon
Aunt Ev .Kay Sable
Anagnos . . . . .Louis Girard
Annie Sullivan . . . . .Arlene Mazure
           Children:
Kim Petrucci, Julie Wisniewski, Elleen Ra-
bideau, Toni Starring Beverly Hiscock
Servant .David Smith
Gwen (the dog) . . . . .Herself

#152
August 7 - 19, 1962
Gypsy
(Suggested by the Memoirs of
Gypsy Rose Lee)
Book by Arthur Laurents
Music by Jule Styne
Lyrics by Stephen Sondheim
Directed by Jack Ragotzy
Choreography by Wayne Lamb
Musical Direction by Maurice Lewis
Set Designed by Lee Fischer
Lighting Designed by Peter Simon
Costumes by Fred Jackson, Betty Vernan
CAST
Uncle Jocko . . . . .Louis Girard
George . . . . .David Hatfield
Miss Christine . . . . .Rucy Jason
Balloon Girl . . . . .Joy Glasheen
           Children:
Diane Ellis, Larry Phelps, Joe Racz
           Mothers:
Ruth Gregory, Jo Ann Wall, Arlene Mazure,
Kay Sable, Betty Vernan
Baby Louise . . . . .Jan English
Baby June . . . . .Donna Marie Hunt
Rose . . . . .Janice Mars
Chowsie (the dog):Willow Creek's
Champion Wee Romeo
Pop . . . . .Arnie Stenseth
Scout Leader . . . . .Steven Vickers
           Scouts:
Larry Phelps, Joe Racz, Jack Houston
Urchin .Dick Lockyer
Rich Man . . . . .David Hatfield
Rich Man's Son . . . . .Tom Lockyer
           Newsboys:
Dick Lockyer, Tom Lockyer, Jack Houston
Weber .Bill Leonard
Herbie .John Varnum
Louise . . . . .Patti Madden
June .Carol Medusky
Tulsa . . . . .Fred Jackson
Yonkers . . . . .Peter Simon

Angie	David Smith
L.A	Wayne Lamb
Kringelein	David Hatfield
Cow	Bill Leonard,
	Arnie Stenseth
Mr. Goldstone	Louis Girard
Waitress	Betty Vernan
Miss Cratchitt	Ruth Gregory

Farm Boys:
Fred Jackson, Peter Simon, David Smith,
Wayne Lamb, Joe Racz, Larry Phelps
Hollywood Blondes (Toreadorables):

"Agnes"	Diane Ellis
"Marjorie May"	Ellen O'Brien
"Delores"	Pat Souza
"Thelma"	Bobbi White
"Edna"	Bev Leonard
"Gail"	Rucy Jason
Announcer	Jack Ragotzy
Pastey	Steven Vickers
Tessie Tura	Betty Ebert
Mazeppa	Betty Vernan
Cigar	Louis Girard
Electra	Arlene Mazure

Showgirls and Strippers:
Ellen O'Brien, Pat Souza, Bobbi Waite,
Bev Leonard, Jo Ann Wall

Maid	Kay Sable
Phil	Arnie Stenseth
Bougeron-Cochon	Wayne Lamb

#153
August 21 - 26, 1962
[World Premiere]
A Hundred Percent Annie
by Susan Slade
Directed by Jack Ragotzy
Set Designed by Lee Fischer
Light Designed by Peter Simon
Costumier - Ellen O'Brien
CAST

Annie	Mollie McCarthy
Fran	Betty Ebert
Jonas Jordan	John Varnum
Felicia	Janice Mars
Mitzy (from downstairs)	Andrea Perejda
Sadie (from downtown)	Ruth Gregory
Warren	Arnie Stenseth

#154
August 28 - September 2, 1962
A Taste of Honey
by Shelagh Delaney
Directed by Louis Girard
Set Designed by Lee Fischer
Lighting Designed by Peter Simon
Costumiere - Carol Medusky
CAST

Helen	Ruth Gregory
Josephine	Arlene Mazure
Peter	John Varnum
The Boy	Bill Leonard
Geoffrey	Fred Jackson

#155
September 3 - 15, 1962
Send Me No Flowers
by Norman Barasch and Carroll Moore
Directed by Jack Ragotzy
Set Designed by Lee Fischer
Lighting Designed by Peter Simon
Costumes by Ellen O'Brien and Fred Jackson

CAST

Judy Kimball	Betty Ebert
George Kimball	John Varnum
Delivery Boy	Don Klovstad
Bert Power	Arnie Stenseth
Doctor Morrissey	Jack Ragotzy
Arnold Nash	Louis Girard
First Passerby	David Hatfield
Second Passerby	Steven M. Vickers
Mr. Akins	Wayne Lamb
Other Woman	Patti Madden

1963 Season

#156
June 2 - 8, 1963
Sunday in New York
by Norman Krasna
Directed by Louis Girard
Set Designed by Curt Senie and Norma Glenn
Lighting by Peter Simon
Costumes by Ora Crofoot
CAST

Adam Taylor	Mike Walsh
Eileen Taylor	Merle Louise Letowt
Mike Mitchell	Dale Helward
Russell Wilson	Arnie Stenseth
Waiter	Mort Siegel
Powder Room Girl	Norma Glenn
Bus Driver	Robert Robinson

Passengers:
Jackie Better, Larry Phelps

Passenger and Masher	Barney Hedges
Passenger and Usherette	Leslie Moulton
Snoopy Woman and Hostess	Pat Morthland
Geisha Girls	Cynthia Redmayne,
	Linda Bruce

#157
June 11 - 23, 1963
Carnival
Music and Lyrics by Bob Merrill
Book by Michael Stewart
Based on material by Helen Deutsch
Directed by Jack Ragotzy
Choreographed by Wayne Lamb
Musical Direction by Maurice Lewis
Set Designed by Richard Gould
Light Designed by Peter Simon
Costumes by Martha Weiss
and Mary Jane Schilling
Puppets created by Ora Crofoot
CAST

Jacquot	Mike Walsh
Roustabout Boss	Wayne Lamb

Roustabouts:
James Barnett, Larry Phelps, Peter Simon

Dog Trainer	Charles Likar
Dog	Folly

Clowns:
Don Westbrook, Ken Andrews
Harem Girls:
Jackie Better, Linda Bruce, Cynthia Redmayne,
Leslie Moulton

Princess Olga	Patricia Morthland
Strong Man	Robert Robinson
Tall Man	Joe Racz
Gladys Zuwicki	Diana Walker
Gloria Zuwicki	Rita Brown
Aerialist	Betty Ebert
Greta	Linda Bruce

Carnival Girls:
Norma Glenn, Martha Weiss, Corinne Allen,
Margaret Fjellestad

B.F. Schlegel	Louis Girard
Rosalie	Karen Jensen
Marco	Dale Helward
Cow	Don Westbrook,
	Arnie Stenseth
Lili	Merle Louise Letowt
Grobert	Arnie Stenseth
Paul Berthalet	Jim Kason

Vendors:
Farrar M. Cobb, Jr., Charles Likar, Robert
Robinson, Joe Racz, Larry Phelps
Volunteers:
Don Westbrook, Corinne Allen,
Mary Jane Schilling
Bluebird Girls:
Rita Brown, Norma Glenn, Diana Walker,
Martha Weiss

1st Card Girl	Cynthia Redmayne
Dr. Wilhelm Glass	Robert Robinson
Armless Beauty	Martha Weiss

#158
June 25 - 30, 1963
The Beauty Part
by S. J. Perelman
Directed by Jack Ragotzy
Set Designed by Don Klovstad
Light Designed by Peter Simon
Costumes - Ora Crofoot and Ken Andrews
CAST

Octavia Weatherwax	Betty Ebert
Mike Mulroy	Mike Walsh
Milo Leotard	Allardyce DuPlessis
Weatherwax	Louis Girard
Lance Weatherwax	Dale Helward
Sam Fussfeld	Ralph Strait
April Monkhood	Merle Louise Letowt
Bunce	Farrar M. Cobb II
Van Lennep	Don Westbrook
Hagerdorn	James Kason
Vishnu	Ken Andrews
Hyacinth Beddoes Laffoon	Louis Girard
Goddard Quagmeyer	Arnie Stenseth
Gloria Krumgold	Karen Jensen
Seymour Grumgold	Charles J. Likar, Jr.
Harry Hubris	Louis Girard
Rob Roy Fruitwell	Peter Simon
Maurice Blount	Don Westbrook
Boris Pickwick	Thomas Hoisveen
Chenille Schreiber	Cynthia Redmayne
Kitty Entrail	Diana Walker
Vernon Equinox	Dick Fogell
Mrs. Younghusband	Diana Walker
Grace Fingerhead	Karen Jensen
Curtis Fingerhead	Mike Walsh
Emmett Stagg	James Barnett
Wormser	Steven M. Vickers
Nelson Smedley	Louis Girard
Rowena Inchcape	Patricia Morthland
Rukeyser	Farrar M. Cobb, Jr.
Wagnerian	Charles Likar
Sherry Quicklime	Martha Weiss
Elmo	Ken Andrews
Hennepin	James Barnett
Poteat	Thomas Hoisveen
Camera Man	Don Westbrook
Henrietta	Rita Brown

Court Stenographer . . . . .Linda Bruce
Policeman . . . . .Bob Robinson
Judge Herman J.
Rinderbrust . . . . .Louis Girard
Baliff . . . . .Dick Fogell
Roxana DeVilbiss . . . . .Mary Jane Schilling
Joe Gourielli . . . . .Mike Walsh
Mrs. Lafcadio Mifflin . . . . .Norma Glenn
1st Photographer . . . . .Margaret Fjellestad
2nd Photographer . . . . .Charles Likar
Misses En Scenes:
Jackie Better, Linda Bruce, Leslie Moulton,
Joan Shields

#159
July 2 - 13, 1963
A Shot in the Dark
Adapted by Harry Kurnitz from the play
by Marcel Achard
Directed by Jack Ragotzy and Louis Girard
Set Designed by Curt Senie
Light Designed by Peter Simon
Costumes by Ora Crofoot and Ken Andrews
CAST
Paul Sevigne . . . . .Dale Helward
Morestan . . . . .Mike Walsh
LaBlache . . . . .Arnie Stenseth
Antoinette Sevigne . . . . .Diana Walker
Josefa Lantenay . . . . .Karen Jensen
Dominique Beaurevers . . . . .Betty Ebert
Benjamin Beaurevers . . . . .Louis Girard
Guard . . . . .Dick Fogell

#160
July 16 - 28, 1963
The Unsinkable Molly Brown
Music and Lyrics by Meredith Willson
Book by Richard Morris
Directed by Jack Ragotzy
Choreographed by Wayne Lamb
Musical Direction by Maurice Lewis
Sets Designed by Curt Senie
Lighting Designed by Peter Simon
Costumes by Ora Crofoot, Ken Andrews
and Sandy Lassila
CAST
Shamus Tobin . . . . .Louis Girard
Michael Tobin . . . . .Peter Simon
Aloysius Tobin . . . . .Ken Andrews
Patrick Tobin . . . . .Farrar Cobb
Molly Tobin . . . . .Merle Louise Letowt
Father Flynn . . . . .Charles Likar
"Leadville" Johnny
Brown . . . . .Barney Hodges
Charlie .Mike Walsh
Christmas Morgan . . . . .Arnie Stenseth
Burt . . . . .Jim Kason
Guitar . . . . .Curt Senie
Sheriff . . . . .Thomas Hoisveen
Miners:
Ken Andrews, Larry Phelps, Farrar Cobb,
Charles Likar, Peter Simon, Robert Robinson,
Dick Fogell, Don Westbrook
Prostitutes . . . . .Diana Walker,
. . . . .Pat Souza,
. . . . .Carol Medusky
Indian Girls:
Linda Bruce, Jackie Better, Rita Brown,
Leslie Moulton
1st Denver Policeman . . . . .Dale Helward
2nd Denver Policeman . . . . .Mike Walsh
3rd Denver Policeman . . . . .Jim Kason

Mrs. McGlone . . . . .Martha Weiss
Monsignor Ryan . . . . .Mike Walsh
Ladies and Gentlemen of Denver:
Patricia Morthland, Rosalie Wheeler, Pat Sousa,
Carol Medusky, Charles Likar, Ken Andrews,
Farrar Cobb
Maids:
Linda Bruce, Jackie Better
Roberts . . . . .Ralph Strait
Professor Gardella . . . . .Robert Robinson
Germaine . . . . .Cynthia Redmayne
Princess DeLong . . . . .Diana Walker
Prince DeLong . . . . .Dale Helward
The Baron and Baroness
of Auld . . . . .Charles Likar,
. . . . .Mary Jane Schilling
Count Ferranti . . . . .Jim Kason
Countess Ethanotous . . . . .Rita Brown
The Duke and Duchess
of Burlingame . . . . .Don Westbrook,
. . . . .Pat Morthland
Malcolm Broderick . . . . .Peter Simon
The Wadlingtons . . . . .Margaret Fjellestad,
. . . . .Thomas Hoisveen

#161
July 30 - August 4, 1963
The Hostage
by Brendan Behan
Directed by Jack Ragotzy
Dance Director - Wayne Lamb
Set Designed by Curt Senie
Light Designed by Peter Simon
Costumes by Ora Crofoot and Ken Andrews
CAST
Pat . . . . .Mike Walsh
Meg Dillon . . . . .Betty Ebert
Colette . . . . .Rita Brown
Bobo . . . . .Cynthia Redmayne
Monsewer . . . . .Louis Girard
Old Ropeen . . . . .Margaret Fjellestad
Russian Sailor . . . . .Charles Likar
Princess Grace . . . . .Barney Hodges
Rio Rita . . . . .Don Westbrook
Mr. Mulleady . . . . .Jim Kason
Miss Gilchrist . . . . .Diana Walker
Leslie . . . . .Dale Helward
Teresal . . . . .Leslie Moulton
I.R.A. Officer . . . . .Arnie Stenseth
Volunteer . . . . .Peter Simon
Ladies of the lodging
house . . . . .Joan Shields,
. . . . .Pat Morthland
Larry, the piano player . . . . .Larry Wolfe

#162
August 6 - 17, 1963
Come Blow Your Horn
by Neil Simon
Directed by Jack Ragotzy
Set Designed by Don Klovstad
Light Designed by Peter Simon
Costumes by Ora Crofoot, Ken Andrews
CAST
Alan Baker . . . . .Dale Helward
Peggy Evans . . . . .Mary Jane Schilling
Buddy Baker . . . . .Jim Kason
Mr. Baker . . . . .Louis Girard
Connie Dayton . . . . .Diana Walker
Mrs. Baker . . . . .Betty Ebert
A Visitor . . . . .Martha Weiss

#163
August 20 - September 1, 1963
Bye Bye Birdie
Book by Michael Stewart
Music by Charles Strouse
Lyrics by Lee Adams
Directed by Louis Girard
Choreographed by Wayne Lamb
Musical Director - Larry Wolfe
Vocal Coach - Tom Kasdorf
Set Designed by Curt Senie
Light Designed by Peter Simon
Costumes by Ora Crofoot, Ken Andrews
and Sandy Lassila
CAST
Albert Peterson . . . . .Dale Helward
Rose Alvarez . . . . .Merle Louise Letowt
Teen Agers:
Margaret Fjellestad, Lou Ann Knudsen,
Susan Reynolds, Pat McDonald, Barbara
Kreling, Linda Bruce, Carol Nowacki, Jackie
Better, Jan English, Dave Smith, Ken Andrews,
Jack Howard, Joe Racz, Bob Black,
Michael Miller, Jon Dykema
Ursula Merkle . . . . .Cynthia Redmayne
Kim MacAfee . . . . .Leslie Moulton
Mrs. MacAfee . . . . .Martha Weiss
Mr. MacAfee . . . . .Ralph Strait
Teen Trio (Margie, Helen, and Martha):
Pat McDonald, Margaret Fjellestad,
Carol Nowacki
Sad Girl .Lynn Denison
Another Sad Girl . . . . .Jackie Better
Policemen . . . . .Dick Fogell,
. . . . .Thomas Hoisveen
Mae Peterson . . . . .Norma Glenn
Reporters . . . . .Don Westbrook,
. . . . .Barney Hodges,
. . . . .Jim Kason
Conrad Birdie . . . . .Peter Simon
Guitar Man . . . . .Curt Senie
Conductor . . . . .Bill Lampe
Mayor . . . . .Mike Walsh
Mayor's Wife . . . . .Joan Shields
Hugo Peabody . . . . .Farrar Cobb
Randolph MacAfee . . . . .Jack Houston
Mrs. Merkle . . . . .Jane Courtney
Neighbors:
Joan Shields, Margaret Fjellestad,
Smith .Pat McDonald
Gloria Rasputin . . . . .Rosemary Brady
100 Ways Ballet Dancers:
Don Westbrook, Mike Walsh, Bill Lampe,
Jim Kason
T.V. Stage Manager . . . . .Bill Lampe
Stage Hands:
Joe Racz, Dave Smith, Bob Black, Jon Dykema
Audio Man . . . . .Thomas Hoisveen
Wardrobe Women . . . . .Jackie Better,
. . . . .Margaret Fjellestad
Quartette:
Marcel Achard, Barney Hodges, Jim Kason,
Ken Andrews, Don Westbrook
Harvey Johnson . . . . .Ken Andrews
Mr. Johnson . . . . .Bill Lampe
Charles F. Maude . . . . .Barney Hodges
Shriners:
Wayne Lamb, Louis Girard, Mike Walsh,
Jim Kason, Bill Lampe, Barney Hodges,
Don Westbrook

#164
September 3 - 15, 1963
In One Bed. . .And Out the Other
A Boulevard Comedy by
Mawby Green and Ed Feilbert
(Adopted from the Paris success,
Une Nuit Chez Vous... Madame!
by Jean de Letraz)
Directed by Jack Ragotzy
Set Designed by Richard Jackson
Light Designed by Peter Simon
Costumes by Ora Crofoot, Ken Andrews
CAST
Maurice . . . . .Jim Kason
Huguette Dubois . . . . .Betty Ebert
Gaston Dubois . . . . .Ralph Strait
Didier . . . . .Dale Helward
Clara . . . . .Merle Louise Letowt
Rosine . . . . .Sigrid Nelsson
Aunt Alice . . . . .Louis Girard

1964 Season

#165
June 9 - 21, 1964
Take Her, She's Mine
by Phoebe and Henry Ephron
Directed by Jack Ragotzy
Set Designed by Lee Fischer
Lights Designed by George McDaniel
Costumes by Ora Crofoot and Ken Andrews
CAST
Principal .Mike Walsh
Mollie Michaelson . . . . .Elizabeth Berger
Frank Michaelson . . . . .John Newton
Anne Michaelson . . . . .Betty Ebert
Liz Michaelson . . . . .Susanne Kopit
Airline Clerk . . . . .Ann Henderson
Emmett . . . . .Ken Andrews
Adele McDougall . . . . .Jane Lyman
Sarah Walker . . . . .Carol Miller
Donn Bowdry . . . . .George McDaniel
A Freshman . . . . .Charles Potts
Richard Gluck . . . . .Harold Smith
Alfred Grieffinger . . . . .Del Lewis
Alex Loomis . . . . .Frank Coleman
Mr. Whitmeyer . . . . .Louis Girard
Linda Lehman . . . . .Dulcie Creasey
Clancy Sussman . . . . .Mike Walsh
Mr. Hibbetts . . . . .Del Lewis

#166
June 23 - July 19, 1964
My Fair Lady
Book and Lyrics by Alan Jay Lerner
Music by Frederick Loewe
Adapted from
George Bernard Shaw's *Pygmalion*
Produced on the Screen by Gabriel Pascal
Directed by Jack Ragotzy
Musical Direction by John White
Choreographed by Wayne Lamb
Scenery Designed by Lee Fischer
Lights Designed by John Flegel and Bruce Mills
Costumes by Ora Crofoot and Ken Andrews
CAST
Buskers:
Elizabeth Berger, Wayne Lamb, Bobbi Waite
A Child . . . . .John Reeds
Mrs. Eynsford-Hill . . . . .Dulcie Creasy
Freddy Eynsford Hill . . . . .Frank Coleman
Eliza Doolittle . . . . .Janet Hayes
Col. Pickering . . . . .Louis Girard
A Prostitute . . . . .Stephanie Moss
Henry Higgins . . . . .John Newton
Selsey Man . . . . .Don Westbrook
Hoxton Man . . . . .Art Sellers
1st Cockney . . . . .Ken Andrews
2nd Cockney . . . . .Hal Smith
Bartender . . . . .Charles Potts
Harry . . . . .Del Lewis
Jamie . . . . .George McDaniel
Alfred P. Doolittle . . . . .Alfred Hinckley
Mrs. Pearce . . . . .Carol Miller
Mrs. Hopkins . . . . .Elizabeth Berger
Butler . . . . .Don Westbrook
Servants:
Dulcie Creasy, Judy Noble, Ken Andrews,
Penne Stansell, Mary Eva Reque
Mrs. Higgins . . . . .Dusty Reeds
Chauffeur . . . . .Charles Potts
Footmen .Hal Smith,
. . . . .Art Sellers
Lord Boxington . . . . .Del Lewis
Lady Boxington . . . . .Penne Stansell
Constable . . . . .Charles Potts
Flower Girl . . . . .Jane Lyman
Duchess of Peltingham . . . . .Sheila Galvin
Zoltan Karpathy . . . . .Don Westbrook
Queen of Transylvania . . . . .Susanne Kopit
Ambassador . . . . .Hugh McMahon
Mrs. Higgins' Maid . . . . .Ann Henderson

#167
July 21 - 25, 1964
[World Premiere]
Here Come the Butterflies
by Allen Boretz
Directed by Jack Ragotzy
Set Design by Lee Fischer
Lights by George McDaniel
Costumes by Ora Crofoot and Ken Andrews
CAST
Anna McVey, ...Carol Miller
Ned Haven, ...John Newton
Wainwright, ...Louis Girard
Penny . . . . .Andrea Perejda
Kenny .Robin Newton
June Haven, ...Betty Ebert
Aldridge Jackson . . . . .Phillip Lindsay
Ethan Sain . . . . .Frank Coleman
Dr. Zimmerman . . . . .Janet Hayes
Woman . . . . .Judy Noble

#168
July 28 - August 9, 1964
The Sound of Music
Music by Richard Rodgers
Lyrics by Oscar Hammerstein II
Book by Howard Lindsay and Russel Crouse
(Suggested by *The Trapp Family Singers*,
by Maria Augusta Trapp)
Directed by Louis Girard
Choreographed by Wayne Lamb
Musical Direction by John White
Lighting Design by George McDaniel
Costumes by Ora Crofoot and Ken Andrews
CAST
Maria Ranier . . . . .Janet Hayes
Sister Berthe . . . . .Penne Stansell
Sister Margaretta . . . . .Mary Eva Reque
The Mother Abbess . . . . .Mattie Willis
Sister Sophia . . . . .Judy Noble
Captain Georg Von Trapp . . . . .John Newton
Franz, the Butler . . . . .George McDaniel
Frau Schmidt . . . . .Stephanie Moss
Children of Cpt. Von Trapp:
"Liesl" . . . . .Seila Galvin
"Friedrich" . . . . .Ken Andrews
"Louisa" . . . . .Judy Hays
"Kurt" . . . . .Jackie Houston
"Brigitta" . . . . .Jan English
"Marta" . . . . .Andrea Perejda
"Gretl" .Kathy Lutz
Rolf Gruber . . . . .Frank Coleman
Elsa Schraeder . . . . .Dulcie Creasy
Max Detweiler . . . . .Del Lewis
Herr Zeller . . . . .Don Westbrook
Frau Zeller . . . . .Penne Stansell
Baron Elberfeld . . . . .Wayne Lamb
Baroness Elderfeld . . . . .Rosemary Brady
A Postulant . . . . .Carol Miller
Admiral Von Schreiber . . . . .Louis Girard
Neighbors of Captain Von Trapp, Nuns, Novices,
Postulants, Contestants in the Festival Concert:
Ann Henderson, Dale Soules, Joe Racz,
Hal Smith, Charles Potts, Susanne Kopit

#169
August 11 - 15, 1964
Rattle of a Simple Man
by Charles Dyer
Directed by Jack Ragotzy
Set Designed by Dusty Reeds
Lighting by George McDaniel
Costumes by Ora Crofoot and Ken Andrews
CAST
Cyrenne .Janet Hayes
Percy . . . . .John Newton
Richard . . . . .Del Lewis

#170
August 18 - September 6, 1964
Irma La Douce
Original Book and Lyrics
by Alexandre Breffort
English Book and Lyrics by Julian More,
David Heneker and Monty Norman
Music by Marguerite Monnot
Directed by Jack Ragotzy and Wayne Lamb
Choreography and Special Staging
by Wayne Lamb and Angelo Mango
Musical Direction by John White
Set Designed by Lee Fischer
Lighting by George McDaniel
Costumes by Ora Crofoot, Ken Andrews,
Fritz Frurip, Kay Gould
CAST
Bob-Le-Hotu . . . . .Michael Walsh
Irma-La-Douce, A Poule . . . . .Karen Jensen
A Client . . . . .Charles Potts
Jojo-Les-Yeux-Sales,
a mec .Ken Andrews
Roberto-Les-Diams,
a mec . . . . .George McDaniel
Percil-Le-Noir, a mec . . . . .Art Sellers
Frangipane, a mec . . . . .Del Lewis
Polyte-Le-Mou, a mec . . . . . . .Don Westbrook
Police Inspector . . . . .Louis Girard
Nester-Le-Fripe,
a law student . . . . .Frank Coleman
M. Bougne, a ballroom
owner .Wayne Lamb
Counsel for the
Prosecution . . . . .Carol Miller

Counsel for the Defense . . . . . . .Steve Murdock
An Usher .Dale Soules
An Honest Man . . . . .J.A.L. Ramanger
Gendarmes .Hal Smith,
. . . . .Charles Potts
First Warder . . . . .Charles Potts
Second Warder . . . . .Hal Smith
Third Warder . . . . .Joe Racz
A Priest .Steve Murdock
A Tax Inspector . . . . .Charles Potts
2 False Poules . . . . .Sheila Galvin,
. . . . .Stephanie Moss
Poules:
Dulcie Creasy, Ann Henderson, Rosemary Brady,
Judy Noble, Carol Miller
Dancers in "The Arctic Ballet":
Nestor . . . . .Wayne Lamb
Penguins . . . . .Charles Potts,
. . . . .Hal Smith,
. . . . .Don Westbrook
False Irmas . . . . .Dulcie Creasy,
. . . . .Ann Henderson,
. . . . .Judy Noble

#171
September 8 - 13, 1964
**Oh Dad, Poor Dad,
Mamma's Hung You in The Closet
and I'm Feelin' So Sad**
by Arthur L. Kopit
Directed by Louis Girard
Scenery Designed by Lee Fischer
Lights Designed by George McDaniel
Costumes by Ora Crofoot and Kay Gould
CAST
Madame Rosepettle . . . . .Betty Ebert
Jonathan .Ken Andrews
Rosalie . . . . .Susanne Kopit
Commodore Roseaboue . . . . .Louis Girard
Head Bellboy . . . . .Stephen Murdock
Bellboys and Bellgirls:
Charles Potts, Michael Hills, Judy Noble,
Ann Henderson, Rosemary Brady
A Pair of Plants . . . . .Judy Noble,
. . . . .Ann Henderson
Two Waiters . . . . .Stephen Murdock,
. . . . .Michael Hills
A Corpse . . . . .Charles Potts

#172
September 15 - 20, 1964
The Fantasticks
Book and Lyrics by Tom Jones
Music by Harvey L. Schmidt
(Suggested by the play *Les Romanesques*
by Edmund Rostand)
Directed and Choreographed by Wayne Lamb
Musical Direction by John White
Setting Designed by Lee Fischer
Lighting by George McDaniel
Costumes by Ora Crofoot and Ken Andrews
CAST
The Mute .Dale Soules
The Boy's Father
(Hucklebee) . . . . .Del Lewis
The Girl's Father
(Bellamy) . . . . .Michael Walsh
The Girl (Luisa) . . . . .Dulcie Creasy
The Boy (Matt) . . . . .George McDaniel
The Narrator (El Gallo) . . . . . . .Frank Coleman
The Old Actor (Henry) . . . . .Louis Girard
The Man Who Dies (Mortimer) . . .Wayne Lamb

1965 Season

#173
June 1 - 12, 1965
Never Too Late
(No Program on File)
by Arthur Long
Directed by Jack P. Ragotzy
Set Designed by Lee Fischer
Lighting by George McDaniel
Costumes by Ora Crofoot and Ken Andrews
CAST
Grace Kimbrough . . . . .Rowena Balos
Harry Lambert . . . . .Louis Girard
Edith Lambert . . . . .Betty Ebert
Dr. James Kimbrough . . . . . .Craig Vandenburgh
Charlie . . . . .Dale Helward
Kate . . . . .Dulcie Creasy
Mr. Foley . . . . .Armaund Storace,
. . . . .Charlie Potts
Mayor Crane . . . . .Del Lewis
Policeman . . . . .George McDaniel

#174
June 15 - July 4, 1965
Camelot
Book and Lyrics by Alan Jay Lerner
Music by Frederick Loewe
Based on *The Once and Future King*
by T.H. White
Directed by Jack Ragotzy
Choreographed by Wayne Lamb
Musical Direction by Tom Kasdorf
Set Designed by Lee Fischer
Lighting by George McDaniel
Costumes by Ora Crofoot and Ken Andrews
CAST
Sir Dinadan . . . . .George McDaniel
Merlyn . . . . .Del Lewis
Arthur . . . . .John Newton
Guenevere . . . . .Janet Hayes
Morgan Le Fey . . . . .Joan Dunham
Lancelot .Angelo Mango
Squire Dap . . . . .Wayne Lamb
Pellinore .Louis Girard
Sir Lional . . . . .Del Lewis
Sir Sagramore . . . . .Craig Vandenburgh
Mordred .Dale Helward
Tom of Warwick . . . . .Eileen Dietz
Ladies of Camelot:
Lady Sybil . . . . .Dulcie Creasy
Lady Anne . . . . .Rowena Balos
Lady Catherine . . . . .Linda Hessian
Other Ladies of Camelot:
Adrienne Barbeau, Lana Caradimas,
Donna Maloney, Carol Ries
Lords of Camelot:
Ken Andrews, Richard Fuchs, Mikel Hatoff,
Charles Potts, H. Joe Scott
Pages . . . . .Diana Van Patten,
. . . . .Eileen Dietz
Jesters:
Charles Potts, Ken Andrews, Donna Maloney,
Knights of the Round Table:
Giliam . . . . .Wayne Lamb
Blient . . . . .Ken Andrews
Castor:
H. Joe Scott and Richard Fuchs, Michael Hatoff,
Charles Potts
Morgan Le Fey's Court:
Unicorn .Richard Fuchs
Hawk . . . . .Charles Potts
Spider . . . . .Carol Ries
Owl . . . . .Linda Hessian
Others in LeFey's Court:
H. Joe Scott, Mikel Hatoff, Donna Maloney,
Dulcie Creasy, Rowena Balos,
Adrienne Barbeau, Lana Caradimas
Soloist in "Guenevere"
montage . . . . .Adrienne Barbeau

#175
July 6 - 11, 1965
[World Premiere]
Sell Me Down the River, Darling
(No Program on File)
by Theodore Apstein
Directed by Jack P. Ragotzy
Setting Designed by Lee Fischer
Lighting by George McDaniel and Ron Camp
Costumes by Ora Crofoot and Ken Andrews
CAST
Fern Walters . . . . .Joan Dunham
Howard Walters . . . . .John Newton
Addie Borg . . . . .Betty Ebert
Ken Walters . . . . .Mark Dunham
Janice Walters . . . . .Heidi Dunham
Maggie .Linda Hessian
Nora Belmont . . . . .Janet Hayes
Iris Tremoines . . . . .Dusty Reeds
Peter Tremoines . . . . .George McDaniel
Isis Tremoines . . . . .Dulcie Creasy
David Belmont . . . . .Dale Helward
Abner Gold . . . . .Louis Girard
Rosemary Gold . . . . .Lana Caradimas
Frank Swanson . . . . .Phillip Lindsay
Caroline Swanson . . . . .Adrienne Barbeau
Tremoinec Villagers:
Ken Andrews. Elliott Apstein, Susan Apstein,
Rowena Balos, Donna Maloney, Linda Marshall,
Charles Potts, Craig Vandenburgh

#176
July 13 - 18, August 3 - 8, 1965
Stop the World — I Want to Get Off
Book, Music and Lyrics by Leslie Bricusse and
Anthony Newley
Direction by Wayne Lamb
Musical Direction by Tom Kasdorf and
Charles Dodsley Walker
Set Designed by Lee Fischer
Lighting by George McDaniel
Costumes by Ora Crofoot and Ken Andrews
CAST
Littlechap . . . . .Angelo Mango
The Women in His Life . . . . .Joan Dunham
Daughter Susan . . . . .Rowena Balos
Daughter Jane . . . . .Adrienne Barbeau
Chorus:
Lana Caradimas, Dulcie Creasy, Del Lewis,
Donna Maloney, Linda Marshall, George
McDaniel, Penne Sue Stansell, Diana Van Patten,
Peter Walker.

#177
July 20 - August 1, 1965
Mary, Mary
by Jean Kerr
Directed by R. D. Simons
Set Designed by Lee Fischer
Light Designed by George McDaniel

Costumes by Ken Andrews
CAST
Bob McKellaway . . . . .John Newton
Tiffany Richards . . . . .Dulcie Creasy
Oscar Nelson . . . . .Louis Girard
Dirk Winston . . . . .Dale Helward
Mary McKellaway . . . . Janet Hayes

#178
August 10 - 22, 1965
[World Premiere]
Baby Talk
by Mawby Green and Ed Feilbert
Directed by Jack P. Ragotzy
Setting Designed by Lee Fischer
Lighting by George McDaniel
Costumes by Ora Crofoot, Ken Andrews, and Clara Cheneweth
CAST
Aunt Pauline . . . . .Dusty Reeds
Henriette Fontanges . . . . .Betty Ebert
Jacques . . . . .Angelo Mango
Edmond Fontanges . . . . .John Newton
Simone .Joan Dunham
Augustin .Dale Helward
Mariette . . . . .Dulcie Creasy
Gambier .Louis Girard
Loulou .Rowena Balos

#179
August 24 - September 12, 1965
A Funny Thing Happened on the Way to the Forum
A musical comedy based on the plays of Plautus
Book by Burt Shevelove and Larry Gelbart
Music and Lyrics by Stephen Sondheim
Directed by Wayne Lamb
Musical Direction by Tom Kasdorf
Choreography by Wayne Lamb
Set Designed by Lee Fischer
Costume Designed by Ken Andrews
CAST
Prologus . . . . .Dale Helward
The Proteans:
Charles Potts, H. Joe Scott, Ken Andrews
Senex, a citizen of Rome . . . . .Louis Girard
Domina, his wife . . . . .Dulcie Creasy
Hero, his son . . . . .Angelo Mango
Hysterium, slave . . . . .Del Lewis
Lycus, a dealer in
courtesans . . . . .Richard Fuchs
Pseudolus, slave to Hero . . . . .Dale Helward
The Courtesans:
Tintinabula"—Donna Shadden
"Panacea"—Linda Hessian
"The Twins" . . . . .Rowena Balos,
. . . . .Allison Crockett
"Vibrata" . . . . .Adrienne Barbeau
"Gymnasia" . . . . .Lana Caradimas
Attendant . . . . .Mary Jane Voelker
Philia . . . . .Joan Dunham
Erronius, a citizen of
Rome . . . . .Stephen Murdock
Milos Gloriosus,
a warrior . . . . .George McDaniel

#180
September 14 - 19, 1965
The Threepenny Opera
Original Text by Bertold Brecht and Kurt Weill
English adaptation of book and lyrics by Marc Blitzstein
Direction by Wayne Lamb
Musical Direction by Tom Kasdorf
Set Designed by Lee Fischer
Lighting by George McDaniel
Costumes by Ora Crofoot
CAST
Narrator . . . . .George McDaniel
Macheath (Mack-the-
knife) . . . . .Angelo Mango
J.J. Peachum . . . . .Del Lewis
Mrs. Peachum . . . . .Betty Ebert
Filch . . . . .Ralph Strait
Jake . . . . .George McDaniel
Walt . . . . .Stephen Murdock
Polly Peachum . . . . .Joan Dunham
Reverend Kimball . . . . .Wayne Lamb
Commissioner Tiger
Brown .Louis Girard
Jenny . . . . .Dulcie Creasy
Lucy Brown . . . . .Adrienne Barbeau
Warden Smith . . . . .Jeff Click
Constables . . . . .Dan Bernhard,
. . . . .Micheal Jon Conner
Betty . . . . .Linda Cole
Dolly . . . . .Linda Hessian
Molly . . . . .Mary Moltz
Coaxer . . . . .Allison Crockett

#181
September 21 - 26, 1965
In One Bed. . . And Out the Other
(No Program on File)
by Mawby Green and Ed Feilbert
Directed by Jack P. Ragotzy
Set Designed by Jack P. Ragotzy
Lighting by Allison Crockett
Costumes by Ora Crofoot
CAST
Maurice . . . . .Angelo Mango
Didier . . . . .George McDaniel
Huguette Du Bois . . . . .Betty Ebert
Gaston Du Bois . . . . .Ralph Strait
Clara . . . . .Joan Dunham
Rosine . . . . .Dulcie Creasy
Aunt Alice . . . . .Del Lewis

1966 Season

#182
June 7 - 11, 1966
Don Juan in Hell
(No Program on File)
by George Bernard Shaw
Directed by Jack Ragotzy
CAST
Dona Ana de Ulloa . . . . .Dulcie Creasy
Don Juan Tenorio . . . . .George McDaniel
The Statue, Don Gonzalo . . . . . . .Louis Girard
The Devil . . . . .Jack Ragotzy,
. . . . .Del Lewis

#183
June 14 - 26, 1966
Tobacco Road
by Jack Kirkland,
adapted from the novel by Erskine Caldwell
Directed by Jack Ragotzy
Scenery and Lighting Designed by Alan Hedges
Costumes by Ora Crofoot and Abbie Lewis
CAST
Dude Lester . . . . .Angelo Mango
Ada Lester . . . . .Dusty Reeds
Jeeter Lester . . . . .Louis Girard
Ellie May . . . . .Dulcie Creasy
Grandma Lester . . . . .Allison Crockett
Lov Bensey . . . . .George McDaniel
Henry Peabody . . . . .Del Lewis
Sister Bessie Rice . . . . .Betty Ebert
Pearl .Erika Fiebich
Captain Tim . . . . .Perry Mallette
George Payne . . . . .Edward Levey

#184
June 28 - July 10, 1966
Funny Girl
Music by Jule Styne
Lyrics by Bob Merrill
Book by Isobel Lennart from her original story
Directed by Jack Ragotzy
Choreographed by Wayne Lamb
Musical Direction by Tom Kasdorf
Scenery by Dusty Reeds
Lighting by Alan Hedges
Costumes by Ora Crofoot
CAST
Fanny Brice . . . . .Karen Jensen
Emma . . . . .Dulcie Creasy
John, the stage manager . . . . .Perry Mallette
Mrs. Brice . . . . .Betty Ebert
Mrs. Strakosh . . . . .Hope Hommersand
Mrs. Meeker . . . . .Arleen Goldberg
Mrs. O'Malley . . . . .Janet Crowe
Tom Kenney . . . . .Del Lewis
Eddie Ryan . . . . .Angelo Mango
Heckie . . . . .Dick Fuchs
Workmen . . . . .Ed Levey,
. . . . .Darrell Ruhl
Snub Taylor . . . . .Wayne Lamb
Five Finger Finney . . . . .Tony Colby
Bubbles . . . . .Jacquelyn Sonenberg
Polly . . . . .Mary Wakefield
Maude .Susan Baker
Nick Arnstein . . . . .George McDaniel
Florenz Ziegfeld, Jr . . . . .Louis Girard
Mimsey . . . . .Dusty Reeds
Ziegfeld Singer . . . . .Orlando White
Adolph .Edward Jay
Cathy . . . . .Erika Fiebich
Vera .Dale Hopkins
Mr. Renaldi . . . . .Del Lewis
Showgirls:
Erika Fiebich, Dale Hopkins, Alice Reno,
Jacquelyn Sonenberg
Dancers:
Susan Baker, Dulcie Creasy, Hope Hommersand,
Mary Wakefield, Edward Jay, Ed Levey,
Del Lewis, Perry Mallette, Darrell Ruhl,
Orlando White

#185
July 12 - 17, 1966
The Roar of the Greasepaint — The Smell of the Crowd
Book, Music and Lyrics by Leslie Bricusse and Anthony Newley
Directed by Wayne Lamb
Musical Direction by Tom Kasdorf
Sets and Lights Designed by Alan Hedges
Costumes by Ora Crofoot
CAST
Sir . . . . .Del Lewis

Cocky .Angelo Mango
The Kid .Dulcie Creasy
The Girl .Erika Fiebich
The Negro . . . . .Orlando White
The Gang:
Susan Baker, Darrell Ruhl, Hope Hommersand,
Cris Berry, Mary Wakefield, Tony Colby,
Jacquelyn Sonenberg, Ed Levey
The Lost Urchins:
Betty Ebert, Louis Girard, Gayle Hinckley,
George McDaniel, Dusty Reeds, Jack Ragotzy

#186
July 19 - 31, 1966
Who's Afraid of Virginia Woolf?
by Edward Albee
Directed by Jack Ragotzy
Scenery Designed by Dusty Reeds
Lighting Designed by Alan Hedges
Costumes by Ora Crofoot and Dale Hopkins
CAST
Martha . . . . .Betty Ebert
George .Louis Girard
Honey . . . . .Dale Hopkins
Nick . . . . .George McDaniel

#187
August 2 - 19, 1966
**How to Succeed in Business
Without Really Trying**
Book by Abe Barrows, Jack Weinstock,
and Willie Gilbert
Music and Lyrics by Frank Loesser
Based on the novel by Shepherd Mead
Directed by Jack Ragotzy and Wayne Lamb
Choreographed by Wayne Lamb
Musical Direction by Tom Kasdorf
Scenery Designed by Dusty Reeds
Lighting by Alan Hedges
Costumes by Ora Crofoot
CAST
Voice . . . . Jack Ragotzy
Finch . . . . .Angelo Mango
Gatch . . . . .George McDaniel
Jenkins . . . . .Darrell Ruhl
Tackaberry . . . . .Cris Berry
Peterson . . . . .Ed Levey
J.B. Biggley . . . . .Louis Girard
Rosemary . . . . .Dulcie Creasy
Bratt . . . . .Dick Fuchs
Smitty . . . . .Susan Baker
Frump . . . . .Del Lewis
Miss Jones . . . . .Hope Hommersand
Mr. Twimble . . . . .Perry Mallette
Hedy . . . . .Jacquelyn Sonenberg
Scrubwomen . . . . .Dusty Reeds,
. . . . .Janet Crowe,
. . . . .Betty Ebert
Miss Krumholtz . . . . .Mary Wakefield
Toynbee .George McDaniel
Ovington . . . . .Perry Mallette
Policeman . . . . .Dick Cady
Womper .Ed Levey
Matthews . . . . Ed Jay
Johnson . . . . .Dick Cady
Davis . . . . .Ed Jay
Secretaries:
Janet Crowe, Erika Fiebich, Karyn Fisher,
Dale Hopkins, Alice Reno

#188
August 23 - September 4, 1966
Oliver!
Music, Lyrics and Book by Lionel Bart
Directed and Choreographed by Wayne Lamb
Musical Direction by Tom Kasdorf
Scenery Designed by Alan Hedges
Lighting by Ron Camp and George McDaniel
Costumes by Ora Crofoot
London Backdrop by Dusty Reeds
CAST
Oliver Twist . . . . .Jack Houston
At the Workhouse:
Mr. Bumble, the Beadle . . . . .Del Lewis
Mrs. Corney, the Matron . . . . .Mary Wakefield
Old Sally, a Pauper . . . . .Dale Hopkins
At the Undertaker's:
Mr. Sowerberry . . . . .Darrell Ruhl
Mrs. Sowerberry . . . . .Hope Hommersand
Charlotte Sowerberry . . . . .Karyn Fisher
Noah Claypole . . . . .Edward Jay
At the Thieves' Kitchen:
Fagin . . . . .Louis Girard
The Artful Dodger . . . . .Angelo Mango
Nancy . . . . .Dulcie Creasy
Bet . . . . .Erika Fiebich
Bill Sykes . . . . .George McDaniel
Sykes' Dog . . . . .Ming
At Mr. Brownlow's:
Mr. Brownlow . . . . .Perry Mallette
Mrs. Bedwin . . . . .Dusty Reeds
Dr. Grimwig . . . . .Ed Levey
Workhouse Boys and Fagin's Gang:
Don Alles, Neil E. Dale II, Jon Faulkner,
Edward Jay, Richard Harrell, Ed Levey, Bud
Livers, James Mandrell, Brendan Ragotzy,
John Reeds, Robin Reeds, Louis Sinclair,
Scott Thompsett
Londoners:
Susan Baker, Chris Berry, Janet Crowe, Richard
Fuchs, Betsie Gustke, Robin Reeds, Jacquelyn
Sonenberg, Betty Ebert, Jack Ragotzy and
Gayle Hinckley

#189
September 6 - 18, 1966
Any Wednesday
by Muriel Resnick
Directed by Jack Ragotzy and Wayne Lamb
Scenery Designed by Dusty Reeds
Lighting by Alan Hedges
Costumes by Ora Crofoot
CAST
John Cleves . . . . .Louis Girard
Ellen Gordon . . . . .Dulcie Creasy
Cass Henderson . . . . .George McDaniel
Dorothy Cleves . . . . .Betty Ebert

#190
September 20 - 25, 1966
The Owl and the Pussycat
by Bill Manhoff
Directed by Wayne Lamb
Scenery Designed by Dusty Reeds
Lighting by Alan Hedges
Costumes by Ora Crofoot
CAST
F. Sherman . . . . .George McDaniel
Doris W. . . . . .Beverly Todd

1967 Season

#191
June 13 - 25, 1967
Barefoot in the Park
by Neil Simon
Directed by Jack Ragotzy
Setting Designed by George Hedges,
Dusty Reeds
and Jack Ragotzy
Lighting by Alan Hedges
Costumes by Ora Crofoot
CAST
Corie Bratter . . . . .Joan Dunham
Telephone Man . . . . .Joseph Cardinale
Delivery Man . . . . .Darrell Ruhl
Paul Bratter . . . . .George McDaniel
Mrs. Banks . . . . .Dusty Reeds
Victor Velasco . . . . .Louis Girard

#192
June 27 - July 9, 1967
Sweet Charity
(No Program on File)
Book by Neil Simon
Music by Cy Coleman, Lyrics by Dorothy Fields
Staged and Choreographed by Wayne Lamb
Book directed by Louis Girard
Music directed by Tom Kasdorf
Setting by Dusty Reeds and Alan Hedges
Lighting by George Hedges and Fred Ellis
Costumes by Jeanne Kunznik, Ken Andrews
and Bill Meyer
CAST
Charity . . . . .Karen (Jensen) Arthur
Dark Glasses . . . . .Neil Peckett
Bystander . . . . .Robert K. Mott
Married Lady . . . . .Catherine Lake
Woman With Hat . . . . .Jeanne Kunznik
Ice Cream Vendor . . . . .Alan Mehl
Baseball Player . . . . .Fred Ellis
Career Girl . . . . .Sallie Shockley
Man with Dog . . . . .George Spelvin
Dog . . . . .Siren
Young Spanish Man . . . . .Neil Peckett
Dirty Old Man . . . . .Rod Layden
1st Cop .Darrell Ruhl
2nd Cop . . . . Jon Scheer
Helene .Joan Dunham
Nickie . . . . .Nicki Gallas
Herman . . . . .Louis Girard
Fan-Dango Ballroom Dance Hall Girls:
"Frenchy" . . . . .Jacquelyn Sonenberg
"Sally" . . . . .Sallie Shockley
"Elaine" . . . . .Susan Chapman
"Carmen" . . . . .Jeanne Kunznik
"Suzanne" . . . . .Chris Loken
"Betsy" . . . . .Francine Karasik
Marvin . . . . .Wayne Lamb
Doorman . . . . .Jim Bennett
Ursala . . . . .Jacquelyn Sonenberg
Vittorio Vidal . . . . .Joseph Cardinale
Manfred .Jon Scheer
Receptionist . . . . .Francine Karasik
Old Maid . . . . .Catherine Lake
Young Intellectual . . . . .Susan Chapman
Oscar .George McDaniel
Daddy .Johann Sebastian
Brubeck . . . . .Joseph Cardinale
Rosie . . . . .Sallie Shockley
Good Fairy . . . . .Jeanne Kunznik
Lost People of Times Square:
Betty Ebert, Gayle Hinckley, Jack Ragotzy,
Dusty Reeds

#193
July 11 - July 23, 1967
On a Clear Day You Can See Forever
Book and Lyrics by Alan Jay Lerner
Music by Burton Lane
Directed by Jack Ragotzy and Wayne Lamb
Musical Direction by Tom Kasdorf
Sets by Dusty Reeds and Alan Hedges
Lighting by George Hedges and Alan Mehl
Costumes by Ora Crofoot
CAST
The Present:
Dr. Mark Bruckner ....George McDaniel
Mrs. Hatch ....Jeanne Kunznik
Daisy Gamble ....Joan Dunham
Muriel Bunson ....Jacquelyn Sonnenberg
James Preston ....Darrell Ruhl
Warren Smith ....Joseph Cardinale
Patty ....Sallie Shockley
Sally ....Francine Karasik
Scout Leader ....James N. Bernett
Boy and Cub Scouts:
Alan Mehl, Mark Dunham, Brendan Ragotzy
Little Girl ....Heidi Dunham
Dr. Conrad Fuller ....Louis Girard
B.C.A. Official ....Darrell Ruhl
Students and Friends:
Susan Chapman, Fred Ellis, Catherine Lake,
Robert K. Mott, Neil Peckett, Jon Sheer,
Kim Barber, Marsha Lyttle
The Past:
Melinda ....Joan Dunham
Samuel Wells ....Louis Girard
Mrs. Welles ....Dusty Reeds
Sir Hubert Insdale ....Joseph Cardinale
Hubert Insdale ....Rod Layden
The Solicitor ....Darrell Ruhl
Edward Moncrief ....Angelo Mango
Flora ....Francine Karasik
Party Guests and Passengers of the "Trelawney":
James N. Bennett, Kim Barber, Susan Chapman,
Fred Ellis, Marsa Lyttle, Alan Mehl, Robert K.
Mott, John Scheer, Jacquelyn Sonenberg
Stowaways on the "Trelawney":
Betty Ebert, Gayle Hinckley, Wayne Lamb,
Jack Ragotzy

#194
July 25 - August 6, 1967
The Odd Couple
by Neil Simon
Directed by Louis Girard
Settings Designed by Allen Hedges
and Dusty Reeds
Lighting by George Hedges
Costumes by Susan Chapman
CAST
Speed ....Angelo Mango
Murray ....Louis Girard
Roy ....James N. Bennett
Vinnie ....Darrell Ruhl
Oscar Madison ....Joseph Cardinale
Felix Unger ....George McDaniel
Gwendolyn Pigeon ....Jacquelyn Sonenberg
Cecily Pigeon ....Francine Karasik

#195
August 8 - August 20, 1967
Half a Sixpence
Music and Lyrics by David Heneker
Play by Beverley Cross
(from the novel by H.G. Wells)
Directed and Choreographed by Wayne Lamb
Music Direction by Tom Kasdorf
Settings by Dusty Reeds
Lighting by George Hedges
Costumes by Ora Crofoot
CAST
Arthur Kipps ....Angelo Mango
Sid Pornick ....Ken Andrews
Buggins ....Rod Layden
Pearce ....Robert K. Mott
Carshot ....John Scheer
Flo ....Colleen Hill
Victoria ....Jill Ray
Kate ....Francine Karasik
Emma ....Susan Chapman
Shalford ....Louis Girard
Mrs. Walsingham ....Dusty Reeds
Mrs. Botting ....Jeanne Kunznik
Ann ....Sallie Shockley
Helen ....Betty Ebert
Young Walsingham ....Darrell Ruhl
Chitterlow ....Joseph Cardinale
Laura ....Jill Ray
Girl ....Catherine Lake
Boy ....Fred Ellis
Photographer ....Neil Peckett
First Reporter ....Fred Ellis
Second Reporter ....Jon Scheer
Gwendolyn ....Jacquelyn Sonenberg
Guests on Mrs. Botting's Boat:
Jack Ragotzy, Gale Hinckley, Wayne Lamb

#196
August 22 - August 27, 1967
**The Persecution and Assassination of
Jean-Paul Marat
as Performed by the Inmates
of The Asylum of Charenton
under the Direction of the Marquis de Sade**
by Peter Weiss, Music by Richard Peaslee
English Version by Geoffrey Skelton,
Verse Adaptation by Adrian Mitchell
Special Playing Version by Jack Ragotzy
Directed by Wayne Lamb
Musical Director by Tom Kasdorf
Sets and Lights by Alan Hedges
Lighting by Gary Lee McCormick
Costumes by Ora Crofoot
CAST
Nuns ....Susan Chapman,
..........................Catherine Lake
Guards:
George Hedges, Neil Peckett, William Meyers,
James Hooper
Monsieur Coulmier,
Director of the Asylum ...Joseph Cardinale
Inmates of the Asylum of Charenton:
The Musician ....Larry Wolfe
Woman with Baby ....Jacquelyn Sonenberg
Imbecile ....Jon Scheer
Laughing Woman ....Francine Karasik
Homicidal Maniac ....James N. Bennett
Man with Club Foot ....Rod Layden
Thumb-sucker ....Robert K. Mott
Schizophrenic with
Ribbon ....Darrell Ruhl
Erotomaniac ....William Davis
Man in Strait Jacket .....Angelo Mango
Paranoiac ....Dale Helward
Woman with Crutch ....Jeanne Kunznik
Girl with Sleeping
Sickness ....Sallie Shockley
Catatonic Girl ....Margaret Crossman
Young Man with Bugle .....Robin Reeds
Girl with Twitch ....Colleen Hill
Donatien Alphonse
Francois, the Marquis
de Sade ....Louis Girard
The Simpleton ....Ken Andrews
The Hunchback ....Perry Mallette
Cast of "The Persecution and Assassination
of Marat":
Author and
Master of Ceremonies .....The Marquis de Sade
The Jester ....The Simpleton
Jean-Paul Marat ....The Paranoiac
Simonne Evrard ....Woman with Crutch
Duperret ....The Erotomaniac
Charlotte Corday ....Girl w/Sleeping Sickness
Jacques Roux ....Man in Strait Jacket
Cocurucu ....The Schizophrenic
Kokol ....Man with Club Foot
Polpoch ....Thumb-sucker
Rossignol ....Laughing Woman
Chorus ....The Inmates
Tableau "The Faces of Marat":
Marat's Mother ....Woman with Baby
Marat's Father ....Homicidal Maniac
Schoolmistress ....Girl with Twitch
Male Nurse and
Scientists ....New Patient
Newly Rich Woman ....Catatonic Girl
Voltaire ....The Hunchback
Lavoisier ....Imbecile
Understudies for:
Mr. Girard ....Jack Ragotzy
Mr. Mango ....Wayne Lamb

#197
August 29 - September 3, 1967
Luv
by Murray Schisgal
Directed by Louis Girard
Setting by Dusty Reeds
Lighting by George Hedges
Costumes by Ora Crofoot
CAST
Harry Berlin ....Dale Helward
Milt Manville ....Joseph Cardinale
Ellen Manville ....Betty Ebert

1968 Season

#198
June 11 - 13, 1968
The Impossible Years
(No Program on File)
by Bob Fisher and Arthur Marx
Directed by Jack Ragotzy
Setting by Jon Figola
Lights by Michael Vogas
Costume by Ora Crofoot
CAST
Doctor Jack Kingsley .....Louis Girard
Linda Kingsley ....Sallie Shockely
Abby Kingsley ....Jane Stricket
Alice Kingsley ....Betty Ebert
Ricky Fleisher ....Rod Layden
Richard Merrick ....Dale Helward
Miss Hammer ....Dusty Reeds
Francine ....Susie Michael
Wally ....David Aris
Dennis ....Terence Marten

247

Andy . . . . .Roger Rathbun	Duke . . . . .Jon Scheer	Hecklers:
Bartholomew Smuts . . . . .Angelo Mango	Aegean .Louis Girard	Bradley James, Robert Kennedy, Terence Marten
Second Boogalooer . . . . .Sherry Adams	Antipholus of Ephesus . . . . . . .Dale Helward	Nina . . . . .Sherry Adams
Third Boogalooer . . . . .Jon Scheer	Dromio of Ephesus . . . . .Angelo Mango	Floyd . . . . .Douglas Copsey
Doctor Harold Fleisher . . . . . .Robert Kennedy	Tailor . . . . .Robert Kennedy	Sophie . . . . .Susie Michael
Arnold Brecher . . . . .Perry Mallette	Apprentice . . . . .Susie Michael	Bella .Catherine Lake
Irwin Kniberg (boy) . . . . .Jack Baker	Antipholus of Syracuse . . . . . . .Dale Helward	Lena . . . . .Vickie Rose
	Dromio of Syracuse . . . . .Angelo Mango	Thea . . . . .Joan Dunham
	Merchant of Syracuse . . . . .David Aris	Secretary . . . . .Catherine Lake
	Corporal .Robert Mott	Senator . . . . .Bradley James
	Luce .Francine Karasik	Butler . . . . .Robert Kennedy
	Adriana . . . . .Joan Dunham	Judge Carter . . . . .Jon Scheer
	Luciana . . . . .Sallie Shockley	Derby (Commissioner) . . . . .Robert Mott

#199
June 25 - July 7, 1968
Walking Happy
Music by James Van Heusen
Lyrics by Sammy Cahn
Book by Ketti Frings
based on the play *Hobson's Choice*
by Harold Brighouse
Directed by Jack Ragotzy
Choreographed by Wayne Lamb
Musical Direction by Tom Kasdorf
Settings by Dusty Reeds
Costumes by Ora Crofoot
Lighting by Michael Vogas
CAST

Henry Horatio Hobson . . . . .Louis Girard
Minns . . . . .Jon Scheer
Denton . . . . .Rod Layden
Tudsbury . . . . .Richard Barber
Heeler . . . . .Robert Mott
George Beenstock . . . . .Perry Mallette
Maggie Hobson . . . . .Joan Dunham
Vickie Hobson . . . . .Sallie Shockley
Alice Hobson . . . . .Francine Karasik
Albert Beenstock . . . . .Terence Marten
Freddie Beenstock . . . . .Douglas Copsey
Mrs. Hepworth . . . . .Dusty Reeds
Toby Wadlow . . . . .Dale Helward
Will Mossop . . . . .Angelo Mango
Butler . . . . .Robert Mott
Mrs. Figgins . . . . .Carole Oshwaya
Customer .Rea Shawn
Handbill Boys:
"Bertie" .Johnny Reeds
"Algie" . . . . .Brendan Ragotzy
Devils:
Sherry Adams, Colleen Hill, Carole Oshwaysa,
Jane Stricker
Townspeople and "Moonraker" Habitues:
Sherry Adams, Colleen Hill, Francine Karasik,
Carole Oshwaya, Linda Crittenden, Robin Reva,
Vickie Rose, Susie Michael, Richard Barber,
Douglas Copsey, Rod Layden, Terence Marten,
Robert Mott, Brendan Ragotzy, Johnny Reeds,
Jon Scheer, Jack Ragotzy, Wayne Lamb,
David Aris, Robert Kennedy

#200
July 9 - 21, 1968
The Boys From Syracuse
Music by Richard Rogers
Lyrics by Lorenz Hart
Book by George Abbott
(based on *The Comedy of Errors*
by William Shakespeare)
Directed and Choreographed by Wayne Lamb
Musical Direction by Tom Kasdorf
Scenic Design by Dusty Reeds
Lighting Design by Rod Layden
and David Aris
Costumes by Ora Crofoot
CAST

Sergeant . . . . .Richard Barber
Angelo . . . . .Douglas Copsey

Maids:
Sherry Adams, Susie Michael, Vickie Rose
Sorcerer .Louis Girard
Courtesan .Betty Ebert
Fatima . . . . .Jane Stricker
Courtesans . . . . .Jayne Bentzen,
. . . . .Colleen Hill
Merchant of Ephesus . . . . .Terence Marten
Egyptians:
David Aris, Richard Barber, Douglas Copsey,
Jon Scheer
Galatea .Jayne Bentzen
Pygmalion .Robert Mott
Amazons:
Linda Crittenden, Carole Oshwaya, Rea Shawn
Big Brother . . . . .Wayne Lamb
Emilia .Carole Oshwaya

#201
July 23 - August 4, 1968
The Killing of Sister George
by Frank Marcus
Directed by Louis Girard
Scenery by John Figola
Lighting by David Aris
Costumes by Ora Crofoot
CAST

June Buckridge (George) . . . . .Betty Ebert
Alice "Childie" McNaught . . . . .Joan Dunham
Mrs. Mercy Croft . . . . .Dusty Reeds
Madame Zenia . . . . .Carole Oshwaya

#202
August 6 - 18, 1968
Fiorello!
Book by Jerome Weidman and George Abbott
Music by Jerry Bock, Lyrics
by Sheldon Harnick
Directed and Choreographed by Wayne Lamb
Music Direction by Tom Kasdorf
Scenery by Dusty Reeds
Lighting by John Figola
Costumes by Ora Crofoot
CAST

Announcer . . . . .Jack Ragotzy
Fiorello . . . . .Angelo Mango
Neil . . . . .Rod Layden
Morris . . . . .Dale Helward
Mrs. Pomerantz . . . . .Carole Oshwaya
Mr. Lopez .Robert Mott
Mr. Zappatella . . . . .Richard Barber
Dora .Francine Karasik
Marie . . . . .Sallie Shockley
Ben Marino . . . . .Louis Girard
Dealer .Richard Barber
Politicians:
Ken Andrews, Jack Baker, Richard Barber,
Douglas Copsey, Robert Mott, Jon Scheer

Jimmy Walker Girls:
Jayne Bentzen, Linda Crittenden, Colleen Hill,
Rea Shawn
Mitzi Travers . . . . .Jane Stricker
Frank Scarpini . . . . .Terence Marten
Florence .Rea Shawn
Reporter .Robert Mott
Tough Man . . . . .Richard Barber
Passersby:
Jon Scheer, Jack Baker, Susie Michael,
Robert Mott
Frantic Man . . . . .Ken Andrews
Soldiers, Politicians, Gangsters:
Ken Andrews, Richard Barber, Douglas Copsey,
Robert Kennedy, Robert Mott, Jon Scheer, Jack
Baker Strikers, Wives, Cuties. Etc.:
Sherry Adams, Linda Crittenden, Susie Michael,
Carole Oshwaya, Rea Shawn, Jane Stricker,
Gayle Hinckley, Vickie Rose, Colleen Hill,
Jayne Bentzen, Catherine Lake

#203
August 20 - September 1, 1968
[World Premiere]
Angela
by Sumner Arthur Long
Directed by Jack Ragotzy
Scenery by Dusty Reeds and John Figola
Lighting by John Figola
Costumes by Ora Crofoot
CAST

Angela Palmer . . . . .Betty Ebert
Alice . . . . .Dusty Reeds
Jeff Dolan . . . . .Dale Helward
Brian Palmer . . . . .Louis Girard
The Three Girls:
Colleen Hill, Jayne Bentzen, Sallie Shockley
T.V. Repair Man . . . . .Angelo Mango

1969 Season

#204
June 10 - 15, 1969
**You Know I Can't Hear You
When the Water's Running**
by Robert Anderson
Directed by Wayne Lamb
Scenic and Lighting Design by John Figola
Costumes by Ora Crofoot
CAST
I'm Herbert

Herbert . . . . .Dan Yount
Muriel . . . . .Joan Tenenbaum
The Footsteps of Doves:
Salesman .Dick Fuchs
Harriet . . . . .Betty Ebert
George . . . . .Dan Yount
Jill . . . . .Robin Murphy

I'll Be Home for Christmas:
Chuck . . . . .Louis Girard
Edith . . . . .Betty Ebert
Clarice .Susan Granger
The Shock of Recognition:
Herb Miller . . . . .Louis Girard
Jack Barnstable . . . . .Gil Savage
Dorothy . . . . .Betty Ebert
Mr. Pawling . . . . .Angelo Mango

#205
June 17 - 29, 1969
Don't Drink the Water
by Woody Allen
Directed by Jack Ragotzy
Scenic and Lighting Design by John Figola
Costumes by Ora Crofoot
CAST
Father Drobney . . . . .Dick Fuchs
Ambassador Magee . . . . .Stuart White
Kilroy . . . . .Mark Boli
Axel Magee . . . . .Angelo Mango
Marion Hollander . . . . .Betty Ebert
Walter Hollander . . . . .Louis Girard
Susan Hollander . . . . .Sherry Adams
Krojack . . . . .Gil Savage
Burns . . . . .Michael Weil
Chef . . . . .Rod Layden
Sultan of Bashir . . . . .Dan Yount
Sultan's First Wife . . . . .Carol Sue Walker
Sultan's Other Wives:
Roslyn Roseman, Robin Murphy, Susan Granger,
Nan Hunter
Kasnar . . . . .Randolph Roberts
Countess Bordoni . . . . .Mary Ann Collins
Party Guests:
Howard McBride, Jack Hoffman, Clint Weaver,
Michael Weil

#206
July 1 - 20, 1969
George M!
Music and Lyrics by George M. Cohan
Book by Michael Stewart
and John and Fran Pascal
Lyrics and Musical Revisions by Mary Cohan
Directed and Choreographed by Wayne Lamb
Scenery and Lighting by John Figola
Costumes by Ora Crofoot
Musical Direction by Richard Hintz
Special Orchestration by Larry Wolfe
CAST
George M. Cohan . . . . .Angelo Mango
Jerry Cohan . . . . .Howard McBride
Nellie Cohan . . . . .Roslyn Roseman
Josie Cohan . . . . .Nan Hunter
Ethel Levey (Cohan) . . . . .Robin Murphy
Agnes Nolan (Cohan) . . . . .Joan Dunham
Sword Box Assistant,
Pushcart Girl, Yankee
Doodle Girl . . . . .Sherry Adams
Acrobat, Bell Ringer, Deck
Hand, Nelly Kelly Policeman
Judge Anspacker . . . . .Mark Boli
Model . . . . .Mary Ann Collins
Fay Templeton . . . . .Betty Ebert
Minstrel Dancer,
Bell Ringer,
Deck Hand, Nelly
Kelly Policeman . . . . .John Eldridge
Ventriloquist, Freddie the
Designer, Freddie Manager,
Harrigan Boy, Director . . . . .Dick Fuchs
Dr. Webb, E.F. Albee,
Sam Harris . . . . .Louis Girard
Party Guest, Pushcart
Girl . . . . .Gayle Hinckley
Living Statue, Ship's
Captain, Waiter . . . . .Robert Kennedy
Ventriloquist's Dummy,
Bell Ringer, Deck Hand,
Nelly Kelly Policeman,
Harrigan Boy . . . . .Rod Layden
Dog Trainer, Bell Ringer,
Deck Hand, Congressman
Burkhardt, Nelly Kelly
Policeman . . . . .Fred Miller
Little Girl, Sharp-
Shooter's Assistant,
"Erie" Little Girl . . . . .Patrice Murphy
Madame Grimaldi,
Rose, Mrs. Baker . . . . .Carole Oshwaya
Young George M . . . . .Brendan Ragotzy
Party Guest . . . . .Jack Ragotzy
Man on the Curtain,
Sharpshooter, Stage Hand,
Stage Manager,
Mayor Hatry . . . . .Randolph Roberts
Draper, Louis
The Designer . . . . .Gil Savage
Trained Dog .Siren
Little Girl, Mrs. Rose
Deer, Flutist, Ma
Templeton . . . . .Joan Tenenbaum
Party Guest . . . . .Dan Yount
Pushcart Girl, Cohan
Secretary, Yankee
Doodle Girl . . . . .Ellen Zitterbart
Periaktoi Pusher . . . . .Josh Dietrich
Periaktoi Pusher . . . . .Michael Weil
Program Girls . . . . .Elizabeth Kahn
. . . . .Susan Granger

#207
July 22 - 27, 1969
The Apple Tree
(No Program on File)
by Sheldon Harnick and Jerry Bock
(Additional book material
by Jerome Coppersmith)
Directed and Choreographed by Wayne Lamb
Scenery and Lighting by John Figola
Costumes by Ora Crofoot
Musical Direction by Richard Hintz
Special Orchestration by Larry Wolfe
CAST
Diary of Adam and Eve:
Adam . . . . .Dick Fuchs
Eve . . . . .Joan Dunham
Snake . . . . .Angelo Mango
The Lady or the Tiger:
Balladeer .Rod Layden
King Arik .Don Yount
Princess Barbara . . . . .Joan Dunham
Prisoner . . . . .Fred Miller
Prisoner's Bride . . . . .Carol Sue Walker
Tiger . . . . .Roslyn Roseman
Nadjira . . . . .Ellen Zitterbart
Captain Sanjar . . . . .Angelo Mango
Guards . . . . .Mark Boli,
. . . . .John Eldridge
King Arik's Court:
Sherry Adams, Nan Hunter, Elizabeth Kahn,
Susie Michael, Patrice Murphy, Carol Sue
Walker, Josh Dietrich, John Hoffman, Dean
Kennedy, Howard McBride, Fred Miller,
Randolph Roberts, Gil Savage, Clint Weaver,
Michael Weil
Passionella:
Narrator . . . . .Louis Girard
Ella and Passionella . . . . .Joan Dunham
Mr. Fallible . . . . .Dean Kennedy
Movie Producer . . . . .Dan Yount
Flip, the Prince
Charming . . . . .Angelo Mango
Subway Rider, El Morocco Patrons,
Fans, Flip's Following and Movie Set Crew:
Mark Roli, Josh Dietrich, Betty Ebert, John
Eldridge, Gale Hinckley, Nan Hunter,
Elizabeth Kahn, Howard McBride,
Susie Michael, Fred Miller, Jack Ragotzy,
Randolph Roberts, Roslyn Roseman,
Clint Weaver, Michael Weil, Ellen Zitterbart

#208
July 29 - August 10, 1969
Cactus Flower
by Abe Burrows
based on a play by Pierre Barillet
and Jean-Pierre Gredy
Directed by Louis Girard
Scenery and Lighting by John Figola
Costumes by Ora Crofoot
CAST
Toni Simmons . . . . .Elizabeth Kahn
Igor Sullivan . . . . .Gil Savage
Stephanie Dickinson . . . . .Betty Ebert
Mrs. Dixon Durant . . . . .Patrice Murphy
Dr. Julian Winston . . . . .Dale Helward
Harvey Greenfield . . . . .Louis Girard
Senor Arturo Sanchez . . . . .Dan Yount
Customer . . . . .Michael Weil
Waiter . . . . .John Hoffman
Botticelli's Springtime . . . . . . .Roslyn Roseman
Music Lover . . . . .Dean Kennedy

#209
August 12 - 24, 1969
The Most Happy Fella
Music, Lyrics and Libretto by Frank Loesser
Based on Sidney Howard's play
They Knew What They Wanted
Directed and Choreographed by Wayne Lamb
Scenery by Dusty Reeds
Lighting by Rod Layden
Costumes by Ora Crofoot and Ken Andrews
Musical Direction by Richard Hintz
Special Orchestration by Larry Wolfe
CAST
Cashier . . . . .Dean Kennedy
Customers:
Patrice Murphy, Randolph Roberts, Joan
Tenenbaum, Carol Sue Walker, Michael Weil
Cleo .Roslyn Roseman
Rosabella . . . . .Joan Dunham
Waitresses:
Sherry Adams, Nan Hunter, Vickie Rose,
Ellen Zitterbart
Bus Boy .Clint Weaver
Postman .Rod Layden
Tony Esposito . . . . .Angelo Mango
Max . . . . .John Hoffman
Marie . . . . .Betty Ebert
Herman . . . . .Dick Fuchs
Clem . . . . .John Eldridge
Jake . . . . .Ken Andrews

Al . . . . .Josh Dietrich
Girls:
Sherry Adams, Sue Engle, Nan Hunter, Elizabeth Kahn, Susie Michael, Ellen Zitterbart
Sheriff . . . . .Randolph Roberts
Joe . . . . .Dale Helward
Electrician . . . . .Michael Weil
Pasquale .Dan Yount
Guiseppi . . . . .Howard McBride
Ciccio . . . . .Mark Boli
Country Girl . . . . .Susie Michael
City Boy . . . . .Clint Weaver
Doc . . . . .Louis Girard
Priest . . . . .Fred Miller
Tessie .Heidi Dunham
Gussie . . . . .Brendan Ragotzy
Truck Drivers . . . . .Randolph Roberts,
. . . . .Michael Weil
Neighbor Ladies:
Patrice Murphy, Vickie Rose, Joan Tenenbaum
Brakeman . . . . .Michael Weil
Bus Driver . . . . .Randolph Roberts

#210
August 26 - 31, 1969
The Star-Spangled Girl
by Neil Simon
Directed by Louis Girard
Scenery Designed by Dusty Reeds
Lighting by Rod Layden
Costumes by Ora Crofoot
CAST
Andy Hobart . . . . .Dale Helward
Norman Cornell . . . . .Dick Fuchs
Sophie Rauschmeyer . . . . .Joan Dunham

1970 Season
[Twenty-Fifth Anniversary]

#211
June 16 - June 28, 1970
I Do! I Do!
Book and Lyrics by Tom Jones
Music by Harvey Schmidt
Based on *The Fourposter* by Jan de Hartog
Directed and Choreographed by Wayne Lamb
Scenic Design by Dusty Reeds
Lights Designed by John Figola
Costumes by Ora Crofoot
Musical Director, Bob Shephard
Conductor, Larry Wolfe
CAST
He (Michael) . . . . .Angelo Mango
She (Agnes) . . . . .Joan Dunham

#212
June 30 - July 12, 1970
Mame
Book by Jerome Lawrence and Robert E. Lee
Based on the novel *Auntie Mame*
by Patrick Dennis
and the play by Lawrence and Lee
Music and Lyrics by Jerry Herman
Directed by Jack Ragotzy and Wayne Lamb
Choreographed by Wayne Lamb
Scenery and Lighting Designed by John Figola
Costumes by Ora Crofoot and Cathe Lake
Musical Direction by Bob Shephard
Conductor - Larry Wolfe
CAST
Patrick Dennis (Age 10) . . . . . .Mark Cummings
Agnes Gooch . . . . .Roslyn Roseman
Vera Charles . . . . .Joan Dunham
Mame Dennis . . . . .Karen Arthur
Ralph Devine . . . . .William Glen
M. Lindsay Woolsey . . . . .Dick Fuchs
Ito . . . . .Angelo Mango
Doorman . . . . .Michael Reno
Elevator Boy . . . . .Josh Dietrich
Messenger . . . . .Mark O'Connell
Dwight Babcock . . . . .Louis Girard
Stage Manager . . . . .Jack Hoffman
Madame Branislowski . . . . . . .Pamela Hoxsey
Gregor . . . . .James D. Smith
Beauregard Jackson,
Pickett Burnside . . . . .George McDaniel
Uncle Jeff . . . . .Howard McBride
Cousin Fan . . . . .Susie Michael
Sally Cato . . . . .Joan Tenenbaum
Mother Burnside . . . . .Sarah Fahey
Patrick Dennis
(age 19-29) . . . . .Bob Shephard
Junior Babcock . . . . .Jack Hoffman
Mrs. Upson . . . . .Dusty Reeds
Mr. Upson . . . . .Wes Finlay
Gloria Upson . . . . .Shelley Osterloh
Pegeen Ryan . . . . .Cindy Crumlish
Peter Dennis . . . . .Brendan Ragotzy
Mame's Dancing Friends:
Cindy Brumlish, Dana Demonbreun, Jack Hoffman, Pamela Hoxsey, Nan Hunter, Nancy Juvinall, Howard McBride, William Olen, Michael Reno, Vickie Ross, Peter Schneider, James D. Smith
Mame's Other Friends:
Cynthia Ballard, Betty Ebert, Wayne Lamb, Jack Ragotzy

#213
July 14 - July 26, 1970
The Boys in the Band
by Mort Crowley
Directed by Jack Ragotzy
Scenic and Light Design by John Figola
Decor by James Knox
CAST
Michael . . . . .Angelo Mango
Donald . . . . .Bob Shephard
Emory .Dick Fuchs
Larry .William Olen
Hank . . . . .Wes Finlay
Bernardo . . . . .Michael Reno
Alan . . . . .George McDaniel
Cowboy . . . . .James D. Smith
Harold .Louis Girard

#214
July 28 - August 16, 1970
Man of La Mancha
Book by Dale Wasserman
Music by Mitch Leigh
Lyrics by Joe Darion
Directed and Choreographed by Wayne Lamb
Scenic Designer - Dusty Reeds
Lighting Designer - John Figola
Costume Designers -
Ora Crofoot and Cathe Lake
Musical Direction - Bob Shephard
Conductor - Larry Wolfe
CAST
Captain of the Inquisition . . . . . . .William Olen
Guards . . . . .Mark O'Connell,
. . . . .Bradley James
Manservant . . . . .Howard McBride
Miguel de Cervantes . . . . .George McDaniel
Don Quixote . . . . .George McDaniel
Sancho Panza . . . . .Howard McBride
Governor and Innkeeper . . . . .Wes Finlay
Duke and Dr. Carrasco . . . . .Louis Girard
Horse . . . . .Michael Reno
Mule . . . . .Jack Hoffman
Muleteers:
Pedro . . . . .Dick Fuchs
Anselmo . . . . .Bob Shephard
Juan . . . . .Peter Schneider
Jose . . . . .Michael Reno
Paco . . . . .Jack Hoffman
Tenorio . . . . .James D. Smith
Aldonza (Dulcinea) . . . . .Joan Dunham
Maria . . . . .Pamela Hoxsey
Fermina and Moorish
Dancer . . . . .Roslyn Roseman
Antonia . . . . .Cynthia Ballard
Housekeeper . . . . .Sarah Fahey
Padre .Angelo Mango
Barber .Jack Hoffman
Men of the Inquisition:
Jack Ragotzy, Wayne Lamb, G. Hinckley, D. Reeds
Other Prisoners:
Betty Ebert, Dana Demonbreun, Cynthia Crumlish

#215
August 18 - 30, 1970
Cabaret
Book by Joe Masterhoff
Based on a play by John Van Druten
and *Berlin Diaries* by Christopher Isherwood
Music by John Kander, Lyrics by Fred Ebb
Directed by Wayne Lamb and John Weeks
Choreographed by Wayne Lamb
Scenery by Dusty Reeds
Lighting by Peter Schneider
Costumes by Ora Crofoot and Cathe Lake
Musical Direction by Bob Shephard
Conductor, Larry Wolfe;
Kit Kat Band: Arrranger and Conductor - Michael Reno
CAST
Master of Ceremonies
(Emcee) . . . . .Angelo Mango
Clifford Bradshaw . . . . .Dick Fuchs
Ernst Ludwig . . . . .Bob Shepard
Custom's Officer . . . . .Howard McBride
Fraulein Schneider . . . . .Betty Ebert
Fraulein Kost . . . . .Roslyn Roseman
Herr Schultz . . . . .Louis Girard
Telephone Girl . . . . .Shelley Osterloh
Sally Bowles . . . . .Cynthia Crumlish
Kit Kat Band:
Michael Reno, Pam Hoxsey, Cynthia Ballard, Joan Tenenbaum, Vickie Rose
Two Ladies . . . . .Cynthia Ballard,
. . . . .Sarah Fahey
Man . . . . .William Olen
German Sailors:
Jack Hoffman, Howard McBride, William Olen
Bobby .Ken Andrews
Victor . . . . .Mark O'Connell
Kit Kat Kuties:
Joan Tenenbaum, Nan Hunter, Dana Demonbreun, Sally Osterloh, Pamela Hoxsey, Sarah Fahey, Vickie Ross

Kit Kat Waiters:
Howard McBride, Michael Reno, James Smith,
William Olen, Jack Hoffman

#216
September 1 - September 6, 1970
A Flea in Her Ear
by George Feydeau
Directed by Wayne Lamb
Scenery by Dusty Reeds
Lighting by Peter Schneider
Costumes by Ora Crofoot
CAST

Camille Chandebise	Jack Hoffman
Antoinette Plucheux	Pamela Hoxsey
Etienne Plucheux	Howard McBride
Dr. Finache	Louis Girard
Lucienne Homenides de Histangua	Dusty Reeds
Raymonde Chandebise	Betty Ebert
Victor Emmanuel Chandebise	Angelo Mango
Romain Tournel	Dick Fuchs
Carlos Homenides De Histangua	Michael Reno
Eugenie	Joan Tanenbaum
Augustin Feraillon	Mark O'Connell
Olympe	Sarah Fahey
Baptisin	Ken Andrews
Herr Schwartz	James Smith
Poche	Angelo Mango

Guests at the Hotel Coq D'or:
Susan Engle, William Olen, Vickie Rose,
Peter Schneider

1971 Season

#217
June 15 - 27, 1971
Plaza Suite
by Neil Simon
Directed by Jack Ragotzy
Scenery and Lighting by Paul Abe
Costumes by Ora Crofoot
CAST
Visitor From Mamaroneck

Bellhop	Jack Hoffman
Karen Nash	Betty Ebert
Sam Nash	Louis Girard
Waiter	Tad Dynakowski
Jean McCormack	Deborah Cresswell

Visitor From Hollywood

Waiter	Barry Kimble
Jesse Kipplinger	Louis Girard
Muriel Tate	Betty Ebert

Visitor From Forest Hills

Norma Hubley	Betty Ebert
Roy Hubley	Louis Girard
Borden Eisler	Peter Schneider
Mimsey Hubley	Judith Ann Williams

#218
June 29 - July 18, 1971
Hello, Dolly!
Book by Michael Stewart
Music and Lyrics by Jerry Herman
Based on the play,
The Matchmaker by Thornton Wilder
Original Production Directed and
Choreographed by Gower Champion
Produced for the Broadway Stage
by David Merrick
and Champion-Five, Inc.
Directed and Choreographed by Wayne Lamb
Scenic Design by David Potts
Lighting by Paul Abe
Costumes by Ora Crofoot
Musical Direction by Michael Reno
Conductor - Larry Wolfe
CAST

Mrs. Dolly Gallagher Levi	Joan Dunham
Ernestina	Sarah Fahey
Ambrose Kemper	Jack Hoffman
Coachman	Wes Finlay
Horace Vandergelder	Louis Girard
Ermangarde	Martha Lou Torrance
Cornelius Hackl	Angelo Mango
Barnaby Tucker	Dale Helward
Irene Molloy	Roslyn Roseman
Minnie Fay	Pamela Hoxsey
Mrs. Rose	Cynthia Ballard
Rudolph	James Smith
Stanley	William Short
Policemen	Tad Dynakowski, Barry Kimble
Judge	Wes Finlay
Court Clerk	Larry Burash

Members of Yonkers' Band:
Tad Dynakowski, Michael Reno, Pamela Hoxsey,
Cynthia Ballard,
Brendan Ragotzy
Waiters at the Harmonia Gardens:
Ken Andrews, Michael Reno, William Short,
Ken Derby, Jeffrey Kucera, David Robison
Townspeople:
Carole Cotton, Deborah Cresswell, Laura Culver,
Patti Dell, Judith Ann Williams, Margo Hadraba,
Holly Reisenfeld, Margaret Heinze, Tad
Dynakowski, Barry Kimble, Larry Burash,
William Short, Jeffrey Kucera, Michael Reno,
David Robinson

#219
July 20 - August 1, 1971
Forty Carats
Adapted by Jay Allen from a play
by Barillet and Gredy
Directed by Louis Girard
Scenery by Paul Abe and David Potts
Lighting by Dan Hansen
Costumes by Ora Crofoot
CAST

Ann Stanley	Joan Dunham
Peter Latham	Philip Laurenson
Mrs. Adams	Roslyn Roseman
Mrs. Margolin	Carole Cotton
Billy Boylan	Dale Helward
Eddy Edwards	Wes Finlay
Maud Hayes	Betty Ebert
Trina Stanley	Margo Hadraba
Mrs. Latham	Sarah Fahey
Mr. Latham	Louis Girard
Pat	Michael Reno

#220
August 3 - 29, 1971
Fiddler on the Roof
Based on Sholom Aleichem's Stories
by special permission of Arnold Perl
Book by Joseph Stein, Music by Jerry Bock
Lyrics by Sheldon Harnick
Produced on the NY Stage by Harold Prince
Original Production Directed and Choreographed
by Jerome Robbins
Directed and Choreographed by Wayne Lamb
Musical Direction by Michael Reno
Scenery by David Potts
Lighting by Paul Abe
Costumes by Ora Crofoot
Conductor - Larry Wolfe
CAST

Tevye the Dairyman	Angelo Mango
Golde	Betty Ebert
Tzeitel	Roslyn Roseman
Hodel	Patti Dell
Chava	Pamela Hoxsey
Shprintze	Judith Ann Williams
Beilke	Margo Hadraba
Yente, the matchmaker	Sarah Fahey
Motel, the Tailor	Jack Hoffman
Perchik, the Student	Dale Helward
Lazar Wolf, the Butcher	Wes Finlay
Mordcha, the Innkeeper	Louis Girard
Rabbi	David Robison
Mendel, his son	Jeffrey Kucera
Avram, the Bookseller	Michael Reno
Nachum, the Beggar	Larry Burash
Grandma Tzeitel	Martha Lu Torrance
Fruma Sarah	Carole Cotton
Label	Barry Kimble
Fredel	Margaret Heinze
Shaindel, Motel's Mother	Deborah Cresswell

The Bottle Dancers:
Jeffrey Kucera, Michael Reno, William Short,
Chaime Yankel
Boys:
Brendan Ragotzy, Dennis Begnall or
Steve Beadle or Tom Boyle

The Fiddler	David Potts

The Russians:

Constable	Tad Dynakowaki
Priest	Ken Andrews
Fyedka	James Smith
Vladimir	Kenneth Derby
Sasha	William Short

#221
August 31 - September 5, 1971
Play It Again, Sam
by Woody Allen
Directed by Louis Girard
Scenery by Paul Abe
Decor and Properties by James Knox
Lighting by Dan Hansen
Costumes by Ora Crofoot and Ken Andrews
CAST

Allan Felix	Angelo Mango
Nancy	Margaret Heinze
Bogey	Jack Hoffman
Dick Christie	Dale Helward
Linda Christie	Patti Dell
Sharon	Martha Lu Torrance
Sharon Lake	Dana Demonbreun
Gina	Laura Culver
Vanessa	Margo Hadraba
Go-Go Girl	Carole Cotton
Intellectual Girl	Deborah Cresswell
Barbara	Judith Ann Williams

1972 Season

#222
June 13 - 25, 1972
Last of the Red Hot Lovers
by Neil Simon
Directed by Jack Ragotzy
Scenery by Frank Bradley
Lighting by Paul Gregory
CAST
Barney Cashman ....John Newton
Elaine Navazio ....Rosa Morin
Bobbi Michele ....Robin Biffle
Jeanette Fisher ....Betty Ebert

#223
June 27 - July 16, 1972
1776
Book by Peter Stone
Music and Lyrics by Sherman Edwards
Based on a conception of Sherman Edwards
Directed and Choreographed by Wayne Lamb
Musical Direction by Michael Reno
Scenery by David Potts
Lighting by Paul Gregory
Costumes by Ora Crofoot
"Declaration of Independence" Drop
by Dusty Reeds
Conductor - Larry Wolfe
CAST
Members of The Continental Congress:
President John Hancock ....Louis Girard
Dr. Joseph Bartlett ....John Beilock
John Adams ....Angelo Mango
Stephen Hopkins ....Michael McEowen
Roger Sherman ....Michael Reno
Lewis Morris ....Wes Finlay
Robert Livingston ....Jack Hoffman
Rev. Jonathan
  Witherspoon ....Larry E. Burash
Benjamin Franklin ....John Newton
John Dickinson ....Dale Helward
James Wilson ....Ken Andrews
Caesar Rodney ....David Potts
Col. Thomas McKean ....Joseph W. Boles
George Read ....Howard McBride
Samuel Chase ....Steve Feuerstein
Richard Henry Lee ....Timothy Landfield
Thomas Jefferson ....Dick Fuchs
Joseph Hewes ....Stephen Schmidt
Edward Rutledge ....John Eldridge
Dr. Lyman Hall ....Kenneth L. Peck
Charles Thomson ....Thomas Martin
Custodian - Andrew
  McNair ....Jon Faulkner
A Leather Apron ....Randall M. Rothenberg
Courier ....Jeffrey Kucera
Abigail Adams ....Patti Dell
Martha Jefferson ....Marianne Torrance

#224
July 18 - August 6, 1972
Promises, Promises
Book by Neil Simon
Music by Burt Bacharach
Lyrics by Hal David
Based on the screenplay *The Apartment*
by Billy Wilder and I.A.L. Diamond
Directed and Choreographed by Wayne Lamb
Musical Direction and Conductor - Michael Reno
Additional Orchestrations by Michael Reno
Scenery by Frank Bradley
Lighting by Paul Gregory
Costumes Coordinates: Ken Andrews
  and Deborah Cresswell
CAST
Chuck Baxter ....Angelo Mango
J.D. Sheldrake ....Dale Helward
Fran Kubelik ....Daryl Hogue
Mr. Dobitch ....Dick Fuchs
Sylvia Gilhooley ....Janette LaLanne
Mr. Kirkeby ....Howard McBride
Ginger ....Jeanne Detwiler
Mr. Eichelberger ....Jack Hoffman
Vivien ....Christine Cullar
Dr. Dreyfuss ....Louis Girard
Jesse Vanderhof ....Wes Finlay
Miss Kreplinski ....Margo Hadraba
Nurse (office) ....Deborah Cresswell
Doctor (office) ....Ken Andrews
Miss Olson ....Linda Carlson
Lum Ding Hostess ....Deborah Cresswell
Waiter ....Tom Martin
Madison Square Garden
  Watchman ....Steve Feuerstein
Miss Polansky ....Christine Culler
Miss Wong ....Patricia Ward
Miss Della Hoya ....Carole Cotton
Bartender Eugene ....Joseph W. Boles
Marge MacDougal ....Cody Dalton
Karl Kubelik ....John Eldridge
New Young Executive ....Jeffrey Kucera
Interns ....Joseph W. Boles,
       ....Michael McEowen
Patrons, Employees, etc
Linda Ann Carlson, Carole Cotton, Deborah Cresswell, Christine Culler, Margo Hadraba, Jeanne Detwiler, Janette LaLanne, Patricia Ward, John Eldridge, Jeffrey Kucera, Timothy Landfield, Michael McEowen, Tom Martin, Stephen Schmidt

#225
August 9 - 20, 1972
**A Funny Thing Happened on
the Way to the Forum**
A musical comedy based on the plays of Plautus
Book by Burt Shevelove and Larry Gelbart
Music and Lyrics by Stephen Sondheim
Directed and Choreographed by Wayne Lamb
Musical Director - Michael Reno
Conducting at the Grand - Larry Wolfe
Settings by Frank Bradley
Lighting by Paul Gregory
Costumes by Ken Andrews
CAST
Prologus, an actor ....Dale Helward
The Proteans:
  Jack Hoffman, Ken Andrews, Jeff Kucera
Senex, a citizen of Rome ....Louis Girard
Domina, his wife ....Cody Dalton
Hero, his son ....John Eldridge
Hysterium, slave to
  Senex and Domina ....Angelo Mango
Pseudolus, slave to Hero ....Dale Helward
Lycus, a dealer in
  Courtesans ....Dick Fuchs
The Courtesans:
  "Tintinabula", Deborah Cresswell; "Panacea", Janette LaLanne; "The Geminae", Margo Hadraba and Christine Culler; "Vibrata", Jeanne Detwiler; "Gymnasia", Linda Carlso
Philia, a virgin ....Daryl Hogue
Erronius, an old man ....Howard McBride
Miles Gloriosus,
  a warrior ....Wes Finlay
Fan Fari ....Michael McEowen,
       ....Joseph Boles

#226
August 22 - 27, 1972
Company
Music and Lyrics by Stephen Sondheim
Book by George Furth
Directed and Choreographed by Wayne Lamb
Musical Director, Conductor,
and Additional Orchestrations - Michael Reno
Scenery by David Potts
Lighting by Paul Gregory
Costumes by Ora Crofoot
CAST
Robert ....Angelo Mango
Sarah ....Cody Dalton
Harry ....Dale Helward
Susan ....Marianne Torrance
Peter ....Dick Fuchs
Jenny ....Daryl Hogue
David ....Timothy Landfield
Amy ....Judith Ann Williams
Paul ....John Eldridge
Joanne ....Betty Ebert
Larry ....Ken Andrews
Marta ....Deborah Cresswell
Kathy ....Roslyn Roseman
April ....Patricia Ward
Waiters:
Jeffery Kucera, Michael McEowen,
Jack Ragotzy, Wayne Lamb

#227
August 29 - September 3, 1972
Norman, Is That You?
by Ron Clark and Sam Bobrick
Directed by Jack Ragotzy
Scenery by Frank Bradley
Property and Decor Master, Jim Knox
Lighting by Paul Gregory
Costumes by Ora Crofoot
CAST
Norman Chambers ....Dale Helward
Garson Hobart ....Dick Fuchs
Ben Chambers ....Louis Girard
Mary ....Linda Carlson
Beatrice Chambers ....Betty Ebert

1973 Season

#228
June 12 - 17, 1973
The Convertible Girl
(No Program on File)
by Daniel Simon
Directed by Louis Girard
Scenery by Dusty Reeds
Lighting Design by Frank Bradley
Costumes by Ora Crofoot
CAST
Ron Gelson ....Angelo Mango
Christiana ....Linda Carlson
Policeman ....Leon Lueck
Rabbi Goldstein ....Jeff Lee
Driver ....Jim Sprague
Rabbi Rothchild ....Michael McEowen
Rabbi Silverman ....Timothy Landfield
Mrs. Gelson ....Dusty Reeds
Rabbi Hahn ....Louis Girard

#229
June 19 - July 1, 1973
Butterflies Are Free
by Leonard Gershe
Directed by Jack Ragotzy
Scenery by Dusty Reeds
Lighting by Frank Bradley
Costumes by Ora Crofoot
CAST
Don Baker .Dick Fuchs
Jill Tanner . . . . .Megan Messing
Mrs. Baker . . . . .Betty Ebert
Ralph Austin . . . . .Timothy Landfield

#230
July 3 - 15, 1973
Applause
Book by Betty Comden and Adolph Green
Music by Charles Strouse
Lyrics by Lee Adams
Based on the film *All About Eve*
and the original story by Mary Orr
Directed and Choreographed by Wayne Lamb
Book Directed by Louis Girard
Musical Director and Conductor - Michael Reno
Additional Orchestration by Michael Reno
Scenery by Dusty Reeds
Lighting by Earl Hughes
Costumes by Ora Crofoot
CAST
Announcer . . . . .Jim Sprague
Margo Channing . . . . .Natalie Ross
Eve Harrington . . . . .Barbara McKay
Howard Benedict . . . . .Louis Girard
Buzz Richards . . . . .Timothy Landfield
Duane Fox .Dick Fuchs
Bill Sampson . . . . .Angelo Mango
Karen Richards . . . . .Sandra Mack
Peter (agent) . . . . .Michael McEowen
Bob (lawyer) . . . . .David Emmert
Stan Harding (columnist) . . . . .Jim Sprague
Bonnie .Roslyn Roseman
Bert (stage manager) . . . . .Max McGuire
Village Bartender . . . . .Tom Morrissey
Sammy . . . . .Jeff Lee
T.V. Director . . . . .Leon Lueck
Danny Burns .Jeff Lee
Mike . . . . .Max McGuire
Gene . . . . .Mark Schwamberger
Mick . . . . .Michael Reno
Debi . . . . .Vicki Kuppinger
Carol . . . . .Lynn Chamberlin
Joan . . . . .Megan Messing
Script Girl . . . . .Michele Frierson
First Nighters, Gypsies, Guests:
Jan Dorn, Elaine Mixson, Gail Lucas,
Linda Carlson, Henrietta Stone, Hazen Branch

#231
July 17 - 22, 1973
How the Other Half Loves
by Alan Ayckbourn
Directed by Peter Schneider
Scenery Designed by Dusty Reeds
Lighting by Frank Bradley
Costumes by Ora Crofoot
CAST
Fiona Foster . . . . .Betty Ebert
Teresa Phillips . . . . .Natalie Ross
Frank Foster . . . . .Louis Girard
Bob Phillips . . . . .Dick Fuchs
William Detweiler . . . . .Jim Sprague

Mary Detweiler . . . . .Yvette Romero

#232
July 24 - 29, 1973
Stop the World - I Want to Get Off
Book, Music and Lyrics by Leslie Bricusse
and Anthony Newley
Directed and Choreographed by Wayne Lamb
Musical Direction and Conductor - Michael Reno
Scenery by Dusty Reeds
Lighting by Frank Bradley
Costumes by Ora Crofoot
CAST
Littlechap . . . . .Angelo Mango
Evie, Anya, Ilse, Ginnie . . . . . .Megan Messing
Susan . . . . .Vickie Kuppinger
Jane . . . . .Barbara McKay
Boy . . . . .Brendan Ragotzy
Chorus:
Lynn Chamberlin, Jan Dorn, Timothy Landfield,
Jeff Lee, Gail Lucas, Leon Lueck, Sandra Mack,
Michele Frierson, Elaine Mixson, Henrietta
Stone

#233
August 7 - 12, 1973
Pajama Tops
by Mawby Green and Ed Feilbert
Based on the French farce *Moumou*
by Jean de Letraz
Directed by Jack Ragotzy
Setting by Dusty Reeds
Lighting by Frank Bradley
Costumes by Ora Crofoot
CAST
Claudine . . . . .Megan Messing
Inspector Legrand . . . . .Jim Sprague
Yvonne Chauvinet . . . . .Betty Ebert
Georges Chauvinet . . . . .Louis Girard
Leonard Jolijoli . . . . .Dick Fuchs
Babette LaTouche . . . . .Linda Carlson
Jacques . . . . .Timothy Landfield

#234
August 14 - September 9, 1973
Hair
Book and Lyrics by Gerome Ragni
and James Rado
Music by Galt McDermot
Directed and Choreographed by Wayne Lamb
Musical Direction, Arranger and Conductor - Michael Reno
Scenery by Dusty Reeds
Lighting by Earl Hughes
Costumes by Ora Crofoot
CAST
[from August 14 through September 2]
Claude . . . . .Timothy Landfield
Berger . . . . .Dick Fuchs
Hud . . . . .James Peddy
Sheila . . . . .Megan Messing
Woof . . . . .Jeff Lee
Jeanie . . . . .Barbara McKay
Crissy . . . . .Henrietta Stone
Linda . . . . .Linda Carlson
Lynn . . . . .Lynn Chamberlain
Jan . . . . .Jan Dorn
Dave . . . . .David Emmert
Michele . . . . .Michele Frierson
Connie .Connie Gould
Vicki . . . . .Vicki Kuppinger

Leon . . . . .Leon Lueck
Edwina .Edwina Lewis
Gail . . . . .Gail Lucas
Steve . . . . .Stephen Lucas
Sandy . . . . .Sandra Mack
Michael . . . . .Michael McEowen
Max . . . . .Max McGuire
Tom . . . . .Tom Morrissey
Eric . . . . .Eric Riley
Mark . . . . .Mark Schwamberger
Jim . . . . .Jim Sprague
Carolyn . . . . .Carolyn Thornton
Babbette . . . . .Babbette Wilson
Ron . . . . .Ron Wyatt
The Establishment . . . . .Louis Girard,
 . . . . .Angelo Mango
[Cast changes from September 4 - 9, 1973]
Berger . . . . .Jeff Lee
Sheila . . . . .Sandra Mack
Woof . . . . .Mark Schwamberger
Crissy . . . . .Vicki Kuppinger

1974 Season

#235
June 11 - 23, 1974
6 Rms Riv Vu
by Bob Randall
Directed by Jack Ragotzy
Scenery by Earl Hughes and Dusty Reeds
Costumes by Ora Crofoot
CAST
Eddie (the Superintendent) . . . . .Angelo Mango
Pregnant Woman . . . . .Lynn O'Donnell
Larry (her husband) . . . . .Timothy Landfield
Ann Miller . . . . .Natalie Ross
Paul Friedman . . . . .George McDaniel
Woman in 4A . . . . .Roslyn Roseman
Janet Friedman . . . . .Betty Ebert
Richard Miller . . . . .Dick Fuchs

#236
June 25 - July 7, 1974
No, No, Nanette
Book by Otto Harbach, Frank Mandel
Music by Vincent Youmans
Lyrics by Irving Caesar, Otto Harbach
Entire Production Staged by Wayne Lamb
Musical Director and Conductor - Michael Reno
Music Arranged for Two Pianos by Michael
Reno and Jane Gallatin
Scenery Designed by Dusty Reeds
Lighting Designed by Earl Hughes
Costumes Designed by Ora Crofoot
CAST
Pauline .Dusty Reeds
Lucille Early . . . . .Natalie Ross
Sue Smith . . . . .Betty Ebert
Jimmy Smith . . . . .Louis Girard
Bill Early . . . . .Angelo Mango
Tom Trainor . . . . .P. Lang Bethea
Nanette . . . . .Maryann Nagel
Flora Latham . . . . .Lynn O'Donnell
Betty Brown . . . . .Connie Gould
Winnie Wilson . . . . .Lynn Chamberlin
Nanette's Friends
Girls:
Nancy Buttenheim, Judy Hollenbeck, Kris
Koczur, Kathe Mull, Yvette Romero, Roslyn
Roseman, Kathleen Spencer, Patricia Wettig
Boys:

Dick Fuchs, Stephen Gray, Timothy Landfield,
Jeff Lee, Thomas; Morrissey, Eddie Owen,
Jim R. Sprague, Michael Reno, Eric Riley,
Bob Van Amburgh

#237
July 9 - 21, 1974
That Championship Season
by Jason Miller
Directed by Jack Ragotzy
Scenery Designed by Dusty Reeds
Lighting Designed by Earl Hughes
Costumes by Ora Crofoot
CAST
Tom Daly . . . . .Timothy Landfield
George Sikowski . . . . .Jim R. Sprague
James Daley . . . . .Dick Fuchs
Phil Romano . . . . .Angelo Mango
The Coach . . . . .Louis Girard

#238
July 23 - August 4, 1974
Sugar
Book by Peter Stone
Music by Jule Styne
Lyrics by Bob Merrill
Based on the screenplay *Some Like It Hot*
by Billy Wilder and I.A.L. Diamond
Directed and Choreographed by Wayne Lamb
Musical Director - Michael Reno
Scenery Designed by Dusty Reeds
Lighting Designed by Earl R. Hughes
Costumes Designed by Ora Crofoot
CAST
Sweet Sue . . . . .Roslyn Roseman
Bienstock . . . . .Jim R. Sprague
Joe . . . . .Dick Fuchs
Jerry . . . . .Angelo Mango
Spats Palazzo . . . . .Timothy Landfield
Dude . . . . .Jeff Lee
Knuckles Norton . . . . .John F. Scott
Sugar Kane . . . . .Lynn O'Connell
Osgood Fielding, Jr . . . . .Louis Girard
Gangsters, Friends, Millionaries and others:
David Allen, P. Lang Bethea, Stephen Gray,
Wayne Lamb, Thomas Morrissey, Warren Nesbitt, Eddie Owen, Jack Ragotzy, Michael Reno,
Eric Riley, Mark Schwamberger, Alex Valatka,
Bob Van Amburgh
Band Members and Chorus Girls Bathing
Beauties and Others:
Nancy Buttenheim, Lynn Chamberlin, Betty
Ebert, Connie Gould, Gayle Hinckley, Kris
Koczur, Maryann Nagel, Dusty Reeds, Jean Rice,
Yvette Romero,

#239
August 6 - 11, 1974
The Prisoner of Second Avenue
by Neil Simon
Directed by Louis Girard
Scenery by Dusty Reeds
Lighting by Earl Hughes
Costumes by Ora Crofoot
CAST
Mel Edison . . . . .Jack Ragotzy
Eden Edison . . . . .Betty Ebert
Harry Edison . . . . .Louis Girard
Pearl . . . . .Samuelle L. Eskind
Jessie .Yvette Romero
Pauline . . . . .Dusty Reeds

#240
August 13 - September 1, 1974
Jesus Christ, Superstar
Music by Andrew Lloyd Webber
Lyrics by Tim Rice
Orchestrations by Michael Reno
Staging, Musical Directing and Conducting —
Michael Reno
Scenery by Robert Yanez
Lighting by Earl Hughes
Costumes by Ora Crofoot
CAST
Jesus Christ . . . . .Timothy Landfield
Judas Iscariot . . . . .Eric Riley
Mary Magdalene . . . . .Connie Gould
Pontius Pilate . . . . .Angelo Mango
Caiaphas . . . . .Louis Girard
Simon Zealots . . . . .James Watkins
King Herod . . . . .Dick Fuchs
Annas . . . . .P. Lang Bethea
Peter . . . . .Jeff Lee
The Apostles:
David Allen, P. Lang Bethea, Stephan Gray,
Thomas Morrissey, Warran Nesbitt, Eddie Owen,
Alex Valatka, Bob Van Amburgh, Ron Wyatt
The Women:
Nancy Buttenheim, Lynn Chamberlin, Kris
Koczur, Jeri Matteson, Kathe Mull, Maryann
Nagel, Lynn O'Donnel, Roslyn Roseman, Kathleen Spencer, Patricia Wettig, Babbette Wilson
Tourists, Attendants, Soldiers, Priests, Prostitutes,
Lepers, etc:
Richard Atkins, Betty Ebert, Marcia Eddy, Ramdom Gott, Gayle Hinckley, Wayne Lamb, Jeri
Matteson, Mary Pekarske, Brendan Ragotzy,
Jack Ragotzy, Michael Reno, Yvette Romaro,
John F. Scott, Jim R. Sprague, Ron Wyatt

1975 Season

#241
An Evening with Angelo Mango
June 3 - 8, 1975
Starring
Mr. Angelo Mango
with
Marcia Eddy, Becky Gilbert, Barbara Marineau,
Robin Reeds and
David Allen, Margo Smith, Barbara Winnery
At the Piano, Jane Gallatin
Costumes by Jeffrey Lieder
Lights by John Reeds

#242
June 10 -22, 1975
The Sunshine Boys
by Neil Simon
Directed by Wayne Lamb
Scenery by Dusty Reeds
Lighting by Paul Abe
Costumes by Jeri Matteson
CAST
Willie Clark . . . . .Louis Girard
Ben Silverman . . . . .Dale Helward
Al Lewis . . . . .Jack Ragotzy
Patient .David Allen
Eddie . . . . .Eric Riley
Nurse . . . . .Barbara Marineau
Registered Nurse . . . . .Betty Ebert

#243
June 24 - July 6, 1975
Seesaw
Music by Cy Coleman, Lyrics by Dorothy Fields
Book by Michael Bennett
(based on the play *Two For The Seesaw*
by William Gibson)
Staged by Wayne Lamb
Musical Director, Conductor -
John Glenn Lehman
Scenery Designed by Dusty Reeds
Lighting by Paul Abe
Costumes by Ora Crofoot
CAST
Jerry Ryan . . . . .Angelo Mango
Gittel Mosca . . . . .Merle Louise
David . . . . .Dick Fuchs
Sophie . . . . .Barbara Marineau
Oscar Julio . . . . .Dale Helward
Hamlet Scene
Laertes . . . . .Richard Alpers
Gertrude . . . . .Barbara Marineau
Hamlet . . . . .Dale Helward
The King . . . . .Louis Girard
Nurse . . . . .Patricia Wettig
Ethel . . . . .Margo Smith
Neighbors, Friends, Dancers:
David Allen, Jeanie Allen, Richard Alpers, Carole Burt, Michael Dodge, Betty Ebert, Marcia
Eddy, Becky Gilbert, Louis Girard, Connie
Gould, Michael Hassel, Gayle Hinckley, Skip
Holman, Michael Jorgensen, Wayne Lamb, John
Glenn Lehman, Jeri Matteson, Thomas Morrissey, Jack Ragotzy, Dusty Reeds, Penny Schlaf,
Margo Smith, Patricia Wettig, Alex Valatka

#244
July 8 - 27, 1975
[World Premiere]
Move Over, Mrs. Markham
by Ray Cooney and John Chapman
Directed by Jack Ragotzy
Scenery by Dusty Reeds
Lighting by Paul Abe
Costumes by Ora Crofoot
CAST
Joanna Markham . . . . .Betty Ebert
Alistair Spenlow . . . . .Dick Fuchs
Sylvie . . . . .Barbara Marineau
Linda Lodge . . . . .Merle Louise
Philip Markham . . . . .Louis Girard
Henry Lodge . . . . .Dale Helward
Walter Pangbourne . . . . .Angelo Mango
Olive Harriet Smythe . . . . .Dusty Reeds
Miss Wilkinson . . . . .Margo Smith

#245
July 15 - August 3, 1975
Godspell
A musical based upon the gospel
according to St. Matthew
Music and New Lyrics by Stephen Schwartz
Lyrics for "By My Side" by Jay Hamburger
Music by Peggy Gordon
Original Conception by John-Michael Tebelak
Musical Director and Conductor -
John Glenn Lehman
Entire Production Staged by John Glenn Lehman
Costumes by Jeri Matteson
CAST
David Allen, Richard T. Alpers, Becky Gilbert,
Skip Holman, Barbara Marineau, Debbie

254

Moreno, Robin Reeds, Eric Riley, Penny Schlaf,
Patricia Wettig,
(General Understudy, Janie Allen)

#246
August 5 - August 17, 1975
Fiddler on the Roof
Based on Sholom Aleichem's Stories
(by Special Permission of Arnold Perl)
Produced on the NY Stage by Harold Prince
Original Production Directed and Choreographed
by Jerome Robbins
Book by Joseph Stein, Music by Jerry Bock,
Lyrics by Sheldon Harnick
Entire Production Staged by Wayne Lamb
Musical Director and Conductor -
John Glenn Lehman
Scenery by Dusty Reeds
Lighting by Paul Abe
Costumes by Ora Crofoot
CAST
The Fiddler . . . . .Michael Dodge
Tevye the Dairyman . . . . .Angelo Mango
Golde, his wife . . . . .Betty Ebert
Tzeitel .Becky Gilbert
Hodel . . . . .Barbara Marineau
Chava . . . . .Janie Allen
Shprintze . . . . .Barbara Whinnery
Bielke . . . . .Dianne Fraser
Yente, the Matchmaker . . . . .Dusty Reeds
Motel, the Tailor . . . . .Timothy Landfield
Perchik, the Student . . . . .Robin Reeds
Lazar Wolf, the Butcher . . . . . . .Dale Helward
Mordcha, the Innkeeper . . . . . . .Louis Girard
Rabbi .Alex Valatka
Mendel, his son . . . . .Richard T. Alpars
Avram, the Bookseller . . . . .Ted Birke
Nachum, the Beggar . . . . .Jan Mark Stouber
Grandma Tzeitel . . . . .Alice Mott
Fruma Sarah . . . . .Marcia Eddy
Shandel, Motel's Mother . . . . . . .Jeri Matteson
Label . . . . .Eric Riley
Mirala . . . . .Carol Burt
Fredel . . . . .Gayle Hinckley
Surcha . . . . .Debbie Moreno
The Bottle Dancers:
Ted Birke, Wayne Lamb, Richard Alpers,
Richard Bloore
The Russians
Constable . . . . .Jack Ragotay
Priest . . . . .Thomas Morrissey
Fyedka . . . . .Dick Fuchs
Ivan . . . . .John Glenn Lehman

#247
August 19 - August 31, 1975
Hair
Book and Lyrics by Gerome Ragni
and James Rado
Produced for the Broadway Stage
by Michael Butler
Music by Galt McDermot
Originally produced
by The NY Shakespeare Festival
Staged by Wayne Lamb
Musical Director and Conductor
John Glenn Lehman
Scenery by Dusty Reeds
Lighting by Earl H. Hughes
Costumes by Ora Crofoot
CAST
(The Tribe)

Claude . . . . .Timothy Landfield
Berger .Dick Fuchs
Hud . . . . .Eric Riley
Sheila . . . . .Barbara Marineau
Woof . . . . .Robin Reeds
Jeanie . . . . .Margo Smith
Crissy . . . . .Dianne Fraser/Carol Burt
Dionne . . . . .Dee Dee Flood
Steve . . . . .Stephen Lucas
Other Tribe Members:
Becky Gilbert, Richard T. Alpers, Debbie
Moreno, Skip Holman, Marcia Eddy, Aaron
Williams, Lorri Greene, Michael Dodge,
Rochelle McCracklin, Thomas Morrissey,
Patricia Wettig
The Establishment . . . . .Louis Girard
. . . . .Angelo Mango
Rest of the Establishment:
Betty Ebert; Gayle Hinckley, John Glenn
Lehman, Wayne Lamb, Jack Ragotzy

#248
September 2 - September 7, 1975
Not Now, Darling
by Ray Cooney and John Chapman
Directed by Jack Ragotzy
Scenery by Dusty Reeds
Costumes by Ora Crofoot
CAST
Miss Whittington . . . . .Barbara Whinnery
Arnold Crouch . . . . .Angelo Mango
Miss Tipdale . . . . .Barbara Marineau
Mrs. Frencham . . . . .Debbie Moreno
Gilbert Bodley . . . . .Louis Girard
Harry McMichael . . . . .Robin Reeds
Janie McMichael . . . . .Margo Smith
Mr. Frencham . . . . .Alex Valatka
Sue Lawson . . . . .Patricia Wettig
Maude Bodley . . . . .Becky Gilbert
Mr. Lawson . . . . .Jack Ragotzy

#249
An Evening with Angelo Mango
September 9 - September 13, 1975
Starring Mr. Angelo Mango
with Barbara Marineau and Patricia Wettig
and Jane Gallatin at the piano

1976 Season

#250
May 25 - June 6, 1976
Corn Crib Revue
(No Program on File)
Production Created by Wayne Lamb
and Jack Ragotzy
Lighting by Rodney Smith and John Reeds
Costumes by Kevin McGuire
Pianist - Cary Belcher
CAST
Richard T. Alpers, Becky Gelke, Robin Haynes,
Lisby Larson, John J. McCabe III, David Mc-
Grath, Robin Rooney, Eric James Schussler,
Marg Smith, Barbara Whinnery

#251
June 8 - 13, 1976
Habeas Corpus
by Alan Bennett
Directed by Jack Ragotzy
Scenery by Dusty Reeds

Lighting by Rodney J. Smith
Costumes by Kevin McGuire
CAST
Arthur Wicksteed . . . . .Louis Girard
Muriel Wicksteed . . . . .Dusty Reeds
Dennis Wicksteed . . . . .Robin Haynes
Constance Wicksteed . . . . .Teresanne Joseph
Mrs. Swabb . . . . .Betty Ebert
Canon Throbbing . . . . .Dale Helward
Lady Rumpers . . . . .Becky Gelke
Felicity Rumpers . . . . .Lisby Larson
Mr. Shanks . . . . .Richard T. Alpers
Sir Percy Shorter . . . . .Angelo Mango
Mr. Purdue . . . . .Eric James Schussler

#252
June 15 - 20, 1976
Not Now, Darling
by Ray Cooney and John Chapman
Directed by Jack Ragotzy
Scenery by Dusty Reeds
Lighting by Rodney J. Smith
Costumes by Ora Crofoot
CAST
Miss Whittington . . . . .Barbara Whinnery
Arnold Crouch . . . . .Angelo Mango
Miss Tipdale . . . . .Lisby Larson
Mrs. Frencham . . . . .Alice Mott
Gilbert Bodley . . . . .Louis Girard
Harry McMichael . . . . .Robin Haynes
Janice McMichael . . . . .Margo Smith
Mr. Frencham . . . . .Dale Helward
Sue Lawson . . . . .Carol Burt
Maude Bodley . . . . .Becky Gelke
Mr. Lawson . . . . .David McGrath

#253
June 22 - July 4, 1976
1776
Based on a conception of Sherman Edwards
Music and Lyrics by Sherman Edwards
Book by Peter Stone
Staged by Wayne Lamb
Musical Direction and Conductor
Michael Reno
Scenery by Dusty Reeds and David Potts
Lighting by Rodney J. Smith
Costume Supervisor, Ora Crofoot
Costumes Designed by Kevin McGuire
CAST
President - John Hancock . . . .Richard T. Alpers
Dr. Josiah Bartlett . . . . .Douglas Lind
John Adams . . . . .Angelo Mango
Stephen Hopkins . . . . .Jeffery Hal Jimison
Roger Sherman . . . . .Lonnie Vick
Lewis Morris . . . . .Bradley James
Robert Livingston . . . . .David McGrath
Rev. Jonathan Witherspoon . . . .Wilson P. Graham, Jr.
Benjamin Franklin . . . . .Louis Girard
John Dickinson . . . . .Dale Helward
James Wilson . . . . .Brian Lewis
Caesar Rodney . . . . .Kevin McGuire
Col. Thomas McKean . . . . .Rodney J. Smith
George Read . . . . .Richard Pahl
Samuel Chase . . . . .Jerry Bacik
Richard Henry Lee . . . . .Skip Holman
Thomas Jefferson . . . . .Robin Haynes
Edward Rutledge . . . . .Thomas Wopat
Joseph Hewes . . . . .Ted Birke
Dr. Lyman Hall . . . . .Lang Bethea
Secretary -
Charles Thomson . . . . .Eric J. Schussler

Custodian -
Andrew McNair . . . . .Eddie Zaremba
A Leather Apron . . . . .John Reeds
Courier . . . . .John J. McCabe III
Abigail Adams . . . . .Lisby Larson
Martha Jefferson . . . . .Becky Gelke

#254
July 6 - 18, 1976
The Ritz
by Terrence McNally
Directed by Wayne Lamb
Scenery by Dusty Reeds
Lighting by Rodney J. Smith
Costumes by Kevin McGuire
CAST
Prologue
Carmine Vespucci . . . . .Richard T. Alpers
Vivian Proclo . . . . .Mary Conetto
Old Man Vespucci . . . . . . .Eric James Schussler
Aunt Vera . . . . .Mary C. Huntington
Cousin Hortensia . . . . .Cathy O'Gorman
Priest .Douglas Lind
Abe .Thomas Wopat
Claude Perkins . . . . .Louis Girard
Gaetano Proclo . . . . .Angelo Mango
Chris .Dale Helward
Michael Brick . . . . .Robin Haynes
Googie Gomez . . . . .Becky Gelke
Maurine . . . . .Lisby Larson
Tiger . . . . .Brian Lewis
Duff .Michael Reno
Carmine Vespucci . . . . .Richard T. Alpers
Vivian Proclo . . . . .Mary Conetto
The Patrons
Pianist . . . . .Bradley James
Policeman . . . . .David McGrath
Crisco . . . . .Eddie Zaremba
Sheldon Farenthold . . . . .Ted Birke
Patron in Chaps . . . . .John J. McCabe III
Snooty Patron . . . . .Skip Holman
Quickies . . . . .Alfred Hinckley,
. . . . .Jack Ragotzy

#255
July 20 - 25, 1976
You Can't Take It With You
by Moss Hart and George S. Kaufman
Directed by Jack Ragotzy
Scenery by Dusty Reeds
Lighting by Rodney J. Smith
Costumes by Kevin McGuire
CAST
Penelope Sycamore . . . . .Betty Ebert
Essie . . . . .Carrie Nodella
Rita . . . . .Barbara Whinnery
Paul Sycamore . . . . .Angelo Mango
Mr. DePinna . . . . .Richard T. Alpers
Ed . . . . .Eric James Schussler
Donald . . . . .John J. McCabe III
Martin Vanderhof . . . . .Louis Girard
Alice .Lisby Larson
Henderson . . . . .Skip Holman
Tony Kirby . . . . .Robin Haynes
Boris Kolenkhov . . . . .Dale Helward
Gay Wellington . . . . .Keri Lynde
Mr. Kirby . . . . .Bradley James
Mrs. Kirby . . . . .Alice Mott
Three Men . . . . .David McGrath,
. . . . .Brian Lewis,
. . . . .Douglas Lind
Olga .Margo Smith

#256
July 27 - August 8, 1976
Candide
Music by Leonard Bernstein
Book adapted from Voltaire by Hugh Wheeler
Lyrics by Richard Wilbur
Additional Lyrics by Stephen Sondheim
and John Latouche
Staged by Wayne Lamb
Musical Direction by Michael Reno
Scenery by Dusty Reeds
Lighting by Rodney J. Smith
Costumes by Kevin McGuire
CAST
Dr. Voltaire, Dr. Pangloss,
Governor, Host, Sage . . . . .Angelo Mango
Chinese Servant, Westphalian
Soldier, Priest, Spanish Don,
Sailor, Lion, Guest . . . . .Richard T. Alpers
Candide . . . . .Thomas Wopat
Huntsman, Bulgarian Recruiting
Officer, Agent, Spanish Don,
Cartagenian, Priest, Sailor,
Eunuch . . . . .David McGrath
Paquette . . . . .Becky Gelke
Baroness, Penitente,
Houri . . . . .Debbie Moreno
Baron, Grand Inquisitor,
Slave, Driver, Guest . . . . .Louis Girard
Cunegonde . . . . .Lisby Larson
Maximillian . . . . .Robin Haynes
Servant, Bulgarian Soldier,
Agent of the Inquisition,
Spanish Don, Cartagenian,
Sailor . . . . .Eric James Schussler
Bulgarian Recruiting Officer,
Rich Jew, Judge, Merchant,
Pirate, Botanist, Guest . . . . .Dale Helward
Gothic Window Figure,
Guard, Pigmy, Cow . . . . .Ted Birke
Gothic Window Figure, Penitente,
Whore, Houri . . . . .Alice Mott
Gothic Window Figure,
Guard, Pirate, Cow . . . . .Brian Lewis
Gothic Window Figure,
Aristocrat, Whore, Houri . . . . . .Robin Rooney
Bulgarian Soldier, Penitente,
Governor's Aide, Sailor . . . . .Skip Holman
Westphalian Soldier, Agent
of the Inquisition,
Cartagenian, Pirate,
Guest . . . . .John J. McCabe III
Aristocrate, Houri . . . . .Carrie Nodella
Aristocrat, Cartagenian,
1st Sheep . . . . .Kim Conrad
Aristocrat, Carthagenian,
2nd Sheep . . . . .Cathy O'Gorman
Penitente, Cartagenian,
Houri . . . . .Carol Burt
Old Lady . . . . .Mary Conetto
Chinese Stage Hands
Keri Lynde, Robyn A. Helzner, Mary C.
Huntington, Teresanna Joseph
Citizens of the World
Betty Ebert, Gayle Hinckley, Bradley James,
Wayne Lamb, Jack Ragotzy, Dusty Reeds

#257
August 10 - 22, 1976
Guys and Dolls
A musical fable based on a story
by Damon Runyon
Music and Lyrics by Frank Loesser
Book by Jo Swerling and Abe Burrows
Staged by Wayne Lamb
Musical Direction by Michael Reno
Scenery by Dusty Reeds
Lighting by Rodney J. Smith
Costumes by Kevin McGuire
CAST
The Guys:
Nicely Nicely Johnson . . . . . . .Richard T. Alpers
Benny Southstreet . . . . .Robin Haynes
Rusty Charlie . . . . .Thomas Wopat
Nathan Detroit . . . . .Angelo Mango
Angie the Ox . . . . .Skip Holman
Harry the Horse . . . . .Brian Lewis
Sky Masterson . . . . .Dale Helward
Big Julie . . . . .Jerry Bacik
Sight-seeing Guide . . . . .Richard Pahl
Officer McGrath . . . . .David McGrath
Louie the Lens . . . . .Kevin McGuire
Joey the Gyp . . . . .Brendan McGuire
Pick-Pocket Pete . . . . .Douglas Lind
Lt. Brannigan . . . . .Bradley James
Brandy Bottle Bates . . . . .Ted Birke
The Greek . . . . .John J. McCabe III
Society Max . . . . .Eddie Zaremba
Scranton Slim . . . . .Eric James Schussler
The Dolls:
Miss Adelaide . . . . .Becky Gelke
Roslyn . . . . .Roslyn Roseman
Carol .Carol Burt
Margo . . . . .Margo Smith
Kim . . . . .Kim Conrad
Robyn . . . . .Robyn A. Helzner
Carrie . . . . .Carrie Nodella
Bobby Soxer . . . . .Cathy O'Gorman
Sight-seers . . . . .Mary Huntington,
. . . . .Teresanne Joseph
Chorus Girls . . . . .Keri Lynde,
. . . . .Robin Rooney
Street Vendor . . . . .Mary Conetto
From the Save-A-Soul Mission:
Sarah Brown . . . . .Lisby Larson
Arvide Abernathy . . . . .Louis Girard
Calvin . . . . .John Reeds
Agatha . . . . .Debbie Moreno
Priscilla . . . . .Barbara Whinnery
General Matilda B.
Cartwright . . . . .Dusty Reeds

#258
August 24 - 29, 1976
[World Premiere]
Revelation
A New Musical by Michael Reno
Based on the prophecies in the Revelation
of St. John the Divine
Staged by Wayne Lamb
Musical Director - Michael Reno
Scenery by Dusty Reeds
Lighting by Rodney J. Smith
Costumes by Kevin McGuire
Sound Design by Roger Gans
CAST
The Families
Mr. and Mrs. Jackson . . . . . . .Richard T. Alpers,
. . . . .Lisby Larson
David Jackson . . . . .Robin Haynes
Mr. and Mrs. Phillips . . . . . . .Eric J. Schussler,
. . . . .Alice Mott
Chris Phillips . . . . .Thomas Wopat
Mr. and Mrs. Fellman . . . . .Angelo Mango,

......................Becky Gelke
Maxine Fellman (Max) ....Roslyn Roseman
St. John ....Louis Girard
The Four Beasts, the Seven-
headed Beast, Locusts:
Ted Birke, Dale Helward, Robyn Helzner, Skip
Holman, Teresanne Joseph, Brian Lewis, David
McGrath, Debbie Moreno, Robin Rooney,
Barbara Whinnery
The Reverend ....Dale Helward
Tina ....Mary C. Huntington
Railroad Quartette:
Robyn Helzner, Mary C. Huntington,
Debbie Moreno, Robin Rooney
Isis ....Margo Smith
Soldiers (Boris and Phil) ....Skip Holman,
......................David McGrath
Spirit ....Brian Lewis,
......................Robin Rooney
Bananas ....John Reeds,
......................Barbara Whinnery
Toby (as a baby) ....Aaron Reno
Bulldog ....Jerry Bacik
Kline ....Brian Lewis
Toby (as a child) ....Collin Reno
Elijah ....Richard T. Alpers
Moses ....Eric J. Schussler
Prairie Gospel Trio:
Robyn Helzner, Brian Lewis, Robin Rooney
Choir, Congregation, People of the Earth:
Carol Burt, Betty Ebert, Bradley James,
Wayne Lamb, Keri Lynde, Carrie Nodella,
Jack Ragotzy, Eddie Zaremba

[reprise of **You Can't Take It With You**]
August 31 - September 5, 1976

1977 Season

#259
May 27 - June 11, 1977
Mango, Center Stage
Created and Directed by Wayne Lamb
Pianist - James Douglas Kent
Lighting by Jack McCabe and Richard Henson
CAST
Angelo Mango

#260
June 14 - 26, 1977
The Bed Before Yesterday
by Ben Travers
Directed by Jack Ragotzy
Scenery and Lighting Designed
by James K. Culley
Costumes by Margaret R. Curry
CAST
Victor Keene ....Louis Girard
Alma ....Dusty Reeds
Mrs. Holly ....Mimi Huntington
Aubrey ....Robin Haynes
Ella ....Becky Gelke
Lolly Tucker ....Betty Ebert
Felix ....Angelo Mango
Fred Castle ....Dale Helward
Taxi Driver ....Eric Schussler

#261
June 28 - July 10, 1977
One Night With You, Madame
(based on *Une Nuit Chez Vous...Madame!*
by Jean de Letraz)
by Mawby Green and Ed Feilbert
Directed by Jack Ragotzy
Scenery by Dusty Reeds
Lighting by Richard Henson
Costumes by Margaret R. Curry
CAST
Joseph ....Jack Ragotzy
Maurice ....Robin Haynes
Hugette DuBois ....Betty Ebert
Gaston DuBois ....Angelo Mango
Didier ....Dale Helward
Clara ....Becky Gelke
Rosine ....Dana Delany
Aunt Alice ....Louis Girard

#262
July 12 - July 24, 1977
Something's Afoot
Book, Music & Lyrics by James McDonald,
David Vos and Robert Gerlach
Additional Music by Ed Linderman
Staged by Wayne Lamb
Musical Director, Conductor and Special
Orchestrations and Choral arrangements by
James Douglas Kent
Scenery by James K. Culley
Lighting by Jack McCabe
Costumes by Margaret R. Curry
CAST
Lettie ....Betty Ebert
Flint ....Angelo Mango
Clive ....Bradley James
Hope Langdon ....Becky Gelke
Dr. Grayburn ....Dale Helward
Nigel Rancour ....Tom Wopat
Lady Grace Manley-Prowe ....Alice Mott
Col. Gillweather ....Louis Girard
Miss Tweed ....Dusty Reeds
Geoffrey ....Robin Haynes

#263
July 26 - August 7, 1977
Equus
by Peter Shaffer
Directed by Jack Ragotzy
Scenery and Lighting Designed
by James K. Culley
Costumes by Margaret R. Curry
Mime by Wayne Lamb
CAST
Martin Dysart ....Dale Helward
Alan Strang ....Robin Haynes
Nurse ....Alice Mott
Hester Salomon ....Becky Gelke
Frank Strang ....Louis Girard
Dora Strang ....Dusty Reeds
Horseman/Nugget ....Tom Wopat
Harry Dalton ....Angelo Mango
Jill Mason ....Dana Delany
Horses:
Joseph Dellger, Phil Dunn, Wayne Lamb,
John McCabe III, Peter Strong

#264
August 9 - August 21, 1977
Annie Get Your Gun
Music and Lyrics by Irving Berlin
Book by Herbert and Dorothy Fields
Staged by Wayne Lamb
Musical Director, Conductor and
Special Orchestrations by James Douglas Kent
Scenery by Dusty Reeds
Lighting by Richard Henson
Costumes by Margaret R. Curry
CAST
Charlie Davenport ....Angelo Mango
Dolly Tate ....Betty Ebert
Mac ....John McCabe III
Foster Wilson ....Bradley James
Frank Butler ....Tom Wopat
Girls from Town:
Lora Adams, Margaret Ann Conway,
Dana Delany, Shay Gibson, Barbb Louis
Annie Oakley ....Becky Gelke
Brother Jake ....Brendan Ragotzy
Nellie ....Cathy O'Gorman
Jessie ....Margaret R. Curry
Buffalo Bill ....Louis Girard
Iron Tail ....Jeffery Jimison
Yellow Foot ....Ed Zaremba
Mrs. Black Tooth ....Mimi Huntington
Conductor ....Joseph Dellger
Porter ....Jeffery Jimison
Waiter ....Phil Dunn
Pawnee Bill ....John Phane
Gun Club Cowboys:
Joseph Dellger, Phil Dunn, George Procter,
Peter Strong
Sitting Bull ....Eric James Schussler
Wild Horse ....Wayne Lamb
Pawnee's Messenger ....Peter Strong
Mrs. Sylvia Potter-Porter ....Alice Mott

#265
August 23 - September 4, 1977
The Pajama Game
Book by George Abbott and Richard Bissell
Music by Richard Adler and Jerry Ross
Staged by Wayne Lamb
Musical Direction and Conductor -
James Douglas Kent
Scenery by James K. Culley
Lighting by Richard Henson
Costumes by Margaret R. Curry
CAST
Hines ....Angelo Mango
Prez ....Eric Schussler
Joe ....Joe Dellger
Hasler ....Louis Girard
Gladys ....Becky Gelke
Sid Sorokin ....Tom Wopat
Mabel ....Alice Mott
1st Helper ....Peter Strong
2nd Helper ....John Phane
Charley ....John McCabe III
Babe Williams ....Barbara Marineau
Mae ....Barbb Louis
Brenda ....Mimi Huntington
Poopsie ....Cathy O'Gorman
Ann ....Lora Adams
Carmen ....Dana Delany
Sara ....Margaret-Ann Conway
Mara ....Shay Gibson
Mary ....Margaret R. Curry
Eddie ....Ed Zaremba
Max ....Bradley James
Pop ....Jeffery Jimison
Poopsie's Pal ....George Procter
Pat ....Betty Ebert
Rita ....Gayle Hinckley
Leroy ....Wayne Lamb
Davey ....Brendan Ragotzy

1978 Season

#266
May 26 - June 10, 1978
Angelo Mango Sings
Created and Directed by Wayne Lamb
Pianist - James Douglas Kent
Lighting by Bruce Mirken
Costumes by Meg Curry
CAST
Angelo Mango

#267
June 13 - June 25, 1978
Light Up the Sky
by Moss Hart
Directed by Jack Ragotzy
Scenery by James K. Culley
Lighting by Rodney J. Smith
Costumes by Meg Curry
CAST

Miss Lowell	Dana Delany
Carleton Fitzgerald	Dick Fuchs
Frances Black	Betty Ebert
Owen Turner	Louis Girard
Stella Livingston	Dusty Reeds
Peter Sloan	Sal Aiello
Sidney Black	Angelo Mango
Sven	Phil Dunn
Irene Livingston	Jen Wolfe
Tyler Rayburn	Glenn Farnham
Max, a Shriner	Jack Ragotzy
Max's buddy	Michael McEowen
William H. Gallegher	Bradley James
A Plainclothesman	John Evans
1st Shriner, Jack	Ric Shaffer
2nd Shriner, Ed	Phil Buhrman
3rd Shriner, Jim	Kurtis Thiel

STAGE:
Production Stage Manager: Wayne Lamb;
Technical Director James K. Culley;
Assistant Stage Manager: Michael McEowen;
Property Master: Jim Knox

#268
June 27 - July 9, 1978
13 Rue De L'Amour
by George Feydeau
Adapted and Translated by Mawby Green
and Ed Feilbert
Directed by Jack Ragotzy
Scenery by Dusty Reeds
Lighting by Rodney J. Smith
Costumes by Meg Curry
CAST

Leontine	Susan Gordon
Moricet	Dick Fuchs
Duchotel	Louis Girard
Marie	Dana Delaney
Jean-Pierre	Glenn Farnham
Birabeau	Angelo Mango
Madame Spritzer	Dusty Reeds
Inspector of Police	Sal Aiello
First Policeman	Ray Mendonca
Second Policeman	Bruce Evan Mirken

#269
July 11 - 23, 1978
Man of La Mancha
by Dale Wasserman
(Suggested by the life and works of
Miguel de Cervantes y Saavedra)
Music by Mitch Leigh
Lyrics by Joe Darion
Staged by Wayne Lamb
Musical Director, Conductor and
Special Orchestrations
by James Douglas Kent
Scenery by Dusty Reeds
Lighting by Rodney J. Smith
Costumes by Meg Curry
CAST

Cantore	Jeffery Hal Jimison
Guitarist	Philip Buhrman
Flamenco Dancers	Phil Dunn,
	Maryjane Cunningham
Capt. of the Inquisition	Bradley James
Priests of the Inquisition	Jen Wolfe,
	Sherra L. Schick
Guards	Bruce Evan Mirken,
	Ray Mendonca
Manservant	Sal Aiello
Miguel de Cervantes	Frederick Reeder
Don Quixote	Frederick Reeder
Sancho Panza	Sal Aiello
Governor and Innkeeper	Louis Girard
Duke and Dr. Carrasco	Kurtis Thiel
Horse	Wayne Lamb
Mule	Brendan Ragotzy

Muleteers:

Pedro	John Evans
Anselmo	Rodney Jacob Smith
Juan	Brendan Ragotzy
Jose	Phil Dunn
Diego	Wayne Lamb
Paco	Ric Shaffer
Tenorio	Doug Mancheski
Miguel	Lonnie Vick
Aldonza (Dulcinea)	Susan Gordon
Maria	Meg Curry
Fermina and	
Moorish Dancer	Dana Delany
Antonia	Kimberly Scroggins
Housekeeper	Alice Mott
Padre	Angelo Mango
Barber	Ray Mendonca

Prisoners:
Betty Ebert, Michael McEowen, Dusty Reeds

#270
July 25 - July 30, 1978
Count Dracula
by Ted Tiller
(Based on Bram Stoker's
19th Century novel, *Dracula*)
Directed by Wayne Lamb
Scenery by Dusty Reeds
Lighting by Rodney J. Smith
Costumes by Meg Curry
Organist - James Douglas Kent
CAST

Hennessey	John Evans
Sybil Seward	Betty Ebert
Dr. Beatrice Seward	Dusty Reeds
Renfield	Angelo Mango
Wesley	Phil Dunn
Jonathan Harker	Frederick Reeder
Mina	Dana Delany
Count Dracula	Sal Aiello
Henrich Van Helsing	Louis Girard

#271
August 1 - 6, 1978
Vanities
by Jack Heifner
Directed by Jack Ragotzy
Designed by James K. Culley
Lighting by Rodney J. Smith
Musical Interlude Arrangements
by Terry Armbruster
CAST

Kathy	Susan Gordon
Mary	Jen Wolfe
Joanne	Dana Delany

#272
August 8 - 20, 1978
Pippin
by Roger O. Hirson
Music and Lyrics by Stephen Schwartz
Directed by Wayne Lamb
Musical Direction, Conductor
and Special Orchestrations
by James Douglas Kent
Scenery by Dusty Reeds
Lighting by Rodney J. Smith
Costumes by Meg Curry
CAST

Leading Player	Angelo Mango
Pippin	Sal Aiello
Charles	Louis Girard
Lewis	Lonnie Vick
Fastrada	Susan Gordon
The Head	Bradley James
Berthe	Alice Mott
Field Marshall	Rodney Jacob Smith
Catherine	Barbara Marineau
Theo	Christopher Lore

The Players:
Maryjane Cunningham, Meg Curry, Dana Delany, Phil Dunn, Betty Ebert, John Evans, Elizabeth Jacobs, Wayne Lamb, Doug Mancheski, Michael McEowen, Ray Mendonca, Brendan Ragotzy, Dusty Reeds, Doreen Remo, Sherra L. Schick, Ric Shaffer, Rodney Jacob Smith

Flag Bearers	Mary Ambrosavage,
	Donna Reeves

#273
August 22 - September 3, 1978
Anything Goes
by Guy Bolton, P.G. Wodehouse, Howard Linsay
and Russell Crouse
Music and Lyrics by Cole Porter
Staged by Wayne Lamb
Musical Director and Conductor -
James Douglas Kent
Scenery by Dusty Reeds
Lighting by Rodney J. Smith
Costumes by Meg Curry
CAST

Reno Sweeney	Barbara Marineau
Billy Crocker	Sal Aiello
Moonface Martin	Angelo Mango
Hope Harcourt	Kimberly Scroggins
Bonnie	Susan Gordon
Sir Evelyn Oakleigh	Louis Girard
Mrs. Harcourt	Elizabeth Jacobs
Whitney	Bradley James
Bishop	Ric Shaffer
Steward	Jeffery Hal Jimison
Reporter	Philip Buhrman
Photographer	Rodney Jacob Smith

Ching . . . . .Kurtis Thiel
Ling . . . . .Bruce Evan Mirken
Purity . . . . .Maryjane Cunningham
Chastity . . . . .Meg Curry
Charity . . . . Jen Wolfe
Virtue . . . . .Dana Delany
Purser . . . . .Ray Mendonca
Captain . . . . .John Evans
Drunk . . . . .Michael McEowen
Sailors . . . . .Lonnie Vick,
. . . . .Phil Dunn, Ric Shaffer
Girls:
Donna Reeves, Doreen Remo,
Mary Ambrosavage, Randi Rae Arnold

#274
September 5 - 17, 1978
Same Time, Next Year
by Bernard Slade
Directed by Jack Ragotzy
Scenery and Lighting by Rodney J. Smith
Costumes by Meg Curry
CAST
Doris . . . . .Jen Wolfe
George . . . . .Sal Aiello

#275
September 19 - October 1, 1978
An Evening with Angelo Mango, VI
Starring Mr. Angelo Mango
Created and Directed by Wayne Lamb
Lighting by Rodney Smith and Philip Buhrman
Costumes by Ken Andrews
Ric Shaffer at the Piano
Group numbers arranged by Ric Shaffer
With: Sal Aiello, Ken Andrews, Randi Arnold,
Philip Buhrman, Maryjane Cunningham,
John Evans, Sherra Schick, Kimberly Scroggins,
Jen Wolfe

1979 Season

#276
May 22 - June 9, 1979
An Evening with Angelo Mango, VII
Created and Directed by Wayne Lamb
Written by Jack Ragotzy
Lighting by Wayne Scofield
Costumes by Elizabeth Jacobs
Pianist - James Douglas Kent
CAST
Angelo Mango
with
Sandeman Allen, Philip Buhrman, Gina Maria
Ferraro, Jim Freed, Ron Gubin, Elizabeth Jacobs,
Sherra Schick, Kimberly Scroggins, Peter
Strong, Jen Wolfe

#277
June 12 - 24, 1979
California Suite
(No Program on File)
by Neil Simon
Directed by Jack Ragotzy
Scenery by James K. Culley and Dusty Reeds
Lighting by Wayne Scofield
Costumes by Elizabeth Jacobs
CAST
Visitors From NY:
Hannah Warren . . . . .Jen Wolfe
William Warren . . . . .Joe Aiello
Visitors From Philadelphia:
Marvin Michaels . . . . .Louis Girard
Bunny . . . . .Krista Neumann
Millie Michaels . . . . .Betty Ebert
Visitors From London:
Sidney Nichols . . . . .Dick Fuchs
Diana Nichols . . . . .Mollie Collison
Visitors From Chicago:
Morton Hollender . . . . .Angelo Mango
Beth Hollender . . . . .Dusty Reeds
Stu Franklin . . . . .Louis Girard
Gert Franklin . . . . .Betty Ebert

#278
June 26 - July 8, 1979
Chicago
Book by Fred Ebb and Bob Fosse
(Based on the play by Maurine Dallas Wakins)
Music by John Kander
Lyrics by Fred Ebb
Staged by Wayne Lamb
Scenery by Dusty Reeds
Lighting by James K. Culley
Costumes by Cynthia A. Ballard
Musical Direction and Orchestrations
by James Douglas Kent
CAST
Master of Ceremonies . . . . .Raymond Mendonca
Velma Kelly . . . . .Jen Wolfe
Roxie Hart . . . . .Krista Neumann
Fred Casely . . . . .Peter Strong
Sgt. Fogarty . . . . .Louis Girard
Amos Hart .Joe Aiello
Matron .Dusty Reeds
Billy Flynn . . . . .Angelo Mango
Tailor .Philip Buhrman
Mary Sunshine . . . . .Kimberley Scroggins
Reporters:
Sandeman Allen, Jim Freed, Dick Fuchs, Ron L.
Gubin, Wayne Lamb, Michael McEowen, Mark
Paladini, Brendan Ragotzy, Brent L. Varner
Harry . . . . .Dick Fuchs
Kitty Katz . . . . .Elizabeth Jacobs
Doctor .Jay Matthews
Coat Rack Girl . . . . .Betty Ebert
Liz . . . . .Betsy Turner
Annie . . . . .Kani Seifert
June . . . . .Randi Rae Arnold
Mona . . . . .Nancy Coker
Beth . . . . .Sherra Schick
Hunyak . . . . .Mollie Collison
Aaron . . . . .Gregory Mortensen
Bailiff .Bradley James
Court Clerk . . . . .Brendan Ragotzy
Prosecuting Attorney . . . . .Philip Buhrman
Judge . . . . .Bob Cooper, Jr.
Foreman/Jury . . . . .Louis Girard
Uncle Sam . . . . .Wayne Lamb
Justice . . . . .Betty Ebert
Whistler . . . . .Bradley James

#279
July 10 - 22, 1979
No Sex Please, We're British
by Anthony Marriott and Alistair Foot
Directed by Jack Ragotzy
Scenery and Lighting by James K.Culley
Costumes by Elizabeth Jacobs
CAST
Peter Hunter . . . . .Joe Aiello
Frances Hunter . . . . .Krista Neumann
Brian Runnicles . . . . .Dick Fuchs
Eleanor Hunter . . . . .Dusty Reeds
Leslie Bromhead . . . . .Louis Girard
Superintendent Paul . . . . .Bob Cooper, Jr.
B.R.S. Delivery Man . . . . .Peter Strong
2nd Delivery Man . . . . .Jim Freed
Mr. Needham . . . . .Angelo Mango
Susan . . . . .Jen Wolfe
Barbara . . . . .Kani Seifert
Mailman (voice) . . . . .Brendan Ragotzy
Office Girl (voice) . . . . . . .Kimberley Scroggins
Television Newscaster
(voice) . . . . .Jack Ragotzy

#280
July 24 - August 5, 1979
Ballroom
Book by Jerome Kass
Music by Billy Goldenberg
Lyrics by Alan & Marilyn Bergman
Staged by Wayne Lamb
Scenery by Dusty Reeds
Lighting by James K. Culley
Costumes by Cynthia A. Ballard
Musical Direction and Special Orchestrations
by James Douglas Kent
CAST
The Family:
Bea Asher . . . . .Krista Neumann
Helen . . . . .Dusty Reeds
Jack . . . . .Louis Girard
Diane . . . . .Mollie Collison
David . . . . .Jim Freed
At the Stardust Ballroom:
Angie . . . . .Jen Wolfe
Marlene . . . . .Kimberley Scroggins
Nathan . . . . .Joe Aiello
Pauline .Betty Ebert
Al Rossi . . . . .Angelo Mango
Shirley . . . . .Elizabeth Jacobs
Johnny "Lightfeet" . . . . .Wayne Lamb
Harry "The Noodle" . . . . .Dick Fuchs
Waiter . . . . .Gregory Mortensen
Lester .Jay Matthews
The Ballroom Regulars:
Sandeman Allen, Randi Rae Arnold, Betty Ebert,
Jim Freed, Dick Fuchs, Wayne Lamb, Bradley
James, Michael McEowen, Raymond Mendonca,
Mark Paladini, Brendan Ragotzy, Kani Seifert,
Peter Strong, Betsy Turner, Brent L. Varner,
Jen Wolfe
Customers at Bea's Store:
Natalie . . . . .Kimberley Scroggins
Estelle . . . . .Betty Ebert
Martha . . . . .Sherra Schick
Eleanor . . . . .Nancy A. Coker
Kathy .Cheryl Asher

#281
August 7 -19, 1979
Move Over, Mrs. Markham
by Ray Cooney and John Chapman
Directed by Jack Ragotzy
Scenery by Dusty Reeds
Lighting by James K. Culley
Costumes by Elizabeth Jacobs
CAST
Joanna Markham . . . . .Betty Ebert
Alistair Spenlow . . . . .Dick Fuchs
Sylvie . . . . .Jen Wolfe
Linda Lodge . . . . .Kimberley Scroggins
Philip Markham . . . . .Louis Girard
Henry Lodge . . . . .Joe Aiello

Walter Pangbourne . . . . .Angelo Mango
Olive Harriet Smythe . . . . .Dusty Reeds
Miss Wilkinson . . . . .Mollie Collison

#282
August 21 - September 2, 1979
Sugar
Book by Peter Stone
Music by Jule Styne
Lyrics by Bob Merrill
(Based on the Screenplay *Some Like It Hot*
by Billy Wilder & I.A.L. Diamond)
Staged by Wayne Lamb
Musical Director and Special Orchestrations
by James Douglas Kent
Scenery by Dusty Reeds and James K. Culley
Lighting Design by Jon Fruytier
Costumes by Cynthia K. Ballard
CAST
Sweet Sue . . . . .Jen Wolfe
Sugar Kane . . . . .Randi Rae Arnold
Beinstock . . . . .Joe Aiello
Joe . . . . .Dick Fuchs
Jerry . . . . .Angelo Mango
Spats Palozzo . . . . .Peter Strong
Knuckles Norton . . . . .Bradley James
Trainman . . . . .Michael McEowen
Osgood Fielding, Jr. . . . . .Louis Girard
Sweet Sue's Orchestra:
Nancy Coker, Mollie Collison, Betty Ebert,
Elizabeth Jacobs, Sherra Schick, Kimberley
Scroggins, Kani Seifert, Betsy Turner
Gangsters and Hoods:
Sandeman Allen, Jim Freed, Ron Gubin, Raymond Mendonca, Mark Paladini, Brent Varner
Millionaires:
Philip Buhrman, Bob Cooper, Jr., Jay Matthews,
Gregory Mortensen
Friends, Passengers, Employees:
Tom Cummins, Gregory Dean, Jim Freed,
Ron Gubin, Kathryn A. Hastings, Raymond
Mendonca, Mark Paladini, Brendan Ragotzy,
Michaelle Ross

#283
September 4 - 9, 1979
Side by Side by Sondheim
(No Program on File)
Music and Lyrics by Stephen Sondheim
Additional Music by Leonard Bernstein,
Mary Rogers, Richard Rogers, Jule Styne
Continuity by Ned Sherrie
Directed by Wayne Lamb and Jack Ragotzy
Pianist and Musical Direction
by James Douglas Kent
Scenery by Kai Seaforth
Lighting by Jan Fruytier
Costumes by Elizabeth Jacobs
CAST
Angelo Mango
Joe Aiello
Kimberley Scroggins
Jen Wolfe
Randi Rae Arnold
Jim Freed
Chinese Stage Hands:
Bob Cooper, Jr. and Gregory Mortensen

1980 Season

#284
May 27 - June 7, 1980
An Evening with Angelo Mango, VIII
Created and Directed by Wayne Lamb
Written by Jack Ragotzy
Lighting by Michael Meyer, John Reeds,
Peg L. Hess
Costumes by Kent Meredith, Gordon Allen
Pianist - Jeffrey Powell
CAST
Angelo Mango
with
Gordon Allen, Steve Devaney, Ron Gubin,
Marin J. Mazzie, Karesa McElheny, Cheryl
Randolph, Kani Seifert, Susan Spindel, David
Tislow, Betsy Turner, Tom VanderWeele

#285
June 10 - June 22, 1980
Bedroom Farce
by Alan Ayckbourn
Directed by Jack Ragotzy
Scenery and Lighting by James K. Culley
Costumes by Cynthia A. Ballard
CAST
Ernest . . . . .Louis Girard
Delia . . . . .Dusty Reeds
Nick . . . . .Peter Strong
Jan . . . . .Julie Mote
Malcolm . . . . .Joe Aiello
Kate .Pamela Cordova
Trevor . . . . .Dale Helward
Susannah . . . . .Marin Mazzie

#286
June 24 - July 6, 1980
On the Twentieth Century
Book and Lyrics by Betty Comden
and Adolph Green
Music by Cy Coleman
Based on plays by Ben Hecht, Charles
MacArthur and Bruce Milholland
Staged by Wayne Lamb
Scenery by Dusty Reeds
Lighting by James K. Culley
Costumes by Cynthia Ballard
Musical Direction and Special Orchestrations by
Jeffrey Powell
CAST
Priest . . . . .John Reeds
Bishop . . . . .Jonathan Larson
Executioner . . . . .Bradley James
Stage Manager . . . . .Michael McEowen
Joan . . . . .Betty Ebert
Owen O'Malley . . . . .Peter Strong
Oliver Webb . . . . .Louis Girard
Porters:
Gordon Allen, Steve Devaney, David Tislow,
Lonnie Vick.
Conductors . . . . .Scott Burkel,
. . . . .Keith La Pan
Train Secretary . . . . .Betsy Turner
Horatio Primrose . . . . .Angelo Mango
Congressman Lockwood . . . .Tom Vander Weele
Anita . . . . .Kani Seifert
Oscar Jaffee . . . . .Dale Helward
Max Jacobs . . . . .Ron Gubin.
Imelda Thornton . . . . .Marin Mazzie
Maxwell Finch . . . . .Wayne Lamb
Mildred Plotka/
Lily Garland . . . . .Pamela Cordova
Bruce Granit . . . . .Joe Aiello

Reporters . . . . .Jonathan Larson,
. . . . .David Tislow,
. . . . .Betsy Turner
Agnes . . . . .Julie Mote
Hospital Attendants . . . . .David Burgess,
. . . . .John Reeds
Dr. Johnson . . . . .Dusty Reeds
Passengers, Actors, Friends:
David Burgess, Alison Gordon-Creed, Cynthia
Hechter, Karesa McElheny, Cheryl Randolph,
Susan Spindel

#287
July 8 - 20, 1980
Do It for Your Country
(*Shut Your Eyes and Think of England*)
by John Chapman and Anthony Marriott
Directed by Jack Ragotzy
Scenery by James K. Culley
Lighting by Mark Netherland
Costumes by Cynthia A. Ballard
CAST
Sir Justin Holbrook . . . . .Dale Helward
Stella Richards . . . . .Pamela Cordova
Arthur Pullen . . . . .Angelo Mango
Lady Holbrook . . . . .Betty Ebert
The Right Honorable Sir
Frederick Goudhurst . . . . .Louis Girard
His Highness Sheik Marami . . . . . . .Joe Aiello
Mrs. Joyce Pullen . . . . .Dusty Reeds
Mr. Rubinstein . . . . .Peter Strong
Dr. Cornish . . . . .Bradley James

#288
July 22 - August 10, 1980
Grease
Music, Book & Lyrics by Jim Jacobs
and Warren Casey
Staged by Wayne Lamb
Musical Direction by Jeffrey Powell
Scenery by Dusty Reeds
Lighting by Mark Netherland
Costumes by Cynthia A. Ballard
CAST
Mr. Tambourini . . . . .Wayne Lamb
Miss Lynch . . . . .Dusty Reeds
Principal Reeves . . . . .Louis Girard
Patricia Simcox Honeywell . . . . . . .Betty Ebert
Mr. Honeywell . . . . .Angelo Mango
Eugene Florczyk . . . . . . .Tom Vander Weele
*Jan .Cynthia Hachter
*Marty . . . . .Susan Spindel
*Betty Rizzo . . . . .Marin Mazzie
+Doody . . . . .David Burgess
+Roger .Scott Burkel
+Kenickie . . . . .Peter Strong
+Sonny La Tierri . . . . .Richard Marlatt
*Frenchy . . . . .Julie Mote
Sandy Dumbrowski . . . . .Pamela Cordova
Patty Simcox . . . . .Betsy Turner
+Danny Zuko . . . . .Joe Aiello
Bingo . . . . .David Tislow
Eugene Florczyk . . . . .John Reeds
Vince Fontaine . . . . .Randy Riggs
WLDS Announcer . . . . .Karesa McElheny
"It's Raining. . ."
Radio Voice . . . . .Cheryl Randolph
Johnny Casino . . . . .Gordon Allen
Cha Cha Di Gregorio . . . . .Kani Seifert
Teen-Angel . . . . .Lonnie Vick.
"Movie Voices"
Sheila . . . . .Cheryl Randolph

260

Hero . . . . .David Tislow
Scientist . . . . .Ron Gubin.
*Pink Ladies, +Burger Palace Boys

#289
August 12 - August 17, 1980
Chapter Two
by Neil Simon
Directed by Jack Ragotzy
Scenery by James K. Culley
Lighting by Mark Netherland
Costumes by Cynthia A. Ballard
CAST
George Schneider . . . . .Angelo Mango
Leo Schneider . . . . .Joe Aiello
Jennie Malone . . . . .Barbara Marineau
Faye Medwick . . . . .Pamela Cordova

#290
August 19 - August 31, 1980
Oklahoma!
Music by Richard Rogers
Lyrics by Oscar Hammerstein II
Based on Lynn Riggs' *Green Grow the Lilacs*
Staged by Wayne Lamb
Musical Direction and Special Orchestration by
Jeffrey Powell
Scenery by Dusty Reeds
Lighting by Mark Netherland
Costumes by Cynthia A. Ballard
CAST
Aunt Eller . . . . .Betty Ebert
Curly . . . . .Lonnie Vick.
Laurey .Pamela Cordova
Ike Skidmore . . . . .Peter Strong
Slim . . . . .John Reeds
Will Parker . . . . .Gordon Allen
Jud Fry . . . . .Joe Aiello
Ado Annie Carnes . . . . .Marin Mazzie
Ali Hakim . . . . .Angelo Mango
Gertie Cummings . . . . .Betsy Turner
Andrew Carnes . . . . .Louis Girard
Cord Elam . . . . .Tom Vander Weele
The Girls:
Fay . . . . .Elizabeth Ann Gorcey
Ellen . . . . .Julie Mote
Veronica . . . . .Cynthia Hechter
Kate .Cheryl Randolph
Vivian . . . . .Susan Spindel
Sylvie . . . . .Karesa McElheny
Armina . . . . .Kani Seifert
The Boys:
Jess . . . . .David Burgess
Chalmers . . . . .Ron Gubin.
Mike . . . . .Michael Meyer
Joe . . . . .Kent Meredith
Sam . . . . .Scott Burkel
Fred . . . . .Jonathan Larson
Dream Laurie . . . . .Alison Gordon-Creed
Dream Curly . . . . .Steve Devaney
Dream Jud . . . . .David Tislow
Dream Post Card Girls . . . . .Kani Seifert,
. . . . .Karesa McElheny

1981 Season

#291
June 2 - 14, 1981
An Evening with Angelo Mango, IX
Created and Directed by Wayne Lamb

Pianist and Special Arrangements
by James Douglas Kent
Lights by Mark Netherland and Tom Stewart
Costumes by Kevin McGuire
CAST
Angelo Mango
with
Barbara Bicknell, Scott Burkel, Ron Faria, Jon
Larson, Marin Mazzie, Karesa McElheny, Steve
Owsley, Cheryl Randolph, David Tislow,
Suzannah Zody

#292
June 16 - 28, 1981
On Golden Pond
by Ernest Thompson
Directed by Jack Ragotzy
Scenery by James K. Culley
Lighting by Mark Netherland
Costumes by Kevin McGuire
CAST
Norman Thayer, Jr. . . . . .Louis Girard
Ethel Thayer . . . . .Dusty Reeds
Charlie Martin . . . . .Joe Aiello
Chelsea Thayer Wayne . . . . . . .Mariana Rence
Billy Ray . . . . .Christopher Creviston
Bill Ray . . . . .Angelo Mango

#293
July 1 - 19, 1981
Carousel
(Based on Ferenc Molnar's *Lilliom*)
Music by Richard Rodgers
Book and Lyrics by Oscar Hammerstein II
Staged by Wayne Lamb
Musical Director and Orchestrations
by James Douglas Kent
Scenery by Dusty Reeds
Lighting by Mark Netherland
Costumes by Kevin McGuire
CAST
Carrie Pipperidge . . . . .Marin Mazzie
Julie Jordan . . . . .Mariana Rence
Mrs. Mullin . . . . .Karesa McElheny
Billy Bigelow . . . . .Tom Wopat
1st Policeman . . . . .Scott Burkel
David Bascomb . . . . .Ric Shaffer
Mrs. Bascomb . . . . .Dusty Reeds
Nettie Fowler . . . . .Betty Ebert
Enoch Snow . . . . .Angelo Mango
Jigger Craigin . . . . .Joe Aiello
2nd Policeman . . . . .Ken Roberts
Captain . . . . .Arnie Stenseth
Heavenly Friend . . . . .Jack Ragotzy
Star Keeper and Dr. Sheldon . . . . .Louis Girard
Louise . . . . .Karen Wheeler
Enoch Snow, Jr. . . . . .Jon Lee
Principal . . . . .Bradley James
The Snow Children:
Jenny . . . . .Barbara Bicknell
Sadie . . . . .Elizabeth Gorcey
Peter .Tom Kellogg
Betsy . . . . .Beth Kavanaugh
Katie . . . . .Kathy Shields
Joan . . . . .Jody Shields
Ruffian Boy, Tony . . . . .David Tislow
Ruffian Boy, Rick . . . . .Jon Lee
Carnival Boy . . . . .Rick Pallaziol
Sailors, Men, Carnival Troupe:
Peter Colburn, Ron Faria, Jonathan Larson,
Robert Newman, Robin Nuyen, Steve Owsley,
Brendan Ragotzy, Tom Stewart

Wives, Girlfriends, Carnival Troupe:
Jody Abrahams, Shawn Dale, Sherry Handa,
Kristen Holland, Mary Israel, Shel Marie,
Bethanne McGuire, Cheryl Randolph,
Suzanah Zody
Pre-Production Stand-in
for Mr. Wopat . . . . .Robin Nuyen

#294
July 21 - August 2, 1981
Deathtrap
by Ira Levin
Directed by Jack Ragotzy
Scenery by James K. Culley
Lighting by Mark Netherland
Costumes by Kevin McGuire
CAST
Sidney Bruhl . . . . .George McDaniel
Myra Bruhl . . . . .Mariana Rence
Clifford Anderson . . . . .Joe Aiello
Helga ten Drop . . . . .Dusty Reeds
Porter Milgrim . . . . .Louis Girard

#295
August 4 - 16, 1981
My Fair Lady
(Adapted from George Bernard Shaw's
Pygmalion)
Book and Lyrics by Alan Jay Lerner
Music by Frederick Loewe
Staged by Wayne Lamb
Musical Direction and Special Orchestrations
by James Douglas Kent
Designed by Dusty Reeds
Lighting by Mark Netherland
Costumes by Kevin McGuire
CAST
Buskers . . . . .Jon Lee,
. . . . .Shel Marie,
. . . . .Suzannah Zody
Mrs. Eynsford Hill . . . . .Marin Mazzie
Freddy Eynsford Hill . . . . .Robert Newman
Eliza Doolittle . . . . .Mariana Rence
Colonel Pickering . . . . .Louis Girard
Henry Higgins . . . . .George McDaniel
3rd Cockney . . . . .Jon Larson
4th Cockney . . . . .Tom Stewart
Sweeper . . . . .Wayne Lamb
Bartender . . . . .Robin Nuyen
Harry . . . . .David Tislow
Jamie . . . . .Ric Shaffer
Alfred P. Doolittle . . . . .Angelo Mango
Mrs. Pearce . . . . .Mary Israel
Butler .Scott Burkel
Maids:
Barbara Bicknell, Suzannah Zody, Cheryl
Randolph, Marin Mazzie
Footman .Jon Larson
Mrs. Higgins . . . . .Dusty Reeds
Lord Boxington . . . . .Peter Colburn
Lady Boxington . . . . .Karesa McElheny
Zoltan Karpathy . . . . .Joe Aiello
Queen of Transylvania . . . . .Shawn Dale
Ladies, Gentlemen, Cockneys,
and other London Citizens:
Jody Abrahams, Betty Ebert, Ron Faria, Elizabeth Gorcey, Sherry Handa, Kristen Holland,
Bradley James, Wayne Lamb, Karesa McElheny,
Brendan Ragotzy, Jack Ragotzy, Karen Wheeler

#296
August 18 - 23, 1981
Whose Life Is It Anyway?
by Brian Clark
Directed by Jack Ragotzy
Scenery by James K. Culley
Lighting by Jon Fruytier
Costumes by Kevin McGuire
CAST
Ken Harrison . . . . .Joe Aiello
Sister Anderson . . . . .Dusty Reeds
Kay Sadler . . . . .Marin Mazzie
John . . . . .Robin Nuyen
Dr. Scott . . . . .Mariana Rence
Dr. Emerson . . . . .Louis Girard
Mrs. Boyle . . . . .Karesa McElheny
Philip Hill . . . . .Angelo Mango
Dr. Paul Travers . . . . .Ric Shaffer
Peter Kershaw . . . . .Peter Colburn
Dr. Barr . . . . .Jonathan Larson
Andrew Eden . . . . .Ron Faria
Justice Millhouse . . . . .Jack Ragotzy
Night Nurse . . . . .Sherry Handa
Patient . . . . .Elizabeth Ann Gorcey

#297
August 25 - September 6, 1981
Damn Yankees
(Based on the novel *The Year the Yankees Lost the Pennant* by Douglas Wallop)
Book by George Abbott and Douglas Wallop
Music by Richard Adler and Jerry Ross
Staged by Wayne Lamb
Music Direction and Special Orchestrations
by James Douglas Kent
Scenery by Dusty Reeds
Lighting by Jon Fruytier
Costumes by Kevin McGuire
CAST
Joe Boyd . . . . .Louis Girard
Meg Boyd . . . . .Betty Ebert
Mr. Applegate . . . . .Angelo Mango
Sister . . . . .Kristan Holland
Doris . . . . .Mary Israel
Joe Hardy .Joe Aiello
The Washington Senators:
Van Buren (Manager) . . . . .Ric Shaffer
Henry . . . . .Robert Newman
Schovik . . . . .Jonathan Larson
Smokey . . . . .David Tislow
Vernon . . . . .Peter Colburn
Rocky . . . . .Scott Burkel
Bryant . . . . .Jon Lee
Micky .Steve Owsley
Lowe .Tom Stewart
Bouley . . . . .Ron Faria
Gloria .Marin Mazzie
Welch . . . . .Robin Nuyen
Lola . . . . .Mariana Rence
Miss Weston . . . . .Cheryl Randolph
Commissioner . . . . .Bradley James
Fans, Housewives, Husbands:
Jody Abrahams, Shawn Dale, Ron Faria, Elizabeth Ann Gorcey, Sherry Handa, Wayne Lamb, Jon Lee, Shel Marie, Karesa McElheny, Steve Owsley, Tom Stewart, Suzannah Zody

#298
September 8 - 13, 1981
The Elephant Man
by Bernard Pomerance
Directed by Jack Ragotzy
Scenery by Dusty Reeds
Lighting by Jon Fruytier
Costumes by Kevin McGuire
Musical Direction by James Douglas Kent
CAST
Frederick Treves . . . . .Angelo Mango
Carr Gomm . . . . .Ric Shaffer
Ross, Elephant
Man's manager . . . . .Scott Burkel
John Merrick, the
Elephant Man . . . . .Joe Aiello
Pinheads . . . . .Jody Abrahams,
 . . . . .Suzanne Zody
Belgian Policemen . . . . .Jim Kent,
 . . . . .Tom Stewart
London Policeman . . . . .Robin Nuyen
Sideshow Barker,
in Brussels . . . . .Robin Nuyen
Conductor of boat train . . . . .Peter Colburn
Bishop Walsham How . . . . . . .Kevin McGuire
Porter, at the London
Hospital . . . . .Peter Colburn
Snork, also a porter . . . . .David Tislow
Mrs. Kendal, an actress . . . . . . .Mariana Rence
The Duchess . . . . .Betty Ebert
The Countess . . . . .Jody Abrahams
Princess Alexandra . . . . .Karesa McElheny
Lord John . . . . .Robert Newman
Miss Sandwich, a nurse . . . . . .Kristen Holland
Orderly . . . . .Bradley James
Side Show Crowd, Citizens:
Elizabeth Gorcey, Jonathan Larson, Cheryl Randolph

1982 Season

#299
June 1 - 13, 1982
An Evening with Angelo Mango, X
(No Program on File)
Created and Directed by Wayne Lamb
Pianist, Choral Arrangements and Direction
by James Douglas Kent
Lights - Bill Hunter, David Wincek
Costumes - Kevin McGuire
CAST
Angelo Mango
with Marin Mazzie
and Jody Abrahams, Robert Lance Clack, Shawn Dale, Jared Hammond, Marta Hedges, Kristen Holland, Jon Lee, Jay McClure, Shel Marie Miller, Steve Owsley, David Perrine
Production Co-ordinator - Peggy Hess

#300
June 15 - 27, 1982
Morning's at Seven
by Paul Osborn
Directed by Jack Ragotzy
Scenery by James K. Culley
Lighting by Bill Hunter
Costumes Designed by Kevin McGuire
CAST
Theodore Swanson . . . . .Louis Girard
Cora Swanson . . . . .Sue DeLano Parish
Aaronetta Gibbs . . . . .Betty Ebert
Ida Bolton . . . . .Shawn Dale
Carl Bolton . . . . .Ric Shaffer
Homer Bolton . . . . .Dick Fuchs
Myrtle Brown . . . . .Marin Mazzie
Esther Crampton . . . . .Dusty Reeds
David Crampton . . . . .Angelo Mango

#301
June 29 - July 11, 1982
Funny Girl
Book by Isobel Lennart, Jule Styne
and Bob Merrill
Music and Lyrics by Bob Merrill
and Jule Styne
Staged by Wayne Lamb
Music Director and Music Arrangements
and Special Orchestrations
by James Douglas Kent
Scenery by Dusty Reeds
Lighting by Bill Hunter
Costumes by Kevin McGuire
CAST
Fanny Brice . . . . .Barbara Marineau
John, Stage Manager . . . . .Robin Nuyen
Emma . . . . .Marin Mazzie
Mrs. Brice . . . . .Betty Ebert
Mrs. Strakosh . . . . .Dusty Reeds
Mrs. Meeker . . . . .Sheila Moran
Mrs. O'Malley. . . . . .Kristen Holland
Tom Keeney . . . . .Dick Fuchs
Eddie Ryan. . . . . .Angelo Mango
Heckie . . . . .Lance Johnson
Workmen . . . . .Robert Lance Clack,
 . . . . .Dan Jacoby
Nick Arnstein . . . . .James Werner
Actor . . . . .Jon Lee
Mr. Rinaldi. . . . . .Ric Shaffer
Florenz Ziegfeld . . . . .Louis Girard
Ziegfeld Singer . . . . .Jeff Austin
Showgirls:
Mary Marek, Marin Mazzie, Shawn Dale, Marta Hedges
Singer/Dancers:
Jody Abrahams, Kim Black, Betty Ebert, Maria Estrada, Dick Fuchs, Jared Hammond, Nancy Himes, Bradley James, Wayne Lamb, Marin Mazzie, Shel Marie Miller, Jay McClure, Steve Owsley, David Perrine, Dusty Reeds, Michael Stopczynski

#302
July 13 - 15, 1982
Tobacco Road
by Jack Kirkland
from the novel by Erskine Caldwell
Directed by Jack Ragotzy
Scenery by James K. Culley
Lighting by Bill Hunter
Costumes by Kevin McGuire
CAST
Dude Lester . . . . .Robin Nuyen
Ada Lester . . . . .Dusty Reeds
Jeeter Lester . . . . .Louis Girard
Ellie May . . . . .Jody Abrahams
Grandma Lester . . . . .Mary Marek
Lov Bensey. . . . . .James Werner
Henry Peabody . . . . .Angelo Mango
Sister Bessie Rice . . . . .Betty Ebert
Pearl . . . . .Marin Mazzie
Captain Tim . . . . .Dick Fuchs
George Payne . . . . .Ric Shaffer

#303
July 27 - August 8, 1982
The Unsinkable Molly Brown
Book by Richard Morris
Music and Lyrics by Meredith Willson

Directed and Choreographed by Wayne Lamb
Music Director and Arrangement and
Special Orchestration by James Douglas Kent
Scenery by Dusty Reeds
and Kim Edward Black
Lighting by Bill Hunter
Costumes by Kevin McGuire
CAST

Shamus Tobin	Louis Girard
Michael Tobin	Jay McClure
Aloysius Tobin	Robert Lance Clack
Patrick Tobin	Steve Owsley
Molly Tobin	Becky Gelke
Father Flynn	Jared Hammond
"Leadville" Johnny Brown	James Werner
Christmas Morgan	Dick Fuchs
Denver Police	Dan Jacoby,
	Jon Lee,
	Jay McClure
Mrs. McGlone	Dusty Reeds
Monsignor Ryan	Ric Shaffer
Roberts	Robert Lance Clack
Maids	Nancy Himes,
	Mary Marek,
	Sheila Moran
Germaine	Alison Roth
Princess DeLong	Betty Ebert
Prince DeLong	Angelo Mango
Malcolm Broderick	Jeff Austin

Leadville Friends, Beautiful People of Denver and International Set:
Jody Abrahams, Kim Edward Black, Betty Ebert, Maria Estrada, Dick Fuchs, Shawn Dale, Marta Hedges, Kristen Holland, Bradley James, Wayne Lamb, Marin Mazzie, Shel Marie Miller, David Perrine, Brendan Ragotzy, Tia Speros, Michael Stopczynski, David Weincek

#304
August 10 - August 15, 1982
Pajama Tops
by Mawby Green and Ed Feilbert
Based on the French Comedy *Moumou*
by Jean de Letraz
Directed by Jack Ragotzy
Scenic Design and Technical Direction
by James K. Culley
Lighting Design by Bill Hunter
Costumes by Kevin McGuire
CAST

Claudine	Marta Hedges
Inspector LeGrand	Louis Girard
Yvonne Chauvinet	Marin Mazzie
George Chauvinet	Angelo Mango
Leonard Jolijoli	Dick Fuchs
Babette LaTouche	Becky Gelke
Jacques	James Werner

#305
August 17 - August 22, 1982
Nuts
by Tom Toper
Directed by Jack Ragotzy
Scenery by Dusty Reeds
Lighting Design by Bill Hunter
Costumes by Kevin McGuire
CAST

Officer Harry Haggerty	Lance Johnson
Aaron Levinsky	James Werner
Franklin Macmillan	Dick Fuchs
The Recorder	Shawn Dale
Rose Kirk	Dusty Reeds
Arthur Kirk	Louis Girard
Dr. Herbert Rosenthal	Ric Shaffer
Judge Murdoch	Robin Nuyen
Claudia Faith Draper	Becky Gelke

#306
August 24 - September 5, 1982
Fiddler on the Roof
Based on Sholom Aleichem's Stories
(by special permission of Arnold Perl)
Produced on the New York stage
by Harold Prince
Book by Joseph Stein
Music by Jerry Bock
Lyrics by Sheldon Harnick
Directed and Choreographed by Wayne Lamb
Original Production Directed
and Choreographed by Jerome Robbins
Music Director, Arrangements and
Special Orchestration by James Douglas Kent
Scenery by Dusty Reeds
Lighting by Bill Hunter
Costumes by Kevin McGuire
CAST

The Fiddler	Jon Lee
Tevye, the Dairyman	Angelo Mango
Golde, his wife	Betty Ebert
Tzeitel	Tia Speros
Hodel	Marin Mazzie
Chava	Jody Abrahams
Shprintze	Shel Marie Miller
Bielke	Nancy Himes
Yente, The Matchmaker	Shawn Dale
Motel, the Tailor	Jay McClure
Perchick, the Student	James Werner
Lazar Wolf, the Butcher	Ric Shaffer
Mordcha, the Innkeeper	Louis Girard
Rabbi	Kevin McGuire
Mendel, his son	Dan Jacoby
Avram, the Bookseller	Robin Nuyen
Nachum, the Begger	David Weincek
Grandma Tzeitel	Maria Estrada
Fruma-Sarah	Marta Hedges
Shandel, Motel's Mother	Kristen Holland
Rivka	Alison Roth
Mirala	Sheila Moran

Bottle Dancers:
Jared Hammond, Steve Owsley, David Perrine, Michael Stopczynski

Chaim, a boy	Andrew Wallace
Yankel, a boy	Neil Zimmer

The Russians:

The Constable	Bradley James
Priest	Jared Hammond
Fyedka	Jeff Austin
Vladimir	Jared Hammond
Sasha	Steve Owsley

1983 Season

#307
May 31 - June 12, 1983
An Evening with Angelo Mango, XI
Created and Directed by Wayne Lamb
Piano, Choral Direction and Arrangements
by James Douglas Kent
Lighting by Bill Hunter
Costumes by Kevin McGuire
CAST
Angelo Mango
with Scott Burkel and Lynn Amari,
Kevin Costello, Jared Hammond, Marta Hedges,
Wendy Martel, David Matis, James McClure,
Leslie Nipkow, Larry Nye, Mark Paladini,
David Perrine, Brendan Ragotzy, Mary Ann
Simas, Tia Speros, Michael S. Stopczynski

#308
June 14 - 26, 1983
Present Laughter
by Noel Coward
Directed by Jack Ragotzy
Scenery by Erich Zuern
Lighting by Bill Hunter
Costumes by Kevin McGuire
CAST

Daphne Stillington	Marta Hedges
Miss Erickson	Tia Speros
Fred	Angelo Mango
Monica Reed	Dusty Reeds
Garry Essendine	James Pritchett
Liz Essendine	Betty Ebert
Roland Maule	J.T. Lee
Morris Dixon	Joe Aiello
Hugo Lyppiatt	Ric Shaffer
Joanna Lyppiatt	Becky Gelke
Lady Saltburn	Sylvia Stewart

#309
June 28 - July 10, 1983
The Best Little Whorehouse in Texas
Book by Larry L. King and Peter Masterson
Music and Lyrics by Carol Hall
Staged by Wayne Lamb
Music Director - James Douglas Kent
Production Consultant - Becky Gelke
Scenery by Dusty Reeds
Lighting by Bill Hunter
Costumes by Kevin McGuire
CAST

Narrator	Scott Burkel
Miss Wulla Jean	Dusty Reeds

The Girls:

Angel	Marta Hedges
Shy	Christine Sanders
Linda Lou	Wendy Martel
Dawn	Lynn Amari
Ginger	Tia Speros
Beatrice	Leslie Nipkow
Taddy Jo	Mary Ann Simas
Ruby Rae	Deborah R. Koski
Eloise	Beth Bria
Durla	Joy Newhouse
Jewel	Pat Bowie
Mona Stangley	Becky Gelke

The Dogettes:
Kevin Costello, Sherwin Frey, David Perrine, Michael S. Stopczynski

Melvin P. Thorpe	Joe Aiello

Melvin P. Thorpe Singers:
Beth Bria, Scott Burkel, Deborah R. Koski, David Matis, Leslie Nipkow, Mary Ann Simas

Sheriff Ed Earl Dodd	James Pritchett
Doatsey Mae	Sylvie Stewart
Edsel Mackey	Bradley James
Mayor Rufus Poindexter	Ric Shaffer
C.J. Scruggs	Robert Lance Clack,
Angelette Imogene	
Charlene Greene,	Lynn Amari

Angelettes:
Wendy Martel, Mary Ann Simas, Tia Speros

T.V. Colorman	David Perrine

Senator Wingwoah . . . . .J.T. Lee
Aggies:
Jared Hammond, Lance La Shelle, David Matis,
James McClure, Larry Nye, Mark Paladini,
Brendan Ragotzy, Daniel O.Touris
Aggie Trainer . . . . .Wayne Lamb
Governor's Aide . . . . .Andrew Mutnick
Governor .Angelo Mango
Reporters, T.V. Sound and Camera Operators:
Dan Jacoby, Bruce Hart, Matthew Mongillo,
John Speredakos

#310
July 12 - July 24, 1983
Arsenic and Old Lace
by Joseph Kesselring
Directed by Jack Ragotzy
Scenery by Erich Zuern
Lighting by Bill Hunter
Costumes by Kevin McGuire
CAST
Abby Brewster . . . . .Betty Ebert
The Rev. Dr. Harper . . . . .Bradley James
Teddy Brewster . . . . .Louis Girard
Officer Brophy . . . . .Jared Hammond
Officer Klein . . . . .David Perrine
Martha Brewster . . . . .Sue DeLano Parish
Elaine Harper . . . . .Becky Gelke
Mortimer Brewster . . . . .Michael S. Stopczynski
Mr. Gibbs . . . . .J.T. Lee
Jonathan Brewster . . . . .Joe Aiello
Dr. Einstein . . . . .Angelo Mango
Officer O'Hara . . . . .Scott Burkel
Lieutenant Rooney . . . . . . .Robert Lance Clack
Mr. Witherspoon . . . . .Ric Shaffer

#311
July 26 - August 14, 1983
Annie
Book by Thomas Meehan,
Music by Charles Strouse
Lyrics by Martin Charnin
Staged by Wayne Lamb
Music Director - James Douglas Kent
Scenery Dusty Reeds
Lighting by Bill Hunter
Costumes by Kevin McGuire
CAST
Molly . . . . .Jill Asmus
Pepper . . . . .Jill Lindsey
Duffy . . . . .Carol King
July . . . . .Stacy Chichester
Tessie . . . . .Lisa Elliotte
Kate . . . . .Cricket Leigh
Christie . . . . .Christie Hecht
Annie . . . . .Temple Ann Schultz
Miss Hannigan . . . . .Dusty Reeds
Sandy .Molly (Byrnes)
Lt. Ward . . . . .Michael S. Stopczynski
Grace Farrell . . . . .Wendy Martel
Drake . . . . .Scott Burkel
Oliver Warbucks . . . . .Louis Girard
A Star-To-Be . . . . .Tia Speros
Rooster Hanningan . . . . .Joe Aiello
Lily . . . . .Becky Gelke
Bert Healy . . . . .Angelo Mango
F.D.R .Jared Hammond
Ickes . . . . .J.T. Lee
Howe .Lance La Shelle
Morganthau . . . . .Kevin Costello
Hull. . . . . .Ric Shaffer
Perkins . . . . .Betty Ebert

Justice Brandeis . . . . .Bradley James
Hooverville-ites, Policemen, Servants, New Yorkers:
Beth Bria, Robert Lance Clack, Kevin Costello,
Sherwin Frey, Bruce Hart, Marta Hedges, Dan
Jacoby, Deborah R. Koski, Wayne Lamb, Lance
La Shelle, David Matis, James McClure,
Matthew Mongillo, Andrew Mutnick, Joy New-
house, Leslie Nipkow, Larry Nye, Mark Paladini,
David Perrine, Mary Ann Simas, John J.
Speredakos, Sylvie Stewart, Daniel C. Touris,
Shakespeare (Reeds)
Understudy for:
"Annie"—Christie Hecht; "Molly" and "Kate"—
Jennifer Boucher; "Tessie" and "Pepper"—Lori
Thompson; "Judy" and "Duffy"—Sherrie Corey
"Sandy"—Nadia (Cloud), Teddy (Stieglitz), and
Shalom (Reeds)
Dog Trainer . . . . .Daniel C. Touris

#312
August 16 - 28, 1983
They're Playing Our Song
Book by Neil Simon
Music by Marvin Hamlisch
Lyrics by Carole Bayer Sager
Directed by Wayne Lamb and Jack Ragotzy
Choreographed by Wayne Lamb
Music Direction by James Douglas Kent
Scenery by Dusty Reeds
Lighting by Bill Hunter
Costumes by Kevin McGuire
CAST
Vernon Gersch . . . . .Joe Aiello
Sonia Walsk . . . . .Barbara Marineau
The Voices of Vernon Gersch:
Scott Burkel, Michael S. Stopczynski,
James McClure
The Voices of Sonia Walsk:
Marta Hedges, Tia Speros, Wendy Martel
Answering Service Lady . . . . . . .Sheila Moran
Phil, the Engineer . . . . .David Perrine
Voice of Anthony Vale . . . . .Angelo Mango
Disc Jockey . . . . .Robert Lance Clack
Hospital Lady . . . . .Betty Ebert

#313
August 30 - September 4, 1983
**I'm Getting My Act Together
and Taking It on the Road**
(No Program on File)
Book and Lyrics by Gretchen Cryer
Music by Nancy Ford
Directed and Choreographed by Wayne Lamb
Music Direction by James Douglas Kent
Scenery and Lighting by Bill Hunter
Costumes by Tia Speros and Leslie Nipkow
CAST
Heather . . . . .Barbara Marineau
Joe . . . . .Joe Aiello
Alice . . . . .Tia Speros
Cheryl .Marta Hedges
Jake . . . . .Scott Burkel
Electric Piano . . . . .Ric Shaffer
Stage Manager . . . . .Angelo Mango
Assist. Stage Manager . . . . . . .James McClure
Follow Spot . . . . .David Perrine
Sound . . . . .Michael S. Stopczynski
Lights . . . . .Robert Lance Clark

#314
September 6 - 11, 1983
Our Town

by Thornton Wilder
Directed by Jack Ragotzy
Lighting by Bill Hunter
Costumes by Wendy Martel and Larry Nye
CAST
Stage Manager . . . . .Angelo Mango
Assist. Stage Managers . . . . .Bruce Hart,
. . . . .Lance La Shelle
Dr. Gibbs . . . . .Jared Hammond
Joe Crowell . . . . .Chris Sanders
Howie Newsome . . . . .Scott Burkel
Mrs. Gibbs . . . . .Barbara Marineau
Mrs. Webb . . . . .Tia Speros
George Gibbs . . . . .Joe Aiello
Rebecca Gibbs . . . . .Lynn Amari
Wally Webb . . . . .Andrew Mutnick
Emily Webb . . . . .Marta Hedges
Professor Willard . . . . .J. T. Lee
Mr. Webb . . . . .Ric Shaffer
Man in the Auditorium . . . . .David Perrine
Simon Stimson . . . . .Michael S. Stopczynski
Martha Mayberry . . . . .Sheila Moran
Mrs. Soames . . . . .Wendy Martel
Constable Warren . . . . .Bradley James
Si Crowell . . . . .Andrew Mutnick
Sam Craig . . . . .James McClure
Joe Stoddard . . . . .Mark Paladini
Farmer McCarthy . . . . .Matthew Mongillo
Townspeople:
Larry Nye, Betty Ebert, Idella McKay,
Deborah R. Koski

1984 Season

#315
May 29 - June 10, 1984
An Evening with Angelo Mango, XII
Created and Directed by Wayne Lamb
Piano, Choral Direction and Arrangements
by James Douglas Kent
Lights by Bill Hunter and Dan Jacoby
Costumes by Kevin McGuire
CAST
Angelo Mango
with
Lynn Amari, Frank Freeman, Kimberly Gheen,
Britt Gilder, Jared Hammond, Lance Johnson,
Lance LaShelle, Jeff Lettiere, Wendy Martel,
Sandy Mulvihill, Andrew Mutnick,
Leslie Nipkow, Mark Paladini, Brendan Ragotzy,
Dede Rumiez, Peggy Sage, Paul Schneider,
Jamie Short

#316
June 12 - 24, 1984
A Bedfull of Foreigners
by Dave Freeman
Directed by Jack Ragotzy
Scenery by James K. Culley
Lighting by Bill Hunter
Costumes by Kevin McGuire
CAST
Karak . . . . .Angelo Mango
Heinz . . . . .Michael Strauss
Stanley Parker . . . . .Joe Aiello
Brenda Parker . . . . .Barbara Whinnery
Helga Philby . . . . .Barbara Marineau
Claude Philby . . . . .Louis Girard
Simone .Becky Gelke

#317

June 26 - July 15, 1984
The Music Man
Book, Music, and Lyrics by Meredith Willson
Story by Meredith Willson & Franklin Lacey
Directed and Choreographed by Wayne Lamb
Music Director and Special Orchestrations
and Arrangements by James Douglas Kent
Scenery by Dusty Reeds
Lighting by Bill Hunter
Costumes by Kevin McGuire
CAST
Salesmen:
Sherwin Frey, Dan Jacoby, Gregg Koski,
Matthew Mongillo, Mark Paladini,
Danny Roche, Leon Ronzana, Jamie Short
Conductor . . . . Sedric bynum
Charlie Cowell . . . . Joe Aiello
Harold Hill . . . . James Pritchett
Mayor Shinn . . . . Louis Girard
Ewart Dunlop . . . . Frank Freeman
Oliver Hix . . . . Scott Burkel
Jacey Squires . . . . Michael Strauss
Olin Britt . . . . Jared Hammond
Marcellus Washburn . . . . Angelo Mango
Tommy Djilas . . . . Daniel Touris
Marian Paroo . . . . Barbara Marineau
Mrs. Paroo . . . . Betty Ebert
Amaryllis . . . . Libby Wortz
Winthrop . . . . J. Asmus
Eulalie M. Shinn . . . . Dusty Reeds
Zaneeta Shinn . . . . Lynn Amari
Gracie Shinn . . . . Christine Hecht
Alma Hix . . . . Sandy Mulvihill
Maud Dunlop . . . . Leslie Nipkow
Ethel Toffelmeier . . . . Becky Gelke
Mrs. Squires . . . . Deborah Koski
Constable Locke . . . . Bradley James
Teenagers:
Beth Bria, Lance Johnson, Lance LaShelle,
Jeff Lettiere, Wendy Martel, Andrew Mutnick,
Dede Rumiez, Peggy Sage
Townspeople:
Laura Gershowitz, Kimberly Gheen, Britt Gilder,
Wayne Lamb, Jack Ragotzy
Children:
Jennifer Boucher, Brenton Johnson,
Cricket Leigh, Brandon Whitesell

#318
July 17 - 22, 1984
Amadeus
by Peter Shaffer
Directed by Jack Ragotzy
Scenery by Dusty Reeds
Lighting by Bill Hunter
Costumes by Kevin McGuire
Music Arranged and Directed
by James Douglas Kent
CAST
Antonio Salieri . . . . Dale Helward
The "Venticelli" . . . . Michael Strauss,
. . . . Howard McBride
Salieri's Valet . . . . Dan Jacoby
Salieri's Cook . . . . Bradley James
Joseph II, Emperor
of Austria . . . . Scott Burkel
Johann Kilian von Strack . . . . Angelo Mango
Count Orsini-Rosenberg . . . . Louis Girard
Baron van Sweiten . . . . Jared Hammond
Priest . . . . Matthew Mongillo
Giuseppe Bonno . . . . Mark Paladini
Teresa Salieri,
wife of Salieri . . . . Dusty Reeds
Katherine Cavaliere,
Salieri's Pupil . . . . Wendy Martel
Constanze Weber,
wife of Mozart . . . . Becky Gelke
Wolfgang Amadeus Mozart . . . . Joe Aiello
Major Domo . . . . Jamie Short
Citizens of Vienna:
Greg Elson, Laura Gershowitz, Lance Johnson,
Lance LaShelle, Jeff Lettiere, Dan Mathieus,
Matthew Mongillo, Sandy Mulvihill,
Joy Newhouse, Leon Ronzana, Daniel Touris,
Alicia VanderVeer, Yolandi
Valets:
Lance LaShelle, Jeff Lettiere, Daniel Touris,
Leon Ronzana

#319
July 24 - August 5, 1984
The Best Little Whorehouse in Texas
Book by Larry L. King and Peter Masterson
Music and Lyrics by Carol Hall
Staged by Wayne Lamb
Production Consultant - Becky Gelke
Music Direction by James Douglas Kent
Scenery by Dusty Reeds
Lighting by Bill Hunter
Costumes by Keven McGuire
CAST
Narrator . . . . Scott Burkel
Miss Wulla Jean . . . . Dusty Reeds
The Girls
Angel . . . . Wendy Martel
Shy . . . . Dede Rumiez
Linda Lou . . . . Beth Bria
Dawn . . . . Lynn Amari
Ginger . . . . Yolandi
Beatrice . . . . Leslie Nipkow
Taddy Joe . . . . Kimberly Gheen
Ruby Rae . . . . Deborah R. Koski
Eloise . . . . Peggy Sage
Duria . . . . Joy Newhouse
Jewel . . . . Pat Bowie
Mona Stangley . . . . Becky Gelke
The Dogettes:
Frank Freeman, Sherwin Frey, Paul Schneider,
Michael Strauss
Melvin P. Thorpe . . . . Joe Aiello
Melvin P. Thorpe Singers:
Laura Gershowitz, Britt Gilder, Deborah Koski,
Jeff Letttiere, Alicia Van Derveer
Sheriff Ed Earl Dodd . . . . James Pritchett
Doatsey May . . . . Sandy Mulvihill
Edsel Mackey . . . . Bradley James
Mayor Rufus Poindexter . . . . . Howard McBride
C.J. Scruggs . . . . Matthew Mongillo
Angelette Imogene
Charlene Greene . . . . Lynn Amari
Angelettes:
Christine Hecht, Wendy Martel, Peggy Sage
T.V. Colorman . . . . Sherwin Frey
Senator Wingwoah . . . . Louis Girard
Aggies:
Jared Hammond, Lance La Shelle, Andrew
Mutnick, Mark Paladini, Brendan Ragotzy,
Leon Ronzana, Jamie Short, Daniel Touris
Aggie Trainer . . . . Wayne Lamb
Governor's Aide . . . . Dan Mathieus
Governor . . . . Angelo Mango
Reporters, T.V. Crew, Townspeople:
Sedric Bynum, Betty Ebert, Dan Jacoby,
Lance Johnson, Gregg Koski, Jack Ragotzy,
Danny Roche

#320
August 7 - August 12, 1984
Mass Appeal
by Bill C. Davis
Directed by Jack Ragotzy
Scenery by James K. Culley
Lighting by Bill Hunter
Costumes by Kevin McGuire
Music Direction by James Douglas Kent
CAST
Father Tim Alley . . . . Louis Girard
Mark Dolson . . . . Joe Aiello

#321
August 14 - 19, 1984
Beyond Therapy
by Christopher Durang
Directed by Jack Ragotzy
Scenery by James K. Culley
Lighting by Bill Hunter
Costumes by Kevin McGuire
Musical Director - James Douglas Kent
CAST
Bruce . . . . Joe Aiello
Prudence . . . . Becky Gelke
Stuart . . . . Michael Strauss
Charlotte . . . . Dusty Reeds
Bob . . . . Scott Burkel
Andrew:
(playing the role at alternating performances)
Brendan Ragotzy, Daniel Tourism,
Andrew Mutnick

#322
August 21 - September 2, 1984
Camelot
Based on *The Once and Future King*
by T. H. White
Book and Lyrics by Alan J. Lerner
Music by Frederick Loewe
Directed by Dusty Reeds
Choreographer - Becky Gelke
Musical Director - James Douglas Kent
Scenery by James K. Culley
Lighting by Bill Hunter
Costumes by Kevin McGuire
CAST
Sir Dinadan . . . . Sherwin Frey
Merlyn . . . . Jared Hammond
Arthur . . . . Joe Aiello
Guenevere . . . . Barbara Marineau
Morgan Le Fey . . . . Wendy Martel
Lancelot . . . . Scott Burkel
Mordred . . . . Daniel Touris
Squire Dap . . . . Andrew Mutnick
Pellinore . . . . Louis Girard
Horrid . . . . Fido
Heralds . . . . Andrew Mutnick,
. . . . Mark Paladini
Sir Lionel . . . . Jamie Short
Sir Sagramore . . . . Michael Strauss
Ladies of Camelot:
Lady Anne . . . . Britt Gilder
Lady Catherine . . . . Leslie Nipkow
Lady Sybil . . . . Joy Newhouse
and Lynn Amari, Betty Ebert, Kimberly Gheen,
Deborah Koski, Alicia Van Derveer
Lords of Camelot:

Bradley James, Lance La Shelle,
Howard McBride, Paul Schneider
Pages .... Christine Hecht,
.... Laura Gershowitz
Tumblers:
Lynn Amari, Laura Gershotitz, Britt Gilder,
Christine Hecht, Lance La Shelle
Squires:
Frank Freeman, Gregg Koski, Danny Roche
Knights of the Investiture:
Bliant .... Greg Elson
Giliam .... Matthew Mongillo
Castor .... Kevin McGuire
Morgan Le Fey's Court:
Sprites:
Lynn Amari, Kimberly Gheen, Deborah Koski,
Howard McBride, Paul Schneider,
Alicia Van Derveer
Spider .... Christine Hecht
Hawk .... Andrew Mutnick
Owl .... Laura Gershowitz
Unicorn .... Lance La Shelle
Soloist in "Guenevere"
Montage .... Frank Freeman
Tom of Warwick .... Mark Paladini

1985 Season

#323
May 28 - June 9, 1985
An Evening with Angelo Mango, XIII
(No Program on File)
Created and Directed by Wayne Lamb
Lights by Bill Hunter and Craig Nesbit
Costumes by Kevin McGuire
CAST
Angelo Mango
with

Lynn Amari, Kevin Costello, Michael Cymanski,
Lisa Engelken, Katherine Goodwin, Sabrina
Hamble, Doborah Koski, Lance LaShelle, Jeff
Lettiere, Matthew Mongillo, Sandy Mulvihill,
Brendan Ragotzy, Peggy Sage, Paul Schneider,
Jamie Short, Bonnie Swanson

#324
June 11 - 23, 1985
Squabbles
by Marshall Karp
Directed by Jack Ragotzy
Scenery by James K. Culley
Lighting by Bill Hunter
Costumes by Kevin McGuire
CAST
Abe Dreyfus .... Louis Girard
Jerry Sloan .... Joe Aiello
Hector Lopez .... Angelo Mango
Alice Sloan .... Becky Gelke
Mildred Sloan .... Dusty Reeds
Mrs. Fisher .... Betty Ebert

#325
June 25 - July 7, 1985
The Robber Bridegroom
Book and Lyrics by Alfred Uhry
Music by Robert Waldman
Based on the novella by Eudora Welty
Directed by Dusty Reeds
Choreographed by Wayne Lamb
Musical Direction by Glenn Wheaton
Scenery by James K. Culley
Lighting by Michael Panvini
Costumes by Kevin McGuire
CAST
Jamie Lockhart .... Tom Wopat
"Caller" .... Brendan Ragotzy
Fiddle Player .... Peggy Sage
Clement Musgrove .... Angelo Mango
Salome .... Sandy Mulvihill
Rosamund .... Barbar Marineau
Little Harp .... Joe Aiello
Big Harp .... Howard McBride
Goat .... Scott Burkel
Goat's Mother .... Betty Ebert
Raven .... Elizabeth Gacs
Residence of Rodney, Mississippi:
Elisa Camahort, Pamela Carlson, Kevin Costello,
Michael Cymanski, Lisa Engelken, Drew Doolin,
Gig Dyer, Anne Fliotsos, Thomas Grady, Sabrina
Hamble, Bradley James, Deborah Koski,
Lance LaShelle, Jeff Lattiere, Craig Nesbit,
Brendan Ragotzy, Dusty Reeds, Stephanie Roth,
Paul Schneider, Bonnie Swanson
General Understudies:
Matthew Mongillo, Helen Morrison, Jamie Short

#326
July 9 - July 21, 1985
Cat on a Hot Tin Roof
by Tennessee Williams
Directed by Jack Ragotzy
Scenery by Dusty Reeds
Lighting by Michael Panvini
Costumes by Kevin McGuire
Music Director by Glenn Wheaton
CAST
Sookey .... Laura Collins
Lacey .... David Robertson
Margaret .... Kathryn Jaeck
Brick .... Tom Wopat
May .... Sandy Mulvihill
Gooper .... Joe Aiello
Big Mama .... Dusty Reeds
Dixie .... Jill Asmus
Buster .... Ben Lindquist
Trixie .... Lisa Elliotte
Big Daddy .... Louis Girard
Reverend Tooker .... Howard McBride
Doctor Baugh .... Angelo Mango

#327
July 23 - August 11, 1985
Evita
Lyrics by Tim Rice
Music by Andrew Lloyd Webber
Directed and Choreographed by Wayne Lamb
Music Direction by Glenn Wheaton
Scenery by Dusty Reeds
Lighting by Michael Panvini
Costumes by Kevin McGuire
CAST
Eva .... Marin Mazzie
Che .... Scott Burkel
Peron .... Joe Aiello
Magaldi .... Angelo Mango
People of Argentina:
Lynn Amari, Laura Birn, David Callander,
Elisa Camahort, Pamela Carlson, Laura Collins,
Kevin Costello, Michael Cymanski,
Drew Doolin, Betty Ebert, Lisa Engelken,
Anne Fliotsos, Elizabeth Gacs, Louis Girard,
Thomas Grady, Sabrina Hamble, Bradley James,
Deborah Koski, Wayne Lamb, Doug LaBrecque,
Lance LaShelle, Jeff Lettiere, Howard McBride,
Kevin McGuire, Matthew Mongillo,
Helen Morrison, Sandy Mulvihill, Craig Nesbitt,
Larry Nye, Peggy Sage, Paul Schneider,
Jamie Short

#328
August 13 - September 8, 1985
A Chorus Line
Book by James Kirkwood & Nicholas Dante
Music by Marvin Hamlisch
Lyrics by Edward Kleban
Directed and Choreographed by Wayne Lamb
Book Directed by Dusty Reeds
Musical Direction by Glenn Wheaton
Scenery by Dusty Reeds
Tech. Dir./Assoc. Designer - James K. Culley
Lighting by Bill Hunter
Costumes by Kevin McGuire
CAST
Zach .... Joe Aiello
Larry .... Thomas Grady
Al .... Drew Doolin
Bebe .... Bonnie Swanson
Bobby .... Lance La Shelle
Cassie .... Becky Gelke
Connie .... Elisa Camahort
Diana .... Marin Mazzie
Don .... Doug LaBrecque
Greg .... Larry Nye
Judy .... Stephannie Roth
Kristine .... Peggy Sage
Maggie .... Pamela Carlson
Mark .... Michael Cymanski
Mike .... Steve Owsley
Paul .... Jeff Lettiere
Richie .... Reginal Ray-Savage
Val .... Sandy Mulvihill
Sheila .... Helen Morrison
Brenda .... Kelly Ross
Butch .... David Callander
Frank .... Scott Burkel
Gregory .... Gig Dyer
Lois .... Elizabeth Gacs
Lucille .... Betty Ebert
Roy .... Paul Schneider
Tom .... Kevin Costello
Tricia .... Laura Birn
Vickie .... Deborah Koski
Walt .... Kevin Casey

#329
September 10 - 15, 1985
E/R (Emergency Room)
A play conceived by Ronald L. Berman, M.D.,
written by Ronald L. Berman, M.D.,
Zaid Farid, Richard Fire, Stuart Gordon, Gary
Houston, Carolyn Purdy-Gordon, Tom Towles,
and Bruce A. Young
Directed by Gig Dyer
Scenery Designed by Jack Ragotzy
Lighting by Bill Hunter
Costumes by Kevin McGuire
CAST
Maria .... Laura Birn
Rosie .... Helen Morrison
Jerry .... Larry Nye
Dr. Sherman .... Scott Burkel
Thor .... Betty Ebert
Julie .... Sandy Mulvihill
Franklin Cunard .... Drew Doolin
Mrs. Surath .... Elizabeth Gacs

Burton Surath . . . . .Howard McBride
Mrs. Freeman . . . . .Deborah Koski
Sheila . . . . .Lynn Amari
Linda Sue . . . . .Cricket Leigh
Fred the Cop . . . . Jamie Short
Roosevelt Jackson . . . . .Reginal Ray-Savage
James Lewis . . . . .Steve Owsley
Helen . . . . .Elisa Camahort
Dr. Sheinfeld . . . . .Joe Aiello
John McKay . . . . .Jeff Lettiere
Harry McKay . . . . .Kevin Costello
Walter Bourdreaux . . . . .Lance La Shelle
Mitch Renko . . . . .Matthew Mongillo
Bonnie Phillips . . . . .Kelly Ross
Brian Phillips . . . . .Nicholas Jones
Irene . . . . .Sue Delano Parish
Peter Woods . . . . .Drew Doolin
William Reynolds . . . . .Jack Ragotzy
Pizza Man . . . . .Lance La Shelle
Ambulance Driver . . . . .Steve Owsley
Ambulance Attendant . . . . .Jeff Lettiere
Punk . . . . .Michael Cymanski
Overdose Patient . . . . .Elisa Camahort
Float Nurse . . . . .Lynn Amari
Indian Doctor . . . . .Kevin Costello
Woman . . . . .Janet Harper
Daughter . . . . .Cricket Leigh

1986 Season

#330
May 27 - June 8, 1986
An Evening with Angelo Mango, XIV
Created and Directed by Wayne Lamb
Assisted by Steve Owsley
Lighting Design by Bill Hunter
Costumes by Larry Nye
Choral Direction and Arrangements
by Glenn Wheaton
Assisted by Elisa Camahort & Paul Schneider
CAST
Angelo Mango
At the Piano - Glenn Wheaton
Featuring Sandy Mulvihill and Jeff Lettiere
with
Bill Bryan, Elisa Camahort, Kevin Costello,
Johathan Ellers, Elizabeth Gacs, Sue Hurd,
Larry Nye, Kelly Ross, DeDe Rumiez,
Paul Schneider, Bonnie Swanson

#331
June 10 - June 22, 1986
Brighton Beach Memoirs
by Neil Simon
Directed by Jack Ragotzy
Scenery by James K. Culley
Lighting by Bill Hunter
Costumes by Kevin McGuire
CAST
Eugene . . . . .Jeff Lettiere
Blanche .Dusty Reeds
Kate . . . . .Betty Ebert
Laurie .DeDe Rumiez
Nora . . . . .Sandy Mulvihill
Stanley . . . . Scott Burkel
Jack . . . . .Louis Girard

#332
June 24 - July 6, 1986
South Pacific
Music by Richard Rogers
Lyrics by Oscar Hammerstein II
Book by Oscar Hammerstein II
and Joshua Logan
Adapted from James A. Michener's
Tales of the South Pacific
Directed and Choreographed by Wayne Lamb
Music Direction by Glenn Wheaton
Scenery Designed by Dusty Reeds
Lighting Designed by Noemi Ybarra
Costumes Designed by Kevin McGuire
CAST
Ngana . . . . .Margie Hachmester
Jerome . . . . .Robert Moore
Henry .Gary Betsworth
Ensign Nellie Forbush . . . . . . .Barbara Marineau
Emile de Becque . . . . .David Holliday
Bloody Mary . . . . .Laura Collins
Bloody Mary's Assistant . . . . .Kelly Rose
Buzz Adams . . . . .Steve Owsley
Abner . . . . .Larry Nye
Luther Billis . . . . .Joe Aiello
Stewpot . . . . .Angelo Mango
Professor . . . . .Jim Coulter
Lt. Joseph Cable . . . . .Scott Burkel
Capt. George Brackett . . . . .Louis Girard
Cmmdr. Wm. Harbison . . . . . .Howard McBride
Yeoman Herbert Quale . . . . .Jeff Lettiere
Sgt. Ken Johnson . . . . .Kevin Costello
Seabee Richard West . . . . . . .Matthew J. Hook
Seabee Morton Wise . . . . .Darin C. Dailey
Seabee James Hayes . . . . . . .Brendan Ragotzy
Seaman Tom O'Brien . . . . .Gary Betsworth
Radio Operator McCaffrey . . . .Jonathan Ellers
Marine Cpl. Steeves . . . . .Thomas Grady
Staff Sgt. Harsinger . . . . .Randall E. Lake
Pvt. Victor Jerome . . . . .Paul Schneider
Pvt. Sven Larsen . . . . .William Ellis Bryan
Sgt. Jack Waters . . . . .Shole Milos
Sgt. Wayne McGuire . . . . . . .Dennis Charvez
Lt. Genevieve Marshall . . . . . . .Jennifer York
Ensign Lisa Manelle . . . . .Elisa Camahort
Ensign Connie Walewska . . . . .Elizabeth Gacs
Ensign Janet McGregor . . . . . .Sandy Mulvihill
Ensign Katie Jacobson . . . . .Betty Ebert
Ensign Blanche Kraus . . . . .Dusty Reeds
Ensign Bessie Noonan . . . . .DeDe Rumiez
Ensign Pamela Whitmore . . . . . .Janice Paxson
Ensign Sue Yaeger . . . . .Bonnie Swanson
Ensign Betty Pitt . . . . .Suzie Chastang
Ensign Cora McRae . . . . .Kiira Jepson
Ensign Dinah Murphy . . . . .Penelope Issichopoulos
Liat . . . . .Sue Hurd
Native Girl . . . . .Cricket Leigh

#333
July 8 -July 20, 1986
Picnic
by William Inge
Directed by Jack Ragotzy
Scenery by Dusty Reeds
Lighting by Bill Hunter
Costumes by Larry Nye
CAST
Helen Potts . . . . .Dusty Reeds
Hal Carter . . . . .Robert Newman
Millie Owens . . . . .Sandy Mulvihill
Flo Owens . . . . .Betty Ebert
Bomber . . . . .Jeff Lettiere
Madge Owens . . . . .Britt Helfer
Rosemary Sidney . . . . .Barbara Marineau
Alan Seymour . . . . .Scott Burkel
Irma Kronkite . . . . .Jennifer York
Christine Schoenwalder . . . . . . .Suzie Chastang
Linda Sue Breckenridge . . . . . . .Elizabeth Gacs
Howard Bevans . . . . .Joe Aiello

#334
July 22 - August 3, 1986
Little Shop of Horrors
Book and Lyrics by Howard Ashman
Music by Alan Menken
Based on the film by Roger Corman
Screenplay by Charles Griffith
Directed by Dusty Reeds
Music Direction by Douglas Austin
Scenery by James K. Culley
Lighting by Noemi Ybarra
Costumes by Kevin McGuire
CAST
Shirelle . . . . .Elisa Camahort
Crystal . . . . .Sandy Mulvihill
Drifter . . . . .Jeff Lettiere
Mushnik . . . . .Louis Girard
Audrey . . . . .Barbara Marineau
Seymour . . . . .Scott Burkel
Derelict . . . . .Angelo Mango
Orin, Bernstein, Snip, Lace . . . . .Joe Aiello
Audrey II (Manipulation) . . . . . .Bradley James
Audrey II (Voice) . . . . .Angelo Mango
Original designs for Audrey II are by
Martin Robinson of the original production of
Little Shop of Horrors

#335
August 5 - 24, 1986
Sugar Babies
Conceived by Ralph G. Allen and Harry Rigby
Music by Jimmy McHugh
Lyrics by Dorothy Fields and Al Dubin
Sketches by Ralph G. Allen
(based on traditional material)
Additional music and lyrics by Arthur Malvin
Sugar Baby Bounce
by Jay Livingston and Ray Evans
Entire production under the supervision of
Rudy Tronto
Directed by Wayne Lamb
Scenery by Dusty Reeds
Lighting by Bill Hunter
Costumes by Kevin McGuire
The Principal Cast
Angie, 1st Comic . . . . .Angelo Mango
Rudy, 2nd Comic . . . . .Rudy Tronto
Scott, Juvenile . . . . .Scott Burkel
Kevin, Juvenile . . . . .Kevin Costello
Joe, Straight Man . . . . .Joe Aiello
Sandy, Soubrette . . . . .Sandy Mulvihill
Lou, Character Man . . . . .Louis Girard
Ann, Prima Donna . . . . .Ann Hodges
The Sugar Babies:
Janice Paxson, Elizabeth Gacs, Sue Hurd,
Penelope Issichopoulos, Kiira Jepson, Sandy
Mulvihill, DeDe Rumiez, Bonnie Swanson
The Quartet:
Scott Burkel, Kevin Costello, Jeff Lettiere,
Paul Schneider
The Dancing Quartet:
Larry Nye, Doug LaBrecque, Thomas Grady,
Matthew J. Hook
Other Members of the Ensemble:
Gary Betsworth, William Ellis Bryan,
Elisa Camahort, Kevin Casey, Dennis Charvez,
Suzie Chastang, Debbie Cohen, Jim Coulter,
Darin C. Dailey, Betty Ebert, Jonathan Ellers,

Randall E. Lake, Howard McBride,
Jack Ragotzy, Kelly Ross, Jennifer York

#336
August 26 - 31, 1986
The Foreigner
by Larry Shue
Directed by Jack Ragotzy
Scenery by James K. Culley
Lighting by Bill Hunter
CAST
Froggy" LeSueur . . . . Angelo Mango
Charlie Baker . . . . Joe Aiello
Betty Meeks . . . . Elizabeth Gacs
Rev. David Marshall Lee . . . . Kevin Costello
Catherine Simms . . . . Sandy Mulvihill
Owen Musser . . . . Thomas Grady
Ellard Simms . . . . Scott Burkel
Townspeople:
William Ellis Bryan, Dennis Charvez,
Jim Coulter, Darin C. Dailey, Betty Ebert,
Jonathan Ellers, Bradley James, Randall E. Lake,
Howard McBride

#337
September 2 - September 7, 1986
Greater Tuna
by Jaston Williams, Joe Sears, and Ed Howard
Directed by Jack Ragotzy
Scenery by Dusty Reeds
Lighting by Noemi Ybarra
Costumes by Kevin McGuire
CAST
Thurston Wheelis . . . . Scott Burkel
Arles Stuvie . . . . Joe Aiello
DiDi Snavely . . . . Joe Aiello
Harold Dean Lattimer . . . . Joe Aiello
Elmer Watkins . . . . Scott Burkel
Petey Fisk . . . . Joe Aiello
Bertha Bumiller . . . . Scott Burkel
Jody Bumiller . . . . Joe Aiello
Stanley Bumiller . . . . Joe Aiello
Charlene Bumiller . . . . Joe Aiello
Chad Hartford . . . . Joe Aiello
Yippy . . . . Scott Burkel
Leonard Childers . . . . Scott Burkel
Phineas Blye . . . . Joe Aiello
Pearl Burras . . . . Scott Burkel
Vera Carp . . . . Joe Aiello
R.R. Snavely . . . . Jill Walmsley
Reverend Spikes . . . . Scott Burkel
Sheriff Givens . . . . Scott Burkel
Hank Bumiller . . . . Scott Burkel

1987 Season

#338
June 2 - June 14, 1987
An Evening with Angelo Mango, XV
Created and Directed by Wayne Lamb
Assisted by Steve Owsley
Lighting Design by James Michael Kerrigan
Choral Direction and Arrangements
by James Douglas Kent
Assisted by Dennis Charvez, Katie Hershberger
and Michael Sherman
CAST
Angelo Mango
At the Piano, James Douglas Kent
Featuring
Sandy Mulvihill and Jeff Lettiere

with
Steve Bratton, Darin Dailey, Jonathan Ellers,
Hans Friedrichs, Mary Louis Herrold,
Jackie Hildebrand, Penelope Issichopoulos,
Kiira Jepson, Troy Longest, Kurt Meeker,
Dede Rumiez, Kimberly Weiner,
Annie Yarbrough, Todd Zamarripa

#339
June 16 - June 28, 1987
Move Over, Mrs. Markham
by Ray Cooney and John Chapman
Directed by Jack Ragotzy
Scenery Designed by Dusty Reeds
(adapted by Greg Little)
Set Decoration by Jim Knox
Lighting Design by Bill Hunter
Costume Design by Kevin McGuire
CAST
Joanna Markham . . . . Betty Ebert
Alistair Spenlow . . . . Dick Fuchs
Sylvie . . . . Sandy Mulvihill
Linda Lodge . . . . Jill Walmsley
Philip Markham . . . . Louis Girard
Henry Lodge . . . . Joe Aiello
Walter Pangbourne . . . . Scott Burkel
Olive Harriet Smythe . . . . Dusty Reeds
Miss Wilkinson:
Laura Wunderlich, Mary Louise Herrold,
Kiira Jepson

#340
June 30 - July 12, 1987
Brigadoon
Music and Lyrics by Alan Jay Lerner
Music by Frederick Loewe
Directed by Dusty Reeds
Production Supervisor - Wayne Lamb
Choreographer - Steve Owsley
Scenery by Dusty Reeds
Musical Director, Steven D. Bowen
Lighting Design by James Michael Kerrigan
Costumes by Kevin McGuire
CAST
Tommy Albright . . . . Scott Burkel
Jeff Douglas . . . . Joe Aiello
Archie Beaton . . . . Steven Lee Burright
Harry Beaton . . . . Jonathan Ellers
Andrew MacLaren . . . . Angelo Mango
Fiona MacLaren . . . . Jill Walmsley
Jean MacLaren . . . . Kimberly Weiner
Meg Brockie . . . . Sandy Mulvihill
Angus McGuffie . . . . Howard McBride
Charlie Dalrymple . . . . Jeff Lettiere
Mr. Lundie . . . . Louis Girard
Stuart Dalrymple . . . . Dennis Charvez
Sword Dancers . . . . Steve Owsley,
. . . . Steve Bratton
Piper . . . . Joe Barrette
Maggie Anderson . . . . . . Penelope Issichopoulos
Frank . . . . Kurt Meeker
Jane Ashton . . . . Mary Louise Herrold
Townsfolk of Brigadoon:
William Ellis Bryan, Dennis Charvez, Darin C.
Dailey, Brett Baer, Steve Bratton, Hans
Friedrichs, Bradley James, Matthew J. Hook,
Wayne Lamb, Kurt Meeker, Charlie Siedenberg,
Todd Zamarripa, Suzie Chastang, Betty Ebert,
Lauren Graham, Katie Hershberger, Jacqueline
Hildebrand, Kiira Jepson, Aleta Margolis, Janice
Paxson, Dusty Reeds, Dede Rumiez, Laura
Wunderlich, Annie Yarbrough, Jennifer York

#341
July 14 - July 26, 1987
Biloxi Blues
by Neil Simon
Directed by Jack Ragotzy
Scenery by Dusty Reeds
Lighting by James Michael Kerrigan
Costumes by Kevin McGuire
CAST
Roy Selridge . . . . Brett Baer
Joseph Wykowski . . . . William Ellis Bryan
Don Carney . . . . Scott Burkel
Eugene Morris Jerome . . . . Jeff Lettiere
Sgt. Merwin J. Toomey . . . . Joe Aiello
James Hennesey . . . . Darin Dailey
Corporal. . . . . Brendan Ragotzy
Rowena . . . . Jill Walmsley
Daisey . . . . Sandy Mulvihill
U.S.O. Dancer . . . . Steve Owsley
Arnold Epstein . . . . Hans Friedrichs

#342
July 28 - August 9, 1987
**A Funny Thing Happened
on the Way to the Forum**
Book by Burt Shevelove and Larry Gelbart
Music and Lyrics by Stephen Sondheim
Directed and Choreographed by Wayne Lamb
Musical Direction by Steven D. Bowen
Scenery by Dusty Reeds
and Steven Lee Burright
Lighting Designed by James Michael Kerrigan
Costume Designed by Kevin McGuire
CAST
Prologus, an Actor . . . . Joe Aiello
The Proteans:
Gary Betsworth, Jeff Lettiere, Todd Zamarripa
Sene, a citizen of Rome . . . . Louis Girard
Domina, his wife . . . . Sandy Mulvihill
Hero, his son . . . . Scott Burkel
Hysterium, slave to Senex
and Domina . . . . Angelo Mango
Pseudolis, slave to Hero . . . Joe Aiello
Lycus, a dealer in
Courtesans . . . . Jonathan Ellers
The Courtesans:
"Tintinabula"—Penelope Issichopoulos;
"Panacea"— Laurea Wunderlich;
"The Geminae"— Jacqueline Hildebrand,
Dede Rumiez. "Vibrata"—Annie Yarbrough;
"Gymnasia"—Kiira Jepson
Philia, a virgin . . . . Jill Walmsley
Erronius, an old man . . . . Howard McBride
Miles Gloriosus . . . . Kurt Meeker

#343
August 11 - August 30, 1987
42nd Street
The Song and Dance Fable of Broadway
Music by Harry Warren
Lyrics by Al Dubin
Book by Michael Stewart and Mark Bramble
(Based on the novel by Bradford Ropes)
Directed by Dusty Reeds
Choreographer and Co-Director - Steve Owsley
Music Directed by Steven D. Bowen
Scenery by Dusty Reeds
Lighting by James Michael Kerrigan
Costumes by Kevin McGuire
CAST
Andy Lee . . . . Steve Owsley
Oscar . . . . Thomas Glass

Mac . . . . William Ellis Bryan
Annie . . . . Penelope Issichopoulos
Maggie Jones . . . . Betty Ebert
Bert Berry . . . . Angelo Mango
Billy Lawlor . . . . Jeff Lettiere
Peggy Sawyer . . . . Sandy Mulvihill
Lorraine . . . . Dede Rumiez
Phyllis . . . . Annie Yarbrough
Diane . . . . Janice Paxson
Ethel . . . . Kiira Jepson
Julian Marsh . . . . Joe Aiello
Dorothy Brock . . . . Jen Wolfe
Abner Dillon . . . . Louis Girard
Pat Denning . . . . Scott Burkel
Frankie . . . . Christopher Lore
Willard . . . . John Haman
1st Thug . . . . Steve Wertheimer
2nd Thug . . . . Dennis Charvez
Doctor . . . . Dennis Charvez
The Ensemble:
Brett Baer, Steve Bratton, William Ellis Bryan,
Steven Lee Burright, Danny Buskirk,
Suzie Chastang, Darin C. Dailey, Jonathan
Ellers, Hans Friedrichs, Lauren Graham, Mary
Louise Herrold, Jacqueline Hildebrand, Bradley
James, Troy Longest, Christopher Lore, Aleta
Margolis, Howard McBride, Brendan Ragotzy,
Charlie Siedenberg, Kimberly Weiner, Laura
Wunderlich, Jennifer York, Todd Zamarripa

#344
September 1 - September 6, 1987
Crimes of the Heart
by Beth Henley
Directed by Joe Aiello
Scenery by Dusty Reeds
Set Decoration by Jim Knox
Lighting by James Michael Kerrigan
Costumes Designed by Hans Friedrichs
CAST
Lenny McGrath . . . . Mary Louise Herrold
Chick Boyle . . . . Janice Paxson
Doc Porter . . . . Joe Aiello
Meg McGrath . . . . Kiira Jepson
Babe Botrelle . . . . Sandy Mulvihill
Barnette Lloyd . . . . Scott Burkel

#345
September 8 - 13, 1987
Nunsense
Book, Music and Lyrics by Dan Goggin
Directed by Edwina Lewis
Co-Directed and Choreography
by Steve Owsley
Music Direction by Steven D. Bowen
Scenery by Steven Lee Burright
Lighting by James Michael Kerrigan
Costumes by Darin C. Dailey
CAST
Sister Mary Regina . . . . Betty Ebert
Sister Mary Hubert . . . . Edwina Lewis
Sister Mary Leo . . . . . . Penelope Issichopoulos
Sister Robert Anne . . . . Sandy Mulvihill
Sister Mary Amnesia . . . . Dede Rumiez
Sister Jennifer . . . . Jennifer York
Brother Hans . . . . Hans Friedrichs
Brother Brendan . . . . Brendan Ragotzy
Brother Bill . . . . Bill Bryan

1988 Season

#346
May 31 - June 12 - 1988
An Evening with Angelo Mango, XVI
Created and Directed by Wayne Lamb
Assisted by Sandy Mulvihill
Lighting by James Michael Kerrigan
Choral Direction and Arrangements
by James Douglas Kent
CAST
Angelo Mango
At the Piano - James Douglas Kent
Featuring
Sandy Mulvihill
with
Michael Blatt, Steve Bratton, Darin C. Dailey,
Janice DiGietano, Hans Friedrichs, Lauren
Graham, Penelope IssichCopoulos, Kiira Jepson,
Troy Longest, D.Newton Reed, Kimberly
Weiner, Annie Yarbrough

#347
June 14 - 19, 1988
The Nerd
by Larry Shue
Directed by Jack Ragotzy
Scenery by Dusty Reeds
Lighting by James Michael Kerrigan
Costumes by Hans Friedrichs
CAST
Willum Cubbert . . . . Dick Fuchs
Axel Hammond . . . . Joe Aiello
Tansy McGinnis . . . . Sandy Mulvihill
Warnock Waldgrave . . . . Louis Girard
Celia Waldgrave . . . . Dusty Reeds
Thor Waldgrave . . . . Tony Garland
Rich Steadman . . . . Scott Burkell

#348
June 21 - July 3, 1988
Nunsense
Book, Music, and Lyrics by Dan Goggin
Directed by Edwina Lewis
Choreography by Charlie Misovye
Musical Direction by James Douglas Kent
Scenery by Steven Lee Burright
Lighting by James Michael Kerrigan
Costumes by Darin C. Dailey
CAST
Sister Mary Regina . . . . Betty Ebert
Sister Mary Hubert . . . . Edwina Lewis
Sister Mary Leo . . . . Penelope Issichopoulos
Sister Robert Anne . . . . Sandy Mulvihill
Sister Mary Amnesia . . . . Jill Walmsley

#349
July 5 - July 17, 1988
Oklahoma!
Music by Richard Rodgers
Book and Lyrics by Oscar Hammerstein II
(Based on Lynn Riggs' *Green Grow the Lilacs*)
Directed by Dusty Reeds
Choreographed by Charlie Misovye
Musical Direction by James Douglas Kent
Scenery by Dusty Reeds
Lighting by James Michael Kerrigan
Costumes by Hans Friedrichs
and Darin C. Dailey
CAST
Aunt Eller . . . . Betty Ebert
Curly . . . . Tom Wopat
Laurey . . . . Jill Walmsley
Ike Skidmore . . . . Howard McBride
Slim . . . . Steve Bratton
Will Parker . . . . Scott Burkell
Jud Fry . . . . Joe Aiello
Ado Annie Carnes . . . . Sandy Mulvihill
Ali Hakim . . . . Jeff Lettiere
Gertie Cummings . . . . . . Penelope Issichopoulos
Andrew Carnes . . . . Angelo Mango
Cord Elam . . . . Louis Girard
Dream Ballet:
"Curley" . . . . George F. Kretchman
"Laurey" . . . . Annie Yarbrough
"Jud" . . . . Rob Langeder
Dance Hall Girls:
Janice DiGieano, Lauren Graham, Kiira Jepson
Cowboys and Farmers:
Michael Blatt, Steven Lee Burright, Darin Dailey, Tim Eash, Douglass Fraser, Hans Friedrichs,
Joseph Hilsee, Greg Loftus, Troy Longest,
Charlie Misovye, Gregory Rehrig,
Paul Anthony Stewart
Women:
Barbara Brooks, Shauna Lilly, Janet Manley,
Gaby Michel, Vicki Pesetti, Dianc Newton Reed,
Kimberly Weiner

#350
July 19 - July 31, 1988
The Musical Comedy Murders of 1940
by John Bishop
Directed by Jack Ragotzy
Scenery by Jim Manning
Lighting by James Michael Kerrigan
Costumes by Hans Friedrichs
Special Music Composed by James Douglas
Kent
CAST
Helsa Wenzel . . . . Sandy Mulvihill
Elsa von Grossenknueten . . . . Dusty Reeds
Michael Kelly . . . . Louis Girard
Patrick O'Reilly . . . . Jeff Lettiere
Ken de la Maize . . . . Joe Aiello
Nikki Crandall . . . . Jill Walmsley
Eddie McCuen . . . . Scott Burkell
Marjorie Baverstock . . . . Lauren Graham
Rodger Hopewell . . . . Angelo Mango
Bernice Roth . . . . Betty Ebert

#351
August 2 - August 14, 1988
The Most Happy Fella
(Based on Sidney Howard's
They Knew What They Wanted)
Book, Music and Lyrics by Frank Loesser
Directed by Joe Aiello
Choreography by Charlie Misovye
Musical Direction by James Douglas Kent
Scenery by Dusty Reeds
Set Decoration by Jim Knox
Lighting by James Michael Kerrigan
Costumes by Hans Friedrichs, Darin C. Dailey
CAST
Cashier . . . . Steven Lee Burright
Cleo . . . . Sandy Mulvihill
Rosabella . . . . Jill Walmsley
Postman . . . . Greg Loftus
Tony Esposito . . . . Giorgio Tozzi
Marie . . . . Barbara Brooks
Photographer . . . . Charlie Misovye
Herman . . . . Jeff Lettiere
Clem . . . . Joseph Hilsee
Jake . . . . Paul Stewart
Al. . . . . Steve Bratton

Joe . . . . Scott Burkell
Pasquale . . . . Howard McBride
Giuseppe . . . . Rob Langeder
Ciccio . . . . Darin Dailey
Country Girl . . . . Kimberly Weiner
City Boy . . . . Michael Blatt
Doc . . . . Louis Girard
Priest . . . . Hans Friedrichs
Waitresses, Customers, Townswomen:
Lauren Graham, Penelope Issichopoulos,
Kiira Jepson, Shauna Lilly, Gaby Michael,
Janice DiGietano, Vicki Pesetti, Dusty Reeds,
Kimberly Weiner, Annie Yarbrough
Customers, Workmen, Townsmen:
Michael Blatt, Steve Bratton, Steven Lee
Burright, Doughass Fraser, Joseph Hilsee,
Bradley James, Wayne Lamb, Gregory S. Rehrig,
Paul Anthony Stewart

#352
August 16 - September 4, 1988
La Cage aux Folles
Music and Lyrics by Jerry Herman
Book by Harvey Fierstein
(Based on the play *La Cage Aux Folles*
by Jean Poiret)
Directed by Jack Ragotzy
Choreography by Charlie Misovye
Musical Direction by James Douglas Kent
Scenery by Dusty Reeds
Lighting by James Michael Kerrigan
Original Costumes by Mela Hoyt-Heydon
Hair Stylist and Wig Master,
Gary Lee McCormick
Make Up Designed by Gregory S. Rehrig
CAST
Georges . . . . George McDaniel
Les Cagelles:
"Angelique" . . . . Kiira Japson;
"Chantel" . . . . Douglass Fraser
"Derma" . . . . Darin Dailey
"Hanna" . . . . George F. Kretchman
"Mercedes" . . . . Charlie Misovye
"Nicole" . . . . Paul Anthony Stewart
"Phaedra" . . . . Hans Friedrichs
"Lo Singh" . . . . Janice DiGietano
Fantasy Birds:
Michael Blatt, Steve Bratton,
Penelope Issichopoulos, Kimberly Weiner,
Francis . . . . Jeff Lettiere
Jacob . . . . Gordon McClure
Albin . . . . Joe Aiello
Jean-Michel . . . . Scott Burkell
Anne . . . . Jill Walmsley
Jacqueline . . . . Sandy Mulvihill
M. Renaud . . . . Howard McBride
Mme. Renaud . . . . Penelope Issichopoulos
Edouard Dindon . . . . Louis Girard
Mme. Dindon . . . . Betty Ebert
Babbette . . . . Annie Yarbrough
Panther . . . . Diane Newton Reed
Cyclist . . . . Gaby Michel
Paulette . . . . Lauren Graham
Hercule . . . . Brendan Ragotzy
Fishermen . . . . Rob Langeder,
. . . . Michael Blatt
Photographer . . . . Jim Manning
Townspeople:
Barbara Brooks, Shauna Lilly, Gregory S. Rehrig

#353
September 6 - 11, 1988
Some Enchanted Evening
Music by Richard Rodgers
Lyrics by Oscar Hammerstein II
Concept by Jeffrey B. Moss
Directed by Joe Aiello
Musical Direction by James Douglas Kent
Choreography by Charlie Misovye
Costumes by Hans Friedrichs and Darin Dailey
Lighting by James Michael Kerrigan
Sound by Scott Lewis
CAST
The Ensemble:
Scott Burkell, Penelope Issichopoulos, Jeff
Lettiere, Sandy Mulvihill, Jill Walmsley
The Chorus:
Steve Bratton, Steven Lee Burright, Darin
Dailey, Janice DiGietano, Douglass Fraser, Hans
Friedrichs, Lauren Graham, Kiira Jepson,
George F. Kretchman, Rob Langeder,
Gabe Michel, Paul Anthony Stewart
James Douglas Kent at the Grand Piano

1989 Season

#354
May 30 - June 11, 1989
Music! Music! Music!
Directed by Joe Aiello
Choreographed by Charlie Misovye
Musical Direction and Arrangement
by James Douglas Kent
Lighting by Bill Hunter
Costumes by H.W.F.
Hosted by Mr. Joe Aiello
CAST
Starring
Scott Burkell, Sandy Mulvihill, Jeff Lettiere,
Penelope Alex
with
Michael Blatt, Steven Lee Burright, Jessica
Frankel, Denis Jones, Rob Langeder, Gaby
Michel, Annie Yarborough, Heather Morris,
Gregg Rehrig, Andrew Scheer

#355
June 13 - June 18, 1989
Barefoot in the Park
by Neil Simon
Directed by Jack Ragotzy
Scenery by Willard R. Neuert
Lighting by Bill Hunter
Costumes by H.W.F
CAST
Corie Bratter . . . . Britt Helfer
Telephone Repair Man . . . . Scott Burkell
Delivery Man . . . . Bradley James
Paul Bratter . . . . Robert Newman
Mrs. Banks . . . . Dusty Reeds
Victor Velasco . . . . Louis Girard

#356
June 20 - July 2, 1989
The 1940's Radio Hour
by Walton Jones
Directed by Joe Aiello
Special Musical Arrangements and
Orchestrations
by James Douglas Kent
Scenery by Dusty Reeds
Choreography by Charlie Misovye
Lighting by Bill Hunter
Costumes by H.W.F
CAST
Pops Bailey . . . . Louis Girard
Stanley . . . . Steven Lee Burright
Clifton A. Feddington . . . . Richard Reardon
Zoot Doubleman . . . . James Douglas Kent
Wally Fergusson . . . . Michael Blatt
Lou Cohn . . . . Howard McBride
Johnny Canton . . . . Joe Aiello
Ginger Brooks . . . . Sandy Mulvihill
Connie Miller . . . . Penelope Alex
B.J. Gibson . . . . Jeff Lettiere
Neal Tilden . . . . Scott Burkell
Ann Collier . . . . Liz Pazik
Geneva Lee Browne . . . . Laura Collins
Biff Baker . . . . Hans Friedrichs
Singers:
Jessica Frankel, Gaby Michel, Heather Morris,
Marcia Vliet, Annie Yarbough, Kevin Cornelius,
Denis Jones, Rob Langeder, Michael Lazar,
Paul Stewart
Understudy to
Scott Burkell . . . . Douglass Blakeslee

#357
July 4 - 16, 1989
Run for Your Wife
by Ray Cooney
Directed by Dusty Reeds
Scenery by Willard R. Neuert
Lighting by Bill Hunter
Costumes by H.W.F.
CAST
Mary Smith . . . . Liz Pazik
Barbara Smith . . . . Sandy Mulvihill
John Smith . . . . Joe Aiello
Detective Sergeant
Throughton . . . . Scott Burkell
Stanley Gardner . . . . Richard L. Reardon
Newspaper Reporter:
Rob Langeder (or Paul Stewart, Aydin Bengisu,
Dan Dawkins)
Detective Sergeant
Porterhouse . . . . Louis Girard
Bobby Franklyn . . . . Jeff Lettiere

#358
July 18 - August 6, 1989
Hair
Book and Lyrics by Gerome Ragni
and James Rado
Music by Galt MacDermot
Produced for the Broadway Stage
by Michael Butler
Originally Produced by
the NY Shakespeare Festival
Directed by Brendan Ragotzy
Choreographed by Charles Misovye
Musical Direction and Conducting
by James Douglas Kent
Scenery by Dusty Reeds and Bill Hunter
Show Curtain by Dusty Reeds
Lighting and Sound Design by Bill Hunter
Costumes by H.W.F.
CAST
Claude . . . . Scott Burkell
Berger . . . . Joe Aiello
Hud . . . . Jeff Coopwood
Sheila . . . . Sandy Mulvihill
Woof . . . . Jeff Lettiere
Dionne . . . . E. Faye Butler
Ron . . . . Darius de Haas

Jeanie . . . . .Ann Schulman
Crissy . . . . .Penelope Alex
Steve . . . . .Paul Stewart
T.C . . . . .Terrence A. Carson
Leata . . . . .Gaby Michel
Paul . . . . .Denis Jones
Walter . . . . .Rob Langeder
Suzannah . . . . .Nicole M. Fruge
Mary . . . . .Jessica Frankel
Emmaretta . . . . .Anne Harris
Diane . . . . .Heather Morris
Marjorie . . . . .Annie Yarbrough
Mom . . . . .Betty Ebert
Dad . . . . .Louis Girard
Tourist Couple . . . . .Louis Girard,
. . . . .Richard L. Reardon
The Tribe:
Aydin Bengisu, Kevin Cornelius, Alison Mould,
Douglas Blakeslee, Michael Blatt, Michael
Lazar, Nikki Nelson, Katie McHugh, Andrew
Scheer, Steven Lee Burright, Charlie Misovye,
Marcia Vliet

#359
August 8 - 13, 1989
Steel Magnolias
by Robert Harding
Directed by Joe Aiello
Scenery by Willard R. Neuert
Lighting by Bill Hunter
Costumes by Lisa Emerson
CAST
Truvy . . . . .Liz Pazik
Annelle . . . . .Penelope Alex
Clairee . . . . .Marcia Vliet
Shelby . . . . .Sandy Mulvihill
M'Lynn .Betty Ebert
Ouiser .Dusty Reeds

#360
August 15 - September 3, 1989
Hello, Dolly!
Book by Michael Stewart
(Suggested by Thornton Wilder's
The Matchmaker)
Music & Lyrics by Jerry Herman
Directed by Joe Aiello
Choreographed by Charlie Misovye
Music Direction by James Douglas Kent
Scenery by Dusty Reeds
Lighting by Bill Hunter
Costumes by H.W.F
CAST
Mrs. Dolly
Gallagher Levi . . . . .Edwina Lewis
Ambrose Kemper . . . . .Paul Stewart
Horace Vandergelder . . . . .Louis Girard
Ermengarde . . . . .Annie Yarbrough
Cornelius Hackel . . . . .Scott Burkell
Barnaby Tucker . . . . .Jeff Lettiere
Irene Molloy . . . . .Sandy Mulvihill
Minnie Fay . . . . .Penelope Alex
Rudolph . . . . .Hans Friedrichs
Stanley . . . . .Charlie Misovye
Hank .Michael Blatt
Ernestina Money . . . . .Marcia Vliet
Policeman . . . . .Steven Lee Burright
Police Sergeant . . . . .Howard McBride
Sallie .Gabry Michel
Townspeople and Waiters:
Aydin Bengisu, Douglas Blakeslee, Nikki
Nelson, Jessica Frankel, Denis Jones,
Rob Langeder, Michael Lazar, Heather Morris,
Alison Mould, Andrew Scheer
General Understudy . . . . .Ann Schulman

#361
September 5 - September 10, 1989
Les Liaisons Dangereuses
by Christopher Hampton
(from the novel by Choderlos de Laclos)
Directed by Scott Burkell
Scenery by Willard R. Neuert
Music Direction by James Douglas Kent
Lighting by Bill Hunter
Costumes by The Los Angeles
Center Theatre Group
(Based on The Royal Shakespeare Co.
Production of
Les Liaisons Dangereuses)
CAST
Major-domo . . . . .Hans Friedrichs
La Marquise de Merteuil . . . . .Linnea Todd
Mme. de Volanges . . . . .Marcia Vliet
Cecil Volanges . . . . .Alison Mould
Le Vicomte de Valmont . . . . .Joe Aiello
Azolan, Valmont's valet . . . . .Jeff Lettiere
Mme. de Rosemonde . . . . .Betty Ebert
La Presidente de Tourvel . . . . . .Heather Morris
Emilie, a courtesan . . . . .Penelope Alex
Le Chevalier Danceny . . . . .Scott Burkell
Maids:
"Adele" . . . . .Annie Yarbough,
"Marie" . . . . .Ann Schulman
Footmen:
Rob Langeder, Michael Lazar,
Gregory S. Rehrig, Paul Stewart
Dueling Second . . . . .Steven Lee Burright

1990 Season

#362
June 5 - 17, 1990
Romance Romance
Book and Lyrics by Barry Harman
Music by Keith Herrmann
"The Little Comedy" based on a short story by
Arthur Schnitzler; "Summer Share" based on
"Pain de Menage" by Jules Renard
Directed by Joe Aiello
Choreographed by Charlie Misovye
Music Director & Conductor - Glenn Wheaton
Scenery by Willard R. Neuert
Lighting by Bill Hunter
Costumes by John Van Hout
CAST
"The Little Comedy"
Alfred Von Wilmers . . . . .Scott Burkell
Josefine Weninger . . . . .Marin Mazzie
"Him" . . . . .Kelly Williams
"Her" . . . . .Penelope Alex
"Summer Share"
Lenny . . . . .Kelly Williams
Barb . . . . .Penelope Alex
Sam . . . . .Scott Burkell
Monica . . . . .Marin Mazzie

#363
June 19 - July 1, 1990
The Pajama Game
Book by George Abbott and Richard Bissell
Music and Lyrics by Richard Adler
and Jerry Ross
Director and Scenery by Dusty Reeds
Choreographed by Charlie Misovye
Musical Director and Conductor -
Glenn Wheaton, Mark Elliott
Lighting by Bill Hunter
Costumes by John Van Hout
CAST
Hines . . . . .Joe Aiello
Prez . . . . .Scott Burkell
Joe . . . . .James P. Focarile
Hasler .Louis Girard
Gladys . . . . .Penelope Alex
Sid Sorokin . . . . .Tom Wopat
Mabel. .Betty Ebert
Charlie . . . . .Brendan Ragotzy
Babe Williams . . . . .Marin Mazzie
Pop . . . . .Howard McBride
Brenda . . . . .Anne Hartmann
Mae . . . . .Michelle Unger
1st Helper . . . . .Ross Kalling
2nd Helper . . . . .Andrew Scheer
Poopsie . . . . .Rebecca Reyes
Max . . . . .Kelly McAllister
Workers in the Sleep-Tite Pajama Factory:
Julie . . . . .Synthia De Lorenzo
Mary . . . . .Michelle Buttignol
Marie . . . . .Shane Frampton
Sarah . . . . .Annmarie K. Martin
Jack . . . . .Charlie Misovye
Bear .Barry Alden
Lenny .Tim Roehl
Buddy . . . . .Charles J. Siedenburg
Carmen . . . . .Nan Mooney
Fritz. . . . . .Daniel A. Schwartz
Davey .Todd Chelf
Trixie . . . . .Susan McGlynn
Leroy . . . . .Kevin Cornelius
Ned .Craig Hermes
Rich . . . . .Rian Galbreath

#364
July 3 - 15, 1990
Born Yesterday
by Garson Kanin
Directed by Jack Ragotzy
Scenery by Willard R. Neuert
Lighting by Bill Hunter
Costumes by Robin Waytenick
CAST
Billy Dawn . . . . .Marin Mazzie
Harry Brock . . . . .Joe Aiello
Paul Verrall . . . . .Scott Burkell
Ed Devery . . . . .Steven Hauck
Senator Norval Hedges . . . . .Louis Girard
Mrs. Hedges . . . . .Dusty Reeds
Eddie Brock . . . . .Todd Chelf
Assistant Manager . . . .Charles J. Siedenburg
Helen . . . . .Shane Frampton
A Bellhop . . . . .Barry Alden
Another Bellhop . . . . .Charlie Misovye
A Barber . . . . .James P. Focarile
A Manicurist . . . . .Michelle Buttignol
A Bootblack . . . . .Andrew Scheer
A Waiter . . . . .Kevin Cornelius

#365
July 17 - August 5, 1990
The Rocky Horror Show
Book, Music and Lyrics by Richard O'Brien
Produced by Dusty Reeds
Directed by Brendan Ragotzy
Choreography by Charlie Misovye

Music Director and Conductor - Mark Elliott
Scenic Designers - Dusty Reeds
and Brendan Ragotzy
Lighting, Sound and Special Effects
by Bill Hunter
Costume Designers - Amy Rohr Berg Wilson
and John Van Hout

CAST
Janet (A Heroine) . . . . .Penelope Alex
Brad (A Hero) . . . . .Steven Hauck
Narrator . . . . .Louis Girard
Riff-Raff (A Menial) . . . . .Scott Burkell
Columbia (A Groupie) . . . . .Kristie Hannum
Magenta (A Domestic) . . . . .Anne Hartmann
Dr. Frank N. Furter
 (A Scientist) . . . . .Joe Aiello
Rocky (A Creation) . . . . .Todd Chelf
Eddie (Ex-Delivery Boy) . . .Steven Lee Burright
Dr. Scott
 (A Rival Scientist) . . . . .Dale Helward

The Wedding Party
Minister . . . . .Kevin Cornelius
Bride . . . . .Synthia De Lorenzo
Groom . . . . .Daniel A. Schwartz
Photographer . . . . .James P. Focarile
Man #1 . . . . .Craig Hermes
Man #2 .Rian Galbreath
Woman #1 .Nan Mooney
Woman #2 . . . . .Susan McGlynn

Added Members:
Cynthia A. Ballard, Katie McHugh Hunter

Guests at the Castle:
Michelle Buttignol, Kevin Cornelius, Synthia
De Lorenzo, James P. Focarile, Shane Frampton,
Craig Hermes, Annmarie K. Martin, Charlie
Misovye, Tim Roehl, Andrew Scheer,
Charles J. Siedenburg, Michelle Unger

#366
August 7 - 12, 1990
The Man Who Came to Dinner
by Moss Hart and George S. Kaufman
Directed by Joe Aiello
Scenery by Willard R. Neuert
Lighting by Robert Jansen
Costumes by Robin Waytenick
CAST
Mrs. Ernest W. Stanley . . . . .Dusty Reeds
Miss Preen . . . . .Penelope Alex
Richard Stanley . . . . .Barry Alden
June Stanley . . . . .Anne Hartmann
John .Kevin Cornelius
Sarah . . . . .Cynthia A. Ballard
Mrs. Dexter . . . . .Shane Frampton
Mrs. McCutcheon . . . . . . .Annmarie K. Martin
Mr. Stanley . . . . .Dale Helward
Maggie Cutler . . . . .Kristie Hannum
Dr. Bradley . . . . .Ross Kalling
Sheridan Whiteside . . . . .Louis Girard
Harriet Stanley . . . . .Suzie Parish
Bert Jefferson . . . . .Scott Burkell
Professor Metz . . . . .Craig Herme

Luncheon Guests:
Andrew Scheer, Daniel A. Schwartz,
Charles J. Siedenburg
Mr. Baker . . . . .Bradley James
Expressman #1 . . . . .Brendan Ragotzy
Expressman #2 . . . . .Todd Chelf
Lorraine Sheldon . . . . .Katrina Kelley
Sandy . . . . .James P. Focarile
Beverly Carlton . . . . .Steven Hauck
Westcott . . . . .Tim Roehl

Radio Technician #1 . . . . .Todd Chelf
Radio Technician #2 . . . . .Andrew Scheer

The Choir:
Rian Galbreath, Michelle Buttignol, Rebecca
Reyes, Synthia De Lorenzo, Michael Unger
Banjo . . . . .Kelly McAllister
Deputy #1 . . . . .Charles J. Siedenburg
Deputy #2 . . . . .Daniel A. Schwartz
A Plainclothes Man . . . . .Howard McBride

#367
August 14 - 26, 1990
Me and My Girl
Book and Lyrics by L. Arthur Rose
and Douglas Furber
Music by Noel Gay
Book revised by Stephen Fry;
Contributions to revisions by Mick Ockrent
Directed by Scott Burkell
Choreography by Charlie Misovye
Conductor and Musical Direction
by Mark Elliott
Scenery by Dusty Reeds
Lighting by Robert Jansen
Costumes by Robin Waytenick
and John Van Hout
CAST
Lady Jacqueline
Carstone . . . . .Kristie Hannum
The Hon. Gerald
Bolinbroke . . . . .Kevin Cornelius
Lord Battersby . . . . .Dale Helward
Lady Battersby . . . . .Katrina Kelley
Herbert Parchester . . . . .Steven Hauck
Sir Jasper Tring . . . . .Ross Kalling
Maria, Duchess of Dene . . . . .Cynthia A. Ballard
Sir John Tremayne . . . . .Louis Girard
Hethersett . . . . .Tim Roehl
Major Domo . . . . .Charles J. Siedenburg
Bill Snibson .Joe Aiello
Sally Smith . . . . .Penelope Alex
Chef . . . . .Todd Chelf
Barkeep . . . . .Brendan Ragotzy
Pub Pianist . . . . .Daniel A. Schwartz
Mrs. Worthington-
Worthington . . . . .Shane Frampton
Lady Diss .Betty Ebert
May Miles . . . . .Katie McHugh Hunter
Lady Brighton . . . . .Anne Hartmann
Lord Wilmont . . . . .Todd Chelf
Lord French . . . . .Kelly McAllister
Mrs. Brown . . . . .Shane Frampton
Bob Barking . . . . .Andrew Scheer
Telegraph Boy . . . . .James P. Focarile
Constable . . . . .Rian Galbreath
Cockney Girl . . . . .Michaelle Buttignol

The Ensemble:
Barry Alden, Michelle Buttignol, Todd Chelf,
Synthia De Lorenzo, James P. Focarile, Shane
Frampton, Rian Galbreath, Ann Hartmann,
Howard McBride, Charlie Misovye,
Rebecca Reyes, Andrew Scheer

#368
August 28 - September 2, 1990
Driving Miss Daisy
by Alfred Uhry
Directed by Joe Aiello
Scenery by Robert Jansen and
Steven Lee Burright
Lighting and Sound by Bill Hunter
Costumes by Robin Waytenick

CAST
Daisy Werthan . . . . .Betty Ebert
Boolie Werthan . . . . .Scott Burkell
Hoke Coleburn . . . . .Kent Martin

1991 Season
#369
May 28 - June 9, 1991
Music! Music! Music! II
Directed by Joe Aiello
Musical Staging by Charlie Misovye
Music Director and Show Pianist -
David S. Young
Lighting by Ann Marie Loomis
and Frankie J. Krainz
Costumes by Ann Richards
Starring
Joe Aiello, Scott Burkell, Penelope Alex
Featuring
Cynthia Ballard
and the "Barnies"
Erin Downey, Amy C. Frank, Rian Galbreath,
Bruce Hammond, Ann LeSchander, Michelle
Millerick, David Mills, Colleen O'Shaugh-
nessey, Gregory Owen, Laura Reisch, Charlie
Siedenburg, Eric Shea Toth

#370
June 11 - 23, 1991
Romantic Comedy
by Bernard Slade
Directed by Dusty Reeds
Scenery by Robert Jansen
Lighting by Ann Marie Loomis
Costumes by Ann Richards
CAST
Jason Carmichael . . . . .Robert Newman
Blanche Dailey . . . . .Betty Ebert
Phoebe Craddock . . . . .Britt Helfer
Allison St. James . . . . .Penelope Alex
Leo Janowitz. . . . . .Joe Aiello
Kate Mallory . . . . .Joellyn Cox Young

#371
June 25 - July 9, 1991
**How to Succeed in Business
Without Really Trying**
Book by Abe Burrows, Jack Weinstock
and Willie Gilbert
Music and Lyrics by Frank Loesser
Based on the novel by Shepherd Mead
Directed by Joe Aiello
Choreographed by Charlie Misovye
Music Director and Conductor -
David S. Young
Scenery by Dusty Reeds
Lighting by Bill Hunter
Costumes by Ann Richards
CAST
J. Pierrepont Finch . . . . .Scott Burkell
Gatch . . . . .Charlie Misovye
Jenkins . . . . .Charlie King
Toynbee . . . . .Rian Galbreath
Johnson . . . . .Frankie J. Krainz
Matthews . . . . .Gregory Owen
Peterson . . . . .Eric Shea Toth
Tackaberry . . . . .Charles J. Siedenburg
J.B. Biggley . . . . .Louis Girard
Rosemary . . . . .Penelope Alex
Bratt . . . . .Ken Andrews
Smitty . . . . .Joellyn Cox Young

Frump .Steven Hauck
Miss Krumholtz . . . . .Anne Hartmann
Miss Jones . . . . .Cynthia Ballard
Mr. Twimble . . . . .Howard McBride
Hedy La Rue . . . . .Marin Mazzie
Davis . . . . .Timothy Bell
Scrubwomen . . . . .Michelle Millerick,
. . . . .Kelly M. Thompson
Ovington . . . . .Brendan Ragotzy
Policeman . . . . .Bradley James
Womper . . . . .Jack Ragotzy
Voice of the Book . . . . .Robert Cox
Office Personnel of the
World Wide Wicket Company:
Deanna Boyd, Senta Connelly, Sara Cycholl,
Erin Downey, Amy C. Frank, Bruce Hammond,
Bradley James, Se Layne, Anne LeSchander,
Howard McBride, Michelle Millerick, David
Mills, Charles Misovye, Michael Naughton,
Colleen O'Shaughnessey, Brendan Ragotzy,
Laura Reisch, Rachel Songer, Anthony Sparks,
Kelly M. Thompson, Robert W. White,
Suzanne Wilson, Melissa Yonkers

#372
July 9 - 21, 1991
Lend Me a Tenor
by Ken Ludwig
Directed by Steven Hauck
Scenery by Robert Jansen
Lighting by Ann Marie Loomis
Costumes by Scott M. Westervelt
CAST
Max .Scott Burkell
Maggie . . . . .Marin Mazzie
Saunders . . . . .Louis Girard
Tito Merelli . . . . .Joe Aiello
Maria . . . . .Penelope Alex
Bellhop .David Mills
Diana .Sara Cycholl
Julia . . . . .Dusty Reeds

#373
July 23 - August 11, 1991
Jesus Christ, Superstar
Music by Andrew Lloyd Webber
Lyrics by Tim Rice
Directed by Joe Aiello and Scott Burkell
Choreographer - Charlie Misovye
Music Direction/Conductor - David S. Young
Scenery by Dusty Reeds
Lighting, Sound and Special Effects
by Bill Hunter
Costumes by Scott M. Westervelt
CAST
Judas Iscariot . . . . .Scott Burkell
Jesus of Nazareth . . . . .John Sparger
Guards . . . . .Timothy Bell,
. . . . .Eric Shea Toth
Mary Magdalene . . . . .Marin Mazzie
Caiaphas . . . . .Steven Hauck
Annas . . . . .Brendan Ragotzy
Simon Zealotes . . . . .Penelope Alex
Peter . . . . .Bruce Hammond
Pontius Pilate . . . . .Joe Aiello
Herod . . . . .Rian Galbreath
The Council:
Louis Girard, Michelle Millerick,
Charles J. Siedenburg, Robert W. White
The Apostles:
Senta Connolly, Frankie J. Krainz, Ann
LeSchander, Charlie King, David Mills,
Michael Naughton, Colleen O'Shaughnessey,
Rachel Songer, Suzanne Wilson
The Company:
Deanna Boyd, Sara Cycholl, Erin Downey,
Betty Ebert, Amy C. Frank, Anne Hartmann,
Katie McHugh Hunter, Bradley James, Se Layne,
Howard McBride, Charlie Misovye, Gregory
Owen, Laura Reisch, Melissa Yonkers

#374
August 13 - 25, 1991
Anything Goes
Music and Lyrics by Cole Porter
Original Book by Guy Bolton, P.G. Wodehouse,
Howard Lindsay and
Russel Crouse
New book by Timothy Crouse
and John Weidman
Direction by Steven Hauck
and Charlie Misovye
Choreography by Charlie Misovye
Musical Director and Conductor -
David S. Young
Scenery by Dusty Reeds
Lighting by Ann Marie Loomis
Costumes by Scott M. Westervelt
CAST
Elisha Whitney . . . . .Louis Girard
Fred . . . . .Timothy Bell
Billy Crocker . . . . .Scott Burkell
Reno Sweeney . . . . .Marin Mazzie
Young Girl . . . . .Senta Connolly
Purser . . . . .Rian Galbreath
Captain. . . . . .Charles J. Siedenburg
Reporter #1 . . . . .Robert W. White
Photographer . . . . .Charlie King
Reporter #2 . . . . .Eric Shea Toth
Minister . . . . .Howard McBride
Luke . . . . .Michael Naughton
John . . . . .Frankie J. Krainz
Purity .Sara Cycholl
Chastity . . . . .Deanna Boyd
Charity . . . . .Se Layne
Virtue . . . . .Anne Hartmann
Hope Harcourt . . . . .Rachel Songer
Mrs. Evangeline
Harcourt . . . . .Michelle Millerick
Lord Evelyn Oakleigh . . . . .Steven Hauck
G-Man #1 . . . . .Robert W. White
G. Man #2 . . . . .Eric Shea Toth
Erma .Penelope Alex
Moonface Martin . . . . .Joe Aiello
Cheeky Dog . . . . .Equity Dog
Sailors:
Bruce Hammond, David Mills, Charlie Misovye,
Gregory Owen, Scott M. Westervelt
Passengers:
Timothy Bell, Senta Connolly, Erin Downey,
Betty Ebert, Amy C. Frank, Bradley James,
Charlie King, Ann LeSchander, Colleen
O'Shaughnessey, Brendan Ragozy, Eric Shea
Toth, Robert W. White, Melissa Yonkers

#375
August 27 - September 8, 1991
[World Premiere]
Bay House
by Bo Brinkman
Directed by Brendan Ragotzy
Scenery by Dusty Reeds
Lighting by Bill Hunter
Costumes by Scott M. Westervelt
Sound by Anne Marie Loomis
CAST
Grady .Louis Girard
Kane .Bo Brinkman
Ryan . . . . .Joe Aiello
Joan . . . . .Joellyn Cox Young
Shelly . . . . .Penelope Alex
Pam . . . . .Melissa Gilbert-Brinkman
Young Soldier . . . . .Amy C. Frank
Emma . . . . .Betty Ebert
Understudy for the
role of Pam . . . . .Deanna Boyd

1992 Season

#376
May 26 - June 7, 1992
Perfectly Frank
Music and Lyrics by Frank Loesser
with music by
Louis Alter, Hoagy Carmichael, Milton DeLugg,
Fred Hollander, Gene Krupa, Burton Lane, Joe
Lilly, Jimmy McHugh, Joseph Meyer, Victor
Schertzinger, Arthur Schwartz, Jule Styne, and
Lawrence Welk
Conceived by Kenny Solms
Directed and Choreographed
by Charlie Misovye
Music Direction by David S. Young
Starring: Joe Aiello, Penelope Alex,
Joellyn Cox Young
Featuring: Heidi Bauer, Timothy Bell, Deanna
Boyd, L. Kirker Butler, Julie Dingman,
John Jay Espino, Rachel Fischer, Amy C.
Frank, Bruce Hammond, Melanie Kidwell,
Charlie King, Mindy Meyers,
Gregory Owen, Rachel Songer, Ben Wolff,
Dennis M. Wright, Courtney Young
Lighting Designed by Ann Marie Loomis
Costumes Designed by Nettie Fischer
Production Assistants: . . . . .Cari Morrison,
. . . . .Don Stephens
Produced by Brendan Ragotzy

#377
June 9 - 21, 1992
Rumors
by Neil Simon
Directed by Jack Ragotzy
Scenery by Michael E. Baggesi
Lighting Design by Ann Marie Loomis
Costumes by Jan Evans
CAST
Chris Gorman . . . . .Penelope Alex
Ken Gorman . . . . .James A. McCammond
Claire Ganz . . . . .Joellyn Cox Young
Lenny Ganz . . . . .Joe Aiello
Ernie Cusack . . . . .Louis Girard
Cookie Cusack . . . . .Betty Ebert
Glenn Cooper . . . . .Craig Bennett
Cassie Cooper . . . . .Rachel Fischer
Officer Welch . . . . .Howard McBride
Officer Pudney . . . . .Deanna Boyd

#378
June 23 - July 12, 1992
Kiss Me, Kate
Music and Lyrics by Cole Porter
Book by Sam and Bella Spewack
Directed by Jack Ragotzy and Charlie Misovye
Choreographed by Charlie Misovye

Music Director and Conductor -
David S. Young
Scenery by Dusty Reeds
Lighting by Ann Marie Loomis
Costumes by Jan Evans
CAST

Fred Graham	Tom Wopat
Harry Trevor	Louis Girard
Lois Lane	Penelope Alex
Ralph	Brendan Ragotzy
Lilli Vanessi	Kathy Taylor
Hattie	Joellyn Cox Young
Stage Doorman	Charlie King
Paul	Charles J. Siedenburg
Bill Calhoun	Bruce Hammond
Cab Driver	Timothy Bell
First Man	Joe Aiello
Second Man	Scott Burkell
Harrison Howell	Robert Cox

The "*Taming of the Shrew*" Players

Bianca	Penelope Alex
Baptista	Louis Girard
Grumio	Ben Wolfe
Hortensio	Gregory Owen
Lucentio	Bruce Hammond
Katharine	Kathy Taylor
Petruchio	Tom Wopat
Haberdasher	Don Stephens
Innkeeper	Timothy Bell
Waiter	Robert A. Prentice
Nathaniel	L. Kirker Butler
Gregory	John Jay Espino
Phillip	Dennis M. Wright

Ensemble:
Heidi Bauer, Timothy Bell, Deanna Boyd, Jennifer Brown, L. Kirker Butler, Julie Dingman, Betty Ebert, John Jay Espino, Rachel Fischer, Amy C. Frank, Bradley James, Melanie Kidwell, Charlie King, Andrew Ludington, Kelly Marshall, Mitchell K. Matsunaga, Howard McBride, Mindy Meyers, Jane Myer, Gregory Owen, Robert A. Prentice, Rachel Songer, Don Stephens, Ben Wolff, Dennis M. Wright, Courtney Young

#379
July 14 - 26, 1992
M. Butterfly
by David Henry Hwang
Music by Giacomo Puccini and Lucia Hwong
Directed by Jack Ragotzy
Choreographed by Charlie Misovye
Scenery Designed by Michael E. Baggesi
Lighting Designed by Ann Marie Loomis
Costumes Designed by Jan Evans
CAST

Rene Gallimard	Joe Aiello
Song Liling	Dexter Echiverri
Marc/ Counsul Sharpless	Scott Buckell

Renee/Girl in Magazine:
Melanie Kidwell or Rachel Fischer

Comrade Chin/Suzuki/ Shu-fang	Deanna Boyd
Helga	Joellyn Cox Young
M. Toulon/Judge	Louis Girard
Man #1	Gregory Owen
Man #2	John Jay Espino
Woman #1	Rachel Songer
Woman #2	Jane Myer

Kurogo Dancers:
Mitchell K. Matsunaga and Andrew Ludington

Chinese Stagehands:
Kelly Marshall and Jennifer Brown

#380
July 28 - August 9, 1992
Phantom
Book by Arthur Kopit
Music and Lyrics by Maury Yeston
Based on the novel *The Phantom of the Opera*
by Gaston Leroux
Directed by Brendan Ragotzy
Co Director and Choreographed -
Charlie Misovye
Music Director and Conductor -
David S. Young
Scenery by Dusty Reeds
Lighting by Ann Marie Loomis
Costumes by Jan Evans
CAST

Christine Daae	Jill Walmsley
Count Philippe de Chandon	Craig Bennett

Count's Girlfriends:
Jane Myer, Courtney Young

La Carlotta	Joellyn Cox Young
Joseph Buquet	Charlie King
The Phantom	Scott Burkell
Gerard Carriere	Louis Girard
Alain Cholet	Joe Aiello
Minister of Culture	John Jay Espino
Jean-Claude	Howard McBride
Florence	Penelope Alex
Fleure	Deanna Boyd
Flora	Rachel Songer

Opera Staff Designers:
Dennis M. Wright, Don Stephens, Gregory Owen

Inspector Ledoux	Charles J. Siedenburg
1st Policeman	L. Kirker Butler
2nd Policeman	Andrew Ludington

Waiters:
Ben Wolff, Bruce Hammond, Gregory Owen, L. Kirker Butler

Oberon	John Jay Espino
Belladova	Heidi Bauer
Young Carriere	Andrew Ludington
Young Erik	Amy C. Frank

Actors, First Nighters, Ballerinas, Penitents Guests:
Penelope Alex, Jill Asmus, Heidi Bauer, Deanna Boyd, Jennifer Brown, L. Kirker Butler, Betty Ebert, John Jay Espino, Rachel Fischer, Amy C. Frank, Bruce Hammond, Bradley James, Melanie Kidwell, Charlie King, Andrew Ludington, Kelly Marshall, Mitchell K. Matsunaga, Charlie Misovye, Mindy Meyers, Jane Myer, Gregory Owen, Robert A. Prentice, Rachel Songer, Don Stephens, Ben Wolff, Dennis M. Wright, Courtney Young

#381
August 11 - 16, 1992
Social Security
by Andrew Bergman
Directed by Jack Ragotzy
Scenery by Michael E. Baggesi
Lighting by Ann Marie Loomis
Costumes by Nettie Fischer
CAST

David Kahn	Joe Aiello
Barbara Kahn	Penelope Alex
Trudy Heyman	Joellyn Cox Young
Martin Heyman	Scott Burkell
Sophie Greengrass	Betty Ebert
Maurice Koenig	Louis Girard

#382
August 18 - 30, 1992
Man of La Mancha
A Musical Play by Dale Wasserman
Music by Mitch Leigh; Lyrics by Joe Darion
(Suggested by the life and works of
Miguel de Cervantes y Saavedra)
Directed by Dusty Reeds
Choreography by Charlie Misovye
Musical Director and Conductor -
David S. Young
Scenery by Steven Lee Burright
Lighting by Ann Marie Loomis
CAST

Gypsy Dancer	Rachel Fischer
Guitar Player	Charlie King
Captain of the Inquisition	Charles J. Siedenburg
Manservant/Sancho Panza	John Jay Espino
Miguel de Cervantes/ Don Quixote	Del Lewis
Governor/Innkeeper	Louis Girard
Duke/Dr. Carrasco	Joe Aiello
Horse	Dennis M. Wright
Mule	Mindy Meyers

The Muleteers:

"Jose"	Bruce Hammond
"Tenorio"	Timothy Bell
"Paco"	Robert A. Prentice
"Juan"	L. Kirker Butler
"Anselmo"	Eric Parker
"Pedro"	Brendan Ragotzy
Aldonza/Dulcinea	Penelope Alex
Padre	Scott Burkell
Maria	Rachel Songer
Housekeeper	Joellyn Cox Young
Antonia	Heidi Bauer
Barber	Gregory Owen
Fermina	Deanna Boyd
Moorish Dancer	Kelly Marshall

Guards, Prisoners, Inquisition Members, Attendants to the Knight of the Mirrors:
Timothy Bell, L. Kirker Butler, Betty Ebert, Rachel Fischer, Amy C. Frank, Bruce Hammond, Bradley James, Howard McBride, Charlie Misovye, Gregory Owen, Rachel Songer, Dennis M. Wright

#383
September 1 - 13, 1992
The Rocky Horror Show
Book, Music and Lyrics by Richard O'Brien
Directed by Brendan Ragotzy
Choreographed by Charlie Misovye
Music Directed and Conducted
by David S. Young
Scenery by Dusty Reeds and Brendan Ragotzy
Lighting, Sound and Special Effects
by Ann Marie Loomis
Costumes (Original Concept) by
Amy Rohr Berg Wilson and John Van Hout
Costumes Designed by Nettie Fischer
CAST

Janet (A Heroine)	Penelope Alex
Brad (A Hero)	Charlie King
Narrator	John Jay Espino
Riff Raff (A Menial)	Scott Burkell

Columbia (A Groupie) . . . . .Kelly Marshall
Magenta (A Domestic) . . . . .Rachel Songer
Dr. Frank N. Furter
(A Scientist) . . . . .Joe Aiello
Rocky (A Creation) . . . . .John Sparger
Eddie (Ex-Delivery Boy) . . .Steven Lee Burright
Dr. Scott (A Rival
Scientist) . . . . .Howard McBride
The Wedding Party:
Minister .Gregory Owen
Bride . . . . .Mindy Meyers
Groom . . . . .L. Kirker Butler
Photographer . . . . .Timothy Bell
Man #1 . . . . .Bruce Hammond
Man #2 . . . . .Eric Parker
Woman #1 . . . . .Deanna Boyd
Woman #2 . . . . .Rachel Fischer
Guests at the Castle:
Heidi Bauer, Timothy Bell, Deanna Boyd,
L. Kirker Butler, Betty Ebert, Rachel Fischer,
Aimee Francis, Amy C. Frank, Bruce Hammond,
Bradley James, Mindy Meyers, Charlie Misovye,
Gregory Owen, Eric Parker, Robert A. Prentice,
Dennis M. Wright

1993 Season

#384
June 1 - 13, 1993
Music! Music! Music! III
Director and Host - Joe Aiello
Choreographer - James Zager
Music Director and Show Pianist - Paul Loeser
Lighting by Ann Marie Loomis
Costumes by John Kristiansen
CAST
Starring
Joe Aiello, Penelope Alex, Scott Burkell
Featuring
John Jay Espino, Rachel Fischer, Jennifer
Garner, Bruce Hammond, Shelly Jackson,
Charlie King, Stephen Lynch, Kelly Marshall,
Eric Parker, Amy Soucy

#385
June 15 - 27, 1993
The Rainmaker
by N. Richard Nash
Directed by Jack Ragotzy
Scenery by Dusty Reeds
Lighting by Ann Marie Loomis
Costumes by John Kristiansen
CAST
H.C. Curry . . . . .Louis Girard
Noah Curry . . . . .Richard Hawkins
Jim Curry . . . . .Scott Burkell
Lizzie Curry . . . . .Kim Zimmer
File . . . . .Joe Aiello
Sheriff Thomas . . . . .Howard McBride
Bill Starbuck . . . . .Tom Wopat

#386
June 29 - July 18, 1993
City of Angels
Book by Larry Gelbart
Music by Cy Coleman
Lyrics by David Zippel
Directed by Tom Wopat
Assistant Director/Choreographer -
James Zager
Music Director and Conductor -
David S. Young
Scenery by Michael E. Baggesi
Lighting and Sound by Ann Marie Loomis
Costumes by John Kristiansen
CAST
Movie Cast:
Stone . . . . .Tom Wopat
Orderlies:
Holly Eliz Walker, Stephen Lynch
Oolie . . . . .Penelope Alex
Alaura Kingsley . . . . .Rachel Fischer
Big Six . . . . .Charlie King
Sonny . . . . .John Jay Espino
Jimmy Powers . . . . .Eric Parker
The Angel City 4:
Denene Mulay, Jennifer Garner, Paul Loesel,
Bruce Hammond
Munoz . . . . .Richard Hawkins
Officer Pasco . . . . .Lance Michael Barber
Bobbi . . . . .Christine Hunter
Irwin S. Irving . . . . .Joe Aiello
Peter Kingsley . . . . .Kirker Butler
Margaret . . . . .Mindy Meyers
Luther Kingsley . . . . .Joseph P. Klinebriel
Dr. Mandril . . . . .Louis Girard
Mallory Kingsley . . . . .Amy Soucy
Photographer . . . . .Ken Rosen
Mahoney . . . . .Stephen Lynch
Coroner . . . . .Charles J. Siedenburg
Commissioner Gaines . . . . . .Howard McBride
Guard . . . . .Andrew S. Kerr
Madame . . . . .Dusty Reeds
Girls:
Shelley Jackson, Kristin Brigitte Hughes
Bootsie . . . . .Kelly Marshall
Hollywood Cast:
Stine . . . . .Scott Burkell
Buddy Fidler . . . . .Joe Aiello
Shoeshine . . . . .Keith Allen Schneider
Gabby . . . . .Christine Hunter
Barber . . . . .Louis Girard
Donna . . . . .Penelope Alex
Masseuse . . . . .Dusty Reeds
Jimmy Powers . . . . .Eric Parker
The Angel City 4:
Denene Mulay, Jennifer Garner, Paul Loesel,
Bruce Hammond
Carla Haywood . . . . .Rachel Fischer
Del Cacosta . . . . .Stephen Lynch
Pancho Vargas . . . . .Richard Hawkins
Werner Kriegler . . . . .Joseph P. Klinebriel
Gerald Pierce . . . . .Kirker Butler
Avril Raines . . . . .Amy Soucy
Gene . . . . .Lance Michael Barber
Cinematographer . . . . .Charles J. Siedenburg
Stand-In . . . . .Kelly Marshall
Hairdresser . . . . .Mary Jo Agresta
Buddy's Niece . . . . .Amy May Andrews
Studio Cops:
Charlie King, Bradley James, John Jay Espino
Studio Personnel:
Ann Filmer, Betty Ebert, Marvin Graham Lewis,
Damian F. Bowerman, Stephen Lynch, Alison
Reiter, Daniel Whitman, Todd R. Smith
Angel City 4 Swings:
Ann Filmer & Marvin Graham Lewis

#387
July 20 - 25, 1993
A Few Good Men
by Aaron Sorkin
Directed by Brendan Ragotzy
Scenery by Dusty Reeds
Lighting Ann Marie Loomis
Costumes by John Kristiansen
CAST
Sentry .Todd R. Smith
Lance Cpl. Harold
W. Dawson . . . . .Stephen Lynch
Pfc. Louden Downey . . . . .Joseph P. Klinebriel
Lt. j.g. Sam Weinberg . . . . .James Zager
Lt. j.g. Daniel A. Kaffee . . . . .Scott Burkell
Lt. Cmdr. Joanne
Galloway . . . . .Christine Hunter
Capt. Isaac Whitaker . . . . .Charles J. Siedenburg
Dave . . . . .Ken Rosen
Capt. Matthew A.
Markinson . . . . .Richard Hawkins
Lyle . . . . .Keith Allen Schneider
Pfc. William T. Santiago . . . . .Daniel Whitman
Lt. Col. Nathan Jessep . . . . .Joe Aiello
Tom . . . . .Damian F. Bowerman
Lt. Jonathan
James Kendrick . . . . .Eric Parker
Lt. Jack Ross . . . . .Bruce Hammond
Cpl. Dunn . . . . .Lance Michael Barber
Cpl. Thomas . . . . .Kirker Butler
Cpl. Hammaker . . . . .Andrew S. Kerr
Cpl. Jeffrey Owen
Howard .Charlie King
Sergeant at Arms . . . . .Kirker Butler
Capt. Julius
Alexander Randolph . . . . .Louis Girard
Cmdr. Walter Stone . . . . .Howard McBride
Orderly . . . . .Todd R. Smith
Asst. to Ross . . . . .Marvin Graham Lewis
M.P.'s:
Kirker Butler, Lance Michael Barber,
Andrew S. Kerr, Damian F. Bowerman,
Keith Allen Schneider, Ken Rosen

#388
July 27 - August 8, 1993
Nunsense II: The Second Coming...
Book, Music and Lyrics by Dan Goggin
Director Edwina Lewis
Choreographed by James Zager
Music Director and Conductor -
David S. Young
Scenery by Michael E. Baggesi
Lighting by Ann Marie Loomis
Costumes by John Kristiansen
CAST
Sister Mary Regina,
Mother Superior . . . . .Betty Ebert
Sister Mary Hubert,
Mistress of Novices . . . . .Edwina Lewis
Sister Robert Anne . . . . .Penelope Alex
Sister Mary Amnesia . . . . .Rachel Fischer
Sister Mary Leo . . . . .Jennifer Garner
Brother Jim . . . . .James Zager
Franciscan Monk . . . . .Howard McBride
General Understudy . . . . .Mary Jo Agresta

#389
August 10 -22, 1993
Li'l Abner
Book by Norman Panama and Melvin Frank
Music by Gene De Paul,
Lyrics by Johnny Mercer
Based on characters created by Al Capp
Direction and Scenery by Dusty Reeds
Lighting Design by Ann Marie Loomis
Choreography by James Zager

Costumes by John Kristiansen
Music Director/Conductor - David S. Young
CAST
Lonesome Polecat . . . . .Daniel Whitman
Hairless Joe . . . . .Keith Allen Schneider
Romeo Scragg . . . . .Brendan Ragotzy
Clem Scragg . . . . .Lance Michael Barber
Alf Scragg . . . . .Andrew S. Kerr
Moonbeam McSwine . . . . .Shelley Jackson
Marryin' Sam . . . . .John Jay Espino
Earthquake McGoon . . . . .Charlie King
Daisy Mae . . . . .Amy Soucy
Pappy Yokum . . . . .K. Hughes
Mammy Yokum . . . . .Penelope Alex
Li'l Abner . . . . .Scott Burkell
Cronies:
Bruce Hammond, Marvin Lewis, Stephen Lynch,
Eric Parker, and Ken Rosen
Mayor Dawgmeat . . . . .Howard McBride
Senator Jack S.
Phogbound . . . . .Louis Girard
Dr. Rasmussen T.
Finsdale . . . . .Damian F. Bowerman
Government Man . . . . .Todd R. Smith
Available Jones . . . . .Richard Hawkins
Stupenfyin' Jones . . . . .Kelly Marshall
Speedy McRabbit . . . . .Ken Rosen
Colonel .Gregg Rehrig
General Bullmoose . . . . .Joe Aiello
Secretaries:
Damian F. Bowerman, Marvin Lewis,
Ken Rosen, Todd R. Smith
Appassionata Von
Climax . . . . .Rachel Fischer
Evil Eye Fleagle . . . . .Joseph P. Klinebriel
Dr. Smithborn . . . . .Ken Rosen
Dr. Krogmeyer . . . . .Todd R. Smith
Dr. Schleifitz . . . . .Marvin Lewis
Sofia Softwicke . . . . .Aimee Francis
Wives:
Mary Jo Agresta, Amy Mae Andrews,
Ann Filmer, Holly Eliz Walker
Butler . . . . .Daniel Whitman
Dogpatchers:
Lance Michael Barber, Kirker Butler,
Betty Ebert, Jennifer Garner, Bruce Hammond,
Bradley James, Andrew S. Kerr, John
Kristiansen, Marvin Lewis, Stephen Lynch,
Kelly Marshall, Mindy Meyers, Eric Parker,
Dusty Reeds, Alison Reiter, Ken Rosen,
Todd R. Smith, James Zager

#390
August 24 - September 5, 1993
The Best Little Whorehouse in Texas
Book by Larry L. King and Peter Masterson
Music and Lyrics by Carol Hall
Produced by Brendan Ragotzy
Directed by Edwina Lewis
Co-Director and Scenic Designer - Dusty Reeds
Lights - Ann Marie Loomis
Choreographer - James Zager
Costumes - John Kristiansen
Music Director/Conductor - David S. Young
CAST
Narrator . . . . .Charlie King
Farmer . . . . .Richard Hawkins
Shy Kid .Ken Rosen
Miss Wulla Jean . . . . .Dusty Reeds
Traveling Salesman . . . . .John Jay Espino
Slick Dude . . . . .Stephen Lynch

Choir:
Mary Jo Agresta, Kirker Butler, Jennifer Garner,
Bruce Hammond, Eric Parker, Alison Reiter,
Keith Allen Schneider
Angel .Kelly Marshall
Shy . . . . .Ann Filmer
Jewel . . . . .Edwina Lewis
Mona Stangley . . . . .Kim Zimmer
The Girls at Miss Mona's:
"Linda Lou" . . . . .Rachel Fischer
"Dawn" .Amy Soucy
"Ginger" . . . . .Amy Mae Andrews
"Beatrice" . . . . .Shelley Jackson
"Taddy Jo" . . . . .Mindy Meyers
"Ruby Rae" . . . . .Jennifer Garner
"Eloise" . . . . .Holly Eliz Walker
"Durla" . . . . .Mary Jo Agresta
Leroy Sliney . . . . .Joseph P. Klinebriel
The Dogettes:
Marvin Lewis, Stephen Lynch, Ken Rosen,
Keith, Allen Schneider
Melvin P. Thorpe . . . . .Scott Burkell
Soundman . . . . .Todd Smith
Stage Manager . . . . .Eric Parker
Melvin P. Thorpe Singers:
Jennifer Garner, Kristin, Brigitte Hughes,
Shelley Jackson, Alison Reiter
Sheriff Ed Earl Dodd . . . . .Joe Aiello
Church Lady . . . . .Aimee Francis
Cameraman Lance . . . . .Michael Barber
C.J. Scruggs . . . . .John Jay Espino
Mayor Rufus Poindexter . . . .Richard Hawkins
Edsel Mackey . . . . .Bradley James
Doatsey May . . . . .Penelope Alex
Angelette Imogene
Charlene . . . . .Kristin Brigitte Hughes
Angelettes:
Jennifer Garner, Mindy Meyers, Amy Soucy
Chip Brewster . . . . .Bruce Hammond
Senator Wingwoah . . . . .Robert Cox
Aggies:
Kirker Butler, Bruce Hammond, Marvin Lewis,
Stephen Lynch, Eric Parker, Brendan Ragotzy,
Ken Rosen, Todd Smith
Photographers:
Betty Ebert, Marvin Lewis, Stephen Lynch,
Ken Rosen, Keith Allen Schneider
Reporters:
Bradley James, Penelope Alex,
Lance Michael Barber, Joseph P. Klinebriel
Governor's Aide . . . . .Bruce Hammond
Governor . . . . .Howard McBride

#391
September 7 - 12, 1993
Jake's Women
by Neil Simon
Directed by Scott Burkell
Scenery by Michael Baggesi
Lighting by Ann Marie Loomis
Costumes by John Kristiansen
CAST
Jake . . . . .Joe Aiello
Maggie . . . . .Kim Zimmer
Karen . . . . .Penelope Alex
Molly (at 12) . . . . .Kristin Hughes
Molly (at 21) . . . . .Jennifer Garner
Edith . . . . .Betty Ebert
Julie .Rachel Fischer
Shelia . . . . .Amy Mae Andrews

1994 Season
#392
May 31 - June 12, 1994
Music! Music! Music! IV
Music Director and Show Pianist
David S. Young
Choreographer - Steve Owsley
Costumes by John Kristiansen
Lighting by Ann Marie Loomis
"As Time Goes by" Arrangement
by Brian Driscoll
Starring
Joe Aiello, Penelope Alex, Scott Burkell
Featuring:
Jill Asmus, Jeff Compton, Ann Filmer, Kristin
Brigitte Hughes, Charlie King, Michael Letch,
Eric Parker, Rebecca Parry, Ken Rosen, Amy
Soucy
Alternates.....Marvin Lewis, Kelly Jeannine
Moran

#393
June 14 - June 26, 1994
Don't Dress for Dinner
by Marc Camoletti
(Adapted by Robin Hawdon)
Directed amd Scenery by Dusty Reeds
Lighting by Ann Marie Loomis
Costumes by John Kristiansen
CAST
Bernard . . . . .Joe Aiello
Jacqueline, his wife . . . . .Joellyn M. Young
Robert, his friend . . . . .Scott Burkell
Suzanne, his mistress . . . . .Daisy Nystul
Suzette, the cook . . . . .Penelope Alex
George, her husband . . . . .Tom Wopat

#394
June 28 - July 17, 1994
Guys and Dolls
A Musical Fable of Broadway
Based on a Story and Characters
by Damon Runyon
Music and Lyrics by Frank Loesser
Book by Jo Swerling and Abe Burrows
Directed by Tom Wopat
Choreographed by Steve Owsley
Music Director/Conductor - David S. Young
Scenery by Dusty Reeds
Lighting by Ann Marie Loomis
Costumes by John Kristiansen
CAST
The Guys
Nicely-Nicely
Johnson . . . . .Scott Burkell
Benny Southstreet . . . . .Eric Parker
Rusty Charlie . . . . .Ken Rosen
Harry the Horse . . . . .Richard Hawkins
Nathan Detroit . . . . .Joe Aiello
Angie the Ox . . . . .Rod Cone
Sky Masterson . . . . .Tom Wopat
Big Jule . . . . .Charlie King
Lt. Brannigan . . . . .Howard McBride
Master of
Ceremonies . . . . .Randy Taylor
The Dolls
Miss Adelaide . . . . .Joellyn M. Young
The Hot Box Girls:
Katherine Adamenko, Corena Chase,
Ann Filmer, Kristin Brigitte Hughes, Soraya

276

Antoinette Knight, Kelly Jeannine Moran,
Rebecca Parry, Amy Soucy
Mimi . . . . .Soraya Antoinette Knight
Other Dolls:
Jill Asmus, Margaret Hollinbeck
From the Save-A-Soul Mission:
Sarah Brown . . . . .Jennifer Roberts
Arvide Abernathy . . . . .Louis Girard
Agatha . . . . .JoJo Bengel
Calvin .Steve Superak
Priscilla . . . . .Lindsey Van De Kirk
Martha . . . . .Holly Eliz Walker
General Matilda B.
Cartwright . . . . .Dusty Reeds
In Havana:
Guys, Dolls and Dancers:
Jeff Compton, Zeke Farrow, Ann Filmer,
Kristin Brigitte Hughes, Soraya Antoinette
Knight, Michael Letch, Marvin Lewis,
James A. McNulty, Kelly Jeannine Moran,
Steve Owsley, Rebecca Parry, Ken Rosen,
Amy Soucy, Randy Taylor
In the Sewer:
Crap Shooters:
Jeff Compton, Rod Cone, Zeke Farrow, Joe
Klinebriel, Michael Letch, Marvin Lewis, James
A. McNulty, Steve Owsley, Joe Pehrson, Brendan Ragotzy, Ken Rosen, Randy Taylor
General Understudies:
Penelope Alex and Betty Ebert

#395
July 19 - 31, 1994
The Odd Couple
by Neil Simon
Directed by Jack Ragotzy
Scenery by Richard Jorn
Lighting by Ann Marie Loomis
Costumes by Nettie Fischer
CAST
Speed . . . . .Richard Hawkins
Murray .Louis Girard
Roy . . . . .Steve Multer
Vinnie . . . . .Howard McBride
Oscar Madison . . . . .Joe Aiello
Felix Unger . . . . .Scott Burkell
*Gwendolyn Pigeon:
Ann Filmer, Katherine Adamenko or Daisy Nystul
*Cecily Pigeon:
Amy Soucy, Soraya Knight or Margaret Hollinbeck
*These actresses will alternate in the roles of
Gwendolyn and Cecily, and will be announced
before the performance.
Corena Chase is standby for Cecily

#396
August 2 - 14, 1994
[World Premiere]
Billy the Kid
Book and Lyrics by Brendan Ragotzy
Music by David S. Young
Directed by Brendan Ragotzy
Music Director/Conductor - David S. Young
Orchestrations by David S. Young
and Brian Driscoll
Choreography by Steve Owsley
Scenery by Michael E. Baggesi
Lighting by Ann Marie Loomis
Costumes by John Kristiansen
CAST
Brushy Bill Roberts . . . . .Louis Girard
Attorney William Morrison . . . . . Jack Ragotzy
Catherine McCarthy . . . . .Ann Filmer
William H. Antrim. . . . . .Scott Schumacher
Preacher . . . . .Marvin Lewis
Saloon Girl. . . . . .Rebecca Parry
Henry Antrim/
William H. Bonney/
Billy the Kid . . . . .Bruce Hammond
Frank P. "Windy" Cahill . . . . Joe Aiello
M'am Jones . . . . .Dusty Reeds
Tom O'Keefe . . . . .Joe Pehrson
Heraldo Jaramillo . . . . .Michael Letch
Lincoln Woman . . . . . . .Margaret Hollinbeck
Mrs. Maxwell . . . . .Betty Ebert
Paulita Maxwell . . . . .Penelope Alex
Telesfor . . . . .Randy Taylor
Blazer Mill Man #1 . . . . .Joe Pehrson
Blazer Mill Man #2 . . . . . . .James A. McNulty
Harvey Morris . . . . .Randy Taylor
Susan McSween . . . . .Corena Chase
Colonel Nathan Dudley . . . . .Joe Aiello
Governor Lew Wallace . . . . .Scott Burkell
Governor's Aide . . . . .Steve Multer
Huston Chapman . . . . .Joe Pehrson
Dave Rudabaugh . . . . .Charlie King
Flamenco Dancer . . . . .Katherine Adamenko
Billie Wilson . . . . .Zeke Farrow
Godrey Gauss . . . . .Joseph P. Klinebriel
Mexican Woman . . . . .Holly Eliz Walker
Peter Maxwell . . . . .Jeff Compton
Murphy-Dolan Group:
(The Santa Fe Ring or the House)
Lawrence Gustave
Murphy . . . . .Richard Jorn
James Joseph Dolan . . . . .Steve Owsley
Judge Bristol . . . . .James A. McNulty
District Attorney
William L. Ryerson . . . . .Howard McBride
William "Buck" Morton . . . . .Richard Hawkins
Jesse Evans . . . . .Eric Parker
Tom Hill .Rod Cone
Frank Baker . . . . .Patrick McNatt
Buckshot Roberts . . . . .Richard Hawkins
Billy Campbell. . . . . .Richard Hawkins
Tunstall-McSween Group:
(The Regulators)
John Henry Tunstall. . . . . .Ken Rosen
Alexander Anderson
McSween . . . . .Scott Burkell
John Simpson Chisum . . . . . . .John Kristiansen
Fred Waite . . . . .Jeff Compton
William McCloskey . . . . .Zeke Farrow
Robert Windenmann. . . . . .Steve Superak
Dick Brewer . . . . .Steve Multer
John Middleton . . . . .Lance Barber
Josiah Gordon Scurlock . . . .Joseph P. Klinebriel
Charlie Bowdre . . . . .Stephen Lynch
Jim French . . . . .Charlie King
Jose Chavez . . . . .Rod Cone
Frank Coe . . . . .Ken Rosen
George Coe . . . . .Marvin Lewis
Ignacio Gonzales . . . . .Zeke Farrow
Tom O'Folliard . . . . .Eric Parker
Ygenio Salazar . . . . .Michael Letch
The Law:
Sheriff Wood . . . . .Charlie King
Sheriff Brady . . . . .Scott Schumacher
Deputy Sheriff Barrier . . . .Joseph P. Klinebriel
Deputy Hindman . . . . .Michael Letch
Sheriff Peppin . . . . .Richard Hawkins
Deputy . . . . Ken Rosen
Sheriff Kimball . . . . .Lance Barber
Pat Garrett . . . . Joe Aiello
Garrett's Deputies:
Ken Rosen, Randy Taylor
J.W. Bell . . . . .Richard Hawkins
Bob Olinger . . . . .Scott Schumacher
Deputy Poe . . . . .Steve Multer
Deputy . . . . .Joe Pehrson
Townspeople, Gunfighters, Reporters,
Cowhands, Guards:
Melanie Gray Allen, Jill Asmus, Lance Barber,
JoJo Bengel, Corena Chase, Jeff Compton,
Rod Cone, Zeke Farrow, Ann Filmer, Margaret
Hollinbeck, Kristin Brigitte Hughes, Charlie
King, Joseph P. Klinebriel, Soraya Antoinette
Knight, Michael Letch, Marvin Lewis, Stephen
Lynch, James A. McNulty, Kelly Jeannine
Moran, Daisy Nystul, Eric Parker, Joe Pehrson,
Rebecca Parry, Ken Rosen, Amy Soucy, Steve
Superak, Randy Taylor, Lindsey Van de Kirk,
Holly Eliz Walker.

#397
August 16 - August 28, 1994
Damn Yankees
Music and Lyrics by Richard Adler
and Jerry Ross
Book by George Abbott and Douglass Wallop
Based on the novel T*he Year the Yankees Lost
the Pennant* by Douglass Wallop
Directed by Dusty Reeds and Steve Owsley
Choreographer - Steve Owsley
Ass't Choreographer Ann Filmer
Music Director/ Conductor - David S. Young
Additional Music Arrangements
by Brian Driscoll
Scenery by Dusty Reeds
Lighting by Ann Marie Loomis
Costumes by John Kristiansen
CAST
Announcer . . . . .Jack Ragotzy
Joe Boyd . . . . .Scott Schumacher
Meg . . . . .Joellyn M. Young
Mr. Applegate . . . . .Joe Aiello
Sister . . . . .Margaret Hollinbeck
Doris . . . . .Lindsey Van DeKirk
Joe Hardy . . . . .Scott Burkell
The Washington Senators:
Van Buren (Manager) . . . . . . .Howard McBride
Sohovic . . . . .Eric Parker
Smokey . . . . .Ken Rosen
Rocky . . . . .Charlie King
Hawk . . . . .Richard Hawkins
Zeke .Zeke Farrow
Mike . . . . .Michael Letch
Steve . . . . .Stephen Lynch
Randy . . . . .Randy Taylor
Jeff .Jeff Compton
Brendan . . . . .Brendan Ragotzy
Henry (Bat Boy) . . . . .Steve Superak
Gloria . . . . .Penelope Alex
Lynch . . . . .Rod Cone
Welch . . . . .Louis Girard
Lola . . . . .Kim Zimmer
Miss Weston . . . . .Rebecca Parry
Fans, Teenagers, Reporters, Friends & Neighbors
Katherine Adamenko, Melanie Gray Allen, Jill
Asmus, JoJo Bengel, Betty Ebert, Ann Filmer,
Kristin Hughes, Bradley James, Joseph P.
Klinebriel, Marvin Lewis, James A. McNulty,
Kelly Jeannine Moran, Joe Pehrson, Amy Soucy,
Gloria understudy . . . .Soraya Antoinette Knight

277

#398
August 30 - September, 1994
Lost in Yonkers
by Neil Simon
Directed by Joe Aiello
Scenery by Michael E. Baggesi
Lighting by Ann Marie Loomis
Costumes by John Kristiansen
CAST

Jay	Stephen Lynch
Arty	Logan Lipton
Eddie	Joe Aiello
Bella	Kim Zimmer
Grandma Kurnitz	Betty Ebert
Louie	Scott Burkell
Gert	Margaret Hollinbeck

#399
September 6 - September 18, 1994
The Rocky Horror Show
Book, Music and Lyrics by Richard O'Brian
Directed by Brendan Ragotzy
Choreographed by Steve Owsley
Music Director/Conductor - Paul Loesel
Scenery by Dusty Reeds and Brendan Ragotzy
Lighting, Sound and Special Effects
by Ann Marie Loomis
Costumes by John Kristiansen
CAST

Janet (A Heroine)	Amy Soucy
Brad (A Hero)	Charlie King
Narrator	Richard Hawkins
Riff-Raff (A Menial)	Scott Burkell
Columbia (A Groupie)	Ann Filmer
Magenta (A Domestic)	Holly Eliz Walker
Dr. Frank N. Furter (A Scientist)	Joe Aiello
Rocky (A Creation)	Marvin Lewis
Eddie (Ex-Delivery Boy)	Eric Parker
Dr. Scott (A Rival Scientist)	Howard McBride

The Wedding Party:

Minister	James A. McNulty
Bride	Melanie Gray Allen
Groom	Joe Pehrson
Photographer	Randy Taylor
Man #1	Jeff Compton
Man #2	Rod Cone
Woman #1	Katherine Adamenko
Woman #2	JoJo Bengel

Guests at the Castle:
Katherine Adamenko, Melanie Gray Allen, Penelope Alex, JoJo Bengel, Jeff Compton, Rod Cone, Betty Ebert, Aimee Francis, Margaret Hollinbeck, Kristin Brigitte Hughes, Bradley James, Joseph P. Klinebriel, John Kristiansen, Stephen Lynch, James A. McNulty, Rebecca Parry, Joe Pehrson, Brendan Ragotzy, Ken Rosen

1995 Season
[50th Anniversary Season]

#400
May 30 - June 11, 1995
Music! Music! Music! V — 50th Anniversary Tribute to Betty Ebert Ragotzy
Directed by Joe Aiello
Music Director Paul Loesel
Choreographer - Charlie Misovye
Lighting by Ann Marie Loomis
Costumes by John Kristiansen
Starring
Joe Aiello, Scott Burkell, Penelope Alex
Featuring
JoJo Bengel, Michele Dibner, LeighAnna Freeborough, Kristin Hughes, Brennan Johnson, Stephen Lynch, Eric Olm, Rebecca Parry, Eric Parker, Ken Rosen
Alternates:
Jill Asmus, Michael Letch

#401
June 13 - 25, 1995
Pure as the Driven Snow; or A Working Girl's Secret
(A thrilling and educational masterpiece demonstrating the triumph of Virtue over Evil)
by Paul Loomis
Direction and scenery by Dusty Reeds
Music Director - Paul Loesel
Choreographed by Charlie Misovye
Lighting by Ann Marie Loomis
Costumes by John Kristiansen
DRAMATIS PERSONAE

Master of Ceremonies	Rirnifer Roberts
Jonathan Logan, the innkeeper	Louis Girard
Zamah Logan, his keeper	Dusty Reeds
Leander Longfellow, our hero	Scott Burkell
Mortimer Frothingham, the villain	Joe Aiello
Jed Lunn, an ex-convict	Howard McBride
E.Z. Pickens, factory owner	Eric Parker
Imogene Pickens, his snobbish sister	Penelope Alex
Mrs. Ethelinda Hewlitt, a society woman	Maggie Hollinbeck
Alison Hewlitt, her daughter	Kristin Hughes
Mrs. Faith Hogue, a guest	Rebecca Parry
Letty Barber, her maid	Jill Asmus

Nellie Morris, a woman of mystery:
Soraya Knight or Georgina Spelvin
The Company (in order of appearance):
Jill Asmus, Joe Aiello, Michael Sammon, Randy Taylor, Trey Hohman, John C. Brown, Michael Letch, Eric Olm, Michele Dibner, Dana Munshaw, JoJo Bengel, Brennan Johnson, Michael A. Sommese, Brendan Ragotzy, Jack Ragotzy, Stephen Lynch, Ken Rosen, Soraya Knight, Bryan Hage, Greg Winter, Joe Pehrson, Joseph Plummer, LeighAnna Freeborough, Katherine Adamenko, Adaku Cunningham, Kelly Moran, Alisa Dariano, Jennifer M. Fagundes, Maria N. Simos, Rochele A. Tillman, Kristin Hughes

#402
June 27 - July 9, 1995
The Music Man
Book, Music and Lyrics by Meredith Willson
Story by Meredith Willson and Franklin Lacey
Directed by Jack Ragotzy
Music Director - Paul Loesel
Choreographed by Charlie Misovye
Scenery by Dusty Reeds
Lighting by Ann Marie Loomis
Costumes by John Kristiansen
CAST

Traveling Salesmen:
John C. Brown, Bryan Hage, Brennan Johnson, Trey Hohman, Michael Letch, Michael Sammon, Joe Pehrson, Joseph Plummer

Charlie Cowell	Joe Aiello
Conductor	Howard McBride
Harold Hill	Tom Wopat
Major Shinn	Louis Girard
Ewart Dunlop	Stephen Lynch
Oliver Hix	Randy Taylor
Jacey Squires	Eric Parker
Olin Britt	Ken Rosen
Marcellus Washburn	Scott Burkell
Tommy Djilas	Eric Olm
Marian Paroo	Pamela Harden
Mrs. Paroo	Maggie Hollinbeck
Amaryllis	Jill Asmus
Winthrop Paroo	Greg Laux/ Logan Lipton
Eulalie Mackecknie Shinn	Suzie Parish
Zaneeta Shinn	Jennifer M. Fagundes
Gracie Shinn	Kristin Hughes
Maud Dunlop	Rebecca Parry
Ethel Toffelimier	Penelope Alex
Mrs. Squires	Dana Munshaw
Constable Locke	Richard Hawkins

River City Townspeople and Kids:
Katherine Adamenko, JoJo Bengel, John C. Brown, Adaku Cunningham, Alisa Dariano, Michele Dibner, LeighAnna Freeborough, Margie L. Hachmeister, Bryan Hage, Sarah Heckert, Trey Hohman, Bradley James, Brennan Johnson, Greg Laux, Michael Letch, Howard McBride, Charlie Misovye, Kelly Moran, Joe Pehrson, Joseph Plummer, Dusty Reeds, Michael Sammon, Brett Schrier, Maria N. Simos, Michael A. Sommese, Rochele A. Tillman, Greg Winter

#403
July 11 - 23, 1995
Sweeney Todd, The Demon Barber of Fleet Street
Music and Lyrics by Stephen Sondheim
Book by Hugh Wheeler
From an adaptation by Christopher Bond
Directed by Joe Aiello and Scott Burkell
Music Director - Paul Loesel
Choreographed by Charlie Misovye
Scenery by Richard Jorn
Lighting by Ann Marie Loomis
Costumes by John Kristiansen
CAST

Anthony Hope	Scott Burkell
Sweeney Todd	Tom Wopat
Beggar Woman	Penelope Alex
Mrs. Lovett	Barbara Marineau
Judge Turpin	Joe Aiello
The Beadle	Michael Sammon
Birdseller	Richard Hawkins
Johanna	Pamela Harden
Tobias Ragg	Stephen Lynch
Pirelli	Michael A. Sommese
Jonas Fogg	Louis Girard

Ensemble:
Jill Asmus, JoJo Bengel, John C. Brown, Michele Dibner, LeighAnna Freeborough, Trey Hohman, Maggie Hollinbeck, Kristin Hughes, Brennan Johnson, Soraya Knight, Michael Letch, Eric Olm, Eric Parker, Rebecca Parry, Ken Rosen, Randy Taylor
Townspeople:

Katherine Adamenko, Adaku Cunningham, Alisa Dariano, Jennifer M. Fagundes, Margie L. Hachmeister, Bryan Hage, Richard Hawkins, Bradley James, Howard McBride, Charlie Misovye, Kelly Moran, Dana Munshaw, Joe Pehrson, Joseph Plummer, Brendan Ragotzy, Dusty Reeds, Maria N. Simos, Rochele A. Tillman, Greg Winter

#404
July 25 - 30, 1995
Love Letters
by A.R. Gurney
Directed by Jack Ragotzy
Scenery by Dusty Reeds
Lighting by Ann Marie Loomis
Costumes by John Kristiansen
CAST
Andrew Makepeace
Ladd III . . . . .Dick Fuchs
Melissa Gardner . . . . .Adrienne Barbeau

#405
August 1 - 13, 1995
Fiddler on the Roof
Based on Sholom Alecheim's Stories
by Special Permission of Arnold Perl
Book by Joseph Stein,
Music by Jerry Bock,
Lyrics by Sheldon Harnick
Direction and Scenery by Dusty Reeds
Musical Director - Paul Loesel
Choreographed by Charlie Misovye
Lighting by Ann Marie Loomis
Costumes by John Kristiansen
CAST
The Fiddler . . . . .Ken Rosen
Tevye, the Dairyman . . . . .Joe Aiello
Golde, his wife . . . . .Dana Munshaw
Tzeitel, his daughter . . . . .Rebecca Parry
Hodel, his daughter . . . . .Penelope Alex
Chava, his daughter . . . . .Kristin Hughes
Shprintze, his
daughter . . . . .Jennifer M. Fagundes
Bielke, his daughter . . . . .Jill Asmus
Yente, the
Matchmaker . . . . .Dusty Reeds
Motel, the Tailor . . . . .Scott Burkell
Perchik, the Student . . . . .Eric Parker
Lazar Wolf, the
Butcher . . . . .Howard McBride
Mordhca, the
Innkeeper .Louis Girard
Rabbi . . . .Joe Pehrson
Mendel, his son . . . . .Bryan Hage
Avram, the Bookseller . . . . .Randy Taylor
Nachum, the Beggar . . . . Joseph Plummer
Grandma Tzeitel . . . . . .LeighAnna Freeborough
Fruma-Sarah . . . . .Maggie Hollinbeck
Shandel, Motel's
mother . . . . .Maria N. Simos
Rivka . . . . .JoJo Bengel
Mirala . . . .Kelly Moran
The Bottle Dancers:
Eric Olm, Ken Rosen, John C. Brown,
Michael Letch
Chaim, a boy . . . . .Eric Olm
Yankel, a boy . . . . .Greg Winter
The Russians:
"The Constable" . . . . .Charlie Siedenburg
"Priest" . . . . .Trey Hohman
"Fyedka" . . . . .Stephen Lynch
"Vladimir" . . . . .Brennan Johnson
"Sasha" . . . . .Michael Sammon
"Lubov" . . . . .Eric Olm
The Villagers:
JoJo Bengel, John C. Brown, Adaku Cunningham, Alisa Dariano, Michele Dibner, LeighAnna Freeborough, Margie L. Hachmeister, Trey Hohman, Maggie Hollinbeck, Michael Letch, Bradley James, Brennan Johnson, Charlie Misovye, Kelly Moran, Joseph Plummer, Brendan Ragotzy, Rochele A. Tillman, Greg Winter
(A Special Thank You to Larry Lando for his assistance on this production}

#406
August 15 - 27, 1995
Hair
The American Tribal Love-Rock Musical
Book and Lyrics by Gerome Ragni
and James Rado
Music by Galt MacDermot
Produced for the Broadway Stage
by Michael Butler
Originally Produced by
the NY Shakespeare Festival
Directed by Brendan Ragotzy
Choreography by Charlie Misovye
Musical Director - Paul Loesel
Scenery by Dusty Reeds and Bill Hunter
Lighting and Sound Design by Bill Hunter
Costumes Designed by John Kristiansen
CAST
Claude . . . . .Scott Burkell
Berger . . . . .Joe Aiello
Hud .Stanley White
Sheila .Penelope Alex
Woof .Stephen Lynch
Dionne . . . . .E. Faye Butler
Ron . . . . .Ron Wilson
Jeanie . . . . .Katherine Adamenko
Crissy . . . . .Kristin Hughes
Steve . . . . .Ken Rosen
Leata .Rebecca Parry
Paul . . . . .John C. Brown
Walter . . . . .Eric Parker
Suzannah . . . . .Leighanna Freeborough
Mary . . . . .Alisa Dariano
Emmaretta . . . . .Cheridah A. Best
Diane .Maria N. Simos
Marjorie . . . . .Jennifer M. Fagundes
Mom . . . . .Dusty Reeds
Dad . . . . .Louis Girard
Tourist Couple . . . . .Louis Girard,
. . . . .Michael Sammon
The Tribe:
Jill Asmus, JoJo Bengel, Adaku Cunningham, Michele Dibner, Margie L. Hachmeister, Bryan Hage, Maggie Hollinbeck, Bradley James, Brennan Johnson, Michael Letch, Howard McBride, Charlie Misovye, Kelly Moran, Dana Munshaw, Eric Olm, Joe Pehrson, Joseph Plummer, Dusty Reeds, Michael Sammon, Randy Taylor, Rochele A. Tillman, Greg Winter, Byron Willis.

#407
August 29 - September 3, 1995
Out of Order
by Ray Cooney
Directed by Jack Ragotzy
Scenery by Dusty Reeds
Lighting by Ann Marie Loomis
Costumes by John Kristiansen
CAST
Richard Willey . . . . .Joe Aiello
The Manager . . . . .Howard McBride
The Waiter . . . . .Louis Girard
Jane Worthington . . . . .Penelope Alex
A Body . . . . .Ken Rosen
George Pigden . . . . .Scott Burkell
The Maid . . . . .Alisa Dariano
Ronnie . . . . .Stephen Lynch
Pamela . . . . .Maggie Hollinbeck
Gladys . . . . .JoJo Bengel
End of the 50th Season

Index

Note:
-Only the text, not the Appendix, has been indexed.
-Play titles indexed have been limited, of necessity, to those which have specific comments, critiques, or photos included in the text.
-Play titles indexed include all productions of the play (without reference to date) that were presented at the Barn during the first 50 years and in other locales as mentioned in the text. Photos are not dated in the index.
-Playwrights of premieres and world premieres are listed in parentheses after play title.
-(c) after names or publication titles indicates critical review
-(p) or (wp) after play titles indicates premiere or world premiere

Abe, Paul, 125
Actors Studio, 16, 74, 77, 186
Actors' Equity Association, 46-47, 107, 158, 173, 181, 302, 204, 205, 206
AFTRA (American Federation of Television and Radio Artists), 173
AGVA (American Guild of Variety Artists), 173
Ah, Wilderness!, 31, 33
Aiello, Sal/Joe: 144, 146, 149, 150, 151, 157, 159, 162, 163, 164, 167, 168, 170, 173, 177, 178, 182, 183, 184, 185, 189-90, 194, 201, 212, 214, 215, 221; photos, 144, 147, 151, 152, 154, 155, 158, 167, 177, 181, 186, 189, 190, 195
Alex, Penelope: 178, 194, 215; photos, 186, 191, 193, 195, 221
  See also Issichopoulos, Penelope
Allen, Gordon, 151
Allen, Janie, 144
Allen, Vickie, 165
Alpers, Richard T., photo, 138
Alt, Robert (c), 113
Amadeus: 163-64; photo, 165
Ameche, Don, 70
And So, Farewell, 76
Andrews, Ken: 210; photo,125
Angela: 13-16, 113, 115-18, 119-20, 123, 158, 164, 204; photo, 117
Annie, 162-63
Annie Get Your Gun; 57, 58-60, 143; photos 58, 59
Anthony, Rob, 14, 118
APA (Association of Producing Artists), 139
Apple of His Eye, photo, 42
Arnold, Cindy, 55, 57, 69
Arnold, Randi Rae, photo, 149
Arthur, Karen: 91, 111, 142, 209; photos, 100, 111 *See also* Jensen, Karen
Aston, Frank (c), 74, 77, 80
Atkinson, Brooks (c), 49, 73, 77, 80, 81
Atkinson, Clint, 86
Baby Talk, (p) (Mawby Green and Ed Feilbert), 102, 106
Baggesi, Michael E., 193
Bailey, Pearl, 70, 179
Bainter, Fay, 76
Bakal, Sid (c), 81
Baker, Becky Ann, 136, 160, 181, 221 *See also* Gelke, Becky and Gilbert, Becky
Baker, Elliott, 68
Baker, Robert, 23
Bankhead, Tallulah: 70, 136; photo, 69
Barbata, Ray, 57

Barbeau, Adrienne: 102, 104, 151, 201; photo, 102
Barn Theatre: 50th anniversary, 198, 199-200; air-conditioning added, 131; apprentices' pay, 172-73; Augusta exit signs added, 179; college/university relationships, 57, 205; and competition, 206; Congressional Record entry, 181-82; damages to, 142, 148; economic statistics, 202; Equity theatre started, 46-47; future of, 220-22; Inman's Restaurant, relationship with, 101; newspapers' support of, 205-6; Michigan State Register of Historic Sites, listed, 165, 166; opening of, 36; improvements to, 41-43, 52, 89, 94, 169, 187-88; programming statistics, 203; Rehearsal Shed and bar added, 131-32; robbery of, 61-64, 65; road improvements, 85; ticket prices, 29, 30, 154, 178, 202; photos, 35, 36, 40, 57, 141, 166
Barnes, Clive (c),16
Barnie(s): defined, 69
Barr, Richard, 76
Batchelder, H., (c), 86
Baxter, Grant: 23, 26, 29, 30, 31, 34, 208; photos, 24, 34
Bay House (wp) (Bo Brinkman): 184, 186-87; photos, 185, 186
Beauty Part, The: 92, 94; photo, 91
Bedfull of Foreigners: 163; photo, 164
Beilock, John, photo, 125
Bell, Jack (c), 33, 43, 47, 48, 51, 53, 58, 60, 68-69, 71, 82, 99, 136
Ben Ami, Jacob, 81
Bent, 173
Bentzen, Jayne, photo, 115
Berry, Don, 188
Best Little Whorehouse in Texas, The: 144, 146, 159, 162, 163, 192, 194-95; photo, 163
Bethea, Lang, photo, 138
Billy the Kid (wp) (Brendan Ragotzy): 195-98; photo, 197
Birke, Ted, photo, 138
Bockstanz, Louis (c), 71, 76, 82, 83, 85, 86, 89, 94, 99, 102, 104, 105, 106, 115, 137, 150, 160, 162
Boles, Joe, photo, 125
Bondi, Beulah: 82; photo, 79
Bonfoey, Robert, 30
Booth, Shirley, 72, 73, 74
Born Yesterday, photo, 180
Boy Meets Girl, photo, 31
Boys From Syracuse, The, photo, 115
Boys in the Band, The, 121-22, 123; photo, 122
Bradley, Frank, Jr., 23
Bramley, William: 52; photo, 53
Brighton Beach Memoirs, 170
Brinkman, Bo, photo, 186
Broadway: and off-Broadway compared, 76; ticket prices, 76, 159
Brown, Georgia, photo, 89
Brown, John C., 221
Buerger, Evelyn, 23
Burash, Larry E., photo, 125
Burdick, Helen: 18; photo, 46
Burdick, Virginia, 18
Burgess, David: 153; photo, 152
Burkel/Burkell, Scott: 151, 153, 159, 162, 167, 170, 171-72, 178, 181, 182, 183, 184, 185-86, 191, 193, 201, 214-15, 221; photos, 152, 153, 168, 171, 184, 195
Butler, Ruth (c), 179
Butterfield, Ann, photo, 42
Butterflies Are Free, photo, 127

280

Bye Bye Birdie: 92-93, photo, 93
Byers, Bobbie, photo, 80
Cabaret, 121, 123-24, 134, 199
Cadman, Robert (Bob): 63, 72; photo, 65
Cage aux Folles, La: 175-76, 177-78; photo, 177
California Suite, 149, 150
Calta, Louis (c): 74
Camelot: 88, 102-3, 163, 211, 212; photo, 103
Camp, Ron, 101
Can-Can: 82; photo, 80
Candide, 136, 139-41, 216
Capanna, Michael: 49, 205; photo, 48
Capillupo, Rinaldo, 55, 58, 68
Cardinale, Joseph, 112
Carlson, Don (c), 107, 111, 112, 113, 116, 118, 119, 121, 124, 131, 135, 138, 139-40, 142, 143, 146, 148, 155, 159-60
Carnival, 91, 92
Carousel: 153, 154-56, 157, 174, 175; photos, 154, 155, 156
Carradine, David, 14
Carter, Arthur, 84, 85
Carver, Louise, 18
Cass, Robert, photo, 25
Cat on a Hot Tin Roof, 70, 71, 77, 164, 166-67, 181, 187, 209
Chapman, John (c), 15, 77
Charley's Aunt: 26-28, 93; photo, 27
Chenery, Howard: 17-18, 19, 27, 29, 33; photo, 42
Chenery, Ruth, 23
Chicago: 149, 150; photo, 149
Chorus Line, A: 144, 164, 168, 169, 173, 192; photo, 169
Christie, Audrey, 81
City of Angels: 184, 192, 193-94; photos, 193, 194
Clark, Donald, 30
Clason, Earl, 43, 208
Clason, Ruth, photo, 56
Clearing in the Woods, A, 71, 74-75
Clow, David L., III, photo, 130
Cobb, Farrar M., II, photo, 91
Coker, Nancy, photo, 149
Cole, Art, 20
Coleman, Frank, 98, 101
Coleman, Robert (c), 74, 77
Collins, Laura, 170
Collinson, Mollie, photo, 149
Come Share My House (wp) (Theodore Apstein), 75, 76, 80-81, 82, 104
Company, photo, 126
Conetto, Mary, 141
Conn, Charles, photo, 65
Conroy, Frank, 82
Cooreman, Dan (c), 150, 153
Cordova, Pamela: 151, 153; photo, 152
Corn Crib Revue, 136
Corsaro, Frank, 75
Co-Star Record Acting Game, 70, 136
Count Dracula, 144, 146
Country Mile (wp) (Jack Ragotzy): 36, 39-40; photo, 39
Crain, Art: 23, 24, 29, 30, 31, 34, 208; photo, 24
Crawford, Kathryn, photo, 87
Creasy, Dulcie, 101, 102, 104, 107, 111
Creears, Joan, photo, 46
Crist, Judith (c), 74
Crofoot, Ora: 101, 111; profiled, 209-10; photo, 209
Crowley, Mort, 121
Crumlish, Cynthia, 123

CUE magazine, 74, 87
Curious Savage, The, photo, 46
Curran, (Margaret) Ann: 23, 30, 31, 49; photos, 22, 28, 48
Curry, Meg, photo, 147
Cutelli, Louis, photo, 48
Cypher, Jon: 58, 60, 64-65; photos, 58, 59, 60
Dalton, Dorothy Upjohn, 21, 148 *See also* Delano, Dorothy Upjohn
Dame aux Camelias, La, 70
Damn Yankees, 71, 88, 153, 157, 195
Dark at the Top of the Stairs, The, 82, 84, 218, 219
Dean, Jim (c), 157, 160, 161
Deathtrap, 153, 157
DeCrocker, Pauline, 18
DeLano, Dorothy Upjohn, 18 *See also* Dalton, Dorothy Upjohn
DeLano, Sue, 30 *See also* Parish, Sue
Delany, Dana: 143-44, 178; photos, 143, 145
Dennis, Ray (c), 133-34
DeSalvo, Johanna, photo, 80
Desire Is a Season (wp) (Joe Stockdale): 52, 53-55, 174, 211; photo, 53
DeVine, Lawrence (c), 155
Dirty Work at the Crossroads, photo, 28
Distant Bell, A, (wp) (Katherine Morrill), 76-78
Dolliver, George (c), 30, 33, 39, 44, 47, 48-49, 50-51, 53, 54, 60, 68, 69, 71
Don Juan in Hell, 107
Dorman, Harry, photos, 56, 60, 61
Doud, Katherine (c), 173-74, 178, 194
Doughty, Carol: 55, 57, 60, 67, 69, photos, 58, 59
Draper, Margaret: 71; photos, 71, 73
Driving Miss Daisy: 183-84, 182; photo, 183
Dumrose, Boyd, 57, 58, 67, 68, 72, 73, 75
Dunham, Joan: 102, 104, 112, 113, 119, 123, 124; photos, 102, 119
Dutra, John: 50; photo, 51
Ebert, Betty: acting reviews, 30, 38, 43-44, 50, 51, 54, 55, 64, 65, 68, 76, 111, 115, 116, 117, 170, 173-74, 179, 183, 184; Barn directing, 26-27, 29; and Barn robbery, 61-64, 65; and Barn statistics, 216; early years, 21-22; Equity Membership Candidate Program, 218; final illness, 198; funeral, 198-99; and Kalamazoo Civic Theatre apprenticeship, 22, 23, 24; "mothering" of actors, 101-102, 198-99; myths about, 216-18; School of Advanced Theatre Training, plans for, 218; Turnabout Theatre, 21; photos, 21, 22, 23, 29, 37, 39, 45, 46, 50, 51, 55, 56, 61, 63, 65, 67, 82, 90, 92, 96, 104, 108, 109, 115, 116, 117, 124, 155, 156, 166, 174, 183, 186, 207, 215 *See also* Ragotzy, Jack and Betty
Echiverri, Dexter: 189-90; photos, 189, 190
Eckert, Royal, 67-68
Eldridge, John, photos, 125, 126
Elephant Man, The: 153, 157; photo, 158
Elliott, Gerald (c), 119, 125
Elliott, Mark, 182
Ellis, Edward (c), 72
Ellis, Michael (Mike), 13, 116, 117, 118
Encore (magazine), 157
Equity Membership Candidate Program, 215
Equus: 143-44; photo, 142
Evening with Angelo Mango, An, 134-35, 153, 157, 210-11
Evita: 164, 167, 171, 192, 216; photos, 167, 168
F.J.S. *See* Sims, Frances Jane
Fastenrath (Stockdale), Robin: 23, 31, 201, 213; photos, 25, 30, 31

Faust, Nick, 17
Ferraro, Lance: 23; photo, 25
Fiddler on the Roof: 124-25, 126, 134, 144, 153, 159, 161, 199, 201; photo, 124
Field, Rowland, 77
Figola, John, 116
Finian's Rainbow: 48-49, 203, 204; photo, 48
Finley, Robert, 23
Finley, Wes, photo, 122
Fischer, Lee, 98, 106
Fisher, Jack H., 208
Fisher, M. W., 17
Fisher, Rachel, 194
Flatley, William, 48
Ford, Nancy, 162
Forty Carats, 15, 16, 124
42nd Street, 173
Francis, Amy, 188
Franklin, Frances (c), 172
Freedman, Lewis: 81, 82; photo, 78
Freud, Ralph, 22
Frierson, Michele, 127, 128
Fuchs, Dick: 121, 130, 131, 133, 135, 143, 144, 148, 159, 172, 173, 199, 201; photos, 121, 122, 127, 132
Fuller, Paul and Dorothy, 18
Fulmer, Marcie (c), 191, 192, 218
Funke, Louis (c), 65, 118
Gans, Roger: 142, photo, 140
Gardino, Jerome: 43, 44; photo, 46
Garfield, John, 18, 19
Gates, Bill, 70
Gelb, Arthur (c), 73
Gelke, Becky: 136, 137, 138, 141, 144, 146, 159, 160, 161, 162, 163, 168, 175, 181; photos, 137, 160, 163, 164, 165, 207 *See also* Gilbert, Becky and Baker, Becky Ann
Genus, Karl, 69
George M! 118-19
Gianakaris, C.J. (c), 177
Gilbert, Becky, 136 *See also* Gelke, Becky and Baker, Becky Ann
Gilbert, Melissa: 186-87; photos, 185, 186
Gillette, Fred, 221
Gilmore, Sylva, 18
Girard, Louis: 51, 65, 67, 72, 77, 86, 92, 93, 94, 98, 99, 102, 104, 107, 111, 112, 122, 133, 135, 137, 153, 163, 167, 176, 179; profiled, 212-13, 218; photos, 66, 87, 92, 95, 108, 109, 122, 132, 138, 155, 182, 186, 207, 212
Gish, Dorothy, 82
Gleason, Michael (Mike), 72, 77, 98
Glubke, Mark (c), 189
Goddard, Paulette, 70
Golomb, Sheldon, 88
Gordon, Mary Louise, 16
Gordon, Peyton, 17
Gordon, Susan: 144; photo, 145
Grease: 150-53, 206; photos, 151, 152
Greek, Shirley, 179
Green Grow the Lilacs: 30, 36, 134, 204; photo, 29
Green, Mawby and Ed Feilbert: 93, 149; photo, 94
Gregg, Richard, 30
Gregory, Ruth: 88; photo, 89
Grey, Joel, 118
Griffith, Donald: 30; 28, 29
Groat, Marcia L. (c), 173, 179, 184

Guys and Dolls: 55-57, 136, 195; photo, 196
Gypsy: 71, 88, 89, 90, 208, 217; photo, 90
H.B. *See* Batchelder, H.
H.H. *See* Humphrey, Hugh
Habeas Corpus, 136-37
Hahn, Marshall (c), 14
Hair: 113, 128, 129-31, 134, 178, 179, 194, 199, 201, 204; photos 130, 131
Hamerman, Milt: 43, 47; photo, 46
Hammerstein, James (Jim), 13
Hammond, Bruce: 188, 197; photos, 191, 197
Handley, Drew: 31, 34, 40, 201, 205; 37, 38, 39, 43
Harding, Ann: 82; photo, 78
Hardwicke, Cedric, 70, 107
Harris, Julie, 90
Harris, Leonard (c), 16
Hartman, Ruth, 18
Hatcher, Cynthia, photo, 152
Hauck, Steven, 186, 187
Havoc, June, 52, 70
Hawkins, Richard, photo, 196
Hayes, Janet: 88, 89, 98-99, 102, 103, 104, 107, 218; photos, 88, 98, 103, 106
Hayman, Edward (c), 177, 179, 182, 187, 189
Haynes, Robin: 86, 136, 141, 143, 146, 187, 192, 221; photos, 136, 140, 142 *See also* Newton, Robin and Reeds, Robin
Heckert, Eileen, 82
Hedges, Alan, 111
Hedges, Marta, 159
Helfer, Britt, 171, 178-79, 185
Hello Dolly!, 124, 178, 179-81
Helward, Dale: 14, 16, 77, 82, 83, 92, 93, 94, 102, 104, 107, 112-13, 116, 118, 135, 143, 159, 164, 218; photos, 77, 80, 83, 86, 91, 106, 115, 117, 125, 142, 165
Henderson, Jean, 18
Hepburn, Katharine, 72
Here Come the Butterflies (wp) (Allen Boretz), 97, 99, 101, 104
Herridge, Frances (c), 73, 75
Hewes, Henry (c), 75
Hice Crain, Helen, 208
High Fidelity (earlier *Hip, Hip, Hooray!*), 85, 86-87, 88
Hill, Frank (c), 135
Hinckley, Alfred (Al): 67, 72, 82, 98, 146-48; photos, 60, 62
Hinckley, Gayle: 61, 63, 64, 72, 208; photos, 64, 65
Hintz, Richard, 119
Hip, Hip, Hooray!, 84, 85 *See also High Fidelity*
Hobsen, Allan B., 18
Hodges, Ann, 172
Hoffman, Carla (c), 162
Hoger, Dave (c), 193
Holliday, David, 170
Hopkins, Dale, photo, 108
Hostage, The: 92, 94; photo, 92
Houston, Jack, 111
How to Succeed in Business Without Really Trying: 107, 184, 185-86; photo, 184
Howard, Stuart, 122
Hoyt-Heydon, Mela, 178
Hud, James Peddy, 131
Huebing, Craig: 71, 72, 74; photo, 73
Hughes, Christopher (c), 126-27
Hughes, Earl, photo, 130
Hughes, Mike (c), 149
Hull, Henry, 84

282

Humphrey, Hugh (c), 82, 83, 93, 94, 99, 105-6
Hundred Percent Annie, A (wp) (Susan Slade), 88, 89-90 *See also Ready When You Are, C.B.!*
Hunter, Christine: 194; photo, 194
Hunter, Katie, 199
I Am a Camera, 51
In One Bed. . .And Out the Other (p) (Mawby Green and Ed Feilbert): 92, 93-94, 95, 97, 102, 143; photo, 95
Irma La Douce: 97, 99; photo, 100
Issichopoulos, Penelope: 172, 178, 212; photo, 172 *See also* Alex, Penelope
J.F.S. *See* Sims, Frances Jane
Jack Paar Show, The, 75
Jacobs, Emmett, photo, 83
Javelin Catcher, The, 81
Jensen, Karen, 91, 92, 99-101, 107, 111, 142, 209; photos, 100, 111 *See also* Arthur, Karen
Jesus Christ, Superstar: 132, 133-34, 184, 186; photos, 133
Johnson, Carla (c), 197
Johnson, Florence (c), 14
Johnson, Justine: 86; photo, 87
Johnson, Reed (c), 193
Jones, Tom, 18
Jones, Tom (set designer), 118
Kaechele, Lloyd, photo, 25
Kalamazoo Civic Theatre, 18, 19, 20-21, 22, 23, 26, 41, 57, 69, 134, 146, 216, 217
Kasdorf, Tom, 111
Kason, Jim, 92, 94
Kauffman, Elaine, 221
Kean Norman: 52, 54, 55, 139, 159, 174-75; photo, 53
Keil, Donald, 30
Kent, April, 52
Kent, James Douglas, 153, 177
Kerr, Walter (c), 77, 80-81
Kiley, Richard, 85
Killing of Sister George, The: 113, 115; photo, 116
King, Charlie: photos, 191, 196
King of the Whole Damn World, 87-88
Kiss Me, Kate: 82, 188, 189, 207; photo, 188
Kleimenhagen, Gay: 61, 62, 63, 64; photos, 65, 68
Knappen, Charles B., Jr., 179
Knox, Jim (a.k.a. Bradley James): 169, 179; profiled, 208-9; photos, 138, 207, 208
Knuth, Dean (c), 164
Kristiansen, John, 198
Kronenberger, Doris, 76
Krug, Alicia: 48, 204; photo, 48
LaBrecque, Doug: 167-68, 191-92; photo, 169
Ladd, Diane: 67; photo, 66
LaLanne, Jack, 127
LaLanne, Janette E., 127-28
Lamb, Wayne: 55, 58, 67, 68, 86, 93, 98, 99, 101, 106, 111, 112, 119, 121, 122, 124, 129, 131, 136, 139, 140, 141, 146, 150, 153, 154, 162, 168, 170, 173, 175, 210; profiled, 213-14; photos, 67, 128, 166, 207, 213
Landfield, Timothy: 128, 130, 131, 133, 134, 144; photos, 130, 132, 133
Lane, Kit (c), 138, 139
Larson, Jonathan (Jon): 151, 153, 157; photo, 151
Larson, Lisby: 136, 140, 141, 144; photos, 136, 139
Laurents, Arthur: 69, 71, 73, 74, 75, 217, 220; photo, 71
Leavenworth, Roger (c), 124, 124-25
Lee, Gypsy Rose, 52

Lee, Jeff, 128
Lend Me a Tenor, 184, 186
Letowt, Merle Louise: 91-92, 93; photo, 91 *See also* Merle Louise
Lettiere, Jeff, 173, 178
Levitt, Stan, 95
Lewis, Brian, photo, 138
Lewis, Del, 102, 107, 139
Lewis, Edwina: 131, 174, 179-80, 181, 192, 194-95; photos, 132, 174, 195
Lewis, Marvin Graham, photo, 196
Lewis, Maurice, 86
Liaisons Dangereuses, Les, 178, 181
Ligon, Tom, 14, 16
Li'l Abner, 75, 192
Lindemulder, Gerhardt, 18, 21
Lindsay, Phillip: 104, photo, 104
Little Shop of Horrors: 170, 171-72; photo, 171
Lloyd, Mike (c), 140-41
Lloyd, Sherman, 148
Loesel, Paul, 188
Lohmann, Otto, 57
Long, Sumner Arthur, 13, 14, 15, 115, 118, 132
Look Homeward, Angel: 82-84, 219; photo, 83
Lost in Yonkers, 195, 198
Loti, Elisa, 76, 80
M. Butterfly: 189-90; photos, 189, 190
Macgowan, Kenneth, 33, 38
Maguire, Kathleen, 72, 73, 74, 75, 218
Mai, Jin Jin, photo, 85
Main, Stewart, photo, 39
Majority of One, A: 85, 86; photo, 87
Mamba's Daughters, 49, 51, 119, 204
Mango, Angelo: 14, 58, 61, 67, 68, 99, 102, 105, 107, 111, 112, 113, 118, 119, 121, 122, 124, 126, 133, 134, 135, 136, 141, 143, 144, 146, 149, 150, 151, 153, 157, 159, 162, 163, 164, 170, 172, 173, 175, 176, 178; profiled, 210-11, 214, 218; photos, 58, 62, 67, 68, 103, 105, 113, 114, 119, 122, 124, 128, 132, 155, 158, 171, 207, 210
Man of La Mancha, The: 121, 122, 123, 144, 189, 215, 216; photos, 123, 191
Man Who Came To Dinner, The, photo, 182
Marineau, Barbara: 134, 135, 144, 146, 148, 159, 162, 163, 164, 165, 170, 173, 201, 221; photos, 134, 147, 164, 167, 200
Marineau, Ed, 134
Marlatt, Richard, photo, 152
Marshall, Fredye, 49
Martin, Elliott, 13, 116, 117, 118
Martin, Kent: 183, 184; photo, 183
Matthau, Walter, 81
Mayer, Philip (c), 51, 53-54, 57
Mazure, Arlene, photo, 90
Mazzie, Marin: 151, 153, 155, 157, 159, 167, 178, 181, 182, 185, 186, 192, 207, 221; photos, 150, 152, 155, 167, 180
McAllister, Kelly, photo, 182
McArthur, Jane: 57, 60; photo, 60
McBride, Howard: 123, 194, 199, 216; profiled, 215; photos, 125, 214
McCarthy, Molly, 89
McClain, John (c), 74, 77
McClure, Gordon, 177, 178
McCormick, Garrylee/Garry Lee: 178, 199; profiled, 208-9; photo, 209
McDaniel, George: 97-98, 101, 102, 104, 107, 111, 112, 121,

123, 157, 177, 178; photos, 97, 103, 108, 111, 122, 123, 177
McEowen, Michael, photo, 125
McGuire, Kevin, 164
McHarry, Charles, 76
McKay, Barbara, 127, 128
McKenna, Siobhan, 81
McQueen, Ollie S., photo, 38
Member of the Wedding, The, 50, 51
Merle Louise, 91, 92, 93, 94, 97, 107, 134, 135, 146, 218; photo, 91
Messing, Megan, photo, 127
Metts, Wally, Jr. (c), 167
Michael, Paul, 72
Michigan Foundation for the Arts, 148, 202
Miles, William, photo, 43
Miller Auditorium (WMU), 143, 168, 206
Miracle Worker, The, photo, 89
Mishkin, Leo (c), 15
Misovye, Charlie, 177, 179, 190, 191, 221
Mister Roberts, 52, 53
Morning's at Seven, 27, 28, 30, 82, 159, 160, 203
Morrill, Katherine, 76, 77
Morris, Chester, 82
Morrison, Helen, 168
Most Happy Fella, The: 118, 119, 125, 175-77; photos, 119, 176
Mote, Julie: 153; photo, 152
Move Over Mrs. Markham, 134, 135, 148, 149, 173
Mulvihill, Sandy, 167, 168, 173, 178
Munshin, Jules, 97
Music Corporation of America (MCA), 75, 78
Music Man, The, 88, 89, 90, 163, 164, 168, 199, 201
My Fair Lady: 98-99, 153, 157; photo, 98
Nelson, Arvid, photos, 46, 50
Nelson, Peggy (c), 131, 133
Nelsson, Sigrid, 94
Nemer, Virginia, 19
Neumann, Krista, 150
Newman, Edwin (c), 16
Newman, Robert: 157, 159, 170-71, 178, 185, 192; photos, 159, 170
Newton, John: 53, 57, 60, 65, 67, 68, 70, 71, 72, 85, 86, 87, 97, 98, 99, 102, 104, 107, 126, 143, 146, 159, 181, 211, 212, 218; photos, 52, 56, 62, 66, 84, 98, 103, 104, 125
Newton, Robin, 143 See also Haynes, Robin and Reeds, Robin
New York Telegraph (c), 77, 80
Ney, Richard, 69
Nicolette, Dave (c), 92, 94, 105, 106, 110-11, 117, 121, 123, 124, 129-30, 133, 135, 139, 141, 144, 146, 157, 160, 161, 162, 163, 164, 165-66, 170, 173, 178, 187, 191, 197, 201, 217
Noble, Larkin and Ruth, 18
Norrix, Loy: 31; photos, 25, 39, 46
Norrix, Superintendent of Schools Loy, 17
Norton, Elliot (c), 13
Nossen, Bram (c), 18
Nunsense: 173, 175; photo, 174
Nuts: 159, 160, 161-62; photo, 160
Nuyen, Robin, 154, 159
Oakland, Simon, 15
Oates, Mary S. (c), 113
O'Connor, Jim (c), 73-74
Of Mice and Men, photo, 43
Oklahoma!, 30, 144, 151, 175, 204
Olen, William, photo, 122
Oliver!, 107, 111; photo, 110

On a Clear Day You Can See Forever, 111-12
One Night With You, Madame (In One Bed. . .And Out the Other), 143
On Golden Pond, 153
Oppenheimer, George (c), 16
Ornellas, Norman, 82
Osborn, Paul, 28, 50, 82, 160
O'Sullivan, Maureen, 13, 16, 118
Our Town, 50, 51, 57, 162, 163, 216
Owsley, Steve: 153, 168, 173; photo, 196
OyamO, 204
Page, Geraldine, 13, 14, 15, 117, 118, 164, 199
Pahl, Richard, photo, 138
Painted Days, The (wp) (John Byrne): 57, 60; photo, 60
Pajama Game: 67, 68, 143, 144, 182; photo, 67
Pajama Tops, 88, 93, 128, 159
Parish, Sue Delano, 160, 162
Parker, Eric: 221; photo, 191
Parker, Gilbert, 75, 78
Pastene, Robert, 72
Peck, Kenneth L. (c), 110
Pedi, Tom, 87
Peppel, Fred (c), 166, 168, 171-72, 175, 177-78, 185, 187, 188, 189
Perfectly Frank, 188-89
Persecution and Assassination of Jean-Paul Marat as Performed by the Inmates of the Asylum of Charenton under the Direction of the Marquis de Sade, The: 111, 112-13; photo, 112
Phantom, 189, 190-91
Picnic: 70, 72, 170-71, 178; photo, 170
Piece of Blue Sky, A, 75
Pippin: 144, 146; photo, 147
Point of No Return: 50, 65, 205, 217; photo, 51
Portofino, 69
Potts, David, 125, 126-27
Pow, Terry (c), 181, 182-83, 187, 198, 201
Praus, Alexis, photo, 166
Present Laughter, 162
Price, Vincent, 70
Pritchett, James T.: 52, 53, 54, 55, 57, 69, 70, 82, 128, 144, 158, 162, 163, 164; photos, 52, 53, 56, 82
Purdue (U.) Professional Theatre, 107, 112, 125, 128, 144, 150, 208, 212, 218
Pure as the Driven Snow: 27, 29, 36, 199, 201, 213; photo, 37
Ragotzy, Brendan Jack: adoption, 95; Barn crew, 149, 179; Barn acting, 112, 118; and Barn future, 179, 220-22; *Billy the Kid,* 195-98; birth mother, 95-96; Barn directing, 179, 182, 190-91, 201; college, 158, 212; Equity membership, 144; marriage, 178; and Melissa Gilbert, 186; stage debut, 111; photos, 96, 110, 114, 148, 220
Ragotzy, Floyd Charles, 17
Ragotzy, Jack: awards and honors, 31, 75, 148; Barn decision making, 202, 216-17; Barn programming, 203-4; and Barn statistics, 202; business strategies of, 202-6; childhood, 16-17; college career, 23, 24, 30-31, 33, 38-39, 40, 43, 47-48; college teaching, 118; directing reviewed, 14, 16, 29, 30, 41, 47, 49, 53, 60, 65, 68, 69, 72-75, 76, 80-82, 84-85, 86, 87, 89, 106, 110-11, 116-17, 121, 132-33, 135-36, 137, 138-39, 143, 157, 160, 161, 162, 164, 166-67, 177-78, 189-90, 192-93; film acting, 184-85; first stock rights, 41, 43, 61, 68, 111, 113, 121, 123, 124, 129, 134, 139, 143, 146, 150, 151, 161, 164, 168, 172, 186, 190, 192, 204, 206; high school, 17-19; jobs held, 19, 30; and Kalamazoo Civic Theatre, 18-20, 20-21; military career, 20; playwriting, 38-39; producing, focus on, 121-122;

script editing, 50, 69, 84-85, 102-3, 112, 123; television career, 51-52, 81-82, 84-85, 91, 107, 118, 159, 184; photos, 22, 24, 25, 27, 31, 32, 39, 41, 46, 55, 57, 64, 65, 69, 71, 79, 81, 94, 96, 156, 164, 166, 184, 207, 216. *See also* Ragotzy, Jack and Betty

Ragotzy, Jack and Betty: Barn purchase, 52; California, move to, 106-7; community relationships, 205, 206; Congressional Record, entered into, 181-82; incorporation, 33-34; landfill battle,157-58, 158-59, 181-82; London trips, 178, 181; marital relationship, 95-97, 133, 199, 219, 220; marriage, 23; New York, move to, 40; New York trips, 158-59, 187. *See also* Ebert, Betty *and* Ragotzy, Jack

Rainmaker, The: 55, 192-93; photo, 192
Rakoczy, Charles, 17
Rambow, Helen (c) 116, 118, 119, 121
Randolph, Robert, 16
Rasbury (Di Re), Flo, photo, 68
Ray-Savage, Reginal, 168
Ready When You Are, C.B.!, 90
Reeds, Dusty: 53, 58, 61, 63, 67, 70, 85-86, 98, 104, 107, 116, 144, 150, 153, 163, 167, 171, 177, 199, 201, 215; profiled, 211-12; photos, 56, 60, 65, 84, 152, 207, 211
Reeds, John: 151, 153; photos, 114, 138, 152
Reeds, Robin: 143; photo, 84 *See also* Haynes, Robin and Newton, Robin
Rehearsal Shed, photos, 161, 195
Rehrig, Gregg, 221
Remo, Doreen, photo, 147
Rence, Mariana, photo, 155
Reno, Michael: 131, 132, 134, 140, 141-42; photos, 122, 125, 128, 130, 140
Reser, Barbara, photo, 80
Respectful Prostitute, The, photos, 49, 50
Revelation (wp) (Michael Reno): 141-42; photo, 140
Rhom, (wp) (Gordon Russell and Larry Ward), 52, 53
Rice, Don, 193
Rice, Vernon (c), 49
Rich, Frank (c), 184
Riley, Eric: 131, 133, 134, 144, 169, 184, 221; photos, 130, 133
Ritz, The, 136, 137-38
Robber Bridegroom, The: 144, 164, 165-66, 171, 211; photo, 167
Robbins, Paul, 179
Robin, Teri, photo, 48
Rocky Horror Show, The: 141, 182-83, 189, 195; photo, 181
Rose Tattoo, The: 48, 49, 77; photo, 48
Roseman, Roslyn: 141; photo, 140
Rosen, Ken, photo, 196
Rosenbloom, "Slapsie" Maxie, 70
Ross, Natalie: 70-71, 82, 128; photos, 70, 129
Russell, Ginger, photos, 53, 54
Russell, Gordon, photo, 54
SAG (Screen Actors Guild), 173
Satter, Francis, photo, 83
Saturday Review (c), 87
Schacht, Mike, 48
Schick, Sherra, photo, 149
Schneider, Peter: 129; photo, 130
Schultz, Temple Ann, 162
Schussler, Eric: 159; photo, 138
Schwamberger, Mark, 127, 128
Scott, Martha, 77, 84
Seesaw, 134, 135, 144
Seifert, Kani, photo, 149
Sell Me Down the River, Darling (wp)(Theodore Apstein): 102, 103, 104-5, 106; photo, 104

1776: 125-27, 136, 139; photos, 125, 138
Shamp, James (c), 132-33
Shephard, Bob, photo, 122
Sherman, Hiram, 82
Sherwood, John (c), 144, 146, 153, 174
Shoaff, Charlotte, photo, 46
Shockley, Sally, photo, 113
Shrike, The, 50, 51
Siegel, Suzanne Blaine (c), 168
Sikking, Jim (a.k.a. James Barrie): 71-72; photo, 72
Sills, Art (c), 126
Silver Whistle, The: 41, 204; photo, 41
Simon, John (c), 16, 140
Simon, Peter: 92-93, 97, 107, 218; photos, 92, 93
Sims, Frances Jane (c), 49, 76
Sinclair, Bob (c), 135, 136, 137, 138, 139, 141, 143, 146
Six, Ava, 97
Smith, Abbie, 18
Smith, James D., photo, 122
Smith, Margo, 136
Snow, Howard, 18
Snyder, Richard, 30
Sound of Music, 97, 99
South Pacific: 67, 68-69, 88, 170, 173, 177, 185; photo, 68
Spayde, Sidney, 18, 19, 20, 41
Speros, Tia, photo, 161
Spindel, Susan: 151, photo, 152
Sprague, Jim R.: 133; photo, 132
Stanley, Kim, 74, 75
States with Pretty Names (wp) (Elliott Baker), 67, 68
Steel Magnolias, 178, 179, 199
Stevens, Leon B.: 52; photo, 46
Stevenson, Paul, 18
Stock Managers Association, 46
Stockdale, Joe: Barn acting, 27, 31; Barn directing, 82-84, 218; *Desire Is a Season,* 53-55; and Purdue U. Professional Theatre, 107, 208, 212, 218; relationship with Jack and Betty, 216, 218-19; and Saugatuck Summer Theatre, 31; and School of the Arts, SUNY Purchase, 218; and Village Players, 23, 30, 32; photos, 22, 26, 28, 31
Stop the World—I Want to Get Off: 102, 105-6, 128; photos, 105, 128
Stover, Carol Ann, photo, 42
Strait, Ralph, 93, 94, 97
Stratton, Delphine, 30, 33
Stratton, Paxton: 26, 29, 31, 34; profiled, 208; photos, 24, 29, 34
Streetcar Named Desire, A: 39, 43, 47, 57, 64, 77, 96, 175, 203, 204, 216; photos, 45, 46
Strong, Peter: 149, 151; photos, 148, 152
Stroud, Peggy, photo, 25
Stryker, Mark (c), 185-86, 190
Sugar Babies: 170, 172, 192; photo, 171
Summer and Smoke, 50, 51, 77
Summertime, 72, 74
Sunrise at Campobello: 85-86; photo, 84
Sunshine Boys, The, 134, 135
Swank, William J. (c), 93, 99, 101, 103, 106, 111, 112-13, 116, 119, 121, 123, 124
Sweeney Todd, 146, 199, 201; photo, 200
Sweet Charity: 111, 175, 216; photo, 111
Taintor, Marjorie, 23
Take Her, She's Mine, 97, 98, 204
Tallmer, Jerry (c), 74-75, 81
Taylor, Kathy: 189; photo, 188

285

Tea and Sympathy: 57, 61; photo, 61
Teahouse of the August Moon, 82, 83, 204
That Championship Season: 132-33; photo, 132
Theatre Communication Group (TCG), 202
Thrall, Richard, photo, 42
Thyssen, Greta, 97
Time of the Cuckoo, The: 69, 70, 71, 71-74, 75, 217; photo, 73
Tobacco Road, 43, 47, 54, 55, 107, 159, 160, 203; photo, 56
Torn, Rip, 13
Tozzi, Giorgio: 176-77; photo, 176
Travis, Harry, photo, 31
Tronto, Rudy: 172; photo, 171
Tucker, John Bartholomew (c), 16
Turner, Betsy: 151, 206-7; photos, 149, 152
Twain, Norman, 77-78
Two for the Seesaw, 82
Tynan, Kenneth, 75
Unsinkable Molly Brown, The, 92, 159, 160-61
Upjohn, Dr. W. E., 18
Vander Roest, Jerry, photo, 166
Van Fleet, Mary, 52
Vanities, photo, 145
Variety (c), 14, 16, 49, 53, 55, 60, 65, 68, 69, 74, 75, 76, 77, 80, 81, 87, 99, 105, 117, 169
Varnum, John, 88, 89
Verily I Do (wp) (Gladys Charles and George Savage), 36, 38
Vernan, Betty, photo, 90
Vick, Lonnie, 151
Vickers, Steve, photo, 91
Village Players, The: finances, 29, 30; formation of, 23; move to a barn, 33-36; and Richland Community Hall, 23-26; photos, 22, 25, 35, 36
Wales, Dirk, 52
Walker, Charles Dodsley, 102
Walker, Diana, 96
Walker, Holly, 195
Wagner, Walter, photo, 31
Walking Happy: 113-15; photos, 113, 114
Walmsley, Jill, 191

Walsh, Mike: 92, 93; photo, 92
Watt, Stan, 67
Watts, Richard, Jr. (c), 16, 77, 80
Wayne, David, 148
Weeks, John, 122
Werner, James: 160-61; photo, 160
West, Ethel, 18
West Side Story: 52, 71, 85, 86, 220; photo, 85
Wettig, Patricia: 134, 135; photo, 134
Where's Charley?: 57, 61; photo, 62
Whinnery, Barbara: 136, 163; photos, 137, 164
White, John, 98
Who's Afraid of Virginia Woolf?: 107, 108-11, 216; photos, 108, 109
Wickwire, Nancy, 74, 75
Will Success Spoil Rock Hunter?, photo, 66
Williams, Governor G. Mennen: 55; photo, 55
Williams, Judith Ann, photo, 126
Willis, Susan: 82; photo, 80
Wilson, Julie, 87
Winters, Freda B., 23
Winters, Shelley, 75
Wolfe, Jen: 149, 150, 159, 173; photo, 145
Wolfe, Larry, 93, 124
Wolpe, Congressman Howard, 181-82
Wood, Audrey, 75
Wopat, Tom: 139, 140, 141, 144, 146, 153-57, 159, 164-65, 166, 167, 174, 175, 178, 179, 182, 184, 189, 192, 193, 194, 195, 198-99, 201, 221; photos, 138, 139, 140, 142, 154, 155, 156, 157, 167, 188, 192, 193, 194, 196, 200
World of Suzie Wong, The: 85, 86; photo, 86
Wyatt, Ron, 131
York, Zack, 148
You Can't Take It With You, 20, 136, 138-39, 142
Young, David S., 191, 193, 197, 198
Young, Joellyn Cox, photo, 186
Zamarripa, Todd, 184, 219
Zaremba, Jack, 148
Zimmer, Kim: 192, 193, 194, 195; photo, 192

About the Author

When did my passion for the theatre start?

When I was a kid, I saw as many movies as I could rake up the dime for at the Regent Theatre in Allegan, Michigan, my home town. In high school, I went to the Kalamazoo Civic Theatre and remember wonderful productions directed by Sidney Spade. His *The Little Foxes* with Pauline DeCrocker and Ruth Noble will be with me always. At the same time, I saw touring shows such as *Watch on the Rhine* with Paul Lukas, Mady Christians and Lucile Watson at the State Theatre.

But the production I remember most is Ethel Barrymore in *The Corn is Green*. Miss Barrymore toured one night stands and carried her own marquee with her name in lights. I'll never forget that voice – like the sound of a cello floating up to the balcony; never forget the ovation she received as she entered, wheeling a bicycle down toward the footlights.

It was a snowy night, there was no bus back to Allegan and it was too late to try hitching. So I stayed in the bus station and caught the 6 a.m. Did I sleep? My mind's eye was too busy going over the play's movement, the voices, the acting and the story.

My passion never subsided. It drove me to the rehearsals at the newly formed Lincoln Repertory Theatre and to Strasberg's classes at the Actors Studio – although as an undergraduate at Western Michigan University, I learned more from Laura Shaw than from anyone else about Stanislavsky's method. My passion drove me, throughout the century, to see most of the great productions in NY and London. It drove me to direct 140 productions, half with full Equity casts in a regional theatre of my own making, as well as off-B'way and at Woodstock. It took me to Russia, Poland, East and West Berlin, London, and Dublin, seeing productions and interviewing directors, and to the major cities of India observing dance and drama.

Oh, don't get me started. . . .

And I had it both ways! Robin and I met as founding members of Ragotzys' theatre. A year later we were married during the run of a show. The births of our five kids, along with so many other major events of our lives, are marked by some concurrent theatre event.

Now we are retired and live just two blocks from the very theatre where I saw Ethel Barrymore and only 12 miles from the theatre we helped establish, and where, last summer, three-year old Ben, youngest of our five grandsons, saw his first theatrical production.

Talk about coming full circle! And can you believe? The passion is still there.